EMPIRE *of* GUNS

EMPIRE
of GUNS

The Violent Making of the
Industrial Revolution

PRIYA SATIA

PENGUIN PRESS

New York

2018

PENGUIN PRESS

An imprint of Penguin Random House LLC
375 Hudson Street
New York, New York 10014
penguin.com

Image credits appear on page 509.

ISBN: 9780735221864 (hardcover)
ISBN: 9780735221871 (ebook)

Printed in the United States of America
1   3   5   7   9   10   8   6   4   2

DESIGNED BY AMANDA DEWEY

For Kabir and Amann

So she followed her red-coats, whatever they did,
From the heights of Quebec to the plains of Assaye,
From Gibraltar to Acre, Cape Town and Madrid,
And nothing about her was changed on the way;
(But most of the Empire which we now possess
Was won through those years by old-fashioned Brown Bess.)

RUDYARD KIPLING, "Brown Bess: The Army Musket,
1700–1815" (1911)

CONTENTS

Part Three

THE MORAL LIFE OF GUNS

Preface

My father is from Muktsar, Punjab, a town just on the Indian side of the border with Pakistan. That border was drawn in 1947, when he was four years old, as part of the subcontinent's independence from British rule. Through various commercial, industrial, and agricultural pursuits, his father, Des Raj Satia, slowly acquired a great deal of land in and around Muktsar. Indian Punjab was itself divided in 1967 according to new state lines, and Des Raj—"Baoji," we called him—was unsure what would ensue, going by his experience of the Partition of 1947. So, partly to insure against the risk of displacement, he sent one of his five sons to the new state of Haryana, one to neighboring Rajasthan, one to Delhi, and one to the United States: my father. One son, Bharat, stayed in Muktsar, along with Baoji's younger brother Balraj and Balraj's two sons. (This schematic narration condenses into two sentences a host of accidents, acts of personal courage, ambition, and confusions. It also writes out of the story Baoji's two daughters. But in the manner of a fable, we will allow it.)

My brother recently attended the latest court hearing about our family property in Muktsar. He brought back for me a copy of Baoji's will, dated 1970 and signed by Baoji, my grandmother Shanti Devi, and Balraj, each in a different script (Persian, Devanagari, and Roman). Despite this document, upon Baoji's death in 1983, the family fought over the disposition of his property. Bharat claimed everything in and around Muktsar on the basis of having been the only one who had stayed and endured Punjab's descent into nightmarish political and military conflict during the late seventies and eighties. Bharat's brothers, Balraj, and Balraj's sons challenged his claim. As the struggle over hundreds of acres unfolded, the strip of land dividing Bharat's and Balraj's homes in Muktsar became a daily irritant between the households. Guns were part of the martial frontier culture encouraged in this region during British rule, and Bharat had always talked and acted tough as a youth. As tempers boiled, finally, in 1991, he stood in the contested garden and aimed his revolver at Balraj, threatening to shoot. Exactly what followed remains obscure. Certainly, he fired several shots, and Balraj fought for his life for three months in hospital. I have seen photos my father later took of bullet marks in the garden wall. A cold war between the neighboring families unfolded thereafter as a property settlement continued to elude the family.

Bharat's wife and son were at his side when he pulled the trigger. His wife later described to me how he shook as he pointed the gun, insisting that he meant only to intimidate his uncle. To her, he had shot his uncle despite himself. But her own and their son's presence at Bharat's side during the standoff also raises questions: If he was shaking, did they goad him? Or restrain him? I know that my uncle Bharat alone was responsible for nearly killing his uncle, but from what I recall of his temperament, I cannot shake the feeling that he would not have physically assaulted his uncle had he had recourse only to a knife. He was too afraid; he was all bluster, without the malignant emotional energy required for such an intimate attack. But pulling a trigger was thinkable in a different manner. The gun changed what he was capable of; he meant it to terrorize his uncle and keep him off his property. I can imagine him that day, against the backdrop of an increasingly militant Punjab, casting himself in a script in which the gun was a prop that he waved to instantly cast his uncle in the role of common trespasser, alienating their familial bond into a contest between strangers. (In court, to protect his wayward nephew, Balraj said he had shot himself accidentally while cleaning his gun, reaffirming the severed bond.) By shaping his actions, the gun made Bharat, just as someone had made the gun. As I wrote this book, I recalled this scene in the garden time and again. The script by which Bharat's revolver figured in our family land dispute came to him through culture. Through this book, I have found one of its origins in the eighteenth century, when, in some places in the world, guns found their first role in interpersonal violence through contests over property in societies of strangers. This incident, its backdrop of provincial turmoil, its lasting legacy, the cotton industry that produced much of Baoji's wealth—this family history has shaped my investigation of the British gun trade and the industrial revolution in the eighteenth century.

Perhaps my memory of the shooting in the Muktsar garden was subconsciously at play when I stumbled on the curious story of a Quaker arms-making family in the eighteenth century, the Galtons. As I looked through the Galton records in the Birmingham City Archive, I discovered a point of view that seemed to me to upend received wisdom about the industrial revolution, and so, partly by accident and partly by will, I hunkered down for a long spell in the eighteenth century and communion with the troubles of another extended family—every unhappy family being unhappy in its own way, as Tolstoy tells us.

But I have also written this book in a time of mass shootings in the United States. My daughter was in first grade when the Sandy Hook shooting happened, in December 2012. My heart broke like everyone else's, five years into my study of guns in the eighteenth-century British Empire. My investigation into the place of guns in that world showed me that their uses are not fixed, but change with time and place. There were no casual shootings in Britain until suddenly, because of cultural shifts inaugurated by the Napoleonic Wars, there were. Likewise, the shooting in my family was not unrelated to the violence that tore up Punjab in the 1980s, and the mass shootings of our time are not unrelated to the war on terror. Culture and technology produce each other. Like all my work on empire and technologies of violence, this book is against militarism and imperialism. Some might be tempted to take its conclusion—that war was foundational to modern industrial life—as approbation of war, but my point is rather that this finding should give us pause in our embrace of that life and in our tolerance for the vast international trade in arms today.

It raises the question of how far complicity in war stretches in different times and places. When guns became central to eighteenth-century violence in a new way in the 1790s, the Quaker church demanded that the Galtons abandon their century-long investment in the gun trade. Samuel Galton Jr. went to great lengths to explain that it was not so easy to distance oneself from investment in war; apart from the difficulty of passing on his business, almost any other industrial activity he might pursue in its place would be similarly, if less directly, complicit in war. We continue to face such dilemmas. After Sandy Hook, the investment firm Cerberus Capital Management publicly pledged to sell Remington Outdoor, the company that made the Bushmaster rifle that the shooter used. Public pension fund investors like the California State Teachers' Retirement System had long called on the firm to sell the gunmaker. Four years later, as I finish this book, Cerberus has failed to find a buyer and has decided to let its investors sell their stakes in Remington and then move the manufacturer out of its funds into a "special financial vehicle." (All this is quite apart from the relentless boom in gun sales and stocks in these years.) The difficulty Galton perceived in 1795 continues to shape the efforts of capitalists and industrialists seeking to distance themselves from violence. Meanwhile, philanthropic capitalists like Bill Gates have begun to donate money toward the campaign for greater gun control. But given the diversity of investment portfolios, where is the beginning and end of the investment in guns and other arms? And how have those connections shifted since the eighteenth century? These are the questions this book tries to answer.

EMPIRE *of* GUNS

Samuel Galton Jr., 1753–1832.

Introduction

For more than 125 years, between 1688 and 1815, Britain was in a state of more or less constant war. The British gun industry was vital to the kingdom's survival. In 1795, however, during war with revolutionary France, one of the British government's regular gun suppliers, Samuel Galton Jr. of Birmingham, became the subject of scandal. Galton was a Quaker and a prominent, if not *the* prominent, gunmaker in England. The Quaker church, the Religious Society of Friends, had silently accepted his family business for nearly a century, but now suddenly demanded he abandon it. Their censure forced Galton to defend himself publicly. At the core of his defense were two related claims: first, that everyone in the Midlands, including fellow Quakers, in some way contributed to the state's war-making powers; he was no worse than the copper supplier, the taxpayer, or the thousands of skilled workmen manipulating metal into everything from buttons to pistol springs for the king's men. Second, like other metalware, guns were instruments of civilization as much as war, as essential to preserving private property in a society of increasingly mobile strangers as doorknobs and hinges. Galton saw himself as part of a military-industrial society in which there was little, if any, economic space outside the war machine and in which the paraphernalia of war doubled as the paraphernalia of civilization based on property. He took the Society of Friends's easy tolerance of his family business up to 1795 as evidence in support of his case. Was there any merit in Galton's view? Was Britain's emerging industrial economy actually a military economy?

And if it was, why did the Society of Friends suddenly find that reality intolerable in 1795?

The story of Britain's transformation from a predominantly agrarian, handicraft economy to one dominated by industry and machine manufacture—the commonly accepted story of the industrial revolution— is typically anchored in images of cotton factories and steam engines invented by unfettered geniuses. The British state has little to do in this version of the story. For more than two hundred years, that image has powerfully shaped how we think about stimulating sustained economic growth—development—the world over. But it is wrong: state institutions drove Britain's industrial revolution in crucial ways. Galton was right: war made the industrial revolution.

Britain was involved in major military operations for eighty-seven of the years between 1688 and 1815, declaring war against foreign powers no fewer than eight times. At any given time, Britain was either at war, making preparations for war, or recovering from war. Even in peacetime, contemporaries assumed war was imminent, or at least that government should act as if it were so. The Seven Years' War (1756–63) and subsequent conflicts took place on a vastly expanded scale, too, involving entire societies and economies and posing unprecedented logistical problems that utterly dwarfed civilian enterprise. With British troops mobilized for most of the century, Parliament's famed antipathy to a standing army was more or less incidental. War was the norm in this period. And it shaped the economy; that's why radical Britons called military contracting and its system of parasitical elite partnerships with the state "Old Corruption." The state was the single most important factor in the economy, the largest borrower and spender and employer. Its minions advanced into civil society to clothe, feed, and arm the expanding army, stimulating domestic output and innovation. Contractors supplied ships, powder, arms, shot, foodstuffs, uniforms, beer, drivers, horses, and more. The state was a consuming entity, supporting private industry through bulk purchases at critical times. It cut a wide swath as a consumer, literally *investing* Britons in its war making.

And yet no one has explained how constant war impinged on the grand economic narrative of the time, the industrial revolution. The backdrop of the industrial revolution as told here is not the whims of cal-ico fashion but the Nine Years' War, the War of the Spanish Succession, the War of the Austrian Succession, the Seven Years' War, the American War of Independence, and the French Revolutionary and Napoleonic Wars. In the foreground are the members of the Galton family, proprietors of the single biggest gun-manufacturing firm in Britain, the largest suppliers of guns to the British state and major suppliers of the East India Company and the commercial arms trade to West Africa, North America, and other parts of the growing empire.

The Quaker church, known for its belief in the un-Christian nature of war, said nothing about these mammoth pursuits until the sudden rebuke of 1795. This long silence says something about the common sense about guns and gun manufacture up to that year, encapsulated in Galton's public defense of his life as a Quaker gunmaker: in the emerging industrial econ-omy, there was no way to avoid contributing to the state's war-making powers. He was part of an economic universe devoted to war making, in which guns were also essential to the spread of a civilization based on property. But by 1795, that common sense was shifting: guns suddenly had become objectionable commodities to Quakers. This was partly be-cause just then, during Britain's long wars against France between 1793 and 1815, they were acquiring a new role in interpersonal violence that was no longer defensible as preservation of property. Suddenly, guns looked bad, and gunmaking worse. Galton tried in vain to remind fellow Quakers of wider investments in war and of guns' centrality to the rule of property. But there was too much at stake in industrial capitalism by then for him to win the argument about its collectively scandalous nature. The arms maker morphed from a morally unremarkable participant in indus-trialization to a uniquely villainous merchant of death. And our memory of industrial revolution became one of pacific genius unbound. But Gal-ton's defense opens a window onto past convictions, and looking through it helps us understand that the British state's colossal demand for war matériel made it a major driving force of the industrial revolution and helped guns find a central place in modern violence.

By taking Galton's claims seriously, by putting them on trial, in a sense, *Empire of Guns* assembles a new common sense about the industrial revolution. In Part One, to assess whether he was right that everyone around him participated in war manufacturing, the book tells the story of the British gun trade from 1688 to 1815, as it made the guns that enabled British armies, navies, mercenaries, traders, settlers, and adventurers to conquer an immense share of the globe. In Part Two, to assess whether Galton was right that guns were part of the paraphernalia of civilization, the book traces how Britons used guns at home and across the empire, in military and civilian settings, how guns migrated from being an instrument of terror specifically relevant to contests over property to a weapon for new kinds of impersonal violence on the battlefield and in the streets. Part Three takes the story up to the present, showing how our inherited blindness to war's foundational role in the industrial revolution has distorted the theory and practice of economic development and has underwritten our enduring failure to regulate gun manufacture and trade.

The Galtons have long been on the sidelines of history. During Birmingham's infamous Priestley Riots of 1791, we spy Samuel Galton Jr. offering shelter to the Dissenting clergyman and natural philosopher Joseph Priestley, running from a torch-wielding mob. Priestley was a leading advocate of equal rights for religious Dissenters; in the eighteenth century, Protestants who did not adhere to the established Church of England—including Quakers—were barred from most public offices. But the unassuming figure offstage, the Quaker proprietor of the single largest gunmaking firm in Birmingham, was nevertheless indispensable to the British state. His name appears in history books—as Priestley's friend, a minor member of the Lunar Society, where the leading lights of Birmingham's "industrial enlightenment" gathered to dine and share knowledge, and incidental ancestor of the notorious Victorian eugenicist and father of modern statistics Sir Francis Galton. But his very presence on the fringes of history profoundly disturbs standard narratives of the industrial revolution and British Dissent: a Quaker who produced mass quantities of an industrial commodity essential to the state's pursuit of empire. He defies our image of Quakers, certainly, but also our image of an industrial revolution driven by textile production and domestic consumerism.

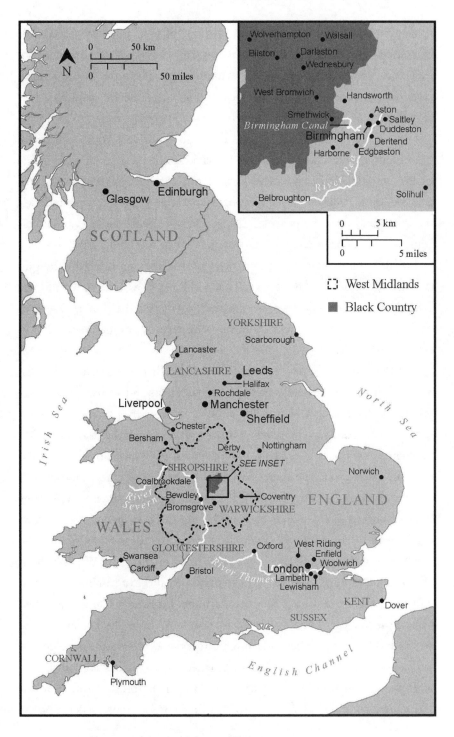

Great Britain and the West Midlands.

During the eighteenth century, millions of guns issued from humble workshops in Birmingham and London into the hands of buyers in Africa, India, the West Indies, the Americas, and Europe. While cotton cloth flowed from Manchester, Birmingham became the capital of the global trade in arms, and Black Country metalworkers forged bonds with a state almost permanently at war. Through family networks, ever more prominent Quaker banking and industrial families were entangled in the Galton gun business. The fortune the family acquired in the gun business laid the foundation for the Galton bank in 1804. They finally abandoned the gun trade after the peace of 1815 ended the Napoleonic Wars. Their bank was later absorbed by what became today's Midland Bank (now part of HSBC). That segment of British wealth is thus founded on the gun trade, but in some measure so, too, are the fortunes that went into the banks founded by Galton's relations, the Lloyds and the Barclays, who in oblique ways were also involved in the gun business, as merchants, bankers, ironmongers.

At the center of these networks stood the British state. It did much more than minimalistically provide the financial and transportation infrastructure for industrial revolution, as traditionally portrayed; it consumed metal goods in the mass quantities that made industrial revolution necessary and possible. Just its bulk demand for guns alone stimulated innovations in industrial organization and metallurgical technology with enormous ripple effects. At the start of the eighteenth century, it contracted for tens of thousands of guns; by the early nineteenth century, its needs were in the millions. That shift in magnitude signifies industrial revolution in the metallurgical world. It was not the result of application of machinery but of state-driven expansion of and experimentation with industrial organization of the artisanal trade. Growing state demand had turned greater Birmingham into a government factory by the end of the century. The entire Midlands metallurgical world became invested in mass production for war. The state learned to set quality standards at a level permitting wider participation, and thus mass production, by mimicking the commercial instincts of trading corporations, especially the

East India Company, that were both bound to it and in competition with it.

Horizontal and vertical linkages between the gun trade, "toy" trades, and mining—all of which the Galtons were involved in—ensured that innovations in one area quickly spilled into others. Tiny revolutions in the workshops in the "Gun Quarter" around Birmingham's St. Mary's Church fueled world-historical change. Gun manufacture overlapped in its techniques, labor supply, and raw materials with manufacture of other metal goods in Birmingham, many of which were also objects of state demand; much of the emerging economic order owed its existence to wars of imperial expansion. In short, guns are an obvious starting point for understanding state participation in the industrial economy, but their material affinities with other metal goods—from coins to buckles—make it possible to imagine a much wider compass of government influence in that economy. This book situates the gun trade within a wider context of manufacturing for war. To Galton, the emerging industrial economy was fully indebted to war; even arms making was so thoroughly diffused through manufacturing, commercial, and financial networks that his role was merely one part in a complex chain of production. He was no more responsible for the manufacture of weapons of war than the Italian woodsman who felled the walnut used in their stocks. He was not alone in perceiving the way war was transforming British productivity: the East India Company permitted voluminous gun sales even to enemies in South Asia partly to enfeeble gunmaking traditions there and thus *prevent* industrial revolution. It understood that arms manufacture was triggering revolutionary change at home, and so it helped create the "great divergence" between East and West.

Galton felt he participated in a wider military-industrial society, a collective of interdependent economic actors tied in varying ways to the state, in which there was no economic space not in some way connected to war. This was different from the "military-industrial complex" of the twentieth century—the cozy, almost conspiratorial "iron triangle" of relationships among governments, the military, and industry, including political approval of industrial research, industrial support for military training, and the arms industry's interest in promoting belligerent policies. The eighteenth-century state spurned such coziness as dangerously susceptible to manipulation by enemies within and without. Its objective was a much *less* exclusive relationship with arms suppliers; it actively encouraged new-comers and intervened in the private market to keep the trade attractive to amateurs even in peacetime. A military-industrial "complex" began to emerge only in the second half of the nineteenth century, when introduc-tion of machine manufacture forced greater concentration in the industry, although wider participation in the prosecution of war remained a fact of economic life.

How did sincere Quakers tolerate their participation in a military-industrial society for so long? Notions of moral responsibility in economic activity shifted after the British defeat in the American Revolutionary War, in 1783—evident in growing investment in abolition of the slave trade (with which the gun trade was notoriously entangled). But Quaker tolerance for its members' involvement in gun manufacture also shifted with understanding about guns. The eighteenth-century gun was a mate-rial object without an exact twentieth-century equivalent. It was mallea-ble, easily morphing into metallic wealth or perishing from rust and rot. Certainly, guns were used in enormous numbers to kill human beings, but they also had other uses and meanings—a wider social life.

For instance, guns were money. The intrinsic metallic value of their brass, silver, steel, and iron components mattered in a period in which consumer goods were often melted into "money," and currency was itself a scarce commodity supplied by contractors. The social and technological worlds of coin manufacture closely overlapped with those of gun manu-facture; bankers and gunmakers were also tightly bound. Guns were a critical currency in global trade, used to purchase commodities (including slaves) and diplomatic loyalty in a competitive arena of European expan-sion. Their commercial value was both intrinsic and symbolic; as minia-ture cannons, they embodied the political power that often enabled commerce in new places. Though mass-produced, the eighteenth-century gun had an aura—the aura of the regime of private property and industrial capitalism it guaranteed. Consumption of any good depends on social and cultural constructs (e.g., sugar consumption depends on social rituals centered on tea and coffee). Gun consumption was tied to the rise of property as *the* social and cultural form of the period. It was an artifact that bound diverse communities and enabled them to build a particular political-economic regime based on property and conquest abroad.

The first European firearms were late-fourteenth-century "hand cannons," essentially tubes mounted on a pole. Shoulder arms, such as muskets, rifles, and shotguns, followed. Pistols could be fired with one hand. The people who made such handheld firearms were called gunmakers or gunsmiths, though *gun* itself might refer to cannons or long guns. *Firearm* usually meant musket. In this book, I use *gun* generically to refer to handheld machines capable of firing missiles that can bore through flesh. But even as weapons, eighteenth-century firearms were radically different from today's—more unreliable, slower, unwieldy, and perishable; the enormous volume of the trade was driven partly by the need for frequent replacement. But the eighteenth-century gun was not merely a cruder version of today's gun; it also functioned differently. The question of its use came up often enough in parliamentary discussion to suggest that it was no settled matter. As a weapon, the eighteenth-century gun commanded obedience not by the threat of a precise mark but by the threat of unpredictable explosion. When a threat was not enough, it removed violence to a clean and comfortable distance; it was (ironically) part of the sanitization of violence that we call the "civilizing process." For the British, the gun's mechanical power, inert among otherwise innocuous springs and locks, made it the weapon of the property holder and the property thief but not of the enraged—such as rioters, who, even within gun factories, preferred rocks and torches, or angry lovers who preferred the sanguinary release of the knife, the former more anonymous and the latter more intimate than the violence permitted by pistol. Guns were for contests over property. In an increasingly mobile society of strangers, guns were the instrument of impersonal, even polite intimidation in the hands of smugglers, highwaymen, poachers, and the property owners and soldiers who defended against such trespassers. Abroad, too, to British explorers, traders, settlers, and conquerors who came to extend the reign of property in the South Pacific or North America, guns were not only a currency but a symbol of civilization. They justified their violent use of these "symbols" with accounts of the abject savagery of the tomahawks and daggers they opposed.

Guns were never simply instruments of mechanical death in the eighteenth century; their multiple uses—their rich social life—made it possible for Quakers to participate in their manufacture without experiencing a contradiction with Quaker principles—until the 1790s. The wars that began in 1793 entailed mass violence on an unprecedented scale, reshaping gun use in civilian life, too. New kinds of impersonal gun violence unrelated to property emerged. Guns did not replace other weapons, like knives, in familiar forms of violence committed in bouts of passion or drunkenness; they made possible new kinds of violence that were neither passionate nor property related. For the first time, we find a discharged teenaged soldier walking on Bristol Bridge waving his musket around until, without notice, he "wantonly drew the trigger" and killed a young man. Abroad, too, guns figured in new kinds of casually exterminative violence just then. Quakers could no longer presume that guns were civilizing objects promoting the protection and acquisition of property the world over. Galton became a scandal.

The great moral question of this time was how the private self, with all its desires, fantasies, and limitless wants, could be made to articulate with the world outside itself, how it could be mobilized for the public good. This was the problem Adam Smith struggled to answer. In 1795, the Society of Friends perceived a scandalous clash between private gain and public good in Galton's business, but Galton saw evidence of wider societal complicity. He argued that by finding particular fault in his activities, the Society avoided facing the reality of wider Quaker and societal participation in an economic system based on war. He lost the debate. My exhumation of his perspective makes a mountain out of this Quaker molehill. I read Galton's failure to persuade his fellow Quakers as a key moment in which war-driven industrial capitalism was normalized by a critical focus on particularly scandalous forms of trade, like the slave trade and the arms trade. The Society's singling him out ironically helped extend the life of the war-based industrial capitalism on which all its members depended.

This remains our way of dealing critically with capitalism: we focus on the problem of particular bad commodities like drugs, slaves, arms—which *seem* to implicate only a few. One of the earliest theorists of imperial capitalism, the early-twentieth-century liberal J. A. Hobson, faulted it for promoting sectional interests like finance, shipping, and armaments. This was the foundation of the theory of a "complex" of military, financial, and industrial interests. Those interests may have been more sectional in the early twentieth century than in Galton's time, but moments like Galton's censure gave us that notion of *sectional* interests and obscured broader *collective* interest and investment in the processes through which empire was acquired. By focusing on the empire's promotion of a few particular business and professional interests at the *expense* of national interests, the Hobsonian critique minimized empire's role in the nation's *overall* economic development. It preserved the old liberal tenet that, in the main, commerce has nothing to do with war or conquest. Hobson was among the political economists who forgot "and did not wish to be reminded what the first industrial nation owed to men of the sword."

The story of the Galtons reveals how, at the very moment in which lethal mechanical violence came to pervade modern existence, it became invisible to those responsible for its spread. The extreme division of labor in gunmaking, the state's efforts to keep the industry diffuse, the intermittent nature of diverse manufacturers' relationship with the state, and guns' place in eighteenth-century violence obscured collective investment in war and made it possible for even a Quaker gunmaker to deny particular culpability for enabling war. To Galton's mind, to be an economic actor in the eighteenth century was to ineluctably support the state's military endeavors. As market relationships across vast distances expanded horizons of moral responsibility, enabling humanitarian movements like abolitionism, a similar awareness of diffuse production relationships dimmed this manufacturer's sense of moral responsibility for producing instruments of global violence. He saw guns and war itself as the products of an entire economy rather than of any individual's moral decision. Recognizing the simultaneous centrality and invisibility of war production to the making of the industrial economy will help us grasp the foundational role of violence in modern industrial and commercial life. Violence committed abroad, in service of imperial expansion, was central to the making of capitalist modernity. But the industrial revolution brought with it new subjectivities that could cope with this moral burden.

The Galton story shows us how the military-industrial economy worked, how its smallest unit, the family, functioned, amoebalike, in the substrate of British society, stretching interest in the gun trade here and there throughout the land. This is a human story; these were no villains, but ordinary men and well-intentioned Quakers. The reckless ambition of Galton Jr.'s uncle James Farmer, Galton Sr.'s unending anxiety, Galton Jr.'s audacious temper bubbling up from beneath his austere Quaker exterior, and the follies and dreams of other members of the cast are the struggles of recognizably modern people. Quaker judgment aside, horrific historical developments are often the result not of egregious individual moral failure but of the incremental decisions of morally unremarkable and even fundamentally decent people in constraining circumstances. The eighteenth-century military-industrial economy was the result not of conspiracy but of such incremental human actions.

H istorians typically treat war as "a historical accident unrelated to the process of industrialization," with a wholly negative impact on the economy. We have just one seminal work on war's impact on the iron industry, by A. H. John. The end of the Cold War at first lowered the ideological stakes in claiming a large developmental role for the state: Historians began to question the habit of treating wars as "stochastic perturbations" to factor *out* of study of the industrial revolution. Economists speculated on civilian spin-offs from military expenditure—improvements in ship design, maps, metallurgy, food preservation, medical care. Others showed how the fiscal-military state spent money, how men, food, weapons, clothing, transport, and all the other paraphernalia of war were acquired and distributed. But before we could come to grips with the implications of this work for the narrative of the industrial revolution, economic historians began demolishing the very idea of an industrial revolution with new quantitative techniques. They began to wonder instead at Britain's *slow* takeoff, speculating that war "crowded out" more productive investments. The notion of revolutionary industrial change was rehabilitated eventually, but the idea that war somehow damaged it stuck. The end of the Cold War ultimately revived an uncontested version of the liberal political economy invented in the eighteenth century, which saw war as abnormal. The rare scholar who acknowledged war's stimulation of eighteenth-century industry distinguished it from "normal conditions."

In fact, there were so many transitions between peace and war that it is difficult to establish what "normal" economic conditions were. Eighteenth-century Europeans accepted war as "inevitable, an ordinary fact of human existence." It was an utterly unexceptional state of affairs. For Britons in particular, war was something that transpired abroad and that kept truly damaging disruption—invasion or rebellion—at bay. Wars that were disruptive elsewhere were understood as preservationist in Britain. When political economy came of age at midcentury, it saw security of the realm and expansion of colonial markets as sustainable returns for increasing burdens on taxpayers. Its mercantilist mainstream saw commercial and colonial resources—metal, specie—as the liquidity needed to acquire a military arsenal and favored policies enabling Britain to acquire more resources than its rivals. Adam Smith's complaints about the costs of war, about the "ruinous expedient" of perpetual funding and high public debt in peacetime, staked out a *contrarian* position; *The Wealth of Nations* (1776) was a work of persuasion. His and other voices in favor of pacific economic development grew louder from the margins. By denormalizing war, liberal political economy raised the stakes of the century's long final wars from 1793 to 1815, which could be stomached only as an exceptional, apocalyptic stage on the way to permanent peace.

In their wake, nineteenth-century Britons packaged their empire as a primarily civilian enterprise focused on liberty, forgetting the earlier collective investment in and profit from the wars that had produced it. Accounts of empire focused on everything but Britain's military might—the navy's admirable role in abolition, failures in the Crimean War. Amnesia about the early arms trade helped reinforce the idea that Britain was "always . . . a peaceful commercial community, only stretching farther afield to increase our trade interests and not solely for conquest and the subjugation of others." These words come from the pen of Charles Ffoulkes, early-twentieth-century curator of the Royal Armouries, who cited as "proof of our pacifist life" the fact that "we have never had great arsenals in this country for accumulating arms, for from the sixteenth century right up to our own times we have imported the larger part of our armour and weapons from Europe." There was "no mass production" in the eighteenth century; gun parts were "all made in local workshops—largely in Germany." He admitted the existence of gunsmiths in the Minories and Dublin but could not conceive of the mass scale of their workshop production. For him, change had come in 1812, with government "takeover" of the factory at Enfield in the face of strong opposition from the trade (in fact, Enfield was always a government factory). Ffoulkes's facts are all wrong but fit well with the myth of peaceable liberal empire. Aggressive war was reduced to an aberration in the history of a polite and commercial people with a charmingly incompetent military; today, even the niche genre of military history barely lets on about the violent expansionism that accompanied commercialization, industrialism, and urbanization. Such is the combined monumental weight of liberal political economy and the liberal myth of empire. And so we continue to celebrate private enterprise and individual genius as creators of the modern world. The popular Victorian author Samuel Smiles published the first "self-help" book, in 1859, and saw the giants of the industrial revolution as exemplars of that ethos: he wrote the first biography of Matthew Boulton, of Boulton & Watt steam engine fame, shortly after, in 1865. The myth of self-help has remained at the heart of our understanding of the industrial revolution.

To be sure, historians have acknowledged war's stimulation of particular industries or its spawning of critical inventions like copper sheathing of hulls. But these nods have not amounted to an *argument* about war's role in the industrial revolution. Such acknowledgments appear as exceptions that led to economic perversions like "excess capacity build-up." In the absence of clear data, scholars lean on theory: during war, "normal patterns" of investment in other industries and foreign sales were "probably" disrupted. War "diverted capital from what Smith considered its natural channel." Whatever war's costs and benefits, it is simply "impossible not to feel" that the final balance "was a negative one." Even if military expenditures caused "possibly significant" growth, war was a less than "optimal environment for development."

This hedging is the result of a collective misunderstanding of what the debate about war and the industrial revolution is about—the question is not whether war was good for the economy, but what role it may have had in economic transformation. If war-driven state procurement transformed the British economy, we might imagine other, more peaceable forms of state procurement producing similar effects. We also confuse "transformation" with "growth." Transformation is neutral. When we think in terms of "growth," we fear arriving at the indigestible conclusion that war is a "good" thing. John, writing in the aftermath of two cataclysmic world wars, was explicitly wary of such an interpretation. T. S. Ashton and John Nef established the peaceful narrative of industrial revolution as a rebuttal to the German sociologist Werner Sombart's 1913 argument that military demand drove capitalism; after World War Two, Sombart's anti-Semitism and support for Hitler raised the stakes for debunking the notion that war was good for the economy. Even those highlighting the way Victorian gun factories fostered industrial practices applied in bicycle and automobile manufacture stress that preparation for war, rather than war itself, was the stimulant. These principled efforts to avoid unseemly enthusiasm for war have distorted our understanding of the remarkable transformation that undoubtedly occurred in eighteenth-century Britain *while war raged*, producing a whitewashed image of a peaceable and innately enterprising industrial kingdom exemplified perfectly by industrial Quakers like Abraham Darby and Sampson Lloyd, whose commitment to "innocent" trades is supposed to have led them to establish businesses based on the "humble domestic market." In fact, both were very much bound up in the world of war supply.

War did not trigger every aspect of industrial revolution, but it was the context in which that revolution took shape. It is impossible to factor that violence out. The international order and the enmity of France and Spain were the "inescapable givens of power politics"; neutrality was no option. There is no counterfactual of a peaceful eighteenth century in which the British economy would have industrialized. The state would not have otherwise devoted public money to education and infrastructure development. The fiscal-military institutions that we refer to as "the state" existed entirely to provide the resources for war; building canals was outside their purview. It was the postwar decline of war industries with the peace of 1815 that finally inspired new kinds of government intervention: the Poor Employment Act of 1817 released funding for public-works schemes like canals, bridges, and roads. The new idea of state expenditure on such projects—of social welfare—emerged from the older sense of partnership between the state and war matériel suppliers. It was also wartime financial structures that enabled private individuals to invest in canals and railroads: war finance made the 1820 capital market substantial enough for entrepreneurs to issue and sell bonds to raise capital for such projects when war no longer needed it. War did not "crowd out" infrastructure development; it produced the financial structures that could fund it. We can't criticize the British government's failure to provide public goods in an era that produced the notion of what a "public good" is.

The line between state and society, public and private, was very blurry in this period. The enmeshment of public and private was what made institutional differentiation of the state as a state conceivable. Apart from taxation for war purposes, one of the earliest purposes of state offices was managing contracts for military supply (overseeing tendering, pricing, quality control). State offices gradually emerged through interaction with the business environment. During the long Napoleonic Wars, contracting and state offices exploded together. The central staff of the Office of Ordnance, the government department charged with small-arms procurement, doubled between 1797 and 1815 (to 227); the department's other offices in the country also grew (353 in 1797 versus 886 in 1815). War increasingly connected men (and, less directly, women) to state institutions, and they remained connected through pensions, invalid support, orphanages, and employment in naval and military installations. Meanwhile, businesses of the increasingly distinct private sector could thank the state for the patronage that had built them up over the century. With this institutional differentiation, the ideology of collective responsibility that war evoked among the state's servants and partners was displaced by new ideas about bureaucratic and industrial organization centered on individual responsibility. The same cultural shift prompted the Society of Friends's perception of Galton's personal accountability; his notions of collective investment had become outdated.

Such notions fueled the growing popular demands for greater separation of "public" and "private" interests and an acknowledgment of a realm of "the economy" with an integrity apart from the state, as liberal political economists were beginning to theorize. The hot mess of government, contractors, finance, and chartered companies became intolerable to the have-nots who demanded reform. Differentiation of public and private spheres would break down the alliance they perceived among elites across the spectrum of state, land, commerce, finance, and industry—which the radical midcentury politician John Wilkes and his followers likened to a gang of robbers plundering society. In 1771, as the British fleet mobilized against Spain in a dispute over the Falkland Islands, the celebrated man of letters Samuel Johnson unleashed a tirade:

If he that shared the danger shared the profit; if he that bled in battle grew rich by the victory, he might show his gains without envy. But at the conclusion of a ten years war how are we recompensed for the death of multitudes, and the expence of millions, but by contemplating the sudden glories of paymasters and agents, contractors and commissaries. . . . These are the men, who, without virtue, labour, or hazard, are growing rich as their country is impoverished; they rejoice when obstinacy or ambition adds another year to slaughter and devastation; and laugh from their desks at bravery and science, while they are adding figure to figure, and cipher to cipher, hoping for a new contract from a new armament and computing the profits of a siege or tempest.

In 1782, Clerke's Act prevented those concerned in contracts from sitting in Parliament. But then contracting exploded during the Napoleonic Wars, prompting the radical reformer William Cobbett's attack on "loan-jobbers, contractors and nabobs." He dubbed the monstrosity created by the entanglement of power, patronage, wealth, and corruption "the THING." Demands for reform were not about *recognizing* the boundaries between public and private sectors; they *produced* the idea of social and political functions divided rationally between distinct private and public sectors. Critiques of corruption aside, the contracting system efficiently laid the foundation of Britain's global power in the nineteenth century. Postwar infrastructure projects and bureaucratic reforms then redefined the role and contours of the state. Supply organizers were no longer amateurs from the business world, but professionals. The state's agenda was still set by propertied society, but its institutions increasingly had their own agency.

In short, this is a story about state making as much as industrial revolution. We cannot attempt to measure the costs and gains of state policy in the eighteenth century as if an alternative set of policies, oriented toward public infrastructure, were available; we do not have data for persuasive use of national accounting methods or counterfactual studies. War was the framework in which eighteenth-century British economic and governmental transformation occurred. Potential for industrialization existed across a wider area of northwestern Europe, but everywhere else, war was not the thing abroad that stimulated industrial resourcefulness at home but a proximate and destructive political struggle. It even slowed diffusion of industrial practice from Britain to the Continent. This story helps us grasp the role imperial warfare played in Britain's industrialization and reflect on what that says about industrial life generally. If we take war as the default context that it was in the eighteenth century, we can begin to assess the way it shaped Britain's economy without abstracting universal truths about the relationship between war and economy across time. Instead, we will discover a particular truth about the way war—and government—shaped the very invention of industrialism. This is no exemplary case to consult in the design of development elsewhere or to use to predict developmental outcomes in other nations at other times. It offers insight into the intellectual history of economics, the expansion of empire, and the place of mechanized violence in modern life.

Given the difficulty of separating the impact of war from that of contemporaneous events, we might accept war as continuous with—rather than a "stochastic perturbation" in—other transformations. The concept of an autonomous sphere of economic relations was a product of this period of war-driven economic transformation when political economists came to disapprove of war; they willfully took the "political" out of political economy. We might now put it back, especially since quantitative assessment of the state's role in the industrial revolution is both methodologically impossible and inappropriate. Guns are a place to start, as one piece in a larger story of militarization—a shift from ad hoc momentary mobilizations of community to permanent and costly impositions on community.

The English gun industry radically changed when it adopted American machine-manufacturing techniques in the 1850s. But it also underwent revolution in the eighteenth century, well before machine manufacture. When machines transformed gunmaking in the 1850s, it was for the sake of increasing not *quantity* but *quality* of output, because interchangeability had acquired its own cachet. Workshop manufacturers were already able to make guns in mass quantities on a scale unimaginable at the start of the eighteenth century.

We typically associate industrial revolution with technological innovation and the replacement of human labor by machine. But this was not the only form it took. It also entailed expansion within existing industrial techniques and know-how. There were many ways to increase efficiency, profitability, and labor discipline, including development of intermediate and hand techniques and wider use of and division of cheap labor. Even factory organization did not always mean physical concentration of machines around a centralized power source, as exemplified by textile mills. Often it meant centralized and hierarchical management and labor discipline—unrelated to machinery. Scale varied, too. The metals world encompassed large-scale works like Ambrose Crowley's nail factory and Boulton's Soho Foundry *and* the extensively divided putting-out framework (by which manufacturing work was "put out" to subcontractors working in their own homes or workshops). Innovative small-scale production was simply more efficient for some purposes, like accommodating frequent change in design and product and preserving trade knowledge. The things people wanted were not always amenable to flow line processes of mass production; flexibility was often more important than economies of scale. Large and small organizations were interdependent, and innovation came to both. Organizational change spilled beyond the factory, transforming workshop production. In the gun trade, large- and medium-scale firms deployed internal contracting and subcontracting to tap the creativity and flexibility of small-scale producers and serve localized tastes. Industrial organization was the site of revolutionary change in the iron sector before 1775; Adam Smith considered the division of labor enabling ten individuals in a Birmingham pin factory to make thousands of pins a day to be the mark of modern production. The majority of the workforce did not have to move into factories for revolutionary change in social relations and the nature of work to occur. It was an uneven process that unfolded over the entire eighteenth century. Handicraft and mechanized production processes coexisted within a single industry for decades; we can't demarcate modern and premodern industries. Particular processes rather than entire industries were transformed. Karl Marx knew that the machine came from the workshop; the steam engine was produced piecemeal in Soho and in John Wilkinson's ironworks. The entanglement of large and small, old and new, is what makes short- or medium-term large rises in productivity the wrong measure of industrial revolution; it is why better data will not help.

So how did the old, hidebound gun trade—"semiskilled men with simple hand tools"—achieve such a leap in productivity over the course of the eighteenth century without machines? Is this evidence of an "astounding capacity for industrious enterprise"? A craft of "wonderful elasticity"? It is. But the state, crucially, stimulated those qualities. The intense division of labor that characterized gun manufacture was the result of government demand for mass quantities. And the state actively directed the trade's expansion and dramatic changes in industrial organization.

The Midlands were able to produce orders of magnitude more guns within the span of a century without major change in technology or design. Whatever we call it, this is a major historical development demanding explanation. The vocabulary of "industrial revolution" originates in a Whiggish habit of defining and contrasting abstract modes of production (e.g., industrial versus preindustrial); in the case of guns, the industrial and preindustrial eras were not dramatically different in anything but output and number of participants. But the effort to tinker with the mode of production, the notion that a particular mode of production was at stake, emerged in that span of time, and that, too, was a revolution of sorts—the objectification of the domain we call "economic." By contrasting industrial with preindustrial modes and invoking the transformative metaphor of "revolution," we obscure the gradual process by which a new age emerged out of its predecessor. Let us expand our definition of the term to encompass the incremental way in which historical change actually takes place, with people blundering into changing times with old baggage that finds new meanings and purposes. Galton was just such a blunderer when he became the subject of Quaker censure of his long-established business. In the half century since the foundation of the family firm, the use of guns as guarantors of property and facilitators of trade and conquest had set the stage for new, more objectionable uses in anonymous mass violence.

By then, my provincial gunmakers had evolved into elites rubbing shoulders with the wealthiest merchants and bankers of their time. The interests and culture of industrialists and of financial and commercial elites were intimately related, bound by marriage, social ties, and complementary interests in banks and bullion. Finance capital and industrial capital were coeval and related. The increasingly dulcet tones of Galton's gentlemanly life deafened the family to the cacophony of gunmaking in the alleys around their home in Steelhouse Lane; in the same manner, we have become amnesiac about the wars that made the British Empire *and* the world's first industrial capitalist economy. Insofar as Francis Galton's theories of eugenics emerged from his study of his own family history, it behooves us to understand that family well. We forget the place of war manufacturing in industrial capitalism like we forget the blood in our veins.

Part One

THE INDUSTRIAL LIFE of GUNS

1

The State and the Gun Industry, Part 1: 1688–1756

The story goes that firearms drove knights from the battlefield, heralding the rise of the modern state. This new state took the form of a continuous public power above the ruler and the ruled; authority was divorced from the personality of the ruler and took an institutional form. Meanwhile, the displaced knights nurtured an aristocratic disdain of firearms as cowardly and ungentlemanly.

This "military revolution" did not happen overnight. The emerging state needed private finances for loans; its war expenditures continually outran tax revenues. It borrowed from goldsmiths who assigned interest on royal debt to their own creditors—a precursor of the national debt. Military entrepreneurs provided the lower-level organization emerging states lacked, raising troops on contract and supporting them with state pay, plunder, and forced contributions. The corporate overseas chartered trading company was a better-financed variant of this system. Such companies—the East India Company, the South Sea Company, and so on—supplanted goldsmiths and moneylenders, marking the corporate embodiment of financial interest. Their shareholders were politically powerful merchants; the companies were granted monopoly trading privileges by royal charter.

States gradually exerted greater control over entrepreneurs, including chartered companies, but in England this transition was stormy and pro-tracted. In the Glorious Revolution of 1689, the landed orders quashed the Stuart king James II's movement toward an autonomous, absolutist cen-tralized state staffed by bureaucrats. A new constitutional monarchy un-der William and Mary partnered with wealth holders, including chartered companies, the new Bank of England, financiers, and contractors. The Bank of England and trading companies now assumed a managerial role akin to fiscal departments of government. For instance, in 1711, naval debts were transferred to South Sea Company stock, and the navy's pri-mary nail contractor, Ambrose Crowley, who had stopped delivering goods for lack of payment, was awarded enough stock to merit a director-ship in the company. Such figures were both inside and outside the state; there was no distinction between public and private. This "corporate state" was an organic collection of interactive institutions, communities, and so-cial networks (including the Crown) with varying degrees of autonomy. Getting from this eighteenth-century agglomeration to the Victorian im-perial state, in which the distinction between public and private, state and market, was naturalized, was a gradual process. The South Sea Company eventually ceased trading and functioned as a branch of the exchequer. Such companies became integrated with the state's administrative ma-chinery, but it took time.

Meanwhile, public and private power were also indistinguishable at the local level. Great landowners and merchant oligarchs were members of Parliament (MPs) but also held wide and unsupervised judicial and administrative powers, hogging powerful unpaid local offices: lord lieu-tenant, sheriff, justice of the peace, an array of committees dealing with increasingly pressing and complex local needs. They commanded the mi-litia. The voluntarism of local "respectable gentlemen" makes it impossible to discern where the state ended and a private sphere began. Unpaid posi-tions layered the status of state power over their holders' local social status. They could secure compliance with the threat of legitimate force, even though they did not always see themselves as preeminently agents of the state and even though their power did not derive solely from their office. Acts of state were cultural and social, rather than fully institutional acts.

Many eighteenth-century British government functions were outsourced or embedded in the social fabric.

This meant that contracting was not a relationship between distinct public and private "sectors." The affairs of gun contractors, the Ordnance Office, and the chartered companies were inextricable. The state cultivated the British gun trade against this backdrop in a time of dynastic insecurity. It feared that a single, concentrated set of domestic gunmakers might be seduced or coerced into throwing its weight, and weapons, behind those who would undo the settlement of 1689—rebels known as Jacobites. And so it worked to multiply the number of domestic producers and to reduce the political leverage of individual gunmakers—not as an explicit grand plan but as a guiding principle in ad hoc decisions. The effort to diffuse arms-making skill was about preventing arms from falling into rebel hands. The resulting competition among gunmakers meant security for the state but low profits for them. The object was not a military-industrial complex, but a steadily expanding military-industrial society. To encourage competition, the state also supported the trade's sales to chartered companies and other customers, particularly those involved in the slave trade. By the 1750s, gunmakers were dependent on the state, though the state had reduced its dependence on any one of them.

B esides procurement of small arms for regiments, the Office of Ordnance was also responsible for artillery, engineers, gunpowder, artillery horses, and transport of these goods. The office was influential with the army; most of its members sat in Parliament. It was headed by a master general, typically a high-ranking military figure. He was one of the few state officers empowered to spend money on unforeseen services for which funds had not already been appropriated by Parliament. The master general commissioned his own officers—those commissions could not be bought or sold. He attended the Privy Council and was principal military adviser to the Crown. The office was simultaneously run by a board consisting of five well-paid principal officers: the lieutenant general, surveyor general, clerk of the ordnance, keeper of stores, and clerk of the deliveries.

The surveyor general oversaw ordering, inspection, proofs, and the engineers. He was treasurer and secretary to the master general. The office's rising stature is reflected in its growth. In 1660, it possessed only nine clerks; in 1703, it had seventeen permanent and twenty-one extraordinary clerks. Its storekeepers, artificers, and laborers increased rapidly, as did salaries. Its staff included dozens in its establishments at the eight outports and ten garrisons, including Jamaica, Barbados, and New York. (A separate board in Dublin handled arms procurement for the Irish colony—another of the partner institutions that made up the corporate state.)

The Ordnance Office contracted for small arms from about two hundred London gunsmiths belonging to a company chartered by the state in 1637: the Worshipful Company of Gunmakers. Its smiths worked in the vicinity of the Tower of London, the national arsenal housing the office. The office's master gunmaker was a member of this company, which described itself as a "body politique." Like other chartered companies, it was a corporate entity related to the state; many of its members were both contractors *and* paid servants of the Ordnance Office, some serving as armorers on naval ships and at Ordnance establishments abroad. The gunmakers determined details of manufacture in wide limits; their muskets were of similar caliber, stood proof (a test of the barrel's soundness), and met a minimum standard of inspection. Typically, a regimental colonel contracted with the office for muskets, returning them afterward. But colonels also might purchase arms at their own discretion on whatever design they preferred (and pocket the savings from the government allotment). The Worshipful Company also served other partners in the corporate state—the monopoly trading companies. That rival custom at times strained its relations with the Ordnance Office, but the office was also bound to encourage it for the sustenance it provided gunsmiths when government demand for arms was low. This was understood from the start as part of the Worshipful Company's purpose and survival plan.

The English began selling guns to Native Americans in the 1620s. The Hudson's Bay Company, founded in 1670, traded them for beaver pelts. From 1675 to 1775, it bought an average of 480 good, proved fusils annually—at times as many as a thousand, plus some pistols—besides guns for factory personnel and ship crews. By the turn of the eighteenth century, the trade was profitable enough for the colony of New York to skim revenue from it with a tariff of six shillings per gun barrel shipped up the Hudson. Competition from independent traders kept prices affordable. Many of the same sorts were made for the East India Company from 1664; London gunsmiths provided guns for it to trade, arm its servants, and present as gifts in Asia. They also supplied merchants trading to Africa, especially after the foundation of the Royal African Company in 1672. Anxiety that such guns might be used against Europeans yielded to fear that abstaining would only enrich rival European sellers. Between 1673 and 1704, the African Company shipped about 66,000 firearms to the Gold and Slave Coasts, Senegambia, Sierra Leone, Ivory Coast, and Angola in exchange for gold, slaves, and ivory. As the season for the African trade ended in the spring, the season for North American orders began.

The British state supported this trade partly because besting European rivals in commerce was essential to mercantilist foreign policy. In 1684, the London artisans protested against the African Company's purchase of cheaper Dutch guns, and the Ordnance Office upheld their complaint. By degrees, the company weaned itself from Dutch goods, purchasing knives and swords in Birmingham instead, starting in 1690. It bought thousands of firearms from John Sibley, a London gunsmith and established supplier of both the Ordnance Office and the Hudson's Bay Company. In North America, Dutch guns became less popular when many were found to be defective in 1684. British workmanship came to be preferred.

The Ordnance Office's own purchases of Dutch guns also began to rankle British gunmakers after the 1689 revolution. In that moment of instability, control of arms supply was crucial. The state turned to Birmingham at the same time that the Royal African Company did. Birmingham had been a center of metalworking since the fourteenth century. In the sixteenth century, its workers had supplied bridle bits, and horseshoes for the army of Henry VIII and nails for Hampton Court and Nonesuch Palace, in Surrey. It had gunmakers, too, known to repair the London-made arms of county squires. More notoriously, in 1643, during the English Civil War, they had supplied guns to the Parliamentarian armies. Royalists had destroyed a mill on the River Rea that turned out swords for Parliamentary forces. Birmingham gunmakers were named in Ordnance records of the late 1670s, but the affair of 1643, having demonstrated the pivotal power of arms makers in a moment of crisis, haunted the new monarchy as William III struggled to defend his claim against the French-backed former Stuart king in the Nine Years' War (1688–97). This was a major conflict between Louis XIV of France and a coalition of the Holy Roman Empire, the Dutch Republic, Spain, Savoy, and Britain. They clashed at sea, in North America (where it was known as "King William's War"), and in Europe, including a contest between William III and James II in Ireland and Scotland.

On his accession, William called a parliament that included Sir Richard Newdigate of Warwickshire County, in the West Midlands. When the king voiced his concern about the kingdom's reliance on Dutch arms, Newdigate volunteered that the men of his constituency could make good guns more affordably, his confidence probably stemming from prior experience—he had had a large armory that had been seized by the Stuarts in 1683. For a staunch Whig like Newdigate, the Glorious Revolution promised to fulfill his party's vision of a state that would protect and encourage English manufacturing as the source of national wealth and prosperity. According to tradition, he boasted, "The men of Birmingham can do whatever skill and metal can do." The king was intrigued and deputed him to ask Birmingham's sword makers whether they could manufacture guns on the Dutch pattern—that was the real question. The Birmingham smiths successfully copied the pattern the government sent. Local legend patriotically hangs the story on the Dutch issue, but cultivating an alternative to the Worshipful Company was also a motivation. That company immediately protested this monarchical violation of its monopoly. Parliament ordered the Ordnance Board to "compose the Matter," but the London contractors remained embattled. In 1691, they met at the Tower to strategize to more "effectually move for the money due to them." The Ordnance Office persisted in its exploration. In March 1692, a trial order was given to Birmingham smiths, and in 1693 a further order to five manufacturers who invoked an instant corporate identity as "The Company of

Gunmakers in Birmingham." They were to make two hundred "snaphance musquets" a month for a year, at seventeen shillings each, plus an allowance for carriage to London. Newdigate extended his personal credit lines to the gunmakers until government payment came through. The "great re-arming of the 1690s," when flintlock muskets with socked bayonets replaced pikes and older matchlocks, depended on exploitation of Birmingham's skills. By the end of the war, in 1697, gun production was well established in the town and its neighboring villages (Harborne, Bilston, Darlaston, Wednesbury). The Worshipful Company petitioned Parliament to strengthen its charter but also found evidence of Birmingham's potential usefulness: in 1700, when local smiths failed on an order for thirty thousand Barbary locks (the part containing the mechanism for igniting the charge), London gunsmiths had them made in Birmingham.

The state continued to carefully tame the London gunmakers' company as the next war, the War of the Spanish Succession (1701–14), began. In this conflict, Louis XIV's grandson vied with the younger son of the Holy Roman Emperor Leopold I for the Spanish throne. Austria and France launched into battle in the spring of 1701. In the fall, the old Stuart king James II died, and Louis recognized his son as "James III," goading the British into war. With France threatening to advance its interests in the Spanish Netherlands, including exclusive rights to the slave trade to New Spain, Britain and the Dutch declared war. This war also extended to the American colonies. The Ordnance Office was beset by orders for firearms. All regiments wanted the latest muskets. Virginia's arms were destroyed by fire, but the governor there refused replacement with old matchlocks. Governors in the Leeward Islands and Jamaica made similar demands. It was probably in 1702, in the midst of this rising demand, that Samuel Galton Jr.'s grandfather, the Quaker ironmonger Joseph Farmer, arrived in Birmingham from the port city of Bristol to participate in the booming gun trade there. London gunsmiths petitioned for contracts, and surviving Ordnance Office records attest to the frequency with which they supplied a range of arms. These were usually group contracts for a specified number of complete arms—muskets, carbines, pistols, and musketoons, typically dozens of each. For instance, in April 1705, the office issued warrants to fifteen gunsmiths for 851 muskets, 160 carbines, 447 pistols, and 75 musketoons. An order for roughly 2,700 muskets went out three weeks later to a longer list of twenty-eight gunsmiths.

But these suppliers were not expeditious enough. Even though the kingdom was at war with the Dutch, the Ordnance Office bought thousands of Dutch guns. In 1707, London gunsmiths complained that the office had done this despite owing them some £30,000. Worse, it had shared trade secrets about manufacture and proofing with the Dutch. Its employment of unskilled workers to repair guns added insult to injury. In a parliamentary hearing, the office explained that the London smiths had charged £11,000 for guns they could get in Holland for £8,000. Moreover, when they had been asked to make guns for Ireland, no one had offered anywhere near the Dutch price of twenty shillings per gun. They had failed even to fulfill orders they had and simply could not turn out the number needed at the right price. The gunsmiths retorted that they might have, given sufficient cash; to make guns as quickly and cheaply as the Dutch, they had to be paid—at least interest, if not the principal—so that they in turn could pay their men and obtain locks. They also blamed slow inspection and proofing. Military witnesses established that English guns were not inferior to Dutch ones. The parliamentary committee resolved to address the queen—Anne had succeeded to the throne in 1702—and ensure that future orders be given to English manufacturers. The law required that troops be equipped from England "as far as is consistent with the service." The hearing forced the government to clarify its obligation to support domestic manufacturers and to turn to foreign sources only as a last resort.

It also revealed the gunsmiths' regard for their other customers. They held up as a model the "Encouragement, as the Merchants give." They also approvingly cited customers like the king of Portugal, an ally for whom they had made forty thousand arms the previous year with the Ordnance Office's permission. An official noted bitterly that the "chief" gunmakers would "rather work for the merchants than the Queen," so the bulk of the arms made for the government came from "younger masters . . . some not yet finished." By charter, they were obliged to apply themselves to the government's service when required. The gunmakers pointed defensively to the merchants' more forgiving standards (and cash resources): the queen's arms were "much better than those made for Portugal or for the merchants." Moreover, however congenial, this alternative custom was not sufficient: while the government ordered guns in Holland, "the Company stood still, and had nothing to do." Humphrey Pickfatt Jr., master of the company, submitted a memorial from the trade requesting greater employment. But they wanted government work on the right terms. When the Ordnance Board suggested Pickfatt breech barrels, he refused, as "there was nothing to be got by them."

The gunmakers' need for cash, particularly for locks, reveals that they were tapping gunmaking skill outside the company to complete their contracts—probably buying locks in Birmingham. The British government was on a stronger footing in 1707, after the Act of Union merged the Scottish and English monarchies and parliaments. It was then that it began to directly source parts in Birmingham, laying the foundation for what became known as the "Ordnance system of manufacture," which permanently undermined the power of the London gunmakers' company. The Ordnance Office broke down gun manufacture into a few major processes, contracting for those rather than for minute parts or the whole finished product. The processes were rough stocking (carving the rough walnut stocks for the guns), engraving and hardening locks, filing barrels, making off (giving the final sandpapering and polish to the stocks), setting up (fitting the barrel, lock, and other parts into the stocks), repairs, and providing major parts—barrels, locks, bayonets, flints, rammers, brass furniture bought by weight (butt plate, trigger guard, rammer pipes, side plate, escutcheon)—and smaller iron parts, or "oddwork" (trigger, screws, loops, sights). With stores of parts, the office strove to prevent breakdowns in production stemming from bottlenecks like a lack of locks; this was not about making guns cheaper or ending foreign imports. Some processes, like stocking, remained London specialties, but the strategy as a whole depended on Birmingham's production of parts. In November 1707, the Ordnance Office contracted with Birmingham's Jacob Austin for two thousand locks to be made to the same standard and at the same price as those ordered from one Moore earlier. A contract with John Green of Solihull, a village outside Birmingham, called for four hundred locks over two years. Joseph Farmer first appears in Ordnance Office papers as a "Gunmaker of Bermingham" contracting for two hundred carbine barrels at the start of 1708, at the same price as an older supplier, John Titten (probably John Tittensor of London). He appeared again in March among a dozen Birmingham gunmakers supplying three hundred barrels and sixty finished muskets. He would remain on the books as a supplier until 1710, and again in 1715 and 1718.

Meanwhile, Birmingham's gunmakers had also joined the trade in guns for North America and Africa, and the London smiths tried to hit them there. In February 1708, a group of Birmingham gunmakers and lockmakers, speaking on behalf of "many Hundreds of Workmen of the said Trades in and about the said Town, and Towns adjacent," complained to Parliament that the London gunsmiths used their monopoly of proof to "put such Hardships upon the Petitioners, and so beat down their Prices, and totally obstruct their Trade to the Plantations, that they (besides their Dependents) being about 400, must remove into some other Nation, unless relieved therein"—implying that their gunmaking skills would then bene-fit another kingdom. Moreover, the Worshipful Company's charter was based on fundamentally "false Suggestions" that London's smiths "made better Guns, and enough to supply all Exigences [sic] of the Government," when, as previous and current wars showed, they could make great quanti-ties in Birmingham, too. They begged relief from these "Discouragements and Hardships." The London company retaliated with its own petition. But diffusion of the trade had deprived both groups of power—no matter how much they bickered or threatened to move elsewhere.

Within weeks of this dispute, the Royal Navy thwarted an invasion of Scotland by the Stuart Pretender (James III), from Dunkirk—a timely reminder of the stakes in keeping the gun trade diffuse. Two days later, Birmingham's gunmakers, cutlers, and other wrought-iron workers peti-tioned Parliament to keep the Africa trade open, as their goods were de-manded in "greater Quantities, than was ever known before." They and the London gunsmiths kept up a steady refrain about the trade's provision of "Employment for great Numbers of poor Families." The Ordnance Office continued to welcome new suppliers. In 1711, London gunsmiths again complained about foreign gun purchases, reminding Parliament of the promises made in 1707, when they had laid out considerable funds to better serve the government. Many could not get bread for their families; others had gone "into foreign Parts for Work, where they meet with better Encouragement." The manufacture was "in danger to be lost, which may be of dangerous Consequence to this Nation," they warned. The friendly potentates they had once served—"the *Muscovites, Swedes, Portuguese, &c.*"—now got their arms from the Dutch, "believing *Great-Britain* can't furnish them, when that Kingdom buy themselves of the *Dutch;* so that in a little time, the Nursery will be spoil'd, and the Art lost, in *Great-Britain.*" But the Ordnance Office had already cultivated a rival nursery. Birmingham smiths were making sporting guns, too, after 1714.

That year, George I acceded to the throne. The war had ended, but the Ordnance Office was determined not to be caught unprepared again—this lesson was applied with deepening commitment after each war of the century. The office calculated that it would take a year to have ten thousand guns ready and contracted for enough to have forty thousand left over in store. Among the profusion of orders was one for two hundred locks and barrels from Farmer, on the same terms as his previous two contracts. London smiths received the new kinds of contracts—to stock and set up barrels with parts supplied by the office.

Meanwhile, the king ordered a search for arms in the Scottish Highlands and assessed the loyalty of his gunmakers. Weeks before rebellion erupted in Scotland and northern England in 1715, the government discovered that London gunsmiths were making 15,500 guns: "the most part are for the South Sea Comp^y & sev^l Merchants, *and about 4000 for Service not Known,* wch they pretend they have given the Government an Acc^t of." On the king's orders, the Ordnance Office asked the Worshipful Company of Gunmakers to detail what arms they were making, for whom, and for what places—and a list of those who dared oppose this command. As this audit proceeded, the Pretender plotted with the Earl of Mar. The earl's troops overran the Highlands, heading into northern England in

September. The government relied on a small force led by the Duke of
Argyll and preemptive arrests in Wales, Devon, and Cornwall while it
built up an army (including six thousand Dutch troops). In Lancashire,
the rebels met a militia armed with pitchforks, and Ordnance Office
records confirm the inadequacy of the arms supply. A clerk went to "hasten the Gunsmiths to bring in the Armes according to Contracts." The
Worshipful Company's wardens explained that they were having difficulty obtaining barrels and asked whether the government could provide
them. The Ordnance Board agreed. Next, the gunsmiths requested
locks. From this point, they time and again requested parts from the
government to complete their contracts, abetting the expansion of parts-
sourcing directly by the government—and establishment of the Ordnance system of manufacture.

Most parts came from Birmingham, but some were manufactured in
the Tower, where firearms had not been made since the sixteenth century.
In 1714, there were eight gunsmiths and one stockmaker in the Tower
employed in assembly and repair work under the Ordnance Office's master furbisher, the gunsmith responsible for viewing arms, producing pattern muskets, and supervising repairs. With the 1715 request from the
London company, the Small Gun Office at the Tower began to employ
gunsmiths to make parts. Three years later, when London gunmakers
complained of "hardships from not being employed by this office as formerly" because of the new Tower manufactory, the board would remind
them that they had not been "shut out from serving the Government as
they alledge but that the Manufacture (as they call it) sett up in the Tower
was occasioned from them not being able to carry on the service unless
furnished with Barrells & Locks by this Board."

Meanwhile, the rebellion overtook these efforts. In November, the
Jacobites moved south into Lancashire. The enormous force raised to defeat them depleted stores. Gunmakers had such "Extraordinary demands
upon them for Armes for the Militia" that they were unable to attend to
their contracts. The Ordnance Office proposed "to get Armes Elsewhere"—the Low Countries again, one surmises. Ultimately, the arrival
of the ill and melancholic Pretender from France in December met with

anemic reception. He thought better of his initial plan to burn villages to hinder Argyll's advance and beat a swift retreat to the coast, fleeing to France on February 4, 1716.

With the situation in hand by April, arms procurement fell into abeyance. But it was clear that London tradesmen had become primarily stockers and setters-up; locks and barrels came from elsewhere. A Minories gunsmith told a regimental agent searching for new matchlocks that there were not a hundred barrels fit for the army in London; all came from Birmingham. This new reality stoked simmering resentments. In 1717, Joseph Farmer was in London and hoped to secure the Worshipful Company's support of his campaign to encourage iron manufacturing in America—which might lower costs for the trade. But he was rebuffed. When he showed his petition to the company's ruling body, the Court of Assistants, they rebuked him for presuming to petition Parliament in their name. As he waited outside, they decided that since the petition had been drawn up without their permission and its contents did not concern the company, they would not sign.

The decision was born of jealousy and bitterness, but also the reality that ironwork had mostly left the company. Among parts contractors, barrel makers and lockmakers were primarily in Birmingham; furniture makers and small-work men were in Birmingham and London. Some London gunsmiths had found more secure jobs in the Tower, where those "who have behaved themselves well" served as daymen earning two shillings and sixpence a day, plus an allowance to the most qualified twenty for the twenty-one holy days. Assistant viewers were appointed from among the eldest and best of them.

The British state was guiding development of the gun industry. The War of the Spanish Succession yielded a broadened set of partnerships for small-arms supply: the Worshipful Company, the Birmingham "company," and the Tower manufactory. The new system narrowed the pool of London contractors from two hundred to fewer than ninety gunsmiths, and fewer and fewer as the century progressed. But many more remained subcontractors or laborers in the processes of stocking, screwing together, and making off. In Birmingham, too, components were made by a multitude of subcontractors. The point of the new system was to reduce dependence on a particular set of gunsmiths so that if one refused work, another would take it. There were fewer individual contractors, but more individuals involved in contracting work. While these contractors negotiated orders independently, they often worked together in filling them.

The new system was inspired partly by the Hudson's Bay Company's procedures. This was merely the first shift in state management of the gun trade to draw on commercial example. It was partly about standardization; the desperate measures to obtain arms during the War of the Spanish Succession had yielded an excessively large number of mixed arms. The state's new arrangements allowed it to mediate the manufacture and assembly of parts to achieve a new objective of more standardized parts for more standardized weapons. The state could inspect and supervise guns at intermediate stages of manufacture. Finishing transpired under virtual direct control of Ordnance Office agents. Pattern guns and Ordnance personnel guided manufacture. In July 1716, Richard Wooldridge, a furbisher and viewer at the Small Gun Office, went to Birmingham to instruct workmen in how to fit locks to the mold. The office periodically sent representatives to view and gauge arms, deducting their expenses from contractors' debentures. Standardizing weapons expedited production and enabled the uniformity of drill practice that was emerging as a military standard. This was a critical step toward development of mass production. The parts may not have been interchangeable, but it was the state, standing at the center of the trade, that perceived the efficiencies that might result from contracting for more standardized parts. The process of gun manufacture was already highly divided; now the state divided the contracts, too, creating a sort of dispersed assembly line. The result was the first truly standard-pattern British infantry firearm: the long land service musket, or the "Brown Bess."

The Brown Bess's final design was the product of compromise between the Ordnance Office and gunmakers. In 1718, the Worshipful Company's wardens complained to the office that the trade "will be distroyed for want of being employed by the Government & y^t their Journey

Flintlock muzzle-loading military musket, 1760.

Men are taken from them to work in the Tower & therefore praying to serve his Maj^y wth Arms, as Cheap as can be Afforded." The Ordnance Office reminded them that they had been on open contract for three years and had "no other Excuse, than that they where [*sic*] fully employed otherwise during the Rebellion, & objecting that the prices were to [*sic*] small for the goodness of the work required." Upon learning that "none of the Chief Company did ever Sign" the open contract of March 1716, the office resolved to prove its willingness "to serve them as much as lay in their power, they would once more order other patterns to be made"—although Parliament would allow no more than twenty-two shillings a musket. The gunsmiths came in to choose new patterns. When they proposed land muskets at twenty-six shillings each, the office repeated that it could not pay such prices and asked whether they could omit any details to reduce them. The wardens specified features they considered mere niceties and agreed to make the best guns they could for twenty-four shillings.

In these guns, precision was sacrificed for the two-shilling margin. Comparing the compromise pattern with one of the twenty thousand Dutch muskets under production, the board judged it less embellished but more effective. Considering the "hardship" the Dutch purchase would cause, the board deemed it "unjustifiable." It agreed to exempt the new-pattern arms from examination against the office's jiggers, for more lenient inspection. It gave out warrants to those willing to fill them, "by which means the whole company may be employed (if they please) as long as their [*sic*] shall be anything to doe." They also complied with gunmakers' request for cash payment. The new muskets began to replace the existing motley mixture (though many of the latter remained in service through the 1740s).

The new Brown Bess was a heavy, large-caliber (.75) smoothbore flintlock musket that fired lead balls. It had a bayonet and, after 1724, a steel rod. It was about forty-six inches in the barrel, with an ornamental raised band at the breech. An artificial oxidation or acid pickling process colored the barrel brown. The furniture was changed from iron to brass in 1725. The barrel length was also later reduced (to forty-two inches in 1760 and thirty-nine in the 1770s), and the shape of the brass mountings and other details changed, but it remained more or less the standard weapon for a century. It was used by infantry and most of the cavalry and required a four-step reloading procedure after each discharge. A skilled infantryman might fire it three times a minute.

The negotiations of 1718 illuminate the government's determination to maintain the London company in decent employment and willingness to compromise on quality to preserve the trade and adopt a pattern more amenable to mass production. It acted out of a paternalistic sense of responsibility toward, and a diplomatic effort to avoid alienating, an industry essential to security. Later that year, when government orders dwindled because of budget constraints, the office parceled out an order for 3,500 muskets among gunmakers asking for work according to "their respective services performed in Times of Exigency—particularly during & since the late Rebellion." Even the paternalism was politically motivated: idle workers (like demobilized troops) were disturbing as potential criminals or followers of rebellion, and the state became increasingly conscious of a responsibility to do something for such victims of peace. Contracts purchased arms makers' loyalty and armed the state.

The new guns came in handy when war was declared against Spain again at the end of the year—the War of the Quadruple Alliance (1718–20). During this war, in 1719, the government again faced down rebellion in the Highlands, backed by Spain. Government forces prevailed at the Battle of Glenshiel, the last close engagement of British and foreign troops on the mainland. But the Ordnance Office remained wary of rebellion— rightly, given the strength of the rebellion that would come in 1745. For the gun industry, this wariness meant continued hope of contracts for a widening set of suppliers.

There would not be another major European war until 1739, but Britain was not at peace. It faced unrest within its colonies and remained at odds with France and Spain, often over those colonies. In India, coastal Maratha forts proved irresistible (yet impregnable) targets. In North America, Native Americans resisted colonial expansion with guerrilla tactics. British colonists suppressed slave rebellions. In Jamaica, the Maroons wrested control of the interior. These clashes produced a steady demand for arms and, perhaps more important for the trade, the perception of a permanent need for arms in an ever-expanding empire facing down insurgent indigenous peoples and European rivals.

The commercial gun trade also prospered. The Royal African Company was outpaced by independent traders and declined steadily until it required an annual subsidy in 1730 to keep up the forts and trading facilities on the African coast. These independent traders had received a boost from the 1713 Treaty of Utrecht, which ended the War of the Spanish Succession and granted the South Sea Company the asiento license to supply five thousand slaves annually to New Spain. By 1730, about 180,000 guns were being imported annually into the Gold and Slave Coasts.

London gunsmiths' assiduous efforts to defend their terrain provide an indication of the industry's dynamism. So many people were breaking into the trade that the Worshipful Company could not prosecute them fast enough. The stocker who illegally set up guns and the man who sold him barrels committed high crimes against "honest trading members," subverting the company's ability to control the quality of Ordnance arms and depriving it of revenue from proving them. The company reprimanded William Brazier for selling two pattern muskets to Joseph Farmer, a "foreigner," "to ye great prejudice of the trade," in 1721. But violations proliferated, evidently with little consequence: Farmer remained a trusted Ordnance Office supplier. Birmingham's emergence as a site of expertise increased the difficulty of recognizing who was legitimately practicing the trade; a suspected "foreigner" might claim an apprenticeship there. In 1735, the company began to keep a "Quarteridge Book" with the names of all those who followed the trade within the limits of the company's charter. It denied the right of the gun engraver Richard Sharp to make guns. It denied the right of those who had taken up the trade "by patrimony"—because their fathers had. The effect was alienating, diluting the company's influence further. In 1722, when Jacobite plots swirled around the unpopular government and the Ordnance Office accordingly audited the company, some insisted on giving their accounts directly to the office rather than submit them to the company wardens. The company remained defensively on the offensive. In 1736, in methodical searches of shops all across London, it seized guns proofed for "foreigners." When it learned that John Johnson daily sold foreign unproved and unserviceable guns, his Holborn shop was searched and the guns seized. Investigators found a Birmingham gun and French and Dutch guns. Johnson was also fined for having "molested and hindered" the company's officials in their search. Seizures continued through 1739. One company member, Stephen Foll, declared that he would go on proving guns for any and all who desired it and refused to pay the £30 fine, doing "great . . . evil to the company," which launched a suit. Gun manufacture boomed in quarters the company could not control. In the 1730s, the London gunmaker Richard Wilson supplied the Hudson's Bay Company, the African trade, and the East India Company. He sold to Charleston merchants and the Georgia Commons House of Assembly.

The trade was bursting at its seams, and this shaped how contracts worked. Just two London gunsmiths did all the government setting-up work for a decade from 1726: Lewis Barbar and Charles Pickfatt, who had taken over his father's Holborn business and was also a major supplier of the Hudson's Bay Company. This was not an outcome the Ordnance Office desired in principle; rather, Pickfatt was "the first and only one, who . . . would comply with the Board's proposals." But the work was not as concentrated as the set of two might suggest. Both drew on the expanding pools of gunmaking labor and subcontractors beyond the company's control. Pickfatt was repeatedly prosecuted for employing "foreigners" and outsourcing work to "foreign" workshops. Birmingham smiths provided parts—including Farmer, who supplied 4,400 barrels and 1,500 locks in 1728–29. In 1730, the office had eight parts contractors, supplying barrels (three), locks (five), brass work (three), small work (one), and bayonets (two). Government work was intertwined with manufacture for the "private" trade. Richard Wooldridge was master furbisher at the Ordnance Office, in charge of inspecting guns. At some point, definitely by 1726, the East India Company and the Royal African Company also hired him to inspect their guns. Government officials commonly enhanced their incomes by engaging in peripheral work related to their main occupation.

The outbreak of war further galvanized the industry. British smugglers in the Spanish West Indies and the loss of Gibraltar (ceded to the British in 1713) were festering thorns in Spain's side. Finally, in 1739, King Philip annulled the asiento license and confiscated British ships in Spanish harbors. Britain declared war. This "War of Jenkins' Ear" acquired a new proportion in 1740, when, on the pretext that a woman could not inherit the Habsburg crown, continental rulers contested Maria Theresa's claim to the throne after the death of her father, Emperor Charles VI. Britain was on Austria's side. The matrix of continental conflicts produced the epic War of the Austrian Succession, involving far-flung colonial and naval theaters through 1748. The Pretender was again a pawn in worldwide struggle for commercial and imperial primacy between France and Britain, civil war shaped by global conflict. The typical Ordnance Office setting-up order increased from 250 in 1737 to 400. In 1740, 10,000 muskets were ordered from Flanders; 20,000 more were ordered the next year.

In 1741, Joseph Farmer died, and his son James took over the business. Ordnance stores were exhausted; purchases outpaced the office's ability to pay artificers. By 1742, it needed £46,000 to pay the East India Company for saltpeter (a major constituent of gunpowder) and the contractors for great guns and small arms. The office anticipated a rise in prices unless the artificers were given at least £30,000. Still, in 1742–43, the office added five new setters-up. In 1745, it purchased Spanish muskets from a Bristol West India merchant. Ten thousand more were ordered from Liège. The office added three more setters-up in 1746–47, including Wilson, who supplied 3,700 muskets and 900 pairs of pistols from 1746 to 1749, and John Hirst, who at one point reported a staff of thirty-four. The government owed £34,000 for small arms at the end of 1747.

Apart from parts, James Farmer, Edward Jordan, and others also supplied more than fifteen thousand complete muskets. Jordan and Farmer partnered from July 1742 to June 1746 to make locks and complete arms. Farmer also provided wall pieces (a type of firearm halfway between a musket and a swivel gun, named for its common use along fortification walls). In 1746, his new brother-in-law, Samuel Galton of Bristol, became his partner. These particular orders for wall pieces and complete arms were merely the tip of an iceberg: at the end of the war, Farmer's leftovers alone stood at five thousand stocks, three thousand musket barrels and locks, and five hundred pairs of pistol barrels and locks, which the Ordnance Office agreed to take off his hands when they next required guns.

The war did not stop pursuit of the private trade. The Worshipful Company was furious to discover, in 1740, that 1,500 Birmingham guns awaited export in a warehouse in Essex, just beyond the limits of their charter and outside the open wharves in London where all goods had to be loaded for export. They contacted the customs office, warning that such arms "must necessarily endanger the lives of all those who use them and others." A customs officer on a ship at Gravesend seized the twenty chests, learning that the guns had been sold to the Royal African Company, which had shipped them without inspection or permission. The gunmakers' company discerned a plot to "monopolize into the hands of a few country smiths and others not duly educated or skilled in . . . gunmaking the whole trade from the port of London," while the London gunmakers "by a due regard to their proof have hitherto supported the credit of the English manufacture of guns in foreign parts." The East India, South Sea, and Hudson's Bay Companies would not buy any guns but those that it had proved, the Worshipful Company affirmed. Indeed, not a merchant in London in a hundred would buy such guns; all would want this practice suppressed to support the "goodness of the manufacture." These indignant protests aside, everyone was buying Birmingham guns. London smiths who supplied the Hudson's Bay and East India Companies relied on Birmingham parts. Alongside his government work, James Farmer was so busy filling "considerable demands" from Liverpool that he could not leave town in September 1742. He installed his brother Joseph (II) in Liverpool to secure orders and convey commercial intelligence. James was adamant that Joseph "leave no stone unturned nor no means unattempted that will promote the sale of guns." He agonized over his rival Thomas Hadley's boasts about *his* guns in Liverpool. John Hardman's *Willowby* and Edward Lowndes's slave ship sought Farmer's goods. In 1744, he secured an order for the Bristol slaver *Recovery*. He knew that as long as the firm dealt rightly with customs and had the guns shipped properly, it was unlikely to encounter difficulties in sending guns to Africa. The Worshipful Company hopelessly decried the "great quantities" of Birmingham guns being brought near London and exported, to the company's "great impoverishment loss and destruction." It formed a committee to stop this activity; among its seizures was a stash of unproved guns with forged company proofmarks in a warehouse at Botolph Wharf.

The Ordnance Office kept a watchful eye on gunmakers' independent activities out of its concern about arms possession. In 1744, it demanded quarterly accounts of firearms made in London and Birmingham and those who had purchased them over the previous two years. Worryingly, Birmingham's sword makers seemed to be executing orders for the army of the Stuart prince Charles (who would invade the next year): a large chest of Birmingham swords was seized in London, followed by twenty chests containing two thousand cutlasses. The French backed the Jacobite rebellion that came at the end of 1745. British forces withdrew from the Continent to fight at home. With the help of Dutch troops, they defeated the rebels in April 1746. Gunmakers were under pressure but also emboldened by their obvious importance: weeks later, barrel filers launched

Birmingham's second-ever trade action, determining to collectively "let their Masters and the Buyers of Gun Barrels know, that if their Prices are lower'd, the Barrels will be as much worse."

When peace came in 1748, the British restored Cape Breton Island to the French; the French restored Madras to them. But government gun work continued. Tower artificers and private contractors repaired arms for at least two years, well after the ink on the Treaty of Aix-la-Chapelle had dried. Replacement of rammers (used to push powder and ball down the barrel) went on even longer. This was no negligible task: repairing a gun required taking it to pieces, smoothing and polishing the brass work, taking out the names on the barrel, smoothing the barrel, fitting a new ramrod, nails, swivels, and so on where needed, and then reassembling and delivering it into store. Cleaning stocks was a separate task. Locks were repaired only by "regular bred gunlock makers." Even manufacture of *new* guns continued: thousands were set up by nine London gunsmiths from December 1748 to March 1749. This work was partly to use up parts in store (before the stocks rotted), partly to replace guns spoiled through rot, rust, or worms. Regiments also ordered particular guns and accoutrements. Through 1770, old Brown Besses were replaced with shorter versions.

The British state had adopted a more permanently belligerent posture; it shifted not from a wartime to a peacetime footing, but from a condition of formal to informal warfare. The midcentury wars militarized British society in a new way, and the state's continual military contracting was a key indicator of that transformation. In South Asia, the Second Carnatic War (1749–1754) picked up where the first one (1746–1748) had left off, pitting the British against the French by proxy. Escalating East India Company demand for guns may have prompted the Ordnance Office's reminder to its smiths not "on any pretence whatever" to do any work for another employer without permission. The office had its own demands: in July 1753, Maryland requested replacement of three hundred guns and accessories issued to men on a Canadian expedition who had kept their arms on disbandment. When Sir Danvers Osborne shipped out to take up his position as governor of New York, the king equipped him with a gift for the "nations of Indians in the British interest bordering upon the province": 380 guns of the "common sort" and 20 of the "best sort," made to a pattern with a long barrel and small bore "judged most proper." Bristling tensions with France generated demands from the Channel Islands of Jersey and Guernsey for 1,000 guns to be distributed among their inhabitants.

The office continued to expand its pool of suppliers. Thomas Nolson was assistant to a regular supplier, Thomas Hollier, and worked at the naval dockyards at Woolwich for thirty-five years. He determined to set up shop in London on his own, offering the Ordnance Office bayonets, ramrods, swords, mantelets, scabbards, springs, brass furniture, and so on. Fearing that Hollier had insinuated that he was merely a scabbard maker, he affirmed that "he would allow no cutler in England to be his superior in workmanship and . . . he could bring the most eminent masters, shopkeepers, and dealers in swords in town to prove the truth of his assertion, even Mr. Hollier himself," whom he had instructed in several areas of the trade. The office gamely asked Hollier to match Nolson's lower prices and asked Nolson to make a trial mantelet. William Sharp, son of the London engraver Richard Sharp, similarly offered the office "rough forged work or pieces of gun locks of sorts" at the same prices as their usual supplier. The gambit worked, and he would serve as a primary contractor for decades (before earning fame as a republican artist-engraver). When he offered brass tips for guns, the office rejected them for Jonathan Buttall's—lessening its dependence on Sharp.

Peacetime continuation of government work was a boon particularly because the private trade was not thriving. British trade to Africa had reached a nadir. The war might have been a factor, but it had been fought partly to protect Britain's position in the global slave trade, and in the early war years, at least, Farmer flourished in it. Farmer, for one, did not think war had caused the depression: he went to the Continent in 1748, presuming that trade from France was better, even though French trade had been disrupted to a greater degree by the war. There he cited accounts circulating from the African coast that "the English arms are bad." The Royal African Company's feckless tending of British forts was probably a factor, too. Farmer's travels gave him some hope: at Dunkirk, he found ships headed for the Gold Coast and Angola and expected to secure orders. But the Africa trade remained dismal in 1749. As his Angola muskets remained unsold at Nantes, he anxiously asked Galton for a clear account of stocks and "all the goods in the toy way." From Rouen, he urged Galton to "reduce everything in the manufacture . . . for our Africa business will never support them." His brother Joseph, in Liverpool, was even keener to abandon the Africa trade. Farmer continued to try to crack continental markets, asking Galton to dispose of their Barbary locks and barrels through Marseilles (the plague having prevented a previous ship from unloading at Smyrna or the Barbary Coast). He hoped they might also unload guns that the Liverpool slave trader Joseph Manesty had refused.

The British state acted to improve this "private" trade. Traders petitioned Parliament to attend to the dilapidated British forts, lest the nation lose more ground to the French. Farmer closely followed the fate of the bill to support expansion of the trade as it passed the House of Commons and was considered in the House of Lords in 1749, aware that it would affect the disposition of his guns. Parliament bailed out the African Company in exchange for control of its coastal properties, which were assigned to a newly chartered Company of Merchants Trading to Africa in 1750–52. The trade picked up enough to tempt gunmakers trading out of Bristol to raise prices (though not Farmer & Galton). In 1750, Farmer, too, described slightly brisker movement of goods for Africa: twenty elephant guns—all "proved and good"—and muskets for a captain; knives, harpoons, and lances on order for Manesty; guns, harpoons, and toys for Clay & Horne. He worked on "well executed" guns and locks for his father-in-law, Thomas Plumsted, presumably for the American market. But three months later, he and Galton shook their heads when Hadley hired more hands, wagering that the more he hired, "the less occasion he will have for them." They could not imagine he had many orders, as "we have none here nor no account of sales from France and no ship fitting out except one for Angola." Remittances were few and far between. "Times were never worse . . . in Liverpool," Joseph affirmed, "and which way to turn myself I know not."

James begged the Ordnance Office to mercifully take the guns he was left with from the war, since he could not use them and would suffer a "total loss" without such indulgence. He smartly reminded the office of his "care and study from the beginning of the late War and at the time of the late unnatural Rebellion to supply the Government . . . at great Emergency," applying his "time and Fortune" and neglecting all other concerns (he claimed) to accumulate this immense stock stored at great expense. He had laid out cash to train workmen to produce guns cheaply "before they could perfect themselves in it," and those now unemployed workmen could not repay him. (The very image of idle men was politically disturbing.) The office curtly regretted his loss but declared that it was too flush with guns to take on more. It was confident enough of Farmer's *relative* inconsequence as a gunsmith, and of the imminent recovery of the commercial trade, to refuse his savvy appeal. It had little to fear from a man who, even while begging for justice to his leftovers, deferentially plied it with new barrels, locks, and guns. (The office did take the half million flints he offered.)

The principle at stake in such decisions is clear in the handling of Pickfatt's similar request, likewise prefaced by a reminder of his twenty-four years of service and unique willingness to serve the Ordnance Office in the 1720s. He asked to clean guns in the Tower, to avoid discharging some of his "very good workmen," and would do it for "a small profit rather than be entirely out of business." The discharge of workmen was again concerning: such men might vanish into the woodwork when the government needed them again or, worse, join the shiftless minions of rebellion. But after serious consideration, the office refused, noting that it would cost £350 more than if the 114,235 arms were cleaned in-house. But the real deal-breaker was the surveyor general's mindfulness of the "extreme hazard the office runs by trusting to one man almost all the serviceable arms of England and the various methods that would be open to him to defeat and render ineffectuall any precautions the government might take against commotions rebellions etc." The concern was total dependence on a single keeper of arms in a time of frequent civil unrest. The office wanted a military-industrial society, not a cozy complex: too great a reliance on any one manufacturer would put too much power in one pair of hands. The office might even be induced into unnecessary purchases. The surveyor general condemned his staff's "most notorious neglect" in allowing Richard Waller to mistakenly stock hundreds of barrels of the wrong sort "during the late hurry of business before the conclusion of the war." Such proceedings dangerously gave "any favourite artificers as much work as they please though the office may have no occasion for their service for it is but to certify afterwards it was a mistake." When William Clarke filed off more barrels than he had warrants for, the surveyor general denounced such "irregularities" and "abuses." When acceding to a request allowed the office to keep regular contractors in business and get work done cheaply, it might comply. But having diffused the work sufficiently to diminish the risks associated with alienating a contractor, it did not have to, especially if doing so risked reconcentrating power over arms supplies.

Expansion of manufacturing within the Tower was part of the diffusion and another way the office supported the industry in peacetime. By 1750, the staff of piece men and daymen—occasionally reaching a hundred—filled a warren of workshops and houses in the Tower and on the Tower wharf. Here, too, political loyalty mattered; the armorer James Coggle successfully petitioned for a job on the grounds that he had borne arms for four months during the rebellion. As the calculations on Pickfatt's proposal show, the office balanced in-house gunsmiths' requests for work against those of contractors. In 1751, six piece men complained that they "oftentimes have no Work for three Weeks or a Month which much impoverishes them and their Familys." The clerks set about finding "necessary, usefull, and wanting" tasks. Together with new regulations established in 1745, the growing staff enabled more cost-effective maintenance of guns as stores also expanded: in 1746, 46,000 arms were in store; in 1747, 63,000; in 1748, 73,000; in 1749, nearly 97,000; and in 1750, 107,000. In the same period, expenses rose from £1,257 in 1746 to £1,570 in 1750. In 1751, 117,000 arms were in store, maintained at a cost of £1,264.

Requests like Farmer's and Pickfatt's find no echoes from 1751 to 1753, partly because the state's efforts to buttress the commercial trade began to take effect. By the end of 1750, Farmer could offer guns and swords to the newly reconstituted African Company, which received a generous government annuity. So, too, did John Brazier of London, among others, affirming that London's proved guns had "always supported the credit of that manufacture on the coast, as is notorious from the late African company till lately sending no others and the India and Hudson's Bay Companys still sending no others." Farmer received a contract to supply, in six weeks, 250 Danish guns slightly longer than his pattern, Tower barrel and proof; fifty walnut birding guns; fifty carbines; and fifty Dutch-pattern guns—the last three items to be London proof. He would also send thirteen buccaneer guns, twenty pairs of pistols, a hundred carved birding guns fuller in the butt than his pattern, and one mounted in silver for a gift, along with hundreds of cutlasses, knives, and fire steels. He knew many of the committee members as private traders and bought shares in the new company, too. He sold 4,000 guns to the company through 1756. Brazier signed a contract for 150 London-proof muskets, on Farmer's pattern but slightly longer, and sixty carbines slightly wider in bore than Farmer's pattern.

The state also supplied guns for the "private" trade—unserviceable or old military guns that gunmakers purchased at auctions and repaired. Less than two months after the Ordnance Office refused to take leftover military guns off Farmer's hands, he bought more than two thousand old and broken guns that the office was expensively storing, paying for them with new barrels and locks valued at wartime prices. They ranged from "Trading Guns with plain Beech Stocks round Locks & Brass Furniture" to "Spanish & French Musquets with Wallnuttree Stocks and Iron Furniture without Locks." Farmer advised Galton against excessive production partly because of this purchase, since old Tower guns "always command the trade and may be a means of procuring sale for others." A month later, he bought Ordnance bayonets "made for the trade" and a mix of unserviceable and repairable French muskets. More purchases followed. In 1754, Farmer bought Tower stores worth £1,000, including a thousand Dutch guns.

Most significant, the government shared its proofing facilities, to keep the trade healthy, in outright defiance of the Worshipful Company of Gunmakers. In March 1750, that company informed the African Company that many of the guns it had received were not London proofed. Outsiders had begun to make and sell unproved guns, to the discredit of the whole industry, courting "total loss" of the trade to the nation. In fact, unproved guns were not being made only by outsiders. In 1751, some company members complained to the Ordnance Office that they had tried since the war to "get a living in the Trading way" but had been "oppressed" by their company's extravagant proofing fees, which prevented them from making cheap arms unless they skipped the proof. As a result, the business had been "Engrossed by 3 or 4 leading Men of the Company," who omitted the proof "to their great detriment." The Ordnance Office gallantly permitted these lesser members of the company, including the loyal Hirst, to prove their guns at the King's Proof House. The prominent traders whose monopoly they now threatened testily reminded the Ordnance Board of the Worshipful Company's exclusive powers to view and prove nonmilitary guns made within its jurisdiction. The Tower's offer to prove guns for all comers would harm the company *and* the state, since the company could detect and punish abuses only in guns bearing its proofs and marks. They ominously reminded the board of their reliability in the country's frequent "dangerous times" and cheerful compliance with the obligation to provide accounts of gun manufacture, behaving "in all Respects as Loyal Subjects." With these chastening words, they called on the board to cease proving nonmilitary guns at the Tower. They presumed that the specter of disloyalty gave them some leverage, but the board had denied them precisely that leverage by opening up the trade ever more widely. Nurturing gunmakers shut out of the African trade was part of that logic; the neophytes vigorously warned the board against discontinuing its indulgence toward them, arguing that doing so would injure business in general, "most Gentlemen being desirous to have their Guns Tower Proof." The Ordnance Office resolved to continue proof at the Tower for "any Person . . . who asks it," willfully violating the company charter to secure its own end of supporting the wider gun industry. Meanwhile, the Worshipful Company of Gunmakers also lost the proving work it did for the East India Company, which shifted its proof to the Tower until 1778.

The Farmer & Galton firm's capital value had declined from £10,000 in 1746 to £8,670 in 1751, but these various state interventions enabled it to recover after 1751. A French buyer brought orders worth £150; Thomas Plumsted's nephew David Barclay ordered 150 muskets, 32 pairs of pistols, and 10 musquetoons—for the American or the African market. Galton sent guns to Liverpool merchants and to London for sale in Africa. They repaired Tower guns. Galton got wind of "several ships about to sail" from Bristol wanting hundreds of guns. Samuel asked his brother John Galton there to "procure large orders." A few months later, he sent hundreds of barrels and locks to Bristol and completed two orders from Lancaster, Angola muskets for others, and an order for Joseph Manesty. He fretted about making just the right number of barrels to avoid surplus, but the frenzy of activity endured through 1754. He sent thousands of guns for Africa to Farmer in London, at times 500 a fortnight. Thousands were readied for Manesty's *African* and the *Duke of Argyle,* captained by the future abolitionist John Newton, who purchased 207 slaves in 1752 with the guns' help. They won orders for his other ships: the *Allen,* the *Adlington,* and the *Byrne.* Many other orders poured in, "all unexpected and in a hurry," for slave ships and their captains.

State support had engineered a business recovery. Now, our protagonists became insecure about their prospects because the trade had become too attractive to too many. Galton begged Farmer to make him an equal partner, not to capitalize on success but to compensate for losses while trade remained "much reduced and likely to be more." He gloomily observed that his share in the firm produced half the profit it once had. Their rivals offered steep discounts for cash payment, pressuring them to do the same. The discounts ran Jordan out of the Liverpool trade. In time,

it would not be worth anyone's while to carry on the trade, Galton foresaw; but they had so much capital invested and dead stock that they had
no option but to press on. Not all their "many competitors" would continue, he anticipated, and then they might see better times. They determined to "pursue our own measures without any consultation with others
or even intention of joining them in advance." They were careful to run
the forges without increasing their stocks; Farmer urged Galton to "do
nothing to increase our stock but all that can be to diminish it." By 1754
they were making 25,000 to 30,000 Africa guns a year and finding it
difficult to meet orders. Galton agonized about the erosion of profit margins, "as many are pushed into the manufactory, the demand for guns
great just now." The discount problem persisted. They could not have
penned a grimmer assessment to their Liverpool agent: "our sales for the
2 last years have been more than heretofore and . . . the orders have been
generally with shorter notice which makes a manufactory far more troublesome and . . . we do it in more parts than any others." Galton almost
suffered a nervous breakdown. His "state of health wont admit of such
constant fatigue," warned his brother, recommending he "relax" for a year
and "drop the too eager pursuit of business." Galton bemoaned "how little
cause we have to push a trade" plagued by fraud and bad debt.

Why all this doom and gloom when business was brisk? Eighteenth-
century trade was bedeviled by risk—insecure sea routes, perpetual doubt
whether a cargo would reach its destination—and the Africa trade was
particularly unpredictable. Galton and Farmer bought shares in the *Alexander;* the ship was lost, and Galton berated his "want of resolution" in
joining that risky proposition. Gun orders involved additional uncertain-
ties. For months, Farmer and Galton remained unsure whether and from
which port (Lancaster or Liverpool) Manesty's *African* would sail—and
the chance for profit hung on that decision (competition was fierce in
Liverpool). Badly managed ships cut into profit margins. And guns were
perishable. That they became useless within a year in Africa was partly
what drove the insistent demand for them, but perishability was also a
major liability in a time of slow and risky commerce. Stoppage of their
guns in France and Lisbon in 1754 was doubly worrisome because of the

risk of rust. Guns awaiting shipment had to be protected from the air and finished well to "prevent . . . worms getting into them." This was also why overstocking was no option. Galton lamented that they could not, like their Manchester counterparts, "keep severally a stock on hand" in anticipation of the next order. Accelerated production offered no relief when they faced a rush of orders: expanding the manufactory to produce 1,500 guns a week would temporarily ease things, but "such demands we have no reason to expect will long subsist," calculated Galton. They would be left with a heavy, perishable stock. Ramping up production and providing impromptu training to new workmen during the war had produced losses; likewise, too vigorous an effort to cope with the boom in the African trade would leave them high and dry.

But more than any of these factors—perishability, risks at sea—the real difficulty in the commercial trade was long credit. Cash shortages were endemic in eighteenth-century business; credit was unavoidable. But in the gun trade, as Farmer lamented, "payments are so long its an article hardly worth following." Galton nagged his Liverpool agent John Parr to collect payments, lest the discount implicit in bills of very long date "destroys the profits." When "ready money" was scarce, Galton confessed he would "rather be without the orders," accepting them grudgingly only to avoid "disgusting" the merchants and losing orders in a future of plentiful cash. In 1752, the firm gave Captain James Birchall sixty guns worth more than £25 on credit to sell in Africa for "teeth wood or gold dust," which Birchall pledged to remit from the West Indies. Five years later, Farmer was still trying to get Birchall's man in Barbados to pay. Rot compounded credit: George Fryer, who managed the victualing contracts of a slave-trading firm in Jamaica, bought guns on credit to sell. When things went wrong, Farmer advanced him £550 more to fit out a vessel for Africa. Galton balked, arguing that Fryer's goods "after lying so long on the coast will be in very bad condition and perhaps some not to be found and guns having lain 4 years after being damaged by salt water will not sell on the coast or be worth bring [*sic*] home." Considering he had "but a small capital can call my own," he preferred not "to be too much embarrassed or run too great risques." But Farmer insisted on throwing more good money after Fryer's bad debt. When, inevitably, Fryer went bankrupt, Galton uselessly pro-tested his reluctant share in the misadventure. In 1754, they hoped for "handsome" compensation from Fryer's bankruptcy proceedings.

The price of parts also made profit elusive. When orders were plenti-ful, parts became scarce. Despite relations with three barrel makers, Farmer and Galton were fresh out of barrels in the spring of 1752 and resorted to pinching some from stores awaiting shipment in Bristol. In 1754, locks were selling at extortionate prices; Galton looked on with dread as competitors offered extravagant prices to lockmakers, who in turn cited rising charges for filing and forging. Galton calculated that the cost of locks would virtually wipe out profits on guns for Liverpool, given the 7 percent discount for cash. He, too, offered more for locks, prompting others to offer even more. He explained to his customers that he would gladly procure locks even at a loss if he could lay his hands on any at all. But this desperate plea met only with obstinate insistence that he fill the order anyway. Demand was high, but, Galton explained to Parr, high prices for parts and predatory discounting had obliterated the profit margin.

For Farmer & Galton, survival depended on quality. The dumping of bad guns in Africa is one of the most notorious dimensions of the slave trade, but for this particular firm, quality—or, at least, the semblance of quality—was a priority for commercial reasons, as Farmer's early concern with the poor reputation of English guns in Africa testifies. Galton was pleased to hear that Hadley used only common barrels for his birding guns for Africa. When forced, on one occasion, to ship shoddy "spliced" guns at short notice, he pledged to avoid that resort in the future so that they might always "excel in the quality of the . . . guns" they sold. They tried to pull out entirely from trade in "common" muskets. Galton re-minded Parr not to "divert us with other orders for common guns as the same finishers must do both and by undertaking too much we are sure to have them worse done as well as be liable to a breach of time and over fa-tigue in the execution." Moreover, the workers would not lower their prices to make a more inferior sort. It simply made better financial sense to sell militia or sea service guns "done in the plainest manner."

This was why the Tower-proof guns supplied by the government were so helpful. In 1754, Farmer agreed not to solicit new orders, out of consideration for Galton's stress, but commercial sense dictated the same strategy. Even their favored clients, Manesty and the Tarletons, specified safe, proved barrels. Galton found among guns he bought at government auction more than a thousand that after repair would be "equal or superior to our best ship stores sold at Liverpoole." They would make up for orders they had forfeited. Old military guns tided over the African supply, just as the African trade tided the industry over in peacetime.

On the whole, for Galton, the Africa trade was paradoxically one "wherein by the Sales of the greatest No^r of Guns on a Calculation farly [sic] stated we are loosers [sic]." Volume offered little advantage at a time when the trade possessed neither the technological nor the organizational potential for high-quality mass production. So the recovery of the "private" trade after 1751 does not help us gauge the trade's relative profitability in peace or war. Low profits were typical of both, structurally embedded in the industry by a government determined to diffuse it as much as possible. High demand from Africa made the trade so hazardous that Galton wished to decrease investment in it and "strike into something else." They launched an iron manufactory, but, predictably, he became exhausted by running two manufactories and saw hope only in the modest production of five hundred guns a week. As his health declined, the partners determined to draw "our affairs in to narrower compass." The firm decided to decrease its stake in the trade because the trade was too *active*.

But it was not to be: demand reached a feverish pitch that left Galton frantic. In September 1754, Farmer secured an order for 800 Bonny muskets from one slave trader. Another big order came from Richard Oswald, who had bought Bance Island, at the mouth of the Sierra Leone River, from Fryer and turned it into an international free port for trading goods (including people). John Peter Blaguier wanted 700 Angola muskets, "very neat, stout barrels proof marked." Galton's men had to complete these, another 1,400 guns for the *Castleton* and the *Duke* at Lancaster, and 450 for the *Swan* in Liverpool. Galton tried in vain to refuse the Lancaster order. He was "at a loss" for what to do first. Farmer insisted he do them all at once, adding an order for one Captain Pickit to his burdens. He had to come up with 6,000 guns within weeks and faced a bleak Christmas of endless gun manufacturing, with supplies as scarce as ever.

Within months, Galton's fear of catastrophe came true—but from an unexpected direction. In London, without consulting him, Farmer had mortgaged the gun firm to join the Lisbon trade. The curtain suddenly fell on that adventure, and a panicked and shocked Galton was forced to beg their agents in Liverpool and Lancaster to secure remittances to free Farmer and him from ruin. He pressed Farmer to extract payments in London, too. Pickit had gotten wind of Farmer's debacle and had to be mollified in person. What ultimately saved the firm from financial perdition was the conflict stirring abroad.

A fter the last war, the British government had given the Ohio Company title to 500,000 acres in the Ohio River Valley. The French challenged the British hold on the region, attacking their Native American allies. In 1752, French allies destroyed a British trading post. The French began to construct forts. Competition stretched north to the domain of the Hudson's Bay Company and east to the seaboard, but the Ohio River Valley remained the sorest point. When Major George Washington's diplomatic efforts to force a French departure failed in the winter of 1753–54, the two sides became locked in conflict. In the spring of 1754, the French forced the British garrison at Fort Prince George to surrender. Washington led a small force of Virginians to defeat an even smaller French Canadian detachment. Next, North Carolina's governor reported that Native peoples allied with the French had attacked Virginia's western settlements, killing several and destroying plantations. He asked the Ordnance Office for a thousand guns not of the pattern used by His Majesty's forces to expeditiously arm the 750 troops raised to "preserve the countrys upon the Ohio." The office sent three thousand of the Liège muskets bought in 1741. Within days, Washington surrendered at Fort Necessity; the French had overwhelmed him with a force almost twice the size of his own, and their Native American allies were raiding British settlements on the seaboard. A new war had begun—two years before it was formally declared, in May 1756.

That summer of 1754, the British had fewer than a thousand troops in North America. The government decided to send an expedition to dislodge the French. The Ordnance Office had been assessing and maintaining its stores in the Tower and magazines around the country. When Tower stores had declined from nearly 140,000 serviceable firearms in 1751 to 115,000 in 1753, in-house workers had set up guns to bring the figure back up and use up walnut stocks before the worms "Eat in so deep that they cannot be Worked out." To maintain them as arms were depleted for the expedition, contracts went out for thousands of arms, parts, and repairs. In February 1755, two thousand stand of arms were readied for the expeditionary force. Another two thousand were prepared for Massachusetts. The Ordnance Office took inventory of outposts and of guns sent to the East Indies, Ireland, the American colonies, "or elsewhere," including those paid for by the East India Company. Contractors set up muskets on a monthly basis at the 1750 price. Pickfatt and Hirst stood out from a "combination" of setters-up who refused that price. Hirst filed barrels for a penny *less* than he had before. Hefty contracts went out, drawing in new contractors, as new companies were raised.

In March 1755, as Farmer's finances crumbled, "Old Jordan" and his son left Birmingham for London in a hurry; Galton darkly assumed that they went to "get into our trade there." Clearly, Jordan knew something Galton did not. The next day, he and the Birmingham gunmaker Joseph Oughton went to the Ordnance Office, offering barrels. The office took two thousand. The looming war began to impinge on Farmer's distracted mind: "While there is any apprehension of a war," he wrote to Galton, "little will be done in the Angola trade." This does not seem to have troubled him. He and Galton exchanged letters frequently in these days, sometimes multiple times a day, and even Galton, never one to repress anxieties, expressed no distress about the possibility of war. Instead they dwelled on the troubles that Farmer's personal misfortunes had created. Soon Richard Heely of Birmingham petitioned the Ordnance Office to supply barrels and locks. In May, Jordan's clerk divulged Jordan's dealings with the Ordnance Office to Galton, who was then despairing of the firm's low credit and capital. He sent his brother in Bristol barrels and locks, begging news of any "prospect of sales." He was anxious that their stocks would rot into losses and Hadley would lure their workmen away. John Galton had no news of ships and feebly hoped his brother had a good share of the Liverpool business. The news from Bristol "staggers the merchants," Samuel reported to Farmer; "there's not one ship about to sail for the coast." He had some hope from the *Swallow* at Lancaster and feelers from France. They secured an order from the African Company, for the sorts they had on hand, fortunately. Galton still deplored orders for "Dutch guns" as the "worst . . . being scarce anything got by them."

War was a welcome disruption to this trying situation. Galton at last got in on that work in July, when we find him briskly sourcing cartouche boxes for the Ordnance Office. The drums of war grew audible after the punishing defeat of the British expeditionary force on the Monongahela River that month, and one of Galton's strategies in softening Farmer's formidable creditor James Johnson was the temptation of massive war profits: "If a war should be declared [*sic*] may expect a large demand for guns of a quite different sort than for the Africa trade and through another hands and perhaps the office of ordnance may give out some orders. Mr. Farmer the last war supplied them with very large contracts and is acquainted with all the clerks." Galton played on his contemporaries' assumption that government war contracts, rather than the peacetime private trade, paved the road to riches for gunmakers.

The desirable private orders Galton received were also tied to the brewing conflict. After a few orders from Bristol assured their creditors that the firm was on solid footing, the creditors and bankruptcy commission members began to purchase guns, too (a thousand for Barclay and more for Champion & Hayley). Initially, these were for the African market, but soon their purpose shifted. In October, Barclay and the Hanburys (customers and iron suppliers of the gun firm) purchased militia-style guns. Both of these Quaker merchants were involved in the slave trade but were also members of the North American Merchants of London, an

organization promoting trade with the colonies. Colonial militias defended their interests as much as the colonists'; the militia-style guns were
likely for the colonies. John Hanbury, a tobacco prince who controlled
200,000 acres in the Ohio River Valley, urged a tougher stance against the
French and advocated arming Native Americans. (He also held a contract
for American remittances from 1745 to 1764.) It is likely that Farmer &
Galton guns found their way to tribes fighting on the British side. Militia
guns became a priority for the firm. Galton was glad for an order for militia muskets for Montserrat, expecting "more orders of same kind which
are very profitable very considerably, if duly paid." The new quasi-military
deals opened doors to fresh commercial opportunities: through Hanbury's
good offices, Galton secured an order for the *Tarleton* at Liverpool. The
firm also delivered guns to leading Lancaster slave traders. Commercial
demand thrived *with* military demand. Galton took this work but expected little from it: while other Birmingham gunsmiths agreed to dis-
allow more than eight-month credits and increase discounts for immediate
payment, he stood aloof, "determined to rest contented wth a very moderate profit such an one as 'twill not be worth the while of others to use the
indirect means heretofore practised."

Contractors, however, could now ask the state to remedy some of the
difficulties posed by the overpopulation it had encouraged in the trade.
Hirst informed the Ordnance Office that he could fulfill their desire for
"utmost Diligence and Expedition in the furnishing of arms" only if no
one troubled his men, i.e., if the office did not continually embrace new
contractors. The Ordnance clerk Thomas Hatcher was charged with
ensuring gunsmiths could complete their work without their men being
poached. He was forbidden to "raise or promote any disturbance either
among the people employed in the SGO [Small Gun Office] or out of
the office among the people of the trade." Nor was he to view "any work
for the EIC [East India Company]" or have "any concerns with gunmakers out in the trade" without permission, "as the King's Service has greatly
suffered thereby and as he will answer the same at his peril." As in the
previous war, the office ordered the Worshipful Company of Gunmakers to provide monthly accounts of firearms made and sold, and their

purchasers, "to prevent any prejudice to His Majesty's Service." It sent Robert Bennet to collect a similar account at Birmingham. Anticipating the usual confluence of internal rebellion with conflict abroad, the office offered a reward in the *London Gazette* to anyone who discovered "any Arms concealed in any part of Great Britain." When accounts came in, the Ordnance Board ordered a further "account of the small arms set up during the last war by the several gunmakers," including names, quantities, and times of each delivery. Issuing warrants for parts to make ten thousand muskets, it called on "the most considerable persons at Birmingham" to report how many barrels and locks they would provide, in how much time, and at what cost. An Ordnance Office lockmaker, Richard Davis, went to places where locks were made "to give the workmen proper directions" and ensure that their tools were made to the same gauge. The war machine was running in high gear six months before the declaration of war.

The demand for accounts was not about monopolizing gunmakers' attention. The Ordnance Office allowed gun production for Africa to go on because the African trade as a whole was "of great consequence to this kingdom and to His Majesty's colonys and plantations in America." Cheap African guns fell outside the compass of wartime prohibitions against arms exports insofar as such prohibitions aimed at preventing enemy acquisition of British guns. Many barely qualified as weapons. This was Galton's defense when one of his consignments was seized en route from Bristol to Liverpool in 1756: his warehouseman had labeled the eighteen boxes of guns "Ironmongery and Birmingham Ware Not Arms," and to their makers this was not far from the truth. The Quaker firm Devonshire & Reeve, which had bought the guns, explained that they were "for the Guinea trade not proved or bored being of the inferior sort sold at 5/10 each." Galton counted on customs commissioners considering them "common African guns not as arms." In the end, Capel Hanbury interceded on his behalf and the guns were released. Such prominent entities, closely concerned with the government and the war effort, were invested in this trade; it could not be prohibited. Farmer & Galton carried on in it, serving others who were critical to the logistics of the war effort, like Oswald, who ran bread supply operations in partnership with Lawrence Dundas and the East India captain Robert Haldane. During the war, another Farmer & Galton customer, the textile merchant and slave trader Samuel Touchet, outfitted five of his own armed vessels at the personal cost of £10,000 to join the king's vessels in the Canaries, with Secretary of State William Pitt's secret support. They took French posts in Senegambia as part of Touchet's scheme to monopolize production of gum, slaves, and other commodities and supplant Indian cloth in Africa. He was an influential member of Parliament in 1761. The Hanburys, Oswald, and Touchet were both inside and outside the state; they were merchants who helped integrate the empire as they integrated their own business operations. "Public" and "private" were inextricable.

News of the catastrophic Lisbon earthquake of November 1, 1755, reached Galton's ears by mid-November, amid all this activity. All hope of Farmer's financial recovery vanished instantly. Just then, Bennet arrived in town. From him Galton learned that the "great drafts of Arms already made & hereafter to be sent out of the Tow^r will occasion fresh Contracts & that more warrants will soon be granted." In short, steady Ordnance work promised to free them from endless solicitation of commercial orders. Demand from Africa remained robust. But whether or not the government allowed them to pursue that "private" trade, gunmakers like Farmer and Galton were happy to pursue military work instead; the switch required no coercion. They did not see war as a disruption to the profitable pursuit of commercial trade. Bennet's news spread in town: the next day, John Willets of Wednesbury offered the Ordnance Office barrels and locks. Jordan requested further orders. Tower stocks had dwindled to about 51,000 serviceable guns, but this was still more than the Ordnance Office had had at the start of war in 1739. The office was learning to smooth supply in a time of frequent war, not least by making contracts even in peace. Now it set about meeting its requirements for necessary parts, determined to control procurement centrally. Contracts for 25,000 barrels went to Oughton, Jordan, Willets, Hadley, Galton, and Farmer, and locks were ordered from Grice & Edge. George Markbee, a London gunmaker who had become an Ordnance viewer, went to Birmingham permanently on four shillings per day, out of which he would defray his expenses and "go wherever the Board shall have occasion to send him." The London company's proofhouse hired a new assistant to cope with the increasing work. Regimental agents were banned from buying arms independently. Contractors knew that sending arms directly to a ship seriously violated protocol.

In this climate, contractors gained leverage on prices. Lockmakers asserted their demand for seven shillings rather than the office's offer of six. In 1756, Galton, too, requested higher prices on the grounds that competition had driven prices up for locks and iron—the very problem that had plagued his commercial sales. But when the customer was the state, there was some chance for amelioration: the Ordnance Board granted Galton's request. In 1757, Farmer & Galton and another firm complained that they could not get locks at the old prices and asked for sixpence more. Ordnance officials validated their claim that lockmakers had raised their prices steeply, and the price book was updated. At the same time, the state's cultivation of a wide array of suppliers and workers put limits on contractors' leverage. When Barker, Pickfatt, and Wilson refused to set up muskets for six shillings and eightpence, the office knew that Hirst would do it at a "reasonable" price. He became virtually the only Ordnance Office setter-up for twenty years, enrolling a sufficient workforce to complete as many as sixty thousand muskets in a year. The continued presence of others in the background ensured that this cozy relationship also did not make the office dependent on him. Plus, the office ordered five thousand muskets from Amsterdam—another means of balancing relations with contractors.

The Hanburys owed Farmer & Galton £1,200, and Oswald owed them £1,000: the African trade had the potential to make arms manufacturers very rich. But all debts are not the same. Farmer's financial crumbling showed that a debt from a merchant could add up to nothing at all. A debt from the government, on the other hand, could have more value than hard currency in the business and monetary environment of this period, as we'll see more fully in chapter five. Contractors' consistent willingness to extend the state credit testifies to their confidence in the state as a reliable customer. Whimsical demand and low profit were intrinsic to gunmaking—partly by government design. The state may have had to compete with other gun purchasers, but contractors' willingness to persist in the often difficult relationship shows they needed the state, too.

The British state steadily guided the gun industry's growth and spread. Its revived demand during the new war unfolding in 1755 seemed likely to redeem Farmer from the financial abyss into which he had fallen as a gunmaker with wider commercial ambitions. The Lisbon earthquake may have delivered divine judgment on his folly, but war, of all things, promised the redemption this Quaker so urgently needed. For, mortifyingly, his fate alone was not at stake. Credit, family, and industrial networks ensured that many more were afflicted along with him; his recovery likewise promised relief to many more besides.

2

Who Made Guns?

Local historians lament that we have no record of the first gun-maker in Birmingham, but the reality is that there was no such thing as a consistently identifiable "gunmaker" until gunmaking had long been established among the town's many varieties of metal manufacturing. The Farmers began as a Quaker ironmonger family in Bristol. Joseph Farmer set up a smith's shop in the Old Square of nearby Birmingham around 1702, dealing in guns but also "toys" and sword blades. He probably made barrels and locks himself (unlike later generations), but his skills were still wide enough to credit the more general label "ironmonger" when he and a few colleagues leased an iron furnace at Rushall in 1717. It is impossible to count "gunmakers" because the people who made guns also made other things, and those who made other things also helped make guns; but gunmaking's ties to the manufacture and sale of other goods help reveal the place of military manufacturing in Britain's growing military-industrial society.

Eventually, the term *gunmaker* referred variously to a parts manufacturer, a retailer, assembler, or entrepreneur, or, occasionally, a manufacturer of complete firearms. As we have seen, some who went by the name "gunmaker" mainly oversaw "setting up" of parts made by specialists running their own small firms—filers, stockmakers, barrel welders, borers, grinders, lockmakers, engravers, polishers, and so on—who in turn depended on outworkers. There were at least thirty subtrades or manual manufacturing processes; those designated as gunmakers might possess experience in one branch but have little technical training in the intricacies of arms fabrication. They were often preoccupied with matters of finance, marketing, and delivery, and the all-important task of constructing a gentlemanly life. Many were also publicans and shopkeepers.

Each gun passed through many highly skilled hands before completion. But many other objects passed through the same hands; polishers and filers hardly confined application of their skill to gun parts. Small masters and workmen with teams of apprentices easily took up other kinds of metalworking, from toymaking to edge-tool manufacture, when necessary; this was why gunmakers' pleas for Ordnance Office work, to hold on to their workmen, were effective. This flexibility meant that arms making involved a wide range of industrial workers but also makes it hard to say who was or was not a gunmaker. Guns were *among* the "toys" at the heart of Birmingham's metals-based industrial enlightenment, including much of what we would term jewelry (bracelets, rings, necklaces, brooches), small articles of plate, sword hilts, dagger furniture, buttons, buckles, seals, chains, chatelains, charms, swivels, bells, hinges, mounts of various kinds, etuis, snuffboxes, patch boxes, and even tools used by carpenters and butchers. These skilled manufacturers displaced the older, more "utilitarian" ironmongery, nailing, and edge-tool manufacture to the outskirts of the town, while maintaining ties to them to cope with fluctuating demand and common needs for raw materials.

Outsourcing of parts manufacture meant that gunmaking also depended on far-flung networks of activity. The Farmer & Galton firm had finishers in Bristol, viewers in Liverpool, stockmakers in London, lockmakers in Wednesbury, and barrel grinders at Duddeston, besides the busy hands at their warehouse in Steelhouse Lane. They bought beechwood for stocks in Gloucester, walnut from Italy and Germany. Iron came from North America, Russia, and Sweden, via Bristol. The diverse parts and materials they needed ensured gunmakers' interest in businesses bearing on supply and carriage—canal construction, banking, trade to Africa and the New World, and so on. Likewise, businessmen from those worlds became invested and involved in the gun trade. Gunmaking was a process spread thinly over a wide area of industrial activity, thanks to the state's efforts *and* because of the very nature of the manufacture.

J oseph Farmer's ambitions took him well beyond his smith's shop, and his success in pursuing diverse activities ensured his gun firm's prominent size and reputation by the 1730s. In 1718, he traveled to America to experiment with iron ore (during a diplomatic breach with Sweden, a primary iron supplier for England in this period). In 1720, he was among a group of Birmingham and London men who established an ironworks, the Principio Company, in Baltimore County. He rented the Town Mill on the River Rea, in Digbeth—the very mill Prince Rupert had destroyed during the Civil War for turning out blades for the Parliamentary forces. By the late 1720s, keeping his house in Old Square, he relocated his business to the developing edge of the city. By 1735, these activities—gun manufacturing, ironworking, and real estate—were successful enough to permit Farmer to shift to the Steelhouse Lane premises that would be the stage of the multigenerational saga of Farmer-Galton gun manufacturing. It was partly the presence of his large firm that drew other gunsmiths to this northern quarter of town, particularly after (sometime before 1756) Farmer & Galton opened a proofhouse around the corner on Weaman Street, where the firm proved its guns and those of colleagues requesting the service. In 1737, Joseph testified before Parliament as "a Manufacturer of Steel Wares at *Birmingham*," in support of importation of American iron. (That year, the Swedes were trying to raise their prices.) He recalled his experiments of 1718, in which he had used Maryland ore to fashion "Springs for Gun-locks, Sword-blades, Files, and Bits to bore Gun-barrels, and Tower Musket-barrels, all of which," he explained, "require the very best Steel." He found it preferable to English and Swedish ore for barrels.

Farmer spoke before the parliamentary committee as one long known to and trusted by the government. But it was not his status as a gunmaker in particular that gave him a claim to that attention. The British state was

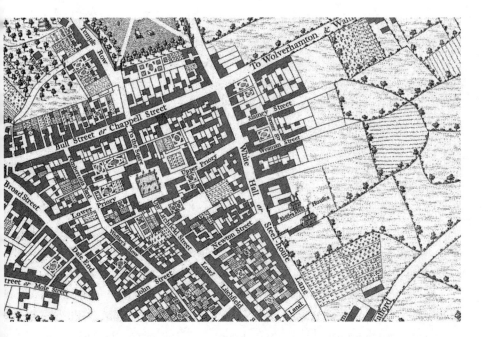

A 1731 map of Birmingham showing the early formation of the Gun Quarter in the corner formed by Steelhouse Lane and Bull Street, heading toward Wolverhampton. Farmer Street, between Slaney and Weaman, is named for the gunmaking business Joseph Farmer first established in this developing part of the city in the late 1720s. He moved his business to Steelhouse Lane shortly after this map was made.

an eager customer of such a range of metal goods that, in effect, the entire metallurgical industry, including other Quaker barons, were its intimates. The Crowleys, Quaker nail makers who supplied the navy, spoke at length, too. In the 1720s, they bought trial lots from the Principio works; they would become the biggest purchasers of Principio iron in England by the 1730s. They were also tied to the Farmers through the Lloyds. In the late seventeenth century, two Quaker brothers, Charles and Sampson Lloyd, had wed Sarah and Mary Crowley (respectively), launching the Lloyd family's career as iron wholesalers. Sampson Lloyd had arrived in Birmingham in 1698, four years before Joseph Farmer. (The Quaker meetinghouse on Bull Street was erected around 1703.) He supplied iron to Birmingham manufacturers on commission for his London-based brother-in-law Ambrose Crowley. After his death, in 1724, his son Sampson II integrated the business backward into slitting mills, forges, and furnaces, investing also in steel, brass, and other ventures. He was an intimate friend of Joseph's who was likely among his early customers and who, in 1728, passed him the tenancy of the Town Mill, which he used for slitting iron for rods. (Joseph's granddaughter would marry Sampson II's son.) The iron industry's evolution depended on such family connections. The subset of Quaker ties was particularly important: Quakers owned or managed between half and three-quarters of the ironworks in operation in the early eighteenth century, most of them interconnected by partnerships and marriages.

Such bonds entwined the Farmer gun business with wider industrial activity in the region. The trust of the Society of Friends was a kind of currency, opening doors to new opportunities in new towns. Joseph's son James proved the power of marriage to develop the family business in multiple directions. On business in London in 1742, a year after his father's death, he found himself an object of special interest to Thomas Plumsted, a wealthy Quaker ironmonger who knew the Crowleys well and also testified about American iron ore in 1737. Plumsted saw in James a promising match for his daughter, Priscilla, "a celebrated beauty with a very large fortune." "Prissy" was already well known to James's cousin Molly Jepson, whose private intelligence he immediately solicited. Assured of her father's immense fortune—some £24,000—and her good character, notably her frugality, James accepted the proposal. Plumsted's fabulous wealth and equally fabulous miserliness turned the engagement into a staple of Friends gossip. James stipulated a £3,000 settlement in hand for the proposal to go forward and was prepared to walk if his terms were not met. He assured his sister Mary that he would "not sacrifice my happiness to any lady . . . as I am not violent hot in love." After prolonged struggle over the settlement, he and Prissy married in 1743, bringing a frisson of London elegance to the Farmer hearth and igniting the envy of their neighbors and kinsmen. Besides the marriage portion of £2,500, they received thousands more of the Plumsted fortune upon Plumsted's death in 1752, when his assets were divided between his daughter and his son.

In 1744, James took out a seventy-year lease on Duddeston Mill, on the River Rea, using it for blade making, gun boring, and metal rolling.

Queen Anne flintlock pocket pistol by Farmer & Galton.

His sister Mary helped him manage the gun business while he shuttled among London, Birmingham, and Liverpool. From 1745, he was also assisted by Samuel Galton, who came to him through a family connection and common mercantile interests. Samuel's brother Robert Galton had married James's cousin Hannah in 1734. He was a "haberdasher of small wares" in Bristol, a term likely indicating Birmingham hardware, for which Bristol was the major port. (Birmingham goods went to Bewdley by wagon, then by trow down the River Severn.) After being apprenticed to Robert, in 1742 Samuel had also emerged as an independent "haberdasher of small wares." He was worth £1,144 in 1743. But he also benefited from Robert's shipping investments related to the slave trade, for which Bristol was the biggest port before 1750. Robert and several prominent Bristol traders bought shares in the *Duke,* trading to North America. In 1745, while Samuel earned £100 after a year helping James, Robert was in Boston dealing with a consignment of slaves worth £54,000 for himself and his brothers. The following year, he advertised "a few boy servants indentured for seven years, and girls for four years," in a Boston paper. This business opened new doors for Samuel. In 1746, he received £1,600 as a marriage settlement. Judging him a "gentleman of good sense sobriety and diligence," James allowed his sister Mary to marry him at the end of that year. The marriage settlement involved James, Samuel, and Samuel's iron-trading brother John Galton. Samuel joined James as his quarter partner in the gun business, at £2,500.

Gunmaking sank roots wherever family ties took it, becoming entangled with new relations' existing interests. John Galton began to manage the Bristol end of the business, obtaining orders from outbound ships and overseeing the setting up of guns in a warehouse there. He bought guns to sell in the Africa trade himself. He supplied the firm with iron. His partner in his iron business was his wife's brother, Graffin Prankard, former partner in Abraham Darby's Coalbrookdale works and exporter of Darby's cast iron pots. Prankard was the major Baltic iron supplier in the West Midlands from the 1720s, supplying Joseph Farmer and Sampson Lloyd in their day, too. These Bristol connections enabled Farmer & Galton to experiment incessantly with iron. The firm sent steel for the gunmakers to try in their springs, which they also passed to lockmakers. The lockmaker Robert Moore Parks found this "Bristol Steel" too "frenzy," faulting the conversion process. He also complained that the evenness of John Galton's iron bars made it difficult for his men to work.

Prompted by such fussiness, James Farmer constantly cast about for new sources of iron. Like his father, he testified in Parliament in favor of American iron imports, easing passage of the Iron Act of 1750, which abolished duties on colonial pig and bar iron. He was intrigued by his toymaker colleague and supplier Henry Horne's recommendation of a particular Siberian iron. In 1751, he and Samuel, whose share in the gun business had increased to two-fifths, began manufacturing iron with John's help. When this news spread, manufacturers inquired whether they would spare metal for purchase by others. They readily assented. Samuel assured Robert Moore Parks that they were setting up their own furnace. He reported to James that a local saw-making firm that consumed fifty tons of steel annually was also unhappy with Siberian iron, perceiving an opportunity to get "the start of the others before any of best marks come in we may sell . . . a great quantity." James, John, and Samuel, with two other Birmingham merchants, Samuel and Randall Bradburne, partnered to make and trade iron and steel. Erecting forges at Belbroughton and other sites (and arranging wood from local landowners), they intended to supply their own needs and saw makers and filers.

This backward linkage was necessitated by local manufacturers' collective dissatisfaction with available iron. Birmingham metalworking firms often diversified into metal processing to generate steady raw material supplies. It is impossible to assess the impact this and other gunmakers' experiments in iron production had on the pace of innovation in iron production—theirs was an old-fashioned charcoal-fueled forge—but certainly the *spirit* of innovation thrived in such enterprises. The possibility of smelting the iron in the newer way, with coke (derived from coal), was broached: Galton reported to Farmer their workers' insistence on "some forrest to work with" (referring to trees used to produce charcoal), because smelting with coke made the pigs draw "hard." In 1755, Galton anticipated a fall in pig iron prices as coke smelting increased; two years later, he bought some from Darby. Five years after that, William and John Wood, father-and-son gunlock makers in Wednesbury, patented a new method of producing malleable iron so good that it was in intense demand by local gun-barrel makers. Wednesbury's horse-driven Adams forge, built in 1760, also produced malleable iron and would be one of the first to adopt steam power. It and Wood's forge produced high-grade iron suitable for gunmaking.

These instances of Birmingham gunmakers' tinkering speak to the breadth of their industrial activities. The first Birmingham man to patent an invention was Richard Baddeley of Old Square, who in 1722 developed a technique for making both "streaks" to bind cart and wagon wheels and box smoothing irons from pig iron. He was described variously as an ironmonger and a gunsmith and had a furnace at Rushall. In 1732, the gunmaker Richard Heely and Matthew Boulton backed John Wyatt's experiments with a file-cutting machine and the spinning rollers he made with Lewis Paul. Of those who took out multiple patents in the town, more than a third changed their occupational designation. The dozens of water mills that powered industrial labor were easily repurposed to support this breadth of activity. Over time, the same mill might be used for corn, paper, making blades, or rolling, slitting, and boring metal, often through subtenancies. During war, many shifted to boring and grinding for gunmakers. Besides the Town Mill, the Farmers held the Duddeston Mill. It was originally a cornmill; in 1756, silver was being rolled there. And so on for other mills held by gunmakers: mills' adaptability reflected their holders' flexibility in a volatile commercial environment.

Farmer and Galton's iron business was typical of this experimental environment and helped diversify their metal manufactures. When the gun spring Galton fashioned from Gottenburg iron broke because of faulty conversion to steel, he made gravers instead and sent samples to saw makers, who found the steel "not only strong but a tough body" and expressed interest in further purchases. The firm's steel sales took off as Galton determined to buy up all the Gottenburg iron in London—unmarked, to keep the source "more secret." Galton now urged Farmer to hire someone to look after the forge full time, as it "interrupts our other business." Without anyone assigned to obtain orders, they would soon have a "large and unsalable stock" on hand. That year, the fortunes of the gun trade were so bad that they took care to produce only as much iron as could be consumed in *other* manufacturing. Farmer tried to charm London ironworkers into using it in shovels and frying pans. Some of the firm's iron went to a nail manufactory in Bromsgrove run by Mary Sowden, who had assigned it to Farmer to avert bankruptcy. (When he, in turn, faced ruin, Galton received the assignment.)

The Farmer & Galton gun firm, like many Birmingham gun firms, also offered other manufactured metalware, such as swords, bayonets, shears, gravers, files, and cutlasses; hence their enduring ties to edge-tool and related trades. Blades, knives, forks, harpoons, and lances were part of their inventory for slave ships and ships sailing for Greenland. Nonmetal accoutrements for small arms were also among their offerings: cartouche boxes, scabbards, and gun belts. The firm also dealt in buckles, curry combs, gilt rings, bells "to put round the necks of sheeps dogs cats," plain and polished buttons—the whole range of Birmingham "toys," many ordered on commission through local suppliers according to patterns. These wares enabled gunmakers to weather the floods and droughts of government and commercial demand for guns. In 1748, when Farmer toured the

Continent in search of customers, he identified himself as a dealer in Birmingham toys and ironwares. Discovering a lively trade in a "prodigious quantity of all sorts of toys of Birm. make" in Lille, he wished he had a "sett of patterns" on him to obtain orders for those. Most of the toys there were gotten off one Mr. Hollier and other London dealers. (This was probably Thomas Hollier, the Ordnance Office supplier mentioned in the previous chapter.) Having secured gun orders at Dunkirk, James resolved to correspond with the town's principal merchants upon his return to get orders for toys. Ships heading to the West Indies with "quantities of ironmongery goods" also promised large orders once he sent out his samples.

The willingness to retail a range of goods was typical, ensuring gunmaking's tight entwinement with other kinds of metal manufacture. In 1818, a local directory listed the gunmaker William Richards's half-century-old shop as "Silversmiths jewellers and cutlers." He made guns at the back and sold them with the other goods. The Ordnance Office furbisher Richard Wooldridge also made tools for building roads in the Highlands. Birmingham gunmakers also engaged in saddlery, whip making, manufacture of candlesticks and snuffers, and selling weights. John Whateley partnered with the button maker Thomas Dobbs out of shared metal interests. Upon the dissolution of their partnership, in 1780, Dobbs acknowledged the "great profit and advantage" it had brought. Whateley continued to ally with toymakers, supplying copper for Boulton's coin press, for instance. He also advised Boulton on working the copper, describing in detail the hammer required. He did business with Boulton's associate, the cannon manufacturer John Wilkinson. Such associations meant that a range of tradesmen and industrialists stood security for gunmakers' Ordnance contracts: merchants, brewers, goldsmiths, and so on.

In short, the gun trade did not grow up *alongside* the toy trade; guns were *part of* that comprehensive category, ensuring that military demand had wide repercussions in what we might wrongly presume to be purely consumer-driven industries. A 1733 poem that a Birmingham mechanic addressed to an architect friend at Warwick in 1751 through *Aris's Birmingham Gazette*, Birmingham's most popular paper, illustrates the seamless grouping of arms with toys:

You'll be convinc'd that Vulcan's Forge is here;
That here Aeneas' Shield divine was made,
Achilles' Armour, Hector's dreadful Blade;
Here Guns and Swords Cyclopean Hands divide,
And here with glittering Arms the World is still supply'd.
Here Implements, and Toys, for distant Parts,
Of various Metals, by mechanic Arts,
Are finely wrought, and by the Artists sold,
Whose touch turns every Metal into Gold . . .

Gunmakers who participated in production and sale of other "toys" were not branching into radically different terrain; these goods shared a common hardware heritage. Other toymakers also made goods for the state: makers of cabinet brass foundry such as hooks, lashing and rope eyes, and hinges provided many articles for the Naval Brassfoundry. The distance between Boulton, maker of engines, buckles, and coins, and Farmer & Galton was not much: the toymaker supplied copper coins and military equipment to the government and manufactured sword hilts and gun furniture; the gunmakers sold buckles and nails to private customers. Indeed, the Galton arms factory was close to Boulton's father's original toy works, in Snow Hill, and Boulton owned property around the corner from Weaman Street.

It was not easy for gunmakers to keep so many balls in the air at once; for Farmer and Galton, the demands of the iron trade forced reconsideration of their commitment to the toy trade. As toy orders dwindled, workmen came around asking for the return of their patterns for buckles and other toys. Their man in charge of toy work, Henry Horne, made noises about leaving. But Farmer resisted burning the bridge; toy goods continued to trickle through their hands, and Horne was still there a year later. Galton continued to play the doomsayer, calling for a simpler, less diversified, more modest trade. He pressed Farmer to return the patterns; some workmen were threatening suit for them. The trade diminished enough to permit conversion of the warehouse's "toy room" into a "complete accompting house" in 1755, but during the Seven Years' War, Galton still advertised his services in providing "anything in the gun or Birmingham toy goods."

Through family, Farmer and Galton were involved in other pursuits, too. John Galton was also a "linen draper" and frequently sent Samuel cloth, particularly baize, to sell in Birmingham. James was involved in his cousin Hannah Galton's effort to break into the linen trade after Robert died in Boston, late in 1748. He also dealt in animal skins and was involved in a London sugar mill. At least one gun shipment Galton packed included a "little parcel of china ware." James had installed his brother Joseph (II) in Liverpool in the 1740s to sell guns on commission, under the wing of the Liverpool merchant John Hardman, a prominent figure in the African and West Indian trades who would be an MP in 1754–55. There, Joseph bought East India goods to sell in West Africa. He also borrowed from the gun firm to buy shares in shipping ventures to Africa, the West Indies, and Lisbon, gambling away his brother's goodwill and cash each year. While joining the Company of Merchants Trading to Africa, he remained drawn to ironmongery as an alternative to frantic pursuit of that trade, dabbling in his cousin Thomas Farmer's Bristol-based ironmongery business. The cotton trade to Ireland was another of his ventures. In all this, he was a perpetual disappointment, not least for his helpless attraction to drink. When he lost more than £1,000 in 1751, his brother pushed him out by appointing a new agent, John Parr, member of a Liverpool family of shipowners, slave traders, and gun merchants. With James's help, Parr got into the "battery" trade—the trade in copper or brass toys. Their man in Bristol, William Gabintass, also engaged in "mercantile affairs on his account to the West Indies" (likely charging his expenses for entertaining his associates to the firm). Meanwhile, the family floated ideas for settling Joseph somewhere, including a place at Cape Coast Castle or as a midshipman aboard a man-of-war, but Hardman feared his conduct would "bring a reflection on the person who recommends him," and Galton worried that on land he would fall into bad company again. In the end, he took to the discipline of army life. After the Seven Years' War, he cleared his debts to the gun firm by assigning it his shares in a ship trading to Africa and another trading to Jamaica.

These were not the partners' only commercial investments. James put more than £2,000 into the Royal African Company in 1747. He and Galton bought shares in other ships. In 1750, when rumors of Farmer's weak credit circulated—the kiss of death to an eighteenth-century merchant— he assured Galton that he was worth more than £28,000, including debt from the African Company, which was "good exclusive of and allowing sufficient to pay everybody and for all bad debts." From London, he charged Galton with resurrecting his reputation in Birmingham, insisting the facts would sound more convincing coming from Galton. The rumors both show the wide net Farmer had cast by then and prefigure the financial doom to which it eventually brought him. The economic horizons of eighteenth-century Englishmen extended well beyond the parish, region, and nation. As producers, consumers, and participants in the web of debt and credit, Farmer and Galton were part of a vast and complex economic order, however rooted they were in Birmingham's Gun Quarter. For most contractors, contracting was part of or a sideline to their normal activities as traders and producers. Whether or not Farmer & Galton is representative of eighteenth-century gun firms, it was large enough by midcentury for its mixed pursuits to have their own significance. Moreover, the systemic reasons that motivated its diversification—the periodic waxing and waning of demand for guns and the common metallurgical processes involved in manufacture of many goods—would have applied equally to other gunmakers.

As emerging gentlemen, Farmer and Galton increasingly attended to the business of their accumulating property, too. James was deeply involved in agricultural labors. Haymaking took a heavy toll on his health. In lean years, he leased his forges, mills, and other properties. In the 1750s, he acquired land and workshop premises all around the Gun Quarter and the mills in the town's neighboring areas. In the 1760s, he bought more property and built several houses in the quarter. He also became a proprietor of the Birmingham Canal Navigation Company, putting the family in close contact with Matthew Boulton, who, as a manufacturer of bulky goods and a large consumer of coal, was deeply interested in canal construction. William Bonnington, who ran the inn in which many of the

Great Barr, the country home of the Galtons, from a photograph of a watercolor drawing in Elizabeth Anne Wheler (Galton)'s manuscript The Galton Family.

The Galton-Farmer house, later the Galton Bank, in Steelhouse Lane, Birmingham.

labor disputes among gun workers were fought out, mortgaged more property in the Gun Quarter to Galton, which he rented out to a victualer and a gunlock maker. In 1770, the seventeen-year-old Samuel Jr. joined the gun firm's countinghouse. The family lived by the workshops in Steelhouse Lane and maintained a country house at Duddeston. In 1786, they built a shop and warehouse in Slaney Street. From 1788, the younger Samuel lived part of the year at Great Barr Hall, a large country house four miles outside the city. In 1794, the family bought Warley estate for £7,300. The Whateleys also acquired hundreds of acres in the posh suburb of Handsworth, abutting the land of the Earl of Dartmouth. Property was not a pursuit unrelated to gunmaking. Agriculture and industry were linked by local capital markets, which shaped the functioning of rural domestic manufacturing. Many in this period raised finance on the security of land in the West Midlands.

Master gunmakers acquired a reputation for wealth and enterprise. Charitable investment in Birmingham's general hospital and library aside, Galton Jr. was a member of the town's exclusive dinner club and learned group, the Lunar Society, from around 1781, putting him at the center of innovative investment. He helped fund his former Warrington Academy teacher Joseph Priestley's experiments with air, and in 1795 (the year of the scandal around him in the Quaker church) he was a trustee for James Watt for the Soho Foundry's investments in the manufacture of steam engines. His father and siblings lent Boulton money on a mortgage on Boulton's shares in the Birmingham Canal Navigation Company. He and Boulton colluded to control canal construction in the city, one of the sticking issues being that competitors were not going to use Boulton's engines. They also worked together to create an assay office in town. Both invested in the Rose Copper Company, in Swansea, in 1802. Galton Jr. assisted Boulton and Watt in steam engine orders and other business matters. The wealth acquired from gunmaking had far-flung and important repercussions in the industrial and commercial economy. Farmer and Galton collaborated and communicated constantly with colleagues in the copper, toy, edge-tool, saw, nail, and other trades; this was an organic community of metalworkers and traders facing similar problems of supply, technique, and labor. As makers of probably the most complex of its products, Galton and Farmer could relate to a large share of it; guns were a point of intersection and contact for metalworkers.

The senior Galton died in 1799, aged eighty, his firm valued at £139,000. In 1804, Samuel Jr., who lived to 1832, passed the gun business to his son, Samuel Tertius (1783–1844). They followed the Lloyds, who had become relations by marriage, in opening a bank in their Steelhouse Lane premises, probably partly to finance the gun trade. Tertius was a banker and a gun contractor until the gun business was wound down at the end of the Napoleonic Wars, in 1814–15; Tertius's brothers Hubert and John Howard were his partners. The family was still invested in coal in South Wales. After the Galton bank closed, in 1831, its capital was absorbed by Midland Bank. When Galton Jr. died the next year, he was worth £300,000; the gun trade had done wonders with his father's original investment of £1,144. This fabulous inheritance afforded Tertius's son Francis Galton (1822–1911) the leisure in which to concoct his fabulous theory of eugenics.

The roads and alleys in the Gun Quarter around St. Mary's Church were thronged with errand boys shouldering baskets loaded with gun parts being passed among the town's various specialists well into the twentieth century. When demand was high, guns moved through specialists' hands so rapidly that gunmakers could hardly account for their stock at a given moment. Craftsmen in these subtrades are hard to identify. Even where their markings exist on gun parts, they are often difficult to decipher and link to particular individuals. Many worked by hand in domestic workshops. Many temporarily hired the use of bench space, a vise, and lighting—a "stand"—from a master whose warehouse was often attached to or part of his home. Specialists like lock engravers, braziers who seamed and jointed goods, founders and casters, and gear makers were called forth by the diversification of metal products at the turn of the century; they made many kinds of objects. To be sure, specifically gun-related specializations also emerged—the first barrel maker is recorded in

1708. But for the most part, specialists like polishers, engravers, and grinders, like their masters, were much more besides makers of guns and gun parts. Directories that began to appear in the 1760s reflect the self-identification of those who considered themselves gunsmiths or found it useful to identify themselves as such in a directory; some avowed gunmakers may actually have been retailers. And some toymakers may also have been gunsmiths. When Galton had to fill vacancies, he turned to skilled workers "in the toy way." Those who applied their technical skill to a range of goods may not have been included in such directories, nor might those whose position within the division of labor (i.e., not at the point of retailing) did not present them with any incentive to publicly market themselves as gunmakers. Directory listings were typically by subscription and included the most important entrepreneurs in the trade. The editors of one catalog note, "A man may have described himself as a blacksmith or whitesmith for ten or fifteen years, and only once during that time have mentioned 'and gunmaker.'" When demand for guns was low, skilled smiths might be busily employed in making buttons, buckles, cutlery, spurs, candlesticks, whip handles, coffee pots, inkstands, bells, carriage fittings, steam engines, snuffboxes, lead pipes, jewelery, lamps, or kitchen tools. They were flexible; they had to be, and it was the nature of metalworking. Birmingham's population of masters of small shops, laborers, and quasi-independent craftsmen earned a collective reputation for being able to leap from trade to trade or pursue multiple trades at once. An old Birmingham song went:

> I'm a roving Jack of all trades,
> Of every trade and all trades,
> And if you want to know my name,
> They call me Jack of all trades . . .
> In Swallow Street made bellows-pipes,
> In Wharf Street was a blacksmith;
> In Beak Street there I did sell tripe,
> In Freeman Street a locksmith.
> In Cherry Street I was a quack,

In Summer Lane sold pancakes;
And then at last I got a knack
To manufacture worm cakes.

The specialized and divided nature of production processes in the gun trade enabled workers to adapt to shifting demand. Master gunmakers with their own diverse pursuits could throw the burden of low demand on workers, and workers, in turn, could use their skills with the file and lathe in other trades. A core base of metalworking skills was adapted across a range of new commodities, besides the older trades of nail, edge-tool, and chain making, which depended increasingly on poor outworkers, especially women and children.

Joining these trades was not difficult. The 1692 joint signature of "The Company of Gunmakers of Birmingham" was no formal trade body, merely an ad hoc association to counteract the London company. Some Birmingham smiths apprenticed their sons to London gunsmiths, but most did not. They were the "foreign" workers increasingly hired by London contractors. The growing trade absorbed even those who had not served an apprenticeship. James and Joseph Farmer plotted in 1743 to hire Thomas Probin before he had completed his apprenticeship to finish guns for them in Liverpool. Lockmaking was the only trade with a relatively high bar to entry; five years of practice was required to produce a skilled lock filer. A determined lockmaker could learn to produce the other parts, too. Lockmakers hesitated to train appentices who in lean times might compete for work; payment in piece rates also made them less inclined to spend time training others. William Sharp, the engraver, made locks and springs, steel rammers and swivels.

The tangle between trades underwrote the ruthless discounting tactics gunmakers used to reduce competition. They knew that, once driven out, rivals would be absorbed by adjacent trades. In 1752, Galton fretted that his nemesis Hadley was discounting his guns to "ruin" the trade before jumping ship for the edge-tool trade. He and Farmer also toyed with discounting, Galton urging that they do it "with every great apparent reluctance," lest they be accused of designing to harm their competitors. But he was sanguine that underselling would not actually run anyone out of a living, only out of a niche in an otherwise inclusive ironware trade. The metal community would find a new equilibrium.

This means we can never know the precise number of hands that contributed to the manufacture of guns. Even gun masters could not correctly estimate the number of workmen they employed, because of the highly subdivided nature of production and the number of outworkers in every branch. In 1708, in their petition requesting parliamentary intervention to end their persecution by their London rivals, Birmingham's gunmakers represented themselves as a group of some four hundred workers and their families, but even they described the figure as an approximation of an unknown number of "many Hundreds." In 1788, John Whateley testified to the Board of Trade that the gun trade employed four to five thousand in Birmingham. Whateley had an incentive to put forward the most generous figure possible, to persuade the board of the folly of constraining the Africa trade. Still, this may be a low estimate, given the multiple identities of those who worked on guns. One scholarly estimate is that Birmingham's toy trades, *including* guns and jewelry, employed about twenty thousand by 1759, an immense proportion of the town's total population. The poet Robert Southey noted in 1807 that every man he met in town "stinks of train-oil and emery."

To be sure, a distinct Gun Quarter emerged in Birmingham for workmen focused on that trade. But until midcentury, all kinds of toymakers intermingled in the lanes of Old Birmingham. After the 1740s, land on the northern and northwestern edge of town and along the main road to Wolverhampton was opened up for building—the angle formed by Snow Hill and Steelhouse Lane. Tradesmen from the city's congested older quarters—gunsmiths, button makers, and various toymakers—took advantage of this opportunity, gunsmiths shifting to the first of the new estates to open up, St. Mary's district. Economies of scale emerged from this collective presence. In the 1760s, Lord Shelburne toured Galton's factory and was astonished to find the gun trade so prosperous in Birmingham after a gestation of a mere twenty-five years. By 1777, about half the gun manufacturers in town were concentrated in the four streets making up St. Mary's district. (The adjacent Jewellery Quarter coalesced only near the century's end.) But the trade remained spread out: half the gun manufacturers were *not* in the district. In 1829, only three-fifths of the trade was located there. Gunlock making remained a specialty of nearby villages like Wednesbury and Darlaston, while water- and, later, steam-power needs for barrel making bound that activity to Aston, Smethwick, West Bromwich, Duddeston, and Deritend. The Farmers' country house was a mile out of town at Duddeston, near their water-powered mill for grinding and polishing barrels and blades. Gunmaking remained fused with the wider industrial and commercial world of the Black Country.

Gunmaking skill had to be summoned when it was needed. The outbreak of war was inevitably hailed by a furious scramble to corral gun workers who had disappeared into other avenues of work. At the start of the Seven Years' War, three regular contractors refused to set up muskets at the Ordnance Office price, because the men they had employed in the previous war had since "got into other business." Advertising drew workers back into the fold. Early in the American war, the Ordnance Office had John York, the barrel-and-bayonet viewer at Birmingham, advertise for bayonet contracts in *Aris's Birmingham Gazette* and spread the word by mouth and handbills. The office advertised in local papers for armorers needed on naval ships and elsewhere. By 1775, *Aris's Birmingham Gazette* had become "the largest in the whole kingdom"; it expanded to accommodate the numerous advertisements submitted. Contractors made contracts conditional on whether they could "get men," but recourse to advertising suggests that they were fairly confident in the attractiveness of government work. In 1778, the bayonet contractor Thomas Gill put out a call in *Aris's Birmingham Gazette*: "Wanted immediately MEN who have been accustomed to forge and file iron, to work at bayonet sockets. They who wish to work at home may be accommodated." Gun masters were aware of the need to prevent workers from disappearing into other hives of activity upon completion of a contract. John Hirst, the London setter-up, consistently requested further orders, "that his men may not be out of employment." At times, rather than stand still, workmen continued production in anticipation of further orders. Flexibility also meant that in a pinch, in most places, local men in metal trades could address gun-maintenance issues. During the American war, the Ordnance Office gunsmith Samuel Spree, inspecting the arms of a militia regiment in Cambridgeshire, engaged "men on the spot" to repair them at office expense.

The elusiveness of skilled labor at the outbreak of war fueled fierce rivalries among contractors. In 1757, Edward Jordan complained that rivals "had got several of his men from him." The Ordnance Office policed these internecine squabbles, to ensure its capacity for belligerence on a global scale. Contractors sought guarantees against harassment of their labor, including supplementary wages and stern warnings to would-be poachers. In 1755, Hirst's low price for setting up depended on the office promising "protection" for his workmen as a reward for his "disinterested behavior." A few months later, he insisted that "no unnecessary difficulties be made to perplex his men at this juncture when good men have many temptations offered them and they will not put up with too much severity." The Ordnance Board assured that inspection would be timely and that they would "shew their Encouragement to all such persons under him, as shall Exert themselves at this juncture for HM's Service as well as shew their severe resentment to all such as shall by any means endeavour to obstruct the said Service." When Jordan's son Thomas offered ten thousand muskets in a year, his contract included a pledge not to "entice or employ any person" employed at the Tower or anyone in Birmingham working either for the board or for one of its other artificers, "particularly Dawes Hervey and Oughton," who were making bayonets and steel rammers for the office. The office knew that "the least interruption . . . would be a plea for [the gunmaker] not performing his contract within the time limited."

Rivalry resulted partly from the fact that the job of gun contractor was as flexible as that of a gun worker. New gun contractors sprang up like mushrooms upon the announcement of war, making straight for workers on other gunmakers' jobs. At least one, Richard Molineux, simultaneously contracted shipping for the Ordnance Office. The office encouraged such gumption as part of its efforts to expand the pool of contractors. The idea of standardization crystallized slowly, and meanwhile the office assumed that any craftsman with a forge and a hammer could make a serviceable firearm. Galton complained about new contractors alarming his men, tempting them with wages in ready money, driving wages up around the town. The distribution of gun masters was thus much wider than that of particular processes like engraving and barrel filing. Workshops may have been small, but they were linked in a geographically diffuse and highly capitalized production chain that drew on and served distant markets. Local and global history evolved together. As one scholar puts it, contractors "referred to themselves as 'gunmakers' when they were simply contractors, running a 'manufactory' which was really a warehouse, employing 'workmen' who were really independent producers, and paying them 'wages' when they actually negotiated prices."

By the American Revolutionary War, some of these rivalries eased. The primary Birmingham contractors—Galton, Whateley, Oughton, Hadley, and a few others—were proprietors of more entrenched firms, an imposing obstacle to any would-be overnight gun contractor. The 1776 issue of contracts included just one avuncular warning to Hadley not to interfere with his colleagues; the systemic problem of poaching had boiled down to the particular hostility between Hadley and the others. The Ordnance Office's regular rough stockers in London, James Waller and Joseph Loder, did complain of "interference" from new contractors, reminding the office that Waller's father (and later Loder) had been contracted to exclusively supply the government from 1740: "Men being very scarce Messrs. Waller with profound secrecy great Trouble and expence did instruct and cause to be instructed 40 men" to fulfill this obligation. In the preceding war, they had rough-stocked nearly 300,000 guns. Now "the increasing number of masters" had made their property more precarious and jeopardized wood supply, since the walnut had to be seasoned for two years. The Ordnance Board called the vexed stockers in, and the meeting ended amicably enough to yield a fresh walnut contract.

The Galton family never succeeded in drawing the firm's business into the "narrower compass" the elder Samuel had envisioned in 1754. Too many had a stake in the firm's affairs. Gunmaking profits spread far and wide in the British economy, and the Quaker network helped, ironically. These far-flung stakeholders in the trade ranged from Quaker elites to Birmingham's industrial tycoons and major transatlantic traders of Liverpool, London, Bristol, and Manchester.

James Farmer's connection with the Plumsted family opened important doors. His marriage to Priscilla was strongly backed by her uncle, the banker John Freame. Freame and his brother-in-law Thomas Gould were goldsmiths who founded the first Quaker bank in London. Among other industrial pursuits, they financed the London Lead Company, of which Freame was governor between 1733 and 1742. (It was known as the Quaker Lead Company because of his investment.) After Gould left in the 1720s, Freame and his son Joseph partnered with James Barclay, son of David Barclay and grandson of the Quaker Apologist Robert Barclay, who was married to John Freame's daughter Sarah. David Barclay took as his second wife Sarah's sister Priscilla. Formerly a linen draper, he had become a general merchant, owning ships trading all over the Atlantic and believed to have been worth £100,000 upon his death. King George III visited his home in 1761. Priscilla and David's two sons joined the Freame & Barclay partnership, merging this Barclay mercantile empire with the bank. The bank invested in many industrial and commercial enterprises, including canals, bridges, the slave trade, and Farmer's gun firm.

James Farmer became utterly absorbed in these new relations, to his sister's consternation. The Plumsteds began to remotely participate in his business. Plumsted conveyed gun orders to Galton for Farmer and bought guns and locks himself. He insured gun shipments for customers. For Earl Daniel, of Montserrat, insurance amounted to £800, and Plumsted considerately paid the freight, too, for which he was later reimbursed. In 1750, the African Company bought from Plumsted casks of copper rivets, copper brads, iron shot, nails, screws, bellows, copper gun ladles, and steel. Galton bought locks and keys for the workshop doors from him. Joseph Freame also bought Farmer & Galton's knives and cutlasses. With Galton managing affairs in Birmingham, Joseph Farmer in Liverpool, agent Nicholas Atkinson in Lancaster, and John Galton in Bristol, James ensconced himself in the financial world of London from 1748 to 1755. His financial failure in 1755 revealed for posterity the strands of capital that he had tied up in the gun trade, which success might otherwise have kept hidden.

In 1754, Farmer felt fairly unapologetic that the gun business "mostly lies on our Samuel Galton." Galton complained about the pressures of running two manufactories and hinted, with diminishing subtlety, that Farmer was not pulling his weight. Worse, their partner in the forge, Bradburne, had proved true to his description as a gentleman of leisure, devoting less than six hours a year to the iron warehouse. Their chief viewer at the gun warehouse was nearly blind, and Galton regularly stayed up all night to complete orders. Futilely, he beseeched Farmer to help, hire help, or drastically reduce their participation in the gun trade.

For Farmer, the gun business had morphed from a daily occupation to collateral in more capricious commercial adventures. Initially for ease of accounting, he had begun purchasing guns from the firm on his own account, selling them onward to other customers in London, but soon bookkeeping became entirely notional as Farmer's independent trade took on a life of its own. His hands were full of London-based investments brokered by his relations and customers in the world of transatlantic and African trade and high finance. In particular, he and one Samuel Montaignt, "a young fellow, a foreigner," with an uncle, Peter Simond, in England, sent to "Lisbon and elsewhere very large quantities of goods which though sold and amount to nigh £30,000 yet can't be paid for" until the ships returned from Brazil. Simond was one of Farmer & Galton's gun customers. He and Montaignt had earlier been involved in the investments that led to the founding of Georgia in the 1730s. Early in 1754, Farmer informed Galton that he was going to borrow £6,500 from Freame & Barclay, because gun remittances were not coming quickly enough. Freame and Barclay, being relations, were convinced of his security, but "as bankers they never did advance on single security," and so he asked Samuel to become bound for him. Samuel met them in Oxford and signed six bonds, worrying that some might deduce from their multiplicity that a large sum had been transacted and make unpleasant inquiries. Freame and Barclay promised not to "distress" him, not least since Farmer would repay them in six months. Galton discovered Farmer's "dubious accounts" later that year as he sat down to make his will. James owed the firm a lot of cash. Farmer gave his bond to Galton for £200 and promised to pay interest for the balance due. In February 1755, Samuel went to London expecting to find the bonds for Freame & Barclay canceled, but they were not.

James's risky behavior was not entirely out of the blue. He had dealt with nasty rumors about his credit in 1750 with remarkable sangfroid, certain that any display of uneasiness would only give his enemies pleasure. And while he disapproved of his brother Joseph's bohemian lifestyle, he admired the brashly heroic exploits of his cousin Benjamin Farmer, a merchant in Lisbon who had spent harrowing years in the West Indies trying to break the Portuguese monopoly on orchilla weed. When his ship had been apprehended and his crew "barbarously used," the gallant Ben "insisted he was in the fault and not them, upon which they put lighted matches . . . betwixt his fingers and tortured him to that degree that inflamed his arm." He and his crew were brought before the governor of Cape Verde and discharged, but their ship and cargo—and clothes—were confiscated. Benjamin smuggled himself home, vowing revenge but in otherwise excellent spirits. His finances were devastated, but Farmer clearly relished the tale, acknowledging that Benjamin's courage was more "madness than solid sense." This coy taste for adventure found expression in Farmer's transactions in the Lisbon trade right then.

This trade, like most foreign trade, relied on long credit and a diversity of goods. Major international merchants became bankers for their clients. One ship, for which Farmer's brother-in-law Robert Plumsted arranged the insurance, carried wheat and corn. Guns, too, were part of the cargo. So were textiles, obtained on credit from James Johnson, a major Manchester- and London-based trader who sold his goods in Africa. Johnson was confident that Farmer had enough assets to secure his investment. Farmer owed him £3,400. Farmer also bought goods from his gun customer Samuel Touchet, another major dealer in textiles for Africa, who was in the House of Commons in 1751 and on the committee of the reconstituted African Company in 1750. In 1753, while brainstorming strategies to extricate the prodigal Joseph from Liverpool, Galton alluded to James's "intimacy and interest" with members of that company. Global commercial networks were entangled with the networks of the gun trade.

Champion & Hayley was also among Farmer's creditors. Alexander Champion was part of a Quaker industrial family that owned the Bristol-based Brass Wire Company. As gunmakers, Farmer & Galton consumed a lot of brass (used in the gun's "furniture") and had an active account with the company, which was founded by Abraham Darby. The Champions were also early investors in Darby's and Graffin Prankard's Coalbrookdale works. Champion and George Hayley traded brassware in North America and Africa and insured ships in the African trade. They also bought Farmer & Galton's guns, probably for Africa. Thus, a supplier of raw material for the manufacture of guns was also a customer for the finished product, a shipper of the product, and an investor in the gunmaker's independent overseas trade in other goods.

The investment of the copper baron George Pengree, another important customer and brass supplier to the firm, was actually secured with guns: he held a stash of guns "as a pledge . . . against a debt due . . . from Farmer." While Galton later tried to resolve their accounts, Pengree bought guns for Africa and Samuel ordered "one hundred of the thinnest bright sheet Latten and a quarter of a hundred rol[l]ed Latten." Farmer also owed £250 to another gun customer, Francis Rybot, a silk mercer and weaver trading to Canada. Credit greased the wheels of eighteenth-century commerce, enhancing collective investment in it. It spun a web that made the British economy an economy, a network of commingled and intertwined economic fates. James Farmer invested a wide mix of business entities in his transatlantic trade and in the gun firm that underwrote it. He testified in Parliament in favor of widening the town's roads, out of an awareness of his firm's implication in complex commercial networks. Galton's later interest in canals arose from the same logic.

By March 1755, James's letters took on an increasingly alarmed tone about his transatlantic venture. Samuel sensitively suggested seeking help from John Galton, "with whom a secret may be reposed with safety." But it was too late. James stopped payment Friday, March 21, 1755, when several bills came due at once and remittances from Lisbon remained a mirage. Freame & Barclay gave notice that they would no longer discount his bills and notes. James Johnson and Champion & Hayley were out of humor, which James interpreted as jealousy at his having first made his "friends secure." He determined not to repent prematurely, certain his venture would still "turn out for the best." He remained confident that "persons of the greatest Cr[edit] on the Exchange" were "desirous of serving me" and that his affairs would soon be in order, despite this "mortifying stroke." Johnson was "one of the best friends I have in the world," he boasted to the utterly shaken Galton. As his material fortune vanished beyond the ocean's horizon, he found an embarrassment of riches at home: "I find every person I owe anything to ready to give to me or come into any reasonable measures." Samuel assured Freame and Barclay that John Galton would ensure the firm's recovery by providing cheap iron. He responded to Farmer's complacency with a stern warning to neither conceal the worst nor exaggerate the best of his circumstances.

Samuel could not get to London, for fear of alarming their creditors in Birmingham and because of his wife's delicate postpartum condition. Instead, he unleashed a river of ink informing his most powerful connections of the situation. He shared with Robert Plumsted his dismay at the wild risks "Brother Farmer" had taken to create "so dismal a crisis." Vouching that James would refrain from such delinquencies in the future, he asked Plumsted to ascertain the true extent of his and the firm's implication in the affair and whether Farmer's creditors could lawfully ask for the debts to be discharged with guns. He hoped Freame & Barclay would take on Farmer's debts until he could get the gun remittances to discharge the bills Farmer drew for on the firm's account—some £20,000 were due to the firm. He assured Plumsted that if Farmer were allowed to return to his work, their shares would be equal and he would attend fully to their joint concerns. Because Farmer had drawn on more than the proportion of his stock in the firm, his stock had been assigned to Galton. Galton was painfully aware that the creditors' leniency toward him was purely a function of their being "relations of Mrs. Farmer." He begged Nicholas Atkinson and John Parr to collect debts due to the firm in Lancaster and Liverpool.

A committee consisting of Johnson, Champion, Hayley, Dr. Joseph Denham, and A. J. Hillhouse investigated Farmer's affairs; they recommended that Farmer get his friends to provide security for his last payments so that he might be discharged. Farmer also applied to Plumsted and Freame, who was still taking up the bills drawn by the gun firm, but he feared that his creditors would run out of patience. The worst happened, with Plumsted and Freame "not hitting it off" with the committee. After a tête-à-tête with Johnson, Farmer blamed Freame and Plumsted and hoped Johnson might be able to redeem him—if Galton would come to London with their accounts.

A commission of bankruptcy was taken out against Farmer. Farmer's optimism proved somewhat justified in that Freame & Barclay did take on his debts until he could gather enough remittances. Freame informed the London banker Andrew Drummond that their bills on Farmer would be paid. Drummond's bank served many army agents and was itself involved in specie contracting for the state. Such banks were invested in the Lisbon trade for its centrality to specie supply (gold and silver arriving from Brazil). Freame's commitment to "securing the gun trade" fueled the creditors' suspicions of family collusion in averting Farmer's bankruptcy. So, too, did Farmer's abrupt assignment of the nail factory to Galton, which Galton explained was merely collateral for Farmer's receipt of cash for guns not yet delivered. The assignees were intent on auctioning off his worldly possessions, but Galton persuaded them to allow him to sell land around Duddeston instead, if needed.

Robert Plumsted, also a transatlantic iron trader, owed money to the nail factory. His investments were bound so tightly with Farmer's that he was compelled to assess the extent to which the latter's failure impinged on his own dealings in Lisbon. This self-absorption may have gotten the better of him; Galton began to feel Plumsted was trying to "entrap" him in a settlement. Whether Plumsted or Farmer exploited relatives for personal advantage, the result of their mutual entanglement was the implication of a range of financial, commercial, and industrial interests in gun production. Farmer's troubles even brought a stop to his aunt Susannah Abrahams's annuity; Galton wrote to her pacifyingly that he had "Effects enough abroad to pay every body and many Thousand Pounds to spare."

Meanwhile, Galton continued to beg Parr and Atkinson to collect on debts to the firm. In explaining the delay, he gave Freame & Barclay an insider view of the gun trade, emphasizing the many big merchants who owed them money, including Richard Oswald and the Hanburys. Through the bonds of debt and credit, Farmer and Galton were drawn into the orbit of such men, whose merchant empires were pillars of the expanding British Empire. When Oswald later needed to borrow from a bank, four times between 1769 and 1778, he, too, turned to the Barclays. In May 1755, Farmer had hopeful news from Lisbon, and his bankruptcy committee examined guns that had been made for Oswald and Earl Daniel and were stored in the firm's London warehouse. Patterns were also arriving from Birmingham, because the committee, too, had decided to buy Farmer & Galton's guns. Farmer kept them in temper by inviting them to dine on a turtle—a West Indian luxury. When the patterns arrived, the committee decided on fifty Dutch-pattern guns and a number of another sort, which they also had priced by John Brazier. Barclay selected from among patterns Galton sent him later that year.

In the end, the familial bonds underlying Farmer's financial and commercial commitments saved him. John Galton met with Freame and his associates in London. He loaned Farmer cash to tide him over, waiting patiently for a dividend from the bankruptcy proceedings. Rybot refrained from prosecution, relying on his optimism, as a "particular acquaintance" of Simond, that Farmer's investments in the Lisbon trade might yet pay off. The Freames and Barclays advanced Farmer £3,000 to recommence a partnership with Galton, on the understanding that he would confine himself to the gun trade and embark on no more foolhardy transcontinental ventures. Galton took advantage of this merciful climate and asked Farmer to prevail on the committee to permit Joseph to go to Africa. But the committee could not overcome its concerns about Joseph drinking there and preferred a post that would subject him to a "regular manner of living." There were limits to family charity.

The new arrangements clicked into place when Galton gave James Johnson, the most temperamental of Farmer's creditors, a new interest in Farmer's release. He proposed that this textile trader act as the gun firm's agent in London, on a commission of 3 percent. This would enable Farmer to return to Birmingham, where, Galton insisted, he was badly needed. He and Farmer had first contemplated asking cousin Plumsted to take on the job, but Galton surmised, "It will not suit him to undertake the business of selling guns." Johnson negotiated a higher commission, on the grounds that he was a large creditor and capable of finding customers they would not otherwise find. Plumsted "would not have the least connection with JJ," but Galton countered that they needed an agent, and who better than "a man of assiduity and good fortune and to whom obligations have been formerly acknowledged." He hoped partnership would turn Johnson into an instrument of Farmer's recovery and persuade him to sign Farmer's certificate of discharge. The expense of his commission would be more than compensated by his help in "pushing on the business briskly," enabling it to be "extended more at the out ports." Farmer was determined to win Johnson over: "If his interest will not do it, I do not know what will." Together they convinced Johnson of the "advantage Mr. Farmer's presence here would be." When Johnson dithered, Galton held out the temptation of big government contracts "if a war should be declared." It would be "desirable" that "Mr. Farmer may be cleared to apply for such orders and be with me at Birmingham to help execute them." A month later, he restated the case, hinting broadly at the profits they would all accrue through "continued connection of interest and friendship."

By then, Johnson had become deeply involved in the business. He was a go-between for guns ordered by Champion & Hayley. Galton confided in him his trouble obtaining payment from another customer and shared the status of orders for the Barclays and Hanburys. Late in 1755, Johnson asked Galton to come to London to form "an agreement between you and me for transacting your business in London." By the end of the year, he was delivering guns to the Hanburys and receiving updates from Galton on other London orders. His nephew purchased guns. He tracked ship arrivals, spoke to captains about cargo and debts, and corresponded with

London customers. He handled payments and made discreet inquiries about the credit of prospective customers. He addressed the surveyor general of the Ordnance Office for Galton. He took on Galton's dispute with customs when a shipment for Africa was seized. He was involved in the nitty-gritty about Ordnance Office prices for Galton's guns. Galton drew on him to pay the Darbys for materials. He called on John Galton at Bristol. So, by degrees, the interrelated interests of overseas traders drew a major Manchester textile merchant into Birmingham's gun trade.

Meanwhile, Farmer returned to Birmingham. Galton had pressed the strategic importance of his settling in Birmingham as "the means of making an agent necessary," but all along he had wanted Farmer by his side in Birmingham. The properties at Duddeston, Saltley, and elsewhere were assigned to Galton, who also inherited an estate at Taunton upon his mother's death. In 1756, Farmer and Galton drew up articles for a new, more equal partnership—the first time they had drawn up articles at all. They specified limits on the partners' ability to mortgage the firm and rewards for greater investment in it. They insisted that the parties "be so settled as to give proper attention" to the business and prohibited either partner from entering into any separate business without the other's approval. With Freame & Barclay covering Farmer's initial investment, the bankers held a clear stake in the firm. In bringing Farmer home and ensuring that they both remained devoted to their narrow pursuit of gun manufacturing, Galton had cast the net of his business wider than ever before, involving London financiers and Manchester merchants deeply in his Birmingham firm.

Even after the fateful Lisbon earthquake wiped out all chance of a return on Farmer's investments, the partners continued to hope they might come aright. As 1756 wore on, Galton begged payment from delinquent customers to recover the costs of Farmer's rescue, occasionally addressing the mysterious Montaigut about gun sales in Lisbon before the quake. He prefaced his deferential request for payment to Manesty with a litany of his recent troubles—the sums he had advanced for Farmer's acquittal, the lack of remittances, his debts to friends who had loaned him money in the

interim. Manesty had done him many favors; he was "so good and obliging a friend." He asked customers in South Carolina and Montserrat to
send in their payments—plus "some allowance for the lapsed time"—while
offering further service in providing more top-quality, affordable wares,
"anything in the gun or Birmingham toy goods." By 1760, these persistent
efforts and the return of war demand restored James to "affluent circumstances." Despite fits of ill health, he was "in high spirits, and full of Business," Galton reported to Freame. With a 1766 agreement, Farmer's and
Galton's shares in the business were set at £13,862 and £22,281, respectively. By 1770, the most important gunmaking businesses in town were
theirs and Thomas Ketland's—which was founded around midcentury
and focused on the American trade.

James Farmer died in 1773. The aftermath of his death, like the 1755
postmortem on his finances, reveals the tight bonds between gun manufacture and other commercial pursuits in this time and place. James's old
friends and colleagues David Barclay and Sampson Lloyd II were execu-
tors of his will. The following year, his daughter "Polly" (Mary) married
Charles, another son of Sampson Lloyd, with a dowry of £30,000. One
of Mary and Charles's daughters would marry a Hanbury, the other a
Barclay. The Hanburys and Lloyds were intermarried, too, and embarked
on a joint banking venture with the Lloyds' new bank in the 1770s. Charles
and Mary Lloyd socialized with the Galtons, the Hanburys, the Gurneys
(Quaker bankers at Norwich), and the Gurneys' relative Samuel Hoare, a
Quaker banker and abolitionist.

John Galton died childless in 1775, leaving his brother more estates.
Barclay took charge of discharging "the old affair," still anticipating surprise returns from Lisbon. His bank was now known simply as Barclays
(partnered with Bevan and Bening). Samuel Galton is a dour and forbidding presence on the margins of Barclay's correspondence on Farmer's
affairs in the 1770s, but the bond between the families soon became even
more intimate. In 1777, Samuel Jr. married Barclay's beautiful daughter
Lucy. (It was difficult to defuse rumors that he had married the king's
daughter.) Barclays remained Galton's bankers. The Lloyds were present

in full force at the small funeral for Mary Galton the same year. The Gurneys were involved in the Galton trade in 1780. Tenuous financial ties
between London and the provinces became stronger after the Seven Years'
War, as we see in miniature in the Farmer-Freame story. By the end of the
century, the Galtons were tied by marriage and capital to the biggest
Quaker banking and commercial families in the country. Even as family
bonds invested more people in the gun business, the gunmakers reoriented their business toward banking. The new Galton bank's London discount house was, of course, Barclays.

In Liverpool, too, the Galton firm was tied to powerful forces. Its
agents were three well-known members of the Liverpool Chamber of
Commerce: William James, Francis Ingram, and Alexander Nottingham.
Nottingham was a distinguished member of the "Unanimous Society,"
attended by "gentlemen of the first families of the town," many later
becoming involved with local government. Thomas Hadley also acquired
a prominent agent in Liverpool: Edward Falkner, son of a prosperous
merchant, soldier, and slave trader and high sheriff of Lancashire in 1788.
Thus, as a 1781 author noted, over the century, gunmakers were "so amply
rewarded that they have rolled in their carriages to this day . . . [T]he same
instrument which is death to one man, is genteel life to another."

The gun trade brought the Galtons shoulder to shoulder with the most
illustrious citizens of eighteenth-century Birmingham, not least through
the Lunar Society. Through that society, the natural philosopher and inventor Erasmus Darwin became a close friend; his daughter Violetta married Samuel Tertius. Tertius's brother John Howard married the daughter
of William Strutt, the Derby industrialist and innovator. Their sister
Adèle's husband, the physician Dr. Booth, showed his gratitude for her
great wealth by recommending Tertius's son Francis Galton as a pupil in
the Birmingham hospital, launching his scientific career. Matthew Boulton
not only took gunmakers' help, he had a stake in their affairs. He leased
land from his frequent colleague and Handsworth neighbor John Whateley. James Watt leased a forge and engine from the Whateleys. Boulton
introduced Whateley to his business associate William Matthews to supply
guns for a ship Matthews was fitting out. Matthews and Boulton also

helped the gunmaker James Alston in his relations with Galton and the Ordnance Office. Boulton introduced Galton to the directors of the East India Company's Shipping Committee in 1802; Galton thanked Boulton profusely when the introduction resulted in a gun contract. Boulton composed the differences between Galton and Thomas Archer when Galton's slow payment for muskets Archer made for the East India Company prompted Archer to try to sell them to another contractor. So obvious was Boulton's intimacy with the trade that in 1802, an MP asked him to help determine the maximum weekly output of Birmingham guns in case of French invasion. Naturally, Boulton immediately discussed the matter with Galton over dinner. Gun orders outside Ordnance Office protocols came through Boulton's intercession: Lord Harrowby asked him to order fifty guns, belts, and cartridge boxes to train his volunteers at Sandon. Boulton got them from Galton. These ties gesture at an unstudied intimacy between war and the renowned makers of the industrial revolution. Of course, Boulton was a military supplier in his own right, too.

Interest in the gun trade was widespread. Guns were the product of an expanding military-industrial society in which much of commercial life was shaped by the vagaries of government custom. There were many reasons for Birmingham's remarkable growth, but government demand for armaments was among them. Farmer's effort to break out of his niche as a provincial manufacturer and enter London's metropolitan financial and commercial world highlights the way eighteenth-century industrial capitalism drew far-flung merchants and manufacturers into a tight network of credit, capital, and raw material, in which state demand played a crucial role. Giants of business and industry and more modest subcontractors came to share an interest in the government's wars. Ordnance officials knew the importance of gun contracts to the wider metallurgical world: they avoided importing firearms during the American war in view of the gun trade's importance to the "publick." The Worshipful Company of Gunmakers noted polemically, as early as 1711, that "*English* Arms, are made all of *English* Materials, and every Penny sent out of the Nation upon that Account, was utterly lost, the *English* Impoverish'd and Discourag'd, and the *Dutch* the Gainers; besides a Scandal to the Kingdom, that *England* (famed for Arms) could not furnish their own Army without being beholden to Foreigners." The nation stood for the gun industry, and the gun industry stood for the nation. In the wars of the second half of the century, in fits and starts, the Ordnance Office shaped revolutionary change in an industry central to the making of the state, the nation, and the empire.

The State and the Gun Industry, Part 2: 1756–1815

I n 1815, Liège was no longer Britain's fallback; Britain was the global arms depot. The British government had an arms factory just outside London, south of the Thames. It also had "view rooms" and a proof-house in Birmingham, where its officials managed a vast array of local workers drafted into the task of gunmaking. This was a kind of virtual factory: a highly subdivided and efficient system of mass production, but too inclusive to house under a single roof. Well before the era of machine production, these factories together produced the standard British military arm in millions. That arm was not the best musket they could make but a replica of the simpler musket used by East India Company soldiers in India.

The government enabled the development of this scale of production over the course of the three major wars Britain fought in the second half of the eighteenth century: the Seven Years' War, the American war, and the French Revolutionary and Napoleonic Wars. As Ordnance Office demand skyrocketed, gunmakers became increasingly dependent on it. The office also worked with them in new ways. Steering a crooked line between alienating domestic manufacturers and offending foreign suppliers, either of whom might unload their wares on Britain's enemies, the office began to play with gun design and industrial organization in the gun trade, in hopes of dramatically expanding the trade's productive capacity to secure the arms the kingdom needed in its ever larger conflicts. These experiments finally succeeded during the Napoleonic Wars, when the East India Company guided the office toward a design that an expanded and reorganized military-industrial society could produce in mass quantities on a new order of magnitude. Revolution had come to the gun industry.

The Seven Years' War is known to Americans as the French and Indian War; it started with tensions in the American colonies but became a global conflict. All the European powers (except the Ottoman Empire) joined opposing coalitions led by France and Britain to settle stakes abroad and within Europe. The coalitions clashed in South Asia, North America, and the West Indies. In the end, the war paved the way for Britain's global supremacy, the rise of Britain's ally Prussia in Central Europe, and the turmoil in France that would lead to revolution. Britain provisioned 96 percent of the "Combined Army" of British, Prussian, and other allied forces west of the Elbe River, numbering more than a hundred thousand, plus seventy thousand British sailors and soldiers at sea and in the Americas. No previous eighteenth-century army had exceeded eighty thousand. Colonial governments in America wanted their soldiers armed like British regulars, not with assorted fowlers, fusils, and trade guns. This enormous operational scale was not anticipated and continually tested the developing state bureaucracy.

The old Jacobite threat was reduced to an increasingly innocuous subplot of this vast drama as Highland clans joined British forces around the world. In February 1759, the French asked the Young Pretender, Charles Stuart, to land in Ireland or Scotland to raise a rebellion, but he refused, insisting on leading rebellion in England itself. But the French doubted he would garner sufficient support there and cut him out of their plan. They abandoned the invasion idea altogether after the Battle of Quiberon Bay, in 1759, dramatically weakened the French navy—although the possibility of reviving it remained on the table. Spies kept the British apprised of these shifting schemes. More to the point for our story, growing Scottish solidarity with the wider British cause made closer government patronage of the gun industry less risky.

At the start of the war, Birmingham's gunmakers knew their fortunes had taken a turn for the better. The Ordnance Office sent Robert Bennet, George Markbee, and Richard Davis to town; contracts went out. Galton waited for Davis to confirm the "exactness" he would require before fixing prices. He showed small lots of rough guns to Markbee to ensure that their work passed muster. The state now rigorously monitored production— both its speed and its quality. Markbee submitted monthly reports of barrels viewed and passed in Birmingham. In May 1756, he refused 81 of Galton's 373 barrels, or about one-fifth. In June, of Farmer & Galton's 457, he passed 385. In July, Farmer & Galton was the single biggest supplier, providing 344 barrels, of which 85 were refused (nearly 25 percent). In August, they were the biggest by a wider margin, providing 476 barrels, of which 87 were refused (18 percent).

The Ordnance Office relied less on foreign arms than in any previous war partly because of the difficulty of finding and shipping arms of the right quality with the French blockading Liège. It was able to purchase five thousand muskets through agents in Amsterdam in August. Then, in 1759, the office contracted for 3,000 muskets from the new Prince of Orange factory at Culemborg, but the arms never arrived. It accepted stranded Dutch arms from a London merchant that proved useless. It later contracted for 10,000 Liège arms through an agent, but by the middle of 1761, fewer than 2,500 had arrived. Less than half of the total was ever delivered, much of it useless.

All this put Birmingham's gunsmiths in a strong position. On Joseph Oughton's request, the office paid in ready money. Old contractors, pointing to new rivals, requested ever higher pay. Galton explained to Surveyor General Charles Frederick that he had altered his forges and mills to make military barrels and had just begun to produce large quantities when his workmen were "alarmed by new contractors" offering cash. He had had to raise wages. Locks also cost more. In short, with the competition, strict proof, and dear iron, government prices were "too low." He had James Johnson follow up with Frederick, certain that "his honor would be willing the manufacturers should have moderate encouragement." He was right: citing representations from "barrel forgers and lockmakers" and a desire "to give them all possible encouragement," the Ordnance Office ordered higher barrel and lock prices, urging "utmost dispatch." It did not raise prices for complete muskets, "the same being sufficient upon the whole and not complained of." Galton was thrilled; the advance would "encourage us to proceed with more vigor as may hope now to get some profit whereas before twas doubtful of any."

The office fulfilled its commitment to take on guns left over from the previous war. It allowed Galton to set up complete muskets with leftover materials. Thomas Hadley and the Jordans also transcended their roles as parts suppliers and did setting-up work or offered complete muskets. While reminding them not to entice the workmen of other contractors in this work, the office itself used the new price Galton had extracted to attract new contractors like John Wood. Within weeks, Jordan was complaining that Wood and others were stealing his men. While Galton brought workmen into his manufactory, Hadley remained "in great want of more hands," carping about warrants granted to "some quite foreign in the business." The Birmingham paper reported missing gun workers, advertising rewards for their return and threatening prosecution of those who employed them. Grice & Edge and William Perry of Wednesbury were new lockmakers. John Whateley offered two hundred barrels a month and received an initial contract for a thousand. Richard Hornbuckle, a bayonet and blade grinder, contracted for a thousand barrels. The Ordnance Office was widening the pool less out of dynastic fears now than out of a desire to speed production. John Hirst and Charles Pickfatt were initially the primary London setters-up, since others, like Richard Wilson, "in combination . . . did refuse to set up any Small Arms at the same price." But they were soon joined by Richard How, John Brazier, John Bumford, Joseph Buckmaster, and Michael Memory.

Many contractors still clung to alternative custom, even if goods were somewhat "more precarious of reaching" the right hands. Farmer & Galton sent arms for the bankruptcy committee, Richard Oswald, Oswald's captain, and a Mr. Bagnall of Liverpool. Galton was keen to reestablish his firm's soundness with old customers in the West Indies, writing to them to request remittances and affirm his continued willingness to serve, especially with Farmer "now settled with me in the gun manufactory at Birmingham." Peter Farmer, an employee of the New York merchant Moses Franks, came to London and inquired about guns. Galton assured him they could make any type "and [I] think [I] may assert none more capable." Laying out his prices, he cautioned that it would likely take extra time in war conditions and referred Peter to a London customer who had bought similar sorts, "little inferior to those sold to the Tower," obligingly offering cheaper sorts, too. Peter was an old customer, "very safe," but, when he ordered £500 worth of goods, Galton asked James Johnson to linger around his favorite coffeehouse to make inquiries "with secrecy." Brisk sales out of Bristol for the West Indies, Africa, and North America continued. John Galton invested in ships, anticipating large gun sales. In Scarborough in 1760, Samuel kept his eye on the "East Country ships" and anticipated sales on ships due in Bristol from Stockholm.

The state's lukewarm embrace encouraged these dalliances, but then a learning process unfolded. Slow barrel production prompted the state to experiment with the instruments at its disposal—design, prices, inspection—to stimulate speedier production. Markbee saw only 1,152 barrels in January 1757 (rejecting 287), and imported arms that arrived that month were so bad that they were returned. Markbee alighted on the problem: 3,000 barrels and locks were under manufacture for Ireland on the same patterns as the Ordnance Office's, but "not quite so good." By April, barrel production for the office had climbed to more than 2,000, holding through the summer. When several contractors fell tardy again, they were threatened with cancellation, but this stick came with a carrot. The office belatedly fulfilled Jordan's earlier appeal for an increase in musketoon, pistol, and carbine barrel prices, citing rising iron prices, higher wages, and stricter inspection. Barrel production improved.

When Hirst contracted to set up the next 20,000, the office solicited proposals for their parts based on contractors' prior work. Finding that Wilson's barrels had stood the proof "extremely well being made of the best sort of iron," Frederick recommended he make and set up

3,000—without interfering with Hirst's work. Such arrangements promised to bring in 34,200 guns inside a year. The office was looking beyond
immediate needs, determining to keep Tower stores constantly at these
levels: 50,000 long land muskets; 10,000 short land muskets; 30,000 short
muskets for marines or militia; 5,000 carbines for artillery or Highlanders; 2,000 carbines for cavalry; 12,000 pairs of land pistols; 20,000 sea
service muskets; 2,000 musketoons; and 10,000 pairs of sea service pistols.
It apportioned contracts by past productivity to Farmer & Galton, Vernon
& Haskins, Whateley, Grice & Edge, and Oughton. Barrel production
shot up that winter to 4,626 barrels. When it fell to 2,100–2,600 in the
spring of 1758, Markbee pointed again to large orders for the East India
Company and Ireland, not required to be "so nice" or viewed so strictly.
(The East India Company, meanwhile, was beset by complaints from
Bengal about quality, particularly brittle locks.) The office decided, as in
1718, to compromise on design. The Ordnance official Thomas Hartwell
suggested manufacture of a "second sort of barrel" for marines and militia,
which would be sixpence cheaper and "not filed to the exactness . . . required of late"—although the difference would be imperceptible to "an
indifferent person." He presented samples, and the Ordnance Board
agreed to alter the standard military firearm for the sake of commercial
expedience. Farmer & Galton was the first firm to make the new barrels.
Rivalry among the many faces of the emerging imperial state—the Ordnance Office, the East India Company, the Irish government—encouraged
movement toward an arm in which function and functionality mattered
more than artistry and artisanal perfection, paving the way toward a mass-
producible gun.

Markbee's reports improved, peaking in September at more than
4,000 barrels. Stocking and setting up proceeded apace in early 1759, but
the barrel makers faltered again. In January, Markbee dropped below
2,000 barrels. Hartwell repaired to Birmingham to "hasten the Barrel
Makers." There he secured more than 4,000 barrels, at one shilling per
barrel less than the office price, by assuring manufacturers that they would
be paid for as soon as they were proved and viewed. He recommended that
another official assist Markbee; John Stewart got the job. The Ordnance

Office learned that the barrel makers could do more, more quickly, if scrupulously watched and provided sufficient incentive. Those 4,000 barrels would have been sold to private customers had Hartwell not come up. Hartwell's design experiment had some salutary effect: in March, Markbee passed 6,602 barrels, many of the new "second sort." The figure fell to 2,800 the next month but was bumped up to nearly 3,500 in May and 4,500 in June.

The Ordnance Office also discovered that timely payment mattered. Gun contractors typically received debentures to present at the Treasury for payment, although at times they got interest-bearing imprests like shipping contractors. In 1759, as Grice & Edge worked diligently on thousands of locks, they were in "great want of money," the office owing them at least £6,600. They asked for £3,000 immediately. The Ordnance Board assured them it would pay as soon as money could be spared. That summer, barrel makers and lockmakers blamed slow production on their being "greatly distressed for the Money." They faced trade action from their artisans. Lockmakers declared that the "masters of the gunlock trade being of a mercenary temper thought their gains not sufficient and have combined to lower and sink the prices." Every journeyman who had "his own and his family's interest at heart will not refuse to meet at the sign of the Swan in the W. B. [West Bromwich] to prevent the combination, for if they [the masters] are suffered to proceed we with our families must soon be sent to the workhouse." This militancy was the result not of low demand but of high iron prices as the war disrupted Baltic imports, causing industrial action in many Birmingham trades from 1759 to 1761. When gunmakers tried other iron, complaints of breakages prompted an Ordnance Office order that all locks be made of the "best Swedish iron." Markbee patrolled the workshops to ensure obedience.

The office began to enforce rules against poaching workers more studiously. Thus, when Wood asked for more orders in 1759, Hartwell advised that he was no lockmaker, nor did he have any men employed in that business, and that giving him orders would interfere with those given to others. Wilson had been judged the best barrel supplier in 1757; in 1759, when he requested orders for more lucrative sorts before completing existing orders, Markbee revealed, "He is no Barrel or Lock Maker but buys them of [*sic*] the trade." Wilson continued to appear in Markbee's monthly reports as he completed outstanding orders, and within a few months he had persuaded the Ordnance Board to grant more. The office did not burn bridges, especially since rivalry worked in its favor.

Price hikes remained a useful instrument. After an abysmal 1,664 barrels passed in January 1760, Farmer & Galton and Whateley requested higher barrel prices and got their wish. Hirst extracted a price hike for setting up carbines, citing proliferation of patterns. The new prices helped. From May through December, Markbee passed between 3,500 and 4,500 barrels almost every month. Barrel production remained erratic, but further crisis was averted, and many barrel makers—William Grice, Thomas Jordan, Richard Edge, Farmer & Galton—filled lock contracts without trouble. As Hirst indicated, the volatility was due partly to the office's continually shifting needs: Farmer and Galton, too, found themselves "frequently obliged to make one sort of Barrels when the Board are in want of them," when they had not quite completed a warrant for another sort, "a great Inconvenience" that "frequently occasions their Warrants not to be completed, so soon as they would have been." Since the barrels were the same price, they asked the board to permit either sort to be received "as they are most wanted[,] and Endorsed on the Warrants as they shall be received." This dialogue between contractors and the state on prices and patterns improved efficiency of mass production.

Awareness that payment of any kind trumped manufacturers' need for just reward emboldened the Ordnance Office to solicit discounts in the war's waning days. Hirst protested working for lower prices, reminding the office of his unique amenability at the start of the war. He positioned himself as a favorite—a new and tenuous claim in the gun-contracting world. It worked. When Wilson swooped in with a discount, the office stood by Hirst, recalling Wilson's refusal to set up guns in 1754—unlike Hirst, who "did throughout all the War, when Arms were extremely wanted . . . at the same reduced price made in time of Peace." Wilson's timing—three days after Hirst's plea—also seemed calculated "to prejudice Mr. Hirst." The office also rejected Wilson's offer of parts, recalling that his firm "were neither Barrel nor Lock Makers" and that he had made "extreamly bad" barrels. Instead, contracts went to Farmer & Galton, Whateley, Oughton, and others for twenty thousand barrels and four thousand locks. "The contract work had now assumed the semblance of a closed shop," a historian notes. "In Birmingham, the manufacture of barrels and locks was under the control of a few families of gunmakers . . . often inter-marrying and forming partnerships. In London, the work of rough stocking and setting up was almost exclusively in the hands of two men": James Waller and Hirst. Nearly 305,000 arms were delivered during the war by forty-seven London contractors.

Birmingham's gunmakers emerged prosperous from the war. In July 1763, Joseph Oughton Jr., "an eminent Gun-Barrel-Maker of this town," married his colleague John Whateley's daughter Dolly, who had "a handsome fortune." They, along with Farmer, Galton, Hadley, and Grice, were among the prominent citizens who subscribed to the town's new general hospital. In 1766, Hadley died "a very considerable Gun-maker." The members of this emerging establishment were well positioned to navigate the shifting terrain of peacetime.

After the Treaty of Paris was signed in February 1763, the signs of an industrial downturn began to gather. Uncompleted gun orders were canceled, and payment for them prorated. Manufacturers tried to settle accounts for parts and guns they had sent over and above their contracts and tried to unload leftovers. By July, Birmingham's industrial prosperity had abruptly ended; bankruptcies were rife. Four gun workers were among the dozen or so unemployed craftsmen who deserted their families in 1765. But, as the British remained in conflict around the globe, gun manufacturing remained somewhat out of step with the general economic slump. Contractors busily maintained existing inventory, repairing and altering thousands of locks for years. Some became piece men and daymen at the Small Gun Office, employed year-round on repairs. William Sharp provided steel rammers, springs, boring bits, musket swivels, wood screws, and "forged work" for locks. Markbee viewed thousands of new barrels in Birmingham, at levels comparable to wartime. Barrel makers could not produce fast enough for Hirst. In 1764, Oughton, Whateley,

Farmer & Galton, and Vernon & Haskins contracted to make 10,000 barrels and 8,000 locks. Contracts went out for setting up rough-stocked arms in store. The Ordnance Office ordered new arms for particular regiments. In 1765, Hirst requested work to employ his men "who would otherwise be likely to leave him" and was allotted arms to set up in advance of his contract for that year. He and Waller went on to set up thousands. He also repaired barrels and borrowed liberally from the Tower to fulfill a Portuguese contract for "a great Number of small Arms," on the understanding that he would replace or pay for the parts when asked. When he produced 3,000 more locks than Portugal needed, the Tower took them. The state was clearly invested in his commercial survival. In both 1764 and 1765, Farmer and Galton estimated a profit of about £3,000. For 1766, the Ordnance Office asked their usual barrel makers to produce 13,000 barrels and 20,500 locks. Hirst set up 15,000 arms. Through 1767–1768, Farmer & Galton and the others supplied barrels and locks in the tens of thousands. The Brown Bess was redesigned in 1768 to improve mobility and ease of use, and this, too, fueled component manufacturing. In 1769, Hirst again successfully requested more orders to keep his men employed. This went on through 1770.

Stores were constantly being depleted because the post-1763 peace was purely notional. The Seven Years' War filliped the British state into a condition of almost permanent warfare for a half century. In North America, French Protestants heading to South Carolina received two hundred muskets. Settlers provoked tensions with Native Americans already rankled by their subordination to the peace settlement, and Pontiac's War followed in 1763–64. British regiments remained in the field in 1764—including Joseph Farmer's, in Pensacola, Florida. In 1767, returning regiments were still storing their guns. Colonial policing also intensified, to enforce the taxation that paid for these arms purchases. The Ordnance Office would never again allow stocks to dwindle unwatched. It anticipated an enduring need for arms, taking measures to ensure that gun workers would not wander into other employment, as in earlier interludes of peace. Its needs were less than the forty to sixty thousand Hirst turned out annually during wartime but considerably more than orders in 1753 or

1752. The tax regime expanded and shifted, giving the state a new capacity to pay for its new attitude toward arms procurement.

Expansion in India was part of this constant activity. In 1763, the East India Company committed to steady continuance of contracts; Calcutta officials prayed "our Want of Arms may be plentifully supplied as our Expence of that Article is very great. We think our Demand will be about five thousand stand annually." In 1766, the company's Madras Council adopted a policy of providing an extra spare musket for each company soldier (sepoy) of the same quality as the arms provided to European troops—thus they had 100 percent reserves of arms. They also needed seventeen thousand new arms, plus more arms for the nawab of Arcot, with whom the company shared power in southern India. The company's capacity to pay for these purchases expanded vastly after its acquisition of the right to collect taxes—Diwani rights—in Bengal in 1765. The need for guns likewise emerged from steady expansion of its forces as it struggled to subdue Bengal, Yusuf Khan in Madurai (1764), and Hyder Ali in Mysore (1767–69), while also expanding into the Northern Circars (1766). Before 1765, its bill for small arms rose above £10,000 on only three occasions, but after 1765, an annual outlay of £20,000 to £50,000 was the norm. In 1767 and 1769, payments were more than £60,000. In 1768–69, nearly 100,000 barrels were proved for the company. Because of the warm and humid climate, guns for India required replacement three times as often as those in the King's Service. The company was also somewhat extravagant, "*too ready* to replace arms . . . abused by the users."

The new tax policies triggered protest at home and abroad. In the spring of 1770, tensions about taxation led to the infamous Boston Massacre, in which British troops guarding the customs house shot into a crowd of civilians, killing five and injuring six. This scandal forced the government to reconsider the revenue mechanisms that sustained contracting. Ordnance Office gun orders abruptly stopped. John Stewart announced that stores were full and returned to the Tower. Gunmakers could not cope with this unexpected turn of events easily. Since warrants were usually granted late, they had, as usual, "proceeded in getting up musket barrels locks and bayonets in order to keep their workmen employed and in order to supply them within the time limited." They pleaded with the office for it to grant warrants at least for arms on hand, lest they be rendered "useless as they are of such a construction as not [to] be vendible elsewhere." The office refused. Only Grice succeeded in unloading six or seven hundred surplus locks. A year later, Farmer & Galton was still trying to unload thousands of parts fit only for government service.

Still, the East India Company's needs remained robust—partly thanks to government support. Frustration with quality prompted the company to alter its pattern in 1770, burdening gunmakers with thousands of old-pattern parts even while securing them new orders. Further changes in 1771 consolidated the classic "India-pattern" musket. Taking stock of the firm, Galton discovered enormous "bad debts" and "dead stock" for the Ordnance Office *and* the East India Company, the latter amounting to £2,500. But the company vigorously kept up demand. These were the years in which it stormed Vellore (1771), besieged Tanjore (1775), and occupied Awadh and Rohilkhand (1772–75). In 1771, it wanted forty thousand muskets for Madras and more for the nawab of Arcot, Bengal, the nawab of Awadh, the Bombay Marine, and the king of Travancore. The company was ever poised on the brink of bankruptcy as it chased more and more revenue-rich territory. Finally, a general credit crisis in 1772 forced it to turn to Parliament for help, triggering the first steps of its institutional merger with other government bodies. Parliament passed the Regulating Act of 1773 to forestall the company's bankruptcy and subjected the company to greater parliamentary control. While Birmingham's trade generally suffered during the crisis, Parliament's efforts to preserve the company sheltered gunmakers from the worst. When the American war started in 1775, the Ordnance Office had difficulty luring Birmingham's smiths away from Indian work.

To be sure, they served African markets, too. In 1765, Lord Shelburne noted prodigious quantities of guns made in Birmingham for Africa. The Ordnance Office still supported this trade by allowing gunmakers to buy Tower materials. But this work did not sustain the trade financially. Competition was ugly. Thomas Hadley II had inherited both his father's firm and its rivalry with Farmer & Galton. In 1772, he faced accusations of undercutting in Bristol, suffering a "clamorous and riotery" attack on his home. In an advertisement in *Aris's Birmingham Gazette,* he warned the band of gun workers behind the violence that a repetition would be vigorously prosecuted. To disprove the charge of undercutting, he extracted a letter from two Bristol merchants explaining that shippers demanded heavy discounts on guns because the Galton firm had lowered its prices and Galton's Bristol agent had claimed that Galton and Hadley were colluding in the discount. Hadley denied this rumor, pledging to expose "every prevaricating Rascal who shall attempt to Father his cringing underhand Tricks and Dealings upon me." Galton deigned to disavow the "obscure and malignant Charge" and explained that he had decided to spare the public further distraction by a private matter by submitting the relevant correspondence to his prominent fellow citizens John Kettle, Samuel Bradburne, and Elias Wallin, who authorized him to state that "they consider me as acquit of such Charge." Hadley considered this "no Answer at all": "TRUTH MAINTAINED," he proclaimed. The nineteen-year-old Samuel Jr., with characteristic readiness for confrontation, now accused Hadley of forging the Bristol merchants' letter. Suspecting the gazette's editor of favoring Galton, Hadley resorted to a handbill rebuking both the editor and Galton. In the name of "the poor workmen employed in the trade," he accused Galton of lying.

Gunmakers were clearly distressed. Galton learned of a club of gun workers attempting to compel Hadley to raise prices to match his. It met at the Nags Head, and the proprietor, William Bonnington, kept him informed. Galton refused to have anything to do with the club, on the grounds that all such "combinations of workmen . . . [were] illegal" and that even a club formed with good intentions "might end in tumult clamour and riot." Moreover, he was loath to sow dissent between Hadley and his men. But the information did prompt him to lower his wages: for an order of several hundred sham Danish guns—typically a losing proposition—he asked the finishers to work at the price he heard Hadley paid, twopence less per gun than he gave. They agreed but joined the club.

Galton heard them out and restored the two pennies. That fall, they refused outwork for nearly a month. These collective protests were part of the making of the English working class—its Midlands metallurgical chapter.

Matters took a turn for the worse when Hadley learned that Galton was discounting prices in Liverpool, too. He accused Galton of deliberately underselling him and incited workmen to violence against Galton and his clerk William Bird. Anonymous threatening letters, attacks on his lodgings, torrents of abuse in public, threats of branding by hot-fired tongs on his way to Wednesbury—these were some of Bird's sufferings. Galton's home was repeatedly attacked, the windows broken by stones flung from Hadley's yard. His guns were stopped from leaving the warehouse, his men forced to send guns back unfinished. Hadley threatened them and his own workmen with unemployment and inspired them with gifts of money, blue ribbons, flags, beer, and incendiary renderings of the latest news of Cornish miners' riots and Scottish corn riots, alternatively promising impunity and martyrdom to secure their participation in this violent campaign.

Galton suspected that Hadley's objective in hijacking the gun workers' club was to keep his firm from completing its orders for sixteen thousand guns. He was certain his attackers were not the workers but "lads of spirit who wished the gun finishers well," since the finishers "had not spirit to do such things themselves." Indeed, Hadley berated gun workers for lacking the spirit to do injury. Many of his prospective henchmen deserted and became witnesses for Galton in the suit the latter launched; two fetched the constables to suppress one of the more unruly meetings. Some tried to go back to work for Galton but were subjected to the routine of broken windows until they rejoined the society. The lines between worker and master were too blurred for Hadley's plot to work without criminal coercion, and misery was too shared, for, despite large orders for Africa, the Galton firm was insecure. The next year, it and other firms again tried in vain to get the Ordnance Office to take their leftovers. When Galton assessed the firm's health upon Farmer's death that summer, he reckoned that £9,000 of the £22,000 debts to the firm could not be repaid because of "distress attending people in the trade." He cited the "the bad state of [the African trade] with the merchants" adding to the dead stock on his hands. Among the fifty to sixty Birmingham craftsmen who abandoned their families to the parish that summer were a dozen definitely belonging to the gun trade. (Others, too, may have been part of it.) For seven years after 1763, the Ordnance Office had remained hungry for arms, but its appetite was sated by 1770, when it pushed up against the limits of its subjects' tolerance for taxation. The war machine kicked into gear enough to lessen the state's interest in supporting the industry but was not yet steady enough to support the gunmakers single-handedly. Gunmakers had become dependent on the state. Left in the lurch from 1771 to 1774, apart from East India Company orders, they had nowhere to turn but against one another.

B ut the trial was not long, for Britain was gearing up for war just a year later. In March 1775, Patrick Henry dared, "Give me Liberty, or give me Death!" urging the Colonial Convention of Virginia to armed resistance against the British governor, Lord Dunmore, who had banned election of delegates to the Continental Congress. Dunmore prudently removed the gunpowder from the local magazine, but the Royal Marines sneaking it out were discovered. Patrick Henry led the Hanover militia to Williamsburg; Dunmore evacuated his family from the Governor's Palace and threatened to destroy the town if they attacked. The local revenue collector paid out royal funds for the gunpowder, and the men left. Dunmore proclaimed Henry a criminal. A month later, he fled to a British warship at Yorktown.

As these portentous events unfolded, the Ordnance Board at last heeded gunmakers offering stock on their hands. John York, a dayman hired after the preceding war, went to Birmingham. Galton unloaded the most, but William Grice, Benjamin Willets, Barker & Harris, Joseph Oughton, John Whateley, and others also sent in portions. By summer, the brewing conflict had altered their destinies more decisively. Galton, Willets, Grice, Edge (contracting separately), Barker & Harris, Oughton, Whateley, Thomas Blakemore, and Henry Nock (in London) received orders for 26,000 barrels and 20,000 locks. Within days, thousands of guns were readied for Dunmore. The board curtly told Thomas Hadley that it had no occasion "for any other contractor at present," likely appeasing collective opinion in the wake of the recent clash.

The reviving trade was constrained by a bottleneck in lockmaking. Lock contractors, including Galton, tried to coax workmen in the villages around Birmingham toward government work, but they were fully employed on East India Company work at a higher price and more forgiving view (not requiring measurement against gauges until 1781). When bayonet makers were similarly busy on India work, contractors and York simply advertised for new workmen, drawing more manufacturers into the Ordnance Office orbit. But lockmaking required skill that took time to acquire. In the previous war, slow barrel production had provoked tentative experiments with inspection and price incentives. Now, lock delays triggered a bolder government effort to tinker with the artisanal order and imagine more collective forms of manufacturing. At first, the Ordnance Board simply refused lockmakers' persistent demands for higher prices and had York report "particularly what Locks are now making in pursuance of the Boards orders." But stubborn vigilance did not stimulate productivity. The office then resorted to the pariah Hadley, who contracted for 1,000 barrels and 2,500 locks and was assured that he might "rely upon further orders." As Virginia broke into full rebellion, the Ordnance Office opened its arms more widely. William Holden of Birmingham received a warrant for six hundred barrels and locks in two months.

The office was braced for "demands we may expect from the nature of this war" and prepared to put the royal arsenals on "the most respectable footing." Galton won a contract for 225 rifles, as one of four contractors deemed most efficient and reliable. Birmingham was prolific in supplying parts, as York regularly reported. A French traveler marveled that the town added three hundred new houses annually as new enterprises flourished. The Tower staff expanded, and daymen worked from 5 a.m. till 8 p.m. Walter Dick, a Loyalist from South Carolina, was hired as a gunsmith for the Small Gun Office. But locks remained a problem. The Ordnance Office contemplated sending an officer to Liège as an "Emergency" measure. The work for the East India Company was not the issue. That company was fully involved in the conflict; its demand for arms inevitably spiked when the Ordnance Office's did, and it was not in the office's interest to sideline company procurement—or "private" sales like the thousand "Indian trading guns" exported to Florida. The Ordnance Board happily obliged the company's requests to prove its barrels at the Tower—more than twenty thousand in 1776 alone. The London gunmakers' company petitioned in vain to have the India proof returned to their proofhouse. Indian guns had to be good; the company's Court of Directors raised prices to ensure that manufacturers used good iron after complaints about "small weak ill-temper'd Locks." The problem was not India but the mass scale of the war, represented by the joint heavy demands of the Ordnance Office and East India Company. The office had to find a way to stimulate mass production.

In May 1776, it decided to engage Galton, Willets, Grice, Blakemore, and Nock "as a Company" to furnish locks on a monthly basis, promising three months' notice before canceling the arrangement. They refused the advance of £1,000–£1,500 offered "to put them all upon one footing in point of stock," presuming "they were paid for what they delivered in six months from the delivery." By making responsibility for locks collective, the office hoped to create a bloc whose influence might rival that of London-based contractors engaged by the East India Company and prevent inflationary internal competition for locks. The only alternative to this experiment was the scheme of a recently bankrupted Wednesbury gunmaker named Thomas Hopkins, who offered to go up "in the country" with an Ordnance Office agent and two lock viewers, to pay lockmakers sixpence extra and put it "out of the power of the India People to get up any." He assured that "the Men would sooner work for him than any of the Contractors" and that he would bring in 20,000 locks by Christmas. The Ordnance Board thought this plan "very uncertain." To give the new lock company a real chance, it kept Holden and Hadley at arm's length, contracting with them for barrels only and rebuking them for sending locks without orders. The board refused William Sharp's locks, too. Only after the "company" had delivered their locks did the board welcome others, firmly reminding Hadley and Holden not to interfere with or obstruct their work. Hadley's request to provide locks "singly and not in connection with other contractors" to better "exert his full power for the service of government" met with cold reception. The office did take locks from Whateley but modestly contracted for only 650 of the 2,500 he promised that year. It also raised lock prices—not as high as lockmakers demanded, but acknowledging that the lock cost them only sixpence less than what they were paid, a slim margin.

This was an experiment in industrial organization for the sake of mass production, led by a state office. But it did not work. By July, Galton, Willets, Grice, and Blakemore confessed "nonperformance" of their contract. The consequent penalty of £1,000 was forgiven, however, when they explained that lockmakers had exploited the knowledge that they were bound in penalty to extort higher prices. Collectivizing lock procurement through master contractors had only given village lockmakers more leverage. For the moment, the office turned to contractors outside the "company": Hadley, Holden, and Sharp. But it also evolved a new plan for collective production. Orders would again be given "in the joint names of the Standing contractors and not separately," but a new general warehouse would receive locks for them. In addition, a viewer, Edward Hines, would inspect locks in Birmingham (and neighboring villages) before the Tower inspection, where an additional viewer was also hired. Galton, Grice, Willets, Blakemore, Holden, and Hadley "highly approve[d]" the plan: "each contractor in consequence will contribute to the general fund his proportion for completing the same." They estimated that they could supply nine to fifteen hundred locks per week, fifty to seventy thousand a year. The arrangement was designed to inhibit inflationary competition: the new warehouse would ensure that locksmiths delivered locks to them rather than to more congenial clients swooping in to take them on easier terms. It would also inhibit locksmiths from playing contractors off one another to extort ever higher prices. Lastly, it would reduce the costs contractors bore for transporting arms rejected at the Tower back to Birmingham (nine days by road and canal). But after two months, Hines still had "no place to inspect the Arms in as the Men object against the general

Warehouse for the Inspection." Galton, Grice, Blakemore, and Willets complained of "other contractors endeavoring to stimulate the workmen against working for the owners of the General Warehouse." As the office accepted some locks from Holden and Sharp and warned contractors against damaging delays, ninety-five lockmakers submitted a petition against the warehouse. The office shared it with Galton, assuring "all the support in their power." It guaranteed the lockmakers' leader, Thomas Parks, that contractors would not lower prices and agreed to let them receive locks at their own warehouses and *from there* send them to the General Warehouse. The petitioners agreed to mend locks found faulty. The Ordnance Board concluded that failure of lock supply resulted not from "Dissatisfaction of the Contractors on account of the Payments but from the Dissensions among themselves and disagreements with their workmen." It insisted that lockmakers "proceed . . . with Harmony," lest the office be forced "much against their Will . . . to take steps that will be disagreeable to them all." It is unclear what ominous steps the board had in mind; consultation with the office solicitor availed nothing. The office allowed a one-off "indulgence" of buying locks from Henry Nock, lest repetition prompt "applications of other contractors for the like." Then the stakes of the dilemma rose dramatically in 1778–79, as France and Spain joined the war.

The office tried to address contractors' other difficulties. When Galton and others complained about "the length of time they lay out their money owing to the slow progress of the proving and viewing of barrels," the office ordered payment from date of delivery before proof. When Galton complained of slow bayonet viewing, the office reprimanded York and let Galton send his bayonets to the Tower for viewing. Galton was increasingly important, judging by the board's frequent reference to its Birmingham contractors as "Galton and the rest of the gunmakers." But continual complaints about lock shortages finally convinced the office to give up on the warehouse experiment in March 1778. Instead, locks would be delivered by the same individuals "from time to time," without any specific agreement. Now it directed the Tower proofhouse not to prove guns for the East India Company or any other customer while guns lay

unproved for His Majesty's Service. The India company reverted to proofing at the Worshipful Company of Gunmakers' proofhouse.

While the Ordnance Office struggled to create industrial breakthrough in a critical war industry, it took temporary recourse to foreign
arms. Birmingham lockmakers tried again for higher prices, but the office
turned to Liège as never before. Thomas Fitzherbert, a Portsmouth contractor for artillery and wagon horses and drivers, was there to get two
thousand carbines made. Now he delivered a musket pattern to Liège
gunsmiths and contracted for twenty thousand to be sent via Ostend on a
specially deployed ship. French diplomats complained. Fitzherbert was
authorized to get another five thousand and then another twenty thousand the next year. A viewer from the Small Gun Office went to Liège.
Then Fitzherbert reported rumors that he could not fill orders because
another agent was sabotaging him. The Ordnance Board reaffirmed its
commitment to him, but in fact George Crawford, a merchant claiming
better Liège contacts, was edging Fitzherbert out. He had engaged the
best workmen so that no one else could contract for good guns there. He
offered the Ordnance Office eight hundred arms a week, a total of twenty
to forty thousand guns. The office paid cash for ten thousand, on the
grounds that they were cheap and it faced a "great deficiency of arms."
Crawford later provided another five thousand and assured more whenever needed. Even after the office was sated, foreign purchases continued,
simply to deny the arms to the French and the Americans. Crawford also
gathered intelligence about enemy arms, sending their patterns to the
Ordnance Office. The master general supported Fitzherbert's procurement of twenty thousand arms in 1779 out of fear that "the Enemy were
intending to buy them up."

In the meantime, the Ordnance Office finally found a way to dramatically expand British gun-manufacturing capacity. It broke the lockmakers' stranglehold by expanding the reach of London contractors, undoing
the Ordnance system of manufacture it had created to check the latter's
power earlier in the century. Early in the war, John Hirst's son was their
regular setter-up (the elder Hirst died in 1776), but the office added many
more, including William Wilson (whose father, Richard, had died in 1766),

Thompson Davis (a former Small Gun Office smith), and John Pratt, a lock viewer at the Small Gun Office and auctioneer at the Tower who resigned in 1777 to enter the gun trade. These new setters-up did not assemble parts from Tower stores, as Hirst had long done; instead they sourced parts independently. They internalized the burden of parts sourcing, freeing the Ordnance Office from managing the division of labor among subcontractors. Thus the office canceled Samuel Oakes's contract upon learning that he wanted only to set up rather than to supply complete muskets. It gave successive contracts to John Harrison, who offered to arrange the stocking, setting up, and finishing of guns he supplied. Michael Memory, a setter-up in the preceding war, had been brushed off in 1777 but now contracted to stock and set up—with his own barrels and locks—five hundred sea muskets. Pratt proposed bayonets but was asked to set up muskets, finding the locks, stocks, and bayonets on his own with his own credit and cash resources. In 1778–79, he did work valued at £47,755 (though he had been paid only £2,000). In the previous war, some Birmingham parts suppliers had evolved into setters-up; now the Ordnance Office encouraged London contractors to break Birmingham's control of parts supply. The Worshipful Company's new strength was evident in its successful bid for livery status just then, aimed at controlling retailers who sold bad guns, excluding inexpert hands from the business, and dignifying the company.

This latest Ordnance Office–driven transformation and the foreign gun purchases together meant a loosening of design strictures. The office traded standardization for mass supply, despite the premium placed on standardization. It accepted Hirst's muskets, with their side plate that was "flat and longer" than that of the standard musket. It accepted Daniel Moore's offer of three thousand muskets in six months according to his own pattern. This system allowed gun workers normally not considered skilled enough for Ordnance Office work to participate, widening the pool of smiths. The new general London contractors now dealt directly with Birmingham's locksmiths. At times they had no better luck than the office. But new lockmaking talent was certainly tapped: Leonard of Lichfield contracted for a thousand locks. Hirst asked Hines and York to view barrels and locks in Birmingham specifically finished for him. The office later decided to have such locks viewed at the Tower instead. Galton was initially surprised at the requests for Tower locks from other contractors, loyally offering to decline if the office desired. He and other contractors routinely began selling locks directly to Pratt and other setters-up. Galton now struggled for payment from the Ordnance Office *and* Pratt. Between this new system of contracting and the foreign purchases, Ordnance Office stores were overflowing by 1780, and contract work dissipated.

The office was abruptly reminded of the stakes of loyalty to gunmakers during the Gordon Riots in June that year. In the wake of legislation allowing Roman Catholics to join the armed forces without swearing the religious oath, Lord George Gordon whipped his Protestant Association into a frenzy of fear about a return to absolutism. On June 6, 1780, he entered Parliament to present a petition against popery, with fifty thousand angry Londoners outside the gates. They broke into riot, attacking peers arriving in their carriages and surging through Newgate Prison. Others joined out of dissatisfaction with the war and the collapse of trade. These were the most destructive riots the city had ever seen. Violence continued through the night, with attacks on Catholic communities and churches. Some feared that the unrest was part of a French invasion plot. Army gunfire killed some three hundred rioters, wounding another two hundred. Five hundred more were arrested, of whom two dozen would be executed.

During the turmoil, gunmakers delivered arms into the Tower to keep them out of rioters' hands. This service weighed on the Ordnance Office. In August, when Crawford offered five thousand foreign guns, he was reminded of the official policy that "nothing but necessity should induce the Ordnance to purchase any foreign arms in preference to those of our own manufacturers which are much superior." The Ordnance Board was "sensible of the complaints which are likely to issue from our manufacturers at home should any further importation of foreign arms of an inferior quality be allowed and for which ready money is paid, whilst our own people are unemployed." For London contractors had just been told that the office was overstocked. The office recognized that it might have to purchase some of Crawford's arms, "to prevent them falling into improper hands," but it also feared that "London tradesmen . . . may be . . . force[d?] through want and necessity to dispose of their work to whoever chooses to become the purchaser." The master general urged some method for restoring "this branch of trade into the hands of our own artificers where work appears to be far superior to that of the Liège manufactory and should it be neglected may fall into improper hands," recalling particularly the "great readiness" with which the gunsmiths had delivered their arms to the Tower "on the late disturbances," meriting encouragement and recognition. Moreover, the Tower was "crowded" with guns, many of dubious quality, and the board would be answerable "to the publick for throwing so important a branch of trade into an improper course especially after the readiness with which they surrendered their arms to government during the late tumults." The old bogey—that gunmakers might throw in their lot with rebels—remained potent. It had earlier inspired a studied effort to keep gunmaking diffuse; now it inspired determination to nurture that diffuse industry.

But stores were full. Pratt offered to set up thousands of arms to fill a new warehouse that he would secure independently, but the Ordnance Office felt that lodging arms there would be "too hazardous." So the office's new resolve did not yield fresh contracts. Galton strained after orders for ramrods piling up in his workshop, "for the sake of the men," and for news of payment, lest they be "reduced to the necessity of overdrawing our bankers." Then the Ordnance officials in town, John York and Joseph Butler, announced a stop to pistol orders. Galton's relations with Butler utterly deteriorated. The inspector faulted the bores of his pistol barrels while accepting others made at the same mill by the same men. Galton's attempts to appease him with a leg of lamb, improve the barrels by working with a filer, demonstrate their fitness with Ordnance gauges, and appeal to other viewers came to no avail. Butler accused him of ungentlemanly conduct. "Such a medley of a fellow as B—r was never known," exclaimed Galton. News of ships fitting out for Africa offered some relief. Galton bought up thousands of "returned Tower stocks" from Joseph Loder and

William Tucker for that. But within days, some "truly afflicting" news undid that promise, and he counseled William Bird, "Times change and we change with them." This may have been news of the Spanish and French naval action of August 9, which ended in the capture of a large British convoy and struck a major blow to British commerce. Doors remained closed at the Ordnance Office, which notified lockmakers that locks would not be received after December 1 without particular orders and told contractors seeking work that it had none. Galton produced a new musketoon barrel, but his and others' entreaties about locks on their hands went unheard. The office put out contracts only for particular needs for the remainder of the war. It took some Liège guns from Crawford in 1782–83, following a guideline to take inferior foreign arms only if they were inexpensive. But many of the 76,000 to 110,000 arms it bought in Liège between 1778 and 1783 were strategic purchases carried out to prevent enemies from buying them. The office's efforts to create sustained, self-sufficient gun production were not entirely successful in this war, but they were creative and purposeful and laid the foundation for later changes.

The war ended in defeat in 1783. York announced his return to the Tower, giving notice that "no more stores will be received." But he dallied, reporting a month later that illness had detained him. Noting that Butler had not received orders to return, he requested that "if any viewer is to remain at Birmingham he [York] might be the person." The Birmingham position had become more attractive than the Tower. The Ordnance Board promptly ordered Butler home and informed York that a viewer in Birmingham was no longer necessary. Contracting had become lucrative at the interface between government officials and contractors, quite apart from government needs. It is possible that Butler's cantankerousness toward Galton had emerged from a desire for more venal blandishment than a leg of lamb. The "bad custom" of viewers taking shillings to pass guns at the Tower had been disallowed in 1778, but the practice continued, even for passing good work. One guilty viewer explained that he had been forced to the recourse in order to cover the costs of *answering* accusations of corruption; workmen volunteered ninepence per gun to help defray the cost of the suit. The Ordnance Office did not allow this military-industrial society to turn into a mutually profiting complex. It summarily dismissed Pratt and others who paid viewers to pass substandard work, deeming them "unworthy" of further employment.

D efeat and overflowing stores dampened the office's willingness to continue purchases into peacetime. More important, the office deferred orders until after it had perfected a new design in cooperation with the gunmakers: the Richmond pattern, named for the Duke of Richmond, the office's master general from 1784 to 1795. But in the meantime, the East India Company routinely had at least 20,000 muskets en route to the subcontinent, in addition to maintaining 75,000 spares in store. In the second half of the century, 150,000 to 200,000 British guns also went to Africa each year. Gunmakers stayed busy.

But they had to contend with the growing abolition movement threatening their African market with increasing force after Britain's humiliating military defeat. In 1788, John Whateley testified to the Board of Trade that the gun trade was critical to Birmingham and that the trade's "whole existence" depended on the African market, to the infinite advantage of the government. For when war broke out, "the best of the artificers" were "immediately collected from every part of the manufactory and employed by government or their agents" to make sixty to eighty thousand superior arms a year, "on lower terms and much more expeditiously . . . than they could possibly be but for the regular support of the African trade." Without that peacetime outlet, the mills and forges the government depended on during war would be "converted to the other manufactures of Birmingham." The African trade also absorbed otherwise worthless unserviceable arms. Whateley spoke strategically; the African trade was very important, but not quite the unique mainstay he made it out to be. In fact, workers flitted in and out of the gun trade in peacetime; the African trade employed the worst rather than the best artificers, and it could not sustain high levels of employment without itself becoming unsustainable. Whateley's own investments were diverse: at that moment he was supplying copper to Matthew Boulton's mint. More notable here is the state's interest in him and in his stakes in the African trade. While Birmingham, like other cities, organized abolitionist meetings and petitions, a counter-organization assembled a petition *against* abolition and *for* regulation of a trade "greatly and extensively beneficial to this town and neighbourhood." Abolitionists led by the ironmaster Samuel Garbett stymied the attempt, arguing that it would be "highly improper" for the town to present a peti-tion directly contradictory to the one then under serious House consider-ation. Corresponding with James Rogers, among the largest Bristol slave merchants at the time, Whateley remarked on the "present precarious & alterd state of the trade."

But ten days after that anxious letter, new opportunity knocked nearby: revolutionaries stormed Paris's Bastille, partly to commandeer the guns it held. In time, the political and economic consequences of the French Revolution erupted in Birmingham. In 1789, Guillaume Foucault, who was involved in French army procurement, visited Boulton's famed Soho manufactory to divulge the rich opportunities the revolution had created for supplying copper buttons and buckle chapes for troops. Soho supplied quantities of buttons to the French National Guard, copper me-dallions depicting heroes of the revolution, and small-denomination token currency (just when Boulton was desperate to gainfully employ the mint he had erected in 1787–88). More advantages would follow. But in 1791, on the second anniversary of the storming of the Bastille, riots broke out in Birmingham against Dissenters whose pretenses to equal civil rights and sympathy for France's revolutionaries earned them the hatred of Church and King supporters. Galton Jr.'s friend Joseph Priestley was a primary target. When his home and church were burned, Galton bravely sheltered him. The homes of other Lunar Society members were attacked, too. Gal-ton saved his by bribing the rioters with ale and money. The next year, France went to war against Austria and Prussia, and gun orders came to Birmingham, given the ruined state of its French counterpart, the artisanal gunmaking town of Saint-Étienne, which had long supplied the French state with an annual capacity of forty thousand to sixty thousand muskets and pairs of pistols (considerably less than British capacity) but had reduced output dramatically in the face of new and costly standards imposed by the state in the 1770s. In 1792, Saint-Étienne's armorers refused to supply the French state. So France turned to Birmingham.

The British government scrutinized these French orders as Jacobins resurrected fear of Jacobites—and not unreasonably: Dr. William Maxwell, of the radical Society for Constitutional Information, met with the French minister of war in Paris, offering to arm and command a French company and urging him to raise irregular French troops. Maxwell ordered thousands of pikes and poniards from Birmingham smiths, including Thomas Gill. When the news emerged, Gill, who was then a high sheriff of Birmingham (with Joseph Oughton), explained that he had sent a sample to the government and had not been told to stop. In a House of Commons debate about limiting French immigration, the famed critic of the revolution Edmund Burke referred to the thousands of daggers "bespoke at Birmingham by an Englishman" for export to France or "home consumption." "This," he said, flourishing one dramatically and throwing it on the floor, "is what you are to gain by an alliance with France." In 1782, as part of wartime crystallization of government institutions, a new Home Office had formed for internal defense; from 1791 it was headed by Lord Dundas, who kept tabs on these arms purchases out of concern that they might be intended for purposes dangerous to the British regime.

The French orders were clearly attractive to British gunmakers. Galton and Whateley were declining African orders because their workmen refused to make beech-stocked muskets that might be left on their hands. His firm was "coutrouled by our Workmen & harassed on every side," Galton explained to an impatient customer. "Our workmen are our masters," Whateley echoed in a letter to Rogers. Asked to do beech work, "they set to work clandestinely for other gunmakers." The Home Office had an attorney named John Brooke and two or three assistants spy on this community. They reported that Birmingham's gunmakers were "very full of Orders" that added a thousand per week to the usual run of business. French agents had ordered three hundred thousand from Galton, two thousand a week from Whateley, a thousand a week from John Parr in Liverpool, and more. They worked with London finishers, and a London banker or merchant underwrote the whole operation. A French inspector superintended the work. They were even boring and fitting up old guns "which have lain rusted for years." Galton and Whateley did make guns for the French state, for they sold several thousand such guns to the British Treasury two years later (through the Home Office), but the concern in 1792 was that these guns were for rebellion against the *British* government. Brooke alleged that they made thousands of light and cheap "short pieces" for Ireland and a new, "most destructive" arm the size of a large blunderbuss that could discharge twenty to thirty balls. Most notably, David Blair was suspected of making rifle-barrel guns for a mysterious Londoner "supposed to be Dr. Maxwell." While inscribing this intelligence, Brooke grew paranoid about being watched himself. An informant in Halifax also wrote to the member of Parliament and abolitionist William Wilberforce that Ketland & Walker of Birmingham was making thousands of arms for the Irish: "I should not wonder if some part of the plundering mad part of the mob of the French army should come over to assist the discontented Irish."

The Home Office informant John Mason put all this to Galton Sr. The "old Gentleman" explained that a few barrels only had been made for France, and they were set up in London. A French merchant did apply often for guns, but Galton could never make them for the price the merchant wanted without sacrificing quality. He did occasionally buy old Irish Ordnance fusils for the African trade or the East India Company, but Parr, in Liverpool, was "the general purchaser," buying tens of thousands for France or Ireland. As for a new gun that could carry several bullets, if anyone had tried to make one, it was "Knock in London," who had openly applied for patents. Galton graciously joined Mason in making inquiries of the town's principal manufacturers, noting particularly William Walker's work on five hundred fusils for a French order and twelve London gunmakers making guns for the French, "'tho possibly said to be for the E. Indies." Mason found Galton "very ingenuous in his declarations." He seemed "to have the good of his Country at heart." If he and others made guns for the French, it was without regard for the politics of their customers, he concluded. Galton, too, wrote to the Home Office to affirm that reports about him and other manufacturers were unfounded.

"The Arms made here exclusive of those for the usual current of Trade, there is ground to believe, are for the French; & I have never heard that any such Guns . . . calculated to carry from 20 to 25 Balls have been manufactured in this place." He sent arms to Liverpool for the African and American trade only, though he knew nothing about guns made in Liverpool—another dig at his old agent Parr.

The investigation did not end here, however. The Home Office deputed William Collins and W. Hurd to unravel a "Liverpool Transaction"—a mystery surrounding two hundred Birmingham guns sold for Ireland via Liverpool. In Birmingham, Collins "pursued the Object of my Inquiry without ceasing." Posing as a customer, he found gunmakers so overwhelmed with orders that there was no risk they would take on his fake one. He learned that Whateley had sold the guns in question. Collins asked a friend at Liverpool customs to track their destination. Though he believed the big orders in town were for the French, contracted by London merchants, Collins was certain they included more for Ireland. For, as he learned from a "most intelligent Gun maker" who had also spoken to "Mr. Brooke," the French service gun had iron mountings, and he had seen guns with brass mountings, which the workmen called "Irish" and which resembled those made the previous year for the Irish Volunteers. There was news also of a Londoner buying guns in town "for no good Purpose" and a "Dissenter of some Consequence" guaranteeing payment for them. Collins described Blair as a former fowling piece maker and "violent Leveller" making old Tower stores for Scotland. He estimated that the region's production capacity of guns was good enough "to go with the Field" at a thousand per week. He called for a search of ports and customs houses to trace the Irish guns, concluding ominously, "While we are looking for Evidence of Facts the Mischief will be done for that Evil is intended cannot be doubted." Inquiry at the Liverpool customs house turned up news of 150 arms on a ship for Dublin, which he deduced were Whateley's 200. From this he drew the rather broad conclusion that "considerable quantities of arms have been sent by one means or other to Ireland & I fear to Scotland also." He, too, exonerated the gunmakers as "more occupied in seducing each others Workmen than in considering the purpose for which the Arms they were making are intended." Hurd likewise stressed that "the Manufacturer may not know where the Guns are intended to go," since agents came around with orders each week claiming to be from France but perhaps intending the arms for elsewhere. Despite this sanguine outlook, Hurd cast suspicion on a huge order Galton & Son worked on "for Government, France or Ireland I cannot tell." He indicted the son in particular as "a violent Democrat & many People here have their Fears with respect to the Use the said Musquets are intended for, especially as they want to keep it very secret from their Workmen." Blair was also "one of the violent Party" occupied with a large order "supposed to be for Scotland," although he had not yet procured many. Men from clubs in Manchester and Sheffield were in town proclaiming "Liberty & Equality. There is to be no King, no Taxes," and every man with three children would have £50 annually. They were forming a local club with the help of a local printer, a "Dissenter & Firebrand."

The Galtons' Dissenting background—enhanced by association with Priestley after 1791—stood out as a political liability in the gunmaking business, though the spies considered the senior Galton trustworthy. More interestingly, broadening of the trade had rendered gunmakers' particular politics less relevant. The spies thought of the trade as essentially apolitical in its acceptance of custom without regard for how the guns might be used. They did not hold gunmakers accountable for those ends— in sharp contrast to the Quaker society in precisely the same moment. To the Home Office, the trade's loyalty was pragmatic rather than principled; it could be purchased with steady demand. No government office judged sales in Africa, either, even when abolition prevailed. In 1807, the year the slave trade became illegal, Robert Southey was appalled that "no secret" was made of the "abominable" sale of bad guns in Africa: "The government never interferes, and the persons concerned in it are not marked and shunned as infamous." The allusions to Blair's and Galton Jr.'s democratic sympathies in 1792 were exceptions to this outlook, and soon even these anxieties were assuaged, for in these waning days of 1792 the British state began to order guns in anticipation of war. When war began in February 1793, gunmakers lost their French customers and were grateful for Ordnance Office demand. A Birmingham gunmaker visited the office and described "Decline in the Gun Trade, which has forced many Families of Workmen to apply to the Parish for Subsistence, and some Hundreds of others to leave the Town." He "solicited Orders for a Supply of Musquets to Government," and they were granted. *Aris's Birmingham Gazette* celebrated the "prospect of removing, at least, one great Evil from this Place." As the Continent closed to Birmingham goods, the gun trade nevertheless thrived. Advertisements promised "constant work" to barrel grinders, gun finishers, and bayonet grinders. The industry's survival and transformation depended on government demand.

These new wars lasted more than two decades. In a context of shifting alliances, Britain and other dynastic European powers struggled to prevent the spread of France's revolution. The French levy en masse, placing all Frenchmen at the army's disposal, made this a contest on an unprecedented scale. Instead of armies of tens of thousands, hundreds of thousands clashed. In the French forces, one army officer's ambitions and genius took him to ever greater heights and a path to absolute power: Napoleon. By the turn of the century, France dominated the Continent, but Britain continued to pose a challenge at sea and in Europe, Egypt, and South Asia. Finally, the Peninsular Campaign of 1811 reopened Spain; Napoleon's foolhardy invasion of Russia failed in 1812 and he withdrew west of the Rhine. After an allied invasion of France in 1814, Napoleon was exiled to the island of Elba. He escaped to fight again and was then finally, irrevocably defeated at Waterloo in 1815. The epic scale and length of these wars would have an enormous impact on British industry.

In 1793, the British Army stood at 38,945 effectives. In 1813, it numbered 330,663. The navy expanded from 16,000 in 1789 to 140,000 in 1812. Volunteer units numbered half a million by 1804; there were militia in Canada and the West Indies. All needed arms. When war began, there were 60,000 muskets in the Tower and other armories, enough for the initial army. Besides the Birmingham orders mentioned above, Henry Nock, in London, received contracts for 5,000 old-pattern muskets and

10,000 of the new Richmond-pattern muskets. The Ordnance Office
hired more contractors for parts, stocking, and setting up and increased
prices. But the supply remained a trickle. In July 1793, the office ordered
10,000 muskets from Liège. The secretary to the board imagined that
they had hit up against the limits of the artisanal trade: "everything that
could induce the Artificers to go has been tried . . . I fear were other Persons to be employed it would not advance the Business for as we have now
no Locks in Store and few Barrels . . . they would have to get all these
Articles from B'ham before they would begin to set up or engage Workmen, and even these Workmen would be decoy'd from other Masters who
are now working for the Ordnance." The Duke of Richmond confided to
Lord Dundas, now occupying the new position of secretary of state for
war (in addition to home secretary and treasurer of the navy), "The People
at Liege are very dilatory," and "all our Workmen have failed us in respect
to the time they had agreed to send in supplies." Gunmakers blamed strict
inspection, but Richmond suspected the real trouble was that "great orders from Ireland and from the East India Company, who do not require
the same precision in work, engages [sic] the least expert and most numerous body of workmen." Now Dundas was also president of the Board of
Control, established in 1784 to supervise the East India Company in another step toward its domestication as part of an increasingly recognizable
set of modern state institutions. The company had steadily acquired arms
since 1783 while the Ordnance Office fussed with design. Richmond suggested to Dundas that the company sell its new arms to the office and refrain from further orders until the government was properly supplied,
especially since the Liège manufacturers could not work "to the pattern . . .
scarce any two of their Musquets are similar." Dundas had just helped renew
the company's charter; he had its goodwill. Within a day he had worked
magic at East India House. The Court of Directors agreed to transfer the
company's arms to the government from its London warehouses and rivers
and canals, where arms were in transit. An East Indiaman in the Channel
was brought back to Portsmouth to give up 5,000. By the end of 1794,
the company handed over 28,920 muskets, 2,680 fusils and carbines,
1,342 pairs of pistols, and 300 wall pieces. (Five thousand muskets were

allowed to reach Madras for the desperate fight for Pondicherry.) Gunmakers also sent in Indian and trade guns they had. Although the Ordnance Office deemed the French guns too shoddy, the Treasury and the secretary of state for war bought up thousands, including Whateley's and Galton's. The Indian army had enough in store and on continual order to spare what it gave up, even with its forces expanding from 88,000 at the end of 1793 to 192,000 by 1805. The military organizations were intimately bound. In 1795, after returning from serving as India's governor general and commander in chief, Lord Cornwallis became master general of the Ordnance Office. (In 1798, he would become lord lieutenant of Ireland—the head of the Irish government.) The intra-imperial rescue sale was pivotal, for the French took Liège in 1795, cutting it off altogether. The company's cash resources made it a proxy procurement agency for purchases in other European markets, too. It also sold the Ordnance Office £20,000 worth of arms in 1808. By the end of the war, the office had bought more than 162,000 company small arms. Though political influence secured them, these were commercial transactions. The company could refuse when its own needs were too great, as in the 1803 effort against the Marathas.

The Brown Bess was thus displaced by cheaper arms of diverse origins, particularly for foreign units and allies. The India-pattern gun had a shorter barrel and was lighter overall and plainer in style than the Ordnance musket. Increasing regulation and oversight since 1773 had enfolded the company more firmly within the state. It was increasingly seen as an "administrative arm of the state," a "limb of the government of the country." In 1798, the company chairman called it and the Bank of England the two "most powerful engines of the state." The industrial metaphor was apposite. This commercially inclined branch of the emerging British state gave it the flexibility to fumble toward a mass-producible small arm. The company taught the Ordnance Office to modify design to get the numbers it needed.

While absorbing this lesson, the office also built on its earlier experiments in breaking artisanal constraints on small-arms production. In 1794, it envisioned a government manufactory that would serve as "a

Checque upon the proceedings of the Gunmakers" and "prevent Combinations among them against Government." This was a *government* plan for factory organization, with the aim of increasing and securing productivity by diffusing the trade to check prices; it was not about introducing machine production. The plan emerged soon after a "loyal subject" informed Prime Minister William Pitt of arms stockpiling in Birmingham for the republican cause in London. In 1795, the Home Office received reports of boxes of Birmingham guns arriving for Jacobins in the West Riding of Yorkshire.

Similar government arms-factory projects were coming up abroad in 1794 out of different motivations. The revolutionary French government launched the Manufacture of Paris, which employed more than five thousand at its peak in thirty government-run workshops—the largest ever "crash" industrial project in Europe, aiming to produce a thousand muskets a day, six times the combined output of the ancien regime's three armories. Uncompromising Enlightenment-minded engineers insisted on interchangeable parts production on principle, in the face of opposition from artisanal gunsmiths and arms merchants. After a year, the governing National Convention closed it, reestablishing the ancien regime "amalgam of private capitalism and statist direction." In 1794, the Spanish government also established a factory in Oviedo, which would average more than eight hundred muskets per month by 1798. Also in 1794, anticipating war with France, George Washington sponsored a bill "for the erecting and repairing of Arsenals and Magazines" in the United States. To that point, American troops had relied on German and British arms and private contractors. This factory experiment was about national autonomy. The first site selected was Springfield, Massachusetts, where a magazine had been established during the Revolutionary War; the second was Harpers Ferry, Virginia. Merchants understood that the government enterprise would create steady demand for iron, coal, files, tools, consumer goods, and toll revenue for the Potomac Company (an interstate company Washington had also created, to promote regional development that would strengthen the new union). The project stalled until undeclared war with France in 1798 and Washington's return as commander in chief of a specially created provisional army. At that point, thousands of guns were ordered from contractors, and construction at Harpers Ferry began. It produced its first arms in 1800, although production became regular only around 1808. Its first superintendent was a Birmingham gunsmith who maintained European-style craft practices, employing individual artisans to manufacture each part. The goal of interchangeable parts was adopted from French military traditions and guided developments, but it took time.

The British government's factory plan stalled until 1805, partly to avoid drawing artisans away from the contractors' work in a desperate time. In the meantime, the Ordnance Office turned Birmingham itself into something of a factory. It began ordering India-pattern arms directly, as the gunmakers could more easily fulfill large orders for its more forgiving design, and it was easier to expand the trade at a lower skill level. Gunmakers and the office advertised for workmen in gunmaking trades. Ordnance viewers persuaded local cabinet makers, wheelers, and carpenters to undertake rough stocking. The office tapped John Parr's business in Liverpool. It was in this moment of dramatic expansion of gunmaking that Galton Jr. defended his business to fellow Quakers by arguing that everyone in some way contributed to war making. The Ordnance Office also expanded its institutional presence in Birmingham. Office viewers staffed an Ordnance proofhouse erected in town in July 1797; the office built view rooms in town. The viewing was made less exacting by official adoption of the India pattern as the standard infantry weapon in 1797 (which it remained until 1840). Birmingham suppliers ran through their materials for the old pattern and switched entirely to the India pattern, with a spare lock for each gun and the promise of higher prices to compensate payment delays. The dumbed-down design loosened the grip of the region's most skilled artisans, making expansion easier. It was a compromise pattern validated by its standing as a mass military arm in its own right, though it was later also validated by favorable comparison with the heavy, clumsy, and more "inconvenient" Ordnance pattern. Soon, the 1801 Act of Union uniting Great Britain and Ireland also ended Irish competition for gunmakers' attention: Ireland's independent ordnance establishment closed, and Irish purchases were amalgamated with England's. This was another strand in the evolution of the corporate state into a more intelligibly imperial one.

The ability to manufacture on a mass scale became critical as Napoleon revolutionized the scale of war, rendering earlier procurement experience irrelevant. Whole nations were pitted against one another and entire magazines lost instantly when a nation switched sides. During the brief Peace of Amiens, from 1802 to 1803, the Ordnance Office toyed again with design, opting for a fairly plain musket incorporating elements of rejected patterns by Nock and the Duke of Richmond into the India pattern. The office sent Major James Miller to Birmingham to procure locks and barrels for it. But the threat of French invasion in 1803 resulted in panicked creation of an enormous force. The Ordnance Office's vast stores of 150,000 guns plus 293,000 foreign guns procured in a hurry were not enough for the more than 600,000 men who now needed them. A hundred thousand men were armed with pikes. India-pattern guns again proved an easier recourse than the new pattern to fill the deficit. The policy of the Ordnance Office and the Cabinet after 1803 was to be "ever prepared with warlike stores; that no event, however unexpected, might occasion a demand for assistance that was not immediately granted, and the opportunity turned to profit by those whose duty it was to be vigilant."

In the panic of 1803, the office permitted infantry corps to buy arms independently. The ensuing scramble produced such confusion and delays that at the start of 1804, the office took full control of Birmingham's arms trade. Contracts for stocking and setting up were signed with eleven local gunmakers, in addition to separate contracts with eighteen barrel makers, twenty lockmakers, seven bayonet makers, and eleven rammer makers. Brownlow Bate, a viewer who had overseen some of Birmingham's production in the previous war, was appointed superintendent of tradesmen. An organization similar to the Tower organization of viewers and furbishers took shape on Ordnance Office premises in Birmingham, under Miller as inspector of small arms. Each contractor pledged not to perform military work for any party other than the East India Company without permission. The Ordnance Office secured a monopoly of arms purchases, ensuring that foreign powers, even allies, could not compete for supply and drive up prices. The decade 1804–15 was the longest stretch of sustained military arms production in Birmingham, resulting in 7,660,229 complete arms and components. In 1808, a new proofhouse was erected. These regulations resembled those the East India Company was using just then to monopolize the product of weavers in India. The Ordnance Office was a mass consumer of an artisanal industrial product in a similar way. The company mimicked the office, too, after 1807 beginning to contract for processes rather than complete guns, which gave it a new, direct interface with Birmingham manufacturers.

The Ordnance Office was now determined to fulfill its vision of a state factory to control prices and supply. In 1805, it created a staff of rough stockers, setters-up, and parts makers at the Tower and began to produce barrels and locks at the Armoury Mills at Lewisham. This factory brought different processes under a single roof specifically to check the power the office was just then stoking in Birmingham—it was not to outproduce Birmingham or make the state independent of Birmingham. Birmingham workers staffed it and were paid the same rates as in Birmingham. The factory was designed to produce 50,000 barrels, locks, rammers, and bayonets annually—significant, but nowhere near the scale of Birmingham. It was water powered, but the River Ravensbourne proved such an unreliable power source that it was replaced with a steam engine. Lathes, grinders, and other machinery were installed; cottages erected for workmen; and bonuses awarded for good work. A proofhouse was added, and the Tower workshops were moved to the site in 1811, just as a new view room went up on Ordnance Office premises in Birmingham. The office thus simultaneously developed two sites at which all stages of manufacture and proof of small arms could take place. In 1812, it purchased land for a water-powered factory at Enfield, to which the Lewisham work was transferred in 1816. Enfield, with its boring, turning, and rifling machinery, could make 26,000 barrels, to Birmingham's 300,000 per year.

Meanwhile, the office continued to nurture the capacity of the

Birmingham trade. Abolition of the slave trade in 1807 forced further compromises on design that abetted mass production. Birmingham's anti-abolitionists dreaded the looming reality. Thwarted in 1789, arms manufacturers in 1805 petitioned the Commons to warn that abolition would destroy "the greatest, and perhaps only, efficient nursery for Artificers in the art of manufacturing of arms." A similar plea came from Liverpool. In 1806, Galton and his colleagues alerted the Ordnance Board that they were about to be "shut from the Market at which they had been enabled to dispose of the Barrels which were rejected by the Ordnance." The board sympathetically increased the price of barrels tenpence and allowed fourpence more for better filing and forging if they would increase supply. Manufacture of these inferior "extra-service" muskets through 1812 helped absorb some of the poorer barrels (and stocks) that would have been unloaded in the slave trade. The war boom thus insulated arms makers from the commercial costs of abolition. In 1807, the Quaker merchant Richard Rathbone, later a prominent Liverpool abolitionist, foresaw a British war with America and "an immense demand for guns, to pop off all the unfortunate wretches, who happen to be on the water at the same time with our British troops." "If you grow very rich and I grow very poor," he teased his friend John Howard Galton, "I shall come and beg from you."

Far from oppressing Birmingham contractors, the Ordnance Office monopoly empowered them. Right around abolition, in 1807, they formed a Committee of the Manufacturers of Arms and Materials for Arms to negotiate collectively—a "contractors' cartel," chaired by Theodore Price. The office called Price in to discuss lock supply, explicitly checking lockmakers' power by explaining that their lack of exertion might force the office to establish an independent manufactory. If they hoped to keep the trade "in their own country," they would use "*unusual* exertion." But the lockmakers were not at the office's mercy. In 1808, the committee resolved to demand sixpence more for locks, and the office agreed. The relationship became more cooperative. The next year, the committee drew two hundred men and apprentices into lockmaking by offering premiums it financed; the office donated a hundred guineas toward this fund. The committee renegotiated the apprenticeship agreements of twenty-seven lockmaking firms so that a person learning forging would get two guineas and the person instructing him three by applying to the committee. This arrangement allowed more to be trained while compensating the skilled person for passing on his trade. Dumbed-down musket design lowered the bar to entry in the skilled trade of lockmaking—as Richmond had noted, the "least expert" were drawn to India work—and the extended duration of the wars eased lockmakers' anxieties about expanding their numbers. The committee reported to the office that negotiation had enabled small firms to overcome their prejudices and that lock supply was increasing. Apprentices entered the trade in modified customary structures. This was part of the general erosion of apprenticeship restrictions late in the war, culminating in repeal of the apprenticeship clauses of the Elizabethan Statute of Artificers in 1814. The Birmingham Chamber of Commerce, in which Galton was a major figure, supported that repeal by arguing that, had the statute been enforced during the war for gunmakers, they would never have been able to supply the arms the kingdom needed.

A new bounty system also increased productivity. Contractors typically got their parts from small masters serving many at once and depending on artisan-workmen with teams of apprentices. To impose greater work discipline on independent artisans, small masters allowed a workman to bind himself to a particular master for a year, in exchange for a weekly bounty of a pound. If a man bound himself to finish fifty a week (the typical figure), he got £50 over and above the price of his work. Reneging triggered legal proceedings. This system provoked self-employed artisans to impose work discipline on themselves and made the small master more like a subcontractor and employer.

The state encouraged the rise of subcontracting through its looser view process, intended to speed production. According to one embittered contractor, subcontracting emerged when contractors found that "unusual quantities of their work began to be rejected, though no alteration had taken place in its quality." Some began to "set their work to sub-contractors" whose work passed more easily, allegedly because, "being workmen," they had no qualms about offering viewers "direct bribes for favor in viewing their work"—even good work. The contractor then received the passed goods and delivered them in his own name to the Ordnance Board.

Subcontracting made machinery more common, particularly for barrel grinding and boring, where risk was lower, since rolling mills were easy to adapt to other functions, too. With capital coming from share ownership, the burden of erecting works for a contract, like the profits it accrued, could be shared. The machines were powered by water until the Ketlands and Whateleys began to use steam, around 1801. A Prussian in town described a barrel-making factory with steam-driven rolling and grinding mills and boring machines, employing hundreds. In 1811, the French traveler Louis Simond visited a Birmingham mill where three hundred men made ten thousand barrels a month with a 120-horsepower steam engine.

Small workshops coexisted with and served the large-scale units, like Galton's, Boulton's, and the Ordnance Office's, that emerged out of government contracting. They worked together toward a single purpose. Division of labor had long existed; the efficiency produced by employing a single workman on a single operation was common knowledge in many trades. An English observer in France in 1802 noted that, unlike in Birmingham,

> each artisan in Paris, working out his own purposes in his own domicile, must in his time "play many parts," and among these many to which he is incompetent, either from want of skills, or want of practice; so that in fact, even supposing French artisans to be of equal ability and industry with English competitors, they are left at least a century behind, by thus being precluded from all the miraculous advantages of the division of labour.

But division of labor did not lead inevitably to the factory in the sense of concentration of production under a single roof, certainly not on the mass scale of gunmaking in this time. Adam Smith had anticipated that "in those great manufactures . . . destined to supply the great wants of the great body of the people, every different branch of the work employs so great a number of workmen, that it is impossible to collect them all into the same workhouse. We can seldom see more, at one time, than those employed in one single branch." This, essentially, was the state of the Birmingham gun trade during the Napoleonic Wars. It was a *virtual* factory. Birmingham's small workshops survived well into the next century, producing diverse products for diverse markets. State contracting fostered the new forms of industrial organization in the gun trade. Machinery, the contractors' cartel, new apprenticeship regulations, and the bounty system adapted internal structures of the artisanal system so that it could produce on a mass scale. Small units expanded production without becoming factories themselves, by participating in the larger, factory-like arrangement of the Birmingham gun trade and responding to an established dynamic of Ordnance Office stimulation of collective forms of production.

The result was a fivefold increase in production, from a capacity of fewer than 3,000 guns per week in 1790 to 14,000 per week after 1803, *without the addition of machinery* beyond that used in barrel making. The town produced more than three million barrels between 1804 and 1815, 250,000 annually, while also producing a million barrels for the East India Company, bringing the twelve-year total to more than four million. They made nearly three million locks, plus a million for the East India Company. More than 1.7 million complete arms were set up in Birmingham from 1804 to 1815. These were apart from the fowling pieces and sporting arms for private consumption and guns for the African trade. The Ordnance India-pattern gun was Britain's most numerous military muzzle-loading weapon ever: more than 2.8 million were produced. Between the government factory and Birmingham, Britain supplied its own needs and those of its allies (Sweden, Russia, Prussia, Spain)—arms worth some £3.3 million. After 1803, the Ordnance Office strove to make Britain the "independent and mighty power" that Napoleon's opponents needed, "an inexhaustible resource." It "put in execution the gigantic plan of being the depot, the manufactory, the place of arms, and the centre of the European war," marveled the French mathematician Baron Dupin afterward. France's ten state-controlled factories in the same period together yielded an average annual output of 190,000 guns. Birmingham exceeded them by more than 600,000. The French government made about 600 a day from 1802 to 1814—as compared with 1,000 a day in England.

The shifts in industrial relations between contractors, small masters, artisan-workmen, and apprentices lasted. The French Committee of Public Safety may have launched bolder experiments overnight, but the Ordnance Office had developed confidence over the century in the adaptive capacity of the existing homegrown, contract-based system. The office itself grew staggeringly to cope with the vastly expanded demands and industries, becoming one of the largest organizations within the British state, employing 886 officials. Richmond reformed its finances and abolished fees and perquisites, transforming it into a disciplined government "department." It offered a model of governance for post-1815 reformers. (Other government departments and industrial establishments also swelled.) The British government's happy dependence on contractors, rather than government factories such as the French used, was not a sign of backwardness or anti-militarism; the contracting system, *because* of its entanglement with the industrial revolution, was simply much more effective. At a critical juncture, the East India Company showed the Ordnance Office what adaptations to make to meet the needs of the wildly mass scale of these wars. It acted as a surrogate for the Ordnance Office toward industry. When Midlands ironmasters complained to the Board of Trade about closing works and mounting stocks during a slackening of demand in 1812, the office persuaded the company to anticipate its munitions orders for the next year to take up four to five thousand tons of their iron.

Gunmaking was the acknowledged heart of Birmingham industry. The town came together to quash an 1813 bill obliging gunmakers to mark their arms with their location, which would "most materially have injured" trade (since a Birmingham mark still lacked the prestige of London). The defeat delighted thousands of "Birmingham mechanics." The gentlemen deputed to oppose the measure were received with "every demonstration of joy"; they had acted out of concern for the *region's* economic health. To further counter London's power, the town's gunmakers raised a fund to erect a public proofhouse that year. Parliament made proving of all barrels at the London Proof House *or* the new Birmingham Proof House compulsory.

In July 1814, the Tower was so full of arms that new guns were diverted for storage at other towns. At the sudden announcement of peace, supplies accumulated quickly in the stores—almost 750,000 muskets. The Ordnance Office staff at Birmingham was halved. The office ordered 84,507 new land-pattern muskets between 1814 and 1817, and then no military arms for a decade. Britain signed a treaty with Spain pledging not to provide arms to the South American colonies in rebellion. Napoleon's escape and return in 1815 triggered momentary reversion to the India pattern, but, with the restoration of peace that summer, all orders were canceled. Thousands who had found employment in Birmingham were reduced to penury. Peace exposed Birmingham's dependence on war demand.

In 1816, the Lewisham works were transferred to Enfield. Fearing that this move spelled their imminent redundancy, prominent townsmen protested in the local paper. Many "industrious manufacturers" had been "reduced" by the "great changes . . . in those branches of trade which were principally dependent upon a state of warfare," they recounted. They were dismayed at the Ordnance Office's preparations

> for removing the manufacture of arms from this district to new establishments in the vicinity of the metropolis, to be conducted altogether by their own Servants. We are at a loss to assign any adequate motive for removing the remains of that manufacture from this town, which, by furnishing to the Government upwards of one thousand musquets per day during many years of the late French war, has proved its ability at any time to supply the exigencies of the State to the greatest possible extent. When we consider the peculiar and natural advantages of this district for the cheap supply of materials requisite for that manufacture, and the evident superiority in point of economy of private factories over those which are placed under the management of a Government, we . . . hope that . . . the public will . . . see the propriety

of seriously remonstrating against a measure so materially affecting the interests of this town and neighbourhood, in no degree called for on the ground of expediency, and which cannot fail to be wastefully expensive in its operation.

Within a week the town was "properly roused to a sense of the injury." The local paper urged the appointment of delegates to convince the government of the injustice and "incalculable injury" that removal of the gun trade would inflict on the region by throwing "so considerable a portion of its population" out of employment and of its impolicy from a national and economic standpoint. Accordingly, at a town meeting, Tertius Galton, Theodore Price (now magistrate), Richard Spooner (the banker), Timothy Smith (brassfounder), and "other eminent merchants and manufacturers" resolved to send a delegation to the Commons, the Treasury, and the Ordnance Office. Seeing "so many gentlemen who had attained large fortunes from the gun trade," one participant proposed a subscription to defray the costs of the effort. Birmingham's elite knew their industrial prosperity was the gift of war. The Ordnance Office met with the delegation after it threatened to petition the Commons. The office pledged to use its factory for repairs only and to rely on the private trade in future wars in "the same proportion . . . as was furnished by them" in the recent war, so long as the trade guaranteed articles as good and at prices as low as the factory. The future was secured, but misery stalked the present. In 1818, the Ordnance Office's Birmingham premises closed. Galton Jr. regretted the "severe privation" caused by the "casualties of trade." Wartime growth in the trade did not extend into the peace, because the trade had expanded not through capital investment but through state-guided shifts in industrial organization.

Gunmakers were right to perceive Enfield's game-changing potential. The Bengal government's suggestion in 1797 that the East India Company set up a gun factory in England met with silence; it was entirely contrary to the company's commercial instincts. Where the state envisioned politically secure efficiency, the company saw unnecessary cost. Still, it is important not to exaggerate the shift Enfield represented. The line between "government" and "private" activity in the gun industry had always been blurry. Enfield was part of the institutional differentiation of government from a private sector, part of the government's effort to fulfill its needs within its own structure. But government-owned industry also undermined that differentiation by collapsing the functional distinction between private and public spheres. Enfield shrank the state's reach into the private economy but expanded the state itself; the state remained an intrusive presence in Birmingham's economy; Enfield depended on it for materials and labor. This widespread investment in the state made Britain an increasingly unlikely scene of armed radical insurrection.

Industrial revolution came to the gun trade as the result of a long history of government efforts to expand and diffuse arms-making skill, collectivize its organization, and compromise on design without intense addition of machinery in an era in which partners in the state *together* monopolized the means of violence. High demand from Africa could not prompt a leap in the scale of production; it took sustained mass government demand. By 1815, the British Empire owed its existence to the Midlands' ability to mass-produce guns, and the Midlands acquired that talent through the long competitive patronage of the East India Company and the Ordnance Office. By contrast, French imperial demand had never been sufficient to prompt intense division of labor in artisanal arms making: French artillery engineers influenced by Enlightenment principles of rationality and republican idealism could not yield on musket design; the French government liquidated the French East India Company in 1793; and war devastated French land. Criticism of contracting as rent-seeking became strongest in Britain, because rent-seeking crumbled elsewhere. All European states harbored ambitions for industrial growth, but British state institutions' ties to and rivalries with chartered companies made it capable of compromising in a manner that allowed it to experiment with industrial organization and make industry capable of cheaply producing mass quantities. War was a dynamic force everywhere, but only Britain raised so much money, underwent industrial revolution, and emerged a global depot of arms.

4

The State, War, and Industrial Revolution

In the late eighteenth century, on any night illuminated by a full moon, Samuel Galton Jr. was likely to be found in deep and convivial discussion about scientific and technical innovations with fellow prominent thinkers and manufacturers in Birmingham. The members of this informal group, the Lunar Society, took turns hosting dinners at their homes, including Galton's home at Great Barr Hall. The close and long friendship and collaboration among these men was solidified by weekly and even daily contact in person or by post. These distinguished neighbors with reputations extending well beyond the town made Birmingham a significant site of scientific experiment and discussion. They placed Galton Jr. at the heart of the social and intellectual networks of the industrial revolution. And yet industrial revolution came to the gun trade in these years without major mechanical transformation. We may never know whether these men wandering at the frontiers of scientific knowledge ever turned their inquiring minds to the science of gunmaking. But many of them were involved in military contracting, and it is clear that their war work shaped the industrial enlightenment they fostered. Government officials may not have joined the moonlit dinners but were integral to their intellectual universe. Innovation was a public-private affair. British state institutions did not employ as many degree-toting engineers as their French counterparts, because tinkering contractors helped solve technical problems. This is how the Ordnance Office stimulated innovation and productivity in the gun industry, and that is only a slice of much wider engagement of government institutions with a range of industries. Farmer & Galton's intermittent ties to the state were not unusual for an eighteenth-century industrial firm.

The British state was involved in technological progress in the gun industry from the start. This was why eighteenth-century English gunsmiths were more concerned with design innovation than their American or continental contemporaries. Certainly, design changes required costly reequipping of the entire army, given the importance of uniformity, and soldiers grew attached to familiar weapons and routines. But the very need to settle on a mass-producible standard arm to uniformly equip the army drove top-down tweaking of design between wars and of production processes during war.

England maintained the largest and most sophisticated Ordnance establishment in Europe. Founded in the fifteenth century, it was loosely administered, embracing private gun foundries and publicly supported armories and administrative offices at the Tower, gun wharves at Woolwich and elsewhere, and research-and-development facilities at the Minories and at Vauxhall, in Lambeth. It had old ties with British science. At the end of the sixteenth century, the master of the Ordnance Office was the Earl of Essex, friend and patron of Francis Bacon, the English philosopher typically hailed as the father of empiricism and the scientific method. Bacon would have been familiar with the office's complex of manufacturing and innovation. Its facilities, with their mechanicians and workmen—jobs that often passed within families to succeeding generations—provided stable niches for unobtrusive experimental projects that might someday produce a militarily useful gadget. In our period, too, this establishment supported scientific and technological experiments. Many military inventions were submitted to the government, and the need to provide masses of goods spurred use of new technologies. Improvements in sailing techniques, for instance, owed much to state experiments. The Royal Brass Foundry—founded at Woolwich in 1716, after a disastrous explosion in the privately managed works at Moorfields—exemplified government participation in rapid technological development. It and the Royal Dockyards were key sites of government cultivation of technical expertise; they produced shipbuilding, sailing, founding, and boring techniques that others emulated.

A similar attitude prevailed with respect to small arms. Attachment to the standard weapon encouraged tweaking, as opposed to wholesale replacement, and tweaking was the driving force of industrial revolution. The Brown Bess was continually adapted. Iron furniture was replaced with brass from 1725. Wooden ramrods were replaced with iron ones after 1730. Those with iron ramrods received a spring in the front guide to prevent rattling. Around 1745, the musket got a stronger cast-brass trigger guard and a trumpet-mouthed upper ramrod guide. The curved bottom profile of the lockplate and its mortise were eliminated. A battery bridle improved the lock's efficacy around 1754. In 1755, the double-bridle lock became standard. Barrel length shrank. The bulbous protrusion on the forestock, ahead of the lock, gradually disappeared by 1770. New designs were introduced, like the short land service musket, around 1750, which in turn influenced development of the sea service and marine/militia muskets in 1755.

The Ordnance Board experimented with arms to extend their life and improve their functioning. The Small Gun Office tested how lacquered (rather than oiled) bayonets stood up to different fluids by washing them with vinegar, urine, and seawater. It got a new carbine pattern made for the Royal Regiment of Artillery, "stronger than the common carbine for Horse." The surveyor general at the time was Charles Frederick, an intensely practical man with considerable personal expertise in manufacturing, especially gunpowder. In 1768, the Small Gun Office ran experiments in firing different kinds of barrels. It searched for ways to permit manufacture of ammunition after daylight at Woolwich, borrowing warship workers' "safe method of making up ammunition by candlelight."

Gunmakers were part of wider local tinkering cultures. They were probably among those who invited the clockmaker Benjamin Huntsman to develop finely tempered steel for clocks and gun springs. Their work was recognized as part of industrial enlightenment. Diderot's *Encyclopédie* of the 1750s included tumbler mills based on files used in gunmaking, hand-powered metal-cutting machines. Gunsmiths lured French drawing masters to Birmingham to help with new patterns. A Birmingham gunsmith discovered how to confirm a barrel's straightness by holding it up to natural light and noting shadows that betrayed inaccuracies in the interior surface. Ordnance Office work was at the heart of this culture. The Scottish army officer Captain Patrick Ferguson had family ties to the Scottish Enlightenment and invented a breech-loading rifle during the American war. He was allowed to patent it to ensure that such rifles would be made only for the government and would not fall into "bad hands." When John Pratt found a way to allow the rammer to go down the short land service musket more easily, the Ordnance Board asked him to use it in setting up. Henry Nock patented a concealed waterproof lock for military arms. While making volley guns for the navy, Nock submitted a prototype with a rifled, rather than smoothbore, barrel. The Ordnance Board let him test the seven-barreled pieces he invented on a warship. Sir John Burgoyne, the playwright–cum–army officer behind the disastrous plan to invade the rebel colonies from Canada during the American war, came up with a successful musketoon design favored by the Small Gun Office; Galton made the barrels.

The need to overcome rust in the small parts of guns inspired much of this tinkering. Rust made it difficult to remove screws, causing serious breakages. Jonathan Hennem, at Lewisham, came forward in May 1781 with a "screwless lock" in which the springs and moving parts were secured by clips and spigots. Impressed, the master general of the Ordnance Office arranged for Hennem to carry on further experiments near Woolwich through 1783, when he ordered four hundred of the locks for £70. Nock was experimenting with his own screwless lock and may have taken Hennem under his wing. He relied on a design by the mathematician George Bolton and used templates or filing jigs to improve interchangeability. This new invention generated the little amount of small-arms contract work that followed the American war; Nock and Hennem were the principal contractors in that decade. In 1784, Hennem proposed setting up muskets by "jigging the Barrel" and using locks of his design, promising "a saving to the Publick." He also proposed to alter some 98,000 locks in store to his new design. He agreed to deliver to each regiment that had new arms locks of his design, a hammer and pin for each lock, twelve main springs for each company, twelve hammer springs, and twelve spring lifters. He also instructed regiments in using the new locks. The Ordnance Board paid Durs Egg, a Swiss-born London gunsmith, to make two "new invented" breech-loading carbines with long bayonets. That year, an "eminent compass maker" and "ingenious artist" of Birmingham reportedly invented a magazine gun that could discharge forty-five balls separately in two and a half minutes with better aim than common fowling guns. Soon Nock improved on Hennem's lock, incorporating it in the .75-caliber musket he made in 1786. His pistols also contained many innovations. Certainly, there were improvements to sporting guns, too, but it was his Ordnance Office work that earned Nock appointment as "gunmaker in ordinary" to the king in 1789. Richmond, the modernizing master general, gave him £100 to design a new standard land musket. He produced a prototype with a screwless lock, the muzzle-loading "Duke of Richmond pattern," arguably the finest martial musket anywhere at the time. He made about a thousand and contracted for ten thousand in 1792, but the outbreak of war forced the Ordnance Office to abandon it in favor of the simpler India pattern. The innovation we associate with industrial revolution did not always move in a direction amenable to the mass production we also associate with industrial revolution. Still, state-led tinkering had impact: some of Nock's innovations were incorporated into the military pattern of 1802, the New Land Series, which had Nock's simple stock and flat keys to hold the barrel to the stock.

Government-sponsored experiments improved quality, quite apart from standardization. The Ordnance Office dispatched bearers of measured expertise among contractors and at Lewisham and Enfield. Their gauges and jiggers made that office an important supporter of instrument manufacture, another Birmingham specialty. Some instruments were made in-house. A mysterious case of a carbine barrel without a touchhole reveals the extent of official management of standards. A series of checks should have ensured that such a gun would never make it out of store: a "very careful and proper person" tried barrels in Birmingham to ensure that they were made to the proper gauges, including touchholes. He marked good ones and sent only those to the proofhouse, where, before proof, the touchhole was again pricked with a wire to ensure that it was not blocked with dirt. Only then was the barrel loaded, in the presence of proof masters and clerks who accounted for each barrel loaded from each maker. After the barrels were fired, they were tried with steel rammers to ensure that they had not missed firing. The touchholes of those that had missed firing were pricked again, and the barrels primed again and laid down again to fire, then retried with a rammer. After this, the barrels stood for some days to ensure that no defects appeared on their outsides. Then the breech pins were turned out and the barrels washed and examined for flaws on the inside. The touchholes were cleared again. Only barrels found to be perfectly sound were marked with the Tower proofmark and stored; others were returned to the makers. If guns lay in store for long, they were examined again before being issued.

By the end of the century, countless small innovations had improved the flintlock's performance significantly. The standard English lock of 1780, with the best gunpowder and a new flint properly adjusted in the cock jaws, could typically discharge two hundred times in succession without misfiring. The ignition speed was much greater than in American gunlocks. Because innovations were driven by the increasing scale of war and fear of French power rather than commercial competition, experimentation continued during the Napoleonic Wars. In 1801, for instance, Henry Osborne of Birmingham made the prototype and first consignments of the sword bayonet designed for the first standard-issue British rifle, the Baker rifle. Few innovations were patented, because patents were expensive and the Ordnance Office typically disallowed them for slowing the spread of innovation. Still, Thomas Gill patented a new rifling method in 1800. J. Hall, of Birmingham, patented a hammer for making locks in 1802. Between 1806 and 1817, the Birmingham gunmakers John Jones, Benjamin Cook, Henry James, John Bradley, and Osborne received several patents for inventing (and then improving on) a method of using grooved rollers to weld barrels—though the technique also changed the way other kinds of iron cylinders and tubes were welded. Osborne began experimenting with such machinery when barrel welders in town went on strike. When he set his steam-powered rollers to work, twelve hundred welders wielding forge hammers appeared at his home, threatening destruction. The military guarded his mill for days—another way in which the government assumed risk associated with innovation. Incremental innovations maximized the quality of flintlocks until the percussion ignition system made them obsolete in the 1840s. Tiny revolutions throughout the processes that made the Brown Bess, many state-supported, were integral to the gun trade's evolution. War promoted the spirit of technical innovation conventionally associated with the industrial revolution.

Many of these technological changes sought to improve hand skills rather than replace them, which placed greater demands on skilled workers. Still, the degree of innovation produced an impression of revolutionary dynamism abroad. Birmingham button makers used hot stamps from 1749, an early instance of the use of tools to achieve standardized products. One of them, Michael Alcock, set up a factory in Roanne in France, which became a local marvel for its stamping machinery, which produced buttons by the millions. In 1764, the French brought Alcock to the nearby gunmaking town of Saint-Étienne to shed light on why ironmongers there were so poor. He answered that Birmingham's ironmongers had more liberty from the violence that threatened those who dared to mechanize production. He then experimented in steel production in Roanne, because he felt it was what Saint-Étienne primarily lacked to make things like files. Intense division of labor, powered polishing equipment, powered rolls to laminate metals, powered grinding wheels, and superior waterwheels distinguished midcentury English gun manufacture from French gunmaking. A visitor to Galton's works marveled at the "incredible" "Cheapness" of his muskets in 1776: "We can only be relieved from our Surprize by observing how little Labour is applied to them, how great a part of the Execution is by Water, and by being informed that Men work at this Business for about 6/- a Week." Not only Adam Smith but also the French *Encyclopédie* admiringly noted the division of labor in Birmingham pin factories. French spies in the 1780s described flying presses for stamping metalwork out of copper, tin, and silver—stamps banned in France for fear of their use in counterfeiting (and which did make Birmingham notorious for counterfeiting). Thousands of British craftsmen were recruited to the Continent in 1792–93 and 1802–3. Honoré Blanc, the Parisian musket contractor credited with inventing a system for interchangeable parts manufacture in 1784, probably with one of Alcock's machine tools, bought out Alcock's stamping factory upon his death in 1794. He used stamping techniques to make gunlocks. The French launched their "crash" industrial project in gunmaking that year partly because of their long-gathering impression that British gun manufacture was heavily mechanized—which it was, relatively speaking. Some British gunsmiths adapted stamping techniques to gunlock production after Blanc did. Isaac Mason was pressing out gunlock parts with a fly press in 1796. In 1818, the Swiss-born inventor John George Bodmer, who had made interchangeable locks for the French government during the war, witnessed locks being made interchangeably (if not well) in a Birmingham shop.

The Birmingham model—the type of incremental, gradual technological change that typified the hardware trades, as historians like Maxine Berg have shown—is probably more typical of eighteenth-century technological advancement than the more dramatic changes in cotton textile production. Gunmaking was at the high-precision end of the hardware trade, like machine building; it produced spin-off effects in other industries, including textiles. Many of the improvements in lathes that allowed the design of sophisticated machine tools were either initially employed in or adapted to firearm manufacture. Improvements in iron and steel triggered by uses in weapons rippled into the vast market of ornaments and jewelry, watch and clock springs, and precision instruments. This was especially true in the early period, when iron manufacturers tended to be under the control of iron producers. Indeed, key inventions even in industries beyond Birmingham had ties to Birmingham's gunmaking trades. John Wyatt had experience developing machinery for boring metal and making files, both essential to gunmaking; he partnered with Lewis Paul in the 1740s to make the first roller-spinning machine to produce cheap yarn for the African trade. The machine failed commercially, but Richard Arkwright later built on it, transforming Manchester's textile industry. Birmingham's William Osborne introduced labor-saving machinery to turn and weld barrels in 1820. He was attacked for this, but his machines found less controversial use in producing the tubes used in gas and water pipes, bedsteads, and steam engines. Surplus government musket barrels were also repurposed as service conduits for gas lighting. Birmingham's gunmakers were in some ways part of the backbone of wider industrial development.

S mall-arms manufacture was not the only arena in which military experiments spawned technological and organizational innovations. Military entanglement in wider intellectual and industrial networks also gave the British government a major role in the creation and employment of arguably the most iconic developments of the industrial revolution, including the steam engine, copper sheathing, and interchangeable-parts manufacturing.

Early changes in iron production owed much to the state and to war demand. The first reverberatory furnace was developed in 1688–98. Abraham Darby began using coal to smelt iron at his Coalbrookdale works in Shropshire in 1708. The Nine Years' War and the War of the Spanish Succession expanded these endeavors. The Lloyds adopted the Darby coke-smelting process in 1721 at Bersham, near Coalbrookdale. The War of the Austrian Succession stimulated improvements in coke-smelting techniques, making it possible to use domestic ores for bar and pig iron and ensuring survival of the nail trade. By increasing demand for metal while constraining importations, war generally quickened the search for ways to use coal to smelt metals. Gunmakers' fussiness stimulated efforts to produce better-quality iron; nailers might have been satisfied with indifferent quality. Gunmakers' diversified investments enabled such risk taking, and the Ordnance Office encouraged their fussiness: Wilson got contracts because his barrels were "made of the best sort of iron"; lockmakers were reprimanded for using "brittle or bad iron." In

1753, Isaac Wilkinson bought the Bersham works to make cannon. During the Seven Years' War, his sons John and William built a thriving trade in cannon, shells, and grenades with the Ordnance Office. They experimented with casting and blast furnaces, taking out several patents. Aside from a brief flirtation during the War of the Austrian Succession, the Darbys remained aloof from military work, but their activities were nevertheless entwined with it. Darby and John Wilkinson built a cast-iron bridge over the River Severn in 1773 because Darby's company depended on communication with Wilkinson's forges.

Ordnance officials who worked with these industrialists saw innovation as a means of coping with perpetual insecurity. Master General George Townshend understood government investment in manufacturing and technological progress as a national obligation in a time of political vulnerability. Complaining of "unexpected obstacles" in the way of producing gun carriages, he explained, "I am sure the public would laugh if it was not too indignant at a difficulty of finding wood or workmen in this country to support the artillery of Great Britain." Wider participation in contracting was the answer: supply of any material should not be confined to two or three contractors, "as it is not a gradual . . . supply our situation requires but the more immediate and ample provision against any emergency which no man can measure." He urged expansion of the Royal Laboratory at Woolwich on the same grounds—calling for fifty additional hands. A sense of permanent threat guided these enhancements: "This country is never secure a moment from insult both abroad and at home." A mathematical instrument maker joined the Ordnance Board. Draftsmen in the office were instructed in shading and perspective in drawing plans.

In this way, the Ordnance Office and John Wilkinson came to play a central role in the history of the steam engine. In 1770, just before Townshend became master general, the office hired Jan Verbruggen, from The Hague, as master founder. Experienced in improving cannon boring technology, he was charged with increasing the precision of cannon production. Townshend agreed to his request for another boring engine at the Royal Brass Foundry to keep up with his furnace capacity. Thus did state establishments "unintentionally nourish" development of the steam engine.

The precision Verbruggen introduced made the steam engine more viable. John Wilkinson improved on his machinery, patenting a cannon lathe in 1774. The Ordnance Board canceled the patent a year later to open up solid boring to more contractors, who also experimented with casting methods. Meanwhile, Wilkinson devised a cylinder lathe based on his cannon lathe, and it alone could accurately bore the cylinders for James Watt's steam engines: its importance to Watt's experiments "cannot be exaggerated." Wilkinson was already the iron supplier for the Boulton & Watt steam engine enterprise. In typical Birmingham style, Boulton, another government contractor (on which more below), was applying the lessons of button manufacture to steam engine manufacture. Wilkinson was also one of the earliest purchasers of Boulton & Watt engines, which he used to raise water from mine shafts. He was the first to purchase their blowing engine, to blow an iron furnace at his works in Broseley, buying four more in a year. He partnered in the steam engine business: he made the main engine parts—cylinder, condenser, and piston—at his ironworks, and Soho took on the more complicated parts. The alliance lasted twenty years, until Boulton's and Watt's sons discovered in 1794 that Wilkinson had been pirating and selling their invention independently—some twenty engines—since 1782. A court injunction closed the Bersham works in 1795, and the parties reached a settlement the next year. (Wilkinson's niece later married Boulton's son.) Without the partnership, Boulton and Watt struggled to get their cylinders made, finally setting up their own boring mill—the beginning of the Soho Foundry. Galton supported their steam engine venture at the turn of the century, too.

In the 1780s and 1790s, Richmond expanded the Ordnance Office's technological pursuits. He originated the Ordnance Survey (the national military mapping project), experimented with gunnery, standardized soldiers' gun-cleaning tools, and oversaw large workforces at government gunpowder mills. He embraced efficiency and quality control on principle. Under the Earl of Chatham (master general from 1801 to 1810), the office created laboratories for restoring aging gunpowder. When walnut supply became scarce, the office tried to grow walnut trees on its stations. There were also experiments in improving artillery and carriages, the invention of shrapnel, and small-arms factories. Before the mills at Lewisham were a government gun factory, they were leased to contractors; state resources were entangled with industry.

The state was part of the apparatus of continual innovation in iron production that made the English iron industry the most advanced in Europe and proved central to the final dramatic invention that led to full industrial takeoff in iron: Henry Cort's puddling process, which reduced the coal needed to produce pig iron, making it easier and cheaper to convert coke pig to wrought iron. Cort's wife's uncle was a major supplier of iron and other naval goods; Cort, too, became a navy agent. When the uncle bequeathed his interest in a Hampshire forge to Cort's wife, he took it over. The forge recycled old iron for the navy. In 1780, Cort had a contract for ironwork for the Victualling Board. His first breakthrough was a new method of turning iron into bars by passing it, at welding heat, through pairs of grooved rolls operated by water power; the grooved rolls allowed him to consolidate the grain of the iron and squeeze out slag. Cort did not cut much of an Enlightenment figure; the Scottish chemist Joseph Black described him as a "plain Englishman, without Science," who made his discovery by "dint of natural ingenuity and a turn for experiment." But crucially, Cort *knew* some Enlightenment figures. In 1782, he went to see Boulton and Watt; they promised to mention his work to their partner John Wilkinson. They corresponded about using a steam engine in his experiments. Boulton and Watt also forwarded Cort's description of his technique to Wilkinson. Cort demonstrated the technique before Midlands ironmasters. He had a contract with the Navy Board in 1782 and was encouraged to try to convert ships' cast-iron ballast into wrought iron. These experiments resulted in the 1784 invention of the puddling process. From this he secured contracts to shape Swedish iron to suitable sizes. By 1789, the Navy Board stipulated that all iron for its contracts be made by Cort's process. Puddling furnaces multiplied. Wilkinson installed fourteen at Bradley, where he produced hundreds of tons of bar iron monthly. In the 1790s, in the course of developing reliable naval cannon, Thomas Blomefield, an old Ordnance Board hand and Woolwich artillery inspector, figured out how to eliminate the sulfur traces that made coke iron brittle. In these stimulating times, Benjamin Farmer was moved to reveal to his niece Mary Farmer his earlier experiments in making bar iron, hoping to benefit her husband, Charles Lloyd. The Cort process freed the Midlands from dependence on Baltic iron, enabling the state to more than double the tariff on foreign bar iron during the wars that had just begun. Foreign iron prices rose 30 percent in 1796, translating into revolutionary gains for English ironmasters, who extended their works and erected more furnaces. Now the processes of iron manufacture— from reduction of ore to production of finished goods—could be collected in a single locality rather than being bound to forests or rivers. Coal-rich areas like Wales, the Midlands, and Scotland profited; new metal-using trades and iron founders thrived.

Steam engines fueled the spread of the puddling furnace. They, too, multiplied as war put pressure on coal mining. In 1796, Boulton determined that little money was to be made in fashion goods and gave up manufacture of "Golden toys or ormolu ornaments, paintings etc." "In lieu thereof," he built "iron furnaces & foundrys which . . . is more perminant [*sic*] & more profitable in proportion to their being more usefull to the publick." He advised his son "to confine his persuits to things usefull rather than ornamental." The war and the expanding market for steam engines underwrote his embrace of utility. After the wars, the influential political economist Thomas Malthus claimed, "In carrying the late war, we were powerfully assisted by our steam-engines." In fact, war had assisted the spread of steam engines. These inventions—steam engines, lathes, the puddling process—facilitated the rise of large-scale industry. They were interdependent and mutually reinforcing, and the state stood at the center of the networks around them. Cort clearly thought of government as *the* patron of technical change. He believed that official adoption of his iron would boost sale of licenses for his process. Work for the state sealed a manufacturer's reputation and prospects. Other big purchasers, like the East India Company, looked to the Ordnance Office for guidance about firms. When a long-standing Birmingham bayonet contractor was shut out from government work, his biggest concern was its effect on his reputation, which alone had made keeping up with government demand worth "unremitting exertions." Artificers who questioned the Ordnance Board or its servants might be exhibited "*in terrorem* to others."

The navy was also the patron of copper sheathing of ship bottoms, often called the period's single most important innovation. The technique was developed to prevent deterioration of ship hulls. The Champions—a family associated with the Galtons—worked with the navy on early trials of brass sheathing in 1740. The practical plan to copper the bottoms of the entire naval fleet was a response to the involvement of France, Spain, and the Netherlands in the American war. Private shippers observing the navy began to sheath their own ship bottoms, too, to reduce their insurance premiums. The technique dramatically boosted copper production and had enormous ripple effects.

Copper sheathing made the iron bolts in hulls susceptible to electrolytic action; a search began for a suitable alloy material. In 1783, technicians at Thomas Williams's factory in Birmingham invented copper alloy bolts. Among these was Williams's partner, John Westwood, an inventor who had developed a new means of proofing cannon. Williams was the principal contractor for sheathing and nails; his establishment dominated the copper industry. Wilkinson was involved in this work, too: he supplied iron for the smelting works in 1780 and a pirated Boulton & Watt engine, and went on to partner in Williams's copper works. Williams controlled the copper mines of Anglesey and had smelting works in Lancashire besides his Birmingham factories. This scale made innovation in bolts possible. In 1786, the navy ordered new bolts for all guard ships; they were three times the price of iron, plus the cost of rebolting. This kind of government support of contractors fueled vehement criticism of corruption. The British public pointed to high copper prices produced by Williams's monopoly. Legislation in 1782 prevented contractors from being elected as MPs, but Williams was nevertheless an MP from 1790 until his death, in 1802. In 1799, he had himself appointed to the select committee investigating the copper trade, thus ensuring that it would not probe into his activities.

Samuel Bentham, as inspector general of naval works from 1796, pushed back against this kind of corruption by innovating new manufacturing methods that might free military agencies from dependence on contractors. His innovations built on his experience in Russia in the 1780s. His brother Jeremy visited him there and began to build on Samuel's ideas of panoptical supervision of workers—the germ of the Panopticon prison Jeremy designed; the problem of mass production for the state inspired a key concept of British liberalism. In Britain in 1791, Samuel and Jeremy promoted the Panopticon scheme. The Admiralty asked Samuel to design ships in 1795, and he included interchangeable parts for masts and spars to enable repair at sea. Then, as inspector general of the naval works, he determined to make the dockyards so efficient that contractors would be unnecessary—an echo of revolutionary France's attempt to apply Enlightenment principles to manufacturing. His vision was to reorganize the dockyards to standardize the measured movement of each woodworker, making personal judgment superfluous. His ideal was an individual at the center of the dockyard directing all the activity around him, responsible to a single supervisor—the Panopticon principle. His techniques—which might have been innovated only in the context of a state operation—were later copied in industry, including introduction of steam power and mechanization of many processes. Steam pumps kept docks dry. Bentham invented bucket-ladder steam dredgers to keep them from silting up. He also built metal-processing mills in the dockyards, to take the supply of copper sheets and bolts back from contractors.

Perhaps most important, he revolutionized production of the wooden pulley blocks used in ships' rigging—to reclaim that work from a monopoly contract long held by Walter Taylor and his son. For this, Bentham worked with Marc Brunel, a French émigré who arrived in Britain from the United States in 1799 upon hearing of the navy's difficulty in obtaining sufficient pulley blocks. Brunel reconnected with and married Sophia Kingdom, whom he had met in France. Sophia's father was a British navy and army contractor, and her brother was chief clerk of the secretary's office in the Navy Office. Brunel got the machine-tool manufacturer Henry Maudslay to make a model of the boring and mortising machines he had designed; Maudslay had worked at the Royal Arsenal, at Woolwich, before setting up his own shop. Through Sophia's brother, Brunel offered his idea to the Taylors. They rejected it, preferring their horse-powered circular saws. Brunel then tried Bentham, who had been working on a similar solution. He took up Brunel's plan enthusiastically, showing the model to the Admiralty Board. The plant was installed at Portsmouth Yard, with machinery built by Maudslay: steam-driven mills to produce blocks more cheaply and quickly than the Taylors could. By 1808, the plant produced 100,000 blocks a year. The Taylors could not take on the risk and the high setup costs required to *revolutionize* production methods. The stakes for the navy—national security—made such risk and cost worth taking on. In 1810, Brunel invented a continuous production method for army boots in a Battersea factory, producing four hundred a day. When he was left with thirty thousand pairs at the end of the war, he petitioned the War Office for relief, but to no avail. He went bankrupt and landed in debtor's prison in 1821. He reached out to Russian contacts, and finally the master general of the Ordnance Office—none other than the hero of Waterloo, the Duke of Wellington—intervened. The government paid his debts, and he restarted his career as an inventor; his son Isambard Kingdom Brunel became a giant of nineteenth-century industry and innovation. In all this, too, the state supported industrial revolution—haltingly, ungraciously, and yet vitally.

M ajor turning points of industrial revolution—the steam engine, puddling, copper sheathing—were triggered by war and produced by networks of contractor-industrialists. Causal relations between science and industry were not direct, unitary, or simple. Formal scientific pursuits were often critical to innovation in the nineteenth century, but in our period, science and industry tended to be parallel pursuits that at times intersected or overlapped. Matthew Boulton puzzled over the connection between the polite, enlightened dissemination of natural knowledge and the transfer of "know-how," which often implied advertisement of trade secrets. Many key figures in the industrial revolution displayed little interest in science for its own sake but were nevertheless within its intellectual orbit. John Wilkinson learned on the job in his father's ironworks, but the family became Unitarians under Joseph Priestley's influence, and John married Priestley's sister. Samuel Garbett had no passion for science but was close to Boulton for a half century. In 1775, the Society for the Encouragement of Arts, Manufactures, and Commerce gave John Bedford, a Birmingham man with works in Wales, a bounty to improve the process of making bar iron from English ore for fine guns and wire and other "capital articles." The rising interest in science and industry together provide evidence of a society that was increasingly curious and on the make, invested in experimentation and continual improvement and the culture of Enlightenment civility. This is the primary significance of organizations and movements that popularized science and technology, including the Lunar Society—what they reveal about the motivations, milieu, values, and approach of eighteenth-century Britons, not about the direct transfer of knowledge to industry.

Practical scientific applications were certainly on the agenda of the Lunar Society; many members were involved in founding the town's general hospital. This community also routinely exchanged information and ideas around steam power, metallurgy, geology, and scientific instruments. Through formal memberships in the Society of Arts—founded in 1754 to encourage practical explorations in the interest of commerce and industry—and the Royal Society, the even older organization devoted to science, they were tied to the intellectual life of the country. They also corresponded with Europe's natural philosophers, their letters serving as the very vehicles of enlightened problem-solving. Dissent was associated with the culture and the political threat that scientific dabbling represented, as the riots of 1791 showed. (In reality, the town's enlightenment pursuits were fairly nonpartisan.) Quakers generally practiced a "culture of apartness," but the lines blurred among these industrial elites. Samuel Galton Jr. was a member of the Lunar Society by 1781. He had a private laboratory, which he loved. He began his experiments in it around 1776, just before he began to manage the gun manufactory. He acquired a range of devices for the lab, including a microscope, Nairn's electric machine, a reflecting telescope, an optical apparatus, a camera obscura, and an orrery.

Priestley was the second name on his certificate for a fellowship of the Royal Society, which he joined in 1785. (Boulton and Watt were fellows, too.) He collected information about nutrition, horses, timber, and so on in a large, alphabetically ordered, multi-volume "Book of Knowledge." It no longer exists; we can never know what he entered under "Iron" or "Guns." He did pursue ornithology and botany, compiling from Linnaeus and Enlightenment authors a book on bird life for the instruction of his children. Most notable was his work on optics and light, yielding a paper on "Experiments on the Prismatic Colors," which showed that if the colors of Newton's prisms were drawn on a wheel in appropriate proportions, the whirling wheel would produce white. He was a subscriber to the lecture tour of the popular inventor and scientist Adam Walker in 1781, when Walker instructed and flattered Birmingham's manufacturers with demonstrations of his mechanical skill.

There may have been little connection between these pursuits and Galton's gun business—although the intellectual assuredness and reputation they yielded likely emboldened his willingness to challenge his church's judgment of that business in the 1790s. In any case, he would certainly have known of the way fellow Lunar Society members' scientific pursuits impinged on *their* contracting work. Boulton's experiments with copper were significantly directed toward government contracts. The Scotsman James Keir arrived in the area around 1770, dreaming of amassing a fortune by experimenting with alkalis. As general manager at Soho, he collaborated with James Watt and other Lunar Society members. His chemical works made key ingredients for pottery, glass, and soap, but he also made metal alloys, specifically out of an ambition to produce nails and bolts compatible with the copper sheathing of ships. He held trials at the navy yards in 1779 and worked closely with Boulton and William Forbes, a copper contractor for the navy who also supplied piping for the Boulton & Watt engines. In 1783, the navy rejected Keir's bolts, preferring Thomas Williams's pure copper bolts. Inspired by Cort's experiments with iron that year, Forbes tried to toughen Keir's bolts by patenting a similar process for copper. But William Collins and Thomas Williams, meanwhile, patented bolts made with grooved rollers.

In the end, Keir's alloy was used only in sash-window frames in Birmingham mansions. He may not have gone down in history as a military contractor, but his story shows that the prospect of state consumption was critical to industrial progress and networks. And the scientific curiosity that was the currency of this social universe was implicated in that ambition. Galton's whole business and family network were involved in war-related contracting or finance—the Champions, Crowleys, Hanburys, Barclays. It was in the context of these intimacies that he concluded, in 1795, that everyone contributed to war. The polite culture of science of which he was part also became more utilitarian in outlook during the Napoleonic Wars—like Boulton's work. Exchange of scientific knowledge without relevance to the war effort seemed increasingly a luxury. The Lunar Society faded away. Instead, Galton Jr. helped found the Philosophical Society, an organization for purveying useful knowledge. His son Tertius was a stalwart of this group. Galton Jr., the longest surviving member of the Lunar Society, admonished his younger son in 1811, "Knowledge is Power."

Quaker family bonds and romances like Sophia Kingdom and Marc Brunel's undergirded this culture, but so, too, did government officials and contracts. These networks made the Birmingham area a prime site for production of useful knowledge; the town outdid Manchester by far in the number of patents recorded from 1760 to 1850. Slight adaptations of techniques and skills enabled new opportunities for profit to be exploited and led to further technical adaptations and innovations. No other provincial town could match Birmingham's artisanal skill and ingenuity, as Adam Smith remarked in 1776, followed by a string of foreign visitors. It was the place where products and raw materials were adapted, where tools and instruments were improved (though the basic tools remained the hammer, lathe, stamp, and press), and where new divisions of labor were introduced. Finding ways to effectively mobilize labor was another way in which Birmingham was particularly inventive, as we have seen in the gun trade. The town's relative lack of institutional regulation, traditions of religious tolerance (apart from the 1791 riots), and traditions of skill and artisanal cooperation, as well as its colonial and overseas markets and regional mining and transport structures, all shaped its industrialism, but so did government war contracts.

A rms were merely the tip of an iceberg of war-driven state purchases from a network of merchants and industrialists. Increasing industrial capacity mattered even more than technological breakthroughs; after all, Napoleon increased *his* resources by conquering more territories. Even skimming the surface of other areas of military purchasing, we begin to grasp the wider impact of war on the British economy during the time of the industrial revolution. In 1776, foreign travelers marveled at the prosperity war had brought to Birmingham, "a fresh flow of new enterprises." The state was a bulk purchaser—a fitful one, but nevertheless one that brought the bounty of mass demand that made industrial trades worth the enormous risk they entailed and made mass production of objects necessary and possible. War was good business, if not always good *for* business, in the eighteenth century. The Birmingham author William Hutton extolled his town's thriving trade as the source of not only private fortune but also "national security." Traders' anxiety to protect their fortunes fueled their support of state security.

Certainly, military departments filled some of their needs internally. Ships were built in the Royal Dockyards on the south coast and around the Thames. These were the first factory-like industrial organizations, producing the most complex artifact of the time, the large sailing warship. Shipbuilding was the country's largest industry in 1688, and the government was the single biggest builder of ships. In 1697, the naval dockyards employed 4,200. Woolwich was the home of the Royal Arsenal for manufacture of brass ordnance, shot, and small-arms ammunition, proofing cannon, and loading transports. The government made its own gunpowder at Faversham from 1759, adding more powder mills at Waltham Abbey in 1787. The 1,500 workers at Woolwich Arsenal in 1800 had expanded to 5,000 by 1814, absorbing convict labor in hulks on the Thames. In 1812, the three inspectorates of artillery, gunpowder, and carriages at Woolwich reached more than 3,500 employees; another thousand were at its powder mills, laboratories, port yards, and magazines. The Victualling Office ran breweries, baked biscuits, and salted and pickled meat. Its slaughterhouses and storage facilities were the biggest meat-production operation in all of Europe, supplying twelve thousand cattle and forty thousand hogs to the navy annually. Only a navy at war could generate demand requiring such a logistical system. The government small-arms factories built on this establishment.

All this amounted to a fraction of wartime needs. The Woolwich brass foundry was mainly a center for testing and maintaining expertise, complementing the Royal Laboratory for testing gunpowder. It did not cast cannon, but proofed and issued contractor-supplied cannon. Even the manufacturing these facilities undertook depended on contractors. Naval dockyards bought ironware from local smiths who sourced their goods from Birmingham. The Crowleys' nail manufactory was virtually a part of the naval establishment from 1693. Contracting work inspired the Crowleys' factory-style organization, arguably the first of its kind, which had nothing to do with mechanized production or economies of scale. Ambrose Crowley wagered that large operations would guarantee further contracts and allow him to address the navy's specialized needs. He wrote in 1705 that, with multiple sets of workmen, he could keep one constantly at work on anchors while others fulfilled other kinds of work. Contracting expanded alongside government industrial establishments. Despite growth in state establishments, the private sector outproduced the state by a greater proportion during the Napoleonic Wars than ever before: cannon, muskets, uniforms, wheat, pigs, cattle, sea transport. Averting invasion involved costly government expenditures, but those expenditures produced long-term gains by increasing the stock of private and public capital.

The Ordnance Office's minute books testify to an insatiable appetite for a stunning array of goods and supplies: copper sheets, sweet oil (for cleaning arms), lamp oil, stationery, tents, bedding, rivets, timber of various sorts, pouches, drums, belts, paper, vises, bellows, wheelbarrows, oars, coal, candles, pickaxes, felling axes, shovels, canvas, chains, forage, spades, weights, tin plates, brooms, canvas filtering bags, copper receiving pans for saltpeter, bar iron, compasses, pencils, harnesses, slings, boxes, scabbards, flints, tarred rope, chests, mattresses, utensils, and more. Beyond the office was the massive effort, with the help of wealthy London merchants involved in the East and West Indian trades, to secure food, clothing, barracks, medicines, bedding, hats, specie, and so on for troops. From 1688 to 1815, roughly 80 percent of public expenditure was for military purchasing. Arms and ammunition accounted for only 4 to 5 percent of that. Whatever eighteenth-century industrial business you were in, you probably made something the government needed for war. We know the broad array of businesspeople with a stake in the gun trade; imagine a similarly wide net for each of these businesses with significant shares of military demand. British military expenditures headed European league tables on a per capita basis, and Britain was the site of the industrial revolution. These were not coincidental but deeply interconnected developments.

Promoting the general health of metal industries was an old government prerogative. In the 1690s, the Royal Mint eased pressure on the Cornish tin industry by buying up enormous quantities and asking merchants to export it instead of cloth. The objective of preserving and nourishing arms-making capacity was never far from this concern with commercial welfare, particularly with respect to the iron industry, which originated with cannonball casting in Sussex in the fifteenth century. Military contracting stoked its expansion over the next centuries well beyond the niche of small-arms manufacturing; indeed, it languished from 1714 to 1740 without the stimulus of war. Early major iron producers of the eighteenth century also made diverse iron goods with military applications: the Sitwells of Derbyshire made nails, guns, iron bullets, and mortars alongside saws, chimney plates, sugar stoves, and cane-crushing rollers. The Crowleys were probably England's largest single consumer of pig iron in the 1730s and "made a mint out of navy contracts." From nails, they went on to supply the government with padlocks, wood screws, tools, files, and stores of iron and steel. In the 1740s and '50s, and possibly later, they supplied big guns to the East India Company. During the Seven Years' War, they competed to supply cannon to the Ordnance Office. Even Abraham Darby's Quaker scruples were breached after a reorganization of the Coalbrookdale Company in 1738, coinciding with the onset of the

War of the Austrian Succession. At that time, the Goldneys, a family heavily involved in the West Indian trade at the heart of the tensions with Spain, held a controlling share of the company, which paid for carriage of cannon patterns up the Severn from Bristol. By April 1740, it had a boring mill; it was making guns by November. Through the end of the war, it made more than two thousand cannon and 182 tons of "guns, heads and fittings," half- to nine-pounders of many sizes. Iron output and profits advanced by leaps and bounds during the Seven Years' War. Eleven new smelting works went up; only four followed in the next eleven years of peace—although there was enough work to sustain existing furnaces. It stimulated construction of water mills in Birmingham for all metal industries and exploitation of new sources of raw materials. Prices rose, and ironworks were fully employed, most obviously the Wilkinson and Carron foundries, which filled a steady stream of military contracts. Wartime government iron purchases did not merely compensate for disrupted civilian demand; they made ironmasters prosperous enough to integrate backward into coal and iron mining. Ironmasters used bigger furnaces and drove them harder. Contracting for the state was "the easiest avenue to wealth that the industry could offer." And wartime gains buoyed firms in peacetime when demand for metal goods was more limited and slow growing. At the end of the American war, Britons apprehensive about the fate of their slitting mills and other manufactories pushed for elimination of duties on Russian iron. The end of the Napoleonic Wars, likewise, caused the closure of half of the Midlands' blast furnaces. The Crowleys abandoned cannon manufacture in the 1790s but remained so generally dependent on war that their firm decayed precipitously after 1815. In Birmingham, the working-class radicalism of those years responded both to war-induced industrial transformation *and* its sudden slowing. Stagnation in ironworks serving home demand—for things like pipes for water and gas-lighting schemes—lasted through the early 1820s.

A similar story might be told about the copper industry, which became valuable only with late-seventeenth-century state purchases and the first copper coinage, in 1717. War demand drove the high coal investments needed to produce copper. Cheap copper, in turn, fueled the rise of

Birmingham's "new Trades"—guns, toys, buttons, and brass goods—over its older industries of textiles, leather, and cutlery. These were at once civilian *and* military goods. Boulton & Fothergill provided buttons, breast-belt plates, muskets, and cartouche boxes for militia and regular troops during the American war. During the Napoleonic Wars, Boulton supplied copper hoops and rivets to the Ordnance Office. He also provided coinage. The buckle-making village of Walsall, near Birmingham, declined overnight when the government's heavy metal purchasing drove metal costs so high that the army was forced to abandon buckles. (Conveniently, the army and the cavalry offered job relief.)

The textile industry also owed a great deal to war. Uniforms first emerged in the eighteenth century. Woolens drapers were among the first major war contractors. Clothier-contractors provided credit to regimental colonels who bought their goods, making them crucial war financiers; some evolved from drapers into bankers this way. Wealth and position acquired through contracting enabled these individuals to expand into other business activities in peacetime, such as insurance, banking, and ship owning. Proto-industrial rural manufacturing activities such as wool spinning and weaving, considered crucial preliminary stages to the industrial revolution, owed much to such war-related opportunities. West Riding textile firms supplied several major combatant forces in Europe, too. Soldiers bought enough to make up for other shortfalls in demand. The armed forces were by far the biggest bulk purchasers of everything from clothing to hats to shoes during war. In the 1720s, when Daniel Defoe visited the West Riding, he knew that places like Halifax and Leeds had risen because of military demand from England and other European states. William Wilson, a London clothier, made £4,000 for supplying Bragg's Regiment of Foot in 1743–45. During the Seven Years' War, the British Linen Company provided shirts for the army; it later supplied the navy with thirty thousand yards of osnaburg—a coarse fabric woven in Scotland (also used for slave garments). From 1760 to 1762, Fullagar and Todd delivered more than seventy thousand clothing pieces to the navy, worth £14,000. Charles James, the navy's primary clothing contractor, received nearly £45,000 in the same period for shirts, drawers, and trousers. Behind these big contractors were a "host of lesser beneficiaries"—the textile manufacturers who provided them with raw materials; suppliers of lace, buttons, cockades, shoes, and more. During the American war, a tartan-manufacturing firm in Bannockburn sold cloth to the army far exceeding the value of its nonmilitary orders, which it turned away. The American war paid "rich dividends" to textile manufacturers in Yorkshire, Lancashire, and the West Country. War eased transformation in the cotton industry, too, quite apart from the Wyatt and Paul spinning machine. High employment rates during the Seven Years' War dampened resentment of the introduction of the flying shuttle, which transformed weaving. The spinning jenny followed as output increased during the war.

Farming benefited, too. The Navy Victualling Office was one of the nation's largest purchasers of agricultural produce, structuring and integrating markets significantly with its bulk-goods transport system. Treasury Board contractors were involved in this work. In 1760, the Navy Board purchased 481,000 pounds of hops, 3,819,200 pounds of flour, 4,636,800 pounds of biscuits, 10,830,400 pounds of beef, 3,628,800 pounds of pork, 2,486,400 pounds of cheese, and 1,064,000 pounds of butter. Grain producers and livestock farmers did well out of war. Brewers prospered. From 1793 to 1815, the Victualling Board made 4,200 contracts with 676 contractors for foodstuffs. The overall number of contracts it signed likely exceeded ten thousand. Apart from a few wealthy City merchants, most were with middle-ranking merchants, tradesmen, farmers, innkeepers, and artisans, such as millers and bakers. The board's ability to replace bankrupt contractors testifies to the mercantile community's size and willingness to undertake this work.

Building, chemicals, engineering, and horse rearing also prospered in war. Despite its massive dockyards, the government was also the single biggest purchaser of ships made in private yards. The end of the Seven Years' War brought "great regret" to the inhabitants of Portsmouth and Gosport, "who find their account much better in war," noted Edward Gibbon. The Duke of Montagu's shipyard in Hampshire launched six naval vessels in 1779 alone. During the Napoleonic Wars, 71 percent of the tonnage of new warships came from private yards. State purchases stimulated production of sailcloth, linen, hemp, turpentine, pitch, tar, and other goods, driving much civilian labor. War was good for some consumer industries, such as silks, linen, glass, pots, and hardwares. Luxury goods like paper, glass, and silk flourished without French competition. Prices *fell* during the Seven Years' War, when spending was highest. Mass production and the consequent lowering of costs were stimulated by government demand.

The government footprint on the economy was extended by the purchases of its partner trading companies. The East India Company created regular work for laborers, retailers, and artisans who provided the goods and services that sustained its operations in Asia: dyers, dressers, pressers, and packers who prepared its woolen exports; lumpers, boatmen, carriers, cartmen, and porters who handled the cargo; dockyard workers who built, serviced, and repaired company ships—some thirty thousand Londoners at the start of the nineteenth century. It hired its own committee members' shipyards to build the largest and most ornate merchant fleet in Britain. It spent heavily on pens, ink, flags, and bunting. In other regions, the company sourced raw materials and manufactures for sale in Asia or for use by its servants, including Birmingham guns. Between 1756 and 1834, it spent more than £70 million on export commodities, crucially stimulating the copper-mining and smelting industries. The impact of all this in regional communities was likely considerable, as key players in this business perceived.

Indeed, eighteenth-century people perceived a causal link between war contracting and acquisition of riches and social status. As early as 1726, Defoe observed contractors acquiring immense estates by supplying troops. Horace Walpole complained of private fortunes acquired overnight during the Seven Years' War. Edmund Burke's and Lord Shelburne's critiques of contractors and the campaign to exclude contractors from the Commons in 1781–82 attacked this system of Old Corruption, which critics began to characterize as the mutual profiting by contractors and members of the government at public expense. But, crucially, *scale* of supply, rather than large profit margins, was the source of this allegedly misbegotten wealth.

Contracting was often about small margins and ambivalent attitudes toward war. Subcontractors were men of modest ambition working hard for moderate financial reward and managing a wider mercantile portfolio. This was a military-industrial society. Contracting was a vast area of British economic activity, and most contractors did not possess high connections. The increasing prominence of contractors over the century reflected the expansion of military activity and its growing importance to the eighteenth-century economy.

The centrality of war purchasing to British industry meant that its cessation in 1815 produced an industrial downturn that extended far beyond the Birmingham gun industry. Textile workers in Derbyshire rioted, too. Mass military participation and high food prices fueled the loud clamor for greater political democracy in the next years, but so, too, did withdrawal of state demand from industries long dependent on it.

Apart from industry and agriculture, the whole imperial financial world was deeply implicated in war. Through midcentury, the London money market, centered around the coffeehouses near Lombard Street, was primarily a market in government securities fueled by war. As ordinary investors converted their bank balances into interest-yielding government papers, bankers financed war expenditure. The most important companies in the stock market were the same institutions that the state depended on for long-term finance: the Bank of England, the East India Company, and (initially) the South Sea Company. An enormous proportion of the country was literally invested in the regime's survival. This financial reality was one reason the breakthrough for Quaker families also came with the war generation of 1740–1763, even for those uninvolved in iron or arms. John Eliot's insurance underwriting business and Samuel Hoare's trading interests flourished. James Farmer's relation, the banker Joseph Freame, was consumed by the "load of business occasioned by this ruinous destructive war." As major bankers to the state, he and David Barclay were closely involved with the public funding of the war. While a committee of two dozen prominent Quaker families waited on the royal family, the royal family honored Barclay's Cheapside home with a visit on Lord Mayor's Day in 1761. The Hanburys, whose businesses included rolling plate, contracted to transport guns and other Ordnance stores across the Atlantic. They were major specie contractors.

Businesses that reached a certain size inevitably turned toward state finance, in default of other investment outlets and in anticipation of political advantage. Great merchants, like industrialists, preferred the state as a debtor over risking capital in commercial ventures. Lending to the state attracted commercial privileges. Among the largest midcentury war financiers were major global merchants like John Boyd, Samuel Touchet, and Richard Oswald, who were also contractors exploiting the overlap between their shipping and trading networks. Their military supply operations stretched from India to Jamaica, and their profits were unprecedented. Touchet was involved in African victualing contracts, remittances to Germany, and distribution of naval prizes. He stood fifth on the list of subscribers who underwrote the government loan of £8 million floated in 1759. Contractors like him helped float loans but were also major subscribers to almost every large issue of government securities. Touchet was even part of naval operations, as we have seen. When he went bankrupt, in the early 1760s, political contacts saved him from total collapse. He advised the government on the peace treaty in 1763 and later advised the chancellor of the exchequer, Charles Townshend, on taxing the Americans, inadvertently helping to pave the way for the next international conflict. He and Oswald were also gunpowder merchants. Oswald became biggest among these contractor-merchants, supplying bread and bread wagons to British and allied forces, hospital and infirmary wagons for British forces, baggage wagons for Prince Ferdinand's Prussian train, and artillery wagons for the Ordnance Board—while keeping up his investments in the slave trade, as we have seen in his engagements with gunmakers. He negotiated the peace after the American war. Meanwhile, the Scottish businessman Lawrence Dundas acquired so much wealth overnight by supplying British troops during the Seven Years' War that he became infamous as the "Nabob of the North."

Leading figures in chartered companies had the expertise to float the kind of loans the government needed in wartime. During the American war, ten Treasury contractors were or had been directors of the East India

Company. Such men directed imperial and industrial expansion simultaneously. The state relied on the financial credit and expertise of individuals like the army agent and banker Henry Drummond, nephew and heir
of Andrew Drummond, who provided access to favorable rates of exchange for specie to pay troops. He and Thomas Harley were specie suppliers earning an annual commission averaging £10,000 from 1770 to
1783. Did they serve, help, or own the state? They took on risk and offered
flexibility; they could purchase in and understand markets the governments could not, such as the wartime international wheat market; they
alone had the logistical skills and resources to cope with the intricacies of
contracts, accounting, foreign currencies, customs, and foreign government offices. The bedding supplier John Trotter bought and warehoused
the army's surplus equipment until he controlled 107 depots in 1807, when
he was appointed storekeeper general. Was Trotter inside or outside the
state? In France, experts formed a state salariat or held military rank; in
Britain, they were self-employed entrepreneurs of expertise—but they
were also integral to the functioning of state institutions.

Contractors gave a city like Birmingham political power well before it
would get formal parliamentary representation in the nineteenth century.
Birmingham submitted five bills from 1773 to 1782 through the influence
of industrial contractors. Their leadership gave the town a powerful lobby;
indeed, it had had a powerful lobby even in 1689, with Newdigate. Galton
and Lloyd were key forces behind the 1813 revival of the Birmingham
Chamber of Commerce, which took on the Corn Laws and the East India
Company monopoly and pushed for the electoral reforms that finally gave
Birmingham parliamentary representation. The assertiveness of Birmingham's merchants and industrialists was founded on their sustained success under state patronage. War-induced prosperity drove Birmingham's
rising political influence into the nineteenth century. Earlier, the claim to
being a "public man" had rested on being a "disinterested gentleman,"
aloof from the base activity of making money. Now men like Matthew
Boulton spoke as "captains of industry," claiming the wisdom of commercial experience, including wartime provisioning; they really were "public"
men. Political economists began to argue for policy based on universal

principles, partly because such "men of movable property" influenced policy by representing *particular* manufacturing concerns—albeit in the name of collective benefit. Government bodies invited these incursions: ministers asked lobbyists for information; parliamentary committees examined experts. The critique of Old Corruption attacked the gentry's abuse of political access *and* the new public men transgressing the new theoretical notion of distinct state and private arenas.

Liberal theory aside, wars were generally fought to preserve and expand Britain's global trading position. Increased carrying capacity was another result of wartime shipbuilding. Re-exports increased during war, merchants earning higher profits, which in turn helped finance war expenses. Weather caused more dislocations than war. Certainly, effects were complicated. When the American Continental Congress refused British imports in 1775, Birmingham merchants petitioned Parliament. But twice as many proclaimed that the lasting welfare of the nation and the empire was more important than the temporary inconvenience caused by American rebellion. Manchester merchants proudly affirmed their immunity from American boycotts, since their trade flowed in so many directions. Contemporary mercantilists were certain that war produced economic growth. If monarchs saw wars as courtly, dynastic struggles, most men saw them as economic in character, aimed at making Britain a certain type of great, commercially prosperous nation. War was popular. Big merchants did not see the machinery of the state as alien or parasitic but as the thing that opened up opportunities, an agent of social and economic change for the public good—enlarging the nation's wealth, supporting industries that enhanced the nation's military power. Its wars were of a piece with the relief of £100,000 that Parliament provided to merchants who had suffered from the Lisbon earthquake and the bounty money it offered in 1781 to those who would grow hemp and flax for five years. When war with France started in 1793, Parliament authorized the issue of £5 million in exchequer bills to support leading merchant houses. Ordinary Britons traced the industrialization and urbanization around them to their nation's closer involvement with the world economy; hence their willingness to pay to expand and defend their interests abroad. They were keenly interested in the progress of each war, not only for the tactical excitement but also to anticipate economic repercussions. They knew that Britain's military success and thriving economy were related. Their lobbying for access to markets was a key *political* condition for industrialization, whatever the accuracy of their economic analysis.

In short, government war demand built up the economic sectors that we know as "private" industry and finance. Contracting was foundational to the first industrial economy. Government-induced investment was critical to the rapid application and development of ideas that had been the subject of experimental interest; it drove substantive progress in heavy-metal industries, steam power, and textiles. British merchants' and manufacturers' ability to provide the ships, cannon, guns, food, transport, and finance that the state needed depended on industrial revolution. Industrial revolution was about reorganization and expansion of industry as much as it was about technological change, often driven by the state.

While military purchasing driven by Britain's aggressive colonial expansion incited industrial revolution at home, British officials abroad intentionally stymied similar transformation in the colonies. Development of the American iron industry, as we have seen, was deeply disturbing to those with influence. In 1737, English iron manufacturers, including the Crowleys and Thomas Plumsted, strongly objected to the manufacture of bar iron in America, fearing that it would stimulate manufacture of iron goods there and ruin English ironworks and iron manufactures at once. The result would be a depopulated "Mother Country." In 1750, James Farmer spoke in favor of the Iron Act, which curbed expansion of American iron manufacturing explicitly to prevent creation of a war machine there. To contemporary Britons, the connection between development of metal industries and war was understood. Its obvious inequity fueled anti-British colonial sentiment.

The Indian subcontinent, by contrast, already possessed excellent gunmaking and metalworking traditions. The ships, guns, cannons, and other objects made there emerged from a "sophisticated and dynamic culture of technical knowledge"; European observers found Indian designs "technically advanced and highly complex." French observers considered Mysore's cannons and firearms equal to the best European arms of the time. In 1787, its ruler, Tipu Sultan, returned five hundred French guns that he found lower in quality than his own. Mysore workshops used local and imported techniques, including a machine to bore cannon, installed with the aid of a French artisan. The machine was adapted to bullock power rather than a waterwheel, itself a feat of craftsmanship. Golconda musket barrels were deemed stronger than those of the French, made of better iron and more reliable. Awadhi and Maratha guns earned similar appraisal. British military men claimed that Indian matchlocks had better range and velocity. Maratha small arms were better suited to the climate and local gunpowder, and Maratha cannon combined iron and brass exteriors in a manner that extended their life and lowered their weight. British military observers also admired the elevating screw used in larger cannon to permit "a certain amount of interchangeability." These observations were among those exchanged in the networks of Britain's industrial enlightenment. William Congreve, controller of the Royal Laboratory at Woolwich, experimented with Mysorean rockets, which had been used very effectively against the British. This led to manufacture of rockets with iron tubes for British forces. In 1818, artillery experts at Woolwich examined Indian-made ordnance from the Fort William foundry in Calcutta and pronounced them superior to those made at the Royal Arsenal.

It was partly to avoid encouraging this local ability that the East India Company insisted on importing its arms from England, mirroring the effort to stifle manufacture of finished iron goods in the American colonies. Suggestions about how to more efficiently source arms locally occasionally surfaced. In the 1770s, when company officials complained about the quality of arms sent from England, their London counterparts urged them to minimize demands for stores that could be manufactured locally. But the Court of Directors frowned on the consequent suggestion to have drums and fifes made in India. A proposal to develop lead, iron, copper, and tin mining in Bengal to avoid import duties was dismissed on the grounds that the company would lose profits and that "the rendering a Colony still more independent of the Mother Country[,] the probable supply to the neighbouring powers of Military Stores[,] and *the teaching of them new means of independence and new Sources of Wealth* are consequences so likely to ensue and so important in their nature and so difficult to limit that they require every attention." To "suffer a colony" to become more independent was "very impolitic and contrary to our government's maxims." It might bring "great and important advantages" to Bengal, "considered as independent," but "considered as parts of the British dominions it must occasion a heavy loss to the nation in point of trade." The proposal was dangerous to the company and national interests precisely because it risked triggering local industrial takeoff, given the evident richness of local resources and technical knowledge: there was every reason to believe that regions bordering Bengal "abound as much in ores," a company official affirmed. "The Natives are not absolutely ignorant of the use of iron ore and if mines of other metals were opened in Bengal and these produced as perfect as those they see brought from Europe and sold at a far lower rate, their curiosity and their avarice would be excited and they would at least proceed to experiment which they would hardly want the means of prosecuting." This official certainly did not consider technical curiosity and a culture of experimentation uniquely European proclivities. He feared that the "impossibility of preventing these people from acquiring knowledge of the European method of conducting each branch of the business they are employed in[,] the facility with which they will be seduced if at liberty[,] the difficulty of confining them and the accidents to which such confinement is liable would certainly contribute to their success." Knowledge of *any* metalworking was risky, given the universal applicability of metalworking skill: "the step from a knowledge of smelting Metals and the manner of casting them into certain forms to that of casting Cannon Shot and Shells is so inconsiderable that if the Natives once acquired the former art they would soon become Masters of the latter." The Court of Directors insisted that the laboratories at Fort William where ammunition was prepared remain a mystery: "No Indian, black or person of mixed breed, nor any Roman Catholic of what nation soever, shall, on any pretence, be admitted or set foot in the Laboratory or any of the military magazines, either out of curiosity or to be employed in them, or to come near them so as to see what is doing or contained therein."

In these ad hoc decisions lie the beginnings of global industrial disparities. The company did use local manufacturers to repair and refurbish arms, but it never manufactured them in India. The deputy commissary of ordnance at Fatehgarh in 1804 sourced tents and tulwars locally. The British also had some brass big guns made in the Fort William foundry, mentioned above. But iron guns were always imported, leaving Indian foundries unprepared to make steel guns in the next century. In 1813, the Court of Directors considered closing the Fort William foundry, out of fear that knowledge about casting might spread. The company's insistence on buying arms in England at once stimulated industrial revolution there and prevented stimulation of "the whole gamut of activities connected to metal working" in the subcontinent. To be sure, Indian states could and did pay other European engineers and officers for expertise in manufacturing arms. British determination not to share industrial and scientific knowledge was also subverted by diplomatic exigencies and independent Indian know-how, as we'll see. The challenge for the British was to at once suppress existing knowledge and skill *and* prevent transfer of European knowledge and skill. That was what empire was about. As British industrialism took off, Indian economic development was reoriented to serve it.

Imperial ambition generated enormous military commitments requiring mass levels of supply. It set Britain on the path of industrial advance and put it in the position to quash industrial advance elsewhere. Metallurgical masters were part of an industrial intellectual community and a network of individuals helping one another broker contracts and finesse manufacturing problems with their biggest customer: British state offices. British industrial growth depended heavily on that stimulant. Government offices led the way in many key innovations in key industries. Isolated, Cort's government contract work appears incidental—trivia—but that association is a common factor behind the pivotal organizational and technological breakthroughs of the time. War demand for mass quantities on standard patterns stimulated forms of production larger in scale, more complex, and more administratively demanding than those in civilian life. It posed organizational challenges that these industries would not otherwise have faced, fueling experimentation and change. Future scholars might plumb each case more deeply, but even these preliminary speculations allow us to confirm that Galton was far from unreasonable in claiming that others were as ineluctably guilty as he was in profiting from war.

Part Two

THE SOCIAL
LIFE of GUNS

Interlude:
A Brief Lesson from African History

I f you looked around eighteenth-century Japan, you might find farmers using firearms to frighten and occasionally kill animals damaging their crops. But only with very great difficulty would you find firearms in any situation of conflict between people, at least up to the 1840s. Although guns came to Japan as weapons in the sixteenth century, their use and meaning changed dramatically over time. In different hands, in different times, guns did different things. Guns had a social life. British gunmakers knew that the object they supplied to the Ordnance Office by the million was a weapon for use in military conflict. But they also knew it had other uses; this is why they so avidly participated in the market for bad and old guns. For eighteenth-century people, the use and meaning of guns depended on context; they might be weapons, but also gifts, ornaments, stewards, and currency. The eighteenth-century gun is the same object as a twenty-first-century gun in only the most trivial of senses; for eighteenth-century Britons, its place in political economy, military practice, and interpersonal conflict made it something very different, not analogous to guns today. Surprisingly, given the apparent obviousness of the gun's purpose—launching an explosive projectile with sufficient force to damage and/or destroy a chosen target—we cannot take for granted their use as weapons.

The Japanese story is not as exotic or anthropologically unique as it seems; guns were multipurpose elsewhere, too. We are used to thinking about guns in eighteenth-century West Africa as having unexpected, multifarious uses. Galton implied as much about British uses with his claim that neither was he strictly an arms maker nor were his arms strictly arms. Indeed, it was the very range of guns' meanings and uses in his time that helped them proliferate in mass numbers even as they became increasingly lethal. Like him, we might take a brief lesson from West Africa in that time.

In West Africa, guns were not only weapons in warfare but also symbols of prestige used in the firing of salutes and other festive and ceremonial occasions, such as funerals, births, marriages, and victory celebrations. They were diplomatic gifts exchanged between African polities. They also had socioeconomic uses related to agriculture and hunting, such as crop protection in newly cleared areas. These nonmilitary uses help explain the African taste for the low-grade trade musket, which was not intended for rapid reloading and was cheap, light, easy to repair, and devoid of delicate parts. More sophisticated military muskets would have required imported parts and cartridges.

Even in warfare in this region, the purpose of a gun was not as straightforward as a twentieth-century observer might expect: they were often used for the noise and smoke they produced, which served as a deterrent in battle. With provision of ammunition being a chronic difficulty, unloaded guns often simply provided a kind of military prestige value. This, too, meant that poor quality mattered less at times: ancient muzzleloaders had value beyond their effectiveness as weapons. Many Africans refused the newest weapons as late as 1900, preferring spears, even if they also carried a rifle, because the customary prestige of highly skilled mounted knights and spearmen was difficult to break down. Oyo cavalrymen preferred their bows and swords to the guns that coastal soldiers wielded, which frightened their horses. This made tactical sense, too, since guns were not necessarily decisive in local warfare: tactics continued to evolve in new ways, and guns were notoriously unreliable and liable to rot. Swords, spears, and the bow and arrow remained central to military

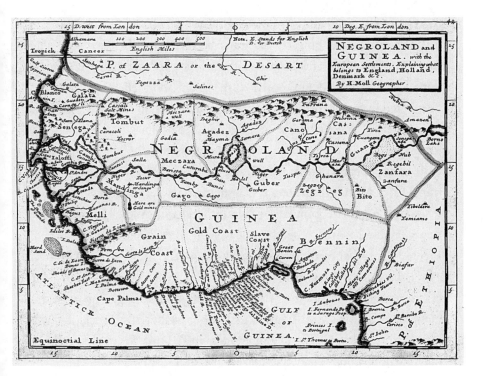

Herman Moll, "Negroland and Guinea, with the European Settlements, Explaining what belongs to England, Holland, Denmark, etc.," 1729.

practice. The Ashanti, near the coast, had musketeer military units, but firearms remained the exception rather than the rule north of them in war and hunting. Gold Coast mercenaries were hired farther inland because they possessed rare skill with firearms. Moreover, in many instances, firearms did not necessarily bestow tactical superiority. They simply did not fit into most eighteenth-century African military practices. In Yorubaland, for instance, they profoundly affected the political-economic balance of power but did not fundamentally alter methods of warfare even by the middle of the nineteenth century.

So how *did* they change power on the western coast of Africa? Despite being rare and ineffective, muskets rendered large, loyal followings of people superfluous to the exercise of power, with radical political-economic effects. Smaller armed bands could command power, though this derived less from their guns' ability to mete out death reliably than from the magical or supernatural powers that guns bestowed on their owners. They were part of rulers' charisma and their followers' morale, even though armies were still made up mostly of spearmen and archers, at most complemented by small corps of musketeers: "The symbolic single volley that began battles . . . could matter more than all the stones, iron slag, and lead shot fired in the course of ensuing struggles actually conducted mostly with bows, spears, and daggers." Accuracy was superfluous. A concentrated stock of guns in the hands of a small group of musketeers could help intimidate an entire population over hundreds of miles. However much they were used to inflict death, they were also ceremonial tokens of homage, power, and obligation that cowed European visitors along slave trails as much as indigenous enemies. As far east as Madagascar, guns were central to warfare as tools of ritual rather than of killing. The most dramatic tactical impact of firearms in most coastal African societies (with important exceptions like Dahomey) was in fighting formation: tight arrangement of troops yielded to looser formations, small, mobile units that often used them to avoid close combat altogether and overwhelm the enemy with gunfire from afar. It was in the interest of gunrunners to peddle minimally lethal guns to customers who would then have to buy replacements sooner rather than later and who might turn better weapons to effective use against their suppliers. Moreover, poor performance would reflect on the warlord rather than the sellers. Thus, although guns were the "very soul of commerce" in the region, "their significance as instruments of death and warfare is less certain than the strong African demand for them might make them appear."

The Ashanti and Dahomey kingdoms, where slaves were the military objective, were important possible exceptions. Europeans notoriously bartered guns for slaves, and African buyers used them in the raids and wars that drove procurement of captives. Growing European shipments of guns were correlated with rising slave exports after 1750. Slave gathering provoked the rise of highly militarized "slaving states." Even in these wars, however, the role of guns was complex. Guns did not make sense as lethal instruments in slaving, since captives had to be in reasonable health to make it to the coast. Among many coastal powers that used them in slaving, smoothbore weapons were too inaccurate for even light wounding of potential slaves; pellets and stones were often substituted for musket balls. African communities also purchased guns to protect themselves *from* slave raids: the gun-slave cycle was complicated. Firearms were also likely used to protect high-value commerce in such commodities as ivory—and captives en route.

The limited reliability of the eighteenth-century gun cautions us against assuming that the enormous numbers of guns shipped to Africa every year indicate an exponentially growing population of African gun owners. The arms were highly perishable and susceptible to disrepair. The average life of a gun sent to West Africa was about one year; much of the purchasing signified replacement of guns rather than a mushrooming gun-owning population. Fewer than 1 percent of the two to four million adult males in touch with the Atlantic trade could raise an operable gun on any given day. Real militarization of the population came later, in the nineteenth century, and those guns were not materially the same (in makeup or effect) as the ones in our period, nor was the political, social, and cultural context in which they functioned the same. Africans' use of guns in warfare at any point in time reflected rational responses to guns' changing material reality and the particular political and social contexts to which Africans adapted them. To be sure, guns figured in European militarization of the West African coast. Rivalries among commercial establishments—Dutch, English, Swedish, Danish, German—obliged each to maintain a strong military position to protect mercantile operations and expand at their rivals' expense. Each formed alliances with coastal and inland rulers and depended on local people as auxiliary troops to defend their forts.

My account of gun use in Africa, based on uncertain and fragmentary evidence, is debatable—and that is the point. Gun use was varied in eighteenth-century West Africa, and there was and is controversy about those uses—beginning in the eighteenth century itself. In England, at the peak of the abolition movement, there was enough doubt—and uneasy conscience—about the use of guns in Africa to provoke parliamentary investigation into the matter. In a 1790 inquiry, Alexander Falconbridge, a surgeon who had been to the African coast four times before abandoning the slave trade for abolitionism, provided critical testimony. Asked whether he had seen in the houses of chiefs "guns in a considerable number, as if kept for the purpose of shew or ornament," he answered that "very few" were "kept for shew," but he had seen "a great number in their houses with different kinds of goods, which I always understood were for trade." The committee pressed, "Did the guns seem to be kept as in store like the other goods, or to be arranged and disposed as if for the ornament of their houses?" He clarified that they lay in a heap with other Indian and European goods. As for quality, the "Black people" told him that "they kill more out of the butt than the muzzle," which he understood to mean that the guns often burst. He added that Africans aboard the canoes that traded with European ships were armed with cutlasses. There were also always plenty of muskets in the canoes, "but for what purpose . . . I cannot tell." His description of slave procurement did not imply a central role for guns: slavers went into a town at night, set fire to it, and caught people as they fled the flames. He had never seen a slave with fresh wounds; they were too wise to go to war "like fools," as white men did, knowing that their enemies were prepared. Europeans, however, used guns to force the slave trade, for instance by firing into or over a town to prompt African traders out of their "slack." The inquiry endeavored to assess the truth of abolitionist claims that bad guns were cruelly dumped on Africa in exchange for slaves. The exchange with Falconbridge highlighted the essentially commercial nature of guns in West Africa and reveals both Britons' generally vague understanding of their uses and confidence that they were not transforming African warfare. Even a convinced abolitionist like Falconbridge did not necessarily consider the trade in bad guns a particular cruelty of the system.

The success of the abolitionist movement in 1807 spelled change for the gun trade to Africa, though the ongoing Napoleonic Wars helped remove some of the initial sting of the loss. Precisely a year after the end of those wars, in 1816, a trader complained to a parliamentary committee that declining gun exports to Africa had crippled the British trade, to the considerable advantage of other European powers. Even then, uncertainty endured about how guns were used there. Asked "for what purposes small arms" were primarily purchased by Africans, the trader replied:

> They are almost wholly expended in amusement and funeral customs.
>
> Not for the purposes of war?—Certainly not; not one barrel in 1000 is expended upon that coast for any other purpose.
>
> Do you recollect, whether the demand for powder and small arms continued to be as large after the abolition of the Slave Trade as before?—Quite as large.

The trader challenged the abolitionist account of the gun-slave cycle, asserting more diverse uses for guns. Oddly, while blaming abolition for damaging gun sales, he insisted that demand for arms was unchanged. Interest distorted such evidence. Still, it is clear that, while integral to the business of slaving, guns also had other uses. More important for our purposes, these inquiries show how reasonable it was to wonder what guns were for in this period; their use was not a foregone conclusion. There was no sort of consensus that the spread of guns around the world implied the spread of lethal weaponry, regardless of whether one thought that was a good thing. Much of the mystery about their use in Africa was grounded in the material reality that on the coast, where they were handed over, they were simply a currency; their use value in the hands of African buyers mattered little to their coastal purveyors, who acquired them only for their further value in exchange.

Uncertainty about African gun use was so general that sales there were considered distinct from arms trading in general. In wartime, we have seen, they carried on with only minor inconvenience, while arms trading elsewhere was prohibited. During the Seven Years' War, the Ordnance Office allowed merchants to ship "ordinary trading musquets," plus pistols, blunderbusses, and gunpowder, to West Africa—and to arm their ships en route. Historians must estimate the number of guns sold annually in Africa (150,000 to 200,000 British guns in the second half of the century, and 150,000 from other European countries) because contemporaries did not record those numbers, instead recording their weight and value as generic "iron ordnance." This says something about how they understood these sales. The quantity of gunpowder and shot sold, by contrast, *was* recorded. When Galton's arms were seized by customs during wartime, he had them freed by explaining that they were merely trade guns for Africa, not arms. Abolition changed that view, just when the Napoleonic Wars also shifted understandings of firearms as strictly weapons. Trade guns became scandalous. In 1807, Robert Southey decried the guns sold in Africa, which "burst when fired, and mangle the wretched negro who has purchased them upon the credit of English faith, and received them most probably as the price of human flesh!" In 1829, chroniclers of the gun trade recounted shamefully, though it might "hardly be believed in the present day," that "fire-arms, if we may so call them," were once made without proof just for the African coast, where they were bartered, "one wretched gun for a human being." The abolition movement established that guns sent to Africa were only guns; it ensured that after the opening of the Birmingham Proof House, in 1813, guns traded for African gums and ivory were "as sound and secure" as those used by English soldiers or sporting gentlemen in the field.

One common feature runs through accounts of gun use in eighteenth-century West Africa: it was not the number or distribution of guns that secured political capital, but their *display*. Their presence in a warlord's hands produced a pervasive atmosphere of formidable power. They were an instrument of terror. Elsewhere, too, in this period, guns were not simply tools of generic offensive violence; this was one reason why Britons were confused about their use in Africa. Their parliamentary investigations came at a moment when their own use of guns was undergoing significant change, as we shall see. They signify not only British assumptions that Africans might use guns in exotic ways but also British *experience* with guns as multipurpose objects. The material reality of guns and political and social contexts shaped gun use in Britain as much as anywhere. Shifting regulation of their use testifies to their shifting role in crime, policing, war, trade, and so on. Eighteenth-century Britons were not entirely sure what guns were for in Africa partly because their uses were so varied at home, too.

5

Guns and Money

ritish guns sold in Africa remained remarkably poor in quality, despite advances in technology: rough-hewn, usually unsigned, often unproved, and increasingly anachronistic in design. This is evidence of both African taste and British merchants' condescension and cruelty. But the constancy of design also signifies guns' use as a medium of exchange and measure of value. It represented *standardization* of an artifact whose continual mutation might have frustrated its uses as a currency. "Trade guns" composed the greatest proportion of guns manufactured from the mid-seventeenth century to the nineteenth century. Their very name gestures to their primary function as an instrument, literally, of *trade*.

Guns were an international currency, but they were also currency at home. The market had not yet become the "cash nexus" of Adam Smith's imagining. Instead, the eighteenth century was a period of extreme currency shortage. Despite the rampantly commercial economy, official commitment to the notion of "intrinsic value" prevented the state from producing sufficient coinage. It did not issue small coins until the early nineteenth century, despite having sufficient bullion. This was not incompetence but the mark of the state's limited sense of its prerogatives and the inchoate nature of eighteenth-century understanding of money.

Leaving currency—paper and metal—to local businesses, bankers, and towns was typical of the state partnership with business in this century. Most Britons used whatever monetary instruments they had, worrying primarily about making ends meet and keeping their personal credit intact while paying down debts whenever they could. Retail depended heavily on gifting, credit, pawning, barter, and other forms of allegedly premodern practices of exchange. Paper substitutes for money included banknotes, bills of exchange, checks, and book credit; metallic and symbolic improvisations included plate, foreign currencies—and guns. Banking's lingering ties to metallurgy made guns integral to the functioning of the financial establishment and the industrial processes for mass production of coin. Guns mattered in socioeconomic relations beyond their purely violent function: they were a currency in a time of scarce cash and risky credit, their production dovetailed with coin manufacture, and their manufacturers were entangled with bankers. Apart from being a key site of industrial revolution, guns were central to the making of the modern British economy in other ways, too. A gunmaker like Galton might then understandably balk at the notion that the objects he made were definitively instruments of violence.

In the seventeenth century, extreme scarcity of currency in the colonies had inspired a turn to certain goods as viable counters and means of exchange—"commodity money." Tobacco and sugar were the usual resorts, but colonial governments at different times designated timber, meats, furs, dairy products, oats, musket balls, and other goods as currencies, too. They were not merely commodities but bona fide currencies. Paper money issued by colonial governments gradually reduced reliance on such commodity money, but the practice continued in some form into the eighteenth century, particularly in the West Indies. Brass wire was also a popular currency in West Africa; most of the brass wire made in Birmingham went there as "guinea rods." Guns were a currency like these. A ship captain pledged to sell Farmer & Galton's muskets on the African coast for "teeth wood or gold dust," which he would remit to the gunmakers from the West Indies. Customers in Montserrat paid for guns with shipments of sugar, cotton, and indigo—or the proceeds of such shipments to London. In 1757, Galton received sugar and a bag of silver on the account of a South Carolina customer. Similarly, his relative David Barclay bartered linens in Philadelphia for tobacco or flour for Ireland, or local produce to trade further for sugar, rum, or bills in the West Indies.

However, guns' particular powers made them a barter good and commodity money unlike any other. They not only could be exchanged for other goods but also endowed the trader with greater power vis-à-vis his object. Thus, infamously, in West Africa, slave gatherers sold slaves for guns that would help them capture more slaves, who would again be paid for in guns. Guns were an *input* as much as a medium of exchange and an intrinsically desirable commodity. They were often bartered for British captives in North Africa, but when ransoming Quaker captives this way, Friends remained unsure whether freedom purchased with guns violated Quaker strictures against the use of arms. They knew that arms were a currency but much more besides.

Our gunmakers manufactured this currency while struggling with the scarcity of money themselves. Credit was a mainstay of eighteenth-century business, a common substitute in everyday financial relations, immersing market relationships in the reciprocal and mutual bonds of community and family. In Quaker networks especially, good credit was a measure of character, of moderation in the pursuit of wealth acquisition, despite many Quakers' accumulation of fortunes through highly speculative overseas trade depending on long credits. Their collective reputation for good credit mitigated some of the risk in such trade. Galton was distressed at Farmer's financial failure in 1755 because it ruined his creditworthiness and thus jeopardized their firm's ability to do business. Credit created its own challenges, too: it was expensive and sometimes stretched so far that business stalled. Cash payment promised speed, and speed was of the essence for customers with schedules bound to seasonal ocean currents. Cash had a value apart from its face value, inspiring creative manipulation: manufacturers complained about merchants who took long credit from them by promising large orders and then, "for the sake of ready money," sold the goods "abroad for less," remitting part of the money to the manufacturers to further enhance their credit and using the rest to import goods for profit to defray the cost of suits against their debts. In this situation, cash was more than a medium of exchange. It was scarce enough that traders, including gunmakers, would sell their goods under value to get their hands on it. In the 1770s, money became so scarce in Birmingham that people paid premiums of 5 percent and higher for the use of it—contrary to the laws against usury, the local paper noted.

Cash hunger created the discounting crisis in the Birmingham gun trade before the Seven Years' War. James Farmer traced his rivals' discounts to the money shortage created by "unreasonable long credits." When Thomas Hadley seemed willing to cancel his discount and increase the regular price, Farmer objected that he might later lower the price just as precipitously, to everyone else's disadvantage. Farmer and Galton felt pressured to match their rivals' discounts for cash. Galton was horrified at the "monstrous" lengths to which his customers took the twelve-month credit he offered, "exceed[ing] it as they please" and consuming even the meager profit the firm could expect. Merchants with cash opted for their competitors' discounted guns, and those who could purchase only on credit could then get even longer credit.

Dealing with other money substitutes often reaped confusion. In 1742, Farmer's Liverpool agent received £200 on Farmer's account for a London bill. He sent it to Farmer, who got cash for it, but then the bill was returned and he had to give other bills for it. The person who originally drew the bill had "failed." Farmer was unsure what to do. A few years later, when Farmer toured the Continent, his wife, in London, turned to Samuel Galton, distraught that she had but one draft remaining for £100 and that a bill that James had given to Peter Simond had come back unfulfilled.

Paper credit was suspect in this era, fictitious in its reference to "mere promises." This was why gunmakers like Galton were more comfortable with being owed by the state than by private traders. A debenture from the state did not accrue interest, nor would it vanish with someone's unexpected failure. Galton & Son even settled direct accounts with Pratt by trading state debentures. More broadly, the web of obligations spun by the credit economy invested ordinary Britons in preserving the status quo. In this sense, the shortage of currency, paradoxically, stabilized the regime.

At times the Ordnance Board could oblige contractors' cash needs, as when it offered ready payment to gunmakers at the mercy of the discounting crisis in 1756. It also understood that timely payment reduced costs overall: egregiously late payment would instigate price hikes; prices were pegged as low as they were "on a presumption we should not generally be more than 6 Months at a time indebted to them." On the whole, the state usually owed contractors money. This credit was crucial to the military effort. The Ordnance Office ran on a Parliament-approved budget, but in wartime, unanticipated purchases proliferated and cash ran short. The difficulties in lock procurement during the American war prompted internal debate about paying artificers. An act of Parliament was required to alter the method, and artificers had petitioned for such a change in 1768, when payments were two years in arrears; then, the Treasury had refused to comply with the request but agreed to bring credit within twelve months. The public was invested in these arrangements. During war, besides government stock, London brokers took orders for short-term government obligations like the debentures, bills, and tallies with which contractors were paid.

Whether dealing with the Ordnance Office or slave traders, gunmakers struggled for money. Credit was not an exact substitute. Another recourse was guns themselves, whose circulation had as much to do with violence as with the scarcity of cash. Selling an old or broken gun to a local blacksmith who might reuse the materials was not unusual. But, as in West Africa, guns could do even more. Because of their use as inputs and their intrinsic metal worth, they not only could be bartered but were a sort of legal tender as a critical military store purchased in mass numbers by states. This endowed them with permanent value in commercial and financial markets, quite different from buttons or cannon. New instruments of currency produced more abstract notions of value in a time of official commitment to the intrinsic value of money, and guns fell somewhere between these competing notions. They were intrinsically valuable *and* represented a capacity to acquire value. They were, paradoxically, a material embodiment of an abstract notion of value.

Guns were a credit substitute and a money substitute; Farmer and Galton used them as security against debts. As his resources grew tight during 1754–55, Farmer "sold and lodged our guns for security where he owed money to the amount of more than £600," Galton discovered, wondering whether guns sold in the firm's name could be seized by someone trying to collect on goods Farmer had bought in his own name. To complicate matters, some of the guns were left with customers who also owed them money. Farmer & Galton had bought brass from George Pengree, and he owed the firm for guns. But he "pretends Mr. Farmer lodged the guns in his hands as a pledge or rather suffered them when not sold to remain so against a debt due to Pengree from Farmer." Pengree had credited Farmer & Galton for part of the guns sent, and Galton wondered whether he might also set off Farmer's separate account. Pengree implied that he had sold some of the guns and set the proceeds against their account. To Galton, this meant that Pengree could no longer claim they were a deposit against future payment. Moreover, Galton could not take the remainder back after they had rotted and rusted in storage. He suggested that Pengree send him the best to repair and sell elsewhere, and he would credit Pengree's account and find mediators to resolve the impasse. The overlap between customers and materials suppliers inspired Farmer and Galton to use guns to pay for supplies that went into their manufacture and to underwrite their expansion into other kinds of trade. But the arrangement was inherently fraught: guns' market value and metallic content made them a practical monetary instrument, but their perishability undermined both those sources of value, reducing them to mere commodities after all. Farmer also compensated the committee of creditors dealing with his bankruptcy case with guns—and James Johnson with an offer to participate in the gun trade.

Gunmakers also used their wares to buy materials from the Ordnance Office, paying for old guns with new guns or parts—again purchasing inputs for their commodity with the commodity itself. Because guns had such a significant social life, old, broken guns could serve as finished goods for sale in Africa *or* raw material for new guns. Rates of exchange—how many new locks per old musket—were carefully specified. The Ordnance Office routinely treated old guns like loose change: when it acquired rusted Dutch guns, it had them valued and paid a third of the value for the salvage. To sell off such material, the office advertised sales at the Tower, where gunmakers bid competitively and often paid with new guns. In a 1715 auction, Richard Jones bid highest for a lot of old barrels—£1,035—paying with guns valued at £1,200. Gunmakers also bought damaged barrels and locks, bushels of iron, and assorted gunstocks by weight, paying in money. Old iron gunmetal was sold to contractors by weight to enable them to fulfill contracts. Guns were both commodity and currency because of their metallic content in a time in which money was the representation of value *and* possessed the intrinsic value of precious metal; money was more important as a system of measurement and communication than as a medium of exchange.

These sales were part of the government's support of the gun industry in peacetime; they purchased loyalty and strengthened the trade above and beyond the payments they reaped. At the end of the American war, the Ordnance Office broke up foreign muskets in store, totting up the total weight of brass and iron and selling them at trade prices as "Old Materials" to stalwarts like William Wilson and John Whateley. Galton and Whateley bid on assorted barrels left unsold at the auction but were outbid by Edward Bate. Bate had given the office information on market prices for the goods and materials. Bearing this and his "conduct at the late sale" in mind, the Ordnance Board also approved his request to retain his debentures as security for the rest of the money he owed for the purchase; wealth included such official assessments of reputation (i.e., creditworthiness) and usefulness. Galton, meanwhile, was allowed to purchase other goods; the office always aimed to please as many gunmakers as possible.

To be sure, the British state could not allow guns to circulate in Britain as freely as money (whatever happened in West Africa). This, too, increased their cachet. A servant to London gunmakers brought king's-pattern muskets to an Ordnance official's house when a man who had bought them at a public auction brought them to the shop to sell. A gun contractor sought Ordnance Board permission before purchasing muskets that a regiment was selling. The board asked him to send one in, along with the identity of the man selling them. Selling old parts and guns to further the global arms trade was one thing, but abetting unlawful armament at home was another. The loyalty the office worked to cultivate among the trade helped it avoid the latter, as these deferential reports from gunmakers show.

Guns' mixed identity and the government's concern to control their flow made their value unstable. When arms on a Spanish prize ship were detained, its captors regretted that they might have sold them for more than £5,000 instead of taking the master furbisher's valuation of some £2,000. A man who received arms from an army captain's widow tried to return them to the Tower, but their rammers and swivels were stolen when they were left overnight in a pub. The good citizen thus lost his right to compensation for cleaning and delivering the arms. There was a continuum of arms; the more deconstructed *or* embellished, the more they functioned as currency. In between were those with the most explicit military function, and the Ordnance Office strove to prevent their slipping into similar use.

Since guns had intrinsic metallic value apart from their value as arms, a sharp eye was kept on those employed in their manufacture. In 1751, Ordnance officials judged that all the small brass work lying about for guns, stored in common chests without fastenings, was at risk of embezzlement. They had special bins and presses made with proper fastenings and began to take regular account of them. During the Seven Years' War, the office discovered that the wife of a Tower artificer was selling brass work bearing the king's mark—evidently stolen. The office deemed its value too small for prosecution and decided to whip the couple instead, commuting the husband's sentence when he "volunteered" to go aboard a ship of war. A Tower employee who stole gunlocks, intending to sell them, was punished. The office prosecuted a Minories gunmaker found in possession of stolen military muskets. As the trial proceeded, the officer in charge of the prosecution was himself charged with stealing gunlocks.

The British state was obsessed with gold and silver as the only metals of sufficient durability and scarcity to serve as coin of the realm, but in a time of burgeoning metallurgical industry, other metals were precious, too. Guns and money could literally be merged: in the seventeenth century, the king of Bantam sent copper coins to buy guns, and William Wightman used them *in* the guns. Guns also contained silver and gold: a 1764 list of those in Birmingham licensed to trade in gold and silver included the gunmakers Thomas Hadley, Barker & Harris, William Holden, and William Grice. But more significantly, as the philosopher David Hume observed, "steel and iron, in such laborious hands, become equal to the gold and rubies of the Indies." As materials of ornament and precision instruments, as well as weapons and machinery, they were the precious metals of this time. A Birmingham mechanic likewise celebrated, "Here Implements, and Toys, for distant Parts, / Of various Metals, by mechanic Arts, / Are finely wrought, and by the Artists sold, / Whose touch turns every Metal into Gold[.]" "Beside the prestige of the goldsmith ranked that of the armourers," writes Maxine Berg. At midcentury, all metals were preciously expensive and worth stealing. Birmingham workshops were plagued by robberies. Boulton & Fothergill lost grain gold to a couple who lined their coats with it each day before leaving the workshop. Workers embezzled iron from furnaces, warehouses, and workshops, like the nailers who helped themselves to iron from their master's workshops in 1770. A warehouse was robbed of eight ounces of rolled silver and four pairs of spurs, another of dozens of watches, silver, and three pairs of pistols. A workshop lost iron bars and several ounces of gold, silver, and tortoiseshell; another lost brass cocks; a third was robbed of nails, tin, and a gun. Button workshops were not spared. Wagons were robbed of parcels of buttons, needles, and buckles. Policing expanded in the town to address these metal thefts.

Gun workshops were also among the targets, not least because a gunmaker often doubled as a general "dealer in metals." In 1767, the Birmingham paper reported the robbery of four unbored barrels from Oughton's mill. The next year, a New Street warehouse was robbed of money, guns, pistols, locks, barrels, and gun furniture. In 1772, the workshop of Thomas

Archer was stripped of a pair of vises, two rough-stocked guns with Spanish barrels, an engraved holster pistol, a small saddle pistol capped with silver, a bunch of pistol locks, a pair of flat brass holster saddle pistols, and a musket lock. In 1789, he again lost half-stocked guns, the top of a brass inkstand, two small rings of silver, and gunlocks. Other gunmakers suffered similarly. Gold dust, "touch-hole gold," silver wire, rolled white copper, and iron were among the materials in gun workshops that routinely exercised a magnetic attraction for burglars, quite apart from guns, gun parts, and tools. Guns were worth their weight in metal, regardless of their quality. Like silver plate, guns were also robbed from homes, for their metallic worth rather than their practical function. Eventually, design, rather than the value of the silver, became the primary attraction for consumers of metal housewares—silversmiths began to display silver plate beside their silver—but more desperate consumers, those left out of that world of consumption, still prioritized an object's intrinsic metal value.

Precious metals conferred wealth in multifaceted ways. Plate was melted down to raise working capital for business. Gold and silver objects and ornaments were also an aesthetic symbol of abundance for social display. They represented a household's standing more unequivocally than "the simple price value of cash," because they helped maintain the liquidity of the owners' credit, enabling them to buy more and expand their business. Paradoxically, the use of precious metal to construct personal value or household reputation, through gifts especially, was a more efficient means of storing wealth than preserving it in the form of money. They symbolized national wealth, too. Guns functioned similarly as symbols and stores of wealth—and guarantors of it, as we shall see in chapter six. The repeated reports of theft of such items reinforced the notion that they *were* money. The mercantilist obsession with bullion was long in leaving eighteenth-century England because the financial instruments that would support a more abstract understanding of money took time to form. Government policing of arms exports was not only for the sake of military security; it stemmed also from a wider concern with metal wealth; the government also prohibited export of metal goods and machinery critical to industrial processes, including stamps and everything needed for them (screws, hammers, anvils, iron rods, iron and steel dies), presses (and their beds and punches), cast iron, wrought iron, lathes, engines, rolled metal of various kinds, certain engines, and materials for drawing and plating metals. These things were valuable to the realm as metal, as tools of industrial revolution, and as the machinery for producing coin *and* arms.

Those who tried to transform plate into coin were not unusual in their bent of mind. Making coin was uppermost in many crafty and craftsmanlike Birmingham minds in this period. Coin was that scarce, and the moral drama around coining that weak. Coins were clipped, bitten, counterfeited, and generally abused. A bewildering variety circulated in each place, their values constantly subject to change. Forgers of coin, both illegal and legal, were among the metallurgical artisans in our gunmakers' social and industrial networks. "Forging," which we take to mean "counterfeiting," also simply means "making"—using a forge to make something. It also means "to coin." In the eighteenth century, "coin" itself had a broader meaning, beyond converting bullion into disks representing standard money units: the Ordnance Office talked of "coining the gun carriages" to prevent guns from breaking loose at sea in bad weather. This is "to coin" in the sense of "to shape or alter the physical properties of (metal) by the application of heavy pressure." By this definition, what gunmakers did and what coiners did were not very different at all. For generations before Queen Anne, the master smith of the Ordnance Office, who made big guns and other ordnance, also served as smith assistant to the Royal Mint, where he undertook the heavy work of raising puncheons and sinking dies for the manufacture of coin. Ties between gunmaking and coining were close and substantive.

Birmingham is as central to the story of money as it is to the story of guns, and the stories are intertwined. Indeed, guns and coin also share common roots in the seventeenth-century trade to Africa: the Royal African Company provided gold to the Royal Mint from 1668 to 1722 for the coin that gave English currency its name: the guinea. These were Britain's first "milled" coins (as opposed to hammered): they were stamped with a screw press from blanks punched from strips of metal flattened in a horse-powered rolling mill. The Royal Mint at Tower Hill, the corporation where the scientist Isaac Newton served as warden (during the Great Recoinage of 1696) and then master (from 1699 until his death, in 1727), was the official site of coin production in the realm, but there were other mints, too. Until 1975, the Royal Mint was not a government-owned company; in our period, it was no less a private firm than the mints around Birmingham that competed with it. This is yet another instance of the corporate partnerships that constituted the eighteenth-century "state." Among Newton's many reformist activities was an effort to punish clippers and counterfeiters, but Birmingham's rich metalworking skills made it a nursery for coiners. Allegations that "all the bad money ever made *must* be manufactured" there were frequent from at least the Restoration, when the technology for coinage shifted from hammering to machine production by rolling mills and presses—the same processes used in button and medal manufacture. "Brummagen" became a "synonym for anything which pretended to be what it is not."

Copper coins were a particular problem, because the Royal Mint did not think of them as its prerogative. As the assay master Joseph Harris said in 1757, copper coins were "not properly money but a kind of token passing by way of exchange instead of parts of the smallest pieces of silver coin." They were a convenience for small home traffic but did not share the magical properties of the two precious metals. This made their manufacture an extraneous duty for contractors for much of the century.

This noncommittal official attitude toward copper currency underwrote tolerance for unofficial copper coins. Despite threatening laws, there was a strange absence of criminality around counterfeiting in the seventeenth century. In the eighteenth century, it remained ubiquitous and at times was condoned as easily, at least by popular opinion. Legally, making such coins was a misdemeanor until 1742 and a felony only in 1771. Striking coins that did not exactly resemble the regal issues remained unpunishable, and possession of counterfeit coin was no offense. By the middle of the century, contemporaries reckoned that half of the copper coin in circulation was counterfeit, most of it made in Birmingham, "where 1,000 halfpennies could be had of the makers for 25s." By 1787, genuine and counterfeit copper currency were roughly equal, about 1,500 tons each.

The mint's complaints about Birmingham forgeries echoed the Worshipful Company of Gunmakers' laments about counterfeit proofmarks on Birmingham guns. Guns and coins were both metallic goods manufactured for the state in which authorship was legally paramount but practically ignored. Both were too marketable and too essential to other commercial transactions. And both kinds of forgery threatened political infraction. Blame for counterfeiting was heaped on Birmingham, one indignant local historian claimed, only because the town had sided with Parliament during the Civil War. That memory shaped the government's relations with the gun trade there, too. Robert Southey sympathetically remarked that dishonesty was inevitable in a town of such intense ingenuity and commercial volatility, but he, too, felt that it made the town intrinsically politically unreliable. Fortunately, in 1791, its fury "by good luck was in favour of the government." These observations about counterfeit coin followed directly after his account of the town's abominable trade in guns for Africa.

Within Birmingham, public warnings against counterfeit coin were frequent. For instance, in 1760, *Aris's Birmingham Gazette* advised against counterfeit guineas dated 1755, which had two highly imperfect fives and a very faint impression of arms; in 1770, it minutely described fraudulent halfpence made of base copper. Scarce money abetted trade in fraudulent credit *and* fraudulent money. Policing of coin and prosecution of counterfeiters intensified, too. In 1761, a resident of Wolverhampton was jailed for "putting off counterfeit half-guineas," while Richard Cardan of Edgbaston was held on suspicion of manufacturing counterfeit money. In 1772, a couple was jailed for making brass coins that they had silvered over. Their home contained sixty-five pieces of unfinished brass, quicksilver, a bottle of aqua fortis, books of leaf silver, "and several Things useful in the Profession of Money making." At times, policing only made conveyance of false coin more surreptitious. In public opinion, Birmingham remained the "Residence of Artists" in the worst sense.

Partly to redeem the town's reputation, Matthew Boulton, in 1772, led a campaign to establish an assay office for guaranteeing purity of gold and silver in the town's manufactures (including guns). Until then, such goods made in Birmingham had to be sent to London or Chester to be assayed and marked; hallmarking plate made outside London was one of the Royal Mint's duties. By midcentury, Birmingham had emerged as the country's largest producer of such objects, and the inconvenience of transporting them for marking was unsustainable. As the campaign for a local assay office encountered vehement protest from London's goldsmiths and plate manufacturers, Samuel Garbett described Birmingham's manufacturers' plight in Parliament, pointing especially to the "important trade" of gunmakers, who, despite their ability to make gun ornaments at half the price, often bought them ready-made from London to avoid the cost of assaying them seventy miles away. Parliament passed the bill establishing the Birmingham Assay Office. To Boulton, the opening of the Assay Office did away with "past associations with counterfeiters and fraudsters, and establish[ed] Birmingham's claim to a new rightful place with the capitals of Europe as a producer of a store of value." Buckle makers, jewelers, bankers, and gunsmiths entered their names in the lists of the new office. Forging assay marks risked a sentence of transportation (banishment to a penal colony abroad). The first Soho objects assayed there were buckles, spoons, knife handles, candlesticks, coffeepots, and sword hilts and gun furniture.

In this sense, gunmaking was part of Boulton's entry into the world of money—and would prove integral to his role in addressing the country's currency shortage. Riding on the Assay Office victory just as the country suffered general financial and commercial collapse in 1772–73, he began to offer advice on the coin problem. Though he called for a return to the silver standard, he still figured centrally in the government's decision to instead recoin light guineas: his firm was among the select few authorized to exchange light gold coin for new coins, with weights adjusted to those at the Royal Mint. The exchange transpired through August 1776. Retailers cooperatively announced that they would not take light coins or Portugal money. The execution of James Duckworth, a grocer and hop factor, for counterfeiting and diminishing the gold coin testified to the new seriousness around the matter.

To be sure, complaints emerged about the changes; the argument that

Portugal coins were not coin of the kingdom was "a very poor Reason," according to one reader of *Aris's Birmingham Gazette,* since they had passed as currency beyond living memory. Business was so badly affected that Birmingham tradesmen reverted to taking Portugal money, with *Aris's Birmingham Gazette* encouragingly reminding readers that the Bank of England's refusal to take Portugal money was irrelevant: "At what time [did] the bank . . . accept the Coin of Portugal in payment!—And yet the Merchants of England . . . not only upheld its Currency, but by the Laws of this Country it is made Felony to counterfeit it." There was no need to scruple over money as long as it was full weight. Counterfeiting, too, went on, despite strenuous moral condemnation. All of this marked the inception of new understandings of money that set the stage for Boulton's intervention in coining: money was increasingly understood as something representative of value, whether or not it possessed intrinsic value. As silver values fell, concerns emerged that the intrinsic value of even good coins was less than their nominal value. Gold coins were current at more than their intrinsic value. A collective leap of faith maintained the value of base silver coin even as the real value of most shillings was hardly fourpence. As legal gold and silver coins fell out of sync with their nominal values, they began to seem little different, substantively, from counterfeits that also possessed only partial intrinsic value. Late-eighteenth-century Britons began to use coins as *representative* symbols of value rather than for their intrinsic value, well before official embrace of that notion. They learned to assume that a particular coin "can be said to *stand for,* even when it does not *embody,* the precious metal it *would have* contained *if* it had actually embodied the gold or silver represented by the stamp on its face."

In this context, Birmingham's industrialists took steps that shaped the government's eventual solution to the problem, finding less scandalous applications for the town's coining skills. As a partner in the Carron Iron Works, Garbett knew firsthand the difficulties in getting sufficient cash for wage payments. In 1782, he and his brother Francis were commissioned to investigate the state of the Royal Mint. He sought Boulton's advice, too. Their report recommended strict enforcement of laws against counterfeiting and official provision of good copper coins. Though the mint remained unreceptive to the notion that coins in the base metal were a proper currency, the investigation sparked Boulton's interest in inventing a mode of coin manufacture that would reduce costs and deter counterfeiters. He would adapt the coining press to the rotative steam engine. Moreover, just then, steam engines had made it possible to mine enormous quantities of copper in Cornwall. (This, too, fueled the counterfeiting disease.) From 1785, Boulton owned his own copper company, undertaking to buy all the copper produced in Cornwall for eleven years. The urgency of putting all that copper to some practical use encouraged his exploration of minting. Thus, in 1787, he began to push the Birmingham area "to petition parliament for a Coinage." In perfecting the "Art of Coining," his object was to "promote the most speedy consumption & greatest quantity of Cornish Copper possible." He knew that if he wanted to secure mass consumption of an industrial metal, the place to turn to was the state.

As with guns, the East India Company set the crucial precedent. Boulton enlisted it to prove the practicability of his system while he angled for a government contract. He made coins for the company's Bencoolen settlement, in Sumatra. Next, thanks to the evolving understanding of the symbolic nature of coin, Boulton made it possible for the emerging large-scale industrial employers to overcome the difficulty of paying their workers. Some had begun to improvise with paper: Wolverhampton's manufacturers, including some in the gun trade, issued their own four-shilling and two-shilling notes. From 1787, privately issued "tokens" became another resort. Roughly four hundred different tokens were produced. Thomas Williams struck the first ones, the Parys Mines Druids, to pay his copper miners. John Westwood and William Collins, of copper bolt fame, worked on them in Williams's Birmingham mint. But soon Boulton began to strike them instead, buying out Williams's presses in 1789. Their common partner John Wilkinson also manufactured tokens for his employees. Many of these were also struck at Soho with steam—another dimension of the Boulton-Wilkinson partnership. Other industrialists followed suit. By the end of the century, private issuers had minted nearly six hundred tons of copper coin, worth more than a hundred thousand guineas. Wilkinson also printed and circulated notes similar to those of any ordinary bank, and other ironmasters emulated him. Williams's and Wilkinson's concentrated and populous industrial organizations, both engaged in government contracting, at once forced and enabled a turn to such expedients. The tokens theoretically possessed value only within such establishments, but their intrinsic value meant that they retained some value even without. Royal Mint engravers profited from the token trend, inventing designs and providing dies for them. With this experience, Boulton's steam press was poised to resolve the coin-starved conditions in which eighteenth-century economic growth was unfolding. In the depressed year of 1787–88, Boulton pointed to mine closings and unemployed men in pressing his case with the prime minister for undertaking a new copper coinage; he understood both the state's paternalism toward industry and habit of partnering with it. As Williams and Wilkinson provided bolts and ordnance, Boulton's coining story was also entangled with guns: he turned to gunmakers for pivotal technical expertise and collaboration.

He and Watt were already collaborating with Galton on the steam engine business, civic affairs, and the Lunar Society. Boulton was also in frequent touch with the Whateleys. They shared common interests and supported one another's work, including Boulton's minting endeavor. Late in the summer of 1787, Boulton had the Galtons over for dinner. Soon after, he was tapping his gunmaker contacts for help with the coinage business. The Whateleys promised to provide the right sort of copper; if Boulton's corner on Cornish copper had inspired his minting ambitions, it was not sufficient to the task. In January 1788, Boulton was in London, dealing with a possible government contract, and John Whateley offered to get him five hundred tons of copper a year if he succeeded. He dealt in copper and leapt at the possibility of "a considerable consumption through your means." Boulton, for his part, helped Whateley get a gun order from his colleague William Matthews. The government contract did not come then, but a few months later, Boulton again corresponded hopefully with the Whateleys about copper. Whateley impressed on his London suppliers that he required their "utmost expedition and attention to the quality of the copper," assuring Boulton that when he had earlier requested "copper cast to particular directions," they had obliged quickly. He hoped that since there was no need for fresh molds, they might be even more prompt now. At the end of that year, Henry Whateley provided Boulton with precise measurements of equipment for the mint. Drawing on networks of expertise and supply that fueled other regional metallurgical trades, especially the gun trade, Boulton turned his mint into an enormous success. From 1787 to 1797, roughly seven hundred tons of copper coin were manufactured in Birmingham—uniform machine-made coins.

Some of these were again for the East India Company: in 1791, Boulton made coins for the Bombay Settlement. Birmingham foresaw an end to counterfeiting (as more were jailed for that crime just then). Erasmus Darwin exclaimed that Boulton deserved a civil crown, as in ancient Rome, for precluding counterfeiting and saving lives from the executioner—an apt depiction of the unofficially official role that he and other key industrialists inhabited. Not everyone rejoiced. Soon after the Priestley Riots that year, Birmingham's workmen nearly rioted over escalating copper prices, accusing Boulton of cornering the market for his coin presses. Meanwhile, Boulton's scheme to set up mints in republican France failed; he instead shipped token coins there, but they were banned after 1792, forcing him to sell his cake copper at a loss and recall the coin in transit. He and Garbett supported a special commission in town to investigate counterfeit foreign coins. When Britain went to war, Williams bought up good copper to fulfill his naval contracts, benefiting Boulton's Cornish mines but hurting his mint.

For decades, the East India Company had bought copper for export markets in India and China. It bought the copper domestically by annual tender, determining the price by the average price over the previous year, which meant that in a rising market, it was lower than the current price. By the 1790s, the company was purchasing 1,310 tons per year, below market prices, provoking complaints of preferential treatment. In 1794, Boulton wrote to the company in time for its annual contract. The market price had risen to more than £100 per ton, and Boulton needed 70 tons more for the company's order of 120 tons of coin. He asked the company to include in its contract 60 or 70 tons of the "best tough cake (not rolld)" for him if their price was around £100 per ton. If their price was higher

than that, he would "take the risk of providing it for myself." He asked the
company to "keep this letter secret, lest copper companies use it to go
against our joint interest." Two years later, he again fulfilled his coin contract for the company with copper it supplied; Williams controlled the
rest. Here, as with guns, the mass consumer of a manufactured metal
good provided raw material for its manufacture. This collaboration, verg-
ing on collusion, put Boulton in the position to obtain for Galton an important contract with the company soon after.

Boulton struck coins for Sierra Leone, Bermuda, and the United States
while continuing his pursuit of a government contract at home. Only that
could prevent his mint from operating at a loss, he felt, especially as rivals
emerged after 1793. The British government remained captive to more
pressing wartime exigencies—until, finally, currency itself became one of
them: in 1797, a farcical daylong French landing in Wales, known as Tate's
Invasion, prompted a government shutdown of cash payments from the
Bank of England and a turn toward banknotes to fulfill the need for cash.
Charles Lloyd was astonished that he could not exchange his banknotes for
cash at the Bank of England. The ensuing financial scare in the midst of
war forced the state to consummate its long dalliance with Boulton. He
received a contract for one-ounce pennies. His was the only mint capable of
producing coins on the scale required—the mass nature of state demand
was critical to industrial coining as much as to arms making. The job was
too large for the Royal Mint. As in the case of gun manufacture, the state's
corporate quality—its network of partnerships among chartered companies, the mint, the Bank of England, and so on—gave it a knack for adapting to and building on standards and practices those entities had developed
for cheaply producing mass quantities of metallic goods. Boulton's initial
contract consumed twelve hundred tons of copper. To get around Williams's monopoly, Boulton had the Rose Copper Company in Swansea, of
which he was a key member, buy out Fenton & Company, copper smelters
bound to sell their goods only to Williams. A fellow Birmingham metal-
lurgist, the Quaker Joseph Gibbins, who had worked with Boulton on the
Assay Office campaign, helped him do this. The state allotted Boulton
£108 per ton (considerably below the market rate), requiring him to charge

the cost of the copper plus fourpence for every pound of coin struck (roughly equivalent to eight twopenny pieces, or sixteen pennies). Weights had to be accurate so the coins could be used as currency *and* weights. The state also budgeted for the cost of distributing the coinage. The coins were distributed from William Matthews's London premises and from the Soho Mint. To promote trust in the new coins, Boulton persuaded the government to supply them to army and navy paymasters; they found their way into British hands through those of colonials, soldiers, sailors, and suppliers of military and naval stores, putting war and contracting squarely at the center of Britain's modernizing economy.

Boulton launched into a decade of producing precision-weight copper pennies, halfpennies, twopennies, and farthings for the British government—the first perfectly rounded and standardized coins (although they did not eliminate counterfeiting). Between 1797 and 1806, he supplied about 4,200 tons of copper coin from Soho—all the copper coinage of George III, which was most of what was in circulation. He also made five-shilling bank tokens in 1804 and coins for Spain and Denmark. He sold an entire mint to Russia in 1799, overriding concern about the propriety of sharing such sensitive technology with another country, and that, too, during war.

His mint took off at a time when those involved in gilding, plating, and jewelry manufacture were facing dim prospects, and demand for specie was rising astronomically. He also supplied the Ordnance Office with copper rivets and hoops. Birmingham and the government blamed inflated copper prices on Williams, but the real cause was skyrocketing government demand. Between the Admiralty, the East India Company, and the coinage, the government swallowed up half of Britain's dwindling copper output in these years.

Boulton next entered the more sacred arena of silver coin. The Royal Mint stopped producing new silver pieces in 1787. In 1804, it asked Boulton to countermark four million captured Spanish dollars. After this, the Bank of England produced a whole range of silver coinage, as did ordinary companies—more tokens. Another Birmingham manufacturer made two million penny tokens for British forces in Spain. Boulton's mint did not curb multiplication of currencies: some four thousand varieties of coin, from the silver dollar to the brass farthing, made mostly in Birmingham, circulated at the turn of the century. Boulton oversaw the modernization and reequipment of the Royal Mint from 1807, a project completed in 1810, a few months after his death. He supplied the steam engine, the bulk of the machinery, *and* the skilled fitters to supervise it. The first coinage of this reformed Royal Mint was a load of copper for the East India Company's settlement near Penang. Hybrid state-industry partnerships transformed gradually into distinct state institutions.

Situated near the eye of this currency storm, Samuel Tertius Galton made the emerging science of economics a field of personal expertise. In 1813, while vigorous debate unfolded about the East India Company trade monopoly, the gun contractor and banker published a tract on currency, anchored by a chart tracking the rise in gold and wheat prices against the increase of banknotes. It was taken seriously enough to merit reference in a parliamentary investigation of depressed agricultural prices in 1821. Its statistical component was much admired by Tertius's son Francis Galton. The tract attempted to understand, empirically, the representational and intrinsic properties of money, concluding that a system of inconvertible paper money would not serve the country, as it would not possess the inherent correctives to excessive issue that coin-based currency possessed—presumably deduced from the deflation caused by wartime overprinting of banknotes. Such defenses of the gold standard carried the day in 1813, but defense of intrinsic value as the only measure of value did not.

The Coinage Act of 1816 inaugurated a standard system of small change, providing for the first time sufficient copper and silver coins of mere representative value. Manufacture of "token money" ceased in 1818 with the passage of the Act of Suppression, which had a grace period of two years for Birmingham and five for Sheffield. Soho made new silver coins in 1817, but for the most part Birmingham's commercial coiners went belly-up along with the iron industry. In 1821, Soho received a contract for halfpennies for the territory of St. Helena. A visiting East India Company engineer charged with equipping a mint in Bombay decided to purchase the mint, and it was shipped to India in 1824—a fitting end to this story of a long dance among the company, Birmingham industrialists, and the emerging institutions of state. The Royal Mint turned to private sources of copper coinage in Birmingham again in the 1850s (and private minters still relied on orders from the expanding empire).

Birmingham's industrialists, including gunmakers, were intimately involved in questions surrounding the manufacture and function of currency. A nineteenth-century minter noted the peculiar quality of coin, which could be legally made only under special restrictions. A coiner's machinery at times worked at its utmost capacity; at other times it stood still and unprofitable for months. Guns were similarly peculiar. In the struggle to enable sufficient production of each, particularly during war, the British state encouraged many of the key processes of the industrial revolution.

G uns could function as money, and gunmakers helped fellow metallurgists accomplish the feat of manufacturing sufficient coin for the realm. But gunmakers also had more literally banklike properties. Early on, a web of ties bound gunsmiths and bankers like Freame, Barclay, and Andrew Drummond. The transatlantic Quaker firms of Barclay, the Hanburys, and Champion & Hayley, through which Farmer & Galton sold guns and toys in North America, doubled as bankers to American Quaker merchants. Insofar as contractors were often owed money, they were essentially bankers to the state. The Galton gun business itself became a bank in 1804, in partnership with Boulton's copper associate Joseph Gibbins. (In 1806, Gibbins left to form another bank.) The emergence of guns (and other metal goods) as everyday objects depended on these tight financial networks binding the metallurgical—and especially the Quaker metallurgical—community. Perhaps unsurprisingly, then, Birmingham became a "financial centre" *while* it rose as an industrial center, "so well endowed with banks that the West Midlands had a lower ratio of population to bank offices than any other region in England including London." Its banks provided local industrial capital but also "addressed a wider commercial world."

The ties between banks and the gun industry appear less odd when we recall that many bankers were only a generation removed from metallurgical work. In the seventeenth century, since reserves were held in plate and bullion, goldsmiths emerged as the early private bankers. Cash was left with goldsmiths, and the receipts circulated as money. They acquired their greatest fortunes from government finance. The creation of the Bank of England made public finance a more specialized endeavor, but private loans to the government continued, including credit from contractors. Drummond and John Freame both began as goldsmiths. Freame, a member of the Grocers' Company, married Priscilla Gould, daughter of a prominent Quaker goldsmith, in 1694. The Freame & Gould bank—the first Quaker bank in London—was launched in 1698. One of its early activities was financing the London Lead Company, with fellow Quaker Edward Wright, in 1704. In 1733, Freame was described as banker and deputy governor of the Lead Corporation. His son Joseph and son-in-law James Barclay succeeded him in partnership. James Barclay was David Barclay's son by his first wife. The family tie predated the marriage, as David Barclay had married John Freame's elder daughter in 1723. *Their* sons David Jr. (the later abolitionist and brewer) and John later entered the bank. Agatha Barclay, David Jr.'s daughter, married Richard Gurney of Norwich, linking the firm to yet another major Quaker banking house. David Sr.'s daughter Lucy married Samuel Galton Jr., drawing him eventually in the banking direction. David Jr.'s second wife was the sister of Charles Lloyd, who married James Farmer's daughter by Priscilla Plumsted, granddaughter of John Freame. The network of family connections is truly indescribable. The point is that this network married finance to industry—and allowed for exchange of business intelligence between them. Joseph Freame shared his worries about the bank after the Seven Years' War with Farmer's daughter "Polly" (Mary), who socialized with the Barclays and the Plumsteds. Agatha Barclay, who became a Gurney in 1773, wrote frequently to Polly, who became a Lloyd in 1774, their correspondence often referring to their parents' exchanges and meetings.

Goldsmiths' business remained inextricable from that of their fellow metallurgists; they dealt in the precious metals that were considered money but also in plated ware and metal toys, which tied them to the hardware trades. Even London goldsmiths dealt extensively with related trades in Birmingham and elsewhere for materials, parts, and subcontracting. Freame & Gould also financed the Welsh Society of Mines Royal Copper. But Quaker banks were inevitably most mixed up in iron, the most common Quaker metallurgical undertaking—witness the Freames' ties with the Farmers and the Plumsteds, the Farmers' with the Lloyds, and so on. These connections among a handful of families were historically significant, forming a kind of industrial aristocracy. Eighteenth-century banks were intimately tied to wealth made in trade and industry, and industrialists commonly became partners in banks.

These partnerships emerged partly from the particular circumstances surrounding private banking. The new Bank of England had a monopoly right to operate as a bank in the country. It was central to the London money market and the major issuer of notes, holding substantial bullion reserves. Private banking partnerships in London also multiplied and expanded, holding more cash reserves in banknotes than specie. To challenge the new institution's intimacy with the state, some used other corporate shells to mask their banking identity. The most notorious case highlights the intimacy of arms making with banking: the goldsmith Stephen Evance founded the Hollow Sword Blades Company to make rapiers in 1691, but after his suicide, in 1702, a group of businessmen turned the company into a bank under cover of the corporate identity of the sword company. This was a stepping-stone to the formation of the South Sea Company, which tried to supplant the Bank of England in its role as banker to the government.

Country banks typically grew out of manufacture. Ironmasters were critical to their growth. From the seventeenth century, traders regularly provided credit and other banking services for customers and business agents. Birmingham, despite its commercial traffic, lacked a bank to circulate cash and bills. Instead, virtually all of the town's drapers and grocers were bankers or cash retailers, and iron industrialists combined iron operations with moneylending and providing credit accommodation to traders (including state offices). Ironmongers often held land and could exchange bills of credit against rent payments in the country. Raising finance on the security of land was crucial to development in the West Midlands. Capital from land and industry was intimately linked in provincial manufacturing firms, as we've seen with Farmer from the start. Insofar as economic power lay in the ability to manipulate money and credit, businessmen acquired influence out of all proportion to their resources. Much business capital in the iron world was in the form of credit provided to clients and in debts owing—as with Farmer & Galton. Galton had to struggle so much to make sense of the firm's accounts during Farmer's crisis in 1755 partly because "almost every workman borrows money on his work to be brought in."

The Lloyds' bank evolved out of precisely such dynamics. The Quaker ironmongers partnered with the Unitarian John Taylor, a manufacturer of buttons and snuffboxes and another victim of Farmer's Lisbon escapade, who determined to confine his trade "entirely with the dealers in England." They founded Taylor & Lloyd in 1765 partly to cope with the downturn in the iron trade after the Seven Years' War. Banking offered escape from the risks of metallurgical production that depended on a war economy. Taylor & Lloyd supplied credit to small manufacturers of the Black Country associated with their businesses. They took deposits without paying interest and issued local notes, which were important during the currency shortage. Other industrialists paid in tokens and notes; Taylor & Lloyd first turned banker and then did essentially the same, providing day-to-day liquidity. Their seven-shilling notes were popular. (Notes smaller than one pound were illegal from 1775.) The bank became more profitable than the iron business—though the Lloyds were dominant in the establishment of the Midland Association of Ironmasters in the 1760s, too. Sampson Lloyd II's sons ran both the iron company and the bank, which funded Boulton's and Galton's enterprises. "Opulent tradesmen," they found that their credit was as good as that of the Bank of England. Other industrialists followed in their steps.

Taylor was formerly a partner of the Birmingham ironmonger and banker John Pemberton, who had married into the Lloyd-Crowley clan. In 1770, the younger Sampson Lloyd led the formation of Taylor, Lloyd,

Hanbury, and Bowman, on Lombard Street in London, one of the five biggest banks of the time. (The Hanburys and the Barclays were both intermarried with the Lloyds.) That same year, the Gurneys expanded from the wool trade to banking with the ironmonger William Alexander. The Spooners evolved from goldsmiths into iron suppliers, partnering in 1791 with the iron-trading Attwood family to found a bank. Later, the Gurney bank became connected with the Spooners'; both ultimately merged with Barclays. Whereas there were two Quaker banks in London in 1738, forty years later there were seven. In 1750, there were no more than a dozen bankers' shops outside London (where there were about thirty then). New country banks sprang up *after* midcentury, numbering about a hundred by 1775 and 370 by 1800. There were about six hundred by the banking crisis of 1825, typically small, averaging about £10,000 in capital. This was the result of war making fields like metallurgy more profitable. Country bankers were tied to London through agents, and London bankers had country clients—as we have seen in the case of Farmer & Galton. The country's financial structure grew increasingly unified as the century of wars went on. Country banks exemplify the heavily networked nature of Britain's entrepreneurial class. They were part of the manufacturing world; many partnered in businesses.

The evolution from industry to banking was a *trend,* shaped by industrialists' efforts to cope with the whimsical nature of the defense contracts that were the mainstay of metallurgical fields (though banking was also bound up in war). The Galton bank began during war, in 1804. In 1811, Tertius's brother Hubert began his apprenticeship there; another brother, John Howard, began working there full time in 1813. Intelligence about a new bank in Manchester, which the Galton boys thought of joining in 1819, came through a friend of the Barclays. Lamenting the recent "casualties of trade," their father gave them permission to fully turn to banking if they chose to.

By the early nineteenth century, many of the largest banks in the country had emerged from businesses that prospered in war. There were six in Birmingham, all private, all sprung from commercial undertakings, when the banking crisis came in 1825; they included Lloyds; Galton,

Galton & James; and Attwoods and Spooners. All but one survived the crisis. In 1826, Parliament allowed the Bank of England to establish branches around the country and made it easy for provincial banks to establish joint stocks. A branch came to Birmingham. It did not compete with the local private banks, discounting at slightly lower rates and charging no commission on current accounts while being more rigid overall in its methods and paying no interest on deposits. Its staffer Charles Geach later managed the Birmingham & Midland Bank, which absorbed Galton's bank. Tertius left the bank in sheer "commercial wearyness" in 1831.

The lines between finance, industry, and state offices were thin. Bankers lent to the state; the state made demands on industry; industrialists became bankers. Henry Drummond joined his family's bank in 1749 while also working as an army agent; the bank handled his agency's affairs relating to regimental purchasing, including arms. After the Seven Years' War, he partnered with Richard Cox, an army agent who, in 1759, had served as secretary to the Ordnance Board and agent to the Royal Regiment of Artillery. He was also banker to General Lord Ligonier, master general of the Ordnance Office. Drummond and Cox were joint paymasters for the Royal Artillery through 1772. Drummond also became a contractor for payment of British forces in North America and went on to contract for specie remittance in the American war. Lloyds Bank took over Cox's agency in 1923. The banker David Barclay was also a merchant and helped arm colonial militias and Native American allies in the Seven Years' War. Tertius Galton was a banker and gun contractor. These various economic activities were linked and heavily driven by war.

Guns and money were intertwined in the eighteenth century in their functions, modes of production, and institutional arrangements. The mercantilist state sought bullion—and the coin made from it—to purchase all it needed to prosecute war as it transitioned into a more modern state. Guns and their makers facilitated that transition, providing representative currency that coins and notes could not yet provide. Money's representative forms eventually produced our idea of "the economy" as the sum of every occasion on which money changed hands, the cumulative product of social processes. The process was just beginning in our period, in the overlap of experts in finance and metallurgy with state functions. Before money became abstract, it was real.

Eighteenth-century Britons struggled with the fictional and intrinsic properties of financial instruments like money and credit, questions forced especially by interaction abroad. Adam Smith pondered the effect of silver imports on silver's value relative to gold in India and the impossibility of sending paper money abroad. Conservatism about monetary form abided even while the lack of specie in the colonial milieu made financial versatility and innovation increasingly urgent. It was a time of competing norms and uncertainty about whether trade could be conducted without sufficient or regular access to bullion. In 1766, a Birmingham resident observed that the recent wartime expansion of paper money and the increase of "real money" through prize-taking had expanded commerce tremendously. This increase of "real and fictitious wealth" had made many lives more luxurious, despite price increases. He wondered at the "nature of the thing"— that the more they abounded in money, the less value it had; as it lost value, prices and wages rose. If currency had this split identity, credit was even more elusive. In Defoe's formulation, it "acts all Substance, yet, is it self Immaterial . . . creates *Forms*, yet, has it self *no Form*." It was *"the essential Shadow of something that is Not."* Eighteenth-century Britons adapted to novelties like paper money, but puzzlement endured; hence the forger's haunting presence in economic life, as an impostor who upset the delicate balance of reality and fiction in money and credit transactions. Our theoretical notion of "the economy" as a realm apart from the state, shaped by the eighteenth-century critical thought of Adam Smith, obstructs our understanding of the ways in which industry, finance, and the state actually overlapped in Smith's time. Guns were currency; gunmakers helped make currency; gunmakers were bankers. These ties help explain why Galton did not think of guns as strictly weapons and did not think of himself as strictly an arms maker. Even as weapons, guns were useful to banks as protection: Drummond bought some to guard the family bank after the Gordon Riots in 1780. Such uses in the defense of property fueled Galton's confidence in the peaceable nature of his work, as we will see next.

6

Guns in Arms,
Part 1: Home

G uns were money, and they were also arms. Their use as arms was distinct from the way we use guns today—as West Africa shows. Though different sorts of guns—plain, ornate, blunderbuss, trade gun, pistol, musket, rifle, and so on—had different applications, a common thread is nevertheless distinguishable among those varying uses across sources from Birmingham, Gloucester, and London. As it turns out, besides functioning as a kind of wealth or currency, guns were deeply bound up with the rise of the very principle of property, the soul of eighteenth-century society. The purpose of government as understood in the eighteenth century was to guarantee property (in land, goods, persons, commissions). And guaranteeing property abetted industrial revolution: Enclosure Acts privatized open fields and common land, funneling rural workers into cities and factories. Industrialism, in turn, provided the materials for property's reign: nails, hinges, anchors, locks, and guns. Guns were the terrorizing instrument of a new kind of impersonal violence perpetrated among new kinds of strangers, arising initially out of efforts to protect or seize property. They figured in contests over mobile and immobile property—money in the pocket as much as land and manor. Certainly, the "propertied" generally meant the class that owned land and engaged in hunting as sport—the exclusive ranks our industrialists worked hard to breach. But shopkeepers and stockholders joined landowners in Associations for the Defence of Property. Whatever form of property was at stake, there was remarkable cultural consensus about guns' appropriateness as props in contests over it, the perception of a link between the particular kind of threat a gun posed and the principle of property it defended or violated.

To assess how guns fit in early modern English violence, we need to know how readily available they were. The British Crown regulated gun ownership and use from the late fourteenth century, and restrictions multiplied in the sixteenth century. Before the Civil War, each county had a magazine, and gentry had arms. The Parliamentarians' New Model Army stoked anti-army sentiment. Then the overarching concern with political stability after the Restoration also made careful monitoring of firearm possession central. Militia Acts of 1661–63 effectively indemnified those engaged in hunting down disloyal subjects and shoring up the Restoration. Arms dumps left over from the Civil War and disbanded soldiers who might use them were a constant source of alarm. Disarmament was effective: in 1666, many felt that a lack of arms had made the Dorset coast vulnerable to attack. A statute of 1670 limited firearms possession to the noble and rich. The 1671 Game Act dramatically reduced the number of people permitted to hunt, empowering gamekeepers to search for unauthorized firearms. Even the wealthy and noble who maintained private arsenals were subject to search and seizure at sensitive moments—such as after news leaked of the Rye House Plot to assassinate the king, in 1683 (when Richard Newdigate lost his arsenal). The arms seized were not returned to their owners, as they might have been earlier, but kept for the militia or handed to the Ordnance Office.

This trend endured after 1689. The concern about rebellion that drove the new government to diffuse the gun industry simultaneously drove it to keep the population disarmed. Article VII of the new Bill of Rights stipulated that "Subjects which are Protestants may have Armes for their defence Suitable to their Condition and as allowed by law." The phrases "Suitable to their Condition" and "allowed by law" indicated that existing laws restricting gun ownership were not suddenly superseded. The framework for game laws laid down in 1671 endured through 1831. Guns were

certainly available. But even when farmers kept them for agricultural purposes, they remained vulnerable to citation for game-law infringement.
Besides laws on possession, there were powers of search and seizure, acts
against going armed at night, and the old common-law prohibition against
going armed in terror of the people.

Regulations against arms possession in Ireland also passed in the
1690s. Searches eventually revealed that "papists," at least, had virtually no
arms; the menace of a numerous, disaffected, and well-armed population
was concentrated in the Scottish Highlands. On his accession in 1714,
George I commanded an arms search there; nevertheless, an insurrection
erupted the following year. After it was put down, laws prohibited Highlanders from owning guns. After every conflict, the Ordnance Office
worked to gather in arms from soldiers. When word came that two gentlemen held arms purchased by the county of Dorset during the 1715 rebellion despite plans to deposit them in the Castle of Portland, the Ordnance
Office sent its master gunner permanently to the castle (charging the
county for upkeep of the arms). The loyalty of such storekeepers was vital.
The office voted a gratuity of £100 to the storekeeper at Benwick for his
"extra services during the late rebellion," christening him barrack master.
This recognition came as the government faced down another rebellion in
the Highlands, backed by Spain. Successive disarmament drives in the
Highlands left the Jacobites of 1745 with a poor assortment of arms until
they looted government arms left by fleeing British soldiers after the Battle of Prestonpans. After this rebellion, too, the government diligently
gathered in arms; the rebellion had shown how easily rebels could arm
themselves by plundering local estates and homes. Highlanders were again
disallowed from gun ownership. Samuel Johnson remarked that the efficiency of this disarmament drive left "every house . . . despoiled of its defence." Meanwhile, the Smuggling Act of 1736 also made carrying arms
grounds for arrest, provoking much protest.

Although the militia existed, in theory, from the Restoration, it was
mainly active through roughly the first decade after the Restoration, as
part of a world of bitter political and religious animosities where any party
quarrel was an incipient civil war and those in power always used force to

suppress their opponents. But that activity was ephemeral. The militia's last real success was in putting down the Exclusionists—those who sought to exclude James II from the succession because of his Catholicism—in the 1680s. In 1690, its arms throughout the land were found defective. Militia bills of the 1690s and 1700s failed. Through the 1740s, state wariness meant that militia arms were locked in royal arsenals and distributed only at assembly. The very success at disarming the civil population was fatal to the militia, whose foundational purpose was to guard against armed rising against the government. It yielded to internal decay caused by monarchical distrust, lack of funds, and its own distaste for the repressive function it was beginning to acquire. Men could be persuaded to fight against invasion or massive rebellion on minimal pay, but not for quotidian forms of repression necessitated by economic grievances generated by continual struggle with France—customs and tax evasion, namely.

Certainly, in rural areas, there were guns in the hands of highwaymen, footpads, and smugglers, often illegally acquired from military deserters or arsenals nearby. Disarming them was an active collective endeavor. Unsanctioned movements of military guns were traced. London gunsmiths took pains to confirm that customers who called on them to clean or repair such guns possessed them legitimately. Around 1748, when the Sussex magistrates heard of suspicious persons attempting to buy hundreds of French muskets from a sailmaker in Portsmouth Point en route to Rowland's Castle, they ordered a troop of dragoons to escort travelers on the road. The sailmaker sold the customer only twenty-five, forfeiting additional sales out of fear that "they were for some desperate case, especially when I found (by their discourse) that they lived somewhere in Sussex."

All of this meant that for a century after the Civil War, firearms were not particularly easy to come by in England. The much maligned ignorance of fresh recruits at the start of each war further supports the claim that firearms were not familiar objects for many Britons. Ordnance Office records contain frequent testimony of guns damaged because young soldiers did not know how to take them apart and reassemble them, clean them, or use them properly. This empirical reality coexisted with widespread belief that a society of armed freemen was the best guarantee against tyranny.

Interest in reviving the militia stirred in the 1750s as dynastic fears receded. Anxiety about a widely armed population lessened, and both the rebels of 1745 and their opponents seemed to model the value of a citizen army. The government sent arms to the inhabitants of the Channel Islands when tensions with France spiked in 1753. In 1755, a Tory polemicist raged against the game laws for depriving people of arms to defend themselves and mount resistance; he was the first to describe them as a violation of the Bill of Rights. Another pamphleteer echoed that, by so depriving "Farmers and Country People," for fear that they should shoot a "paltry Partridge," the state rendered them "incapable of knowing how to make a proper Use of that necessary Weapon, when their country calls upon them for Assistance." This "True-born Englishman" instanced a tradesman who nearly died through such ignorance, placing the butt end of the gun to his breast instead of his shoulder. This pamphlet appeared in 1757, a year into the Seven Years' War and in the midst of parliamentary debate about a militia bill. All the protest helped the bill pass. However, the new militia it created was hardly the nationally armed population that enthusiasts had envisioned. Participation depended on a property qualification in land. There was no question of a general arming of the people; fear of uncontrolled arms possession guided debate about the bill. Decades of disarmament had also encouraged development of other recourses for coping with political, religious, and party differences. Indeed, our "True-born Englishman" validated enduring government mistrust of the population; he threatened that if the bill put arms in all hands, "could it be reasonably expected, that . . . we should turn the Edge of our Swords against the external Foes of *Britain*, when we have internal Enemies, much more obnoxious to every free-born *Englishman?*" He deemed those who supported the game laws as treacherous as the "Association of 1745–6 against our Kingdom and Laws," fancifully exposing them as "Sir Simon Faithless," "Hotspur," "Sir Greedy Partridge," and the like. There was still too much open contest over political legitimacy to entrust all trueborn Englishmen with guns.

Gun ownership did increase in the second half of the century. Shops selling guns proliferated around the Minories and Birmingham. T. Richards, a Birmingham gunmaker, regularly advertised sale of "guns and pistols" in his High Street shop, informing "sporting gentlemen and the public in general" of his "large assortment of guns for the shooting season . . . and pistols of all sorts." He offered wholesale rates for merchants. The Act of Proscription that had disarmed Scotland was also repealed in 1782. A proliferation of accidental gun deaths in the second half of the century testifies to the increasing prevalence of guns, especially for the sport of shooting. The Birmingham newspaper had to warn the public not to "wantonly play with loaded firearms."

Still, the state had hardly become careless of the spread of guns. The Ordnance Office diligently collected arms disbursed during the Seven Years' War and the American war. Demobilized troops left their arms at inns for collection. In moments of political crisis, the state swiftly disarmed the population. During the Gordon Riots of 1780, the lord mayor called for arming all of London, but Lord Jeffrey Amherst, the senior army officer in London, ordered disarmament of all but the militia and others designated to defend the city. When the Ordnance Office's master general, the Duke of Richmond, protested against this violation of the rights of Protestant subjects to arm themselves, Amherst's defenders nevertheless prevailed; moreover, even in his confusion, Richmond spoke of subjects' right to arms "suitable to their conditions, and as allowed by law."

At the start of war in 1793, the British government was still "as afraid of its own people as it was of the enemy." Radicals urging crowds to seize the opportunity for reform by getting arms—daggers, blades, and pikes—were convicted of sedition. In 1795, hearing that the king had been mobbed by a crowd calling for peace and shot at "by some ruffians" in front of the Ordnance Office, the Birmingham builder George Elliott declared, "I wished they had knocked his dammed head off and Pitt's too . . . I hope in a little time [to] carry a musket myself, for it is better to die by a musket than to be starved to death. If there should be an insurrection in Birmingham, I should take pleasure in joining them." He joined one of the city's seven secret societies dreaming of rebellion. In 1797–98, fear of rebellion drove the government to disarm Irish civilians much more effectively than they had Americans twenty years earlier. Even as the government's need for men forced it to trust its people, that trust was qualified. In 1798, when forty thousand armed persons gathered in London independent of the regular troops, to "defend our government and our family and property," the Earl of Warwick urged a similar armed association in Birmingham but insisted that it consist of "none but the known and respectable householders, or persons who can bring at least two such householders to answer for their good behavior." Government arms would be stored for them in a safe depot. Within weeks came alarming news that people without authority had purchased arms in Staffordshire, and illegal training had transpired. The authorities wanted not an armed people but a propertied and respectable home guard to restrain domestic disorder.

By 1800, wall graffiti in Birmingham had changed from "Church and King" to "No War" and "Damn Pitt." Volunteer soldiers joined with local poor in food riots or refused to acquiesce in suppressing such riots. In this atmosphere, for *most* of the period, free possession of small arms in England remained an entitlement of the nobility and segments of the upper middle classes with whom the nobility had come to share political power. Through the 1790s, the British state had a long-established policy of regulating and prohibiting arms possession among avowedly dissident elements and the lower orders of society in general. This is why a strategy of drawing on privately held arms did not work when war restarted in 1803, after the brief Peace of Amiens. With the government scrambling to arm enormous numbers of troops raised overnight, the home secretary confidentially advised the lords lieutenant of the maritime counties, "A good fowling-piece, with a bullet-mould properly adapted to it . . . together with a dagger or bayonet contrived to screw on the muzzle . . . will prove a very efficient equipment for brave and zealous men determined to defend their country." But there were not enough private arms; the government issued pikes while accelerating musket production.

We may never know just how many people in the eighteenth century owned guns. But even if my account underestimates their presence, we are left with the startling absence of their use in certain types of violence. For instance, throughout this period, regardless of shifting availability, rioters wielded farm implements (while faced down by property owners and troops wielding guns). Even in the riots among gun workers in Birmingham caught up in the rivalry between the Galtons and Thomas Hadley in 1772–73, stones were the preferred arm. That drama involved threats of stabbing, hanging, burning William Bird's hair with hot tongs, impalement with a hot poker, and beating to death. Bird and his roommate armed themselves with cutlasses when their house was attacked. Hadley's men threw gunstocks at Bird—the only way guns figured in the whole ugly saga. During the wildly destructive Priestley Riots of 1791, arson and stone throwing were the favored tactics. The rioters wielded crowbars and rails to tear buildings down. I have found but two instances in which rioters used guns before 1795: in Machynlleth, around 1739, one participant in a stone-flinging mob fired a pistol to force the Welsh Methodist Howell Harris to cease preaching in the street, and in Birmingham in 1789, Quaker homes that remained aloof from the illuminations celebrating the king's recovery from illness were shot at. These are exceptions. "Mobs" did not use guns, even when possession was less strictly policed, because guns were not relevant to the particular kind of violence they were perpetrating. Even if we presume, for the sake of argument, that guns were widely owned, we are faced with the interesting fact that, despite having guns, ordinary people almost always took up pitchforks and rocks when angry; this says something profound about the place of the gun in eighteenth-century life.

In one instance in which a crowd took pains to acquire guns, they did not use them in the actual violence. This was the 1736 riot over the hanging of John Porteous, captain of the City Guard of Edinburgh. Porteous was supposed to hang for ordering his men to fire upon a crowd vaulting stones at the executioner terminating the life of the smuggler Andrew Wilson. But Porteous obtained a royal reprieve. The night before his canceled execution, men entered the city and seized the City Guard's firearms, battle-axes, and drums. They burned the entrance to the Tolbooth prison, where Porteous was being held, and forced their way into his cell, where they hanged him while armed men patrolled the streets to prevent surprise by the king's forces. They left the stolen arms at the site of the execution. Magistrates who attempted to disperse the mob were pelted by stones and threatened with firearms. This was a conflict over state power in which guns projected a particular kind of power (but were not used against Porteous himself).

Guns were also generally not used in murder. Going by evidence from Gloucester from the 1720s to 1760, English murder was perpetrated by (usually drunken) beating (the most common means), drowning, strangling (especially of bastard infants), beating with an iron bar and knifing combined, and with a hedge stake, penknives, swords, clubs, staves, sticks, an ax, a hedge bill, a whip, a wool card, shovels, and hangers. Suicides occurred by way of hanging, poisoning, drowning, and stabbing. One shooting death occurred in 1739: two boys fought over a bird both claimed to have shot, three others tried to part them, and a sixth took up a loaded gun and told them to stand back so he could part them. He shot at them; one of the brawlers was killed, and the other badly wounded. Since his intention was to part them *without* killing them, the verdict was accidental death. In this scenario, the gun served as a weapon of intimidation to curb other kinds of violence. In the 1740s came the first nonaccidental killings with guns. First, a dispute between two men out shooting ended with one of them using his fowling piece to shoot the other in the back. Second, a gentleman shot his brother "through his body in the bed," robbing him of some money. He then broke his brother's skull with the butt end of the gun "so that his Brains came out." In the 1750s, besides one accidental death from a half-cocked gun on a rack, there was a gun suicide: the steward to Lord Bathurst, insisting on his innocence on a sodomy charge, shot himself through the head.

In London, too, from 1700 to 1760, only 3 to 8 percent of killing indictments involved deliberate shootings—two to five cases per decade. The vast majority of indictments involved other weapons, usually improvised (e.g., scissors, sticks, farm tools), or beating. Pistols were often present in violent situations but were seldom the actual instrument of violence. When they were, they were often used as blunt instruments for beating rather than projectile launchers. Data from Coventry for 1755–63 bears out this trend: murder by throat cutting, strangling, stabbing (between soldiers), accidental death of a farmer out shooting, suicides by drowning.

Though gun possession seems to have increased in the second half of the century, there was no corresponding increase in their use in homicide through the 1780s. In 1760–'80s Gloucester, murders went on with kicking, brawling, strangling, beating, poisoning, drowning, and wielding knives, stakes, plow paddles, hammers, a stool, a hatchet, a double cord, and one mysterious "murder attended with the most barbarous and most unmanly instance of brutality that was ever heard of in any age or nation." Suicides turned to hanging and drowning. In Birmingham, reported murders involved iron rods, a mowing scythe, knives, swords, penknives, a mattock, bare hands, feet, and a pair of tongs. A recruiting sergeant murderously frustrated in his effort to enlist a barrel borer in a pub resorted to his sword. There was one accidental gun slaying when a woman died intervening between her farmer son and the servant he threatened with his gun.

So, one or two incidents apart, the effort to correlate gun ownership with homicide rates is based on a misunderstanding about what guns were for in the eighteenth century. Guns did not have much to do with murder in this period, when murders were about face-to-face violence. (This says nothing about their role in homicide in other periods.) The homicide rate remained fairly consistent from the Middle Ages to 1800; there is no significant correlation with poverty or gun proliferation or any such trend. The British were not too different from the contemporary Japanese villagers described by David Howell, who "brawled, . . . flew into drunken rages, . . . killed each other in fits of passion and stupidity, . . . rose by the thousands in violent protest," but "did not shoot each other, even when it might have seemed reasonable to do so." Guns did not occupy the conceptual category of weaponry for Tokugawa peasants. They did occupy that category (and others) for English villagers, but not for emotionally motivated violence. Most homicides took place during heated arguments or brawls; those involved took recourse to whatever was at hand. Hence the prevalence of knives, sticks, stones, pitchforks, and axes, or simply hands and feet. The sheer inefficiency of eighteenth-century guns may have made them less appealing instruments of violent emotional gratification. But they also simply had different connotations—like bows, which were understood as a weapon of ambush and were not used in murder, either. When anger raged, an intimate form of violence was threatened and demanded; the gun removed violence to too impersonal a distance, in this time and place. The very nature of the slow, mechanical process for loading and triggering made it a weapon of cool threat rather than hot-blooded violence. In one midcentury account, a man endeavoring to discover the whereabouts of his kidnapped lover pointed a gun at her aunt, threatening to "blow thy brains out, instantly; and then my own." The terrified aunt "begg'd him to turn away the muzzle of the gun from her, and to moderate his fury." He begged her pardon for his rage, put the gun away, and spoke to her. The gun could be used as a prop in a gentlemanly tale of passion but was rarely actually used in the heat of passion; its use was typically more calculated, and the result less certain. More characteristic was the incident later in the account when robbers stabbed the lady of the house while her husband was out shooting. Having "at his first shot split the flint of his gun to shivers," he returned home, discovered the mayhem, and rode out after the villains.

So what kind of weapons were guns, then? Though mostly absent from the annals of homicide, they were waved around in intimidation on roads, in fields, out of windows, and in forests. As in West Africa, they were seen to possess a deterrent power different from the power embodied in a sword: mechanical, latent in a series of springs, gears, locks, and inert charge— and, crucially, dangerously unpredictable in impact (unlike today's gun). This relative unpredictability made the gun a poor recourse for the determined murderer but, paradoxically, more effective as an instrument of intimidation. In Birmingham in 1765, when a highwayman snapped his pistol at a corporal and it only flashed in the pan, the corporal drew his sword and cut the robber on the side of his face. A second highwayman hit him violently on the head, and the villains rode off. In another instance, six robbers entered a man's house and, after firing pistols, stabbed him to death with swords. At times, the robber used his pistol to strike rather than shoot the victim. In one instance when the threat of "instant Death" by pistol did not compel the victim to surrender her money, the robbers threw her on the floor repeatedly, leaving her bleeding and disabled, before they ransacked the house. In some instances, they resorted to fists despite carrying pistols. The gun was an accessory in these crimes, the loose cannon that might stave off conflict or the opening salvo to a fight in which swords and bare hands still did the real work. In 1796, a prosecutor explained to a jury in a lethal property dispute that if the shooter had desired to simply "terrify" the alleged trespasser, as was within his rights, he might have used an empty pistol or might have let the trespasser know the pistol was loaded. But he had kept his gun "out of sight," in which case its presence had no legitimate purpose. Those who wielded pistols explicitly did so "to intimidate" another.

Even on the battlefield, guns did not simply replace blades. The flintlock's more efficient ignition process permitted faster firing than the older matchlock, fueling the popularity of shooting for sport, but also the seventeenth-century rise of military musketry and European linear tactics. Training, coordination, and command structure became crucial. The army was deployed in two or three ranks for volley firing plus a rank a few paces back to replace casualties in front. Sheer number compensated for the relatively slow rate of fire. All foot soldiers came to possess muskets with attached bayonets, making the division between musketeers and pikemen obsolete. Indeed, flintlocks were so unreliable, failing to fire even under the best conditions, and hardly at all in rain or damp, that soldiers just as often used them as pikes. When they were used to shoot, rate of fire was more important than accuracy. As in West Africa, noise was crucial. Adam Smith recognized the power of the "noise of fire-arms, the smoke, and the invisible death to which every man feels himself every moment exposed . . . a long time before the battle can be well said to be engaged." These effects disrupted the regularity and order that firearms made essential, and the terror they produced made modern war utterly different from "ancient battle," in which "Every man, till some mortal weapon actually did approach him, saw clearly that no such weapon was near him." Since this terrorizing effect was what really mattered, guns were pointed but not aimed; soldiers loaded and fired in unison on command. Experienced officers had low expectations of their men's accuracy, considering aiming in the main line of battle a waste of time. The order to fire came when soldiers were about fifty yards from the enemy—point-blank range—since flintlocks were accurate only at that range. As the men closed in with a second and third volley, the bayonet became crucial. The bayonet charge *after* firing (and clubbing with muskets) caused most battlefield deaths and usually decided the outcome. Linear tactics were about precision of command, not marksmanship; firing struck the enemy at random. Colonel George Hanger wryly observed,

> A soldier's musket, if not exceeding badly bored, and *very crooked, as many are,* will strike the figure of a man at 80 yards, it may even at 100 yards; but a soldier *must be very unfortunate indeed* who shall be wounded by a *common musket* at 150 yards, PROVIDED HIS ANTAGONIST AIMS AT HIM; and as to firing at a man at 200 yards with a common musket, you may just as well fire at the moon, and have the same hopes of hitting your object. I do maintain, and I will prove, whenever called on, that NO MAN WAS EVER KILLED AT TWO HUNDRED YARDS by a common soldier's musket, BY THE PERSON WHO AIMED AT HIM.

Hanger wrote these words in 1808, when aim was becoming a British objective. Until then, on the European battlefield, guns had other uses. Guns kept combat at closer quarters than the longbow, but more impersonally, since they were not aimed and the battlefield ceased to be a collection of single combats. As late as 1792, Lieutenant Colonel Lee of the 44th Regiment advocated a return to the longbow on the grounds that men could aim and reload them more easily and that a flight of arrows could terrorize as well as a rain of ball and shot. In 1945, an ex-master of the Tower Armouries classified the flintlock among long-distance weapons like longbows and later muskets only reluctantly, given its awkward fit in that category. Eighteenth-century firearms were for terrorizing at a distance with *unpredictable* fire, not precise targeting.

As the robbery incidents above illustrate, such terror became increasingly useful with the rise of private property. In Birmingham from 1760 to 1799, when only a few murders involved guns, highwaymen and burglars routinely put pistols to the heads or breasts of their victims (two cases resulting in death and two more in which the robber was killed). Perpetrators of new crimes of extortion relied on the image of the coolheaded villain willing to shoot if necessary. A gentleman in Ayrshire received an anonymous letter conjuring an image of six men armed with good pistols, demanding £50 and ready to shoot if he attempted to discover their identities. The gun's intimidating force was equally central to deterring threats to property by highwaymen, who were often demobilized soldiers. "People of property" braced themselves for such threats after the Seven Years' War by providing "themselves with firearms," noted *Gentleman's Magazine*. A reader of the Birmingham newspaper suggested that stagecoach owners arm their carriages with firearms affixed for easy and safe use. When carriages were "known to be thus guarded, few would be so hardy as to attack them." The paper later blamed a coach robbery on the fact that the guard next to the coachman did not have pistols and had stored his blunderbuss in a case at the back of the coach. As a popular contemporary historian of Birmingham observed, guns were essential to every man who had something to lose or gain—"No property will protect itself." The Birmingham newspaper hoped, after an intrusion into Dr. Priestley's home in 1790, "that persons living in the country, will . . . provide themselves with a sufficient quantity of fire arms." Colonel Hanger published an influential pamphlet of shooting advice for sportsmen and gamekeepers in which he insisted that there was "no better defence for a house, than a double-gun, nor against robbers on the road." He always kept a loaded duck gun by his bed. Homeowners waved their guns through windows at robbers, drunken passersby, and other undesirable elements. Samuel Johnson insisted that Highlanders needed firearms to defend against the "gang of robbers" confederating in the region; thus would firearms enable "commercial" values to subdue the "ferocity" that had underwritten this martial people's violent ways of settling differences.

It was through contests over property that guns found a role in English homicide. From 1760 to 1799, the Birmingham area saw nineteen nonaccidental deaths involving firearms. Nine directly involved property disputes. Two others involved military men: a deserter who killed a sergeant apprehending him and a soldier who committed suicide with his pistol. Three occurred in quarrel-like situations: A group of young men trying to snatch a girl from the arms of another man fired over his head in warning and, when that failed to intimidate, fired straight into his chest. A man resisting military recruitment shot a member of the gang impressing him into service. An affray between two ship crews ended with one shot. The circumstances of the remaining five are less clear: three suicides; a man capitally convicted for shooting another; a man who shot another "feloniously (but not of his malice afore-thought)." In reported nonlethal shootings, a man stealing rabbits shot the warrener's servant; two military officers were wounded while dueling; two burglars were wounded by their victims; a Birmingham seller fired on someone who stole his fowl. Three other cases seem idiosyncratic: Three drunk men went to a Birmingham earthenware seller's home and "discharged a pistol loaded with powder . . . full in his face" when he opened the door. A young man masquerading as a duke came to town with an underage girl. When her father came with the constable to fetch her, the impostor fired at the constable's son. He apologized afterward, adding that "if he had been a Bow-Street runner he should not have lamented shooting him." He understood shooting as a legitimate means of dealing with a thief (and perhaps inappropriate in emotional circumstances). Finally, in 1793, a man shot his wife in a "fit of jealousy," though the pistol misfired. He then wounded her twice on the head with a cleaver and swallowed mercury. All but six of these incidents involved property crimes and/or military men. One incident in Wales reached the Birmingham paper because it utterly broke the mold of gun violence: in 1788, a gentleman living in Carnarvon with a young woman returned there from a trip and "shot her with a brace of pistols," bringing a verdict of willful murder.

Similar patterns prevailed elsewhere; this was a general culture. In Kent in 1778, a man was acquitted for shooting a young man stealing apples from his orchard when he explained that he had not realized the gun was loaded. In 1772, when burglars entered a yeoman's house, he and his servant chased them out with pistols, shooting one in the back—justifiable homicide by law. Most gun deaths in London from 1700 to 1760 related to violent theft or disputes among soldiers. From 1760 to 1800, London trials involving guns increased slightly, to between 8 and 10 percent of total murder indictments (which fell by about a third from the first half of the century), but again these related almost exclusively to situations of property crime (besides accidents). In the 1760s, among twelve cases involving guns, five were related to robberies, one to trespass, and three to instances in which guns were used to ward off riotous supporters of the radical politician John Wilkes. There were just two other cases—a tavern brawl (yielding a verdict of manslaughter) and one lowly love triangle (willful murder). Instances in which a gun figured prominently in a crime of passion were sensational because they were relatively rare: In 1779, James Hackman, a clergyman and, notably, former army officer, shot and killed Martha Ray, longtime mistress of the Earl of Sandwich and mother of many of his children, as she got into her coach outside the Covent Garden Theatre. She had refused Hackman's heart and hand. Hackman was hanged. In 1797 in Staffordshire, Thomas Oliver shot a man whose daughter had disappointed him in love. These were exceptions in a trend of property-related gun violence. To understand why guns made sense primarily in the category of property-related crime in this period, we need to grasp their place in the emotional and cultural landscape of eighteenth-century Britain.

O bjects do not merely signify and represent us but enhance our capacity as human beings, creating new kinds of humanity and human agency. As we make objects, they make us. Bruno Latour explains, "You are different with a gun in your hand; the gun is different with you holding it. You are another subject because you hold the gun; the gun is another object because it has entered into a relationship with you." The gun in the hand shaped what eighteenth-century people could do. The tension and fear of physical conflict is almost entirely debilitating at close range without intense emotional motivation; it takes that kind of emotional motivation to violently wield instruments of intimate violence, like swords, knives, clubs, or the hands. The firearm, however, could be wielded from afar; it required no intimacy. Thus, it made less emotionally motivated violence possible. The greater the distance, the more depersonalized the target and the greater the ease of firing at it. (Archery required too much skill and strength for everyday violence.) Guns were an early innovation in the technological distancing of violence that has culminated in killer drones, which transform killing into a science rather than a response to immediate behavioral clues. They enabled the "relative restraint" of eighteenth-century wars (before the 1790s): mechanized killing allowed a break from the intense and immediate "affective discharge . . . of the medieval phase," explained the sociologist Norbert Elias in his foundational theory of the eighteenth-century "civilizing process." The individual "can no longer give free rein to his pleasure, spurred on by the sight of the enemy, but must fight, no matter how he may feel, according to the commands of invisible or only indirectly visible leaders, against a frequently invisible or only indirectly visible enemy." The eighteenth-century gun allowed a dispassionate kind of violence partly *because* it could not promise precision. Its theoretical purpose was that of a stern deterrent, the greater ease of perpetrating violence and aloofness from its impact serving to inhibit defiance. This was the source of its power as an instrument of terror in England. Some worked to make guns maximally destructive to enhance their use as deterrents. The inventor of a double-shot firearm defended his work by arguing that "in proportion as the weapons of war have become efficient and terrific, the quantity of carnage attending hostility has been diminished." This tactical logic would echo through history, in defenses of aerial bombardment, nuclear bombs, and American gun possession.

Such a deterrent became generally required as part of the eighteenth-century commitment to property. The gun communicated a particular threat: *I am at enough of a distance that I can overcome my revulsion against physical violence to protect my property, which I might not have had the courage to do if I were armed only with a knife. That type of violence—up close, with a knife—I would engage in only if your attack was upon my life rather than upon my property.* The unpredictability of the eighteenth-century gun ensured the impersonal nature of this threat. The hand pulled the trigger without knowing what the result would be, making the result the impersonal product of chance: *I pull a trigger that unleashes a multistep mechanical process that may or may not result in harm to you. The multiple steps produce a distance between intention (protecting my property) and the result (anything from terrifying you to wounding you to killing you). I am not responsible for the result; it is the product of an impersonal mechanical process.* The bow and arrow, on the other hand, produced a reliably predictable result and lacked the distancing steps of mechanical power; a sword threatened but without the cover of impersonality. The gun was the exemplary instrument of unintended consequence. Adam Smith observed,

> He who shoots a bird, and he who shoots a man, both of them perform the same external movement: each of them draws the trigger of a gun. The consequences which actually, and in fact, happen to proceed from any action, are, if possible, still more indifferent either to praise or blame, than even the external movement of the body. As they depend, not upon the agent, but upon fortune, they cannot be the proper foundation for any sentiment, of which his character and conduct are the objects. The only consequences for which he can be answerable . . . are those which were someway or other intended.

This was why crimes that failed in execution were treated mercifully: no country punished the man who fired at his enemy and missed, though the mere attempt, Smith thought, should be a capital offense. Would a failed stabbing inspire the same degree of mercy? This was the age of the "polite and commercial people," and guns helped propertied people build that reputation of politeness even while they were antagonistically engaged against the propertyless. Emotion was invested in the property they defended but actively denied in the relationship to the person threatening it. The gun's threat was as impersonal, like the new mode of social discipline embodied by Smith's "invisible hand." Capitalism alienates nature as private property, but property also helps people identify with a place. Guns ensured that physical identification between property owner and place, keeping threats at a polite distance. If property is the power to exclude others from taking or using certain things, the gun was the handheld instrument that made it effective (along with the law). The sword expressed the personal, aristocratic quality of chivalry; the gun, the impersonal, bourgeois quality of private property.

Feudal values gave way to bourgeois values through the "civilizing process": civility, manners, and humanitarian sentiment filtered down through society, collectively sensitizing it to violence. Crimes were directed against property more than the person as feudal values of honor and status gave way to bourgeois values of money and market relationships. Birmingham's "toys" were critical to the new rituals and hallmarks of civility: "Forks transformed table manners; curtain rods and rings allowed privacy in the home; buttons and hooks and eyes meant clothes were securely fastened . . . ; bells meant servants could be called; locks and keys meant property could be protected." And guns politely kept threats to that property at bay. The nobility evolved into courtiers rather than warriors; from a people quick to draw their knives, shifting easily from joviality to fierce aggression, evolved a people marked by the self-restraint enabled by the growth of a more coherent, centralized state authority and social interaction across distances—a society of strangers. As war became more spatially and temporally contained, and anger was less often expressed through physical attack, people became more sensitive to anything even reminiscent of an attack—hence sensitivities to passing knives at table without pointing the sharp end toward another. This new alertness to the "gesture of attack" opened up a space for terrorizing through distant display of a dangerous weapon.

Violence did not decline; it changed. The new aversion to overtly violent behavior was accompanied by tolerance of more discreet forms of violence. The ideal even for punishment was what the moral philosopher William Paley described as "a mode of execution . . . which would augment the horror of punishment, without offending or impairing the public sensibility by cruel or unseemly exhibitions of death." Gruesome public executions at Tyburn ended in 1783, not least because they had become more carnivalesque than terrifying. Instead, more shockingly efficient hanging took place at Newgate Prison. The number of capital crimes was reduced, and more impersonally terrorizing forms of punishment emerged: transportation and imprisonment, in which, as with guns, physical intimacy—*touching*—was unnecessary. Imprisonment was rarely used before 1775. In the era of the penitentiary and discreet execution, power acquired a new shape, less prone to participative spectacle and more grimly institutional. The violence of firearms was in this same mode. However inhuman and imposing, it was more *polite*, or at least coldly impersonal.

It is no coincidence that by the 1780s, pistols were adapted to the duel, a custom central to the taming of upper-class violence. Pistols made it easier for those unskilled at swordplay to participate but also made this eminently choreographed form of violence more polite. Rules of engagement required duelers to raise their weapons and fire in a single movement without pausing to aim. Parties took to firing into the air as a pragmatic and honorable way of terminating the conflict. Some fought with only powder and no ball. Pistols did not make duels less deadly, but they allowed the custom to evolve with notions of gentlemanly honor. A man killed in a pistol duel near York fell "victim to modern honour." Quarreling sailors used a pistol duel to settle things "like *gentlemen*," i.e., more politely than with the usual brawl. The technical and cultural constraints against aiming made the gun a weapon of general, impersonal intimidation rather than targeted animosity. It became more prominent in interpersonal violence when interpersonal violence changed and expanded, when brawls in pubs or among relatives were not the setting for murder, when immediate passions were not the trigger, when property rather than persons were at stake. It removed violence to a comfortable distance, leaving the hands of the perpetrator cleaner, even if at times it left its victim's body savagely mangled.

The gun was, paradigmatically, the weapon of the landholder, whose exclusive right to his land encompassed an exclusive right to shoot animals within it and ward off trespass with the same fowling piece. Gamekeepers were licensed to kill poachers. Property, in the form of sheep or game, was exposed to such easy violation that the terror of death seemed the only effective deterrent. But a political point was also at stake in that defense. The

gun was a miniaturized cannon, instantly militarizing any setting, transforming it into a battlefield over the settlement of 1689. This is why the
state feared rioters' possessing them: a bread rioter with a gun in hand
morphed into a Jacobite, a challenger of the regime of property rather than
a mere protestor for just prices. The disarmament provisions of game laws
and smuggling laws were likewise part of that struggle: in this period,
poachers and smugglers carried the stigma of Jacobitism, their offenses
against property being, sometimes rightly, presumed as offenses against
the regime that had ushered in the freedom not of men but of men of property. Certainly, not all poachers were protesting the rise of property and
demanding restoration of customary rights, but *some* rural laborers or
tenant farmers who engaged in this kind of activity were. Some insisted
that there could be no private property in wild animals and pointed to the
corruption of property owners and the regime supporting them. Guns were
central to the contest over game because of the political point at stake,
above and beyond their use in shooting game. Following a series of poaching raids, the Black Act of 1723 introduced the death penalty for more than
fifty criminal offenses, including going disguised in a forest, but ferocious
encounters between keepers and poachers followed, and keepers' right to
search for and confiscate the arms of suspected poachers annoyed enough
people that juries routinely refused to convict in capital cases involving
poaching unless the poacher was styled as a Jacobite. Poaching remained
rampant. Later in the century, poachers also risked tripping spring guns
rigged to shoot automatically. By the 1790s, keepers' determination to protect property also made them national symbols: awaiting French invasion
in 1796, the Birmingham paper noted that as "excellent marksmen . . . well
acquainted with the country in which they live," keepers "would form an
useful, as well as numerous body of men (about 7,000)."

Smuggling communities also lived in a state of war with the authorities,
the smuggler often symbolizing resistance to authority in general, feted for
defying the hated exciseman. Many questioned why free imports were a
crime when the politician Horace Walpole used an Admiralty barge to run
smuggled wine up the Thames. A radical advertisement of 1769 depicted
a gang of notorious robbers infesting the aristocratic neighborhoods of

Edward Haytley,
A Sportsman, *1752.*

St. James and the Treasury, plundering the public of millions. Criticism of the partnerships on which the state's war-making powers depended produced a positive image of armed outlaws. The army policed smuggling, and many smugglers declared their allegiance to the Pretender and helped Jacobites traveling to and from France.

Highwaymen, too, possessed a romantic and heroic aura and flair—glimmers of Robin Hood—despite their depredations against the innocent and their frequent lack of social objective. Many of these "gentlemen of the road" or "captains" of martial bearing were demobilized military men. They may have been brutalized by military experience, confident in their martial skills, suffering dislocations produced by war, or enacting the breakdown of social deference that often accompanied the experience of war. At the end of the Seven Years' War, Walpole remarked, "We swarm with highwaymen who have been heroes." By choking off outlets for emigration and transportation and producing soldiers disgruntled by defeat, the American war yielded the greatest spike in highway robbery. Convicted robbers liberated from Newgate during the Gordon Riots added to the mayhem. When deserters escaped the soldiers who held them, taking the soldiers' pistols, the Birmingham paper presumed that "they would have been that night depredating on the highway." In theory, the highwayman treated his victims with civility and humanity. He was, according to myth, part of the polite and commercial culture, and his pistol helped produce that image, with its impersonal threat perpetrated at a distance with an uncalculated effect. He was a mobile stranger among other mobile strangers on the roads that proliferated as state power expanded, carrying excisemen, soldiers, members of Parliament, postboys, surveyors, communities of Methodists and artisans displaced by industrial change, and the poor heading to the Midlands for mining and manufacturing. Despite their evident greed, many notorious highwaymen also possessed a "Jacobite flavor." Jacobites contrasted the fuss over highway robberies (like smuggling) with the nonchalance toward speculation and corruption on an enormous scale, holding the highwayman up as the heroic social criminal who exposed the illegitimacy of the post-1689 regime. He merely reclaimed a fraction of what the establishment had stolen. Highwaymen and smugglers, like pirates and bandits, contested the state's exclusive right to tax and exercise coercive power. Their use of firearms to that end symbolized their political challenge to the state's assertion of its singular legitimacy, including a monopoly on violence. The footpad wielding knives, maiming his victim while rifling through his pockets, was an "inhuman miscreant"; no such epithet attached to highwaymen who wielded pistols and left the consequence to fate.

The propertyless crowd was not polite and did not use guns. Its (usually) drunken fury helped individuals overcome inhibitions against wielding stones, knives, and torches in intimately violent ways. The crowd insisted on the legitimacy of the *personal* paternalistic social relations eroded by the impersonal relations of the emerging market economy. Even when defying local authority, its purpose was to secure redress of specific

Everett and Bird robbing a Stage-Coach on Hounslow Heath.

John Everett and Richmond Bird rob a coach on Hounslow Heath, circa 1720.

grievances, not to turn the world upside down or threaten the basic structure of society. Crowd action was about preservation of community, an
affirmation of personal and social bonds. The state, however, presumed
that all rioters wanted guns, and, indeed, some riots were more political
than others. But even during the Gordon Riots, which the state saw as
either a conspiracy against the American war or a general attack on the
regime, the crowd relied on arson and ransacking; some who attacked the
Old Bailey used bludgeons, crowbars, and chisels. The troops that extin-
guished the incendiary chaos, on the other hand, relied heavily on guns,
adapting this, like all riots, to the script of property defense. Most of the
more than three hundred rioters who were killed died of gunshot wounds;
many more were wounded. There was not a single casualty among the
soldiers or property victims. Crowd violence was authored by a commu-

nity rather than an individual but was nevertheless personal in its claims on a moral economy and paternalistic relations.

If a homeowner could legitimately ward off a single trespasser, troops took on that duty for such larger-scale assaults. Despite Britain's famed lack of a regular standing peacetime army, there were always sufficient troops on hand to restore order—in smuggling areas, areas with industrial disorders, and the Scottish Lowlands. Under the Mutiny Act, passed year after year in peacetime, Parliament voted to retain a peacetime army of about seventeen thousand in Britain and twelve thousand in Ireland, and most of the time the kingdom was mobilized for war anyway. The militarization of riot control was complete during the last wars against France. In 1795, when a crowd of mostly women attacked a cornmill, the troops protecting it tried to wound them with their bayonets, then fired over their heads, but "this instead of intimidating, seemed only to increase their violence." Finally, a dragoon fired on the crowd, killing two and dispersing the mob. Two months later, troops fired on a food riot at Rochdale, killing two elderly bystanders and splintering a boy's arm. The "humane conduct" of the major of the Worcestershire militia who put down a miners' insurrection without casualties warranted exceptional notice. A month later, troops shot a boy in the leg while suppressing a grain riot in Nottingham.

In this period, the idea of a "military" world with its own distinctive rules, values, and experiences, apart from the "civilian" realm, was just emerging. A violation of a private home was a violation of the kingdom. Frederick John Robinson (later Viscount Goderich) sponsored the protectionist Corn Law, which artificially raised wheat prices in 1815. A private soldier defending his home against rioters protesting the new law shot an innocent woman. His successful defense was that, by law, a man's house was "his castle of defence" and that he thus stood in the same situation as the soldiers called upon to protect life, property, and houses during the Gordon Riots. Guns were the individual-scale equivalent of the armed ships defending British property around the world, a technology for deterring seizure and intrusion. They projected power even at rest.

These incidents occurred during and just after the Napoleonic Wars, a conflict that armed an entire nation in fear of invasion and that was understood as defense of property on a national scale. To eighteenth-century Britons, war was a zero-sum game to protect state property *and* the property relations ushered in by 1689. This was why disarmament was so galling to many: by denying Englishmen the means of defending their property, the game laws deprived them of both the means of defending king and country and of any *motivation* for doing so. A people stripped of their ancient liberties would hardly take up arms to defend those who had stripped them or the regime that did not allow them to preserve their own properties:

> A Man is not suffered to keep a Gun in his House, to insure what little he has by his Diligence acquired; he is not permitted to defend himself, and Family, against Thieves and Robbers, but as soon as these Noblemen and Gentlemen Associators [members of the Association for the Preservation of Game] observe the least Degree of Danger towards themselves, he is compelled to bear Arms, *to protect their Effects,* neglecting both his Family and Business to secure them in their tyrannical Power.

Defending the House of Hanover depended on the ability to defend one's own house. War with France was, after all, a contest between two *houses*: Hanover and Bourbon. The Birmingham newspaper praised a "patriotic British Heroine" at Plymouth who ordered a light fusil and bayonet from a Birmingham gunsmith "for the Defence of her country" against the "hostile designs of the insidious House of Bourbon." The Napoleonic Wars generalized the defense of property as a national commitment. Mass volunteers fought for the principle of property itself, which Jacobinism threatened ideologically and practically. Edmund Burke saw in revolutionary France "the dreadful energy of a State, in which the property has nothing to do with the Government." The British citizen fought for property whether or not he had any of his own. Guns were a weapon for a society made up of greater numbers of strangers and determined to defend property as a point of national pride. *In this moment,* they were not the weapon of the angry and passionate or the weapon of the mob; they were the weapon a man of property might (legally) use to fend off an angry mob and the weapon a practiced highway-man might (illegally) wield to snatch that property.

Eighteenth-century law was also designed to terrorize the population against infractions of property. The draconian Black Act, the centerpiece of the Bloody Code, marked the rise of legal terror. The legal sanction of death replaced the whipping post and the stocks as the category of crime underwent a paradigmatic shift: "What was now to be punished was not an offence between men . . . but an offence against property," which was an offense against the post-1689 regime. Civil government, insofar as it secured property, was "really instituted for the defence of the rich against the poor," wrote Adam Smith. By drastically expanding the number of capital crimes for property offenses, the Black Act was not supposed to actually kill more offenders but to deter them, so that they would "not suffer at all," explained the barrister Sir Matthew Hale. Punishment was "more for example and to prevent evils, than to punish." There were fifty capital offenses in 1689 and four times as many by 1800, for petty thefts, food riots, forgery, violent resistance of enclosure, and so on. The law, like the gun, deterred "by *unpredictable* example."

Legal terror allowed the state to address property violations without expending many resources; privately owned guns were part of that cheap solution, part of the partnership between public and private power at the local level. The Riot Act of 1715 indemnified *civilians* for shooting rioters in aid of troops. "If we diminish the terror of house-breakers," Justice Christian of Ely wrote in 1819, "the terror of the innocent inhabitants must be increased." He counted on the death sentence to deter those who would steal his plate *and* took a brace of double-barreled pistols to bed with him nightly. A regular police force was anathema to a Francophobic gentry traumatized by memories of the Stuarts; legal terror and the gun at the property holder's bedside were acceptable substitutes. From the 1770s, private citizens formed associations for nightly policing of their own towns to preserve property and peace. In a period in which the line between crime and rebellion was so thin, with the regime's legitimacy at stake in property, guns militarized "private" clashes over that principle. The state did not have a monopoly on violence, because it was not yet institutionally coherent enough to have one. It existed in tension and continuity with semiautonomous sources of legitimate authority at the regional level. Gun possession among the propertied classes within a wider context of general disarmament was the result: a distribution of miniature cannon militarizing the ostensibly private sector to defend the private property that was the post-1689 regime's raison d'être. This *was* state monopoly of violence, if we work with a corporate definition of the state. The farming out of property protection to volunteers sits awkwardly against the assumption that secure property rights are the foundation of a sophisticated economy. But economic development depended more on the ability to "*signal credibly* that property rights would be protected than to enact them into formal law," explains the economic historian Joel Mokyr. The gun was that signal, as theoretically impersonal in its dispensation of justice as the "rule of law," though both enabled class exploitation by securing property.

The law fully sanctioned civilian use of guns to defend property. Gun fatalities transpiring in the course of theft were deemed willful murders, but those resulting from the defense of property typically ended in acquittal. Such was the outcome when, on two separate occasions, John Green fired out of his window in 1768, killing a cobbler and a soldier, while Wilkes supporters attacked his home with stones and brickbats. Likewise in the 1784 case of Porter Ridout, who killed a thirteen-year-old boy and wounded others while dispersing a crowd around his house that had begun to fire squibs and crackers as part of a Jewish festival in the neighborhood. The prosecutor urged that an act showing "wanton disregard for the safety of others . . . is equally immoral" as murder motivated by "malignity directed against an individual." But when Ridout explained that the crowd had robbed him of his money and "knew I had a great deal of property in the house," he was deemed "not guilty." In May 1791, a mob stoned the home of a Wiltshire clothier, wanting to burn the carding machine he was experimenting with. He threatened to fire. The mob persisted, and the clothier and his friends shot into the crowd, killing three: "justifiable defence." Death by a gun fired with intent to frighten was considered "chancel-medley." The unpredictability of the result made clear the impersonality of the action, justifying it before the law as reasonable defense of property—and the risk of death as something of which every trespasser must be aware. To be sure, it was not always clear how far the right to kill for property extended. When a Birmingham gamekeeper was tried for shooting a dog, the local paper explained, "No man has a right to take the executive part of the law into his own hands, except in cases where his life and property are in danger and the danger cannot be avoided without an immediate exertion of the party." The paper shared this information, "as these matters are not generally known."

Homicide verdicts evolved to accommodate the new kinds of violence made possible by guns. Initially, "manslaughter" was the verdict attached to homicides occurring when a bout of intense passion or fury overrode a person's usual capacity for reason and moral judgment. It carried milder sentences—typically a few months of imprisonment and burning in the hand—than "willful murder," which was the result of premeditative malice and which earned punishments like death plus dissection. Chance-medley obtained in accidental homicides devoid of passion and malice. For most of the century, most murders were classified as manslaughter, forgivably transpiring in the heat of passion, usually between family members. The Bloody Code did not even try to deter such acts of obvious irrationality, directing its terror against new crimes against property. Guns wreaked havoc with this system. Juries assigned manslaughter in instances of accidental shooting *and* duels, in neither of which immediate passion ruled. In vain did judges and prosecutors remind them that duels always transpired after "reason has assumed its office." Most gun-related deaths in this period were the result of impersonal conflict or accident. By degrees, a "manslaughter" verdict became a means of arriving at a more merciful sentence for those caught somewhere between these categories, especially as the compassion that underwrote verdicts of manslaughter for emotional crimes also came into criticism for eradicating altogether the concept of *mens rea*, criminal intent.

This culture surrounding gun use began to shift during the 1790s. Guns found a new relevance in interpersonal civilian crime as British society's exposure to them radically changed at the turn of the century.

In part one, I argued that continual warfare shaped the British economy; war also shaped understandings of what guns were for.

Mass armament expanded through the 1790s. By 1803, when war restarted after the Peace of Amiens, even the great enemy of radicalism William Pitt conceded, "There was a time . . . when it would have been dangerous to entrust arms with a great portion of the people of this country . . . *But that time is now past.*" Men joined the war effort for different reasons—out of military ardor, love of country, or novelty, but also impoverishment and the effort to avoid "being drawn in the militia." After 1803, enlisted men made up 11 to 14 percent of the adult male population, three times the ratio in France. Half a million civilians, mostly working men, were drawn into civil defense and given arms. The result of mass arming, according to Henry Addington, prime minister from 1801 to 1804, was a renewed contract between the government and the governed:

> A determination on the part of the government to put arms into the hands of a whole people, and a resolution on the part of the people to accept them . . . proved a double security, a double pledge. It was a pledge on the part of the government, that they should never attempt anything hostile to the constitution. It was a pledge on the part of the people that they valued as well as understood its excellence; that they were steadily attached to it, and determined to preserve it.

Average enrollment during the Nine Years' War was 76,400; it had been 108,400 during the American war, but 300,000 in 1809. The hundreds of thousands of Volunteers incorporated from 1808 into Local Militia under commissioned gentry officers and military discipline withdrew an enormous population of men from the ranks of potential food rioters. Thousands guarded the six naval dockyards. The Home Guard, furnished with uniforms, officers, arms, and weekly drill pay, faced down food rioters.

Guns became pervasive. Availability and experience *together* shifted understandings and uses of guns. As in much of Europe, training in arms for the state became "the most common collective working class experience." The Volunteer army did not use their weapons to revolt or extort political concessions, proving that they preferred their own unreformed state to French invasion. But the experience did transform their lives, ideas, and expectations. New kinds of people, well beyond gentlemanly sportsmen, became intimate with guns. Village artisans became well-traveled soldiers; ex-soldiers became artisans. This was a military experience on an unprecedented, seemingly apocalyptic scale of magnitude and duration, opening up the possibility of a major cultural shift in understandings about guns and violent death. Mass arming exposed an entire generation to the business of impersonal killing to an entirely new degree. The experience of bureaucratically rationalized violence taught an entire generation to suppress personal inclinations to accomplish a collective purpose. The mass-produced gun made mass casualties possible—not, initially, because of its technological superiority to pikes or swords, but because of the impersonality with which it allowed death to be dispensed.

Gun use shifted on the battlefield, even as the Duke of Wellington extended the life of eighteenth-century aristocratic military ideals with his careful maneuvering of small bodies of highly trained professional soldiers rather than Napoleonic mass assault. "Effective fire" emerged as a peculiarly British occupation. Aim had long been an impossible objective, partly because the thought of firing on others while also being fired at made it difficult for the infantryman to hold still long enough. But in some contexts, British soldiers did achieve higher levels of accuracy. Madras Army soldiers aiming at a roughly man-size target two hundred yards away could hit it in one out of thirteen shots. Toward the end of the century, East India Company forces generally embraced the idea of aimed fire (hence their slow adoption of steel rammers, which sped up firing). British soldiers elsewhere also overcame the squeamishness that made aim so difficult. The emphasis on unaimed rapid fire yielded to an emphasis on accuracy. The 1800 military manual instructed infantry in aim: "Look along the barrel with the right eye from the breach [*sic*] pin to the muzzle end and remain steady. Pull the trigger strong with the forefinger." There was no mention of the sight, and the advice on pressing the trigger was calculated more for volleys than for accurate shots. They still fired in unison by word of command, pressing the trigger without setting aim. Then, in 1803, a general order for Horse Guards introduced the habit of pausing after triggering, to avoid spoiling the aim and to give the soldier the habit of "precision and coolness." The pause was mentioned three times in the 1804 *Manual and Platoon Exercises,* explicitly to ensure precision and effective fire. More substantial change came when the order "Fire" was dropped in the light infantry in 1807 and then for the line infantry. Men were supposed to trigger whenever they, as individuals, arrived at a correct aim. The emphasis on effective fire made the British rate of fire slower than that of other European armies, who noted its special deadliness, especially as compared with the rapid-firing Prussians. Soldiers received medals for proficiency in marksmanship. As invasion was expected daily after 1803, military thinkers brainstormed musket improvements that might strengthen aim, some out of a sense that British soldiers required a technical crutch against a German foe deeply practiced in war. By contrast, in 1805, Napoleon banned breech-loading rifles with better accuracy because of their slow rate of fire, and Prussians continued to make muskets without a proper sight and stock so that infantrymen would not try to aim and would simply fire from the hip with mechanical speed.

The unique British interest in accuracy may have been at least partly due to British encounters in the expanding empire with populations (like Native Americans and Marathas) who had already mastered the art of gun marksmanship. However it transpired, it was a *shift.* The gun did not change so much as understandings about it. British military manuals' attempts at minute choreography of the body to achieve aim evidence the discipline of time and the body that was the hallmark of the industrial age. The practice of aim required segmentation of time and intense bodily drill. Mass demand for military muskets helped drive industrialism, and industrialism, in turn, helped make them an effective agent of mass death.

This shift in military use mattered beyond the battlefield. State violence was mirrored throughout society. Guns began to appear in reports of untimely death with startling frequency. Their increased availability is evident from the leap in accidental gun deaths. In vain, newspapers reminded readers of the "impropriety of leaving loaded firearms" within reach of those "ignorant of the danger of handling them." Celebrations of national military prowess fueled some of the danger. In 1805 in Gloucester, a boy was found dead after watching celebrations of the naval victories, having been "frightened to death by the firing, as he often fell into fits at the firing of a gun." Despite official precautions to prevent firing of arms in Bristol's streets on the anniversary of the Gunpowder Plot in 1807, a girl was shot and killed from an unknown direction. The years 1811–15 produced ten accidental gun deaths in Gloucester, their circumstances revealing the enduringly diverse uses of guns: besides accidents among men out shooting and children playing with guns, there was a sheep thief shooting sheep, a young man firing while watching the illumination at Upton-upon-Severn in 1814, a farmer firing to frighten rooks from his newly sown barley, a man firing to celebrate the peace, and a man shooting fish. Guns also remained central in property-related crimes, not least because the period saw dramatic ups and downs in employment.

But there was something different even in that familiar category of gun violence. A Gloucester yeoman shot and killed the parish tax collector. The local paper explained that the yeoman was an "old man of considerable property, but generally very litigious in his disposition, and gave much trouble to the persons appointed to receive his taxes." On his execution, the paper made him an example to those who would resist officers performing their duty and give way to "those unbridled passions which generally terminate in their own destruction." But the incident appears less an emotional stand against taxes than a whimsical exercise of power.

This shooting was a harbinger of a change in gun violence near the turn of the century. Guns were implicated in new kinds of deliberate homicides unrelated to property, passions, or duels. In the Birmingham area in 1794, a man was sentenced to death for shooting a woman "without even knowing her person." In Liverpool, a man stopped a woman, took her calash, and fired a pistol in her face. When the gun misfired, he tried again and wounded her. When caught, he appeared "quite collected" and told bystanders that he *"had twenty more to shoot yet!"* In Bath in 1795, a young man spurned by the schoolteacher he loved shot her "with coolness and deliberation" in her schoolroom. This was neither property-related nor impassioned violence, but the disturbed man's way of meting out justice. In Gloucester in 1797, a sentinel of the Royal Buckingham Militia shot a Frenchman (justifiable homicide). In 1802, one currier shot another. The same year, a fifteen-year-old discharged from a marine corps walked with his musket "imprudently pointed towards several persons, saying to them that the piece was loaded and threatening to fire, to intimidate them." On Bristol Bridge, without any notice to passersby, he "wantonly drew the trigger" and shot the whole charge into the legs of a young man, killing him. The local paper judged this an "unpardonable instance of wanton wickedness." A Birmingham man was hanged in 1806 for shooting a night constable on duty. (The constable lived.) When a coal carrier refused to tell his name to a passing gentleman who judged him ready to strike with a whip, the gentleman shot him, killing him instantly. His quick provision of medical help to the victim and assurance that he had acted only after being assaulted fetched him a verdict of manslaughter. In Greater London between 1800 and 1810, there were four killings unrelated to property and duels. The subsequent five years brought eight such cases (including the notorious shooting of a woman in front of the home of the Corn Law sponsor and the assassination of the prime minister, on which more below). Gun-related deaths constituted 12 percent of killing indictments in that half decade, a higher proportion than ever. The massive wars that had begun in 1793 were changing the way guns were used in civilian violence, too. An entire generation had been made familiar with and capable of impersonal gun violence unrelated to property.

Rioters took up firearms, too. The novelty was clear from news reports: in Leicestershire in 1795, rioters pelted the Volunteer cavalry, "even fired on them," wounding one in the knee. Troops returned fire, killing three and wounding eight more, perhaps fatally. Navvies and colliers from Shackerstone, near Leicester, also committed "daring outrages" with firearms. In 1797, the radical John Thelwall escaped a riot at his lecture at Derby by waving his pistol and threatening to "shoot any person who molested him." In Carlisle in 1812, rioters armed with guns and pitchforks seized £500 worth of meat and flour from a warehouse.

The period's two most sensational shootings showcase the new role guns were acquiring in British culture: the attempted assassination of King George III in 1800 and the assassination of Spencer Perceval in 1812—the first and only assassination of a British prime minister. It is worth recalling as a baseline the 1763 attempt by a Scottish marine to kill John Wilkes with a penknife—the Scotsman was a member of a gang that had sworn to slay their national enemy, sufficiently emotionally motivated to wield a penknife. The affair of 1800 was different. Dressed in his officer's uniform, James Hadfield, a silversmith severely wounded and disfigured in the wars, fired at the king as he entered the royal box at the Drury Lane Theatre. He missed. Hadfield claimed no personal animosity toward the king; he was proud of his recent service in the king's name. He told his interrogators he "had not attempted to kill the king. He had fired his pistol over the royal box. He was as good a shot as any in England; but he was himself weary of life—he wished for death, but not to die by his own hands. He was desirous to raise an alarm; and wished the spectators might fall upon him. He hoped that his life was forfeited." He was acquitted as insane. Hadfield wanted to provoke general terror, and the pistol served him to that end of committing a crime that was premeditated but *without* malice (and unrelated to property)—a new sort of crime. These features neatly foreshadow John Bellingham's bitter logic. Bellingham had been imprisoned while doing business in Russia when a Russian ship was lost at sea and he was accused of sabotaging the shipowners' efforts to claim on their insurance. His appeals to the British government fell on deaf ears, as did his attempts at obtaining government compensation for his imprisonment when he returned to Britain. As his finances and family crumbled, he embarked on a bolder course: he waited in the lobby of the House of Commons and shot the prime minister. He later explained in court, "Mr. Perceval has unfortunately fallen the victim of my desperate resolution. No man, I am sure, laments the calamitous event more than I do. If I had met Lord Gower [former ambassador to Russia, who had declined to assist him and was present in court] he would have received the ball, and not Mr. Perceval." "What," he asked, "is my crime to the crime of government itself? It is no more than a mite to a mountain, unless it was proved that I had malice propense towards the unfortunate gentleman for whose death I am now upon my trial. I disclaim all personal or intentional malice against Mr. Perceval." This disavowal of personal malice was not enough to stave off a verdict of willful murder, given the national trauma, but does usefully signify for us what Bellingham thought he was doing by taking up a gun, a miniature cannon with which to impersonally defy the increasingly impersonal power of the state. It is no coincidence that Bellingham and Hadfield were both military men. Soldiers were prominent in many gun incidents cited above, and among highwaymen, too.

To be sure, most murders involved throat cutting, fighting, stabbing, strangling, beating, poisoning, or murder by dung fork, razor, poker, scythe, shovel, hammer, knife, and so on. In Kent, bladed weapons and guns accounted for only 13 percent of violent deaths from 1800 to 1850. Hitting and kicking grew in proportion. A fatal contest between a gamekeeper and poachers could still transpire with sticks. Soldiers still scuffled with swords; land disputes were still resolved with drowning and hitting; robberies were still committed with hatchets. But at the same time, guns had a role that they had not possessed in 1750 or 1790. After a period in which their use was confined to the impersonal defense or seizure of property, they found a role in a new kind of *impersonal violence against the person*. The appearance of that coldly clinical form of interpersonal violence coincided with expansion of the state's destructive power during the Napoleonic Wars. Guns had proliferated in Britain in the second half of the century while remaining tethered to property-related violence. Perhaps culture shifted when proliferation hit a certain "critical mass" during the Napoleonic Wars, but apart from sheer number, the mass experience and *practice* of using guns to kill impersonally mattered. Mass exposure to military gun violence produced new kinds of civilian gun violence. That was the cultural work of war.

Softening sensibilities produced revulsion against mutilating forms of bodily punishment at precisely this moment. Guns gave violence a polite form suitable to modern sensibilities while expanding its scale to truly barbaric levels. Before they became the "emotionally repressed nation of the twentieth century," the British were a "drunken, passionate, melancholy, romantic, and tearful" people, as one historian notes. The French Revolution pivotally exposed the dangers of a cult of feeling and grounded British national character in the practice of emotional restraint. The gun, operating outside the domain of the passions, was an important tool of the creation of that bounded self possessing bounded property. At the end of the wars, Jane Austen could write of a character in her novel *Persuasion* that "he sometimes took out a gun, but never killed; quite the gentleman." Gentlemanliness was embodied in the authority and restraint implied by possessing but not using a gun. The eighteenth-century legal vocabulary of mental excuse—the plea of temporary fury—that was part of the old cult of feeling gave way to the concept of a controlled and controllable self. This new, modern subject epitomized middle-class British masculinity, displacing the emotion and empathy of the eighteenth-century "man of feeling." The French Revolution's threats to the nation and property could not be met with sudden, impassioned revenge, but with the coldly intimi-dating mass of trained citizen-soldiers armed with guns. English self-representation became one of unique surface calm masking a readiness to defend oneself at the quick.

The British government's trust in an armed people was ephemeral. Demobilization, high food prices, and the postwar industrial downturn triggered radicalism that threatened the existing order. In 1819, Parlia-ment passed the Six Acts, forbidding arming and meeting for arms training—justified two months later by the unraveling of the Cato Street Conspiracy to murder the entire British Cabinet. The state reverted to forestalling armed insurrection. Victorian citizenry surrendered to state bodies (policemen, courts) much of their predecessors' autonomy in deal-ing with thieves, the state promising, in theory, to use its monopoly of violence for their benefit. "Public" and "private" became more defined. The strategy for property protection also shifted from building a wall around property owners to building a wall around criminals. Guns in the hands of property owners disappeared. With dress, house address, domes-tic interiors, and club memberships increasingly indicating social position, they became a less urgent defense among strangers. Highwaymen also disappeared, and travel was shaped as a zone of middle-class respectability in which strangers could be avoided altogether. When Emily Brontë sat down in 1845 to depict the Yorkshire of 1801–2 in *Wuthering Heights*, Hareton Earnshaw's obsession with guns, which he used in uneconomical pursuit of pheasant, epitomized the uncivilized savagery to which his vengeful master Heathcliff had reduced him. They seemed less the handmaiden of the civilization of property than a symbol of the Moors' stubborn remoteness from the modern world. Still, in 1934, a Greek character in an Agatha Christie novel could declare, "The English, they do not stab," and plausibly evoke the image of the British gentleman—or highwayman—who killed impersonally and dispassionately with a gun. That image found its ultimate apotheosis in the British Cold War spy. It lived on largely because, in the empire, the gun maintained its role as the commonsense, modern, and impersonal equipment of the civilizing Briton, as we shall see in the next chapter.

P olite or not, guns made ghastly wounds. Many observed the "shocking" manner in which they tore the flesh. The "horrid spectacle" of the victim's rent face was central to news of a gun death. The Birmingham paper detailed the way a robber's pistol took off his victim's cheek and ear, leaving his neck "quite open to the windpipe." The highwayman's signature threat of blowing the victim's "brains out" was duly noted for its literal relevance. When a gamekeeper accidentally shot a farmer, the paper reported, astonished, that "he received the entire contents of his own piece in the groin and it came out the back!" Guns tore holes in the flesh and smashed bones in new ways. Surgeons had to deal with the "mystery in the business of gunshot wounds," the unprecedented combination of laceration, bruising, and gangrenous bleeding caused by the ball and powder. Harder to repair than the wounds caused by sword and bayonet, they evolved into a distinct branch of surgery.

How was this mutilating power reconciled with "politeness"? First, mutilation was mediated by distance (no touching); second, the gun, ideally, was not to go off at all, and the threat of its great mutilating power was supposed to prevent such violence. The highwayman's "blow your brains out" threat built on the older threat of "beating your brains out," which required much more motivating anger than the average highwayman possessed. Guns allowed villainous talk to be tougher than the villain. Third, the gun's mass-manufactured nature normalized its presence and perforating function—an early chapter in the anesthetization of human sensibilities by the overstimulation of modern industrial life and mechanized warfare. Individuals learned to insulate themselves, to cheat themselves out of sensory response (in Walter Benjamin's terms) to protect the human psyche from the trauma of perpetual shock. Technological advances helped: as guns became more sophisticated, their wounds became increasingly surgical and less offensive to the eye.

If most became reconciled to the wounds, a few did express concern about the gratuitous way in which guns could kill, unlike weapons requiring the exertion borne of genuine emotional motivation. In 1767, John Aldington, an "Experienced Fowler," broke with the tradition of poetry celebrating the art of shooting and openly lamented the prey's powerlessness in the face of the gun's metallic, engineered power. In "A Poem on the Various Scenes of Shooting," he dwelled on the "*Gunner's* Cruelty," stalking his prey like a "stern Monster," bringing death as the "pond'rous Lead o'rtakes her wounding Wings." A hare falls victim to the "roaring Tube," "breathless, bleeding on the Ground." Linnets yield to a "Huge massy Ball," which "wide tears their tender carcasses, and lop whole limbs away." Upon the hunter's return, his family praises his "Mighty Deeds and Goodness: His lovely Gun." He "glories in the Murder of the Day." Aldington sought to expose the cruelty masked by the gun's modernity, impersonality, and sporting role. A later verse shifts to the "hideous Din of War," where men kill with bayoneted muskets "devoid of Malice."

Where fallen Cruelty, (frightful indeed!)
Rob'd in complete Steel, with crimson Horror,
Stalks along the daring Lines, where Thousands meet,
Far from their native Home, in rueful Conflict;
Man to kill Man; devoid of Malice, stab
Their fellow Creatures, and drench th' sun-pierc'd wide

Inhospitable Plains, with human Gore,—
The peaceful Muse, shrinks from the shocking Scene,
Agast! Which Words were never made to paint.

The 1768 edition opened with a lyric about a young man pursued "like a fearful frighted fawn by ruffians." Shot, "the harmless stripling drop'd, dead to the ground." Aldington reflected on the sheer volume of death a gun could produce: "in murder'd Heaps, the hapless Strangers fall." He asked "wretched man" to recollect how

Thy bloody Hand, hard ram'd the mighty Piece
With desperate, enormous, fatal Ball;
And, like a Murder stanch, the thun'ring Ruin
Right level'd at a tender Brother's Heart.
Thus in this Life, or that which is to come,
The great and mighty GOD of *Heav'n* will
Repay our Cruelties; and justly he,
Who late no Mercy felt, now for it begs,
With shrieking, mournful Tone, and is denied.

The powerlessness of the victim and cold-bloodedness of the perpetrator set death by gun apart. The weapon's industrial nature—that it was a complex combination of many metallic parts propelling a bullet like an "Engine" rather than a single piece of metal like a bladed instrument—made it cruel, and cruelly capable of killing on an industrial scale without implicating human conscience. It made killing sport. Man's nature had fallen: "A wretched Animal, to Reason tack'd," sunken "in Character, below the Brute!" In 1817, the "vulgar" advantages of the new percussion lock similarly exercised a reader of *Gentleman's Magazine,* who discerned that true sportsmen were skillful enough with flintlocks, and gentlemen would not care for its advantages in bad weather, since gentlemen did not shoot in bad weather. This meant the invention was really intended to make war "so frightful as to exceed all bounds of imagination, and . . . civilization itself."

In the eighteenth century, such critiques were rare. More typical was the perspective of Henry James Pye, member of Parliament for Berkshire, who published "Shooting, a Poem" in 1784. Coming just after national defeat at the hands of American rebels, the poem offered patriotic affirmation. "The ambition of the Sportsman," he pronounced, "lies more in the certain shot than bleeding prize." Sure aim required "steady care" and "quickness." Poachers, on the other hand, inflicted "random slaughter" among the covey. Pye's classist views were rewarded in 1790 when he was appointed poet laureate. Idealization of the gun's *potential* precision long coexisted with obvious evidence of its use in perpetrating mass violence— which Pye easily dismissed as vulgarity. Even robbers saw in the wielding of a gun a kind of honor and blunt honesty: at the end of his life, in 1726, the ruthless gangster Edward Burnworth proclaimed that "as he had liv'd with a pistol in his hand, so would he scorn to die with a Lye in his Mouth." What made the gun straightforward was the power it embodied; picking one up was a blunt avowal and, for some, disavowal of established power.

Abolitionist depictions of guns were less forgiving. Besides the shoddy guns traded for slaves, the movement also criticized guns' uses in the "extraordinary punishments" typical of slavery. Evidence submitted to Parliament in 1790–91 included an account of a runaway slave in Tortola whose overseer found him sleeping and *"shot him through the body."* The slave jumped up and said, "What, you kill me asleep" and dropped dead. The overseer *"took off his head,* and carried it to the owner." The barbarism of decapitation was coupled with the callous shooting of a sleeping man. In another incident, a planter offended by his mulatto servant "stepped suddenly to *his gun,* on which the man ran off, but his master *shot him through the head with a single ball."* The gun made capricious killing possible. Abolitionist evidence in 1805 included the case of a slave boy in Bermuda shot at by the estate's overseer and "not quite dead when he was buried." This was whimsical violence, requiring little physical effort and fueling the unfeeling wastefulness of the slave system.

The gun in the hand of the eighteenth-century Englishman was not merely a more efficient substitute for the knife or the sword but served entirely new purposes. That is how it made its place in the world, but over time it would substitute for other instruments of violence as culture and technology both shifted. In the nineteenth century, guns were used in passion as much as cold calculation and were rationalized in new ways against a backdrop of even more remote ways of killing. The impersonal, casual violence they enabled at the start of that century remained part of common understandings of their uses, enabling the ordinary person to kill "types" rather than individuals—on the battlefield, in conquest, in counterinsurgency, and in riot. Guns mediated the rise of a particular regime of property and the social relations it rested upon. They were a tool of violence for a society of new kinds of strangers—especially abroad.

7

Guns in Arms, Part 2: Abroad

In 1689, ten Quakers were among the English merchants and crew caught at sea and held captive by pirates at Mequinez, in Morocco. Some had been there several years. The Society of Friends wrote them a letter reminding them not to resort to weapons to attain their freedom. But, the captives asked, what if the merchants to whom they had entrusted their money to obtain their liberty *purchased* it with arms? Sure enough, within days, a captive wrote to his father that guns were about to procure their freedom—but by barter rather than violence: an English merchant had agreed to exchange four thousand musket barrels, plus gunpowder and "30 Moors," for the thirty English captives. In the event, the deal fell through, and the prisoners languished for another decade until the survivors were ransomed. But at other times, guns and gun parts were used to redeem English captives on the Barbary coast. Barbary military capacity kept the British at bay but depended on trading Britons for armaments.

Similarly complicated dynamics unfolded elsewhere in the world. British colonialism was a larger instance of the spread of private property in which guns figured centrally. Property was not an abstract principle the British brought into benighted parts of the world but something actively made in particular places through appropriation and violence. As currency, commodities, weapons, symbols of power, and more, guns were critical to eighteenth-century colonialism—to British trespass abroad. A basic tension gradually unfolded between guns' uses as currency and as weapons. British efforts to use guns as a diplomatic and commercial currency to open doors to trade and conquest undermined the effort to prohibit rivals and enemies from obtaining dangerous weapons. These conflicting goals together made guns central to the making of foreign lands into British territory and private property. Guns for trade were the primary category of gun manufacture; second were guns understood as tools for survival in "unsettled and unstable" areas; last were military arms. All three made empire.

Abroad, the gun's impersonality acquired a different twist: the British intruder shook off the implication of trespass by advertising the abject savagery of the worlds in which he interloped. In countless narratives hungrily consumed at home, those contexts not only licensed an aggressive posture but transformed it into a humbly defensive one: the intrepid Briton's entry could only improve such places. In this script, the gun in hand was an instrument for ushering backward places into the modern age. Indeed, the modern age can be said to have begun in 1719, with Robinson Crusoe's resourceful fictional survival on a Caribbean island with but a few implements of civilization salvaged from his shipwreck, including muskets. Abroad, the gun was understood as the impersonally civilizing instrument with which to oppose the more intimate violence threatened by tomahawks and daggers. The image of solitary courage in hostile environs most substantiates the eighteenth-century reading of the gun as essentially a deterrent, reasonable armor against unreasonable enemies and unknown barbarities. The armed adventurer in exotic terrain remains central to our collective imagination about what guns are for.

The search for trade—styled as the benevolent spread of civilization—justified his trespass. In some places, guns were the sine qua non of trade. West African financial institutions could not accommodate British banknotes and stock certificates. The Royal African Company's charge was to bring gold and silver from the Guinea coast to London to alleviate the currency shortage; the British government could not countenance expenditure of specie there. To buy African goods, the company engaged in "assortment bargaining," trading bundles of goods, among which guns were essential; there had to be at least one as a token of connection or recognition. Barbary corsairs traded British captives for guns, and the British traded guns for African captives. The Ordnance Office allowed the sales even in wartime, because it understood guns' currency function there. To concerns about arms in Africa being used against the British, defenders of the trade replied that abstaining would merely forfeit profits to rivals. The Royal African Company also armed itself against that eventuality by fortifying its position on the coast and arming slaving ships— the onerous expenses that brought it to financial collapse by midcentury while individual traders carried on with lighter arms requirements. This trade-off between commerce and security shaped British expansion elsewhere, too.

One of Samuel Galton Jr.'s friends was the botanist Joseph Banks. Banks rose to fame after his adventures exploring the South Pacific with Captain Cook. Guns were central to their encounters. In 1769, on Cook's first great voyage, Banks customarily escaped the morning heat in Tahiti by wandering into the woods with his gun. One morning, upon returning, he found Tubourai Tamaide near his house. They walked together, until the latter suddenly took Banks's gun and "cocked it and holding it up in the air drew the trigger, fortunately for him it flashed in the pan." Banks rebuked him severely "and even threatened to shoot him," wondering where he "had got so much knowledge of the use of a gun," particularly since Banks had "upon all occasions taught him and the rest of the Indians that they could not offend me so much as even to touch it." Tubourai was so hurt that he and his family promptly left their home, and Banks went to some trouble to persuade his useful friend to return. His description of this effort included an account of a nighttime ritual he witnessed in which an old woman struck a shark's tooth into her head until it foamed with blood and another native attempted to scale the fort walls, "no doubt to steal whatever he could find." This context established the

gun's civilized, if unpredictable, power among gratuitously violent customs performed by a people insensible to notions of property. Part of its
elegance was its enduring mystery, to the islanders at least: an early chron-
icler of the voyage explained that Tubourai's actions offended Banks so
much because of "the necessity of keeping the Indians ignorant of the
management of fire-arms." Abroad, guns terrorized people the British
encountered by giving an impression of almost magical destructive power.
In a setting that the British intruder perceived as rife with unexpected
dangers and cruelties, preserving that aura was essential.

In theory, the Briton needed only demonstrate the gun's power occasionally to establish its awing effect. When four hundred natives sur-
rounded their ship in canoes, and a few boarded to receive presents, Cook's
crew was secure in the knowledge that some of them "had been about the
ship when she was off at sea, and knew the power of our fire-arms, for
when they saw a gun, it threw them into manifest confusion: under this
impression they traded very fairly." Terror alone was not always effective:
some attempted to tow away a buoy, and a musket fired over them did not
dissuade them. So, as they put the buoy into their canoe, Cook "was
obliged to fire a musket at them with ball, which hit one of them, and they
immediately threw the buoy over board." After this disciplinary measure,
the rogues agreed to behave and were again welcomed onto the ship. Incidents abound during these voyages of guns fired to intimidate natives who
did not appear docile enough before engaging in trade or other activities.
On Pulo Condore Island (near present-day Vietnam), British travelers
found that, though the temple was ornamented with old firearms, cutlasses, and daggers, local people "were not accustomed to the use of firearms, as they appeared to consider these warlike instruments as objects of
adoration." They then produced "alarm and astonishment" among the local people by discharging a musket at the trunk of a tree, securing an
agreement to purchase buffalo.

The mystique could wear off, however, and many indigenous peoples
remained both indomitable and fully alive to the political and practical
advantages bestowed by gun ownership (not least for its metal value). In
one instance at Nomuka Island, a native approached the British launch,

seized a cartouche box full of ammunition, and wrested a fowling piece from the second lieutenant on board. The crew fired, to no avail. The British raconteur observed, "They seemed . . . in less fear of fire-arms than any savages they had met with yet." The explorers got their stolen goods back by seizing a native canoe, which prompted their antagonist to attack the captain with a "desperate weapon over his head," until the captain presented his piece and the offender dropped his weapon. The instant the gun left the captain's shoulder, he took his weapon up again and advanced, obliging the captain "in his own defence to fire." The good captain aimed at the thighs, "being unwilling to kill so brave a fellow." The swan shot hit the aggressor's hand. He ran, howling, into the woods, his companions following to offer succor. The surgeon then "very humanely dressed his wounds," using a local remedy of "scraped sugar-cane spread upon a certain leaf." Peace was restored, and the fowling piece returned. The tone of this account is that of a parental lesson to an overzealous child. No hard feelings, no malice, no intense emotion—not even fear—is at play. The gun is the well-intentioned teacher; it, like the surgeon, is humane—for the gift of trade it brought and the sparingly instructive wound it gave those too naïve to recognize commerce's advantages. Explorer-authors often protested that they used their firearms only reluctantly; firearms were merely the reasonable and fairly humane recourse for self-preservation against more savage native weapons.

Narratives about travels to the South Seas were popular. The Earl of Shaftesbury considered them central to imaginary life, the "chief materials to furnish out a library." They were to his generation what books of chivalry were to their forefathers, he felt, conjuring an analogy between the sword-clutching knight and the pistol-clasping explorer. Visits by Pacific Islanders to Britain—along with specimens of Pacific plants and animals—fueled this imaginative engagement, promoting at once curiosity about peoples abroad and an appreciation of the unity of mankind. Middle-class ire was quickly aroused by news of brutal treatment of primitive men abroad. The explorer's gun fit in this context as a polite and primarily self-defensive arm. But however insistently defensive its use was in narrative accounts, a certain amount of hedging may have alerted the astute reader otherwise. In 1767, the explorer Philip Carteret sent the ship's master and some men in a cutter to obtain supplies from the coast of one of the islands that would be named after him. A party of "Indians" suddenly shot them with four-foot arrows. They defended themselves by firing, but the master wound up with three arrows in his body and died, along with three seamen. Having related this much, the narrator belatedly reveals that the master "had been more to blame upon this occasion than he had acknowledged," for the Indians had been welcoming enough until he ordered a cocoa tree chopped down and they deserted him in anger. Instead of backing down, the master fired a pistol; hence the ensuing melee. The gun had been a weapon of *offense,* fired intimidatingly to defy the Indians' wishes and claim the tree. On Wallis's Island, when an Indian snatched a sentinel's musket, the midshipman ordered the marines to fire into the crowd. They shot the thief dead, persuading the rest that no injury would be done to them if they behaved. The midshipman earned the name Matte, meaning "dead." The British saw their use of the gun as defensive, but the very presence of the gun in the first place was a provocation, especially once the people they encountered knew it to be a dispenser of death.

Its terrorizing function in opening up new lands to trade and occupation helped produce its polite image even while it enabled a new kind of casual exterminative violence abroad, just as it did at home. British settlement at Risdon, on the island of Tasmania, began in 1803. A year later, the Risdon massacre opened the first chapter of an exterminatory campaign against the island's population. The officer in charge claimed motives of self-defense, but the group of three hundred Aborigines he attacked on May 3 were merely chasing game. The real cause of violence was alcohol and his "desire for a few minutes' rifle practice with the added entertainment of a live and moving target"—in his words, "his wish 'to see the Niggers run.'" His colleague advised that the best way to open relations with the Aborigines was with "grapeshot and cannon." Aim was irrelevant. The massacre claimed at least fifty Aboriginal lives and launched a long history of antagonism between the indigenous population and the colonists in which the gun figured prominently. The contest was ultimately about seizure of property. And so was the larger project of settling the South Pacific colonies, including Tasmania, with convicts starting in the 1780s. Those convict colonies emerged out of the eighteenth-century anxiety about property. Petty thieves and other violators of property were turned *into* property, even while being cut off from society as transported convicts. The lands they were transported to were themselves seized from an indigenous population not invested in notions of private property. Ex-convict bushrangers shot Aborigines for sport—precisely when casual gun violence was also being discovered at home. Bushrangers, the lowest of the low in colonial society, clutched (often stolen) arms to hunt the meat that settlers depended on, but their leisure sport of shooting included human prey. One claimed he would "as leave shoot them [the Aborigines] as so many sparrows." Others fed their dogs on Aborigines shot specifically for that purpose. Despised though bushrangers were by the rest of colonial society, no one was ever tried for murdering an Aborigine.

C olonial settlers were produced by the tectonic social transformations of the eighteenth century: the consolidation of private property abetted by the gun produced new kinds of thieves and itinerant people, and many of them tried their luck abroad. There, the struggle for land also depended on the musket as a defense against unknown threats, scarcities, and barbarities. It was not unusual for a group aspiring to settlement abroad to approach the Ordnance Office for arms, as members of the Moravian Church heading to the coast of Labrador did in 1771. In North America, guns were the weapon and tool of the settler and the currency of trade among Europeans, colonists, and indigenous populations.

Consider the foundational story of Jamestown. In 1607, the Virginia Company sent out a party. It built a fortified base, immediately provoking clashes with the Powhatan Confederacy. Their instructions said nothing about negotiating with local inhabitants about land use; conflict was presumed. This was why they were told to trade for local grain *before* the local population understood their intention to stay. Here, too, promoting fear of firearms was the strategy. Colonists were instructed never to allow Native Americans to handle their muskets or see any but the best marksmen fire. But desperation forced departure from this strategy. As the colony dwindled, Powhatan corn prices and demands for gifts escalated. They had acquired hundreds of hatchets and many swords. Now they refused to trade corn for anything but muskets. The colonists tried approaching the confederacy's enemies, but this only halted all grain trade. John Smith had been a mercenary in Europe and against the Turks; now he led raids to extort corn from the Powhatan. In one raid, he held a loaded pistol to the head of the chief's brother, Opechancanough, until he was ransomed with boatloads of corn. He trained other colonists to fight in the woods, but hungry ones defected and taught the Powhatan how to use their stolen muskets. In 1609, an English fleet brought new muskets. The first Anglo-Powhatan war began. Heavy armor protected the English from the Powhatan bows during their killing expeditions. In 1613–14, the Powhatan returned seven colonial deserters and some broken muskets but refused to pay the corn ransom for the captive princess Pocahontas or give up their functional muskets. The tobacco planter John Rolfe married Pocahontas, and both sides claimed victory. As the new tobacco crop succeeded, the two communities began to interact in new ways. The new chief Opechancanough tolerated Christian instruction as the price of instruction in musket use. This well-known story captures the many ways in which guns mediated settler-Native relations in the American colonies: they were instruments of terror and discipline, currency, a civilizing art, weapons of war, and objects of trade.

A few years later, Myles Standish, the sole experienced soldier among the Pilgrims at Plymouth, stood outfitted like a soldier of the 1620s with a snaphance musket, sword, dagger, armor, and helmet. There were four other snaphances and some cheaper matchlocks among the party. Like the Jamestown settlers, the pilgrims stepped ashore at Cape Cod ready to "presume and provoke unfriendliness," primed muskets in hand. They stole the corn of local Nauset, who hid for three weeks before attacking. Their arrows were answered immediately with snaphances while the matchlocks were readied. No one was killed. Settlers typically used firearms to engage an enemy at a distance but, when within arm's reach, relied on edged weapons (swords and, later, bayonets), given the time required to load firearms. Firearms did not always decide the outcome, but they did dramatically shape interactions on the continent.

Colonial narratives traded in paranoia, in a vision of the New World as a place of infinite insecurity and danger where a gun could comfort, if not guarantee safety. A Quaker in Maryland struggled with fears of "our public enemy" during the Seven Years' War, while awaiting "fresh alarms" from the frontiers and enduring terrifying summer thunderstorms. Coupled with news of "dire calamities" befalling thousands abroad (including the Lisbon earthquake), she presumed that "the Great day of Accounts" was approaching. Guns were but an understandable—and lamentably skimpy—defense at the end of times. For colonials, they, and fortifications generally, were considered essential to security of person, food, and property. The presence of Native Americans was a context requiring constant vigilance and readiness, especially because they had many guns, too.

In 1609, while the affair at Jamestown unfolded, Henry Hudson sailed up the river that now bears his name to begin the fur trade that eventually brought guns to Native Americans throughout the region—despite the early effort to keep them ignorant of firearms. Dutch and English competition shaped the arms trade in North America, as it did in Africa. The promise of profit overcame scruples about protecting the military superiority of colonists. After several attempts at prohibiting the trade, even on pain of death, by 1650 the Dutch government had grown resigned that it had reached a level at which forbidding it was the riskier proposition, since the Native peoples would fight to continue it. The government tried instead to limit Dutch settlers to matchlocks, to keep more sophisticated weapons out of Native hands. Once the British turned New Amsterdam into New York, in 1664, they pushed the trade on to secure the support of the Seneca against the French. Arming Native Americans served commercial and diplomatic ends. The St. Lawrence–Great Lakes network offered a waterway to the heart of the continent, fortified by peace with the Five Nations. French missionaries and traders competed with Hudson's Bay Company traders for beaver pelts from the Cree. Firearms became

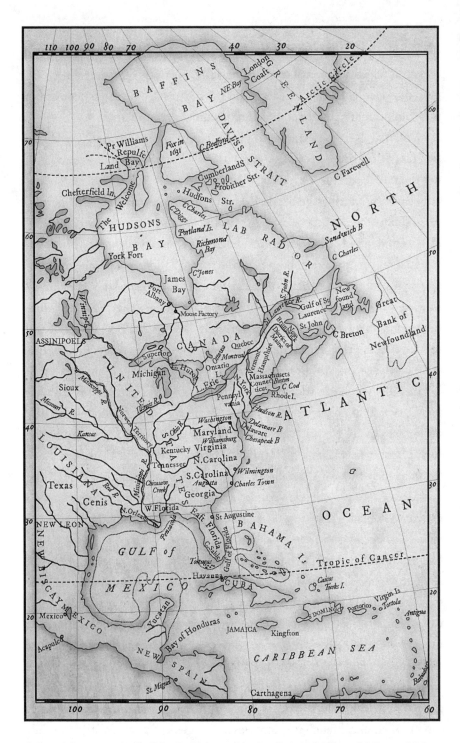

Map of the eastern half of North America, based on Jedidiah Morse, "A General Map of North America from the best Authorities," 1796 (engraved by Amos Doolittle).

central to the contest. From 1670 to 1689, the company traded 10,100 flintlock fusils to the Cree. The French and English also supplied the Ojibwa, who strove to deprive the Fox and the Sioux, from the upper Great Lakes, of access to firearms. The Sioux got arms from other Native brokers. The powerful Illinois Confederation migrated east, seeking furs and French weapons in the Ohio Valley. In the 1670s, King Philip's War, in New England, was fought with flintlocks on all sides. From 1685, Carolina traders traveled to the Upper Creek center of Coweta, launching into fifteen years of trading monopoly that armed the Creek with muskets bought with deerskins, horses, and slaves. The Spanish withdrew after futile military efforts to stop the trade. Their allies the Apalachee demanded payment from the Creek in English guns; war broke out in 1701, forming part of the War of the Spanish Succession. In the 1720s, Carolina traders distributed flintlocks so thoroughly to Spanish and Native American customers that they destroyed their own earlier military advantage.

From 1713 to 1730, the Hudson's Bay trade was a seller's market. Inland, Native Americans traded furs for light goods and luxuries from the French and then exchanged whatever was left at the bay for English guns, shot, cloth, ironwork, and heavier blankets. Guns also purchased tobacco. In the early years of the York Factory, on the bay's southwestern shore, firearms and accoutrements were the main items traded with Native populations. Furs were often brought to the trading posts by intermediaries who purchased them inland with ironware (old axes, knives), guns, and ammunition obtained at the bay. Guns were thus an internal and coastal medium of exchange. Native American purchases remained roughly constant through the 1770s, despite increases in fur prices. In 1805, when Lewis and Clark were at the mouth of the Columbia River, they encountered Native people who knew the English words *musket, powder, shot, knife, file, damned rascal,* and *son of a bitch.* The Ordnance Office contractor Richard Wilson, in London, was a major supplier of the Hudson's Bay Company and Charleston buyers. Trustees of Georgia bought his Indian trading guns. His rival Thomas Williams also sent trading guns to Charleston.

The line between commerce and diplomacy was blurry, since provision of firearms and repair service helped colonial officials gain and retain the allegiance of Native Americans. Each trading post had an armorer to maintain guns. Guns forged long-term ties between traders and Native peoples. By their very nature, they required constant repair and supply of ammunition and flints. Commercial expansion also almost always entailed military conflict, and trade guns doubled for both purposes. Hudson's Bay Company officials and traders and their arsenals, like Native Americans, were presumed to be part of every military struggle. At the outbreak of conflict, the company committee instructed its chief factors to set their cannon and keep their small arms in good order and at hand. They were also told to keep enough trading guns close, in case of attack and to employ trustworthy Native Americans in the task.

Many guns were gifted outright as part of New World military diplomacy (as elsewhere). The Dutch armed the Mohawk to fight French allies in the 1640s. The English again armed them in King Philip's War. In 1754, the British Board of Trade created a unified Indian Department to deal with frontier diplomacy, with superintendents in charge of the northern and southern districts. This imperial structure existed alongside commercial structures. The department bought guns to give as gifts to Native peoples starting in 1756, as war began: £4,000 worth of gifts, including 700 "Indian guns" made by Richard Wilson, brought with Lord Loudon, the newly appointed commander in chief, who arrived in New York City in June. Colonies also bought guns from London agents to use as gifts. In 1755, under an older agreement with the Board of Trade, Georgia's colonial agent submitted a list of "Indian presents" to be sent that spring, including 150 of Wilson's guns and 40 fowling pieces. The Indian Department's presents for the southern district in 1757 included 800 Wilson guns and 50 pairs of pistols. South Carolina's colonial agent purchased 800 trading guns from Wilson in 1758. Over the course of the war, nearly nineteen thousand trading guns were sent, mostly by Wilson. In 1764, another firm sent 200 trading guns to Charleston, for the superintendent of the southern district, and 300 more for Pensacola, plus some finer arms. The next year, hoping to economize, the superintendent requested trading guns only, but expensive guns continued to trickle in. Rifles were also popular. When officials discontinued gifts in the northwest after the war, Chief Pontiac of Ottawa created a confederation to oust the British. The British sent an expedition and ultimately won Pontiac's War, but they lost the war against arms proliferation: unregulated British traders entered the newly secured Illinois area to sell guns. Northern areas supplied by the Hudson's Bay Company also saw competition from independent traders.

During the American War of Independence, English guns flowed more purposefully toward Native Americans. Arms—including military muskets—were sent by packtrain to secure alliances with the Cherokee, who had long bought guns from Virginia trading centers. The Choctaw, Creek, Chickasaw, and others obtained guns from river routes. Wilson supplied rifles for this trade. The governor of East Florida requested a hundred trading guns in 1776. In 1777, £2,000 worth of presents went to the southern district. The next year, the southern superintendent asked for 1,000 guns for the Choctaw congress at Pensacola and another 1,200 for others. Wilson sent to West Florida fifty-three chests containing 1,325 guns. In 1780, the government sent 2,400 guns there. Wilson's invoice for 1781 was his largest and most diverse of the war: 4,000 Indian fusils, 100 fowling pieces, 45 fine fowling pieces, 156 rifles, 108 other rifle guns, and many pairs of pistols, valued at £5,700. Government accounts list nearly 44,000 Indian guns supplied during the war, plus 1,700 rifles and 1,600 pistols, all from Wilson.

Britain lost this time, but English guns continued to sell. As old alliance structures fell apart, British trade shifted to the margins— Quebec, St. Augustine, Pensacola—where goods could be sent to government representatives and loyal merchants directly from London or via New York. The northern and southern superintendents distributed them. Wilson remained a major supplier through at least the 1790s, as did private merchants now accountable to the imperial licensing structure. New players were also evident. Many guns entered the United States through Canada. John Jay's Treaty of 1794 gave Canadians rights to enter the United States to trade with former British allies, including the right to carry furs back to Canada tax-free. Their goods included English guns, at times even East India Company guns, despite American protests. This was one of the provocations for the War of 1812. The last British gifts of guns to Native Americans in the United States came at the end of that war, in 1815, although English traders in the southeast quietly continued selling guns for years afterward. English traders also sold guns in the northwest through 1846, in accordance with the joint occupation agreement of 1818.

Until the 1770s, Native Americans bought and used the same cheap, light fowling pieces ("birding guns") used by settlers and traders. They refused obsolete guns even as gifts. They pressured the Hudson's Bay Company to supply particular types. At the start of the century, Woodland Native Americans persuaded the company to import three-and-a-half-foot guns, over the older four-foot ones at Fort Albany, for easier handling in hunting. In the 1740s, they, like African buyers, grumbled about poor quality. The company ordered manufacturers to repair defective guns shipped back, while also pointing to the harsh climate and suggesting that Native Americans did not use guns properly. Anticipating the African scandal, the company's detractors alleged that North America was a dumping ground for shoddy guns sold for extravagant profits. Rumors abounded that traders stacked beaver skins to the height of the gun to conclude a price. These allegations circulating in pamphlets triggered a parliamentary inquiry in 1749. Enoch Alsop, the armorer at Moose, explained that the muskets "frequently burst, not from the Fault of the Gun, but by overcharging, or from Snow getting into the Muzzle." Of the numerous guns sent home in 1751, the company deemed only four actually unfit. But decades later, English traders feared death at the hands of Native Americans seeking vengeance for compatriots "killed by the bursting of a gun . . . sold to them," as one officer sympathetically related. This account appeared in 1789, when the dumping of bad guns in Africa was becoming part of the abolitionist case. But by the end of the century, English arms were the most favored by Native Americans, known for their lightness, compactness, and locks that did not freeze.

In the meantime, the Hudson's Bay Company's defense of its goods shaped British notions about guns' civilizing uses in North America. In 1726, to ensure continuance of its government charter, the company argued that its failure would amount to a travesty of the civilizing mission:

"Many thousand Families of the Natives for want of the supply they Annually receive from us, of Guns, Powder, and Shott, wherewith they kill the Beavor, Buffalo and several other Beasts of that Country, the Flesh whereof is their food, will by the disappointment of the not arrival of the said ships, be starved before the next Year." Within a generation of contact with the fur trader, the company claimed, the Native American had become dependent on European firearms. Much later, in 1809, the company again justified its petition for government funds by pointing to the hundreds of European families and thousands of Native Americans depending on its presence, even though continual war had stymied trade and exhausted its resources. These "nations of hunters" had for a century and a half been so dependent on firearms that they could not revert to the use of the bow or javelin for subsistence. Even the British-made hatchet was indispensable; they could hardly be expected to resort to stone for building and other purposes. They would starve, and their race would be destroyed. The company asserted its moral obligation to continue to offer the religious advantages, civilizing influence, and education it diffused among Native peoples. The petition failed, and the company found new policies that enabled its survival, but the question remains whether this commercially motivated image of gun use among Native Americans was true.

Guns did replace the bow and arrow and the spear for some purposes, such as hunting small game and waterfowl. Shorter guns (three and a half feet) were ideal for hunting geese and for heavily forested areas where animals could be shot at short range. In more open areas and in warfare, the four-foot gun was preferred. But, as in Africa and England, change was only partial: traditional weapons remained more effective for large game. A simplistic version of the fur-gun cycle is as problematic as the overly simple gun–slave cycle: guns were not used to hunt animals with valuable pelts. Moreover, Native Americans had other sources besides the British for firearms.

Gun use in Native American warfare was also complex. Guns provided a kind of symbolic power, particularly for men. Like West Africans and the English, indigenous Americans attributed supernatural powers to guns: their bulk and deadly aura imparted confidence in the wielder, and their noise and uncertainty inspired terror in the potential victim. Knowledge of their wounding power redoubled that terror, for they created wounds that could not be stitched up neatly like blade or arrow wounds. Native Americans valued them for both their psychological impact *and* the wounds they produced. They often used them against opponents who did not have them to take advantage of that psychological impact; the point was to make the opponents flee. When both sides had guns, reliable arrows were a common recourse. Native Americans might lure a European enemy into firing an initial volley and then attack with arrows while the Europeans reloaded. Alternatively, they used surprise so that Europeans did not have time to ready their guns. When they intended fire to be deadly, they used muskets differently. In New England, Native Americans' distinct tactical uses included emphasis on accuracy and undetectability, which led them to seek flintlocks well before they were in general use in Europe. Because they did not always distinguish between hunting and warfare, they trained to achieve accurate marksmanship in both and became more skilled marksmen than their European opponents—though, to be sure, most accounts of Native American marksmanship are culled from colonial sources with a stake in portraying indigenous peoples as dangerous foes.

Native Americans may not have become entirely dependent on guns, but the company was right that guns had come to shape their tactical thinking and commercial reality, and Native societies were heavily armed. Parts of useless guns were used to repair other firearms, but butt plates, side plates, heel caps, and trigger guards were also transformed into hide scrapers, knives, awls, and personal ornaments. In one instance, a Native American left behind on the Juan Fernández Islands by Captain Watling in 1681 survived for three years with a knife, a gun, a horn of powder, and a little shot—a real Crusoe. When his ammunition ran out, he turned his knife into a saw and used it to divide the gun barrel into small pieces. Kindling a fire with his flint, he turned the pieces into a lance, fishhooks, and harpoons. He had learned to do all this from an English smith, he later explained. Guns had multiple uses and meanings in North America, as elsewhere.

England's gunmakers also sold guns in enormous quantities to European colonists and traders in America. The Virginia Company and the Massachusetts Bay Company shipped arms to settlers from the seventeenth century. Wilson sold to settlers and colonial governments. In 1737 and 1741, he billed the Georgia Commons House of Assembly for muskets. In 1744–45, South Carolina ordered hundreds for its militia. Charleston merchants also dealt with him. To arm provincial soldiers, the Massachusetts government bought 500 Tower mark arms from England and impressed good, privately owned arms, compensating owners. It bought 2,500 English military muskets in 1754. Galton also supplied firearms to the colonies as war began. Wilson's wartime sales included more than 40,000 muskets that were *not* Indian trading guns. Colonial imports of his arms were high in the South, especially after the war, even as militias decayed between 1764 and 1775. His son William took over the business in 1766; they emerged as the most important single supplier of Indian and military-style guns in British North America from the 1740s to 1783. The Ketlands later overtook them.

Gun ownership was widespread in colonial society, about half of all households owning at least one working gun (with some exceptions like Maine and areas with high Quaker populations). The average colonist was probably more familiar with firearms and better at using them than his European counterpart. Still, colonial governments made panicked purchases of military-caliber guns at the start of war (1739, 1754), because most privately owned arms were lighter and smaller, intended for pest control, hunting, and self-defense. Widespread ownership did not mean that *militias* were properly armed. Many privately held arms were also simply in bad condition, and some militiamen were too poor to buy them. Wealthy South Carolina had particularly high ownership rates, to confront Spanish and Native foes and police its enslaved population; it was the only colony with a credible militia in 1755. (Most of its militiamen policed slaves during the war.) Many in the colonies had never seen a large-caliber military firearm like the Brown Bess in the 1750s. Publicly owned arms were stored, not distributed, until militiamen were called to active service, as in Britain. The enhanced sense of security after 1763 made militias seem less urgent, and some public arms became private again. But by the third quarter of the century, colonial governments wanted to arm militias properly with military-style muskets. During the Revolutionary War, rebelling colonies grew desperate for such arms. Most private arms moved into public stores. (Loyalists were disarmed.) The regulation British Army musket provided the pattern for guns made by Committees of Safety in rebelling colonies. Seizures of local arsenals also kept plenty of British arms in American hands, although rebels also used French muskets. By the end of the war, many military muskets were lost to decay or waste. There were fewer guns in private hands than earlier. Recession made it harder to buy new arms, and independence made defensive arming seem less urgent. British military guns continued to come in, along with trade guns; in 1794, the United States purchased thousands. In 1823, the U.S. Army Ordnance Department still had nearly three thousand British-pattern muskets.

As in England, American newspapers recount numerous fatal accidents in the course of repairing, cleaning, and testing guns or while hunting, practicing, or playing with guns. There, too, the gun figured prominently in property conflicts. On the eve of the Boston Tea Party, in 1773, disregarding warnings, Richard Clarke determined to receive the controversial tea consignment. A mob came whistling, shouting, and beating at his door, and one of the Clarke men shot into the crowd, fearing a break-in. Guns were also important in everyday activities like fowling and vermin control. The American long rifle evolved specifically for hunting. (It was slow to reload and lacked a bayonet, limiting its usefulness in battle.) Homicide rates were at times correlated with high levels of gun violence, but not always; it was a complex relationship shaped by politics, culture, the law, and other factors. Some uses were particular to the frontier context. Exploring parties always carried guns; venturing into unknown terrain without them was unthinkable. They might be displayed prominently to ward off rival intruders (the French) or fired at night as exhausted adventurers drank to one another's health. They might attract friendly attention when a party needed help. The return of long-lost exploring parties might be announced with a general discharge of firearms expressing recognition, relief, welcome, and triumph. Guns' inaccuracy and unreliability meant that frontiersmen also subscribed to superstitious beliefs about them as tools for survival, leaving a rich linguistic heritage. Pistols were the personal sidearm of the fur trader and the trapper. Fur traders later kept up steady orders for the lightest, cheapest hunting muskets. These "Northwest Guns" flowed into Montreal—the earliest known reference to one dates from 1777, made by William Grice. Most were made in Birmingham until 1800, when London firms became active. The North West Company, formed in Montreal in 1779 to compete against the Hudson's Bay Company in the fur trade, bought them. Certainly from the 1770s, firearms also acquired political symbolism vis-à-vis the British Crown. Here was the rebellious armed population the British state had long feared. The Coercive Acts of 1774, following the Boston Tea Party, made the ideal of the citizen-soldier important to American republicanism—although militias had trouble getting military muskets, not least because, in 1775, imperial authorities seized public and royal arms in New York City.

With both Native Americans and colonials heavily armed, guns shaped their interactions. Here again, Europeans understood their own guns as defensive arms. James Adair, an "English Chikkasaw," deduced a Choctaw's "base intentions" from the way he snatched up a gun each time Adair neared, for "no friendly Indians were ever known to do the like," and "innocence is not suspicious." He dismissed the notion that the man's conduct resulted from fear. This was a land in which an explorer might stumble upon the dreadful scene of thirty bodies found slain and scalped by knives and arrows. In 1754, Peter Williamson, a plantation owner in Pennsylvania who had come to America from Scotland as a slave, took up his gun before a throng of Native Americans threatening his home: "How vain and fruitless are the efforts of one man against the united force of so many bloodthirsty monsters!" They threatened to burn him alive if he refused to come out. When he emerged, they disarmed him and tied him to a tree, proceeding to rob and burn his house. They next threatened him with a tomahawk, which, Williamson explained to his readers, was a kind of hatchet Native Americans used *after* firing their guns to cleave the skull. He agreed to accompany them, and they again tied him to a tree and then forced the blood out of the ends of his fingers before building a fire and dancing around him. Such narratives offered a pornography of real or invented Native violence that attracted readers while allowing them to feel properly repelled.

Adair offered similar shiver-inducing accounts of Native punishment. One night, as the Chickasaw accompanied their French prisoners, he went out with his gun to sweep the area for Choctaw while his allies prepared for battle. Suddenly, a Chickasaw companion rode out into the ambuscade and was shot below the heart. This was but the merciful opening to the real torments that Adair witnessed next: the "barbarians" struck a tomahawk into his head, "just between his eyes, and jerked off a piece of scalp." Adair let out a war whoop, summoning his companions, who faced fire as they chased the enemy, until at last they buried their friend. Others told of Native drumheads made of human skins. In colonial depictions, Native Americans used guns as wanton prologue to crueler violence. They were often portrayed as the amoral henchmen of French evil, viciously skilled in all forms of murder. When a famed Native marksman was captured, Adair described, with chilling irony, the great "civility" with which he was treated: women and children beat and whipped him, and he was condemned to die. In the world Adair conjured, where "civility" merely meant no punishment worse than whipping, carrying a gun was only polite. In trader settlements, "beds are always hung round with various arms of defence." Guns were but feeble defense against people who could, with the skilled toss of a tomahawk, instantly slice off the fingers desperately seeking a trigger. In instances in which a *European* resorted to more intimate violence, as with a knife, narratives emphasized desperate circumstances and the perpetrators' civilized temperament: after burying a knife in a Native person's bowels, the settler returns, removes the knife, and dresses the wound.

In reality, the cycle of violence was a spiral of brutality launched by the armed European effort to turn North America into private property. In regions like the Pacific Northwest, Native peoples and traders consumed with mistrust expected the worst from one another, visiting their earlier rough treatment on the next comer. Stories of Native American massacres led to American reprisals against other Native Americans, and so on. White-on-white violence was savage, too, the gun similarly functioning there as the introduction to crueler punishments. Conflict between the Hudson's Bay Company and the North West Company was particularly ugly. North West Company men broke into a Hudson's Bay Company warehouse near Lake Winnipeg in 1806, knocking down the guard and striking the trader staffing the building with the butt of a gun until he fell to the ground bleeding. Then the group leader stabbed a trader in the arm. The intruders stole liberally from the warehouse—flour, pork, a canoe, and other goods. Hudson's Bay Company men saw the resort to daggers and clubbing as evidence of the brutishness of their Canadian rivals.

In war, colonists borrowed from Native American tactics. They knew that the purpose of Native American gunfire was often psychological. An explorer from Winnipeg noted that, seeking to frighten more than kill, the Native enemy approached, mounted and in full war paint, in line of battle, but launched a desultory fire. It was equally clear when fire was intended to be deadly. For colonials, too, guns' psychological impact was important—the confidence they bestowed, their terrifying sound. The theory was that guns were best for facing unknown threats in unknown terrain from behind entrenched positions, given the time required for re-loading; hence the fortifications that invariably accompanied Europeans abroad. But Native Americans rarely attacked fortified sites. In forests and situations of ambush, contests between settlers and Native Americans took the form of close combat in which pistols were more useful than muskets (although reloading still took minutes). Parade-ground tactics were no help against an enemy hidden in thickly wooded, mountainous country, as was immediately evident after the British defeat at Mononga-hela in 1755. Carbines became particularly important for a mobile infan-try. British soldiers (including many American recruits) fighting the French and Native Americans in forests had to move quickly and relied heavily on cavalry carrying muskets and pistols. Rifles were well suited to such warfare, permitting a measure of accuracy. Guns were adapted to the new conditions by Tower gunsmiths working overtime by candlelight. A new short musket was introduced, as we have seen. Light infantry units were introduced, and by the summer of 1758 all regiments were trained to deal with ambushes, and rifles were provided to the ten best marksmen in each battalion. In the Revolutionary War, British soldiers were in the line of fire of rifle-wielding American woodsmen and requested their own. Grice fashioned a rifle barrel for the Ordnance Office, promising two hundred. He, Barker, Willets, and Galton supplied a thousand rifles based on a Hanover pattern. The Ordnance Office inspector in Birmingham ensured that rifle barrel production proceeded "with the utmost expedition." Others arrived to proof them under the direction of the rifle designer Captain Patrick Ferguson, whose design was adopted by his experimental rifle corps. But many British officers continued to set store by regular troops, since riflemen lacked bayonets, which still carried the day on the battlefield.

American merchants also used British guns as currency in their own oceanic trading networks, exchanging them in Sulu and Polynesia for furs, sandalwood, and bird's nests (to sell in China). The British governor in Java, Stamford Raffles, complained in 1811 about unscrupulous Americans selling firearms all over the Pacific, as far as Manila and Fiji, for exorbitant profits. There, unlike in North America, the British saw the spread of guns as a political menace. Especially after the loss of the American colonies, British authorities grew concerned about the global spread of firearms they had so enthusiastically enabled until then. The American war showed that in rebels' hands, guns could prove fatal to the empire. Guns' rich social life in America had long obscured that potential danger, disguising them as many things besides potential threats to the state. The British commander General Amherst had briefly abandoned gifts to Native Americans during the Seven Years' War, but that was an exception motivated by his belief that their obedience ought simply to be commanded as that of a conquered subject population. Belated British attempts to seize arms stores outside Boston on the eve of the Revolutionary

War were disastrous, ending in the portentous defeats at Lexington and Concord. Elsewhere, where gun use perhaps appeared more singular and the population less obviously reliable, the British tried more consistently to limit the availability of arms, even at the cost of diplomatic and commercial advantages. Thus Jamaica's Maroons showed early in the century that the spread of arms on the island risked British control of it: several thousand Maroons fought long against British suppression, with firearms either stolen or purchased on the "black market," perhaps through Spanish agents. Colonial authorities came to terms with them militarily only in 1739, guaranteeing their freedom and surrendering tenure to 1,500 acres and the right to engage in trade, in return for which the Maroons promised to return runaways and help defend the island. Such experiences ensured that the Ordnance Office later readily agreed to the expense of maintaining one white man and two "trusty negroes" as watchmen at Antigua's arms storehouse, to raise the alarm "should the natives attempt to rise and seize" them. In 1795, a report emerged that a Birmingham major had been assailed in the West Indies by "three negroes, armed with muskets and bayonets." The Birmingham paper's account put the major's consequent violence in a thoroughly defensive frame: "Though he had only his sword and a brace of pistols, he refused to surrender, but defended himself with such bravery, as to kill two of his antagonists, and to oblige the third to save himself by flight." The possibility of American collusion in rebellion by other armed colonial societies was intense in this moment of global war. The next year, capture of the *Olive Branch*, carrying twenty thousand French arms purchased by a Vermont businessman for the Vermont militia, unleashed fervent suspicion that they were destined for Ireland or Canada as part of an American-French conspiracy.

In the South Asian colonial arena, British concern about gun distribution was in continual tension with the East India Company's commercial objectives in the subcontinent. The company also had an army made up of Indians and officered by Britons, which enabled its territorial expansion and was the primary source of its constantly growing demand for

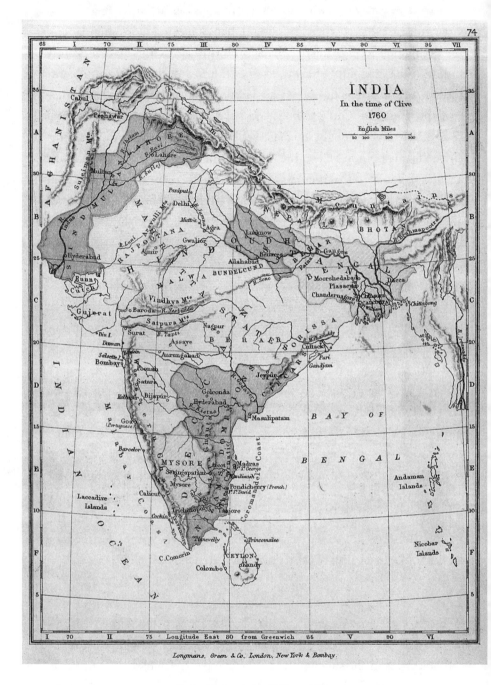

India in the time of Clive, 1760.

guns from England. But the priority of ensuring that company soldiers and allies alone had English arms conflicted constantly with the goal of edging out commercial rivals like the French and *making* allies among local rulers in a complex political environment. That tension shaped the spread of arms in the subcontinent.

Guns were part of Indian Ocean trade even before the company's arrival in the region. The Ottoman government manufactured muskets equal in quality to the best in Europe and helped diffuse small-arms technology in the region from the sixteenth century. The Ottomans traded guns (also many of European origin) and other military equipment for spices in Aceh and elsewhere, a trade that enabled them at once to prop up key allies (Turkestan, Crimea, Gujarat, Aceh, Ethiopia) against the Safavids and Mamluks, who adopted European handgun technology. Babur, the first Mughal emperor in South Asia, brought Turkish matchlocks in 1526, which in turn were adopted by Mughal adversaries, the Rajputs and the Afghans. The subcontinent's exchanges with the Portuguese (for instance, through the Vijayanagara Empire of the Deccan Plateau) and Mamluk Egypt also established the technology in the region. Later in the sixteenth century, the Mughal emperor Akbar was keenly interested in matchlock manufacture and drew several master gunmakers to his court, among whom Ottoman influence was great. By the next century, the Mughals had established state foundries and arsenals. Other kingdoms, from Malabar to Bihar, also cultivated arms manufacture, as did Burma and Aceh. Indian craftsmen also copied European firearms from at least the seventeenth century as intensifying European involvement in local political conflicts heightened demand for arms.

The Mughals used guns to control local nobles and king's officers. Musketeers also helped control peasants of disturbed tracts and enforced payment of land tax more cheaply than cavalry troops. But the technology spread beyond the state. Peasants of the Gangetic plains used cheap handguns made by local blacksmiths to defy revenue collection. The late-seventeenth-century Mughal emperor Aurangzeb forbade blacksmiths from making guns. Rebellious landowners (zamindars) also turned Mughal musketeering corps into their retainers. These dynamics emerged on the margins of Mughal power, in Orissa and the Deccan, and in the Mughal heartland of Agra and Delhi. Here, too, guns worked through their symbolic power as much as their violence. If the Mughals used them to overawe their opponents and draw them into their fiscal-military ambit, nobles defiantly retained their own corps of musketeers as a status symbol. The center responded by creating mounted musketeer corps (probably recruiting from Ottoman lands, where they brought the flintlocks suited to firing on horseback). In Mughal combat, precision and range were *more* important than rate of fire, in contrast to European tactics. Europeans commented on Indians' superior marksmanship with local matchlocks, which were used by individuals rather than in drill formation. Guns also had ceremonial purposes: they were fired to mark the birth of a son; scare off evil spirits; announce the start of Ramadan, an important arrival, or a victory; and so on. Their uses multiplied as interactions with Europeans intensified.

The East India Company bought English arms to trade and present as gifts—often with a view to obtaining trading privileges. In 1615, Sir Thomas Roe, the first British ambassador to the Mughal court, presented a prince with a Liège firelock to secure trading options for the company; in 1618, the ruler of Jakarta accepted two culverins and money in exchange for trading privileges; in 1647, the East India Company's Madras Council gave Mir Jumlah, general to the king of Golconda, a brass gun valued at 641 pagodas instead of paying the 2,350 it owed as interest on a loan of 10,000 pagodas. In 1663, the king of Bantam sent King Charles II a gift of ginger and pepper, which Charles sold through the company, using the proceeds to pay seven London gunmakers for a hundred muskets for the king of Bantam. Trading guns helped elbow out competition. In 1671, the company's Madras officials tried to break the Dutch monopoly in Ceylon by offering the king English arms "to resist his enemies in return for his cinnamon and other commodities." In the mid-eighteenth century, the Dutch sent arms from Batavia to Mir Jafar, the British-backed nawab of Bengal, to take advantage of his conflict with his British master, Robert Clive, and improve their own trading prospects; Clive destroyed the shipment. Lacking sufficient manpower and military resources, the French and the British used arms exports as a proxy to challenge one another in the region. State-sponsored arms exports and cash subsidies were a major component of military diplomacy in Europe; similarly, French and English trading companies supplied massive arms shipments to South Asian allies.

Guns were a profitable trade commodity. By the 1690s, the East India Company exported nearly a thousand tons of small arms per year for profit, including military-grade weapons. "Hardly a ship came" in the 1760s "that did not sell them cannon and small arms," a colonel testified in Parliament. In 1815, the Board of Customs reported an annual export of 151,572 guns to South Asia, the Indonesian archipelago, and China worth £103,463.

Meanwhile, the company also purchased English guns for its "defense" (or aggression). Muskets were ordered for Bombay, Calcutta, and Madras in the 1660s–'80s. They were provided to Indian peons and soldiers in the company's Madras garrison. The company's Court of Directors shipped out light muskets especially, ordering native peons and other trusted inhabitants to be armed and trained in their use to provide balance "against the Sumatrians, Madagascar Blacks or Mutinous drunken English, if we should have the misfortune to entertain any such, as we have formerly been troubled w[i]th." In moments of crisis, native militia were given arms from the English fort to defend the "Black Town" that grew up around the Madras fort. In the late seventeenth century, they kept these arms at home as long as the threat existed. English officials organized groups of hundreds of peons into regular companies, armed and drilled in European fashion. European rivalries turned the subcontinent's cosmopolitan port cities into armed battle zones.

From these footholds, the company provided arms to Indians incorporated into its growing formal military ranks. The Court of Directors initiated formation of the first cavalry troop at Madras in 1684–85: "If you could perswade all ye rich men in Fort St George to ye number of 100 English, Jews, Portuguez, & Gentues, to keep each of them a Horse & Arms at their own charge . . . it might be a brave addiconal strength upon any sudden occasion, And you may appoint a Captain & Officers to

exercise that Troop once in 2 or 3 Mo[nth]s as a Militia or Citty Troop."
They were most likely armed from the company's stores. In 1692, a shipment of cavalry arms arrived for these stores. The volunteer cavalry troop
lasted a few decades. As the eighteenth century began, shipments of cavalry guns continued, some for sale and some for the company's forces. In
western India in the 1670s, small armed and mounted parties of Englishmen were employed—without pay—to escort gold sent from Bombay to
Surat, and in other such tasks.

The company defeated Mughal forces at the Battle of Buxar in 1764,
gaining secure control of its first major territorial stake in the subcontinent, from Awadh to Bengal. The line between volunteer or civilian soldier and professional soldier now became more defined. The company
began to radically expand and professionalize its troops, which required
massive gun shipments. In 1765, the Select Committee at Calcutta asked
London headquarters for ten thousand stand of arms plus four thousand
more each subsequent year, to be supplied by the same manufacturers who
supplied the home government. British Army units often stayed in India
for decades at a time and also had to replace their Ordnance-issued arms
with company arms. The company hired the Ordnance Office's inspector
to inspect their firearms on a freelance basis. In 1771, it hired its own
salaried inspector.

The company's bureaucracy for managing arms expanded, establishing arsenals in Calcutta and Madras. In 1775, the Bengal Army's enormous expenditure on military stores prompted creation of a new Board of
Ordnance to manage that activity. Bombay, too, formed a Board of Ordnance (1779) and built an arsenal in 1794. In 1785, the company's Court
of Directors ordered each of these three main trading settlements, known
as "presidencies," to create a Military Board composed of senior officers to
scrutinize expenditures. Depots were scattered across the region well into
the nineteenth century. As in Britain, theft plagued these stores.

Company gun orders for more informal military organizations and
allies also took off. A short-lived European militia formed at Calcutta in
1770 received a thousand stand of arms to store in their homes. Similar
groups, both European and native, were frequently formed and disbanded

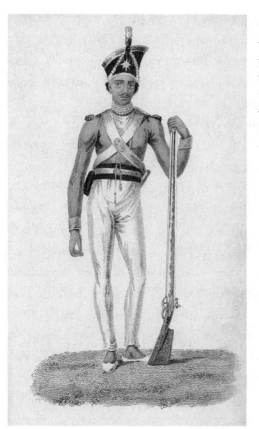

Sepoy, sipahee, or native Indian soldier. Handcolored copperplate engraving by an unknown artist, from Asiatic Costumes, *(London: Ackermann, 1828).*

in the late eighteenth century. British arms were provided to European cavalries *and* cavalries belonging to the nawab of Arcot during the sieges of Tanjore in 1771 and 1773. They were part of the diplomacy that expanded British power—as in North America. British allies required enormous supplies as successor states to the Mughals began to adopt European tactics and drill. With European arms and officers, the nawab of Arcot's men served two masters. During the Second Anglo-Mysore War of 1780–84, four regiments were temporarily taken into company service to ensure their regular pay and forestall mutiny. Company arms and drill techniques acquired ever more cachet among Indian powers with each British success, making arms an ever more effective medium of diplomatic exchange for the British. The company's commitment to European tactics was continually validated, even though conflicts were often drawn out, and contingent political factors ultimately enabled success. The Marathas struggled to get even condemned company arms in the 1790s, despite having their own manufacturing capacity. This provides a measure of Maratha esteem for British muskets and proof that possession of guns was about confidence as much as firepower.

Indian powers leveraged loyalty and trade access to obtain arms. In 1763, Hyder Ali of Mysore bought 500 muskets from the British government at Bombay. The resulting profits then secured exclusive access to pepper produced in his area. Soon after, Hyder Ali purchased 400 stand of arms and other military assistance, agreeing to continue the pepper trade and ward off the Marathas. By 1765, the Bombay government was regretting these exchanges. The First Anglo-Mysore War lasted from 1767 to 1769, ending in a defensive military treaty between the British and Hyder Ali. Thus, Bombay again provided him guns in 1771. The Court of Directors repeatedly warned local officials of the danger these sales courted, but Bombay munificently supplied 6,000 more in 1777, promising 3,000 more annually. Hyder Ali was then recovering Coorg and Malabar from the Marathas and buying guns from the French and the Spanish, too. In 1778, he sent Bombay 357 candies of pepper for 2,092 muskets. The following year, he again received muskets for pepper and cardamom. From the British perspective, selling guns to Hyder Ali brought both profit and his goodwill as he brought down their common enemies.

Company arsenals also sold guns for private purchase. In Calcutta, ships' captains and merchants who needed to arm peons guarding their warehouses and convoys bought them. Officers heading up-country bought them to arm their servants. Thus, in 1723, fourteen carbines were sold to Harry Moore, Mr. Eyre, Jethre, Santose, and Gopechund. Three years later, 431 were sold in a similar manner, Indian buyers outnumbering Europeans. Local officials granted such indulgences to encourage commerce. Auctions of old guns were also common, although many were shipped to London as ballast from as early as 1615. Sales dwindled in the nineteenth century as company settlements expanded and independent shopkeepers catered to expatriates' everyday needs.

The company was concerned about the spread of arms but could not keep them out of enemy hands. It refused Mir Jafar's demands for guns in 1763, but his officers at Monghyr then stopped five hundred arms en route to Patna. When the British ambassador at Mir Jafar's court pressed for their release, the nawab tried to extort political concessions. When that failed, war began. In 1765, the Madras government urged steps to prevent arms from "falling into Hands who may turn them against Us," especially since "Continual Military Operations . . . have diffused the European discipline in a very great degree among the Natives." Precaution had to be taken to ensure that arms supplied to the trusted nawab of Arcot would not reach "improper hands." While ordering thousands of arms for company troops in the 1760s, Calcutta urged London to stop ship captains from engaging in illegal private gun sales to Indians. This plea faltered on the logic that doing so would merely push buyers to obtain guns from rival European powers, forfeiting both British profit and influence. Indian demands for English guns were increasing partly because the British were actively quashing indigenous gunmaking.

The company manufactured a range of military goods in its arsenals but not small arms, out of fear of stimulating industry and rebellion but also because of profitable relationships between London gunmakers and military storekeepers in India (drawn from that world) and English guns' uses as a diplomatic and commercial currency. The company did purchase some swords and perhaps guns from existing South Asian small-arms industries. More important, indigenous gun manufacture revived out of an attempt to *arrest* British expansion. In the early 1760s, Mir Qasim (who replaced Mir Jafar, with British support, from 1760 to 1763) began to manufacture firelocks at the fort at Monghyr, where guns had been manufactured by Raja Todar Mal in the late sixteenth century. The manufacturing continued after his defeat at Buxar, as Clive turned the fort into a company arms depot. Its guns were said to be better than the best Tower-proof muskets, especially in the barrel metal and flints made of agates from the Rajmahal Hills. As French fortunes declined after the Seven Years' War, indigenous manufactories absorbed scattering French expertise. European mercenaries started manufactories for princely employers in Agra and elsewhere. State arsenals and magazines across the former Mughal heartland (Agra, Delhi, Gwalior) produced munitions of the same standard as Europe's. Most of the guns used by powers challenging the Mughals and the British were made in factories in Lucknow, Pondicherry, Hyderabad, Lahore, and Seringapatam. Travancore, Kashmir, Rajasthan, and Sindh also possessed sites of arms manufacture. The rising Sikh kingdom relied on imports but also arms made in Lahore, Amritsar, and Peshawar, sometimes modeled on European arms. Indian guns and gun parts were also sold in Persia, Oman, and elsewhere in the Indian Ocean.

The British balanced the risk of sales to unfriendly powers against the risk of encouraging this indigenous manufacture. After Buxar, the nawab of Awadh, Shuja-ud-Daula, was repeatedly refused arms on the formal grounds of policy, though the British were in fact specifically anxious over Shuja's reviving ambitions, evident in his enterprise in manufacturing arms. Captain Richard Smith visited the site in the capital city of Faizabad, where Shuja cast big guns and small arms, finding an excellent eight-pounder brass gun molded from a Dutch model. Nearly a thousand new matchlocks with bayonets had been made. Good firelocks were being made slowly. Two Bengalis directed casting of the big guns, and a French engineer made carriages and mounted them. This Frenchman was improving all processes of manufacture, instructing workers in the use of a machine to bore guns flawlessly. He had brought the nawab a plan for a furnace, too. Smith suspected that the nawab had lured him from among French deserters from Pondicherry who had joined the company army earlier, many of whom had gunsmithing experience. Rumors flew that the nawab intended to take advantage of impending war in the Deccan to break with the English. He was raising an infantry on the company's model.

Shuja also employed an Armenian agent to secretly purchase five hundred arms from Calcutta. The agent bought a few at a time from a French settlement north of Calcutta, concealing them beneath the planks of a boat after having a former company sergeant check them. (Many were old and bad.) The boat passed all the checkpoints on the Ganges until Ensign

George Wallen discovered them. The nawab claimed them and expressed outrage at his boats' being stopped. Like Hyder Ali, he threatened a break to get arms. The threat was credible, since British officers on the spot knew he had well-paid trained troops and a larger treasury than the company. Shuja expressed surprise at English jealousy of his obtaining a few arms. The governor in Calcutta diplomatically blamed the "folly and evil imaginations" of the nawab's agent while asserting that for the nawab's people to carry away arms "in this clandestine manner . . . has a very ill appearance between friends." He was sure that the nawab would punish the parties involved to make an example of them, for a repetition might create a difference between friends. Within five years the British had established greater control in Awadh, appointing a resident to Faizabad; Calcutta now amiably supplied Shuja with two thousand muskets. When he died, in 1775, the company took advantage of the vulnerable moment of succession to secure its objectives: monopoly of Awadh's plentiful saltpeter, the primary ingredient in gunpowder. Awadhi need for British guns was pressed into service of the British need for gunpowder. When Asaf-ud-Daula succeeded his father, the company threatened to withdraw military support unless he dismissed the Frenchmen in his service. If he agreed, the company would itself supply him with arms. Asaf took the deal. He received five thousand company guns repaired by armorers hired at his expense. The company also sold him fourteen thousand guns for *company* battalions stationed in his territory under their defensive alliance. This began to grate, and in 1778 Asaf-ud-Daula refused to buy more until those he had purchased were accounted for. Some of his troops were then transferred to company service, with their arms. The company co-opted Awadhi military strength.

It did the same with Awadhi gun manufacturing. The Frenchmen left, and the British took over the local gun industry. They allowed construction of a new arsenal in Asaf's new capital, Lucknow, in 1776, at his expense. A company man was superintendent (the former French deserter and company soldier Claude Martin). The guns produced were modeled on British guns. The French mercenary Benoit de Boigne bought arms for the Maratha leader Mahadji Scindia there in 1784. When Martin retired in 1787, the company had depots up-country and no longer needed either the Lucknow armory or the nawab's troops. It put a final stop to Awadhi gun manufacture, officially prohibiting Europeans from making and selling arms for native rulers. In 1790 in Agra, de Boigne employed a Scottish mercenary, George Sangster, to establish an arsenal for Scindia, but when Sangster died in 1792, the resident at Lucknow prevented his son from carrying on. Asaf-ud-Daula remained fascinated by arms, amassing an enormous personal collection.

A similar dynamic unfolded in Mysore. In the Second Anglo-Mysore War, in 1780, Hyder's men had company arms. The company finally grew wary of reengaging in that trade. But then twenty new iron-smelting furnaces went up in Mysore, and upon Hyder Ali's death in 1782, his son Tipu Sultan built gun manufactories emulating European techniques. In nearly a dozen armories, he produced arms of comparable quality, involving foreign workers, too. There were also cannon foundries and four large arsenals. After the British victory following the siege of Seringapatam in 1799, during the Fourth Anglo-Mysore War, in which Tipu was killed, the British seized nearly one hundred thousand of his flintlocks, only half of which were European-made (both English and French). They shut down his small-arms manufactories, dislodging (and probably deporting) the Europeans. After the British restored a friendly monarchy, company arms again flowed into Mysore (and Tipu's weapons became European collectors' prizes).

After the defeat of Mysore, the British turned to the Marathas, who also had sophisticated gun-manufacturing capacity. By 1785, Scindia had established ordnance factories in the Agra area, using indigenous technology and expertise. Maratha military culture derived from this elaborate "military economy," including skilled metalsmiths who might as easily craft temple ornaments as cast artillery. In Indian towns recalling contemporary Birmingham, "metal workers were often found in proximity to local wheelwrights making parts for bullock carts and both groups found employment in manufacturing artillery." Scindia also had high-quality flintlocks made locally. As in England, the civilian labor market profited from defense procurement contracts.

Scindia also had British guns. He bought surplus guns after the Third Anglo-Mysore War, in 1792, and rebuilt decommissioned company guns he bought in Bombay. The British tried to prevent this possibility by cutting condemned company arms in two before auctioning them off for local smiths to use in the manufacture of nails and bolts. But buyers complained that this devalued the metal, so the company instead stripped the guns down, beat the barrels flat, kept the locks intact, and parted with other elements en masse. This system worked until the post of military store-keeper was abolished: in 1792, hundreds of muskets were quietly transferred intact to another warehouse. The smuggled guns were auctioned at Bombay, and the Marathas got them. The middlemen in this clandestine supply chain were a mix of Indians and Europeans. In the late 1790s, chests of company muskets were also found in the possession of the mercenary Captain Peter Gossan, who died in Maratha service in 1797, resulting in charges against company employees for illegal arms trafficking. These are just two known incidents. The company began to require return of all unserviceable arms to Europe. One mercenary foresaw that this new regulation "may for a time prevent the increase of native infantry corps, but then it will drive them to the expedient of making their own firelocks, as Scindeah has done, and his are very excellent ones, far superior to the ordinary Europe arms to be met with in the bazars." After defeating the Marathas in 1805, the British withered local artillery-manufacturing capacity and co-opted small-arms manufacturing. (It would still require a third war to definitively defeat the Marathas, in 1818.)

The British victory of 1805 was thanks to the bayonet charge, not superior firepower. Before the introduction of breech-loading guns later in the nineteenth century, Britain and its major Indian rivals were at near parity in small-arms technology; this was why indigenous small-arms manufacture was so problematic for the British and why the conquest of the subcontinent was so slow, costly, and difficult. It was not better guns but the systems in which they were used, and the way they were used, that mattered; the shock effect of inaccurate firelocks was important. British arms sales were partly about effacing indigenous manufacturing capacity while at once reaping diplomatic and commercial gains. Company arms spread as far as Persia and Cochinchina. Shipping bad guns to London proved no guarantee against their reappearing in Asian hands. Nearly all of the European guns among the Chin tribes of Burma in the nineteenth century were English-made flintlocks, a quarter of them late-eighteenth-century company arms and the bulk old Ordnance Office arms probably from London. A few had been cut and rejoined, evidently formerly condemned company guns. Ammunition could be improvised in these old muzzleloaders. As late as the 1990s, company gunlocks were sold in towns like Kanpur for use in cheap muzzle-loading shotguns. From the subcontinent, British guns reached other margins of the empire. From the 1790s, gifts of arms flowed to the sultans of Nzwani Island, off Africa, in gratitude for assistance to company ships. The sultanate became deeply dependent on these arms. Guns spread with British power despite British wariness of their potential danger: they were coin, symbols of British industrialism, diplomatic tools, and a source of profit. Jealous as the East India Company was of its arms, it was more jealous of its sway in the subcontinent and willing to sacrifice the former for the latter.

Given the pervasiveness of guns in the subcontinent and the existence of indigenous gun manufacture (unlike in the South Pacific and North America), British representations of their use there were framed somewhat differently. There the gun was less the skimpy armor against unknown medieval horrors and more the common symbol of masculine self-preservation in a competitive arena. In 1792, when Thomas Twining traveled through Rohilla territory, he was wary of becoming the target of anger at its recent conqueror, Robert Abercromby. His admiration for this "fierce" people was obvious. He and his men were on their guard, arms at the ready even while he engaged in "conciliatory intercourse," draped, native fashion, in a shawl. His group requested the protection of a Rohilla police chief, who asked them to stay at his office rather than in the serai. There Twining set up a table to write, and his accompanying soldiers brought their spears and matchlocks to the courtyard, to prevent their being seized while they ate. To Twining, "the solicitude which these brave men always showed to have their arms near was no sign of fear but of their determination to make a good use of them—*Da soldato morir coll' arme in mani.*" He laid his own pistols on the writing table and another gun in the corner behind him. As he wrote, he saw a stranger advancing, with a hand poised to draw out a pistol. Twining immediately seized his own. The surprised intruder protested his innocence, but Twining shrewdly kept the pistol aimed until the intruder put his down to explain that it was a foreign make, out of repair, and that he had brought it in hopes of having it fixed when he heard a foreign traveler was in town. On examination, Twining found it scarcely usable. He obligingly repaired it as best he could, revising his opinion of the stranger—from Rohilla assassin to "a very intelligent and respectable man." The gun was a ubiquitous defense for the European in the subcontinent; the Rohilla rightly assumed (per Twining) that a traveling foreigner would possess skill at gun repair. Their shared familiarity with guns endowed them with a common masculine respectability. The gun was also handy against more "primitive" Indian weapons: when Twining, walking in a grove after breakfast, confronted a surly sepoy attempting to stir up trouble among his men, he presented the man with the butt of his gun. The sepoy put his hand to his tulwar, and Twining instantly turned the gun to point the muzzle at him. The offender muttered a few words and retreated to his companions. In a seamier episode the same year, three British men forced their way into the compound of an Indian woman, Aura Marguard, armed with blunderbusses, muskets, pistols, swords, and sticks. They attempted to break into her bungalow, where she had locked herself into a room, shooting and injuring one of the servants. There was also William Tucker, who, armed with guns and backed by sepoys, attacked boats passing through Goalpara, in Assam, stealing their goods until local business came to a halt and company officials ordered him to Calcutta for disciplining. The British did not bring the rule of law to India but produced islands of lawlessness among competing strangers on a scale beyond that of any contemporary English county. Gratuitous shooting was as much a part of this time and place as it was elsewhere. In 1893, an Indian journalist observed of Englishmen, "Here shooting of tigers and bears is not sufficient sport; there can be no full sporting without occasional indulgence in native shooting."

English guns reached well beyond Africa, the South Pacific, North

America, and South Asia. The British and the Dutch split a healthy trade with the Levant. North Africa, Iberia, and other parts of the Mediterranean were also British arms markets. Even the arms grants to Spain during the Napoleonic Wars fulfilled more than military objectives, securing commercial privileges in Spanish America and control over the Peninsular War. By the start of the nineteenth century, the British arms trade was undisputedly the largest in the world. English arms were standard trade items in Muscat and Zanzibar, fueling trade in ivory and slaves from East Africa to the Middle East. They brought diplomatic advantage in the Persian Gulf and the Red Sea—critical routes to India. In South Africa, British merchants and missionaries encouraged Africans to use firearms to secure the frontier and kill so much game that they would be forced to adopt modern agriculture; in 1812, the explorer-botanist William Burchell wished that guns would spread more extensively, to speed that civilizing process. In Southeast Asia, too, guns spread as a currency of economic and political power. Pirates adapted them to a range of cultural, ceremonial, political, and violent uses.

Guns played many parts in the story of imperial expansion and exploration. Eighteenth-century English guns may not have been a superior technology, but they were confidence-boosting and were understood as an everyday necessity for facing the rude reality of foreign lands. They shaped relations with indigenous peoples as instruments of immediate terror and confident masculinity, currency, a crucial commodity, a source of metal, a reason for prohibiting industrial development, and more. Imperial expansion was fundamentally about seizure of land, and the imperialist gathered the confidence to make that seizure by displaying his gun before the native inhabitant, styling it as the instrument of civilization countering barbaric native instruments. The poet laureate, Henry James Pye, who wrote paeans to shooting, also praised "The Progress of Refinement" (1783). His contemporary theorist of progress, Adam Smith, overcame his instinctive doubts to affirm that guns were part of that process: the expense of firearms gave an advantage to an "opulent and civilized over a poor and barbarous nation." So, while their invention might at first appear "pernicious," he reasoned, it favored permanency and "the extension of civilization." This conclusion sits awkwardly with his admission that the natives of the East and West Indies did not reap commercial benefits from the discovery of America and the Cape of Good Hope, because of the "dreadful misfortunes" occasioned by the "accident" that "the superiority of force happened to be so great on the side of the Europeans, that they were enabled to commit with impunity every sort of injustice in those re-mote countries." He hoped those natives would grow stronger, or those of Europe weaker, so that all the world's inhabitants would arrive at "that equality of courage and force which, by inspiring mutual fear, can alone overawe the injustice of independent nations into some sort of respect for the rights of one another." This mutually terrorized world would come about through the sharing of knowledge and improvements that com-merce naturally produced. Many Cold War survivors might reasonably question the comforts of Smith's vision of a mutually terrorized world (hardly a utopia of liberal self-governance); but, more pressingly, one won-ders what Smith would have said had he known how hard his contempo-raries were working to prevent knowledge sharing in South Asia. Perhaps this news would merely have fueled his already vehement criticism of the East India Company. His fleeting perception of how context shapes his-tory vanished, eclipselike; by the nineteenth century, the notion that "civility and humanity" were the "companions of trade" was a well-worn shibboleth entirely unrelated to guns. The controversy around Galton in 1795 was pivotal to that forgetting.

Part Three

THE MORAL
LIFE of GUNS

Interlude:
A Brief Account of the Society of Friends

Seventeenth-century England was a place of violent political struggle over religion. During the Civil War, in the 1640s, George Fox, the son of a Leicestershire weaver, began to preach about the contradiction between the spirit of war and the spirit of Christ. His influence spread, among soldiers and ex-soldiers especially. After the Restoration, the inchoate and persecuted Quaker sect developed its structure of local meeting groups. Fox went to the Americas, too. In 1676, one of his Scottish adherents, Robert Barclay, penned the *Apology for the True Christian Divinity*, which became the foundational text of Quaker doctrine and practice, including the testimony against all wars. Quakers were forbidden to bear arms or send others in their place or give money for the purchase of military equipment or attire. Rejection of war was foundational to the Quaker sect. And yet, as Galton Jr. pointed out in his defense of 1795, the sect had passed no comment on his family business as it had unfolded over generations. Why not? And what changed in the 1790s to make the Society suddenly oppose it then? The sect's concern about members' conformity with principle grew in fits and starts over the century as war increasingly shaped economic opportunity in the country.

From the start, the sect's refusal to pay tithe in support of the state church, to take oaths of allegiance, and to participate in military preparations made its members a close-knit community in tension with the broader social and political framework of their time. Self-policing ensured conformity with Society principles. From 1682, the Society's Yearly Meeting in London posed three queries to all regional Quarterly Meetings, the first two relating to deaths of Friends and the third inquiring how "Truth has prospered among them." Over the next half century, the list of queries expanded. In 1742, a query alluding to warlike activities appeared: "Do you bear a faithful and Christian testimony against the [*sic*] receiving or paying tithes? And against bearing arms? And do you admonish such as are unfaithful therein?" Until then, most Friends in most places were rarely at risk on the last two counts: the militia was embodied only once, in 1715. The query emerged out of a *new* concern, that Friends were not following the principle against participation in war, not least because it was virtually impossible to participate in overseas trade without arming vessels during wartime. In 1743, answers indicated that Friends were mostly clear of bearing arms, but in 1744 the Yearly Meeting feared that "all are not duly careful." The Derby Meeting confessed that "several . . . are the reverse in their conduct." Bristol "sorrowfully" acknowledged that some were concerned in privateers. The Yearly Meeting reminded local meetings of the sufferings of their ancient Friends and of the Society's condemnations of the arming of ships. The sect's faith was to confide in the protection of God, "not in weapons of war." It admonished local meetings to reclaim such individuals or, where that failed, disown them.

Individual conscience aside, a *trend* of participation in war prompted the new query—though the Society did not yet stake out a position on contracting specifically. The opportunity to profit from war was great, and so, then, was the concern that the community's success was increasingly bound up in it. In that moment in the middle of the War of the Austrian Succession, many were becoming successful bankers, traders, and industrialists. The state was actively tapping Quaker networks, drawn, like others traders, to their collective reputation for honesty. Even Abraham Darby II broke with his father's refusal to make weapons of war and helped equip the state, although he soon gave it up. Ambrose Crowley III was an apostate from his Quaker faith from the day he left home for training in London, but the Crowley family, too, overcame vestigial qualms about arms production only in the 1740s. Another apostate, the mathematician Benjamin Robins, published *New Principles of Gunnery* in 1742, substantially influencing development of artillery. The Hanburys also transported guns and other Ordnance stores in the 1740s, fueling much of the Society's new concern—while also contracting for remittances and other military supplies. The Quaker banker Samuel Hoare said that war was a necessary evil, and defense of country a duty. In 1745, William Cookworthy, the ingenious Quaker porcelain manufacturer, was astonished that it was "a settled maxim, that Friends may deal in Prize-Goods." Many Quaker fortunes went into the six figures with this "war generation."

These delinquencies were motivated by growing patriotism as much as profit. In 1745, the Society instructed local meetings to remain aloof from the effort to put down the rebellion, despite their regard for the king. By then, its principle against bearing arms was well known enough that such aloofness was less misconstrued than it had been earlier. Still, many Friends paid taxes in support of the militia, and some bore arms, including James Farmer's brother, Joseph. A Quaker gift of woolens to the Duke of Cumberland's army, encamped near Coventry, elicited the observation that although Quakers did not bear arms, "yet they contribute to them that do." Joseph Farmer protested to his sister that he would not stay in the army longer than necessary and that "love of one's country ought to prevail over all self interested views and motives." Most of the young gentlemen in Liverpool had joined, he explained—palpable peer pressure. In this "critical conjuncture," it was the "indispensible duty of every man to do all that he could to secure the liberties of this country . . . though he runs ever so great a risk of his own life or fortune. This is the reason I am turned soldier for the present though there's no way of life I've greater dislike to." His family was far from scandalized; his cousin Thomas Farmer, in Bristol, wished him success in engaging "the rebels . . . for they have been the disturbers of this Nation for some time." He hoped they would "meet wth their rewards" and asked Joseph to write frequently with army news. Dr. John Fothergill in London welcomed peace in 1748 as a Quaker but, "as an Englishman," hoped war would be pursued "with vigour" until "a solid peace" was secured. By the 1740s, the community had become invested enough in the regime, and taxation in the service of its defense had become normalized enough, that even the Society's new efforts to discipline its members were not fully effective.

Joseph reappeared in uniform in the Seven Years' War; army life gave him the discipline and adventure he sought. The Society's increased vigilance during that war testifies to the growing difficulty of standing aloof from war as it became the central and defining fact of eighteenth-century British life and national identity. It reminded Friends not to participate in public rejoicing over military victories or be concerned in privateers or armed ships. By 1757, the query about warlike activity was decoupled from questions about the tithe: "Do you bear a faithful testimony against bearing arms or paying Trophy Money, or being in any way concerned in privateers, letters of Marque, or in dealing in prize goods as such?" Freame's financial assistance to the state was perfectly acceptable according to the terms of the query, but Robert Plumsted was reluctant to ship arms to America, partly because of scruples against accepting "any gain or advantage from articles purposed for the destruction of mankind." He explained to a colleague,

> You know, wee [*sic*] as a people, are in principle against everything that tends to war and bloodshed, and consistent with this belief can neither be active therein or partake of the profit arising from the sale of goods the use whereof is for *de*structive purposes. This lays me under a difficulty, which there seems but one expedient for. The demand for these things are but temporary they cease in time of peace and now are but a verry [*sic*] small part of your busyness, would it be any great illconvenience to you to let them drop. It would ease me from a scruple that at present I cannot divest myself of, tho at the same time am far from judging those who do not profess with us, for acting as they may find freedom, and here I must leave it to your Christian consideration.

He did covertly ship sword blades and a gun for a ship's captain. He also sent out arms under the charge of Captain Adams, albeit abstaining from charging profit or commission. And he did not scruple about shipping guns in years of peace, like 1750, when he purchased guns himself, nor did he judge his in-law James Farmer's livelihood. Joseph Farmer's military career also endured: in 1764, he was in Somerset, in command of a company, complaining about "little dirty disagreeable things in a military life" like being "quarter'd by ones self in one of these little dirty Towns." "A Man might live with almost as much Comfort & Satisfaction in the Wilds of America," he wagered, and soon enough his corps embarked for those wilds. He protested to his sister-in-law that he would have gladly quit the army and "gone into some more elligible employment," but, with his regiment under orders for Pensacola, "it wou'd be a mean cowardly action" now. And so he would trust to Providence and take his chance with his "brother soldiers."

The wider context of disregard for Society admonitions may explain why no complaint emerged about the Farmer & Galton business, whose crumbling fortunes were resurrected by war in 1756. Another part of the explanation may be the families' involvement in diverse pursuits and the diverse uses of guns, which together may have obscured awareness of their work for the Ordnance Board or reduced it in proportion to a merely incidental accompaniment of their wider industrial activity. Gun possession was not inherently incompatible with membership in the sect. Gun ownership rates in American colonies with high Quaker populations—West Jersey, Pennsylvania, and Delaware—were lower than in other colonies, but Quakers did own firearms for hunting and killing vermin. In England, Quaker acquisition of country estates included a taste for country pastimes like shooting. The Gurneys had guns to guard their Norwich bank, displaying them prominently after a robbery in 1786. In 1765, Lord and Lady Shelburne "went to a Quaker's to see the making of guns" (Galton's factory), without noting any incongruity in the phrase—and despite being alive to moral issues about unproved guns traded to Africa. An American Quaker at Galton's Duddeston home in 1776 was full of admiration for the environs, the garden, the tastefully done "artificial Cascades," *and* the "very capital Manufactury of Muskets."

The one expression of concern about the family came from Ann Mercy Bell, who troubled over Farmer's attendance at meetings for worship in 1756. (He was then, self-confessedly, the "most unhappy man living.") There is no record of censure of his bankruptcy, though he had arguably violated core Quaker injunctions against "overtrading" and risky ventures rooted in greed—which brought reproach to the entire society (even though the very security of the Quaker network, with its rigorous communal scrutiny and collective reputation for honesty, thrift, and a tight credit network, also encouraged such ventures). Despite the general view of bankruptcy as the result of personal failure even among non-Quakers, Farmer, too, felt innocent: he had not dragged Galton into the mess "intendedly," and his actions had been guided by certain "necessities." He had committed no "mean actions or premeditated designs." Moreover, a fine profit might still await him. The Society's leniency may have partly resulted from the fact that old Charles Lloyd had endured a scandalous and stressful bankruptcy himself in 1727, which had left him in purgatory until 1742. The senior Galton expressed doubt about his brother-in-law's moral soundness but reserved his severest condemnation for the "foreigner" who had led him astray. "My Brother Farmer not contented with the moderate profits of the gun trade carried on at London a separate trade in company with . . . a foreigner who . . . spent a large sum of money and took up large sums in the name of Farmer and himself which Mr. Farmer was forced to pay," he recounted to his agents. His wife (Farmer's sister) also blamed Farmer's naïveté. Joseph Freame did hope Farmer would "sit down with the Loss of 10,000 to teach you to be cautious for future," but Galton in turn decried his and the Plumsteds' "sinister" insistence on enormous securities before assisting Farmer.

As Quakers, but also as eighteenth-century men, these men were highly self-conscious about their moral sentiments, framing their actions with phrases attesting to their integrity, character, or honor in the letters that were the mainstay of their social and business exchanges. They were *interested* in their own consciences and aware of the moral risks at stake in business decisions. But that concern did not impinge on their assessments of the product that Farmer & Galton manufactured. The moral test, for the senior Galton, lay not in what he produced but in how well he navigated the treacherous waters of eighteenth-century commerce and finance. After all, credit was the automatic measure of character. His moral arrogance was well known, irking Thomas Hadley and David Barclay, who felt little pleasure communicating "with a man of his Cast" and advised Farmer's son-in-law Charles Lloyd to tread carefully. Gun manufacture did nothing to weaken or taint this reputation for moral arrogance. Galton, like Lloyd, was a leading figure in the campaign against the theater license in Birmingham. It may be that this and other good works the Galtons undertook as emerging local eminences helped stifle questions about their trade. Samuel Sr. was "Chosen Overseer of the poor in Birmingham" in 1750. He and Farmer contributed to the town's general hospital in 1765 alongside Samuel Garbett, Boulton & Fothergill, and the Lloyds. Other gunmakers followed, including Thomas Hadley, Joseph Oughton, John Whateley, and William Grice, perhaps perceiving the public relations advantages in this good work. The 1769 Improvement Act to make Birmingham's streets cleaner and safer named fifty commissioners, including Samuel Galton, John Taylor, and Sampson Lloyd. Galton was also involved in canal construction. His civic conscience and interest in the public good were above question.

The American war raised the stakes of all these matters. In 1776, the radical author Thomas Paine, son of a Quaker, publicly accused the sect of hypocrisy in its criticism of American rebellion. Theirs were "pretended scruples": they exclaimed "against the mammon of this world" while "hunting after it with a step as steady as Time, and an appetite as keen as Death." Perhaps these sharp words figured in the cultural shift that marked the Society from that point. Its concern about members' contributions to war now went beyond investment in armed vessels as awareness grew of the more general way that war increasingly impinged on economic activity: Adam Smith noted that military equipment had become the state's biggest expense. Still, nothing was mentioned about the Galton business. Whatever the earlier ignorance of the Birmingham Meeting's members about Galton's contracting work, such ignorance was impossible by 1780, given the volume of output, presence of state inspectors, and visible experiments in industrial organization in town. This says something about the continued confusion about guns as objects, but also perhaps about the influence of particular eminences in local meetings.

After the war, the Yearly Meeting became newly assertive over local meetings, making it impossible for Birmingham Friends to continue to turn a blind eye to the Galton trade. This new assertiveness was bound up with the way defeat transformed the abolition movement, in which Quakers were virtually the only force from 1783 to 1787. Abolitionism was part of the Age of Contract, a cultural and institutional trend for enforcement of promises regardless of circumstances. The law made promisors generally liable for whatever expectations their promises created, endowing individuals with a greater sense of moral and legal liability. Intensified scrupulousness in fulfillment of ethical maxims fueled humanitarianism, just when military defeat politicized slavery in a new way, providing a means of denigrating the colonial rebels as moral hypocrites (while American abolitionists sought to undermine the British pose of innocence). Both sides together invented the notion of complicity in slavery, producing new conventions about moral responsibility according to which specific villains, rather than uncontrollable systems, could be held accountable for immoral activity. Earlier in the century, high public pride in the empire and its unique benevolence had helped quiet intimations of exploitative or aggressive British actions abroad. The worst abuses could be excused as singular lapses uncharacteristic of the larger endeavor, and excessive scrupulousness in the pursuit of wealth could appear as "unsophisticated carping against the public good." Critics of corruption were muffled by the sense of the greater public good war supported even when driven by corruption. Investigation into East India Company affairs—the long impeachment trial of Governor Warren Hastings on corruption charges from 1788 to 1795—was part of the new moment of reflection on imperial practices as a legitimate area of public inquiry. So, too, was the outcry against contractors as vulgar warmongers. Their immodest profits were especially unseemly in their indifference to national defeat. Campaigns demanding an end to exclusion of religious Dissenters from office holding were part of this ferment; Joseph Priestley, the target of the 1791 Birmingham riots against such campaigns, was deeply involved in abolitionism. The abolition movement was part of this intense moral questioning about the very mainstays of eighteenth-century economic activity after defeat.

The Society of Friends's new efforts to enforce discipline among its members were part of this intense concern with promises and accountability. In 1779, it recirculated a minute about overtrading from a meeting held in 1732, which called on Friends to be "exact in performing promises," particularly for the sake of the Society's collective credit and reputation. Galton, too, became accountable in a new way to his Quaker fraternity as Quakers took the lead in the abolition movement. Taking up this political crusade was entirely out of character with the quieter ethos of withdrawal the sect had long adopted. It had prohibited participation in the slave trade after the Seven Years' War, but without any sense of trying to end it; rather, it aimed to impose discipline among its own members to enforce their separateness from a world that it presumed would persist in the sinful trade. Like the effort to police participation in war, the prohibition was not effective: most Quakers *did not* abstain from investing in the slave trade or holding slaves. Prominent Quakers were heavily invested in the Atlantic economy, including David Barclay and the Hanburys—at least until the American war disrupted those ties. The move toward ending the slave trade altogether, toward reform *outside* the Society, was new in the 1780s.

Barclay emerged as a key figure in the movement. He had already revealed himself to be a Quaker willing, for the sake of business, to blur the otherwise firm boundaries Friends drew between religion and politics. In 1766, he had joined the campaign to repeal the Stamp Act, which imposed a tax on all paper documents in the colonies in an effort to pull the British government out of debt after the Seven Years' War. In 1781, he launched his brewing works at Southwark, perhaps to disinvest from the increasingly troublesome Atlantic trade. This move provoked in him a strenuous need to prove his moral bona fides. The new venture was rawly ambitious, and he asked his cousin Priscilla Farmer to be his "monitor," as the "natural impetuousity" of his temper "often carries me beyond that line of moderation which I admire in others though I cannot attain it." He also asked her to be his advocate to ensure that his peers did not misjudge his intentions, explaining that he had embarked on this "immense concern" out of depression and a feeling of uselessness after misfortunes experienced by his relatives at Norwich (the Gurneys, presumably). When his nephew Robert Barclay was offered the new "mighty affair," he had considered it "coolly and quietly" and concluded that it would benefit all of his family. Thus had he launched into brewing "in the belief of its being right." This timely need to prove his earnestness coincided with tactical accident to put him at the center of the new cause. In 1783, he led a delegation of Quakers in a closed-door meeting with the Board of Trade to encourage consideration of antislavery petitions, hoping that an optimistic report might forestall more aggressive campaigning by American Friends. His investments in the Atlantic trade made it difficult for him to unequivocally support limiting slave supply to Virginia, but he also worried that an entirely futile campaign would stir disputes and damage the Society's reputation. In the end, the petition was favorably received, and he was appointed to a standing committee to promote abolition.

Once Parliament began to encourage the movement, Quakers took up the difficult cause, partly for the way it marked them off as "unusually virtuous, as distinctively philanthropic," regardless of its potential for success. It helped restore the sect's tradition of conscientious Christian witness. Conflicts within the Society made the cost of not acting against the slave trade unbearable. The long struggle to avoid profiting from war perhaps roused Friends to the ways in which economic activity could produce violence in other spheres, too. Nine of the twelve members of the Abolition Society, formed in 1787, were Quakers. The movement injected new energy and visibility into the Yearly Meeting, leading it to pursue its other objectives with new vigor and determination as a reputation for ethical consistency became crucial in a new way. If wealthy families like the Barclays had abetted the slackening of Quaker discipline, their tight-knit network also accelerated the movement for self-purification and Quaker revival. The need was evident; the Birmingham Meeting of 1789 noted its "low" state and the lukewarmness of many Friends. Several meetings reported violations of testimony. The Society's General Epistle of 1790 noted that, the cause of slavery being before Parliament, it was a time for salutary discipline, a time to "preserve and edify the body in love" and clear the Society's reputation "from the scandal that might arise from the disorderly walking of any professing with us." The Society's determination to discipline its fold on the count of arms manufacturing was part of this new activism and concern for collective reputation. The Yearly Meeting's Written Epistle emphatically condemned all warlike practices, citing the "warlike preparations . . . making in this country." "As the Ambition of Nations is even now slaughtering its Thousands," it warned, "let none amst [amongst] us, whose Principle is Peace, be employed to prepare the means. . . . We have been publickly charged with some under our name fabricating or selling Instruments of War." The epistle thus called for an inquiry so that those involved with a practice so "inconsistent" might with love be reclaimed or, failing that, disowned.

Crucially, this directive coincided with the moment in which guns began to be conceptually associated with interpersonal violence in a new way. In 1795, the Society also explicitly proclaimed itself against hunting and shooting. Meetings in Ireland called on Friends who had sporting guns to destroy them, "to prevent . . . their being made use of to the destruction of any of our fellow creatures, and more fully and clearly to support our peaceable and Christian testimony in these perilous times." A Friend appointed to an enforcement committee in Wexford broke his own fowling piece in the street outside his door and found that most Friends had done or were willing to do the same. Irish Quakers had come to see their guns as weapons first and foremost.

The epistle's 1790 recommendation did not trigger any formal action or comment in Birmingham, this nonchalance providing a measure of the Galtons' local importance and influence—they were plainly and anomalously the largest gunmakers in town and the only Quaker ones. But the growing popularity of abolitionism and shifting views of guns eventually trumped that influence. In 1792 came the first local objection to the Galton trade on those grounds. A collection was being made to enlarge the meetinghouse on Bull Street. Joseph Robinson wrote to committee member Joseph Gibbins to protest Galton's contribution (without naming Galton explicitly)—because of his role in the African trade. Galton supplied an article "likely to be very hurtful to them (the natives), for," Robinson explained, "I cannot think they are only made a bauble of and hung up to their houses for ornament, and if applied to birding, being so slightly proved, are a kind of snare to them, but the worst of it is many of them are used in their wars with each other." The meeting must not accept any part of the "thousands . . . accumulated by a forty years' commerce in these articles." Robinson did not remark on the Society's forty-year silence about this trade; for him, it was controversial because of its ties to the slave trade, not because of the article itself. He did not even mention arms supply to the government. There is no record of the Monthly Meeting acting on these strenuous objections. The next year, the Birmingham Meeting pointedly responded to the query about arms: "We believe Friends are clear in respect of <u>bearing</u> arms and being concerned in the militia." The underlining suggests their awareness of individuals *making* arms. Galton evidently brushed off the "animadversions" made and the "private admonition" given to him in these years before formal allegations were charged in 1795. His distinction was such that even those formal allegations were put in the most forgiving terms possible: in his understanding, the "*sole, and entire*" charge against him was that he was "engaged in a Manufactory of Arms, some of which are applicable to military purposes." At least one reader of his printed defense saw the claim's modesty as evidence of his fellow Friends' care not to "exceed the bounds of Truth & Moderation, in their charge respecting his Manufactory," proof of their courteous concern to mitigate the accusation as much as possible. After all, the Galtons were entwined with leading Quaker families and leading personalities of Birmingham society. They were the very picture of provincial respectability, "a genteel family."

The start of the war in 1793 made it impossible for the Birmingham Meeting to avoid confronting Galton any longer. It was difficult, given their financial, industrial, and commercial roles, for Quakers to avoid participating in the long military contest that followed; the Society grew disunited, especially because of emerging distinctions of wealth. Its members required frequent admonishment against paying rates for raising navy men and aiding in the conveyance of soldiers and their equipment. Birmingham Friends were disowned for enlisting. Meanwhile, guns steadily acquired a more sinister profile. Thus, at some point in 1794–95, a conversation stirred about the Galton business. Now the objection was to not only its role in the slave trade but also its disunity with the testimony against war. The first minute of the Monthly Meeting on the matter, on April 8, 1795, confirms that "Mention" had been made "at this and some former sittings respecting the case of Samuel Galton and Samuel Galton, Jr., Members of this meeting, who are in the practice of fabricating and selling instruments of war." Moreover, "divers opportunities have been had with the parties by several Friends under the direction of the overseers and others, to some satisfaction." The meeting now appointed three Friends to continue the visitation: Sampson Lloyd, Joseph Gibbins, and James Baker. As Galton Jr. perceived, this process was "adopted reluctantly," his friends feeling "obliged in compliance with the" epistle of 1790. The Yearly Meeting sent a further epistle regretting that the testimony against war was being violated for the sake of gain, and calling for vigilance. The Birmingham Meeting pursued the Galton case, taking "several opportunities" to counsel the family. In July came the happy announcement that "Samuel Galton the elder has relinquished the business and declined receiving any further emolument from it." But the fate of the son remained uncertain. Friends were deputed to "continue their care towards" him.

8

Galton's Disownment

By the 1790s, the Society of Friends was in earnest about the Galton family business, but the pressures shaping that new agenda did not necessarily resonate with its members. The elder Galton fell in line, but his quick passing of the business to his son suggests that he hardly felt doing so would implicate his son's soul; there was nothing newly damning about the business in his eyes. The son's defense also made much of his innocent inheritance of the business, leaving the question of original sin unanswered. His father's action smacks of expedience, perhaps expected from this eternal worrier, who must have borne the Society's admonitions with a great deal of anxiety. His son was made of stiffer stuff and determined to engage in an analytical contest with his judges.

Some of his self-assertion, bordering on arrogance, stemmed from his consciousness of his cultural stature as a scientist and fellow of the Royal Society—as a practitioner of Enlightenment civility. His pose in engaging with the Society's complaints was self-consciously analytical and modern. The distinction was temperamental, too. Galton Jr. had long experience in defending himself and his principles in public squabbles since his youthful clash with Thomas Hadley. He mediated a dispute over management of the town's poor in 1790. During the riots of 1791, when the Priestleys fled their home ahead of a torch-wielding mob, Galton offered them shelter, courting danger himself. Later, he pressed Priestley for news of his return from London, promising to meet him and show his attachment to him publicly. He asked Priestley to come to the next Lunar meeting, which he would be hosting; Boulton, by contrast, did not attend when he heard that Priestley might be there. (In the end, Priestley was not.) Once, finding a doctor courting one of his daughters in his carriage drive, Galton asked whether he had come to see one of the servants, a calculated gesture of snobbery. From the bankruptcy of the 1750s through the battle with Hadley and the heroism of 1791, moral indignation and the sense of being unjustly persecuted had become a genuine Galton trait.

This was the formidable creature the Birmingham Meeting contended with in 1795. The minute relating to his case was continued month to month. Then, in January 1796, he sent the meeting a letter—his defense. Acknowledging the "candid and liberal conduct" of his worthy friends (Lloyd, Baker, and Gibbins) who had vilified him on the meeting's behalf, he sought to answer the accusation, disrupt the process of disownment, and clear the smudge on his character. He requested that the meeting preserve his letter in their records. It was printed for ease of circulation, but also preservation. Though it was addressed to the meeting, he intended it also as a legacy for his "children or others who may feel an interest in the event." He was concerned with posterity's judgment and confident of the substance of his argument. This is an essential point. To the extent that rationalization was at work, it was felt deeply enough to merit serious consideration for how it allowed him to sustain his actions. He felt that his arguments shed important light on the real-life limits of living a life disconnected from war in his time.

As a participant in the provincial enlightenment, Galton would have been aware of such works as Adam Smith's *Theory of Moral Sentiments* (1759) and its scrutiny of the processes of self-analysis and self-governance. Looking back on his life in 1815, he affirmed the value of happiness arising from religion, explaining to his son John Howard that "pure religion includes the purest morality, the most active benevolence, and beneficence towards others, purity of mind, humility, a sense of constant dependence upon God, and gratitude to him, and devotedness of will to every article both of

To the Friends of the Monthly Meeting at Birmingham :—

RESPECTED FRIENDS,

I have been visited on the part of your Monthly Meeting, by my worthy Friends, Sampson Lloyd, Samuel Baker, and Joseph Gibbins; whose candid, and liberal conduct to me, on this occasion, I acknowledge :—They left with my Father, a Copy of your Minute, dated 8th of the 4th Month, 1795, and a Narrative of Obfervations, that were made in the Yearly Meeting of 1795, on the fubject of the Bufinefs, in which I am engaged :—And, I underftand, that a Procefs is inftituted, tending to the difownment of me, as a Member of your Society, in confequence of a Minute made at the Yearly Meeting of 1790; a Copy of which Minute, together with that of your Meeting, accompany this Addrefs.

In this Procefs, adopted, reluctantly, I believe, on your parts (but to which I prefume you conceive yourfelves obliged, in compliance with the Minute of the Yearly Meeting of 1790) this is perhaps the only ftage, in which I can claim your attention, to the following Statement of FACTS, and OBSERVATIONS;—or in which, I fhall have an opportunity of requefting you, to preferve this letter, and to refer to it in that record, which you will have occafion to make in my Cafe. I am very folicitous that you fhould comply with this requeft, in order that my Children, or others, who may feel an interest in the Event, may have an opportunity hereafter, of informing themfelves of the Circumftances, and of the Motives of my conduct; and becaufe, from the rules of your difcipline, I am precluded from every other Mode of Defence.

F A C T S.

1ft. The fole, and entire caufe alledged for this procefs, is, that I am engaged in a Manufactory of Arms, fome of which are applicable to military purpofes.

2d. My Grandfather,—afterwards my Uncle;—then my Father and my Uncle,—and laftly, my Father and myfelf, have been engaged in this Manufactory for a period of 70 Years, without having before received any Animadverfions on the part of the Society.

3d. The Trade devolved upon me, as if it were an Inheritance, and the whole, or nearly the whole of the Fortune which I received from my Father, was a Capital invefted in the Manufactory; a part of which, confifts in appropriated Mills, Erections, and Apparatus, not eafily affignable, or convertible to other purpofes.

4th. I have, at various times, during my carrying on the faid bufinefs, performed many Acts, with the Concurrence, and at the Inftance of the Society, which alone would have conftituted me a Member.

5th. I have been engaged in this bufinefs from the Year 1777, and it was not until the Year 1790, that the Minute was made, on which this Procefs against me is founded.

6th. My Engagements in the Bufinefs were not a matter of choice, in the firft inftance; and there has never been a time, when I would not have withdrawn from it, could I have found a proper Opportunity of transferring the Concern.

OBSERVATIONS.

1ft. I am convinced by my Feelings, and my Reafon,—(*)THAT THE MANUFACTURE OF ARMS IMPLIES NO APPROBATION OF OFFENSIVE WAR—(‖)THAT THE DEGREE OF RESPONSIBILITY THAT HAS BEEN IMPUTED TO THAT MANUFACTURE DOES NOT ATTACH—(§)AND THAT IN ITS OBJECT, OR ITS TENDENCIES, IT NEITHER PROMOTES WAR, OR INCREASES ITS CALAMITIES.

(*) Will any Perfon, for a moment fuppofe, that as a Manufacturer, it is my object to encourage the Practice, or the Principle of War, or that I propofe to myfelf any other end, than that which all commercial Perfons propofe, viz. the acquifition of Property?—And although it be true (and I lament the fact) that in too many Inftances Fire Arms are employed in Offenfive War, yet it ought in candor to be confidered, that they are equally applicable to the purpofes of DEFENSIVE WAR, to the Support of the CIVIL POWER, to the PREVENTION OF WAR, and to the PRESERVATION OF PEACE.

(‖)If Arguments from the Abufe, are to be admitted against the Ufe, and the Exiftence of things, Objections may be made against almoft every Inftitution, fince almoft every Inftitution, is fufceptible of Abufe. Is the Farmer who fows Barley,—the Brewer who makes it into Beverage,—the Merchant who imports Rum, or the Diftiller who makes Spirits;—are they refponfible for the Intemperance, the Difeafe, the Vice, and Mifery, which may enfue from their Abufe?—Upon this Principle, who would be innocent?

(§)No reflecting Perfon will contend, that the Manufacture of Fire Arms has ever been the Caufe, or Occafion of any War; it is a confequence only, but not a Caufe :—Neither can it be admitted that the Calamities of War have been increafed thereby,—all Hiftory, both facred, and profane, prove the reverfe.— Thofe horrid Contefts, fince the invention of Fire Arms, are univerfally allowed to have been lefs fanguinary, and lefs ferocious.

2d. I know

First page of "Address to the Friends of the Monthly Meeting of Birmingham,"
by Samuel Galton Jr., 1795 (presented to the meeting in January 1796).

faith and conduct which we believe to be true and acceptable to him."
Mindfulness of the Deity's constant presence and accountability to it were
habits he sought to inculcate in his son, noting that Napoleon's godless
pursuit of power had gained him the world but cost him his soul. He
confided to his daughter Adèle that he had "invariably found that my
plans have succeeded in proportion to the Correctness of the Motives
under which they were undertaken & pursued." When pleasure was the
sole object, he had met with disappointment; where duty was the motive,
he had experienced "unforeseen Pleasure during the Pursuit." The "Pleasure of Retrospect & Reflection" offered the surest path to happiness.
These are the reflections of an older man, couched with paternalistic
care, but together they suggest a piety and sincerity of character that makes
it difficult to dismiss the 1795 defense as mere rationalization. It is easy
to identify and condemn hypocrisy, but much more interesting to grasp
how the hypocrite lives with a clear conscience or how what appears hypocritical might have *felt* ethically consistent in a different imagining of
the world.

A ffirming his deep affection for the Society, Galton offered a summary statement of six "facts":

> 1st. The *sole,* and *entire cause* alledged for this process, is, that I am
> engaged in a Manufactory of Arms, some of which are applicable to
> military purposes.
> 2nd. My Grandfather,—afterwards my uncle;—then my Father
> and my Uncle,—and lastly, my Father and myself, have been engaged
> in this Manufactory for a period of *70 Years, without having before
> received any Animadversions on the part of the Society.*
> 3rd. The Trade devolved upon me as if it were *an Inheritance,* and
> the *whole,* or *nearly the whole* of the Fortune which I received from my
> Father, was a Capital *invested in the Manufactory;* a part of which,
> consists in appropriated Mills, Erections and Apparatus, not easily
> assignable, or convertible to other purposes.

4th. I have, at various times, *during my carrying on the said business,* performed many Acts, with the *Concurrence,* and at the *Instance* of the Society, which alone would have *constituted me a Member.*

5th. I have engaged in this business *from the year 1777,* and it was not until the Year 1790, that the Minute was made, on which this Process against me is founded.

6th. My Engagements in the Business were not a matter of *choice,* in the first instance; and there has *never been a time,* when I would not have withdrawn from it, could I have found a proper Opportunity of transferring the Concern.

Next followed six "observations." First, both his reason and feelings convinced him that arms manufacture implied no approbation of offensive war; the industry neither promoted war nor increased its calamities. If firearms were unfortunately used in offensive war, they were equally useful for defensive war, supporting the civil power, preventing war, and preserving the peace. He had no control over the end for which his product was used; his only object as a manufacturer was the typical one of "acquisition of Property." Otherwise, "upon this Principle, *who would be innocent?*" He instanced the brewing industry, in which many Quakers were prominent: "Is the Farmer who sows Barley,—the Brewer who makes it into Beverage,—the Merchant who imports Rum, or the Distiller who makes spirits;—are *they* responsible for the *Intemperance,* the *Disease,* the *Vice,* and *Misery,* which may ensue from their Abuse?" Manufacture of firearms was a consequence, not a cause, of war. Moreover, their invention had made war "*less sanguinary,* and *less ferocious.*"

His second observation took on the scriptural basis of the Society's condemnation of violent resistance—despite his denial of the necessary connection between firearms and war. He cited instances in which Christ sanctioned raising of the sword (still affirming his personal abhorrence of offensive war). He also questioned how literally they were intended to take scriptural prescriptions: when smote on the cheek, did they *actually* turn the other? Did they *never* turn away some who asked to borrow of them? "If an armed Assassin were to aim a Stroke at my *Parent,* my *Wife,* or my

Child, ought I not to *repel* him with whatever Weapon were the most effectual? When your Houses are beset, and invaded by *Thieves* and *Murderers,* do you not call on the Civil Magistrate, and is he not obliged to *use Arms* against armed Ruffians[?]" This last perhaps played on recent memories of the violence of 1791—and the Galton family's gallantry during those events.

Third, Galton cited earlier Quakers who manufactured war munitions, including his grandfather, "a *convinced Quaker.*" He mentioned George Robinson, a Birmingham Friend and son of a minister, who was apprenticed to a gunmaker without censure. The Admiralty had employed Robert Grassingham of Harwich, who was imprisoned with George Fox, on repair of a royal frigate. Another late minister had long worked at the King's Yard in Chatham. The seventeenth-century Quaker Isaac Pennington had approved use of the sword in defense against foreign invasion or suppression of evildoers at home, "and while there is need of a *Sword,*" he wrote, "the Lord will not suffer . . . the Government . . . to want fitting Instruments . . . for the managing thereof."

Fourth, Galton raised the matter of wider financial investment in war: "Do you, not *all* in many ways *contribute* to the War, by supplying Government directly, or indirectly, with *Money,* which is so necessary, that it is called proverbially the *Sinews* of War?" The Friends invested in East India stock, subscribed to government loans, purchased lottery tickets, and participated in navy victualing or exchequer bills—did not all such activities directly and "as *voluntarily*" furnish the means of war as his own business? If they refused compliance with the tithe, why did they comply with taxation? Similarly, despite the Society's strict censure of slavery, most Friends used the produce of slave labor—tobacco, rum, sugar, rice, indigo, cotton— which made them more direct promoters of the slave trade than "the *Vender of Arms* is the Promoter of War," since consumption of those goods caused slavery while manufacture of arms did not cause war. How could they expect him to sacrifice the livelihood on which his family depended when they could not contemplate sacrificing even slave-produced luxuries? To be consistent with principle, they ought to abstain from all taxed commodities, "for, you may be well assured, that every Cup of Beer you drink, and every

Morsel of Bread you eat, has furnished Resources for carrying on this War." This exercise in logical consistency proved that "the *Practice* of your principles, is not compatible with the situation in which Providence has placed us." They had unfairly singled him out when the room for anyone to maneuver in contemporary economic circumstances was limited.

The answer, he observed with a fifth item, was not to disown everyone, but to respect "THE RIGHT AND DUTY OF PRIVATE JUDGEMENT." Ecclesiastical censure was incompatible with the true spirit of Christian discipline, he argued. If a Friend paid tithes without feeling "any conscientious Conviction of Impropriety" of doing so, why should he be excommunicated by Friends who paid taxes on the same principle? He called for general reconsideration of excommunication as a policy.

Finally, he affirmed that his object was to prove that the Society's law was too strict for practical and fair implementation. He preferred the Society "before any other religious Sect," but rather than pledge to abandon his business, he reserved to himself *"perfect Independence . . .* to act as Circumstances may suggest.—So that whenever I may have an Opportunity of withdrawing myself from these Engagements consistently with my Judgement, I shall have the satisfaction to feel that I act from *spontaneous Sentiment only,* and not from unworthy Influence." Since his relationship with the Society had not changed because of any action by him, he saw no reason to withdraw. "If I should be disowned," he concluded, "I shall not think that *I* have abandoned the Society, *but that the Society have withdrawn themselves from their antient, tolerant Spirit, and Practice."*

In the end, Galton's main arguments were that guns were not necessarily instruments of war and that every contemporary economic actor contributed to the state's war making in some incremental way. There is much in the history of eighteenth-century guns to recommend Galton's point of view as more than self-serving rationalization. The record laid out in this book supports his claims in facts 1, 2, and 5 that only some of the arms he produced were used in warfare and that the Society had mutely accepted his family's business for seventy years. Fact 4, concerning his other worthy acts, is uncontroversial. His claims about his limited range of action (facts 3 and 6) are likewise supported by the story in this

book: the Farmer & Galton business depended on heavy capital investment, provided a modest stream of profits much of the time, and was often cash-starved. The last part of fact 6, that Galton would have left the
business whenever decent opportunity arose, makes less sense, given his
defense of the trade as generally harmless—his only concession to its objectionable nature. That said, his uncle James Farmer's ill-fated attempts
to shift capital into a different line of business attest to the difficulty of
such a move. His father's complaints to the Ordnance Board about the
difficulty of converting manufactories established for particular guns to
other purposes lends further support. Still, it might have been easy to sell
out a gun business during a war. Galton's phenomenal wealth certainly
seems to support his critics' presumption that he persisted in it purely out
of greed, that he simply did not want to transfer his capital to a less profitable concern. But the timing of its accumulation—and the limits of Galton's subjective understanding of it—mitigate against that presumption.

Galton Jr. was worth £35,716 in 1783, £43,049 in 1788, more than
£180,000 in 1803, and more than £300,000 upon his death in 1832. His
wealth increased at a fairly moderate pace before the 1790s (accumulation
over several generations was typical among Quakers, partly because of
the absence of primogeniture and the emphasis on just division of estates); it skyrocketed *after* the controversy of 1795. Moreover, cash shortages and long credit "significantly complicated—and not infrequently
compromised—individuals' perceptions of economic profit and loss in
their market transactions." As we have seen, wealth was a continual process of ethical judgment about credit, something much more complex and
volatile than simple possession of large amounts of cash in a stable banking
system. Indeed, hoarding money would threaten trust and the circulation
of social capital on which credit and exchange depended. Nor did wealth
necessarily provide a measure of profit, which possessed a temporal quality. Accounting practices did not readily lend themselves to assessments of
profitability. Galton Jr. considered his profits modest, aiming to keep them
steady more than large, like his father, who continually urged James
Farmer to moderation and fretted that his own request for an equal share in
the partnership might incite suspicions of an "engrossing temper." Indeed,

his calls to reduce production and his reluctance to engage in discounting were the result of his "being determined to rest contented wth a very moderate profit." The gun's perishability made modesty imperative, too; greedy overproduction would result in the excess rotting in storage. A windfall of custom only made the senior Galton anxious about "hurrying guns through finishers hands." Farmer & Galton remained the humble refuge to which Farmer hoped to return after his speculative adventures. The state's efforts to keep the trade diffuse reinforced the modesty of profits. Complicity in gun production was both wide and modest, to those considering their own contribution to it. Eighteenth-century people generally did not use a language stressing "private desire for profit over mutual interdependence" to interpret what they were doing. That the gun business eventuated in a great deal of personal wealth did not, for Galton Jr., mean that it was particularly profitable; rather, this was evidence of a complex array of other factors—prudence, providence, persistence, and so on.

Even fantastically successful Quakers understood their wealth as unsought fruit of the pursuit of modest returns (as we have seen with Barclay). They were also wary of how easily all could be lost again, given the fickleness of eighteenth-century fortune. Agatha Barclay reminded her cousin Mary Farmer, upon Mary's marriage into the Lloyd family, that "those apparently in a prosperous state may in a future day want that sympathy they have bestowed on others." War being a frequent source of this erratic prosperity, Quakers spoke resignedly of financial participation in it. During the Seven Years' War, Freame bemoaned that "we are overwhelmed with a multitude of business," concluding sagely that "what can't be cured must be endured"—an adage designed to clear the conscience. He complained frequently of "our hurry in business" while entertaining "hopes of peace . . . which . . . will set us a little more at liberty than we have had for a considerable time past." Oddly, from any but an eighteenth-century-Quaker perspective, he longed for the leisure that came with peace rather than the profits that came with war. This outlook could result in some convoluted sentiments: he grumbled in 1762 about the "disagreeable" work of raising supplies for the war, the cause of "all our hurry and confinement during the war, which I hope will be the last that I shall live to see, notwithstanding the badness of the peace, which indeed considering our glorious successes is bad enough." Charles Lloyd complained in a similar vein in the next war.

In this world, failure to amass easily transferable wealth despite a prosperous trade was entirely acceptable, if not an explicit aim. Lloyd praised his grandfather for being "too good a man to be an amasser of riches." Galton Jr. could tolerate his enormous fortune partly because his family's circumstances remained constrained: as he explained to his sons in 1819, his father had appointed most of the family property to Tertius, severely restricting his power to provide for all of his children as he would have liked. The gradual, intergenerational nature of Quaker wealth accumulation and resignation about the bounty of war shielded individual Quakers from the guilt of excessive greed. Context mattered tremendously; their wealth accumulation was as nothing compared with the notorious overnight richesse of nabobs and other kinds of contractors loudly disparaged in these years. Galton's conviction of the modesty of his trade and profits was honest.

His argument that he merely filled an independently existing demand for guns was as crucial to his self-exculpation and echoed the judgment of the Home Office spies of 1792 who did not hold gunmakers accountable for the destination of their goods. Instead, the gun consumer (the state) was accountable, just as consumers of slave-produced goods were accountable for the slave trade. Somewhat missing the abolitionist point, he argued that no commodity was inherently objectionable. He may have invoked the comparison to brewing with the irreproachable Barclay in mind; it was also an industry known for long partnership in the state's fiscal-military arrangements, implicating agriculture in that project. Of course, guns themselves were just then beginning to lose their neutral image and become an inherently bad good; the controversy of 1795 hung on that shift.

Galton's first observation—that guns did not promote war but, if anything, reduced its calamities—is not borne out by the facts in terms of number of military deaths but is of a piece with contemporary thinking about the deterrent or at least sanitizing role of guns in war vis-à-vis more intimately brutal weapons of the past. His second observation, about their usefulness in warding off ruffians (also armed with lesser and more ghastly weapons), likewise invoked the contemporary understanding of guns as deterrent instruments for the entirely justified defense of property. His related argument that he was no more responsible for the violent purposes to which guns were often put than the distiller or brewer was responsible for the abuse of alcohol carried a germ of truth, too: gun production was a complex and diffuse process, making it difficult to apportion blame or responsibility for the existence of firearms. As far as he could see, all of Midlands society was complicit in production of war matériel or financing. Indeed, Birmingham's general dependence on state custom was a great source of civic pride. In 1752, the city petitioned for local courts of conscience partly on the grounds that it employed "above Twenty thousand Hands, in useful Manufactures, . . . greatly serviceable to the Government." Sampson Lloyd, assigned to visit Galton as part of the disownment process, was the scion of a family that had long supplied and financed his manufactory. From Galton's point of view, guns were collectively—even socially—produced objects. Grand authorities had made this point, as we have seen: Adam Smith described "great manufactures" supplying the "great wants of the great body of people," which employed too many to collect in a single workhouse, precluding anyone from seeing more "at one time, than those employed in one single branch." Galton, too, perceived how division of labor alienated the manufacturer from his product; to him, this released the manufacturer from responsibility for what it became or the uses to which it was put. His father had always agonized over stocktaking, because of the difficulty of keeping up with the incremental progress of a highly divided production process that added value almost alchemically. With the emergence of complicated mechanical objects like the gun came a process of incremental manufacture, and the universal alienation from the final product made modern war making possible, made everyone complicit in it, made it the product of a system rather than of individual moral choice. Galton Jr. felt no more responsible than the manufacturer of the springs for his triggers. By launching a sugar boycott, the abolition movement illuminated the remote effects of market decisions, sensitizing eighteenth-century Britons to their complicity in slavery, but Galton turned that awareness on its head, arguing that complicity in gun production was so general that it rendered individual acts of abstinence futile. He imagined himself a cog in an enormous, inescapable wheel of highly divided industrial production in which many individuals earned profits too modest to impinge on any conscience. Cognizance of the impersonal efficiency of the "invisible hand" inhibited perception of a need for radical individual action; the system was always already in an optimal equilibrium. Opponents of abolition similarly considered the "intricate web of mutual dependencies" between buyers and sellers an insuperable obstacle. Competing views of market relationships coexisted: in some, the market enabled new understandings of complicity and possibilities for individual remedial action; in others, the market freed all from particular responsibility and constrained their scope of action as individuals. Galton's was the latter view; it emerged from the social relations that were his everyday experience of the market. The very networks of credit in which he was immersed implicated everyone and no one at once. Eighteenth-century businesspeople were painfully aware of their interdependence.

The Napoleonic Wars would soon damage popular faith in war as a crucial driver of trade. But from his vantage point in the Midlands at the start of those wars, Galton could not conceive of an alternative universe in which the state's primary expenditure was on peaceable "development." Commerce itself seemed impossible without the currency of guns. From Galton's perspective, *especially* in the Quaker network in which he and his business were enmeshed, it was difficult to envision an economy not dependent on war. His views were not eccentric for his time. Despite seeing war as mostly intolerable, he saw no way to end it. If he did not provide guns, the state would acquire them elsewhere or pursue war by what he envisioned as more brutal means. So, as Freame had put it, "what can't be cured must be endured."

Galton's third and fourth observations further articulated his sense of the inescapable nature of economic contribution to military activity. The Society's efforts to proscribe certain activities acknowledged the indirect ways in which an individual's economic activity might support warfare. Galton felt that its list of objectionable activities was arbitrary, shaped by convention (e.g., tithes were disallowed, but taxes were not), especially since seemingly unobjectionable actions—like consuming malt or beer—also inevitably fueled military power. Thus, only private judgment could determine which pernicious activities one was obligated to abstain from. By shifting to banking, the Lloyds had not escaped war-related activity; bankers underwrote government issues of stock and negotiated contracts for the payment and provisioning of British troops. The quandary faced by prominent Quakers was that their proud origins were in persecution and rejection of warfare, rank, and friends in high places, and yet their resulting industriousness had put them at the center of the maelstrom of power.

Galton pointed out that all Friends supported war through their taxes, not to advocate tax resistance but to highlight the impossibility of avoiding complicity in war in "the situation in which Providence has placed us." To be sure, tax resistance was a common form of popular rebellion—recall the smugglers of chapter six—but it was beyond the pale of the respectable industrial society Galton addressed. The Society of Friends routinely urged its members to comply with taxation. Given that reality, it was up to consumers, not producers, to exercise moral principle in the economy. (He supported his daughters' participation in the sugar boycott.) It is easy to fault Galton for refusing to recognize the difference in *degree* of complicity between consuming malt and supplying guns to the state. But his point was that if *principle* was at stake, degree did not matter. Only individual conscience mattered—a subjective rather than objective assessment of guilt, the only kind possible when complicity was systemic. He was like the abolitionist of the 1740s who argued that a slaveholder's conduct was not immoral as long as he did not see "the relation of one thing to another and the necessary tendency of each"; persisting *after* being convinced of these connections was the problem.

In acknowledging the practical impossibility of fully abstaining from economic participation in war, and in distinguishing defensive warfare as morally legitimate, Galton's defense reflected the power of eighteenth-century patriotism. Prominent Quakers were Britons first, he knew; they paid their taxes and supported Britain against the aggressor, France. Longing for peace in 1762, Freame knew it had become "more distant" since "we had the good fortune to take Havana and retake Newfoundland for these conquests intitle us to insist on better terms." Remaining aloof from public rejoicings over victories became increasingly difficult as war became the nation's central cultural activity. In 1782, Quaker homes were stoned for their self-exclusion from such activities. In 1789, they were again attacked for abstaining from public celebrations of the king's recovery from illness. Such were the tensions in which Quakers increasingly lived, and Galton's defense presumed a Society used to making compromises with the nation.

Hence his emphasis on private conscience, which governed his position on the abolition movement, too. His family had long been involved in the slave trade, but their kinsmen and friends (the Lloyds, Priestley, Garbett) had made Birmingham a capital of abolitionism. The town's abolition petition pointed particularly to the way the slave trade stoked war in Africa, directly implicating the gun trade. Meanwhile, John Whateley testified to the Board of Trade about the importance of the slave trade to Birmingham's gunmakers. Did Galton stand with his fellow gunmakers or his fellow Quakers (and sugar-boycotting daughters)? He dined with plantation owners interested in exploring steam as a substitute for horsepower; perhaps he favored the compromise position of the manufacturers who in 1789 called for regulating rather than abolishing the slave trade? Galton was also part of the deputation that welcomed the freed slave and abolitionist Olaudah Equiano to town that year. Equiano thanked the Lloyds for subscribing to the celebrated autobiography he published that year, acknowledging also the kindness of other "famous Birmingham names," including Galton, Boulton, Priestley, and Garbett. A year later, Galton and James Watt corresponded with a Liverpool slave trader about supplying engines for Trinidad. Galton was not alone in searching for a way to simultaneously pursue the African trade and abolitionism. Priestley's sermons envisioned an African trade in which Britons traded manufactures for sugar instead of slaves. David Barclay also juggled Atlantic business interests with abolitionism. As Galton and his friends picked their way through the moral and financial minefield of the slave trade, he saw his involvement in the gun trade as something the Society ought likewise to trust him to find a way to reconcile with his principles on his own terms rather than through the threat of excommunication.

The ultimate test of Galton's sincerity is perhaps the extent to which he remained committed to Quaker theology, whatever his ecclesiastical defiance. His family's ties to the Society were old and deep. His grandfather John Galton (1671–1743) had joined the Quakers early in the century by marrying into the Quaker Button family. Galton Jr.'s marriage in 1777 to a descendant of the Apologist strengthened the bond. He had attended the prominent Dissenting academy at Warrington, and he and Lucy Barclay raised their children strictly as Quakers. To be sure, his eldest daughter, the author Mary Anne Schimmelpenninck, experienced doubts from an early age, eventually converting to the Moravian Church and flirting briefly with Roman Catholicism, too. Tertius Galton would attend Cambridge University (unusual for a Quaker—he matriculated but did not graduate) and left the Quaker church in 1807 through his marriage to Violetta Darwin, daughter of the illustrious scientist Erasmus Darwin, Galton's Lunar Society colleague. Francis Galton's protégé the eugenicist Karl Pearson later described Galton Jr. as practically a Deist; and, theologically, perhaps as a result of long engagement with Lunar Society associates like Priestley and Enlightenment thought, he may have been. Fashionable education was important to the family. Considering his son John Howard's future education, Galton expressed particular admiration for the "habits of regularity and industry" the University of Glasgow cultivated, especially "as business is the ultimate object in view." But in 1795, much of this lay in the future; there is little reason to doubt Galton's claim that he was a devoted member of the Society of Friends, as evidenced by his stubborn attendance at and participation in its many activities despite the charges against him. The controversy did perhaps make it easier for subsequent generations to leave the fold: Galton's experience with the visiting process rankled enough that he advised John Howard not to accept such visits when the latter engaged to marry outside the fold in 1819. Sampson Lloyd III also broke with the Quakers over the Galton affair.

This attrition is a reminder that Galton's questioning of Quaker principle was part of a broader loosening of theological precision in this time, even as the sect was reinvigorated by abolitionism—which itself broke with tradition. Assimilation was a wider trend, particularly among wealthy Quakers. Alternative religious organizations proliferated in the wake of the evangelical movement (as exemplified by Schimmelpenninck's experiments). The Society dwindled from about sixty thousand effectives in 1680 to twenty thousand in 1800 and perhaps sixteen thousand at the start of Victoria's reign. Besides education, marriage took many from the sect, including the Gurneys, Barclays, and Hoares. Patriotism also caused disownments during the Napoleonic Wars, through enlistment and other forms of participation. The Galton case was one among this spate of wartime disownments, but it was perhaps unique in Galton's stubborn attachment to the sect regardless. The vigor of the abolition movement and the enhanced social selectness of the group as its numbers declined also helped many stay within the fold. The success, in 1828, of the movement to remove political disabilities applying to Dissenters also opened up more opportunities for Quakers. As religious conviction across sects diminished, cultural and sentimental attachment to a sect may have been strengthened, as in Galton's case. The family curated its Quaker heritage, particularly memory of the Apologist. Galton Jr. had his ancestors' headstones recut and freshly engraved with verses. The family cellars were full of fine bottles, and the house and grounds were "enchanting," but their opulent lifestyle remained restrained. The drawing room at Duddeston was still unadorned in 1827—neither pictures nor mirrors on the walls.

Distinctions of Quaker costume also became less meaningful as dress became less crucial to construction of the turn-of-the-century self. As Schimmelpenninck deduced, disguise could not make one into something one was not. Identity was not so mutable from the outside; and this, too, put a premium on private judgment. Galton's defense was partly an attempt at carving out a unique interpretation of his identity as a Quaker and industrialist, a way to be a Quaker without following the diktat of a Society that failed to grasp the final accountability to *individual* conscience. He asserted his capacity to remain a Quaker, socially and culturally, while theologically straying into personal interpretations of the faith encouraged by the evangelical trend. He wanted to have his cake and eat it too. He was part of a wider cultural focus on private moral judgment: churches no longer gave commandments, and the "shrine of morality" was understood to move within the self. Affluence and intellectual networks made this Galton's cultural milieu.

How convinced was Galton by his own arguments? That the family remained entrenched in the gun trade even after joining banking in 1804 suggests a fairly easy conscience. The gun business was wound down in 1815, when Tertius had already left the Quaker fold and preferred living off the revenue of his estate. The decision was governed more by the commercial reality that peace and the end of the slave trade promised a tough road ahead for gunmakers. What about earlier? Had the Galtons' consciences about gun manufacturing been as clear up to 1795 as the Society's collective conscience was, going by its ninety-year silence? Did the threat of disownment prompt Galton Jr. to undertake the scriptural researches included in his defense, or had curiosity and a clouded conscience led him to pursue such reassurance earlier? His astonishment at the Society's sudden censure seems genuine enough, and it seems likely that he assembled the facts for his defense only after the conversation had begun within the Birmingham Meeting. He may thus be accused of retroactively finding rationalizations for actions he had never found reason to closely examine until then, but we are left with the reality that his business had not perturbed his conscience anytime earlier. The fact that it was an inheritance loomed large in his mind; he described himself as "engaged in" manufacture of arms rather than simply a manufacturer of arms. He felt entrenched in that business, whether or not he objectively was—a more difficult matter to assess.

Smithian political economy has overpowered other sophisticated eighteenth-century views like Galton's. Francis Galton later (self-servingly) described his grandfather as possessed of a "decidedly statistical bent, loving to arrange all kinds of data in parallel lines of corresponding lengths, and frequently using colour for distinction. My father . . . inherited this taste." Indeed, Tertius, besides being a banker, made economics a field of personal expertise. Such thinkers helped produce new ways of thinking about economic activity and create "the idea of a distinctive space, or territory, of economic relationships" encompassing the production and distribution of wealth. Galton may have been on the wrong side of these developments, but more important is the fact that he was among those who thought in terms of those relationships, seeing them as constraining his own actions and potential for moral perfectionism. The eighteenth-century mind-set had only an inchoate sense of the distinctness of economic and political life. Concepts like "state" and "economy" were the objects of anxious and contested reflection, impinging on business decisions, including whether to invest in the slave trade or provide arms to the state. While Smith condemned the East India Company's combination of commercial and military power, others saw that combination as the secret of its success. They were skeptical of the notion of trade without force and of Smith's premise that individuals pursue their interests solely through economic competition. Smithian political economy trusted too much to individual judgment, critics worried; individuals were rarely so wise; their decisions were colored by political influence, including recommendations, taxes, and regulations. Such pre- and anti-Smithian understandings of the government's right and obligation to regulate the economy for the public good (e.g., by promoting exports, encouraging import substitution, supporting industries that enhanced military power) shaped the perspective of individuals like Galton. It was difficult for eighteenth-century people to think of their own behavior in terms of Smithian self-interest, given their intense interdependence through community-based networks of trust and credit. Certainly, the Age of Contract enabled more exchanges between strangers, but Smith's celebration of self-interest gained more purchase only after important shifts in the structure of and discourse about credit networks that made credit less dependent on individual morality and a more abstract and calculated attribute of larger-scale businesses. Those shifts were occurring around 1795 (becoming sweeping only after industrialization), but the Quaker network that Galton inhabited obscured that emerging reality for him in particular.

Accurate as many of Galton's observations were when set against the realities of eighteenth-century gun use and trade, the Society of Friends remained skeptical. They considered his letter formally at the Birmingham Meeting in February 1796 and informed him that they had not found his arguments substantial and were concerned that he "should attempt to vindicate a practice which we conceive to be so inconsistent with our religious principles." The Preparative Meeting of Birmingham was instructed not to receive his collection.

The London Friend Morris Birkbeck's response to Galton's broadside was perhaps typical among those situated outside the Midlands. His copy of Galton's defense is annotated with his marginalia of doubt. He questioned the modest terms of the allegation (fact 1) as the result of excessive deference to Galton, underlining "some" and "applicable" and noting, "Are not all arms so applicable?" In fact, he countered, the "chief or principal part are not applicable only but designedly made for, intended, and actually applied to those purposes." Galton's disingenuousness on this point was "designed rather to mislead in the outset." The second fact he found equally objectionable, countering that the Society's judgments were clearly expressed in its minutes and read publicly at meetings, and animadversions had been made; Galton could not justly plead "ignorance of or not timely receiving any animadversion" before the public process began. He had mistaken the Society's "too great lenity and long forbearance." Galton's larger point—that the Society had not objected to his family's manufactory for a very long time—remained, however.

To Galton's third fact—the difficulty of converting the capital he had inherited to other purposes—Birkbeck asserted that it could "very easily" have been done. Moreover, it was immaterial to the Society whether he sustained a loss in converting his capital. The bottom line was that arms manufacturing was inconsistent with Society principles, "especially seeing . . . so many other honorable and eligible means open to choice." For Birkbeck, Galton's arguments that nearly all economic occupations and activities ultimately contributed to war held no water. He did not comment on them, seeing any attempt at defending arms manufacturing as sophistry. The sixth fact—that Galton would embark on a different trade given the opportunity—he likewise dismissed as "corrupt & unsound," alleging that Galton would quit only for a manufactory offering greater profit.

To the first observation, Birkbeck predictably pointed out the false distinction between defensive and offensive war, for "there can be no <u>war</u> without opposition, <u>murder</u> only." Galton had anticipated such objections with his scriptural arguments, but Birkbeck did not address the cases he invoked—use of guns for preserving the peace, supporting the civil power, preventing war. He considered the entire segment "illusory or inconsistent." He agreed on the guilt of distillers, but not in the sense of the reductio ad absurdum that Galton intended. The argument that guns made war less sanguinary he considered "weak, foolish talk." He sneered at Galton's claims of humility in his scriptural interpretations, finding them of a piece with the "eccentricity of the whole performance, address or apology* which ever it may be called." (The asterisk led to a footnote affirming that the letter was a performance, and a poor one.) On the roll call of Quakers who had made arms before, Birkbeck noted, "So have many Quakers carried arms till they became too <u>heavy</u> for them." In short, to Birkbeck the document was totally insincere and cynical, a hypocritical offering of weak rationalizations by a man "<u>who</u> can also furnish <u>arms</u> for the <u>slave</u> <u>trade</u>." The use of arms in war was no "abuse" of those objects, since that was the very use for which they were made and bought—even though possession of guns had been acceptable among Quakers up to this moment. Galton's defense patronized the Birmingham Meeting "as mere machines or puppets; having neither <u>feelings nor reason</u>." "Happily," he concluded, that meeting was actuated by superior sentiments. As an address to the Society at large, it was insolent and egotistical. His vehemence revealed the gap between the Midlands and London as much as a dispute between Quakers. Birkbeck picked up an odor of pragmatism in Galton's position, and pragmatism was untenable in the new age of principle.

After the unenthusiastic response, in March, during a home visit by Friends, Galton merely affirmed that his letter had not sought to attack

Quaker principles and that his opinion remained unchanged. He would not pledge to quit his business. The consequences were swift. The meeting declined "to receive any further Collection from him or to admit his attending our Meetings for discipline, as a testimony of our decided disunity with the practice of fabricating & selling Instruments of War." The minute reminded all members to "not only avoid engaging in personal Service and the fabrication of Instruments of destruction, but also in any other concern whereby our testimony against war may not be supported."

The last reminder may have been a concession to Galton's argument that he was far from alone in profiting from war. The evidence suggests that Birmingham Friends continued to see Galton's situation sympathetically, certainly more so than their London counterparts, as disownment proceeded. They were clearly eager to keep Galton in their midst. Perhaps because of this local sympathy, in April, hearing that the arms manufactory remained open, the regional Quarterly Meeting appointed five Friends to "visit & assist" the Monthly Meeting in their task. Gibbins, Baker, and Lloyd took two of them to visit Galton, again without appreciable results. In July, the Birmingham Meeting approved William Lythall's request to see Galton again, in company with other interested Friends. In August, one of these reported that Galton still found it impractical to relinquish "that part of the concern" which made the Society uneasy. Within weeks, the meeting had concluded that there was no excuse for further postponement, after the "great labour" that had been bestowed; the Society had to be clear "from an imputation of a practice so inconsistent as that of fabricating Instruments for the destruction of mankind." The Birmingham Meeting declared Galton "not in unity with" the Society "& hereby disowns him," hoping "nevertheless" that "he may experience such a conviction of the rectitude of our Principles & a practice correspondent therewith as may induce Friends to restore him again into unity with them." Lloyd and Gibbins read him the minute.

Karl Pearson, who thought Galton's defense "excellent common sense," noted Galton's "characteristic stubbornness" in persisting in his business almost because of the meeting's interference. Galton also disregarded the disownment, as promised: he and his wife continued to attend the worship, although he could not take part in business meetings. He continued to donate heavily to the Society's Ackworth School, outdoing the Lloyds, and engaged in other visible philanthropic works, earning public praise for donating another £300 to the hospital. While the controversy unfolded, he had helped found a humane society for rescuing the drowned (by rewarding rescuers and establishing treatment houses), raised funds for relief for the poor, donated to famine relief, and joined the committee in charge of subscriptions for corn and wheat relief. In 1798, he promoted the Birmingham Library and donated funds to the Overseers of the Poor. He subscribed to the "National Stock"—the Society of Friends' fund for the poor—outdoing Gibbins and Lloyd. He participated in the plan to enlarge the meetinghouse in 1796—while in conversation with the Ordnance Board about erecting a proofhouse in Birmingham. No wonder, then, that his good works did not seem to impress in London. In 1798, the Yearly Meeting dwelled on the failure of the third abolition petition in the Commons, affirming the sect's commitment to the rights of Africans and peace among men, "especially" the need to avoid seeking or accepting "profit by any concern in the preparations so extensively making for war," for it would be "reproachfully inconsistent" to "refuse an active compliance with warlike measures and, at the same time, not to hesitate to enrich ourselves by the commerce and other circumstances dependent on war."

Perhaps this was a swipe at Galton. Nevertheless, when the senior Galton died the following year, at the age of eighty, his reputation was intact. The local paper memorialized a "gentleman peculiarly distinguished by his numerous charities, and who, we are well assured, failed not every year to distribute, with his own hand, among the poorest classes, a sum of *Five Hundred Pounds*, besides performing other great acts of benevolence." *Gentleman's Magazine* celebrated his qualities: "A sound and acute understanding, a quick and clear conception, extended views and a mind active and firm, joined to the habit of unremitting industry, commanded success with regard to the improvement of his fortune. The same talents were ever ready to be employed in giving advice and assistance to those who asked and in forming and directing charitable institutions." No mention was made of the commodity upon which he had founded his fortune. The notice remarked on his "great hospitality," which was enhanced by "the urbanity and courtesy of his manners, by an agreeable, well-formed person, and a countenance expressive of the intelligence of his mind and the cheerfulness of his disposition." It acknowledged the "uncommon dignity" and "powerful mind" that had enabled him to "support those trials which related to himself, without relaxing in his attention to the distresses of others" (including the early deaths of six of his seven children). At his burial, noted one account, "a larger concourse of spectators attended than we ever remember to have seen on a similar occasion."

Galton Jr.'s reputation also proved resilient. Perhaps his father's passing, his own charitable works, and his continued attendance together were too much to gainsay within his immediate Quaker community, for, in 1803, the Birmingham Meeting accepted his donation toward an enlargement of the burial ground that had received his father's remains—perhaps ensuring future space for himself and his wife. In June, he engaged workshops in London and obtained an Ordnance Office contract to repair Tower guns. Through Matthew Boulton, he obtained an East India Company contract. Then, in 1804, he passed the business to Tertius, who had come of age, although his money remained in the partnership (as his father's had in 1795). In November, the family launched into banking, possibly at Barclay's suggestion. Rising fortunes in town were calling rivals to the Lloyds' bank into existence; Wilkinson, Startin & Smith had opened in January. Galton and son partnered in their bank with Joseph Gibbins, one of the Friends who had been charged with Galton's disownment case and who was related to the Lloyds. Gibbins had abandoned the button trade out of principle in 1797, when many began to sell fraudulent double-plated buttons. He joined the copper business through a loan from Boulton, becoming proprietor of the Rose Copper Company, which supplied Boulton's mint. Galton had invested in that company in 1802. Despite his principled nature, Gibbins evidently felt no qualms about working with a man still invested in the gun business, whose banking capital emerged from that tainted source. When Gibbins left the bank in 1806, the Galtons were joined by Paul Moon James, Charles Lloyd's son-in-law, in a partnership that lasted twenty years. (Gibbins joined a bank in Swansea. In

1829, his son would open the Birmingham Banking Company, which later absorbed the Galton bank, becoming the nucleus of today's Midland Bank.) Barclays & Co. also readily served as the Galton bank's London discount house.

The family remained associated with the gun trade and its war profits. Galton may have been among those Birmingham individuals "concerned in the making and manufacturing of Arms" who in 1805 petitioned Parliament against abolition. In 1806, he persuaded the Ordnance Board to grant him a price hike by complaining that abolition was about to shut them out of a key market for rejected Ordnance barrels. This was when the Galton fortune skyrocketed into six figures and John Howard Galton's friend Richard Rathbone teased from Liverpool that gun sales were making him "very rich." Touching on news of the Gurneys and the Barclays, Rathbone concluded, "As I really am a good Quaker you would oblige me by directing all my letters, merely Richard Rathbone, Liverpool"—without further embellishment. He then signed off by cheekily affirming friendship with "Mr. J. H. Galton Esq." Quaker bonds were as tight as ever, but also, among the new generation, lighter. Their parents had been patriots, and this generation assimilated the militarism of their time. Hubert wrote playfully to his brother John Howard that he and his army were preparing to occupy Oxford's suburbs, scribbling at the top, "Burn this."

It is hard to tell whether the Galton family's civic achievements in this time tactically insulated them from ill repute or built on an actually unmarred reputation. They were typical of Quakers who contained the contradiction of growing affluence and the principle of modesty through philanthropy. In 1809, Tertius held the title of overseer of the poor, and his father chaired the Lancasterian Society for promoting new kinds of public education. (Paul Moon James was secretary, and Sampson Lloyd treasurer.) They guided foundation of a Lancasterian Free School in Birmingham. In 1811, Galton Jr. helped found the Birmingham Philosophical Society. He and Tertius served on the town's first committee to support and teach deaf-mute children. Tertius was high bailiff of Birmingham in 1813 and chaired the town's Commercial Committee from its inauguration that year through 1830. Later, he was town magistrate and deputy lieutenant. He was not involved in the town meetings that led to establishment of a proofhouse in 1813, nor was he a subscriber to the proofhouse—perhaps because the Galtons had their own. But in 1815, when controversy over its management erupted in an effort (led by their old nemesis Hadley) to disestablish it, Tertius chaired a meeting calling for it to be run by independents rather than gunmakers, obtaining an act of Parliament for the change. His firm did not sign the resolution (perhaps because it was closing just then?), but his trade loyalties were strong enough that he participated in the 1816 meeting at which gunmakers resolved to protest the Ordnance Office's rumored plans to remove gunmaking from the town. He was also chosen to take Birmingham's addresses to the prince regent upon the restoration of the peace and the marriage of Princess Charlotte, in 1815 and 1816. In 1796, Galton Jr. lost the debate with the Society of Friends, but he won the larger battle to remain within its fold without altering his family business, until it suited him to alter it.

He did so despite the Society's hardening attitude toward guns themselves. In 1812, upon hearing that some Friends had followed their neighbors in securing armed protection for their property, the Yearly Meeting urged trust in divine protection. It cautioned "Friends everywhere against keeping guns or arms of any kind in their houses, or on their premises, or in any manner uniting in armed associations, that so, whatever trials may take place, our Society may not by thus becoming liable to contribute to the destruction of their fellow creatures, violate our peaceable principles." Guns were now purely weapons, a "bad good," like slaves, without civilizing justification. That view was consolidated with the Society's outright rejection of Galton's claim otherwise in 1796. Galton's rationalization had been part of a collective rationalization evidenced by the Society's long silence on his business until that point. That long indulgence was shaped by a more open-ended understanding of guns as something besides weapons and a more restrictive understanding of economic life as intensely constrained by circumstance. Only when both of those notions shifted did Galton's business begin to appear odd to all but Galton himself, who remained convinced of—or deceived by—both guns' wider uses and his limited range of action as an economic actor. Galton's defense may betray the man's overweening spiritual, social, and intellectual conceit, but it also possessed analytical merit.

By insisting on the particular perniciousness of Galton's trade and evading the questions he raised about collective, societal complicity, the Society fell victim to another kind of false consciousness, which endures today: avoiding the truth that modern life is founded, intrinsically, on militarism and that industrial life has historically depended on it. Galton's grasp of his circumstances shielded him from any sense of complicity in a social or moral wrong; the Society's condemnation of him shielded its members from any sense of their own complicity in social and moral wrongs, too. In a sense, with abolition's notion of complicity, industrial society invented a means of scapegoating particularly toxic activities attached to it in order to ensure survival of the whole. The scandal became Galton's arms manufactory rather than the entire Midlands economy's dependence on government contracts. Just as virtuously boycotting sugar enabled uninterrupted consumption of rum and tobacco, so disownment of Galton normalized a provincial banking industry founded on fortunes from war. Industrial-capitalist society survives by focusing critical energy on elimination of particular evils and abuses rather than on the perniciousness of that entire mode of existence. In the nineteenth century, Marx reopened the question of systemic wrong, as did Henry David Thoreau with his advocacy of tax resistance. But the targeted tactic of boycott has endured better than ecumenical critiques requiring revolutionary change. There is perhaps poetic irony in the way the verb *bore*—referring to making or drilling a hole—also came to mean "tiresome or dull" in the eighteenth century: the repetitive mechanical movements of industry came to stand for a new kind of numbed mind.

Galton's arguments about universal investment in war did find validation later in other quarters. In 1815, protestors in Manchester claimed, "The great importance of trade and manufacture in this country has been fully evinced during the . . . war, by enabling us to call forth resources impracticable in any state that was merely agricultural." In 1857 in

Birmingham, the Quaker John Bright's candidacy as a Liberal was challenged (unsuccessfully) on the grounds that his pacifism fit awkwardly in a town whose trade depended on war—including guns and "the other paraphernalia of military metallic supplies." The stakes in acknowledging wider complicity in arms making are not merely Galton's innocence or guilt, but our own understanding of the way imperial wars produced the structures of modern finance, commerce, industry, and governance. The fiscal-military state and the consumer revolution were coeval *and* joint developments. By criticizing gun manufacture, the Society of Friends avoided criticizing war and conquest. It did not try to affect war in the manner that it sought to change the slave trade. It was content to let arms manufacturing go on so long as its own members were not implicated. Though it framed participation in war making as voluntary, it did not see war as disruptable. Galton, meanwhile, saw himself as powerless to effect change. Despite the promise-keeping culture of his time, he pleaded circumstantial obstacles to living the kind of life that, as a Quaker, he had promised to live. The abolition movement took off when slavery was understood as the fault of specific groups—planters or traders—and specific laws and policies. The Galton case reveals the tenuousness of such notions of particular complicity and individual responsibility in an actual world of interdependent economic actors and networks. Even Adam Smith, while urging the self-governance necessary for free trade, acknowledged systemic limitations. His critique of the East India Company blamed the entire "system of government" constraining its agents; he conceded that those who would criticize them would "not have acted better themselves" in the same situation. Nineteenth-century evangelicals, like nineteenth-century socialists, expected more; they insisted on individual responsibility even in a context of complex processes.

Private judgment, individual responsibility—these are terms for the assertion of agency, the free exercise of self-willed behavior. Galton insisted on exercising his own agency as the judge and arranger of his moral conscience while also insisting on his lack of agency as a businessman, given social and historical circumstances. (Despite the debate's religious stakes, he did not invoke spiritual constraints on his agency—God's will.)

He articulated an understanding of compromised agency that a historian would feel entirely comfortable with, an elite British industrialist-capitalist's version of "Man makes his own history, but not in circumstances of his own choosing."

Modern as this subjectivity was, up to his death at age seventy-nine, in 1832, a year after his bank closed, Galton wore a powdered wig and pigtail. He was a genteel man of the eighteenth century, remembered as "an old Birmingham worthy" among "those men whose names and memory we should not let die . . . active in all the good works of the time," taking "great interest in everything which could advance the intellectual and spiritual, as well as the material well-being of the town," a "member of the famous Lunar Society, . . . friend of Watt, Boulton, and other leading men of the time," and father of "the celebrated Mrs. Schimmelpenninck." His adoring children felt they had lost "their friend, their companion, their everything . . . In all troubles . . . our adviser and sympathiser. We felt alone in the world." They and their descendants curated his memory, making this book possible. The family archive that began with detailed exchanges about gun sales fell silent on such matters in later decades, yielding to a steady account of births, deaths, weddings, and the transfers of wealth pertinent to such occasions. But Galton did succeed in preserving for posterity his defense of that increasingly invisible trade. Resurrecting its vision of industrial capitalism's dependence on warfare does not so much exonerate him as implicate *us*. Quaker values and networks were good for banking and commerce; they also supported the foundation of the warfare state. Quakers may have been hesitant in embracing modernity, but an elite subset proved central to its very making.

Later Quakers looked back on Galton's defense more favorably. Edward Hicks, an American Friend and editor of *Quakeriana*, thought it "very able." Samuel Lloyd, whose 1907 family history devoted a chapter to the Galtons, called it a "clear, argumentative, and able statement," particularly validating its claims about early Quaker principle. He referred to a document sent to Sampson Lloyd in 1757 proving that, in early times, leading Friends had thought force might be used to preserve the peace, as Galton still believed in 1795. Such had also been the views of the generation that had raised him, explained Samuel Lloyd. He recalled a tea party in 1858 at the home of the "great philanthropist" the Quaker abolitionist Joseph Sturge, where he met the missionary-explorer David Livingstone, about to leave for Africa. Asked whether, as a peaceable man, he carried weapons of defense, Livingstone had replied that the only weapon he carried was a gun. It was easy to question doing so from a drawing room in Edgbaston, Livingstone conceded, but alone among the natives of Africa, it was a different thing: "When the natives saw that he could bring down a bird useful for food by his mysterious weapon, those not friendly to him felt some awe; otherwise . . . one would come near and touch him; another, seeing no harm resulted, would take something from him; others would then do the same, and he would soon be deprived of everything of any value." Sturge asked what Livingstone would do if someone stole his watch in the streets of Birmingham; would he not call on the police to get it back? Livingstone would not commit. (In fact, he reported on missionary and merchant gun sales in southern Africa.) Lloyd traced his adult convictions to this scene. The imperial excuse for guns had become Quaker-proof. Against those who would threaten property in Africa, if not on the well-policed streets of Victorian Birmingham, guns were common sense. Still, he opposed war between *Christian* nations, citing Prime Minister Henry Campbell-Bannerman's recent speech blaming the policy of large armaments for raising that specter and calling on statesmen to adjust armaments to "new and happier conditions." Where were such statesmen? he asked. Like Galton, he blamed the arms buildup of his time on their purchasers rather than their manufacturers. But the very same year, two gunmakers publicly criticized the British government's cavalier treatment of their industry to explain its dramatic "decay." Over the course of the nineteenth century, the government struggled to at once maintain productive partnerships with its arms industries and limit the spread of arms in its constantly expanding empire.

The Gun Trade after 1815

The Napoleonic Wars secured British imperial power and the Galton family's prosperity for the coming century. Tertius carried on his forefathers' philanthropic tradition and invested in his scientific pursuits. He was a major provincial banker until the family bank closed in 1831. The Steelhouse Lane premises were let and then sold in 1844. His father had been the single most successful businessman among the Lunar Society associates. James Keir and Matthew Boulton invented more; but Galton outdid them in sheer wealth. Galton Bridge, in Smethwick, was named for Tertius in 1829—the second feature of the regional canal network named for the family. (The other was Farmer's Bridge Locks.) Tertius's brother John Howard married into the Strutt textile family. His son Sir Douglas Strutt Galton was a Birmingham Council Chamber member of considerable literary gifts, a member of the British Association and the Royal Society, and an engineer. His daughter's husband died in a shooting accident, ironically, but her second husband was governor of the Bank of England, president of the Hudson's Bay Company, and a major investor in Harrods. Douglas collaborated closely with his wife's cousin Florence Nightingale in improving the safety of hospitals and barracks; she lobbied for his appointment as assistant undersecretary at the War Office in 1862. Another cousin of Francis Galton, Arthur

Galton, attended Oxford and was a vicar in Lincolnshire, author of many books on history and poetry, and mentor to the novelist Frederic Manning, whom he brought from Australia after serving as secretary to the governor of New South Wales. Tertius's and John Howard's marriages severed their bonds with the Quaker church but bound the Galton family to the main currents of nineteenth-century British history. By midcentury, most of the descendants of prominent Quaker families had become Anglicans. Assimilation often entailed acquisition of country estates and pastimes, including shooting. It was perhaps only in Francis's anxieties about breeding that the lapsed principle of endogamy remained influential.

Other gunmakers did well, too. John Whateley left large legacies and property to his children and a life of leisure to his eldest, Henry Piddock Whateley. John Parr, Galton's erstwhile agent and later an independent gun manufacturer, left large workshops and properties in Liverpool. He invested some of his profits in a steam-powered cotton factory. His children carried on the gun business. Of thirty-one men who called themselves gunmakers whose wills were proved in Birmingham between 1820 and 1840, fifteen left personal estates worth £1,000 to £10,000; ten, probably small masters, left estates worth less than £500. Gunmaking was profitable over the long eighteenth century, fueling not only banking but also cotton and other horizontally and vertically linked endeavors. Britain's historic prosperity depended heavily on war and slavery. The Fabian sociologist Beatrice Webb recognized the monied class dominating London in the late nineteenth century as the "old-established families of bankers and brewers, often of Quaker descent."

Apart from gunmakers, Birmingham as a whole continued to prosper as the source of "nearly the whole of the hardware wants of the world." As the empire expanded, the domain of private property—in contemporary language, "civilization"—stretched, and doorknobs, padlocks, and keys found large markets in Australia, New Zealand, India, Canada, the Cape Colony (in southern Africa), and the West Indies. Chains, cables, anchors, hollowware, jewelry, nails, and hinges were exported all over. Having supplied the guns to conquer the empire, the city retained a crucial imperial role. It remains wealthy today, but the gun industry is nearly gone. Before it declined, however, it changed—and its transformation, characteristically, altered adjacent industries, too.

I n 1816, the trade extracted a pledge from the Ordnance Office to rely on it in future wars in "the same proportion" as in the previous war. Enfield could not turn out a large order: the storekeeper George Lovell often suspended production of one type of arm to focus resources on another. Still, the trade's immediate prospects were not encouraging. Continuing friction with Spain resulted in passage of the Foreign Enlistment Act in 1819, which prohibited sale of war vessels to foreign states, blocking sale of small arms for them, too. In 1827, Egypt bought vessels and arms from Marseilles, Trieste, and Venice, despite hoping to get them in England. An order-in-council in 1825 prevented British gunmakers from supplying the Ottoman-Greek conflict; guns for the Greeks were seized in the Thames. The careless supply of the previous century, when Britain had been an empire on the make, yielded to a more cautious effort to preserve diplomatic relations and maintain moral prestige, even at the expense of domestic industry and trade. At home, fear of revolution constrained markets. Besides the Six Acts of 1819, the Seizure of Arms Act of 1820 empowered justices of the peace to seize and detain arms that might be used by revolutionaries. In Ireland, annual Coercive Acts restricted arms possession. The 1820 law lapsed, but others later sought to limit arms possession.

The Ordnance Board issued a few gun orders: cadet muskets for the military academy in 1818–19; 450 infantry rifles contracted in 1820; 300 pairs of sea service pistols recut and adapted by contractors in 1821; and contracts for 1,700 pairs of new land service pistols. Some of this work may have aimed at establishing the trade price for the work to fix prices at Enfield, where more may have been made. The trade also produced, jointly with Enfield, 10,000 of the 1823-pattern infantry rifle through 1827; Enfield made only half. Several contractors also made components for Enfield: side-nails, rammers, ribs. In 1828 came an order for locks from nine contractors. Guns also remained an important currency and a barter good for West African commodities such as palm oil—a crucial industrial lubricant. Establishment of the Birmingham Proof House, in 1813, bolstered the reputation of Birmingham guns used in that trade. A contemporary account reports 100,000 to 150,000 Birmingham guns exported to Africa annually. Britain dominated this trade through the 1840s. British gunmakers also supplied the Anglo-Burmese War of 1824. Some established businesses in India, where they forged hybrid guns with Indian stocks and English locks. The Birmingham trade was prosperous enough to inspire the French general Marshal Soult when he visited in 1828. Two years later, London and Birmingham were supplying the French National Guard; a large order in London for the Russian government followed in 1831. The "Musket Wars" fought in New Zealand among Maori consumed large quantities of British guns, killing a third to half the Maori population.

But as the state remained ambivalent, the gun trade felt threatened. In the midst of this spate of international orders, in 1829, the anonymously authored *Observations on the Manufacture of Fire-Arms for Military Purposes* called attention to the trade's importance to the Birmingham region and the state, and the risk posed by Enfield and the Foreign Enlistment Act. The Ordnance Office sold muskets instead of buying them, the author complained, citing government sales to Spain in 1831–32. The office also had unfounded faith in Enfield's abilities when the trade's spirit of competition and exertion enabled it to make the best and cheapest goods in a way no public body could. Moreover, "general opinion" dictated that government should not establish manufactures except when industries indispensable to public service were not practiced sufficiently to supply the country. The Ordnance Board claimed that Enfield would secure it against combinations, but it could acquire a workforce only by enticing workmen from the trade, compromising the trade's ability to meet supply objectives. He urged faith in market equilibrium: given sufficient demand, private makers would, from their own interest, train new workmen: "In a manufacturing country like England, the demand for every article will soon produce a corresponding supply and demand and supply will soon find a level." The board had seduced some of its best workmen to the Tower, raising their wages by nominally enlisting them in regiments. By spreading contracts among thirty or forty masters in London and Birmingham, rather than among a few large suppliers, it had enhanced the risk of combination. Still, he assured, no combination would last a month if the board acted "with common prudence." Furthermore, the private trade could do much more in the area of experiment, as governments are "proverbially supposed to be the last to deviate from the old beaten track and to improve upon articles of manufacture." If economy was its object, why did the board's factories manufacture barrels and locks when the necessary raw materials did not exist at Lewisham? In 1813, when "everyone with common sense knew the war was ending" and stores were full, it had extravagantly erected this factory. Its calculations of economies omitted the tens of thousands spent on buildings and machinery. And it did all this while the private trade was fully meeting demand: lock provision had increased steadily, from 81,000 in 1804 to 234,773 in 1809. Lewisham had, in fact, retarded supply by making it harder to keep workmen. After the war, Enfield had wastefully turned old barrels into nails—exchanging silver for iron. Competition from the state factories had driven walnut prices up. In short, the state's factories harmed the private trade, the public purse, and supply itself. Meanwhile, the Foreign Enlistment Act unjustly extended control on exports into peacetime. The gun trade, like others, should be left free and unfettered, not least since other European states did not restrict their arms makers.

This liberal critique was the beginning of *our* forgetting of the state's role in industrial change in the eighteenth century. The trade forgot how crucial the state had been to its survival; the state factories were merely the latest chapter in the long story of state intervention in the trade. Implicit in this critique was the Galtonesque argument that there was nothing particularly bad or dangerous about guns as commodities. The uses to which they were put were not manufacturers' concern; better they should profit than others. As the state began to prioritize diplomacy abroad over diplomacy toward the trade, gunmakers resorted to reminding it of the risk of "ingratitude," especially since there was no guarantee that foreign powers could or would supply them as they had in the past. The government must enable England to once again "become the manufactory and depot for the supply of the whole Globe." But the very existence of the state factories enfeebled such threats, as was their design.

A decade later, adoption of the percussion principle reopened the debate. Stores were low; the Ordnance Office had indeed sold many arms. In 1838, British forces were rearmed with percussion-style muskets based on a design by Lovell. The Ordnance Office had the new arms made by contract rather than in its own factories. Enfield could produce and assemble parts, but its output was considerably less than the trade's warren of workshops. Birmingham remained "the great school in which the Royal Manufactory must always seek its hands," Lovell held; workers often preferred returning to it after just weeks in Enfield's rural marshland. He reopened and refurbished the Ordnance premises in Birmingham, serving as inspector of small arms there starting in 1840. The old system was in full swing by 1841, when a fire destroyed thousands more arms in the Tower, making supply more urgent. The need to cultivate the trade had also become more politically persuasive after the mass working-class movement for political reform known as Chartism began in 1838, raising fears of armed rebellion. The home secretary took the trouble to confirm from the trade that the bulk of the arms they had made lately had been for export.

Birmingham masters used machinery for barrel boring, but not much in other parts. The trade thwarted Lovell's attempts to introduce machinery expressly to break up unions. Enfield adopted machinery for certain processes, including a lock plate driller in 1842 and percussioning machines in 1845. Stock making remained free of automation: stock-making machines used at Springfield, Massachusetts, were offered and rejected in 1841. Complete guns were still fitted rather than assembled. (Enough machinery was in use in Birmingham on the whole that a movement to revive vanishing metalworking arts began in 1838.) Price negotiations between contractors, small masters, and artisans continued to structure the trade and its ability to complete contracts on time. Strikes were frequent, and the local press warned gunmakers to resolve disputes, lest the government turn to Enfield. Government representatives again intervened in industrial relationships: Lovell mediated price fixing between masters and work-men, despite the Ordnance Office's insistence on the impropriety of such interference. He claimed to act in his private capacity, to prevent masters from exploiting or poaching workmen in order to ensure steady supply, but the trade perceived him as acting in his official capacity. The agreed-upon prices were posted in the view rooms in Birmingham, signed by Lovell, as inspector. Strikes ceased for a few years. At least one gunmaker consid-ered Ordnance Office regulation of prices standard practice since the war, a mechanism for providing certainty that workers and masters otherwise lacked. Complaining workmen were referred to the posted list, putting the matter out of the master's hands.

The Ordnance Office worried that Lovell's intervention would en-courage gun workers to blame the office for their troubles, for, as these universal wage arrangements show, its old tactic of playing London against Birmingham had unraveled. Railways had brought the two groups to-gether, breaking down loyalty to locality in favor of loyalty to the wider trade. Together they accused Lovell of buying stocks from the Continent and taking "contracts out of the English people's hands." (Lovell insisted that walnut was scarce in England.) They accused the office of undersell-ing them in international markets. The Birmingham gunmaker William Greener testified before a government committee in 1849 that the office had sold arms to the Imam of Muscat, at a loss to the public. When the committee wondered at his credulity, he merely added that many aston-ishing things transpired. To gunmakers, their problems were caused by the state's bad faith as a partner and customer; after all, they produced masses of guns for the East India Company, Portugal, and the kingdoms of Sardinia and Denmark without so much difficulty.

The government committee had formed to address the difficulties that emerged in the rearmament plan. In July 1848, the Ordnance Office observed bitterly that either the trade's manufacturing powers were much less than was supposed or there was a tremendous lack of energy in calling them forth. Lovell threatened noncompliant contractors with exclusion from future contracts. But the well-organized gunmakers complained to *his* superiors. The Chartist disturbances of 1848 (and the revolutions then sweeping the Continent) were also a factor: newspapers were alarmingly reporting open sale of "war like weapons" in London. London's Metropolitan Police reassuringly provided the Home Office with an account of arms sold in the city. In February 1849, the Ordnance Office announced that contracts would be advertised for competitive tender without restrictions on rates paid to workmen. This, too, failed. "In some Cases Advertizing may prevent or break Combinations, in others it may form and strengthen them," the office learned. "By Advertizing you are tied down to admitt the cheapest without regard to Credit or substance, but by the other method you treat with none but reputable and Substantial People, and it is apprehended that by advertizing a door would be open to more abuses, than by the other method mostly Practised by the Office." As the office resorted to the very threats of exclusion that it had reprimanded Lovell for, a Select Committee of the Commons investigated whether there was a way to improve the mode of contracting for guns— the first of three major government inquiries into the private trade over the next century.

Many of those consulted criticized the office's strict inspection and granting of contracts for parts, rather than complete weapons. Rejected work fell entirely upon the workmen. "Men report . . . that they have worked for a fortnight and have but a very few shillings to take," Greener testified. But not all agreed that the inspection system was the problem. The committee decided against altering it but criticized Lovell's interference in wages, which Lovell justified by pointing to East India Company rivalry. William Sargeant and John Wheeler, also contractors, insisted that there was no way to improve the existing system.

To the state, the problem remained one of industrial organization; it needed to re-create the competition that had guaranteed cheaper prices in the past. There was no question of depending solely on government production. Lovell insisted that spreading production among Enfield, London, and Birmingham was key; they had to keep up the lock trade in London "in opposition to the trade in the country; as a check against it." He registered that "London and Birmingham, by means of the railway, are become one place, and the gunmakers . . . are in constant communication to settle the price . . . demanded of the Government." Enfield would keep that combination in check. Likewise, having all guns manufactured there would be risky, as "we should then have no check upon our own men." Lovell had long perceived the "evil tendency" of a system in which small arms were made only in Birmingham and London, in which government demand was irregular, sudden, and often enormous, and in which reliance on a few masters encouraged competition for workers, which workers exploited by combining. The remedy, he thought, was to equalize and regulate demand—spread it over a long period (at least three years) and across the entire trade. There should be only so many contractors—albeit with unlimited workers—to guarantee that each could profit through volume, keeping margins small. In the eighteenth century, diffusion had aimed to prevent Jacobites from capturing the kingdom's arms-making capacity and to purchase the loyalty of arms makers; now it was about ensuring affordability and supply. The outcome was the same: the state became invested in encouraging the health of the trade.

Meanwhile, techniques of gun manufacture were changing in the United States. Artisan ways prevailed in government factories on both sides of the Atlantic through the turn of the century. The manner of welding barrels remained the same in Harpers Ferry in 1807 and 1829. But the U.S. Army had absorbed the French goal of designing a uniform weapon whose parts could be replaced in the field. Lieutenant General Jean-Baptiste Vaquette de Gribeauval's ideas had wide influence from the 1760s; he promoted Honoré Blanc's efforts at making guns with uniform parts in the 1780s. Blanc's shops hosted American visitors, including Thomas Jefferson, ambassador at Versailles in 1785, who personally assembled fifty locks by taking pieces at hazard as they came to hand. He wrote home about it, and tried in vain to persuade Blanc to immigrate to the United States. He shipped six of Blanc's muskets to Philadelphia. In England, Henry Nock made screwless locks on a similar principle, and the Taylors used interchangeable-parts manufacturing to make pulley blocks for the navy. The objective of mass warfare produced the industrial principle of interchangeability, whose purpose shifted from easy repair to lower units of production. In 1793, Eli Whitney built a cotton gin to quickly separate seed from cotton fiber, revolutionizing raw cotton production. In 1798, the U.S. government was desperate for guns and hired contractors to make forty thousand—including Whitney, who accepted an advance to deliver four thousand muskets in 1799 and six thousand more in 1800. Legal battles around his gin kept him from completing his contract until 1809. But in the meantime, he learned of Blanc's work (possibly through Jefferson) and became a zealous advocate of uniformity, deeply influencing the first chief of the U.S. Army Ordnance Department, established in 1812 (during the war against Britain) to oversee the arsenals at Springfield and Harpers Ferry. Decius Wadsworth was a military engineer who knew French military engineers well; he prioritized uniformity especially because American ordnance was then so randomly assorted. In 1813, the Connecticut contractor Simeon North made pistol locks with interchangeable parts, and in 1815 the Ordnance Department acquired the teeth to implement uniformity as a general objective. It took time, however, not least because of resistance from artisans at Harpers Ferry. In 1819, the Harpers Ferry gunsmith John Hancock Hall contracted to make a breech-loading rifle he had patented in 1811. He used dozens of gauges and much machinery, showing definitively, in 1826, that his rifles could be made with interchangeable parts—the first of their kind. Legally, arms for militias had to be made by contractors, so the War Department had Hall share his technology with North. By 1834, North could make rifles that could be exchanged with Hall's. Ordnance policy was that contractors had to share their inventions without royalty, which helped innovation spread; few changes of this period were patented. The scale expanded in the 1840s, and interchangeable-parts manufacturing was adopted in the machine-tool and sewing-machine industries. This "American system of manufacture" was the result of long state investment in and direction of new techniques of arms manufacture aimed at fulfilling specific American military objectives. Military sponsorship enabled the technique to evolve over decades, despite unfavorable macroeconomic conditions, until it became attractive to private manufacturers later in the century. Only the federal government could have financed and organized this sustained, complex affair. Only it could give out the contracts that enabled private manufacturers like North and Whitney to make large investments in factories with machinery for interchangeable-parts manufacturing. These American developments soon impinged on the British debate about arms making.

In 1850, tenders for British government arms came in at the same price, indicating combination. Strikes caused delays. Adoption of a new pattern in 1851 triggered a fresh call for tenders and more evidence of combination and delays. The gun trade nevertheless prospered as exports expanded, including parts for the American machine-manufacture system. The Ordnance Office grew frustrated with its inability to *control* this thriving trade. It was the year of the Great Exhibition at the Crystal Palace in London—the first world fair. Birmingham's guns were proudly displayed and recognized for their beautiful design and excellent workmanship; barrel welders won a certificate of merit and a gold medal for the perfection of their work. But the exhibition included American guns with interchangeable parts. With help from the American government, Samuel Colt had also established a pistol factory in London, since England was "the greatest mart of fire-arms in the world." At these two sites, British Ordnance officials witnessed the wonder of the "American system of manufacture" up close.

Enfield was just then moving toward a more machine-driven structure. James Nasmyth's steam hammer was installed in 1851, and Lovell's rifling machine and a planing machine in 1852. Steam-powered machines (run by boys) jointed and percussioned arms and fit cocks to locks. The Ordnance Office turned to machines to subvert suspected "combination" behind barrel makers' tenders. Private barrel makers, in turn, complained in 1852, explaining that they had agreed to a price before they knew what they were contracting for, while facing a strike from the underpopulated grinding trade. They themselves had substituted costly grinding machinery to avoid a stoppage. They affirmed their willingness and capacity to make all the barrels needed, but the Ordnance Office insisted on the machinery. The barrel makers demanded an inquiry. Lovell affirmed that Enfield muskets passed the view more frequently because of the better "character and supervision" of workers and better housing and machinery.

The master general minuted this note as useful for answering attacks in Parliament. Setters-up, meanwhile, complained that parties who had not gotten contracts egged the workers on to demand higher prices. They asked for an official to settle inspection disputes, and for Enfield's wages to be posted in Birmingham to prove to workers there that they were getting the best prices possible. They asked that no price hikes be made at Enfield until "fair competition" had been achieved. They admitted to feeling intimidated by Lovell. Similar problems occurred with adoption of a new pattern in 1853. The insights of the Great Exhibition acquired greater purchase as the Crimean War began, pitting Russia against Britain, France, and the Ottoman Empire.

In 1853, a government commission visited the next world exhibition, in New York. It also visited American factories, including, only incidentally, the arms factory at Springfield. Among the commissioners was the eminent engineer and machine manufacturer Joseph Whitworth, who would give evidence the following year to a parliamentary committee considering the "Cheapest, most Expeditious, and most Efficient Mode of providing SMALL ARMS for HER MAJESTY'S SERVICE." In December 1853, the Ordnance Office sent the machine maker John Anderson, a proponent of machine adoption in Birmingham, to see Colt about his use of anthracite coal; he incidentally reported on machine production of guns there. As the committee investigated, an Ordnance officer visiting the United States inquired about government-run machine manufacture of arms. A memorandum of February 1854 also recalled how in 1803 the state had, with "great exertion and almost lavish expenditure," increased output of small arms. Prompt supply had delivered Europe from France, though the arms had been on the inferior Indian pattern.

The crux for the master general of the Ordnance Office, Lord Raglan, was that the office have at its command the means to supply the government "at any moment with a sufficient quantity of arms." He recalled 1814, when they had 800,000 men under arms and awaited "war near home," which would have required calling upon countless volunteer corps, all needing arms. Recent delays proved that the contract system could not fulfill such sudden large demands. Together, Colt's factory, the Great

Exhibition, and the commission in the United States triggered a new appreciation for machine production in the early 1850s. The office proposed construction of a large government factory at Woolwich for machine manufacture of arms, to make the office totally independent of contractors. Lord Seymour assured the rest of the committee that this would not controvert the 1849 decision against a government factory, because machine production had not been on the table then. Captain Sir Thomas Hastings, storekeeper of the Ordnance Board, explained his overnight conversion to machine manufacture: earlier he had urged manufacturers to improve their supply, lest the government turn to the United States, Liège, or a government factory, but after visiting Colt's factory, he had become convinced of the wisdom of a government factory, where strikes would be rare, since there would be little skilled labor, and all of it well paid. If workers did combine, the state could turn to artisans anywhere in the world or get a "few clever men" from Liège. Such epiphanies testify to Colt's skills not only as an industrialist but as a publicist and proselytizer. Besides displaying his guns at the exhibition, he had lectured to the Institute of Civil Engineers, where his friend and agent was secretary. His lecture on the application of machinery to the manufacture of firearms and their interchangeability, which he likely exaggerated, attracted great interest for two evenings.

The nature of the supply problem had also shifted for the Ordnance Office. The question was not whether gunmakers could make sufficient arms, but whether they could make sufficient high-quality arms. All of Birmingham's gunmakers—makers of superior fowling pieces, military arms, or more inferior trade guns—might together be able to make four to five thousand arms per week, but the military arms of the time—the 1853-pattern musket—were now of a superior sort. To the concern that a government factory would destroy the country trade, the office admitted that military musket making might suffer, but the rest of the trade would continue to thrive on foreign orders.

Those calling for a factory were also influenced by increasingly current notions about rationality in production. Several pointed to the trade's irrational organization. A delegation that had visited Birmingham reckoned it was fifty years behind the country's other branches of manufacturing, like cotton and machine making. A machine maker contended that division of labor was all to the good, but having barrels made in one part of town and locks in another was not division of labor in the right sense. Carrying baskets of parts through Birmingham's lanes was wasteful, explained Anderson, who made machines for making percussion caps—everything should be made in the same room. Anderson had also made machines for the cotton industry and pointed to the way cotton went in and product came out in Manchester cotton factories. When his interviewers pointed out that weaving, printing, and dyeing happened elsewhere, he insisted that the business was still done in a more "wholesale" manner, by wagonloads rather than basketfuls. He pointed to the layout of cotton factories, machines in rows performing incremental tasks. His questioners noted that cotton factories pulled together just two trades, spinning and weaving, while the gun industry comprised at least ten, but he dismissed their distinctions as remnants of a bygone era, conceding only that guns were made up of many more materials than cotton. Besides Colt's scornful testimony against hand manufacture, others, too, professed general faith in machinery as liable to improve production of almost anything, citing also the wretched conditions in which Birmingham workers labored, in cellars and garrets. A machine maker who had supplied Russia's Tula arms factory claimed that England's gunmakers groaned "under a kind of tyranny resulting from their dependence entirely upon the dexterity of their men; so much so, that those very gun masters themselves would hail it as an emancipation most desirable to be attained; they . . . are afraid to introduce the most obvious improvements, lest the men should . . . strike."

This raised the question of why the proposed factory had to be government-owned, particularly since Colt himself had just supplied the British Baltic naval fleet with pistols on short notice and offered a million arms for the government. Hastings explained that accepting that offer would award profits to Colt that would otherwise go into the pockets of the public. A machine maker added that government auspices would foster "unity of design," a single spirit, object, and system of governance. But, one gunmaker argued, a government factory would lack the fundamental drive of self-interest. Others cited as evidence against government-run small-arms manufacture Lovell's partiality toward viewers and Enfield and his abuse of his position to help his son set up a factory at Liège. The Ordnance Office repudiated this personal attack, not least since Lovell had just retired and was desperately ill. (He died that year.) Gunmakers also defended their trade: far from inefficient and declining, it was thriving, asserted John Goodman, who exported guns from Birmingham to the United States. His manufactory supplied all the locks to the American industry and the "Northwest" guns the American government provided to Native Americans. (They had recently shifted to a Philadelphia supplier but showed signs of reverting, and the Philadelphia supplier relied on Birmingham locks and furniture.) England also supplied the Hudson's Bay Company. Others tallied fowling pieces sent to America, cheaper guns for Africa, the countless foreign governments supplied—including, recently, Peru and Spain—the East India Company, and other Indian customers. Spanish war steamers got arms from London. Birmingham guns were reputed to be superior to any in the world; a Wolverhampton contractor's locks had been proudly displayed at the 1851 exhibition, too. Goodman reckoned that exports to America had increased five times in the past decade, that eight to ten other houses exported guns there, and that the workers who made them could make military guns, too. They opted for lower-quality trade work only out of frustration with the uncertainty of government work. Colonel Bonner, who superintended musket supply for the East India Company, avowed that its army of 200,000 had always relied on contractors and had never experienced difficulty, nor any sense that the contractors would take advantage of an emergency to raise prices.

Some argued by principle. Westley Richards of Birmingham made fowling pieces but also sights for the Ordnance Office. In 1852, he also improved the Minié rifle, a rapid muzzle-loading infantry rifle, for the government for £1,000—creating the Enfield rifle. He urged the flexibility of private contracting over a government factory. When a private arms trade existed, it could be called on in wartime to supply allies or stop the supply to enemies. By encouraging it, the government would both ensure

its own supply and exercise some control over the supply of other countries. He was also skeptical about the quality and interchangeability of
Colt pistols. Others argued that machine-made guns would be poorly finished, not entirely interchangeable, and wasteful. Moreover, gunmakers
already used a great deal of machinery—for rolling and boring barrels,
rifling, turning the iron, making the rod, cock, and lock, making sights,
and making materials, and for most aspects of revolver manufacture. It
was not all "made to appear in one place, but it is in various parts of the
town, and seldom seen by strangers." The trade knew when machinery or
hand labor was most efficient. The delays in 1851 were the fault of the
inspection process. A gunmaker who had served as an Ordnance Office
viewer in 1838 and a contractor from 1843 to 1851 explained that he had
tried and rejected a stocking machine and had not had sufficient government orders to invest in further experiments with machinery. Others
reported bad experiences with stock-making machines—in Belgium,
too. The pro-machine contingent replied that the latest machines were
more capable.

Some gunmakers conceded that more machinery would help. Lock
contractors expressed their desire to set up a factory like what the state
envisioned, and more cheaply. But they needed large, continual orders to
invest in it. Richards explained that adoption of machinery depended on
the size of the contractor pool: with half a dozen contractors, prices would
be lower and the incentive to invest in machinery greater; with twice as
many, when government demand declined, each would suffer only frac-
tionally and stood a greater chance of making up the loss with private
orders. The state countered that large, continual orders were unwise in an
age of rapid invention: the 1851 military musket had been entirely superseded in 1853. Some gunmakers insisted that large, continual orders did
not require identity of pattern and recalled the way they had supplied the
East India Company and the Ordnance Office in the 1840s while also
supplying foreign governments on short notice. Without large, continual
orders, it was difficult to complete a single large order, since labor dissipated into other channels. They met sudden demand by getting men from
the trades they had moved to; some even went without work until they

were induced to come back. They did not mind machinery so long as they had work. "Many . . . are in different parts of the country in different occupations," explained one gunmaker, "but they would gladly come back if they could find occupation in my manufactory."

The plight of men in the trade was a running theme in the debate. Many had had nothing to do since 1851 and were destitute and miserable. Sixteen London houses making guns for the Ordnance Office and the East India Company stood idle. A London contractor who had not made Ordnance Office guns since 1849 described many "walking about and leaving the trade." Stockers did carpentry at higher wages. Many were in wool warehouses or at the docks, some fixed rifle sights at the Tower, some were at Colt's. They no longer employed their children in their work, out of fear of passing on their fate of uncertainty. A former Birmingham contractor who had worked ten years at Enfield ultimately left the trade because contract prices were too low, as had others.

No one knew how many skilled men were at stake. Most agreed that four thousand was too low an estimate. Goodman said there were too many outworkers to say how many were actually employed. The elusiveness of such figures was a result of the long state effort to keep the trade diffuse. Government interest in them now emerged from concern about skilled labor for the proposed factory; the superintendent at Enfield, James Gunner, doubted that the government could get five hundred for a factory outside Birmingham, since workers there hated leaving the town—contradicting earlier assertions that workers preferred Enfield. Asked whether the Ordnance Office routinely poached men from the private trade, Gunner replied evasively that contractors poached his men. While shortage of hands was a continual refrain, so, too, was sudden competitive increase in hands. Hastings called for regulations to "counteract the growing evil of admitting fresh hands into the trade without some restrictions."

All points remained contested, but the gunmakers' pleas had significant impact. Committee members ultimately were not persuaded that machine production of long-barreled guns would work and worried about the effect of a loss of government orders on the trade. A certain pride in the nation's skill also came to bear. After all, Birmingham exported enormous numbers of guns to the United States, by now the capital of machine manufacture. Joseph Whitworth, impressed as he was by Springfield, insisted that ironworking was superior in England and that musket parts were better there than in the United States. He advised against erection of a large government factory in favor of a smaller, ideal establishment "to produce a limited number, and to set an example to other gunmakers." Even the American government relied on a mix of government factories and private manufacturers. Colt, too, urged the advantage of sacrificing some "cheapness" for the sake of maintaining the private industry: "Any person who has to negotiate with another [must] always . . . hold within himself the power to produce that which he requires of another." The American government could "produce at the national armouries double what they now do; they do not do so; they wish to encourage the artisans of the country." The committee concluded that "the advantage of an increased use of machinery and the expediency of making all muskets in a government factory are not . . . in any way necessarily connected." It recommended continuation of the old contract system and establishment of a limited government factory at Enfield, to test the gains from extensive application of machinery and act "as a check upon the price of contractors, and as a resource in times of emergency." The more ambitious original plan would have forced manufacturers to conclude that their employment was about to cease, and the public would have lost the advantage of their skill, capital, and enterprise. The recent supply problems were put down to overly strict inspection and delays in providing patterns to manufacturers. Birmingham possessed rolling machinery to make 300,000 barrels a year; clearly its gunmakers found more remunerative occupation in selling quantities abroad. The committee requested the Ordnance Office both to send enough patterns to accommodate all contractors and subcontractors and to date contracts from the time of pattern delivery. Contracts would be given only to men who had the means and capital to fulfill them, and an official would be appointed to whom contractors could appeal in conflicts over inspection.

Thus, the British state did not end its partnership with the private arms industry. The old political risk became entangled with the Victorian concern for industrial welfare. The need to keep the industry diffuse remained paramount. Besides Colt's articulation of the practical importance of multiple sources of production, the idea that the country "must wholly depend for the supply of materials upon Birmingham and its neighbourhood" remained concerning. Critics spoke of a barrel-making "monopoly." Lovell's 1851 warning that they "must always remember that military barrels are not made at any other place in the United Kingdom" was invoked. In 1829, Birmingham's gunmakers had held up as a great advantage the fact that during the wars, the government had been able to procure most of the arms it needed from a single town in the center of England, while the French government's manufactories were spread all over—"on the banks of the Rhine, at the foot of the Pyrenees, and amidst the Alps." But the government continued to see concentration through a glass darkly—finding validation soon after, in the seizure of Harpers Ferry during John Brown's raid in 1859.

In 1854, the Ordnance Office selected twenty firms to supply arms for the Crimean War. They united as an association to cope with competition for skilled workmen and regulate wages, akin to the cartel/committee formed during the Napoleonic Wars. Those who carried on the trade within ten miles of Birmingham borough and paid poor rates of a certain level belonged to this Birmingham Small Arms Trade Association, on an annual registration of a guinea. This body shaped the Gun Barrel Proof Act of 1855, another part of the appraisal of the trade, which aimed to increase safety for gun users. The association elected the proofhouse's managers. It regulated output, ensured constant supplies at fair prices, fixed wages, and determined selling prices. Workmen did not like it; the War Department eyed it with suspicion. Meanwhile, scandalous inefficiencies affecting the Crimean War led to the abolishment of the Board of Ordnance; small-arms procurement became the responsibility of a new committee. (A new board was formed in 1881.)

The supply scandals brought debates about gun production into the press. The *Times* of London challenged the trade's competence, denouncing the "absurdity" of the contract system, which had forced troops in the

Crimea to resort to bayonet charges and hand-to-hand encounters. The paper welcomed news that engineers were helping the trade progress: Whitworth had created a shooting gallery in Manchester for experiments with boring accuracy. Other Manchester machinists experimented in improvements, while bayonet, shell, mortar, and rifle-sight manufacture also came to Manchester: "The obstinacy of the Birmingham manufacturers in resisting the introduction of machinery is rapidly transferring an important branch of trade to the great centre of northern industry." John Goodman, as chairman of the small-arms association, replied that Birmingham was supplying rifles rapidly, two to four thousand per week; after the government had addressed problems with inspection, the city's gunmakers had proved that they could make the thousands required faster than ever anticipated. They knew best when machinery was appropriate and saw Manchester as no threat: "When I see . . . the ring of the anvil in our streets exchanged for the sound of the spindle, I will then begin to believe in the possibility of Manchester making guns or teaching Birmingham how to make them." The *Birmingham Journal* proffered similarly proud testimony. The trade reached its zenith of prosperity. One contractor established sawing mills in Turin, Italy, to convert 100,000 walnut trees into stocks, nearly denuding the area. Still, these debates helped concretize the belief that mechanization produced moral and economic advance, obscuring the trade's proven ability to meet sudden increases in demand by adapting internal structures.

A commission had left for the United States to inspect Springfield and Harpers Ferry and bring back machinery for stock- and lockmaking for Enfield. They persuaded the master armorer at Harpers Ferry to take charge of Enfield. The factory made locks and bayonets; its waterwheels were replaced by steam engines. It went into full production mode in 1856 as the Royal Small Arms Factory (as Colt's factory closed in failure). The sixty-odd parts of the 1853-pattern musket were made by machine; the total number of processes was greater than six hundred. The factory could make 130,000 complete muskets.

In 1856, the musket was introduced to soldiers of the East India Company army. Rumors that its paper-wrapped cartridges were greased with tallow derived from beef, offensive to Hindus, and pork, offensive to Muslims, "triggered" mutiny among Indian soldiers in 1857, which escalated into a widespread military and civilian rebellion that seriously threatened British rule on the subcontinent. These events intensified gathering interest in changing small-arm design. Percussion caps, rifling, oblong bullets, and paper cartridges had maximized the muzzle-loading musket's capabilities. Its turn-of-the-century range of fifty to seventy-five yards increased to three hundred yards. Army officers drew on lessons from wars in the Cape Colony in South Africa, and gunmakers cited game expeditions in India as crucial arenas of experimentation that benefited their work for the Ordnance Office. In 1858, Westley Richards's carbine became the first breechloader adopted by the government. By the 1860s, breech-loading bolt-action rifles had replaced muzzleloaders, increasing range and cutting reloading time.

The end of the Crimean War and the government's declaration that it would no longer accept noninterchangeable arms forced the gun trade to adapt. In 1860, the London Armoury Company used machine-production techniques to make guns that were fully interchangeable with Enfield's. That year, fifteen of the largest contractors in the Birmingham Small Arms Trade Association formed the Birmingham Small Arms Company (BSA). This joint-stock company erected a factory along the canal at Small Heath for machine manufacture of rifles. Much of the machinery came from Leeds. Its first gun was an Enfield rifle for Turkey, in 1865. It could produce a thousand per week. It still depended on the workshop sector, contracting out to smaller firms for many parts. Its first government contract was for converting thousands of 1853-pattern muskets to breechloaders in the 1870s.

The American Civil War allowed the old workshop system to prosper a little longer. The northern states and private speculators commissioned Birmingham guns, buying up whatever was in store in town and placing large orders for new arms until the U.S. government suspended orders, late in 1863, and began relying on its own factories. By then, Birmingham and London had supplied a million rifles. Setting up remained subdivided, with only a few larger establishments housing the various branches in a single location. Outworkers were important in every branch, employing assistants and working for multiple masters—hence the continued difficulty of knowing exactly how many were engaged in the trade. Goodman repeated in 1865 that "no master can tell how many hands he is employing at any given time." He supposed the number had increased, perhaps even doubled, since the 1854 commission. Machines had caused many branches to disappear, such as jiggers, makers-off, break-off fitters, percussioners, and barrel welders. A staff of sixty to seventy government viewers in town checked and marked parts and guns.

Goodman predicted that the machine style of production would preserve the town's position in the global trade and attract the "highest class of military work." But the Gun Quarter declined after the Civil War. New competition emerged on the Continent, especially in cheaper weapons. Those who produced diverse products could not compete for military contracts after the Ordnance Office committed to interchangeable parts only. Many small masters were driven out or drafted into other branches with better prospects. Much skilled labor remained unemployed. The London Armoury Company was reorganized as the London Small Arms Company in 1867, pooling agreements with BSA. Many employers allowed their men to take on work for other firms. New factories emerged as new industrial rings of Birmingham were built up; military manufacturing deserted the quarter. Street improvements demolished houses in St. Mary's district, where outworkers rented workshops, pushing them into factories or retirement. The Birmingham School of Gunmaking could not fill its classes. The manual trade became focused on sporting guns known for handcrafted quality. In his 1866 history of Midlands hardwares, Thomas Phipson noted wryly that the old habitual reference to the pin trade to exemplify the division of labor had passed out of use since an American had patented a pin-making machine in 1824. American technophilia had displaced English workers and workmanship in this view. It did not make economic (or cultural) sense for sporting-arms and African-gun makers to adopt interchangeability. Military-arms makers adopted it "as a response to economic pressure from the War Office, rather than firm conviction of its benefits." This outlook was logical, given English gunmakers' objective of supplying a market requiring diversity; it was the Ordnance Office that sought standardization, making it the logical initiator of American practices. This state institution's desperate need for mass-produced small arms, rather than the trade's own quest for greater profits or love of innovation and efficiency, fueled revolution in the gun industry.

Interchangeable-parts manufacturing had a wide impact on the economy, as in the United States. The capital needs of large factories dramatically altered the structure of the industry, part of the wider trend of corporatization in the late nineteenth century. It changed the industry's relationship to the state. The old system had spread participation in production for war far and wide, creating a "warfare society." The twentieth century, by contrast, saw the emergence of a "warfare state" that created and commanded the preeminent military-industrial-scientific complex of its time. The leading exporter of arms, it had intimate ties to business and regularly intervened in the organization of industry. The path from the old formation to the new one winds through an era of intense European imperial rivalry and two world wars.

A s breechloaders were adopted in Britain, outmoded flintlocks were dumped in Africa. The Cape and Natal received 308,512 arms from 1857 to 1881, not counting those illegally imported and coming via Mozambique—enough to arm nearly half the able-bodied men south of the Limpopo River, despite settler concerns about security. British missionaries sold guns for ivory (other sellers at times sold them for slaves), to the annoyance of the Boers, though they, too, traded guns for ivory. David Livingstone's father-in-law, Robert Moffat, of the London Missionary Society, gifted guns to the chief of the Ndebele. His son John deemed "gun-mending" the most "potent" means of "gaining influence . . . in South Africa," converting the Ndebele to Christianity by that means. Between the 1860s and the 1890s, Birmingham still exported an annual average of 100,000 to 150,000 African trade muskets, although barrels were increasingly being set up in Liège. An 1874 report by the lieutenant governor of Griqualand West discouraged gun control as dangerous:

Kimberley's workers needed guns to shoot elephants, ostriches, and other large animals whose teeth, skin, and feathers they sold or bartered for manufactures—a trade that advanced civilization. New tariffs undermining the sporting-gun market in America in 1890 made Africa even more important.

The guns in African hands could not defend against the new European firearms: automatics like the Maxim gun, which were materially different in use and effect from flintlocks. There was now a clear technological hierarchy between colonizer and colonized; crushingly superior firepower trumped army size and superior knowledge of terrain, enabling conquest of large swaths of Asia and Africa in the late nineteenth century. European states dispensed death on an industrial scale.

Hiram Maxim's gun company was financed by the Vickers steel family, which later absorbed it. This family's rise—and steel more generally—helps connect the dots between the warfare society and the warfare state. The imperial conflicts of the mid-nineteenth century prompted changes well beyond small-arms production and design, in which steel was crucial. The Crimean War inspired the inventor Henry Bessemer to turn his attention to artillery guns. In 1853, he patented an automatic breech-loading gun powered by steam, a smoothbore gun that could fire self-rotating shot. After trials at Vincennes sponsored by Napoleon III, Bessemer decided it had to be made of material stronger than iron. Within weeks he patented a process to make tougher iron; soon he also discovered a way to use air to remove impurities from melted iron. This led to invention of the Bessemer process for making steel; it was the product of an effort to build a gun powerful enough to fire self-rotating shot. Steel became mass-producible. Journalists seized on its potential for producing masses of cannon inexpensively, to outnumber the vast continental arsenals. Bessemer spoke of eighteen-pounders cast cheaply by 11 a.m. and ready for boring by 7 p.m.

Meanwhile, the first armor plate was rolled for the floating battery the *Terror*, for the Crimean War, at Parkgate Ironworks. John Brown of Sheffield partnered with two Birmingham manufacturers (J. D. Ellis and William Briggs) to make wrought iron at Atlas Works. The works expanded quickly as Brown got into production of armor plate from 1859. He was the first steelmaster to adopt the Bessemer process, in 1860. Steel weaponry—artillery firing armor-piercing shells, armor plate—made Sheffield a center of large-scale metal industry. The Newcastle manufacturer of hydraulic machinery William Armstrong also got into cannon manufacture during the war, designing breech-loading artillery in 1857. The British government took over his patents in exchange for appointing him "engineer for rifled ordnance." In this position, he organized the Elswick Ordnance Company, outside Newcastle, which contracted with the War Department to make his gun and supply it exclusively. By 1861, it had produced sixteen hundred. They did not work flawlessly, and critics complained about Armstrong's abuse of his official position to monopolize contracts for Elswick. Joseph Whitworth now designed muzzle-loading guns that he claimed were better than Armstrong's breechloaders. Others, too, touted designs, but Whitworth and Armstrong already had close ties to the state and could test prototypes. The government remained enmeshed in war-inspired "private" entrepreneurship and innovation. It decided on a muzzle-loading gun but found Whitworth's too difficult to produce, instead reverting to obtaining artillery only from Woolwich, as it had before 1859. Armstrong and Whitworth sold their guns to the Americans during the Civil War and to other foreign customers. Meanwhile, having visited Sheffield in 1839 to learn about steel manufacturing, Alfred Krupp was establishing his German arms empire. He showed off his large guns at the 1851 exhibition, including a steel gun. He corresponded with Bessemer, too.

These various players came into their own in the 1880s. In 1884, Britain's shipyards were idle and the economy depressed. The navy leaked information to the sensationalist newspaper editor W. T. Stead about the end of British naval supremacy, and Stead's scaremongering triggered higher naval appropriations. The debate about naval estimates ran parallel to questions about aid for the unemployed. Journalists connected the topics, calling for private dockyards to be enrolled in providing work and thus achieving national and social security in a single stroke. The first lord of the Admiralty adopted this idea, requesting extra funds for contracts with private shipyards. The franchise reform of 1884, which doubled the electorate, passed just two weeks before revision of the naval estimates. This act forced Parliament to abandon its former obedience to taxpaying voters' priority of reducing government expenses during trade depression in favor of the priorities of the now larger, non-taxpaying portion of the electorate—backed by entrepreneurs eager for contracts. Costly naval bills now became urgent and attractive; arms contracts promised to restore wages, profits, and imperial security. As in the eighteenth century, state concern for security and the welfare of workers drove the expansion of contracting.

A handful of technically proficient naval officers inaugurated intimate collaboration with private arms manufacturers. Captain John Fisher, commander of the naval gunnery school at Portsmouth in 1883, hoped that rivalry between Woolwich and private manufacturers would yield the best outcome for the navy—echoing the logic that had guided the creation of Lewisham and Enfield. In 1886, as director of naval ordnance, he obtained the right to purchase from private firms any article that Woolwich could not supply quickly or cheaply, effectively giving private arms makers a monopoly on heavy naval weapons, since Woolwich never caught up with the scale of capital investment needed to make large steel guns and other complex armaments. William Armstrong, meanwhile, learned from Krupp's demonstrations to install machinery to make big steel breechloaders. Those demonstrations altered Admiralty perceptions, too. By 1886, Armstrong had added the navy to his list of customers again. (He had merged with the Mitchell shipbuilding firm.) Vickers followed in 1888. Woolwich had just begun to convert to making breechloaders; the gap remained unbridged for three decades. In 1897, Armstrong merged with Whitworth's company, producing cars and trucks, too; Vickers bought the Barrow Shipbuilding Company, including its subsidiary, the Maxim Gun Company. They, too, made cars and civilian machinery, besides the full suite of arms technology. The spin-off effects of the arms revolution of this period of the "second industrial revolution" included use of Bessemer steel in viaducts and bridges, industrial chemistry, electrical machinery, radio, turbines, diesel, optics, hydraulic machinery, and so on. In June

The Birmingham Small Arms Factory, Small Heath, Birmingham, February 1917.

1899, *Arms & Explosives* noted, "Practically all mechanical progress in the light department of engineering has originated from the organisation of methods which Government arms orders render possible and make necessary." A "complex" began to take shape, a structure of state-private industry relations both echoing and departing radically from the partnerships of the earlier period. (Armstrong and Vickers would merge in 1927.)

Small-arms firms also fostered modern industrial practices applied in the manufacture of bicycles and automobiles. Government contracting created an elite group of firms, especially in the rifle industry, that spun off ideas and innovations into general industry. Though much government work shifted to Enfield, in 1891 Birmingham factories were fully employed producing the new army rifle. BSA was the largest privately owned rifle manufactory in Europe until German factories surpassed it in the 1890s, though it remained the biggest private manufacturer of military small arms in the United Kingdom through the First World War. In 1896, the Birmingham and Provincial Gunmakers' Association was established to further the trade, the next incarnation of trade organization formed to negotiate with the government. By 1901, the South African War had drawn more workers into the government factories. (Two gunmakers analyzing the industry in 1907, under the pseudonyms "Artifex" and "Opifex," noted that at each census year, it was in better health than usual because of coincidental shocks: the 1871 Franco-Prussian War, army rifle orders in 1891, the South African War at the turn of the century. In those years, machinists, engineers, and others temporarily employed in gun factories called themselves gunmakers, inflating census figures.) In 1912, the Birmingham association merged with the London group to form the Gunmakers' Association, to deal with fraudulent proof-marks and promote British registered trademarks.

State arsenals remained the main suppliers for European governments, but private firms dominated export markets. Government aid fostered private gun manufacturing in France—using the best British machinery—focused on East Asian and South American markets. Birmingham's manufacturers did not benefit as much as Liège's from the wars of the period: the Turko-Russian conflict, the Egyptian campaigns, the South African wars, the first Sino-Japanese War, the Philippine and Cuban campaigns, the Boxer Rebellion, the Somaliland Campaign, and the Russo-Japanese War. European states unloaded old guns in Africa and the Balkans, where the Ottoman Empire was in conflict with its Christian territories—to gain influence more than profit. This meant that states at times undersold their own private merchants. British diplomats opposed British sales in the Balkans and South America, but the British dominated the naval arms trade all over, remaining the most powerful force in the global arms market. The most valuable part of the British arms trade gravitated toward the Indian Ocean, including East Africa.

Ottoman tensions spilled into East Africa, where Ethiopia clashed with Ottoman Egypt. Britain futilely opposed French and Italian arms sales in

the region; the ensuing scramble for Africa exacerbated Great Power rivalries. British complaints about arms sales met with unanswerable French
reminders that Britain had only recently led arms sales to the Continent.
Rebels in British territories had French rifles. After the Ottoman Empire's
failure to pay caused collapse of American rifle firms, arms companies obtained banking partners that gave loans to client states. Cartels formed as
business alliances emerged to divide up world markets. The British concluded that the best way to stop the flow of arms into Ethiopia was to
manufacture arms there themselves, so they progressed, slowly, in building
a factory there. (They also finally set up a rifle factory in Ishapore, India, in
1905.) Meanwhile, the arms trade supported the cost of the colonial administration in French Somaliland, a precious fiscal resource and source of
private wealth for French merchants and officials. Arms firms engaged in
their own informal imperialism, with or without approval from their governments, working with local elites. Consumers from the Middle East to
the North-West Frontier also used firearms to new political, commercial,
and social ends. Many continental firms received aggressive government
support while the British policed the region in the name of imperial security. European states insisted on the right to sell arms in client states: France
in Russia, Germany in Turkey, Austria in Serbia.

It was in this context that "Artifex and Opifex" protested the British
government's comparatively cavalier treatment of its gun manufacturers in
their 1907 account *The Causes of Decay in a British Industry*, accusing it of
abetting the decline of "one of the most productive crafts" of Britain, on
which millions depended. While attempting to tame that industry, the
government itself sold arms to the Indian and colonial governments and
to the new chartered companies exploring Africa, and "probably would
not refuse to dispose of its arms to any corporate body such as the Shang-
hai Volunteers, the League of Frontiersmen." It armed the native states of
India and police forces across the empire, who could, at any time, sell
those arms on the open market.

The First World War mooted such complaints, generating enormous
demand for small arms; machine guns caused the most carnage. Afterward,
BSA was left with enormous stockpiles. Building on prewar experience,

it diversified—into cars, bicycles, machine tools, and steel—just as an eighteenth-century gun firm might have. By 1930, it was almost out of the small-arms business. To maintain BSA's arms-producing capacity, the War Office made the company a deal: BSA would be sole global agent for selling government surplus stocks of Lewis LMGs and Enfield P1914 rifles. BSA hired John Ball, a former Royal Flying Corps officer with wide experience selling British surplus arms around the world since 1919 on behalf of the Disposals Board and the War Office. In 1927, he had created the Soley Company, with a factory in Liège where he made unsalable rifles salable, drawing on the stocks of continental governments. In 1919, Birmingham gunmakers formed a limited company, the Birmingham Registered Gunmakers, to buy materials and parts cooperatively and mass-produce the hammerless gun in town. It lasted until 1935. In the early thirties, the United Kingdom remained the world's largest exporter of arms, while struggling to contain arms smuggling in sensitive areas like the Middle East. Meanwhile, defeat forced German arms makers to focus exclusively on spin-offs. American Quakers showed journalists around Krupp's factory in Essen. It reminded the British journalist Vera Brittain of the Black Country. She witnessed swords being made into plowshares "in their modern guise of typewriters and surgical instruments and household pipes and cinematograph machines." Rearmament in the 1930s and during World War Two ended this trend. The ten years following that war proved a golden age of British arms exporting. Senior businessmen in the Ministry of Supply ran firms in the Midlands and were at the helm of state interventions in industry. With a virtual monopoly over international arms sales (shared with the United States), Britain hawked its wares to new customers emerging from the rubble of its empire during the Cold War. The British-based arms trader and former CIA officer Samuel Cummings controlled 90 percent of the world's small-arms trade through the 1960s. His firm, the International Armament Corporation, or Interarms, traded surplus World War Two European weapons. Agreements like the 1972 Strategic Arms Limitation Treaty did not stem the flow of arms *not* specified in them; military spending continued to increase around the world. As the British attempted to ration arms without taking sides in postcolonial disputes—in South Asia, the Middle East, Ireland, and elsewhere—it again evolved into an unprejudiced arms dealer willing to supply all comers, as long as they could pay. In the 1960s, Raymond Brown was appointed to a post that made him chief arms salesman of the British government, for which he drew on his experience as chairman of the Racal group of companies, which had exported electronic equipment for civil and military purposes. Brown's British Defence Sales Organisation promoted arms sales by commercial firms and sold weapons made in government factories—a source of revenue to the state. Capitalist governments were politically, economically, and financially interested in arms sales abroad, stepping into the realm of distribution as weapons became more complex and expensive. In Britain, protestations of concern about spawning arms races around the world were inevitably coupled with the unanswerable eighteenth-century rationale that too moral a posture would only send the unscrupulous customer elsewhere. In 1980, surplus weapons were all over the world, thanks to both licit and illicit traffic.

British Aerospace (BAe), determined to become an internationally competitive manufacturer of rifles and machine guns, bought the Enfield factories in 1987. The Royal Small Arms Factory was a relatively old and high-cost unit and was closed in 1988. The Ministry of Defence adopted a policy of competitive tendering and buying less equipment. The chief executive of the Royal Ordnance wanted that department to become competitive enough to secure overseas markets rather than dangerously rely on Ministry of Defence purchases. The global small-arms market became fiercely competitive as postcolonial states set up their own industries.

Small arms—pistols, revolvers, carbines, handheld machine guns, rifles, shotguns, and hand grenades—remain the most abundant and most massively destructive category of weapons *and* the only category that continues to proliferate virtually unregulated. They inflict greatest suffering in former European colonies. There are roughly 640 million small arms in the world—mostly in private hands—increasing by 8 million each year and causing the death of one human being per minute. They are responsible for the vast majority of deaths in armed conflicts since 1945. While massive production and dumping of these long-lasting weapons during the Cold War continues to fulfill demand in the unhappiest parts of the world, the war on terror has accelerated their spread. In 2003, there were more guns than people in Iraq, to be had for as little as $10. Recent regional crises and ethno-religious conflicts make the international arms trade a matter of increasing concern. Global arms exports reached $72 billion in 2014. Even as sales of large high-tech weapons systems have declined, the small-arms trade remains robust. It is managed by a network of brokering and shipping agents who exploit the lack of controls, working on a global stage that renders approval by particular governments superfluous. The new arms race ignited by drone warfare includes a new kind of "small arm": nano drones, tiny weapons designed to attack in swarms. The Pentagon is also fielding the Switchblade, a 5.5-pound precision-attack drone that can be carried and fired by one person.

Britain is the world's second-biggest arms supplier. Its annual international weapons fair represents the public face of the industry. After Foreign Minister Robin Cook's brief nod to a more "ethical" stance toward the arms trade, Tony Blair's government reverted to the old ways, the scandalous secret deals with Suharto's Indonesia echoing Mark Thatcher's ignominious role in earlier deals with Saudi Arabia. British brokers arrange shipments to paramilitary and guerrilla forces around the world, particularly in former parts of the empire. The trade is as dependent on "men of mystery" as the intelligence world—many arms companies' agents are former intelligence agents. Under David Cameron, arms sales to Saudi Arabia continued, despite evidence of Saudi breaches of humanitarian law in Yemen and European Union arms-export laws. Industry spokesmen continue to remind the public that such exports enable them to employ "150,000 highly skilled people" in Britain and "thousands more . . . through the extended supply chain," and to invest "huge sums in research and development."

In the early nineteenth century, William Cobbett called the corrupt nexus of capitalism and landed power, backed by the monster oligarchic state, "the THING." In the twentieth century, Cold War arms deals activated the historian E. P. Thompson's perception of a "new, and entirely different, predatory complex" occupying the state, a "new Thing" distinguished by:

its interpenetration of private industry and the State (Government contracts, especially for war materials, of an unprecedented size, subsidies, municipal indebtedness to private finance, etc.), its control over major media of communication, its blackmail by the City, its reduction of the public sector to subordinate roles, and its capacity to dictate the conditions within which a Labour Government must operate . . . its vast influence reaching into the Civil Service, the professions, and into the trade union and labour movement itself.

The route from Cobbett's THING to Thompson's Thing—from a military-industrial society to a complex—was long and complicated. Future scholars may more fully trace its contours—and assess whether they perhaps coexist in our time, the latter distracting attention from the former.

In the 2012 "jobs for generals" scandal, the president of the Royal British Legion resigned in the face of claims that he had boasted that he could use his position to help defense companies lobby ministers and key British military figures; he was also fired from his role in the British defense-and-engineering company Babcock. The scandal revealed the extent of links between the Ministry of Defence and the arms industry. Senior military officers and ministry officials had taken up more than 3,500 jobs in arms companies in sixteen years; a revolving door still connects the public and private sectors.

C old War ideological priorities helped shape our understanding of the industrial revolution as the product of innovation rather than mass production for the state. We accordingly remember the innovators Priestley, Boulton, Watt, and Keir more than the wealthier Galton, who sponsored much of their work. In 1907, even the shrilly libertarian Artifex and Opifex were certain that "no manufacturing industry, such being an artificial and not a natural product, can originate or progress without some sort of protection." This opinion was hardly controversial as part of liberal ideology up to that date. In 1854, too, the superiority of private over state manufacture was by no means obvious: the parliamentary committee on small arms recalled that the Admiralty's biscuit factory produced better and cheaper biscuits than private contractors. Colt acknowledged that government manufacture of guns had produced great improvement in tools and machines and that the private sector depended on the state. He had launched into machine manufacture of guns specifically to supply the government, "as all new mechanics think that Government patronage is valuable . . . it is an advertisement." But later in the twentieth century, a more extreme interpretation of an Adam Smithian theory of state intervention in trade supplanted our understanding of the practical reality that that theory critiqued. That myth of pacific British industrialism was the other side of the coin of the myth of Asian despotism. We must give up both and understand how capital and state institutions interacted in the organization of society, military strategy, the state, industry, and empire. The British state forged conditions conducive to industrialization: it legally, bureaucratically, infrastructurally, and militarily penetrated its own territory; created markets; protected industry; created tools to create revenues; policed borders; fostered changes that allowed mobilization of wage workers; *and* furnished a market for key commodities, stimulating demand, innovation, and experiments in industrial organization well beyond suppression of worker upheaval. It inaugurated factory organization in the small-workshop world of Birmingham; its superintendents brought military discipline to the workplace to ensure uniform production.

This narrative does not leave us confronting the inconvenient truth that war is "good" for the economy (not least because it suggests that government purchasing for other ends might prove similarly stimulating). Rather, we learn that war was crucial in forming perceptions of a sphere of mutually interdependent relationships that came to be called "the economy," in which the state was a major participant. War had a fundamental historical role in creating the economy and our sense of our role in it. Just as the slave trade enriched specific interests and industries while imposing enormous costs, human and economic, on others, the gun trade came with profits and costs. The eighteenth-century state's important role in driving the industrial revolution was also different from later episodes of autocratic government direction of total war in the twentieth century; it was part of a series of partnerships that deepened over the century. The industrial revolution was caused by "state" action, but the "state" was a porous entity driven partly by businesspeople and industrialists.

In ancient Europe, the necessities of war were maintained by the people or their lords; the state had few expenses besides the family and household of the sovereign himself. In the modern era, however, firearms made war much more costly. With a moderate increase in taxes, explained Adam Smith in 1776, the state could raise enough money to carry on war without inconveniencing those remote from the scene of action, compensating them for the increase with the amusement of newspaper accounts of battles. "They are commonly dissatisfied with the return of peace," Smith observed, for it ended the amusement and "visionary hopes of conquest and national glory." He knew that war shaped the modern economy and modern sensibilities but did not recognize wider popular investment in it beyond taxation. Edward Gibbon's *History of the Decline and Fall of the Roman Empire* appeared the same year, recounting the story of an empire's loss of military capacity to show that an affluent society needed a cohesive army to sustain a mighty, far-flung empire. Gibbon reminds us that Smith did not represent eighteenth-century realities and perceptions; he challenged a mainstream view of war as the foundation of economic and imperial progress.

As I type, I am aware of my own debt to arms makers' efforts to navigate the peaks and troughs of government demand. Eliphalet Remington first mass-produced the typewriter when his arms business hit a slump after the Civil War. He struck a deal with Christopher Sholes, inventor of the modern keyboard, in 1868, producing the first Remington typewriter in 1874, a "discursive machine-gun" whose strikes and triggers echo the ammunitions transport in a revolver or machine gun. Electronic writing revolutionized communication; like the gun, it alters us fundamentally.

10

Opposition to the Gun Trade after 1815

Before he explained the wealth of nations, Adam Smith wrote about the moral sentiments necessary for judicious economic behavior, especially the capacity to survey one's own sentiments "with the eyes of other people." His *Theory of Moral Sentiments* appeared in 1759–61, when the doubling of identity was the norm—when exercising one's conscience involved an almost literal division of the self into the judge and the self being judged. As a man shaped by that time, Galton Jr. could tolerate his split self: Quaker and gunmaker. It was modern enough, relative to earlier, God-driven Protestant understandings of conscience. But late-century Britons required a more internally consistent self. The final version of Smith's text, from 1790, presents the impartial spectator, the conscience, not as a distinct internal character but a more metaphorical allusion. The eighteenth-century man was archetypally a man of principle, a promise keeper willing to act on principle no matter how inconvenient, but Galton saw little point in acting in the name of principles that were impossible to preserve more than superficially. Did this make him even more modern than his peers?

If later Quakers revised their opinion of his defense, his own descendants proved virtually blind to his faults. Their carefully curated family history fueled his grandson Francis Galton's theory of (his) "hereditary genius." Meticulous study of his own ancestors helped Francis arrive at his eugenicist notions, his own evident genius proving the efficacy of careful intermarriage. The younger Lloyd likewise credited Francis's successes to his inheritance of his grandfather's thoroughness. The gunmaker's son provided the theory that rationalized the racist elimination of life that guns made possible—a dark example of Noel Annan's aphoristic observation that "family connections are part of the poetry of history." Francis may have had himself or his cousin Charles Darwin in mind when he wrote that men who left their mark on the world, "being gifted and full of nervous power" and "haunted and driven by a dominant idea," were "within a measurable distance of insanity." But the invocation of insanity carries a more sinister charge if we reflect on his family's and Britain's eighteenth-century history—the sheer insanity of mass production of arms and the uses to which they were put. There is a strange poetry in the fact that the Galton home at Duddeston became a private lunatic asylum in the 1840s. The Galton case launched a long history of painting arms making as villainous madness, distinct from "normal" industrial and economic pursuits, with important consequences for current American debates about gun control.

B esides being a capital of the global arms trade, Britain is also a capital of the global effort to regulate the arms trade, which began with eighteenth-century Quaker pacifism and the moral critique of Old Corruption in which contractors were caricatured as "animals of a greedy nature, always craving and never satisfied, their appetites for dishonest lucre and foul gain . . . as insatiable as their consciences were easily satisfied." Arms contractors were not particularly targeted in these critiques because profit margins were small and contracts widely distributed, but abolitionist debates planted the seed of the modern concern with arms trafficking as a moral problem. Meanwhile, early efforts to limit arms trafficking were about ensuring arms supply for the home government during wartime. Then, in the nineteenth century, imperial-diplomatic concerns drove departures from permissiveness toward arms trading—tactical and practical rather than principled objections to arms trading. Controls on domestic firearm possession were also about promoting security. Laws such as the Vagrancy Act of 1824, which policed armed men roaming the country after the wars, and the spate of legislation against use of firearms for poaching (1828, 1830, 1844, 1862) were in the same vein. (The Gun License Act of 1870 was a revenue-raising measure.) But by the late nineteenth century, the objectives of security and imperial moral prestige began to blend, and an ethical critique of arms trading emerged. As arms races accelerated, the British government opposed some sales as potentially threatening to imperial security (for instance, in the Balkans and South America), even when British firms stood to benefit from them. As they were appointed in successive posts across the empire, British officials brought their experiences of rebellion in one place to the next, propagating ideas about arms control. Henry Bartle Frere developed his ideas about firearms regulation between 1851 and 1859 as chief commissioner of the Indian province of Sind (today Sindh), where he licensed firearms and restricted the arms trade. The strategy was vindicated when the province remained tranquil during the 1857 rebellion. The viceroy then promulgated an Arms Act throughout India, instituting licenses for gun ownership and restricting the trade. When it was due for renewal in 1860, Chief Justice Sir Barnes Peacock suggested disarming the entire population, with the exception of Europeans, Americans, and Eurasians. Frere, now on the Viceroy's Council, disagreed, arguing that such a policy would be perceived as oppressive and unjust and would encourage rebellion while also proving ineffectual. He persuaded the council to reject the revision and renew existing restrictions. In 1877, he departed for South Africa, where arms regulation was a divisive issue. Perhaps the Indian experience had changed his mind by then, or perhaps he saw the Cape differently, for, as governor, he advocated total disarmament of the African population, going above and beyond controls settlers asked for.

Earlier, British officials had pushed back against settlers' calls to ban arms sales to Africans. As the trade grew, some had joined the settler chorus, not least because the Cape governor from 1855 to 1861, George Grey, was formerly governor in New Zealand (1845–54), where there had been de facto discrimination against Maori in firearms regulations through the Arms Importation Ordinance of 1845, which empowered the governor to regulate firearms sales in certain districts. In 1846, concern about Maori purchases prompted Ordinance 18, which required licensing of arms traders; loyal Maori got around it. By the 1870s, intensified racism fueled calls to disarm Africans, even as missionaries, free traders, and philanthropists defended the gun trade as part of the spread of civilization. In 1878, the Cape Parliament passed the Peace Preservation Act, authored by the Irish attorney general, Thomas Upington, who based it on disarmament legislation imposed on Ireland (despite many pointing out that Ireland showed the futility of such legislation). Uprisings erupted. In Basutoland, which was administered by the Cape, the Sotho insisted that they held their guns at the pleasure of the queen. When they refused to surrender their arms, a "gun war" ensued in 1880–81. Sotho chiefs lost eight thousand soldiers and much property but still controlled the country and refused to disarm. Basutoland became a Crown colony, with the British ruling indirectly through local chiefs. When the Peace Preservation Act passed in the Cape in 1878, a new Arms Act passed in India under Viceroy Lord Lytton, permitting only Indians who could demonstrate loyalty and pay a fee to possess arms, the idea being that few such licenses would be granted. It remained in place until 1959; even today, Indian gun laws are very restrictive. This is probably a good thing from the point of view of public safety, yet it is nevertheless the outcome of colonial and racial politics, which also govern debates about gun control in other postcolonial societies, including the United States.

In Africa, concern about arming potential rebels merged with the effort to control the slave trade. The arms trade's intimacy with the slave trade helped fuse and confuse ethical and security motivations behind controlling it. In 1890, the Brussels Convention focused on rivalrous European arms flows to Africa, though stopping the slave trade was the explicit rationale. Imperial authorities also blamed the flood of weapons for the surge in crime, unrest—and, from 1905, political terror—in the Middle East and South Asia. They strained to control it. They had long paid the Afridi tribe to guard the Khyber Pass at the Indian frontier; the Afridi revolted in 1897. The British suppressed the revolt and then sought

Muscat's permission to search vessels in its waters, to prevent tribes on the North-West Frontier from obtaining guns. This led to massive seizures in the Persian Gulf in 1898, when a naval ship seized arms headed for Muscat, killing a thriving trade overnight. Birmingham gunmakers saw this incident as proof of their government's utter fecklessness toward them. The government cited pleas from rulers in Persia and Muscat and their own concern about the North-West Frontier. The *Times of India* proclaimed, "British influence in the Persian Gulf has not been maintained for centuries in order that the gunmakers of Birmingham should wax wealthy by the stealthy encouragement of the foes of order and good government." The 1900 Exportation of Arms Act placed the industry at the mercy of the government of the day; it was immediately enforced by a proclamation prohibiting arms exports to China—even without concerted action from rival suppliers. As the Indian government began to regulate firearms imports more aggressively, a government representative enlarged on the "paradox of Empire" in the *Times of India*: "Government maintains warships in the Gulf to preserve peace, and the Birmingham manufacturers and London exporters ship out whole cargoes of rifles and cartridges which can only destroy peace." Birmingham gunmakers and importers and distributors in India suffered from these changes. Gunmakers complained that ignorance resulted in overly broad exclusions—ordinary rifles were automatically prohibited alongside military ones, with no attempt to bar rivals from filling the void. (The Indian government ultimately righted this wrong.) Within the United Kingdom, too, efforts at firearms control launched in the 1890s culminated in the Pistols Act of 1903, limiting children's and alcoholics' access to pistols, albeit without abridging private sales between individuals. Pistol sales peaked as it went into effect.

These restrictions unfolded as arms trafficking was blamed for generally destabilizing peace. Freshly returned from his critical coverage of the South African War for the *Guardian*, the liberal economist J. A. Hobson took sharp aim at arms makers in his classic work *Imperialism* (1902), which explained imperialism as the product of the expansionist forces of capitalism. In 1905, Prime Minister Campbell-Bannerman blamed the policy of large armaments for the reliance on force for solving internal differences—the speech Samuel Lloyd recalled and echoed in his 1907 family history. Lloyd pointed to the absence of statesmen to fulfill the prime minister's vision, but others blamed arms manufacturers. In *Major Barbara* (first performed in 1905 and published in 1907), George Bernard Shaw caricatured the arms trader in the form of Andrew Undershaft, a wicked, amoral character inspired partly by Basil Zaharoff, the notorious international arms dealer who worked for Vickers and was a crucial figure in the prewar arms buildup. Undershaft, like Galton, likens the arms trader to the whiskey distiller and sees immoral economic activity as systemic. The whole industrial economy depended on alcohol, "a very necessary article. It heals the sick . . . It assists the doctor . . . It makes life bearable to millions of people who could not endure their existence if they were quite sober. It enables Parliament to do things at eleven at night that no sane person would do at eleven in the morning." But Shaw did not share this perception. To him, arms making was not a collective endeavor; rather, Undershaft wielded special power as part of a closeted elite deciding national policy: "I am the government of your country . . . you will do what pays us. You will make war when it suits us." Awareness of widespread, systemic complicity in arms production was repeatedly obscured by focus on the particular moral failure of the arms maker, the fall guy of industrial capitalism.

"Artifex and Opifex" wrote their public defense of the gun trade in precisely this moment, billing it as crucial for "all who wish to see Great Britain maintain her position in international commerce." They denied that Birmingham's manufacturers supplied England's enemies, asserting that they were "the most law-abiding men within the six seas that girth Britain. . . . Their loyalty is so thorough and constant that it cannot count for righteousness: it has ceased to be a virtue, and become merely a habit. Did they show more sturdy independence they would be treated more considerately by the legislature." The pitiable state of the industry proved that they were no gunrunners. They complained of the many restrictions affecting the production, sale, use, and export of firearms at home and abroad and rehearsed the trade's long service and loyalty to the state, warning that the state might not be able to depend on its support in the future if it were allowed to fall into neglect.

But they had little purchase on public opinion, which was increasingly captive to the moral liabilities surrounding the arms trade in the context of imperial security. That same year, J. G. Lorimer, a colonial administrator charged with producing a comprehensive handbook for British diplomats in the Persian Gulf area, the *Gazetteer of the Persian Gulf, Oman, and Central Arabia,* condemned the arms trade as "at least as great a public evil as the slave trade," arguing that, "besides intensifying anarchy and bloodshed in Central Arabia and in some of the smaller states, it has weakened the authority of the Persian and Turkish Governments and threatens in the end to produce widespread and incurable disorder." The arms trade fueled slowly building paranoia about the specter of Islamic revolt in the region. It was no longer merely tainted by association with the slave trade; it had become equally morally objectionable in its own right, threatening that most sacred construct, the Pax Britannica.

That year, the Hague Convention also determined that neutral powers that furnished arms to belligerents forfeited their neutrality. (This applied to government sales.) Despite such measures, that year, thirty thousand rifles were run through to Kandahar—they were guns from the South African War that the New Zealand and Australian governments had disposed of a year before. The British called another convention at Brussels in 1908, but it ended in deadlock over arms trading in the Persian Gulf and the Red Sea. It reconvened the following year, again conceding failure in 1910. The British resorted to unilateral force—a naval blockade and inland operations—to disrupt the arms trade from Oman to the North-West Frontier, ending in the Battle of Dubai, which cost many Arab lives. To secure public support, Arnold Keppel published a book the following year explaining how this crisis had resulted from the effort to suppress arms traffic in the Persian Gulf. He affirmed the peaceful effect of the blockading squadron on the Indian frontier, where its work helped contain the tribal threat and the Afghani emir, for, with modern rifles, the Afghan army would prove a formidable opponent. He explained the logic behind the 1898 Persian Gulf arms seizures and recounted the futile efforts to secure French cooperation in controlling arms traffic. Although secret channels of egress remained, the violent policing effort worked well enough

Rifles surrendered by the Sheikh of Dubai, displayed
on the deck of HMS Fox, circa 1910.

to secure French acquiescence in a deal in 1914, including compensation for their arms dealers. In the eighteenth century, British arms sales to enemies had not threatened the entire edifice of empire, nor was British power enough to prevent rivals from stepping in. By the twentieth century, the threat at the North-West Frontier, acknowledged linchpin of the empire, and British naval capacity had rendered concerns about profit sectional and selfish. Support of the gun trade was also less necessary from the state's point of view, as it could now rely on one or two major corporate producers, like BSA and Vickers, and its own manufactories. Moreover, the arms trade's treasonous potential was made undeniably clear in 1914, when Irish Unionists smuggled thousands of German Mauser rifles into Ulster in preparation for militant resistance against the imposition of Irish Home Rule—a civil war narrowly averted by the start of the First World War.

Meanwhile, firearms legislation expanded at home, too. In 1911, a bill involving protracted negotiations between the Home Office and the gun trade required a police certificate before purchase. Two shocking shooting incidents sealed the deal, the first involving Russian anarchists in a London jewelry shop shooting at the police, in December 1910, and the second, the subsequent army siege of the gang in Sidney Street, in January 1911. Instead of the Pistols Bill, an Aliens Bill passed, prohibiting aliens from possessing pistols without police permission. During the First World War, the Defence of the Realm Act included regulations on firearms sales and carrying them in certain areas, particularly in Ireland. (Many uniformed men bought pistols through private channels.) Manufacture and import of guns was also regulated to serve war needs.

The horrors of the war led to criticism of the arms industry. Many saw the prewar arms race and pileup as its cause. In 1914, Labour MP Philip Snowden pointed to the high number of MPs who were shareholders in arms companies. He noted Vickers's high profits that year. The leftist Quaker J. T. Walton Newbold published *How Europe Armed for War* in 1916, focusing on small arms and criticizing the mainstream arms-control movement for its preoccupation with Krupp and other makers of heavy weapons, which he felt camouflaged more sinister figures in the trade, like Loewe & Company, makers of the Mauser. The Loewes and Vickers had formed an alliance in the 1890s, sabotaging the operations of Britain's state factories and delivering the country into the hands of American capital. The Union for Democratic Control, formed in 1914 to press for a more democratically shaped foreign policy, found Newbold's ideas persuasive, but so, too, did the Liberal minister of munitions, David Lloyd George, who made his department the biggest buyer, seller, and employer in the country. Liberal appointees came to distrust small-arms manufacturers. Lloyd George became prime minister in 1916; his government's investigations confirmed the suspicions of the left as major arms seizures unfolded at sea. In 1917, a Committee of Imperial Defence subcommittee on the arms traffic gathered, chaired by Lord Islington. It brooded over the political and financial costs of unilateral operations, noting the erosion of the sultan's power in Oman since the blockade. The Middle East expert Mark Sykes spelled out to the committee the obsoleteness of prewar principles. Smokeless magazine rifles were all over the world, enough to "arm every black man who wants a rifle." The real problem now was the automatic pistol, like the Loewe Broomhandle Mauser of 1896, which could fire ten bullets in seconds and had earned prominence from its role in the Sidney Street siege. The Belgian Browning pistol had fired the shot that started the world war by killing the Austro-Hungarian archduke. Such small, cheap arms had revolutionized conflict; Sykes foresaw a world in which unrest took the form of terrorism by pistol-armed anticolonial individuals capable of wreaking more havoc than insurrectionary soldiers. Any fool could shoot a viceroy. The committee determined to renew efforts to create an international agreement. Guns had made impersonal property violence possible in the eighteenth century; now the automatic pistol made new kinds of colonial rebellion possible. The imperial anxieties it awakened stimulated the invention of new, violent systems of colonial surveillance and collective punishment, such as air control in the Middle East.

In 1918, at the prompting of the Islington Committee, the Blackwell Committee was formed to deal with the large number of guns in private hands after the war, particularly the concern Sykes had so hauntingly articulated: that they might reach the hands of "savage tribesmen" or "anarchists" in the empire. Ireland was a particular concern. The committee considered domestic controls on possession, manufacture, sale, and import/export of firearms. It consulted with the chief constable of Birmingham, concluding that laws to limit firearms were needed. Imperial and domestic concerns about firearms merged. (Nevertheless, at this very moment, John Ball began his work selling surplus arms for the Disposals Board and the War Office.)

The arms convention in Paris in 1919 intended to address the nightmare scenario of pistol-armed anticolonial revolutionaries by imposing controls on the export of arms to certain parts of the world. Sir Edward Grey, the foreign minister before the war, blamed arms makers for fueling belligerence and causing the war. The war changed the consensus at The Hague, in 1907, that only government sales could be subject to international regulation. Restriction of the private trade was now framed as a "high moral issue." The immorality of arms trading blended with the immorality of colonial rebellion; it helped to delegitimize and depoliticize rebellion. British aims were to prevent dumping of surplus arms in the empire and to regulate pistol manufacture and sales. Accordingly, the convention forbade export licenses to any country refusing to accept the "tutelage" under which it had been placed and defined a prohibited zone for the trade encompassing Africa (except Algeria, Libya, and South Africa), Persia, Transcaucasia, Gwadar, the Arabian Peninsula, parts of Asia formerly under the Turkish Empire, and a maritime zone around Southwest Asia, with rules laid out for search and seizure of native vessels. Manufacture, assembly, or repair of arms in these areas was also prohibited, except at government arsenals. The convention built on wartime rationing by establishing a licensing system for exports and called for published accounts of licenses granted.

Representatives of France, Italy, Japan, and Britain did not wait for ratification, meeting in Paris in 1920 and agreeing to informally carry out its provisions in Africa and the Middle East, as a "moral duty of all civilised States." The new League of Nations approved the convention; its Temporary Mixed Commission on the arms trade, in 1921, also saw problems and dangers in the private manufacture of arms. Allegations against the private trade generally dominated discourse, drawing on testimony of the prewar left. Meanwhile, as each signee of the 1919 protocol waited for the others to ratify, it remained a dead letter. The United States recognized that its purpose was to protect European empires and worried that it would harm exports to Latin America, and thus American private manufacturers and American national security.

Even in this abortive effort, the gun's multiple uses also created loopholes. Firearms "adapted both to warlike and also to other purposes" were excluded from regulation at the discretion of the contracting parties, who would decide on the basis of the "size, destination, and other circumstances of each shipment for what uses it is intended." Exports to the prohibited zone were permitted if the authorities in question were satisfied about the safety of the particular shipment. The exporter would ensure deposit of the arms in a government-supervised warehouse from which withdrawal would be authorized only for places where they were needed for defense against "robbers or rebels" or individuals requiring them for "legitimate personal use." All the signees of the informal protocol other than the British at various times chose to view firearms as not being "arms and munitions of war," granting licenses for exports to the prohibited zone. Still, the British felt that it helped in the Middle East and Africa.

The Blackwell Committee's recommendations about control of the domestic market as the step toward more general control shaped postwar domestic firearms control. After the war, pistols had also become worryingly common in riots in Britain (e.g., race riots at Cardiff, Liverpool, and London), likely because of unprecedented levels of brutalization. Against this backdrop, the Firearms Bill passed into law in 1920. Anyone wanting to purchase or possess a firearm or ammunition needed a firearm certificate, which lasted three years and specified both the arm and the ammunition that the holder could buy or possess. Certification was at the discretion of local chief constables, and applicants had to demonstrate good reason for needing the certificate. The Home Office provided chief constables with classified directives on good reasons for granting certificates.

Meanwhile, the League brought the United States back to the table for a new convention on arms trafficking—the Geneva Convention of 1925. The Americans wanted to negotiate an international arrangement that included much more than small arms. This convention failed, too. Small, new, non-arms-producing European states brought crippling objections out of concern that overly tight control would limit their ability to purchase arms to defend their hard-won sovereignty. Small arms may not have been the convention's primary focus, but they helped it to fail. Belgian representatives argued that controls would disproportionately affect their country's manufacturers and that small arms were for sporting and personal defense. (In fact, there was no difference between the military and sporting versions of the replica Mauser rifle then made by the Belgian Fabrique Nationale.) Small arms' multiple identities helped them sabotage the international effort to regulate arms and ensured that when arms regulation succeeded, small arms fell outside its scope. Britain asked how the convention could achieve meaningful control if it excluded arms with potential military value from licensing (despite British recourse to precisely the same reasoning in the past). Britain's evident lack of concern about the fate of *its* small-arms manufacturers is noteworthy. The British government was satisfied with ensuring the health of one or two major corporate suppliers alongside state factories. It no longer needed to worry about supporting a wide array of smaller producers. In the end, the Belgians carried the day, and the agreement was altered to apply to weapons "exclusively designed and intended for . . . warfare." The British also quarreled with the Persians, who wanted the Persian Gulf excluded from the prohibited zone, but the British delegate Percy Cox, who had long experience in India, Iraq, and Iran, would have none of that. The Persians walked out. The United States rejected controls on private manufacture. Nearly forty nations signed the convention, but only a third ratified it, and nothing was done to make it effective.

Britain reversed even its own 1924 ban on disposal of government stocks within a year. Its Middle East experts were concerned about arms flows, while the British public's suspicion about corrupt arms trading fueled paranoia about their government's activity in the Middle East. Echoes of the Union for Democratic Control's critique of the arms industry's corruption of government could be heard in parliamentary questions about Britain knavishly subsidizing both its Sharifian allies in the Hejaz and the Sharifians' enemy Ibn Saud, until the latter's victory in 1925. Then the leftist MP Joseph Kenworthy began to fear that British arms supplied to Saud would be used against the British. Memory of the war colored such anxieties: in 1926 in the Commons, Hugh Dalton recalled Vickers's supply of the guns that the Turks used against the British in the Dardanelles, condemning "directors of armament firms" as "the highest and completest embodiment of capitalist morality." During the debate on that year's air force estimates, which touted development of civil aviation, Clement Attlee asked why they allowed aircraft parts to be traded if they were committed to disarmament.

In 1929, the government again banned disposal of government stocks and again canceled the order the following year. In 1931, an order-in-council established government control over arms exports, prohibiting it without license. That year, H. G. Wells's *The Work, Wealth and Happiness of Mankind* depicted collective public investment in the arms trade. The science of warfare, he argued, was a perversion of scientific advance, skewing it toward murderous ends, to the profit of figures like Zaharoff but also "thousands of persons of all ranks of life who, as lesser shareholders, play no part in policy." Vickers's eighty thousand shareholders encompassed every class of society, all of whom stood to profit from arms sales, though most were "quite innocent of any desire to slaughter their neighbours." Workers joined the League of Nations Union and held shares in arms firms without being "conscious of any inconsistency." Many held them out of patriotic devotion. Workers at arms firms also benefited from the trade; disarmament would require finding them new work. The shareholders, Wells presumed, would be so horrified to learn that they were part of an "armament class" that they would hardly oppose disarmament. Only the big capitalists, that international organization of crooks, posed a problem. Galton had seen collective complicity as paralyzing—no one had any choice but to go on profiting from war—but because it focused on share-holding (rather than a wider array of consumption habits and fiscal and financial investments), Wells's vision of collective complicity required only the sacrifice of a fraction of wealth or profit from most individuals to achieve real change. The new concentration of state arms-making power in a few factories and corporations also narrowed perception of the field of complicity, and perhaps the field itself.

For this postwar generation, arms makers' immorality lay in their willingness to sell their goods to foreigners and bribe officials at home and abroad. They fomented war scares, spread rumors of the intentions of hostile powers, influenced public opinion in favor of rearmament, drove international rivalries to raise their profits, and exploited their workers. The 1929 stock market crash intensified criticism of capitalist arms production. In 1932, the Union for Democratic Control published an exposé on the "secret international," a complex of arms firms and government. The group described the World Disarmament Conference then transpiring at Geneva under the auspices of the League of the Nations as a sinister cabal where arms firms would ensure rejection of all worthy proposals. It saw the arms industry as unique in offering huge inducements toward combination. Since it produced a commodity for which there was no "real human need," each firm stood to gain from the others' expansion as they collectively encouraged an international arms race and then charged extortionate prices. The group noted Vickers's close relationship with government departments and the high-grade staff experts with military and naval titles serving on its board. The firm had no loyalties; its works were all over the world. Zaharoff, the "Mystery Man of Europe," had been a good friend of Lloyd George when the latter was minister of munitions and prime minister. The industry was intertwined with banking, too, abetted by the state, which supplied allies with enormous loans to buy arms when war began. Certainly, Vickers also made ships, rail equipment, sewing machines, speedboats—an enormous range of civilian and military goods. The government had both an interest and a role in keeping it and similar firms prosperous and allowed them to develop large peacetime exports. These features—diverse pursuits, ties to banking, state support—had been true of the eighteenth-century gun industry, but now the number of players had shrunk and become more corporate in structure. The Union for Democratic Control called for abolition of private arms manufacturing, warning that if the industry again brought the country to the brink of war, workers might refuse to take up arms and opt for revolution instead.

The World Disarmament Conference at Geneva, where private manufacture and big weapons systems were the main issues, failed when Germany, under Nazi leadership, pulled out in 1933. Other countries (Belgium, Sweden, the United States, France, Italy) followed Britain in establishing an export licensing system, but no international agreement to regulate the arms trade emerged. The issue remained on the table, and the data the League assembled for 1925–38 proved crucial in later inquiries in the United Kingdom and the United States. Meanwhile, the Chaco War between Bolivia and Paraguay erupted, with sordid tales of arms firms supplying both sides.

The writing of the history of the eighteenth-century industrial revolution was shaped by these struggles over arms trading. In 1924, the British historian T. S. Ashton acknowledged war's role in fueling the iron industry through demand for cannon, gun carriages, shot, and firearms. Ordnance contracts were like "Food of the Gods." By the early 1930s, that reality had acquired a moral charge, not least because of the rise of Nazism. The

American historian Lewis Mumford's 1934 work *Technics and Civilization* argued that industrialism emerged from militarism but saw that reality negatively, as an indictment of industrialism. This systemic critique emerged just as British public opinion began to sharply condemn the conspicuous villainy of arms firms—perhaps the interwar peace movement's greatest campaign. The British leftist Fenner Brockway published *The Bloody Traffic,* with cartoons by David Low. The book's attack on Vickers and Imperial Chemical Industries heralded a flood of such works. The Labour Party pushed the issue as the League of Nations disarmament conference adjourned that year. The Home Office's 1934 Bodkin Committee, although noting the adverse impact of the 1920 Firearms Act on the gun trade (which bore the losses "with resignation and loyally cooperated with the authorities to help restrict firearms"), also recommended further restrictions on firearms. All existing firearms legislation was consolidated under the Firearms Act of 1937, which stood for the next quarter century.

Meanwhile, the United States Senate launched the Nye Committee to investigate the American arms trade and explore the case for government monopoly of arms production. The committee's evidence on the international trade attracted much attention in Britain, particularly its revelations about arms companies' profits during the war and the international ties that enabled them to supply both sides of the conflict. The committee did not change much in the American arms industry, but its revelations about Vickers incited demand for investigation in Britain. Attlee, leader of the Labour opposition, called on Britain to set an example to the world by prohibiting private manufacture of arms. Sir John Simon answered for the government that, given Attlee's likening of the arms trade to the slave trade and prostitution, his call for nationalization was peculiar. Should they have nationalized the slave trade instead of suppressing it? The interwar focus on the private nature of the arms trade as a moral problem obscured the historical state-industry partnership that had nurtured arms manufacturing. If the arms trade was morally objectionable, like the slave trade, it was because of the thing it produced—arms—not because of who produced it. But critics avoided that tack; the recent war had exposed not only the dangers of an arms race but the danger of a lack of arms. Some may have been pacifists, but most were too patriotic to contemplate total abandonment of arms production.

Christopher Addison (minister of munitions, 1916–17) and the Liberal leader Archibald Sinclair continued to push for an inquiry. The government also began to see its potential use in shielding the growing demand for rearmament from public criticism. Maurice Hankey, secretary to the Cabinet and the Committee of Imperial Defence, saw private manufacture as central to rearmament. But Edward Grey's analysis of the pileup before the previous war rang in critics' ears. In October 1934, the government agreed to the inquiry; at least it would allow the arms makers to answer the allegations against them. The high-ranking Conservative politician Lord Halifax acknowledged the "sincere and profound feeling in the minds of our people" about private arms making: "Rightly or wrongly, a great majority believe it to be directly connected to great issues of peace and war, on which they feel more deeply than about anything else."

And so, in February 1935, another government investigation of arms supply began, eighty years after the last: the Royal Commission on the Private Manufacture of and Trading in Arms. This time the question was not efficiency but ethics. A massive public outpouring of evidence accumulated against the private arms trade, particularly from church groups, including a memorandum signed by Anglican and nonconformist religious leaders. The vocabulary of "abolition" retained a particular moral charge. Communist Party General Secretary Harry Pollitt gave evidence on export figures (based on League data) showing (accurately) that Britain was the greatest contributor to international arms traffic, with a third of the world's arms originating there. Private firms had armed both sides of the unfolding Sino-Japanese conflict and the Chaco War. The Communists also publicized the rising share prices of armorers, the coincidence of pro-Nazi and pro-rearmament sentiment, and the politics of the leadership of the service leagues. The Union for Democratic Control presented an extensive case. Addison and Lloyd George added that private arms makers were also inefficient and unreliable; in the war, the state had coordinated their work with national armaments to make them effective.

The government responded, questioning Pollitt's and Addison's data and asserting the industry's commercial value and its support of national defense at a relatively lower cost than a nationalized industry. If exporting meant that at times they would face an enemy armed with British guns, as in the Dardanelles in 1915, they also benefited from knowing everything about their enemy's munitions—and from the profits and prestige. By 1936, the commission concluded that there was not convincing evidence that British firms promoted belligerent policies, bribed their own government (even if they bribed others), conspired in price hikes, or controlled the press. Nor did profits make the trade morally questionable, since government factories would presumably make profits, too—the morality of arms making was on the user, not the producer. Most important, abolition of private manufacture would not enhance prospects for peace, since the causes of war were much deeper. The supply of arms followed demand; it did not create demand. (Charles Craven of Vickers testified that other commercial goods were as dangerous: he had nearly lost an eye to a firecracker but had never been injured by a gun.) Abolition would also harm preparation for war: the navy relied on peacetime private enterprise; its ships were built in government dockyards, but from articles supplied by private firms, which had nonmilitary uses, too (e.g., steel ribs, engines, boilers, electrical machinery, and so on). The army was already ordering tanks and shells from the trade. The Air Ministry depended entirely on private enterprise. The policy had long been to maintain a healthy private industry to meet peacetime needs and preserve reserve manufacturing capacity for wartime. Without it, the government would lose the ability to expand capacity in war. Prohibiting private manufacture in Britain alone would harm the nation's security and commerce. The commissioners reverted to the eighteenth-century mode of thinking about the state's relationship to the private trade. It saw the relationship between government and wider industry as one of partnership. It believed in private arms manufacturing in principle even if it had not always supported gunmakers' interests in practice when imperial security was at stake.

The commission report put responsibility for maintaining the private arms trade squarely on the government. Licensing gave government control of exports, so it was unfair to blame the private traders. Like Galton more than a century earlier, it argued that a coherent plan to obviate the evils of the system of private manufacture was practically impossible, for it would have to cover "the whole field of industrial activity in which the motive of private profit can be stimulated in relation to arms production," a field much vaster than arms manufacture, extending to "industries producing components and essential materials to a wide ramification of trades," including "producers of many of the essential requisites of peace," such as fuel, oil, and civil aircraft. Nationalization of industries closely associated with manufacture of warlike needs would work only as part of a "general scheme of nationalisation of industry as a whole." The League of Nations Union had in fact proposed state monopoly of the stage of industrial production at which a product was converted into something with lethal capacity, administered by an armaments board that would thus control subsidiary industries. Addison had submitted a similar proposal for a peacetime public department monopolizing manufacture of specified products. But the commission concluded that such schemes presented too many practical difficulties and would cause serious delays. State organization could rapidly mobilize manufacture but also had its limits. The state could not make commercial products unrelated to armaments or participate in export trade; the private trade, however, could use its plant to serve other peacetime markets. Moreover, those who supplied metals and other materials for arms and those who supplied food, medical stores, and clothing to the services profited as much, if not more, from war. There was thus no justification for singling out one industry for special treatment. The commissioners more or less reproduced Galton's analysis as a defense of private arms making in general. They, too, implicated the entire industrial economy as ineluctably involved with war production. This time the defense worked; all but the Communist Party greeted the idea of nationalizing all industry as the absurdity the commissioners intended it to be—akin to Galton's suggestion of tax resistance. (The Labour Party's interest in nationalizing the "commanding heights" of industry stemmed from different concerns.)

The commission recognized the public's own awareness of collective complicity in arms production, "the fact that under the existing economic system large numbers of people, of all classes of the community, by reason of their employment, their business interests or by the holding of shares, may have a financial interest in war or the preparation for war." This was a point the Union for Democratic Control and others had made, too. The commissioners conceded that this collective investment induced in the public an "unconscious tendency" in favor of warlike policies but argued that people were also subject to stronger influences tending in the opposite direction. They reiterated their respect for the good faith and earnestness of those who objected to private manufacture of arms. But the only practical concession was the recommendation that an appropriate minister approve employment of retired officials by arms firms. The commission also criticized the sale of surplus guns abroad, disapproving particularly of John Ball, whose sordid and pugnacious image was undented by War Office attempts to defend him. Such secondhand trade damaged national prestige and empowered Britain's enemies with British weapons without producing any financial, military, or technological advantage. Less scrupulous dealers could easily evade restrictions on exports. But the government disagreed with the recommendation to end the secondhand trade, as it was already subject to license. The commission also recommended creation of a ministry to control arms supply and assured the public that in war, private firms would be brought under strict control and prevented from making excessive profits. Within six weeks, the report was buried; the government proceeded with rearmament as German forces occupied the Rhineland.

By the 1930s, the issue of private manufacture, particularly of planes and warships, rather than arms trafficking more generally and small arms in particular, was the dominant concern of those invested in arms control. Even the Royal Commission, while including small arms, was more concerned with makers of big weapons systems. Tensions on the Indian frontier had been defused by suppression of the small-arms trade there. In 1935, the subsidy to ensure the sultan of Muscat's cooperation in that suppression ended without fuss. Fears of colonials armed with automatic pistols had been vanquished partly by the development of heavier weapons systems like air control; those systems appeared more threatening and demanding of regulation. Small arms ceased to be the decisive weapons they had been in the late nineteenth century, deadly though they proved in World War Two. The lack of dramatic advance in small-arms technology since the 1890s was a factor in this view. In 1934, the War Office brought in a Czech design for the new army light machine gun, over protests from Vickers and BSA. After World War Two, the Ministry of Defence considered it impracticable and uneconomical to maintain an R&D team for designing small arms; BSA closed down as a result of a government decision to let them go.

In 1936, the politician Philip Noel-Baker, who had been closely involved in the formation of the League of Nations, published a treatise against private manufacture of arms, building on his testimony at the commission. He remarked on the public's preoccupation with the greed and dishonesty of arms makers as individuals rather than the systemic roots of the evil, in which they were all enmeshed through their support of government policies. Unlike the commissioners, he perceived not collective profits from war, but a system that produced conflict between the public interest in peace and the private interests of individuals and firms who stood to profit from war. If the state saw collective participation as an argument against change, Noel-Baker saw it as a reason for greater democratic assertiveness, approvingly quoting the French arms maker Paul Allard (of the Schneider-Creusot firm), who asked his critics to examine his factories' century-long industrial history, always oriented toward the "whole industry of metallurgy and mechanical construction," with only periodic focus on war matériel at the government's behest. Noel-Baker ignored the implication that arms firms had been critical to industrialism generally, insisting instead that responsibility for the system lay with governments that promoted development of the private manufacture of arms, deliberately "spreading" orders among different establishments. He got most of the story right, even if he avoided acknowledging that a wider swath of industry depended on the trade than his narrow indictment of large firms allowed—the shift from an earlier period of "spreading" orders to the twentieth-century reliance on a few corporations that did have different relations with the state than, say, suppliers of paper, ink, and furniture (e.g., collusion in loans to foreign governments, nominations of ex-officers as agents for firms). The ripple effects of the arms industry's partnership with the state remained arguably the same, however, as the commissioners of 1935 saw. The intimacy between banking and the arms industry was not new. Interwar critics never fully grasped wider complicity in the production of war matériel, remaining focused on the particular moral bankruptcy of arms makers, despite the Royal Commission's perception of broader economic investment in war. The scandal of the arms maker continued to obscure the scandal of modern industrial life's debts to war.

The Nazi state easily took over gunmaking firms in 1938, showing that states dominated arms firms rather than vice versa. In May 1939, on the eve of war, the British state imposed controls on its arms industry's profits, signaling collapse of voluntary cooperation between the government and arms firms when it was most needed. The Ministry of Supply emerged to reconcile the conflicting needs of a profit-driven industry and the country's defenses. After the war, thousands of arms in ex-soldiers' hands were surrendered. As the British emerged as major global arms suppliers in the sixties, the 1937 Firearms Act was amended three times and reconsolidated as the Firearms Act of 1968. Self-defense ceased to be valid grounds for firearm possession. The law continued to require dealers to register, imposing high security standards on their premises and requiring a full record of all dealings. Arms critics focused on nuclear weapons. The "Thing" that E. P. Thompson perceived in this time was wider and vaguer than a military-industrial complex. Part of its power was its lack of ideological charge, ensuring its appeal to the right and the left, both of which were nationalistic about technology and industry. The long history of state partnership with military industrialism helps explain the origins of this Cold War Thing.

In 1959, Noel-Baker won the Nobel Peace Prize, validation of his indictment of the state, rather than arms firms, as primarily responsible for arms proliferation. Of course, the Nobel Foundation is itself the product of the arms industry, thanks to Alfred Nobel, the inventor of dynamite, who transformed the Swedish Bofors Company from an iron-and-steel producer into a major arms manufacturer. "Nobel" has been normalized as a philanthropic brand, just as the industry has been normalized as a primarily civilian enterprise occasionally hijacked by states' war needs. Still, popular opinion continues to villainize arms makers even while criticizing the military-industrial complex, a theory that got legs during the Vietnam War as many Americans became mistrustful of the military and its relationship with the world of high tech.

It may be impossible to abolish the sale of small arms; even where export controls are effective, forgery, imposture, and extortion of official approval enable smuggling. Their size makes small arms liable to illicit trafficking. In the 1980s, however, Britain itself experienced a major reduction in arms possession. After the Hungerford massacre of 1987, in which a lone gunman killed sixteen, the Firearms (Amendment) Act of 1988 prohibited semi-automatic and pump-action guns and tightened registration and storage requirements for shotguns. The Dunblane massacre of 1997 prompted greater restrictions: the Firearms (Amendment) (No. 2) Act of 1997, which banned private possession of handguns, including small-bore pistols and rifles used by target shooters, almost entirely, with some exceptions for antique guns—radically different objects going by the same name. Britain, the world's second largest supplier of small arms, passed some of the toughest anti-gun legislation in the world. The 1988 and 1997 laws were accompanied by the surrender of thousands of firearms and rounds of ammunition. Britain now has one of the lowest rates of gun homicide in the world. Outside of Northern Ireland, United Kingdom police are not armed with firearms (apart from a small subset of specially trained firearms officers). Shooting sports remain an important pastime. Mass shootings have stopped, apart from the 2010 case in Cumbria in which a taxi driver went on a shooting spree, killing twelve people.

In 1998, Birmingham was the site of the first major international discussion about small arms proliferation, at the annual meeting of the G8. That year, the United States passed a law requiring a license for sales abroad, even while domestic laws remained lax. Other governments began using licensing and registration to regulate the business in the name of public safety and open trading. In Britain, successive reviews of arms export controls have urged proper implementation of existing laws and closure of enduring legal loopholes, especially regulation of arms brokers. But such efforts have continued to confront the paralyzing logic that loose controls in other countries make tight control in any one place pointless. The idea of an internationally coordinated effort has gained greater traction in this context, not least because the global war on terror has fueled concern about small arms in the hands of terrorists and insurgents— echoing the concerns of the Islington Committee in 1917–18. The collapse of the Soviet Union and ties between the Russian arms industry and its former party organs have flooded the world with Kalashnikovs.

Against this backdrop, in 2006 the United Nations convened a conference on illicit small-arms trafficking, giving legal force to action initiated in 2001. The conference ended without agreement. Of the 140 states that voted on the resolution to start work on a treaty, only one voted in the negative: the United States, where the gun lobby, led by the National Rifle Association (NRA), fears that any attempt to control international trade is the first step in a plot to ban private gun ownership. Another conference was convened in 2012. Failing to reach agreement, it met again in 2013 to attempt to regulate the $70-billion-a-year global market in conventional weapons, including tanks, armored combat vehicles, large-caliber weapons, combat aircraft, attack helicopters, warships, missiles and launchers, *and* small arms and light weapons. In April 2013, the United Nations General Assembly adopted the Arms Trade Treaty, which requires states to review cross-border arms contracts, establish national control systems, and deny exports to purchasers who might use weapons for terrorism or violations of humanitarian law. It entered into force in December 2014; the United States, the world's biggest arms exporter, signed the treaty but has not ratified it.

We have inherited the old suspicion of "merchants of death" and a robust critique of the military-industrial complex, but we have lost a sense of the larger, more dispersed military-industrial society in which they thrive. The American Revolution politicized slavery in a new way as Americans and Britons competed for the moral higher ground, indicting entire societies for complicity in slavery rather than pinning it on a few villains who could be called on to desist. The reform of East India Company affairs was part of that moment of reflection on systemic evils. But the trial of Warren Hastings found a scapegoat for the system; likewise, criticism of contractor greed distracted from wider economic investment in war, and abolition deflected attention from the wider scandal of exploited labor in Britain and all over the empire. Today, too, the effort to regulate arms trading can tend to obscure collective investment in it—not that this makes it any less worth pursuing. Even as we recognize wide arenas of complicity, we avoid indicting the mode of industrial-capitalist imperialism in which these iniquities have flourished—at least since the collapse of Marxism.

Galton's defense of the neutrality of his commodity—his attempt to abstract his economic acts from other moral and social commitments—helped produce the episteme of economics. To him, serving demand was a morally neutral activity. In a sense, the history of modern capitalism has been precisely the struggle to extract something called "the economy" from inherited notions of "moral economy" in which the very idea of an "economic price" for grain was a cultural outrage. Bourgeois culture disguises social relations as a system free from obligatory power relations; all are instead bound by innocent relations to things—and the impersonal gun helped assert those new bonds. This cultural shift faces continual challenge from other kinds of claims humans make on one another. The Society of Friends did not buy Galton's claims about the moral neutrality of guns. Around the same time, the Romantics began to criticize the dehumanized intellectual universe of "political economy" and the dehumanizing effects of industrialism. Periodic efforts to moralize debate about the arms trade were part of this recurring rebellion, even though, by focusing outrage on a particular commodity, they helped distract attention from wider systemic iniquity and alienation.

Liberalism came with such mechanisms for managing guilt. It is "constitutively guilty in conscience"; hence the need to govern sentiment. By identifying sentiment as a sufficient internal governing constraint on the greater excesses of the market and the systemic suffering it breeds, Smith's *Theory of Moral Sentiments* preemptively offered a rejoinder to conscience's moral objections to the system he would lay out in *The Wealth of Nations*. He insisted on the need to refuse the vision of the "miseries we never saw" and limit ourselves to the immediate, local, and visible effects of capitalism as it emerged; global knowledge of its effects would paralyze its progress, throwing its agents into gloomy dejection. The more global capital became, the more it required a parochial moral vision. Smith prescribed for capital's agents a restrained habit of sympathizing with a limited set of others, and for its subjects a stoic response to the fact of their own suffering. He called for an internal economy of sentiment, an ability to distribute the passions within the bounds of propriety. Propriety determined the magnitude of society's response to unjust suffering. The Society of Friends felt that Galton's role as arms maker was beyond propriety, while perhaps the Lloyds' financial involvement in war was not. Galton felt the Society's expectation that he give up his business was a disproportionate and thus inappropriate moral response that entailed splitting hairs over the reality that they were all involved in war-driven industrial capitalism. He suggested mass tax resistance as the absurd end of the Society's moral logic, and the royal commissioners of 1936 suggested nationalization of all industry as the absurd end of the moral logic of critics of arms manufacturing then: both strove to expose the illusion of wider innocence created by an overly parochial moral vision. As Marx observed, "To call on them to give up their illusions about their condition is to call on them to give up a condition that requires illusions." These words were about religion, but they apply well to liberalism itself, whose morality was rooted in eighteenth-century religion.

I n October 2013, the *New York Times* urged the United States to ratify the United Nations Arms Trade Treaty. This was a rehearsal of 1919, not 1936: it was about keeping guns out of the wrong hands—militants, bad regimes, criminals—not about the ethical dubiousness of the trade itself. The editors instanced the role of the trade in conventional weapons in the conflicts in Syria, Sudan, and the Congo, depicting them as senseless civil wars devoid of political content and unrelated to a colonial past. I point this out not to question the good sense of regulating the arms trade—the fewer guns that are available in those places, the quicker the political conflict can be addressed—but to show how efforts to regulate the arms trade continue to entail depoliticization and delegitimization of certain kinds of violence and evasion of the reality that providing arms to such conflicts helps maintain the peacetime arms-manufacturing capacity of countries like the United States and the United Kingdom.

The *Times* editors complained about NRA interference against a treaty that would have no impact on the domestic gun market, especially since American manufacturers are already legally obligated to comply with an export control system designed to keep weapons out of the hands of human rights abusers and other unsavory actors; the treaty's main effect would be in countries where such standards were not in place, and its only enforcement mechanism was shame. Yet the NRA persuaded a third of the Senate to oppose ratification. The editors were adamant: "In a world where virtually every major commodity is subject to international agreements, allowing weapons to avoid any review or regulation is irresponsible and unacceptable." Guns' rich social life continues to enable them to escape such regulation. In the United States, they have even been exempted from regulation by the Consumer Product Safety Commission since its inception. Alongside the *New York Times* editorial were letters to the editor about the paper's recent investigation of the systematically underreported number of children accidentally killed by guns in the United States—toddlers playing with guns hidden under sofas or kept handy to ward off coyotes, or accidents occurring while cleaning a gun or hunting. The newspaper challenged the low figures in the NRA's fact sheet opposing safe-storage laws and documented the magnetic attraction of firearms among boys—the shooters in almost all instances. Culture shapes the meaning and use of objects like guns, whose role has evolved in disturbing ways in the United States. In literature, they remain ubiquitous as part of the paraphernalia of civilization, providing easy plot fixes even in juvenile fiction, where they appear as blunt representations of power requiring little verbal elaboration, as ubiquitous as forks and spoons. Meanwhile, in real life, barbaric mass public shootings, often in school settings and by mentally disturbed individuals, have pushed gun control to the forefront of national debate.

The push for greater controls on who can possess guns and what sorts of guns civilians should be allowed to possess encounters opposition couched as defense of the Second Amendment, written in 1791, just when the controversy around Galton was heating up within the Society of Friends. The British certainly had an image of a well-armed American society by the Victorian era. In 1854, a British gun manufacturer explained the large market there for Birmingham guns: "Everybody wants a gun in America, and of course every man wants one as cheap as he can get it." Lord Raglan, head of the Ordnance Board, explained that the American government could support both its own factories and private manufacturers, because "in America every man is armed, so that the supply is endless almost." But as we have seen, all guns are not the same: a gun in 1791 worked differently and was used for different ends than guns in 1701 or guns today, even if they all go by the same name. The most formidable firearm of 1791, a muzzle-loading single-shot firearm, is hardly comparable in use, effect, cultural status, or purpose to the semi-automatic weapons many hope to regulate now.

Guns alter human agency, in different ways at different times. We use smartphones to record and share things we would not have recorded and shared in the past, even though we had other cameras and recording devices. Guns are not merely alternatives to knives and other weapons; they make particular kinds of violence possible. Eighteenth-century England was a place where guns were used not in crimes of passion, but in new kinds of property crimes. At the end of the century, as all Britain mobilized for war and masses of people became familiar with guns in a new way, they figured in new kinds of impersonal and casual violence that would not have been committed with any other weapon. Over time, guns have enabled entirely new forms of violence. The mass shootings of our time are historically specific; they need not go on. It is not true that without guns, the same "bad people" would commit the same acts with a knife or some other weapon. The American gun lobby draws on arguments similar to Galton's to defend the innocence of the gun and point to other causes of violence, like mental health. When Galton made such arguments, they made a kind of sense, since guns were not used much in interpersonal violence in Britain and had other commercial and symbolic uses. But since then guns have changed, and the way they are used has changed. They frequently facilitate types of violence that would not otherwise occur. The NRA's defense of the neutrality of the gun as a commodity rings false.

In 1939, the Supreme Court ruled that the Second Amendment did not guarantee individual householders a right to own whatever guns they liked outside the context of a militia. More recent rulings have overturned this understanding. In the *Heller* decision of 2008, the court ruled that the Second Amendment protected the individual right to possess firearms unconnected with militia service—based on the myth that in early America all adult males owned firearms. Gun ownership was widespread, but mostly not of military quality. In Virginia, those who had arms had "such firelocks as they had provided to destroy the noxious animals which infest their farms," wrote Thomas Jefferson. In Pennsylvania, militiamen protested state recall of their publicly supplied muskets in 1787. Shays' Rebellion, in Massachusetts in 1786–87, ended in confrontation at the Springfield arsenal, where both sides struggled to control the seven thousand muskets housed there. The Second Amendment was not about protecting Americans from federal government seizure of their fowlers; it addressed the practical danger that militias might be disarmed by federal *in*action, providing reassurance that if the federal government neglected to arm the militia, state governments might do so. The issue was not self-defense, but national defense. Our gun-control debate should not be so tightly anchored to that debate about military muskets for state militias—not least because no right is unlimited or immune from reasonable regulation. That old debate itself highlights the importance of attending to material differences in guns; eighteenth-century Americans made distinctions about the appropriate uses of different types of firearms, and so should we.

Advocates of gun control often point to other "developed" nations that have tightened laws to reduce gun violence, including Japan, Britain, Australia, and Canada. Three of these four are pieces of the old British Empire whose love affair with guns was shaped by the period covered in this book. The fourth, Japan, in its past already proved the possibility that a technology—the firearm—can be rejected, discontinued, and forgotten. In the seventeenth century, Tokugawa Japan obliged its army to renounce firearms and exorcise all knowledge of gunmaking, eliminating firearms from two centuries of Japanese history without giving up on technological progress in other fields. Even France forgot its invention of interchangeable parts. We might even reinvent guns as stores of metal and money value, in the manner of the Mexican artist Pedro Reyes, who recently melted 1,527 guns and turned them into shovels to demonstrate "how an agent of death can become an agent of life." He distributed the shovels to art institutions and schools to plant 1,527 trees and asked people in his town of Culiacán, the city with the highest rate of gun deaths in Mexico, to give him their guns in exchange for coupons to buy electronics or household appliances. We do not have to be the passive victims of our own knowledge and skills. Progress is not a force beyond human control; it emerges from human actions and what we choose to remember or forget.

In 1907, Artifex and Opifex rehearsed the British gun trade's role in the expansion of the empire:

The fire-arms industry established in London by Henry VIII allowed of England's expansion during the reign of Elizabeth. . . . [T]he guns Elizabeth sent to Russia stayed the Tartar invasions and brought Siberia under the dominion of the Tsars of Muscovy. The Parliamentarians owed their successes to their good, Birmingham "O. C." blades, and the care they took to keep their powder dry. But for Birmingham arms the Jacobites might have succeeded. The two million muskets supplied by Birmingham enabled England and her allies to wage a successful war against Napoleon later; British arms conquered India.

The 1908 history of Warwickshire County traced the remarkably expensive shooting there to the proximity of "prosperous gunmakers, naturally interested in and addicted to shooting." The best guns in the world still came from the "Hardware City." Artifex and Opifex were proud gunmakers; Birmingham was proud of its gunmaking past. The Galtons had been proud, too. They did not suffer pangs of conscience, nor, evidently, did Craven, Zaharoff, or the other Undershafts of history. In recent liability lawsuits—before 2005, when the U.S. Congress passed a law shielding gunmakers from such suits—the world's gunmakers staunchly denied responsibility for improper sales of guns. Paul Jannuzzo, then an executive at Glock, asked why his company should police its sales: "There's nothing intrinsically evil about these things." Indeed, Smith & Wesson's attempt to adopt changes, such as designing a handgun that couldn't be operated by children, produced an industry backlash and a sharp drop in sales, until the company was taken over in 2001 and began to toe the NRA line again.

There is one story of an arms maker's bad conscience bearing on the history of the very place in which I write. In 1862, the son of the Connecticut manufacturer of the Winchester repeating rifle, the gun that won the West, married Sarah Pardee. Sarah lost her baby daughter in 1866 and her husband in 1881. Falling into a deep depression, she sought help from a spiritualist, who told her that she was being haunted by the spirits of Native Americans, Civil War soldiers, and others killed by the Winchester rifle. They had caused the untimely deaths of her daughter and husband. She could escape a similar fate if she moved west and built a great house for the spirits. As long as construction did not cease, she would remain safe. Sarah came to Menlo Park, California, where her niece lived, and from there she found the site for her new home in San Jose. She began building in 1884, and over the next thirty-eight years she produced the "Winchester Mystery House." She also owned homes in Atherton, Los Altos, and Palo Alto. Her financial resources were virtually inexhaustible, thanks to the thousands of shares she still held in the Winchester Repeating Arms Company—just under 50 percent of the company's capital stock, producing an income of $1,000 a day. The Mystery House stands today in the heart of Silicon Valley, whose growth has been fueled by the security and defense needs of the Cold War and the war on terror, although we like to think of it as a story of entrepreneurship unbound, akin to the old story of the British industrial revolution. Sarah Winchester was haunted but remained invested in the arms business, which funded her unending and purposeless construction project; like her, we remain haunted yet invested.

ACKNOWLEDGMENTS

Writing this book has been a long and often solitary pursuit, but many individuals have helped along the way. Indeed, complicity has been so widespread that I hope I will be forgiven if I do forget a name here or there. So many of you have helped, by chatting about industrial revolution, passing on references about Quakers and guns, answering queries about slavery and homicide, providing voluminous feedback on drafts, offering penetrating questions at workshops, and more. Some of you I have never met, and yet you generously shared your expertise by e-mail. Thank you, Ken Alder, Sascha Auerbach, Gordon Bannerman, Huw Bowen, Michael Collins, Christopher Brown, Vincent Brown, Patrick Charles, Arianne Chernock, Carl Chinn, Sakura Christmas, Deborah Cohen, Randolf Cooper, John Craig, Edward Davies, Jan de Vries, Mark Dincecco, Jonathan Eisenberg, John Essex, Hannah Farber, Margot Finn, Kate Fullagar, Stefanos Geroulanos, Evan Haefeli, Sudheendra Hangal, Frederick Hoxie, Joseph Inikori, Penny Ismay, Maya Jasanoff, Roderick Jones, Patrick Joyce, Elizabeth Kolsky, Michael Kwass, Elizabeth Lambourn, David Lieberman, Jennifer Luff, Marc Matera, Tom Metcalf, Alan Mikhail, Joseph Miller, Patrick O'Brien, Guy Ortolano, Anthony Page, Steven Pincus, Lucy Suchman, Susan Pedersen, Mark Peterson, Giorgio Riello, Andrew Sartori, Tehila Sasson, Lois Schwoerer, Junaid Shaikh, Rivka Shenhav, Simon Smith, Philip Stern, Kevin Sweeney, Jennifer Tucker, Melissa Turoff, Ilya Vinkovetsky, Carl Wennerlind, Warren Whatley, Nicholas Wilson, and Aaron Windel.

I particularly want to thank Brian DeLay for his generous and sharp critical feedback on key portions and for being an inspiring "comrade in arms" whose intellectual enthusiasm for the history of the gun trade has buoyed my own. I have learned a great deal about "economic sentiments" and family history from Emma Rothschild, whose support of this project has been essential. I am also deeply grateful to Roger Louis for his belief in me and in this project. My Berkeley past continues to shape all that I research and write: James Vernon has been a treasured and steadfast friend and mentor in the nine years that I have been immersed in this project. Tom Laqueur remains the cherished angel on my shoulder, guiding, lovingly encouraging, and, most of all, continually inspiring me to make my historical inquiry as human and humane as I possibly can.

I am grateful to have had the opportunity to present parts of this work at workshops and seminars at Columbia University, New York University, Harvard University, the University of Chicago, the University of California at Santa Cruz, Simon Fraser University, the University of Virginia, the University of California at San Diego, the University of Illinois at Urbana-Champaign, the Newberry Seminar in British History in Chicago, the University of California at Berkeley, Yale University, and the Aspen Institute. I thank the wonderful colleagues who invited me and the generous scholars who attended and shed much-needed light on many aspects of the work. I also thank those who attended a panel at which I presented the first fruit of this study, at the North American Conference on British Studies in Baltimore in 2010.

This has been a Stanford book, and I have been fortunate to share my results at critical moments with my department (first in the original Junior Faculty Reading Group), as well as the Social Science History Workshop and the Clayman Institute for Gender Research, and in halls and parking lots. Warm thanks to Ran Abramitzky, Keith Baker, Richard Bell, David Como, Jon Connolly, Arie Dubnov, Paula Findlen, Zephyr Frank, Allyson Hobbs, Nick Jenkins, Yumi Moon, Tom Mullaney, Jennifer Pegg, Erica Plambeck, Jessica Riskin, Richard Roberts, Peter Samuels, Londa Schiebinger, Jane Shaw, Matt Sommer, Peter Stansky, Laura Stokes, Jun Uchida, Gil-li Vardi, Ali Yaycioglu, Richard White, Caroline

Winterer, and Gavin Wright. I particularly want to thank Avner Greif and Jack Rakove, for sharing wise insights from their long thinking about economic history and the Second Amendment, respectively. Lisa Surwillo generously provided close readings of several draft chapters. Sean Hanretta imparted crucial early lessons from African history.

I learned a great deal from the students in my Capital and Empire seminar each year from 2010 to 2013. Brianna Rego, Benjamin Hein, and Boris Atanassov provided impeccable research assistance. Research and writing of this book depended on support from the staff and administration at Stanford, particularly in our wonderful History Corner. The librarians and staff at Cecil H. Green Library at Stanford have been exceedingly tolerant and generous. I also want to thank Benjamin Stone for his unending indulgence of my archival requests.

Several external agencies have been indispensable to my ability to write this book. The National Endowment for the Humanities, the American Philosophical Society, and the American Council of Learned Societies provided essential resources. I thank Ankur Day School in Shimla, India, for permitting my children to enroll temporarily so that I could write chapter eight. I am indebted also to the archivists and librarians at the Huntington Library, the National Archives of India, the Guildhall Library, the Birmingham City Archive (Fiona Tait, Angela Skitt, Peter Doré), University College London Special Collections (Dan Mitchell), the Friends House Library, the Bull Street Meeting House (Alison Ironside), and the U.K. National Archives. I also want to thank C. W. Harding, historian and archivist at the Birmingham Proof House, and Derek Stimpson, archivist at the Worshipful Company of Gunmakers, who offered a great deal of help by e-mail and phone, as did Malcolm Reid of the Internet Gun Club and Paulette Burkhill of the Handsworth Historical Society.

Thank you to Meg Jacobs for her encouragement and support of this book years ago and to Scott Moyers at Penguin Press for his early belief in its potential. My agent, Don Fehr, helped me to realize that potential further and make the book a practical reality. My wonderfully wise and meticulous editor, Emily Cunningham, gently and smartly helped me get the manuscript in shape for public consumption. I am grateful, too, to the talented design and editorial team at Penguin that shepherded it through production.

I want to thank Socorro Reyes for her constant care and tolerance for my at times insane moods while writing (or, worse, not writing). It has been years since I acquired the debt, but I am glad to at last be able to thank Vivek Ramachandran and Karen Loh for their hospitality in London, and my dear friend Adrienne Copithorne for hers in Cambridge. I also want to record here my deep gratitude to all my friends, who share their lives with me out of choice. I have loved laughing with you while awaiting the horrendously delayed gratification of this completed book. Sunil Khanna was a vital companion in parts of the journey.

All my family, in the U.S. and in India, have been a great support. My brother, Rishi Satia, especially, shared references and cheered me on. I thank my parents, Jagat and Indira Satia, as always, for making it possible for me to make a career of reading, writing, and thinking, and for the gentle understanding with which they have always related our own family stories. I cherish the discussions I had about this book with my father, with his face all lit up—unforgettable moments in this long undertaking. My dear parents-in-law, C. P. Sujaya and S. K. Alok, swooped in with characteristic generosity to make my early research and writing possible. My children, Amann and Kabir, also provided research assistance—helping Mama carry books, reading a paragraph here and there, reminding me about the Winchester Mystery House, believing I would get it all done, even as it has stretched into each new year of their lives. Aprajit Mahajan has been there with me, with his love, throughout. My economist mirror, he gallantly read the tomelike first draft and helped me believe that I actually had a book. Understanding inequality has been something we have both, with our different languages and sensibilities, pursued since we met as college freshmen. Thank you for daily forcing me to confront the discipline of economics and for helping me through the most difficult phases. But thank you, most of all, for filling our life together with enough sunshine to make writing about guns a tolerable occupation.

Even though so many are complicit, unlike Galton, I take full responsibility for the final product. And like everything I write, this book is for my children. In 2010, when Amann was four, she asked a policeman sitting at our local taqueria why he had a gun. The policeman explained that he had it to protect everyone from bad guys, and Amann bravely replied, "But if you have a gun, then *you* are a bad guy." She was certain. Writing this book, I have found all certainties fall away, but there remains a wisdom in her preschool insight about guns and how we decide what is "bad." I hope, dear Amann, you are proud of this book, which you have watched me write from start to finish as you developed into a remarkable writer yourself. And Kabir—at last. Here it is. You were born two weeks shy of the publication of *Spies in Arabia* and did not get to see your name on the dedication page. How patiently you have waited for your name in this second book, and how sweetly and precociously you decided to learn about Galton yourself. Of all the workshops where I shared Galton's story, I loved most your kindergarten class. In the end, you wrote about him before I did, for your first-grade writing assignment. I hope you are proud of the book that I wrote and that it was worth the long wait. Infinite love to you both.

NOTES

Key to Abbreviations
Birmingham City Archives: BCA
The National Archives (UK): TNA
Guildhall Library: GL
National Archives of India: NAI
Friends House Library: FHL
Bull Street Meeting House (Birmingham): BSMH
Proceedings of the Old Bailey: POB
University College London Special Collections: UCL
Historical Violence Database, Ohio State University: HVD
Parliamentary Papers: PP
Ordnance Minutes: OM
Court Minutes: CM
James Farmer: JF
Samuel Galton: SG
Samuel Galton Jr.: SGII
PP: *Report from the Select Committee on Small Arms* 18, May 12, 1854: *RSCSA*

Preface
xiv **Cerberus has failed:** Michael J. de la Merced, "Remington Investors Get Chance to Cash Out," *New York Times,* May 16, 2015, B1; Julie Creswell, "After Mass Shootings, Some on Wall St. See Gold in Gun Makers," *New York Times,* January 7, 2016, A1. Cerberus's founder, Stephen Feinberg, is an avid hunter, but his father lived near Sandy Hook. Large providers of 401(k)s are also large shareholders in gun manufacturers. Campaign to Unload is calling on them to divest from these stocks. Andrew Ross Sorkin, "Gun Shares Have Done Well, but Divestment Push Grows," *New York Times,* December 8, 2015, B1.

Introduction
2 **The state was the single most:** Brewer, *The Sinews of Power,* xvii, 27, 29, 31, 34. The capital assets of a large eighteenth-century business rarely exceeded £10,000. The army and the navy nearly tripled in size from 1680 to 1780. The army doubled during the Nine Years' War, reaching 87,500, then 144,650 during the War of the Spanish Succession. After a brief dip during the War of the Austrian Succession, the upward trend resumed.
2 **no one has explained:** We do have a sophisticated grasp of how commercial, demographic, geological, technological, agricultural, and cultural developments made it possible. See de Vries, "The Industrial Revolution and the Industrious Revolution"; M. Berg, *Luxury and Pleasure in Eighteenth-Century Britain* and *The Age of Manufactures, 1700–1820,* 116–17; Macfarlane, *Marriage and Love in*

England; Mokyr, *The Enlightened Economy;* P. Jones, *Industrial Enlightenment;* Hobsbawm, *Industry and Empire;* Inikori, *Africans and the Industrial Revolution in England;* Landes, *The Unbound Prometheus;* R. Allen, *The British Industrial Revolution in Global Perspective.* But cultural and technological accounts that do not reckon with the presence of state officials and contractors in the networks of the British Enlightenment remain incomplete; likewise for commercial accounts that do not attend to the massive military purchasing that made markets abroad accessible.

4 **Birmingham's "industrial enlightenment":** Mokyr, *The Enlightened Economy,* chap. 2.

7 **guns are an obvious starting point:** To be clear, I am not claiming that the gun industry drove the industrial revolution, or that the consumer cotton industry was unimportant. I use the gun industry as a window onto understanding how state purchasing figured in the transformations that made up the industrial revolution—tethering that story to the Midlands to understand how war shaped the metallurgical industries that were the backbone of industrial transformation everywhere. The Galton story, in turn, offers a generous window onto the gun industry.

8 **wider social life:** Guns are "socially and politically situated objects whose function and meaning changed over time." Howell, "The Social Life of Firearms in Tokugawa Japan," 65.

8 **gun had an aura:** One might think of that aura in terms of fetishism, in the Marxist sense, or, following Hegel, as part of the inherently contradictory nature of the process of objectification, which binds even as it alienates.

9 **Consumption of any good:** On sugar, see Austen and Smith, "Private Tooth Decay as Public Economic Virtue," 185–86.

9 **Abroad, too, to British:** This is not an argument about superior military technology enabling European conquest of the world; in this period, Europeans and indigenous populations were often armed with the same weapons, and technological innovation was not a uniquely European phenomenon. Guns altered British agency abroad; the particular ways in which the British used guns mattered. See also Raudzens, "War-Winning Weapons"; "Military Revolution or Maritime Evolution?"; Cooper, *The Anglo-Maratha Campaigns,* 6, 310–11. From the nineteenth century, technology played a different role in conquest. See Headrick, *Tools of Empire.*

10 **great moral question:** Laqueur, *Solitary Sex,* 21, 235, 280, 291.

11 **One of the earliest:** Hobson, *Imperialism,* 150.

11 **political economists who forgot:** E. Silbener, 1972, quoted in O'Brien, *Power with Profit,* 32–33.

11 **market relationships across vast:** Thomas Haskell, "Capitalism and the Origins of the Humanitarian Sensibility, Part 1" and "Capitalism and the Origins of the Humanitarian Sensibility, Part 2," in *The Antislavery Debate,* ed. Bender.

12 **members of the cast:** Unfortunately, the sources on the Galton family do not permit even modest reflection on how the intimate sphere of family life—such as relations between husbands and wives—might have shaped this history.

12 **"a historical accident":** Hueckel, "War and the British Economy," 365, 368, 371.

12 **one seminal work:** John, "War and the English Economy." See also J. Anderson, "Aspects of the Effect on the British Economy of the Wars against France." In a recent working paper, Patrick O'Brien has also proposed that the wars from 1793–1815 shaped industrial transformation in that period. "The Contributions of Warfare with Revolutionary and Napoleonic France to the Consolidation and Progress of the British Industrial Revolution."

12 **as "stochastic perturbations":** O'Brien, "Introduction," 12. See also Brewer, *The Sinews of Power,* 37, 196; Hudson, *The Industrial Revolution,* 63.

12 **Economists speculated on:** See, for instance, O'Brien, *Power with Profit,* 2–3, 15, 20, 24–27.

12 **fiscal-military state spent:** See, for instance, van Creveld, *Supplying War;* Pool, *Navy Board Contracts;* Knight and Wilcox, *Sustaining the Fleet;* Knight, *Britain Against Napoleon;* Bowen and Enciso, eds., *Mobilising Resources for War;* Cole, *Arming the Royal Navy;* Bowen, *War and British Society;* Baker, *Government and Contractors;* Bannerman, *Merchants and the Military.*

13 **industrial change was rehabilitated:** Key texts in these debates were Crafts, *British Economic Growth;* "British Economic Growth"; Mokyr, "Has the Industrial Revolution Been Crowded Out?"; Williamson, "Why Was British Growth So Slow during the Industrial Revolution?"; Berg and Hudson, "Rehabilitating the Industrial Revolution"; M. Berg, *The Age of Manufactures.* Sven Beckert recently argued that states had a large role in the industrial revolution, but state purchasing does not figure in his book (except on 161, instancing Russia). *Empire of Cotton,* xv, xvii, 76, 155. Generally, see R. Harris, "Government and the Economy."

13 from "normal conditions": P. Langford, *A Polite and Commercial People*, 635.
13 "inevitable, an ordinary fact": D. Bell, *The First Total War*, 5, 30. Eighteenth-century wars were horrific but, relative to other periods, among the least horrific in European history. It was a period of virtually permanent but restrained warfare, a theater of the aristocracy and its values—until the Napoleonic Wars.
13 the "ruinous expedient": A. Smith, *The Wealth of Nations*, 998.
14 These words come from: Ffoulkes, *Arms & Armament*, 55, 147.
14 popular Victorian author: Smiles, *Self-Help; Lives of Boulton and Watt*. See also Roll, *An Early Experiment in Industrial Organisation*.
14 historians have acknowledged: See Thompson, *The Making of the English Working Class*, 252; Flinn, *Men of Iron*, 147–48; Birch, *The Economic History of the British Iron and Steel Industry*, 45–47; Hyde, *Technological Change and the British Iron Industry*, 114–16; J. Anderson, "Aspects of the Effect on the British Economy of the Wars against France"; Deane, "War and Industrialisation"; McNeill, *The Pursuit of Power*, 211; P. Langford, *A Polite and Commercial People*, 539, 634–35; M. Anderson, *War and Society in Europe*, 149–52.
15 "excess capacity build-up": Birch, *The Economic History of the British Iron and Steel Industry*, 47–52. On the problem with the excess capacity argument, see also J. Anderson, "Aspects of the Effect on the British Economy of the Wars against France," 12–13.
15 during war, "normal patterns": Hyde, *Technological Change and the British Iron Industry*, 112–16.
15 "diverted capital from": P. Langford, *A Polite and Commercial People*, 634–36.
15 "impossible not to feel": M. Anderson, *War and Society in Europe*, 155.
15 "possibly significant" growth: O'Brien, *Power with Profit*, 13, 20. Some more usefully speak of "winners and losers." Conway, *War, State, and Society*, 110–14. Clive Trebilcock excludes the eighteenth century from the general trend of civilian "spin-offs" from military production. "'Spin-off' in British Economic History." John cautioned that his conclusions did not necessarily apply to the second half of the century and later argued that agricultural productivity and home demand drove industrial revolution. "Farming in Wartime." Philip Hoffman argues that war canceled out the growth it produced, dating industrialization to the onset of peace in the nineteenth century. "Prices, the Military Revolution, and Western Europe's Comparative Advantage in Violence," 56–57; *Why Did Europe Conquer the World?*. But Britain was uniquely protected from war damage, fighting abroad.
15 We also confuse: Ashton implies that those who would present war as being "possibly productive of national wealth" are not merely in error but in sin. J. Anderson, "Aspects of the Effect on the British Economy of the Wars against France," 1. On the way theory has stymied understanding of how war shaped the industrial revolution, see also O'Brien, "The Contributions of Warfare with Revolutionary and Napoleonic France to the Consolidation and Progress of the British Industrial Revolution," 3–6.
15 two cataclysmic world wars: John, "War and the English Economy," 329.
15 T. S. Ashton and John Nef: See Merritt Roe Smith, "Introduction," in *Military Enterprise and Technological Change*, 28–32; Gutmann, "War and Industrial Development," 157–61. World War Two's role in enabling American recovery from the Great Depression perhaps seems correspondingly less controversial in light of the United States's defensive entry into the war, and on the good side.
15 Even those highlighting: Trebilcock, "'Spin-off' in British Economic History."
15 commitment to "innocent" trades: Raistrick, *Quakers in Science and Industry*, 42, 44, 338, 344. Beckert helps correct the image of British peaceableness but insists that cotton was "the launching pad" for the industrial revolution. *Empire of Cotton*, xiv, xvii, 63, 73. Bowen knows "all aspects of life in Britain were touched by war during a century in which a wide range of economic and social institutions, processes, and structures were transformed," but he refrains from blunt causal statement: "The economy and society that supported the war efforts was slowly and fitfully transformed by the various processes associated with industrialization. The early years of the industrial revolution were in the second half of this war period." *War and British Society*, 71, 77, 78, 80.
16 "inescapable givens" of: O'Brien, *Power with Profit*, 13–14.
16 the postwar decline: Knight, *Britain Against Napoleon*, 469. It was not effective.
16 war finance made: Mokyr, *The Enlightened Economy*, 434–35.
16 War did not "crowd out": "The empirical question of where the stock of British capital . . . might have stood in 1815 . . . continues to be difficult for historians . . . to specify, let alone measure," writes

O'Brien. He further explains that while the turn-of-the-century wars against France imposed heavy burdens related to taxation and state borrowing, their other "positive legacies" did contribute to Britain's industrial transformation. "The Contributions of Warfare with Revolutionary and Napoleonic France to the Consolidation and Progress of the British Industrial Revolution," 14–15, 22. See also 29–35.

16 **central staff of the Office:** Woolwich Arsenal had fifteen hundred workers in 1800 and five thousand by 1814. Knight, *Britain Against Napoleon*, 315–16.

16 **War increasingly connected men:** B. Collins, *War and Empire*, 400.

17 **ideology of collective responsibility:** Morriss, *The Foundations of British Maritime Ascendancy*, 14, 221–22.

17 **Wilkes and his followers:** Porter, *English Society in the Eighteenth Century*, 115, 130.

17 **Samuel Johnson unleashed:** Cited in Knight and Wilcox, *Sustaining the Fleet*, 1.

18 **He dubbed the monstrosity:** Quoted in Knight and Wilcox, *Sustaining the Fleet*, 2, and Porter, *English Society in the Eighteenth Century*, 378.

18 **Postwar infrastructure projects:** In the nineteenth century in Europe, the British state had the least proportionate expenditures in the economy. Harling and Mandler, "From 'Fiscal-Military' State to Laissez-Faire State," 59.

18 **we do not have data:** Hudson, *The Industrial Revolution*, 58–60; O'Brien, "Central Government and the Economy," 215–16; "Introduction," 17; "The Impact of the Revolutionary and Napoleonic Wars," 339; M. Berg, "Factories, Workshops and Industrial Organisation," 124. As O'Brien explains, fiscal and financial data reflecting the costs of war bias investigations against consideration of benefits that flowed from money efficiently spent by the state. "The Contributions of Warfare with Revolutionary and Napoleonic France to the Consolidation and Progress of the British Industrial Revolution," 15. Current data allow us to say only that war is as likely to have had a growth-promoting effect as a growth-retarding one. Deane, "War and Industrialisation," 91–102.

19 **But it also underwent:** Contrary to previous assessments: Chew, *Arming the Periphery*, 60; Bowen, *War and British Society*, 71; Alder, *Engineering the Revolution*, 222; B. Smith, "The Galtons of Birmingham," 140–41.

19 **But this was not:** The assumption that machinery must lie at the core of industrial revolution is partly a product of the eighteenth-century effort to distinguish British techniques from Asian ones, which were also based on sophisticated division of labor. M. Berg, "In Pursuit of Luxury," 129–30.

19 **many ways to increase:** Hudson, *The Industrial Revolution*, 121–26.

20 **The metals world:** M. Berg, "Factories, Workshops and Industrial Organisation," 128–29, 136–39, 147.

20 **Industrial organization was:** The iron industry switched to coal-burning methods only late in the century, when wartime tariff policies suddenly rendered uncompetitive the foreign iron that had effectively been meeting rising demand. Evans et al., "Baltic Iron and the British Iron Industry," 662.

20 **Adam Smith considered:** A. Smith, *The Wealth of Nations*, 4–5.

20 **Handicraft and mechanized production:** M. Berg, "Revisions and Revolutions."

20 **Karl Marx knew:** M. Berg, *The Age of Manufactures*, 194–98, 204, 255.

20 **short- or medium-term large rises:** Hudson, *The Industrial Revolution*, 45.

20 **"semiskilled men with":** Collier, *Arms and the Men*, 29.

20 **an "astounding capacity":** Chew, *Arming the Periphery*, 64.

21 **Finance capital and industrial capital:** Such a view may help reconcile older accounts of industrially driven imperialism with Cain and Hopkins's more recent theory of financially driven expansion in *British Imperialism*.

22 **We forget the place:** George Orwell described manual labor as so "vitally necessary and yet so remote from our experience, so invisible . . . that we are capable of forgetting it as we forget the blood in our veins." *The Road to Wigan Pier*, 34.

Chapter One: The State and the Gun Industry, Part 1: 1688–1756

25 **Such companies—the East India:** Duffy, "Introduction: The Military Revolution and the State, 1500–1800," in *Military Revolution and the State*, 2–6.

26 **naval debts were transferred:** Flinn, *Men of Iron*, 159–62, 166.

26 **This "corporate state":** P. Stern, *The Company-State*.

26 The South Sea Company: Brewer, *The Sinews of Power*, 120, 126. Other European states evolved differently; see Carruthers, *City of Capital*, chap. 4.

26 Acts of state: Braddick, "The Early Modern English State," 95–99.

27 it worked to multiply: In the early seventeenth century, lack of skilled gunmakers was not alarming in this way; the government knew enough blacksmiths could be trained, in comparatively little time, to make small arms quickly (which was not the case for large ordnance). State demand was enough to call forth gunsmiths from the ranks of blacksmiths. In 1620, only twelve gunmakers were found to fill government contracts for small arms, but within a year they had more than doubled, to twenty-six, of whom only five had been in the trade in 1605. By 1631, there were thirty-one. This quick expansion prompted the formation of the Worshipful Company of Gunmakers in 1637 (see below), when sixty-three craftsmen were making muskets in London alone. Stewart, *The English Ordnance Office*, 99–101.

27 Besides procurement of: It was founded in 1414 as a department of state separate from the king's household. It also administered and maintained fortifications and barracks. Its varied activities included supplying candles at Chelsea, firing the Tower guns on state occasions, caring for fortifications, and supplying oil to Jamaica. The Admiralty, the Treasury, the Navy Board, and the Victualling Board engaged in other kinds of military contracting. In a reorganization in 1683, the Ordnance Board took over provision of all munitions, from small arms to heavy armaments, ammunition, and other warlike stores for the army and navy. Forbes, *A History of the Army Ordnance Services*, 1:131.

27 He was one of: Scouller, *The Armies of Queen Anne*, 36–37, 41. The Ordnance Board was subordinate only to the Treasury and the Auditors of Imprest for accounting, and to the secretary of state for the issue of military equipment. The Navy Board was more junior. The master general was a member of the Cabinet until 1798 but was not as senior as the first lord of the Admiralty, who belonged to an inner group of Cabinet members who set strategy and policy. The engineers he commanded supported operations for which he was not politically responsible. The first lord wielded extensive naval patronage, appointing admirals and captains, who gained access to great wealth in the form of prize money. The Ordnance Board remained relatively free of political trouble. It had a kind of local autonomy, with less of its business being referred to London than in the case of the navy. Knight, *Britain Against Napoleon*, 41–42.

28 In 1660, it possessed: Tomlinson, *Guns and Government*, 14–15; West, *Gunpowder, Government and War*, 10. Its military personnel also expanded. A separate body of engineers emerged in place of the select band appointed randomly by the Crown. There were distinct and enlarged civil and military establishments. In 1667, 175 officers were attached to the office; in 1692, 268.

28 a "body politique": Gunsmiths in the Armourers' and Blacksmiths' Companies petitioned for a separate charter to prevent unskilled smiths from making guns that damaged the reputation and livelihood of those who had "attayned more exquisite skill in that Mistery then in former times" and endangered "sundry of our Loyall Subjects" who bought their guns. GL: MS05229 Charter and Ordinance Book: Charter of the Company of Gunmakers of London, granted 1637, 2.

28 Like other chartered companies: Guns were kept at castles, garrisons, and magazines such as Chatham, Woolwich, Sheerness, Scarborough Castle, Edinburgh, Stirling Castle, Chester, Carlisle, and Berwick. The state also had gunsmiths in its pay at depots in the colonies.

28 This was understood: GL: MS05229 Charter and Ordinance Book: 1670 ordinances, 16.

28 The English began: Russell, *Guns on the Early Frontiers*, 40–41, 301n58.

28 The Hudson's Bay Company: Willson, *The Great Company*, 1:65–66.

28 From 1675 to 1775: N. Brown, *British Gunmakers*, 2:130, 156–57.

29 Many of the same: Hanson, *The Northwest Gun*, 13. Other companies bought fusils from arms merchants who sourced them from independent gunsmiths on renewable short-term contracts. The French and the Dutch also sold guns. The Hudson's Bay Company sent four ships each spring. West, *Gunpowder, Government and War*, 135.

29 Between 1673 and 1704: Chew, *Arming the Periphery*, 26. Firearms were part of Dutch cargo when the Dutch began trading with the Gold Coast in the late sixteenth century. They appear in English trade accounts from about the 1640s. The numbers became significant from the 1660s for both, not least because of the Anglo-Dutch war in the Gold Coast in 1664–65. Kea, "Firearms and Warfare on the Gold and Slave Coasts," 185–94.

29 **In 1684, the London:** Davies, *The Royal African Company,* 173, 175, 177, 178; Neal and Black, *Great British Gunmakers,* 326. After English guns sent in 1692 provoked complaint, the committee employed a proof master to test the guns before shipment.

29 **In North America, Dutch:** Rich, *The History of the Hudson's Bay Company,* 1:190.

29 **In the sixteenth century:** Rowlands, *Masters and Men,* 1.

30 **Royalists had destroyed:** Stephens, ed., *The Victoria History of the County of Warwick,* 7:263.

30 **Birmingham gunmakers were:** Bailey and Nie, *English Gunmakers,* 15.

30 **Newdigate volunteered that the men:** His father had been a chief justice under Oliver Cromwell and a member of Parliament during the Restoration. The younger Newdigate first succeeded in securing a seat in 1681, but that Parliament met for only a week before Charles II gave up on Parliament entirely. When William of Orange recalled it in 1688, Newdigate was probably there. He was reelected in 1689. Newdegate-Newdigate, *Cavalier and Puritan in the Days of the Stuarts;* BCA: ZZ33 245341: Goodwin, "Notes on the History of Birmingham."

30 **"men of Birmingham":** Timmins, "The Industrial History of Birmingham," in *The Resources, Products, and Industrial History of Birmingham and the Midland Hardware District,* 210–11.

30 **"compose the Matter":** PP: *Journals of the House of Commons* X, July 11, 1689, 214.

30 **In 1691, they met:** GL: MS5220/6: CM, 1691–1704, March 3, 1691, 11.

30 **In March 1692:** Goodman, "The Birmingham Gun Trade," in *The Resources, Products, and Industrial History of Birmingham and the Midland Hardware District,* ed. Timmins, 408–11. The term "snaphance" derived from the sixteenth-century mechanism for firing the gun. The trigger was pulled to drive a flint (held in a clamp at the end of a bent, spring-loaded lever called the cock) onto a piece of steel to create a shower of sparks that ignited the main charge (no match needed). The name reflects its Dutch origins: *Snap Haan* translates roughly as "snapping lever." Hoff, "The Term Snaphaunce."

31 **Newdigate extended his:** Stephens, ed., *The Victoria History of the County of Warwick,* 7:85.

31 **The "great re-arming":** Black, *Britain as a Military Power,* 47. All regiments raised after 1689 were armed with flintlocks that fired at least twice a minute and weighed one pound less than the old matchlocks.

31 **in 1700, when:** GL: MS5220/6: CM, February 2, 1698, 137, and July 22–October 3, 1700, 157–67.

31 **Virginia's arms were:** Blackmore, *British Military Firearms,* 38–39.

31 **in April 1705:** TNA: WO 47/22: OM, April 23, 1705, 73.

32 **An order for roughly:** TNA: WO 47/22: OM, May 12, 1705, 131–32.

32 **The law required:** PP: *Journals of the House of Commons* XV, March 5 and 19, 1706/7, 323, 348–50; Scouller, *The Armies of Queen Anne,* 195–97. The queen decided that half the required arms not already contracted for would be made in Ireland. The relevant law was the Act of Parliament for punishing Officers or Soldiers who shall Mutiny or Desert, *Anno Primo Anne Regina,* Fol. 539, and *Anno Tertio & Quarto Anne Regina,* Fol. 259, containing the clause "Provided always, and be it further Enacted, That all Clothes, Arms and Accutrements of War, belonging to the Horse, Foot and Dragoons, in Her Majesties Pay and Service, who receive English Pay, shall be bought in the Kingdom of England, Dominion of Wales, and Town of Berwick upon Tweed, and not elsewhere; and every Officer or Person, who shall offend herein (upon Proof made in that behalf) shall be Cashiered." Still, the Dutch order for Ireland remained in place. Six months later, the Ordnance Office urged that the guns be obtained with haste, lest "gunsmiths here . . . renew their clamour in Parliament under pretence that they could have made them in less time." This was justified legally by the fact that they had been ordered by the Master of Ordnance in Ireland with a warrant from the queen and paid for out of Irish revenues. TNA: WO 46/6: Ordnance to Marlborough, August 8[?], 1707, 57, and Board to Marlborough, August 22, 1707, 59.

33 **"the Company stood still":** Worshipful Company of Gunmakers, *The Case of the Company of Gun-Makers.*

33 **"there was nothing":** TNA: WO 47/24: OM, May 17, 1707, 448.

33 **this was not about:** Reduced costs may have been an effect of the change but were not the impetus behind it. Foreign imports remained a frequent recourse.

33 **In November 1707:** TNA: WO 47/25: OM, November 4, 1707, 170.

34 **A contract with:** TNA: WO 47/25: OM, November 15, 1707, 192.

34 **Farmer first appears:** TNA: WO 47/26: OM, January 27, 1707/8, 296.

34 **He appeared again in:** TNA: WO 47/26: OM, March 4, 1707/8, 354.

34 **He would remain:** TNA: WO 47/30: OM, March 7, 1718, 60; Bailey, *British Board of Ordnance Small Arms Contractors*, 43.

34 **In February 1708:** PP: *Journals of the House of Commons* XV, February 18, 1707/8, 550.

34 **The London company:** PP: *Journals of the House of Commons* XV, February 20, 1707/8, 556–57, and February 27, 170[7]8, 577.

34 **in "greater Quantities":** PP: Petition of Gun-makers, Cutlers, and other Artificers, of Birmingham, *Journals of the House of Commons* XV, March 25, 1708, 630–31; *Journals of the House of Commons* XVI, January, 28, 1708/9, 74 and Mar. 15, 1710/11, 549.

35 **"into foreign Parts":** PP: *Journals of the House of Commons* XVI, February 26, 1710/11, 519.

35 **The friendly potentates:** Worshipful Company of Gunmakers, *The Case of the Company of Gun-Makers*.

35 **Birmingham smiths were:** G. Allen, *The Industrial Development of Birmingham*, 17.

35 **The office calculated:** TNA: WO 47/28: OM, February 1, 1714/15, 28, and February 8, 1714/15, 36.

35 **Among the profusion:** TNA: WO 47/28: OM, March 29, 1715, 88.

35 **London smiths received:** Bailey, *British Board of Ordnance Small Arms Contractors*, 16.

35 **"the most part":** TNA: WO 47/28: OM, July 26, 1715, 203 (italics added).

35 **On the king's orders:** See TNA: WO 47/28: OM, August 16, 1715, 232, and August 26, 1715, 245; WO 47/20B: OM, July 26, 1722, 117. By 1722, these accounts included Birmingham makers. The South Sea Company guns were likely for the slave trade in Spanish America, which had opened up thanks to the "asiento" Spain granted Britain after the war in 1713 (see p. 41).

36 **"hasten the Gunsmiths":** TNA: WO 47/28: OM, September 13, 1715, 263, September 20, 1715, 264, September 27, 1715, 271.

36 **The Worshipful Company's wardens:** TNA: WO 47/28: OM, September 29, 1715, 272.

36 **gunsmiths requested locks:** TNA: WO 47/28: OM, October 11, 1715, 291.

36 **From this point:** See, for instance, TNA: WO 47/28: OM, December 2, 1715, 343; WO 47/29: OM, March 20, 1716, 66.

36 **In 1714, there were:** TNA: WO 47/20A: OM, n.d., 5.

36 **With the 1715 request:** TNA: WO 47/20B: OM, January 16, 1721, 25.

36 **"hardships from not being":** TNA: WO 47/30: OM, January 31, 1718/9, 39, and February 17, 1718/9, 64.

36 **"to get Armes Elsewhere":** TNA: WO 47/28: OM, November 4, 1715, 317.

37 **A Minories gunsmith:** TNA: WO 47/30: OM, February 27, 1716/7, 50; WO 47/30 generally.

37 **As he waited:** GL: MS5220/7: CM, 1716–32, February 27, 1717, 26.

37 **"who have behaved":** Blackmore, *British Military Firearms*, 49. Daymen were permanent staff, earning benefits; piece men were paid by the piece and hired and fired as needed.

37 **Assistant viewers were:** TNA: WO 47/30: OM, March 21, 1718, 72.

37 **two hundred to fewer than:** Bailey, *British Board of Ordnance Small Arms Contractors*, 17.

38 **The new system was:** N. Brown, *British Gunmakers*, 156–57, 227. Its governing committee decided how many fusils to purchase based on projected factory requirements. This regulated the number of gunsmiths it employed each year, which at times reached forty. Company inspectors ensured quality, forwarding the guns to warehouses for crating and shipment.

38 **the desperate measures:** In 1715, when the controversial Dutch guns for Ireland were finally ready, the Irish Ordnance Office refused them because of inconsistent design and quality. Bailey, "Liège Muskets in the British Army," 283–84. They were returned to England by 1718, and many were later sent to the colonies.

38 **Richard Wooldridge, a furbisher:** TNA: WO 47/29: OM, July 20, 1716, 172. Wooldridge had had his own workshop in 1705 but was almost immediately appointed to the Small Gun Office. In Ordnance records, he is described as a gunsmith on an annual salary of £50 for assisting in the viewing and proving of small arms. Neal and Black, *Great British Gunmakers*, 366–67.

38 **Standardizing weapons expedited:** In 1722, a new regulation required inspection of soldiers' muskets before purchase to encourage standardization; colonels were disallowed from buying arms on the private market. Darling, *Red Coat and Brown Bess*, 19. The 1722 order was mostly ignored until the rearming of 1740–41. Bailey, *British Board of Ordnance Small Arms Contractors*, 17.

38 **"will be distroyed":** TNA: WO 47/30: OM, August 19, 1718, 232.
39 **"none of the Chief Company":** TNA: WO 47/30: OM, August 22, 1718, 233.
39 **The wardens specified:** TNA: WO 47/30: OM, September 2, 1718, 250.
39 **Considering the "hardship":** TNA: WO 47/30: OM, October 7, 1718, 284–85.
39 **They also complied:** TNA: WO 47/30: OM, November 7, 1718, 330; WO 47/30: OM, October 17, 1718, 302.
40 **The new Brown Bess:** Darling, *Red Coat and Brown Bess*, 19. Perhaps 7.8 million Brown Besses were manufactured for distribution all over the globe. Chandler, *The Art of Warfare in the Age of Marlborough*, 81.
40 **It was used by:** R. Browning, *The War of the Austrian Succession*, 4–5.
40 **government orders dwindled:** TNA: WO 47/30: OM, October 17, 1718, 303, and October 31, 1718, 326.
40 **"their respective services":** TNA: WO 47/30: OM, November 14, 1718, 339.
41 **The Royal African Company:** The subsidy lasted through 1746.
41 **By 1730, about 180,000:** Chew, *Arming the Periphery*, 26.
41 **"honest trading members":** GL: MS5220/7: CM, October 3, 1719, 44–45. See also April 7, 1720, 51–52.
41 **The company reprimanded:** GL: MS5220/7: CM, June 29, 1721, 77.
41 **Farmer remained a trusted:** He made the office 190 muskets in 1723. Williams, "James Farmer and Samuel Galton," 121–22; Bailey, *British Board of Ordnance Small Arms Contractors*, 43.
41 **Birmingham's emergence as:** See, for instance, GL: MS5220/7: CM, December 11, 1729, 202.
42 **keep a "Quarteridge Book":** GL: MS5220/8: CM, January 9, 173[5], 45.
42 **engraver Richard Sharp:** GL: MS5220/8: CM, February 6, 173[5], 52.
42 **the trade "by patrimony":** GL: MS5220/8: CM, February 6, 173[5], 49.
42 **some insisted on giving:** GL: MS5220/7: CM, May 21, 1722, 92.
42 **methodical searches of shops:** GL: MS5220/8: CM, April 1, 1736, 80.
42 **John Johnson daily sold:** GL: MS5220/8: CM, March 31, 1737, 93–96.
42 **"molested and hindered":** GL: MS5220/8: CM, June 30, 1737, 97.
42 **"evil to the company":** GL: MS5220/8: CM, August 30, 1739, 137–38. The suit was launched June 27, 1740, 151–52. In many of these cases, the seized foreign arms were given to the king. Johnson's fines were mitigated when he pleaded ignorance of the laws.
42 **Charleston merchants and:** Bailey, "The Wilsons."
42 **Lewis Barbar and Charles Pickfatt:** Neal and Black, *Great British Gunmakers*, 288–89, 310–13. Barbar was a French Protestant who arrived in England in the 1680s.
42 **"the first and only one":** TNA: WO 47/35: Pickfatt to Board, June 25, quoted in OM, June 26, 1750, 559–60.
43 **Pickfatt was repeatedly:** See, for instance, GL: MS5220/8: CM, February 6, 173[5], 52; August 31, 1738, 119–20; December 7, 1738, 125.
43 **Birmingham smiths provided:** Williams, "James Farmer and Samuel Galton," 121–22.
43 **eight parts contractors:** Bailey, *British Board of Ordnance Small Arms Contractors*, 17, 43.
43 **At some point:** Harding, *Smallarms of the East India Company*, 1:6–7. The Ordnance Office tried to sell the Dutch guns purchased earlier for Ireland to the East India and South Sea Companies. Bailey, "Liège Muskets in the British Army," 283.
43 **This "War of Jenkins' Ear":** The War of Jenkins' Ear was named after Captain Robert Jenkins, who in 1738 recounted before Parliament an incident of 1731 when his ship had been boarded by the Spanish coast guard, and a Spanish official, accusing him of piracy, had cut off his left ear and threatened to do the same to the king himself—one of the many "Spanish Depredations upon the British Subjects" that provided the casus belli. R. Browning, *The War of the Austrian Succession*, chap. 2.
43 **The Pretender was:** The Jacobites needed foreign help to achieve their goal. They waited for Britain to go to war and deploy its army abroad, hoping that one of the opposing states would pour men and money into an invasion on the Stuarts' behalf. Colley, *Britons*, 73, 79.
43 **The typical Ordnance Office:** Neal and Black, *Great British Gunmakers*, 288–89.
43 **In 1740, 10,000 muskets:** Bailey, "Liège Muskets in the British Army," 283; TNA: WO 46/7: Ordnance Office to Treasury, August 14, 1741.
43 **By 1742, it needed:** TNA: WO 46/7: Ordnance Office to Treasury, April 14, 1741, April 27, 1742, and February 15, 1742.

44 **the office added:** Bailey, *British Board of Ordnance Small Arms Contractors*, 18, 43, 51–52.

44 **In 1745, it purchased:** Blackmore, *British Military Firearms*, 47.

44 **Ten thousand more:** Bailey, "Liège Muskets in the British Army," 283.

44 **Wilson, who supplied:** Bailey, "The Wilsons"; Blackmore, *British Military Firearms*, 57.

44 **The government owed:** TNA: WO 47/34: OM, March 10, 1748; WO 46/7: Ordnance Office to Treasury, February 19, 1747.

44 **Apart from parts:** Darling, *Red Coat and Brown Bess*, 23; Bailey, *British Board of Ordnance Small Arms Contractors*, 51. Farmer was a contractor from 1741 to 1751 and supplied locks, barrels, and complete arms (the latter particularly from March 1746 to September 1748). Jordan was principal supplier of barrels and locks and also supplied complete arms from 1746 to 1748. Williams, "James Farmer and Samuel Galton," 122.

44 **Farmer also provided wall pieces:** Blackmore, *British Military Firearms*, 48.

44 **Farmer's leftovers alone:** TNA: WO 47/34: OM, January 27, 1748.

44 **"must necessarily endanger":** GL: MS5220/8: CM, March 27, 1740, 145–49.

45 **filling "considerable demands":** BCA: MS3101/C/D/14/2/6: JF to Mary Farmer [later Galton], September 13, 1742.

45 **"leave no stone unturned":** BCA: MS3101/C/C/2/1/6: JF to Joseph Farmer, November 16, 1743.

45 **He agonized over:** BCA: MS3101/C/C/2/1/13: JF to Joseph Farmer, December 31, 1743.

45 **John Hardman's *Willowby*:** BCA: MS3101/C/C/2/1/18: JF to Joseph Farmer, February 18, 1744.

45 **he secured an order:** BCA: MS3101/C/C/2/1/19: JF to Joseph Farmer, February 25, 1744.

45 **decried the "great quantities":** GL: MS5220/8: CM, April 14, 1743, 190–91.

45 **at Botolph Wharf:** GL: MS5220/8: CM, October 3, 1745, 234–36.

45 **In 1744, it demanded:** GL: MS5220/8: CM, March 1, 1743/4, 199–206; March 31, 1743, 201; June 28, 1744, 208–10; December 6, 1744, 218–19; August 29, 1745, 230–32; October 3, 1745, 234–36; January 16, 1746, 240.

45 **a large chest:** Timmins, "The Industrial History of Birmingham," 214.

46 **"let their Masters":** *Aris's Birmingham Gazette*, May 19, 1746, quoted in J. Langford, *A Century of Birmingham Life*, 1:25–26. In 1733, shoemakers had engaged in similar action.

46 **Replacement of rammers:** See orders in OM in TNA: WO 47/34–37 and WO 47/39: OM, April 10, 1752, 331–32, and May 1, 1752, 383.

46 **"regular bred gunlock":** TNA: WO 47/34: OM, February 21, 1748, n.d.

46 **thousands were set up:** See OM for February to April 1749 in TNA: WO 47/34.

46 **Regiments also ordered:** See OM for March to April 1751 in TNA: WO 47/37. The Brown Bess had a life expectancy of about eight years; the army recalled about 10 percent of them every year.

46 **Through 1770, old Brown Besses:** Farmer & Galton's name appears frequently on locks of this period. Locks were engraved with contractors' names until 1764. Williams, "James Farmer and Samuel Galton."

46 **the Second Carnatic War:** Chanda Sahib, nawab of the Carnatic, was part of the system of allied rulers the French governor in India, Joseph-François Dupleix, made across the south. The East India Company supported a rival claimant to the Carnatic, Muhammad Ali, helping him at Trichinopoly. In 1751, Chanda Sahib besieged Trichinopoly, and the British commander, Robert Clive, led a diversionary force to capture Arcot by surprise. They held against the siege and pursued the besiegers, defeating them at Arni. In 1752, Chanda Sahib and the French surrendered. The war continued until Dupleix was recalled to France in 1754.

46 **"on any pretence":** TNA: WO 47/36: OM, August 14, 1750, 76.

46 **Maryland requested replacement:** TNA: WO 47/42: OM, July 2, 1753, 1, and August 9, 1753, 78.

47 **"nations of Indians":** TNA: WO 47/42: OM, August 23, 1753, 103; August 31, 1753, 110; and November 29, 1753, 295.

47 **Bristling tensions with:** TNA: WO 47/42: OM, August 3, 1753, 60, and August 17, 1753, 100–101.

47 **Thomas Nolson was assistant:** Nolson's letters, quoted in TNA: WO 47/35: OM, January 10, [1750]; 26–27; February 19, 1750, 129–30; February 23, [1750], 143–45; and February 27, [1750], 152.

47 **William Sharp, son of:** TNA: WO 47/40: OM, July 13, 1752, 31.

47 **When he offered:** TNA: WO 47/40: OM, December 15, 1752, 305–6.

47 **"the English arms are":** BCA: MS3101/C/D/15/5/3: JF to SG, January 3, 1749.

48 **at Dunkirk, he found:** BCA: MS3101/C/D/15/5/2: JF to SG, October 14, 1748.
48 **"all the goods":** BCA: MS 3101/C/D/15/5/3: JF to SG, January 3, 1749.
48 **their Barbary locks:** BCA: MS3101/C/D/15/5/6: JF to SG, January 8, 1750.
48 **Farmer closely followed:** BCA: MS3101/C/D/15/5/4: JF to SG, November 17, 1749.
48 **Parliament bailed out:** PP: *Journals of the House of Commons* XXV, February 9, 1748/9, 732; May 5, 1749, 857; May 9, 1749, 861–62; May 24, 1749, 874 and 876–77; June 1, 2, 5, and 6, 1749, 885–86; "A Bill, Intitled, an Act for Extending and Improving the Trade to Africa," *Journals of the House of Commons* XXVI, March 6, 1750, 96.
48 **"proved and good":** BCA: MS3101/C/D/15/5/8: JF to SG, February 5, 1750. See also MS3101/C/D/14/2/19: JF to Mary Galton, March 3, 1750.
48 **"the less occasion he":** BCA: MS3101/C/D/15/5/10: JF to SG, April 27, 1750.
48–49 **"Times were never worse":** BCA: MS3101/C/D/15/5/11: Joseph Farmer to SG, September 5, 1750.
49 **James begged the Ordnance Office:** JF, memorial quoted in TNA: WO 47/35: OM, February 23, [1750], 140–41.
49 **It had little to:** See TNA: WO 47/35: OM, April 18, 1750, 299–300; WO 47/36: OM, August 14, 1750, 97–99, and September 28, 1750, 174–75; WO 47/38: OM, August 2, 1751, 102–3.
49 **The office did:** TNA: WO 47/40: OM, July 20, 1751, 60.
49 **"very good workmen":** TNA: WO 47/35: Pickfatt to Ordnance Board, June 25, 1750, quoted in OM, June 26, 1750, 559–60.
49 **the office refused:** TNA: WO 47/36: Pickfatt, letter, July 29, 1750, quoted in OM, July 31, 1750, 57.
49 **"extreme hazard the office":** TNA: WO 47/36: Surveyor General, letter, quoted in OM, August 14, 1750, 77–78.
50 **"most notorious neglect":** WO 47/35: Waller, letter, April 2, 1750, quoted in OM, April 6, 1750, 262–63, and Surveyor General, letter, quoted in OM, June 26, 1750, 541.
50 **When William Clarke:** TNA: WO 47/35: OM, April 18, 1750, 309–10; May 8, 1750, 362; June 29, 1750, 555–60; June 26, 1750, 533–34; WO 47/36: OM, August 14, 1750, 82–83; August 17, 1750, 103. Paying off Clarke, he reprimanded two board officers for having "industriously and unwarrantably concealed" Clarke's declaration for a year. In 1751, new regulations clarified the cleaning-and-repair process in-house. WO 47/38: OM, October 8, 1751, 222–27.
50 **By 1750, the staff:** In June, there were forty-seven daymen on the books, with daily pay ranging from one shilling sixpence to three shillings. The Small Gun Office resolved to better regulate them and to superannuate nine. TNA: WO 47/35: OM, June 19, 1750, 495–98; February 1 and 6, [1750], 85.
50 **the armorer James Coggle:** TNA: WO 47/37: OM, June 14, 1751, 583–84. See also TNA: WO 47/39: OM, February 11, 1752, 119–20.
50 **"oftentimes have no Work":** TNA: WO 47/35: OM, April 27, 1750, 330–31. They cleaned and repaired a thousand pistols, the warrant going to those longest in service and the ablest workers. May 18, 1750, 391–92.
50 **in 1746, 46,000 arms:** TNA: WO 47/38: OM, October 8, 1751, 222–27.
51 **"always supported the credit":** TNA: T70/1516: Brazier to new African Company committee, December 5, 1750. See also JF to committee, November 27, 1750; Farmer's prices and particulars, December 12, 1750; Brazier contract with committee, December 18, [1750]; Farmer's contract, December 18, 1750, January 25, [1751], and January 16, [1751]; T70/143: minutes of meeting of Committee of the Company of Merchants Trading to Africa, December 14 and 18, 1750, 23–24. Farmer's other orders for 1750–60 are given in Richards, "The Birmingham Gun Manufactory of Farmer and Galton," 41–42. There is evidence that Farmer's guns bore London proofmarks and were intended for use at the fort rather than in the trade itself. BCA: MS3101/C/D/15/1/1: SG to JF, November 2, 1751.
51 **he bought more than two thousand:** TNA: WO 47/35: JF to Ordnance Office, April 12, 1750, quoted in OM, April 18, 1750, 299–300.
51 **"Trading Guns with plain Beech Stocks":** TNA: WO 47/36: OM, August 14, 1750, 97–99.
51 **"always command the trade":** BCA: MS3101/C/D/15/5/10: JF to SG, April 27, 1750.
52 **"made for the trade":** TNA: WO 47/36: OM, September 28, 1750, 174–75.
52 **In 1754, Farmer bought:** BCA: MS3101/C/D/15/1/1: SG to JF, August 24, 1754.

52 **courting "total loss":** TNA: T70/1516: Gunmakers' Company to African Company, March 8, [1751].

52 **some company members:** TNA: WO 47/38: Company of Gunmakers, letter, September 27, 1751, in OM, October 8, 1751, 222–27.

53 **lost the proving work:** Blackmore, *British Military Firearms*, 266–67.

53 **firm's capital value:** Richards, "The Birmingham Gun Manufactory of Farmer and Galton," 10.

53 **A French buyer:** BCA: MS3101/C/D/15/1/1: SG to JF, July 4, 1751, July 10, 1751, July 16, 1751, July 17, 1751, and July 21, 1751; SG to John Parr, July 6, 1751; MS3101/C/D/15/5/11: JF to SG, July 8, 1751.

53 **"several ships about":** BCA: MS3101/C/D/15/1/1: SG to JF, July 24, 1751.

53 **"procure large orders":** BCA: MS3101/C/D/15/1/1: SG to John Galton, July 28, 1751.

53 **A few months later:** BCA: MS3101/C/D/15/1/1: SG to JF, October 12, 1751, October 20, 1751, October 31, 1751.

53 **He fretted about:** BCA: MS3101/C/D/15/1/1: SG to JF, March 15, 1752, June 27, 1752, July 27, 1754, September 22, 1754, [c. December 6–10, 1754], and December 9, 1754; SG to John Parr, March 18, 1752, February 20, 1754, and July 13, 1754; MS3101/C/D/15/5/14: JF to SG, January 5, 1754.

53 **He sent thousands:** BCA: MS3101/C/D/15/1/1: SG to John Parr, March 11, 1752, March 18, 1752, March 22, 1752; SG to JF, May [?], 1752; SG to John Parr, May 20, 1752; MS3101/C/D/15/5/13: JF to SG, December 10, 1753; MS3101/C/D/15/5/16: JF to SG, September 10, 1754. See also Richards, "The Birmingham Gun Manufactory of Farmer and Galton," 14, 50–57; "The Import of Firearms into West Africa," 44–45.

53 **"all unexpected and in a hurry":** BCA: MS3101/C/D/15/1/1: SG to JF, April 19, 1752.

53 **"much reduced and likely":** Ibid.

54 **their "many competitors":** BCA: MS3101/C/D/15/1/1: SG to JF, June 14, 1752.

54 **"do nothing to increase":** BCA: MS3101/C/D/15/5/52: JF to SG, [February 1753?].

54 **"as many are pushed":** BCA: MS3101/C/D/15/1/1: SG to JF, March [?], 1754.

54 **"our sales for":** BCA: MS3101/C/D/15/1/1: [SG] to John Parr, July 20, 1754. This letter is in Galton's letter book but seems to have been a draft of a letter he wanted John Galton or James Farmer to send on his behalf.

54 **"how little cause":** BCA: MS3101/C/D/15/1/1: SG to John Parr, February 20, 1754.

54 **"want of resolution":** BCA: MS3101/C/D/15/1/1: SG to JF, December 23, 1754. See also SG to JF, March [?], 1754, and March 22, 1755.

54 **For months, Farmer:** BCA: MS3101/C/D/15/1/1: SG to JF, August 8, 1752.

54 **they became useless:** J. Miller, *Way of Death*, 91.

55 **"worms getting into them":** BCA: MS3101/C/D/15/1/1: [SG] to John Parr, July 20, 1754. See also SG to JF, October 20, 1751, and July 27, 1754. Unlike perishables like sugar and wheat, however, guns were not subject to a deductible by insurance companies. Personal communication from Hannah Farber, March 6, 2012.

55 **"keep severally a stock":** BCA: MS3101/C/D/15/1/1: SG to JF, [c. December 6 to 10, 1754].

55 **Ramping up production:** BCA: MS3101/C/D/15/1/1: JF to SG, January 5, 1754.

55 **"payments are so long":** Ibid.

55 **"destroys the profits":** BCA: MS3101/C/D/15/1/1: SG to John Parr, February 20, 1754. See also July 13, 1754.

55 **"rather be without":** BCA: MS3101/C/D/15/1/1: SG to JF, June 3, 1754.

55 **Africa for "teeth wood or gold dust":** James Birchall, promissory note, February 14, 1752, enclosed in BCA: MS3101/C/D/15/1/2: SG to Nicholas Atkinson, April 6, 1757. See also October 27, 1757, and MS3101/C/D/15/5/33: JF to SG, June 2, 1755.

55 **"after lying so long":** BCA: MS3101/C/D/15/1/1: SG to JF, April 27, 1752. See also SG to JF, April 19, 1752, and December 23, 1754.

55 **"but a small capital":** BCA: MS3101/C/D/15/1/1: SG to JF, July 11, 1752. See also July 4, 1752, July 18, 1752, and December 11, 1754.

56 **"handsome" compensation from Fryer's:** BCA: MS3101/C/D/15/1/1: SG to JF, December 23, 1754.

56 **Despite relations with:** BCA: MS3101/C/D/15/1/1: SG to JF, March 15, 1752, and March 22, 1752.

56 **looked on with dread:** BCA: MS3101/C/D/15/1/1: SG to JF, March 9, 1754, [c. March 15–May 20, 1754], and June 3, 1754; SG to Parr, February 20, 1754.

56 **"excel in the quality":** SG to JF, March 15, 1752.

56   **"divert us with other orders"**: [SG] to Parr, July 20, 1754.
56   **"done in the plainest manner"**: BCA: MS3101/C/D/15/1/1: SG to JF, [c. March 15–May 20, 1754]. See also May 30, 1754.
57   **"equal or superior"**: BCA: MS3101/C/D/15/1/1: SG to JF, August 24, 1754. See also JF to SG, September 10, 1754; SG to JF, May 30, 1754, March 22, 1752, and September 22, 1754; MS3101/C/D/15/1/2: SG to Parr, December 17, 1755.
57   **"wherein by the Sales"**: SG to Parr, July 13, 1754.
57   **"strike into something"**: SG to JF, March [?], 1754.
57   **"to narrower compass"**: BCA: MS3101/C/D/15/1/1: [SG] to Parr, July 20, 1754. See also SG to JF, September 19, 1754.
57   **In September 1754**: Richards, "The Birmingham Gun Manufactory of Farmer and Galton," 56; Hancock, *Citizens of the World*, 80.
57   **"very neat, stout barrels"**: BCA: MS3101/C/D/15/1/1: JF to SG, September 10, 1754.
57   **"at a loss"**: BCA: MS3101/C/D/15/1/1: SG to JF, December 23, 1754.
58   **He had to come**: BCA: MS3101/C/D/15/1/1: SG to JF, [c. December 6 to 10] and December 12, 1754.
58   **The curtain suddenly fell**: See BCA: MS3101/C/D/15/1/1: SG to Nicholas Atkinson, March 22, 1755; SG to John Parr, March 22, 1755; SG to JF, March 22, 1755; MS3101/C/D/15/5/23: JF to SG, March 25, 1755; MS3101/C/D/15/5/24: JF to SG, March 26, 1755.
58   **Pickit had gotten wind**: BCA: MS3101/C/D/15/5/22: JF to SG, March 24, 1755.
58   **"preserve the countrys"**: TNA: WO 47/43: OM, June 25, 1754, 369. See also OM, June 28, 1754, 373; WO 47/44: OM, July 2, 1754, 1.
59   **"Eat in so deep"**: TNA: WO 47/43: OM, February 18, 1754, 101. For figures, see WO 47/37: OM, January 8, [1751], 17; WO 47/41: OM, January 9, 1753, 25–28.
59   **To maintain them**: See orders recorded in OM for September to December 1754 in TNA: WO 47/44; January to June 1755 in WO 47/45; July to December 1755 in WO 47/46.
59   **two thousand stand**: TNA: WO 47/45: OM, February 7, 1755, 91; March 5, 1755, 169–70; and March 6, 1755, 171.
59   **American colonies, "or elsewhere"**: TNA: WO 47/46: OM, September 6, 1755, 219. See also WO 47/46: OM, August 14, 1755, 156.
59   **on a monthly basis**: TNA: WO 47/45: OM, March 17, 1755, 227[?]; WO 47/46: OM, September 4, 1755, 212, and September 16, 1755, 230–31. See also WO 47/45: OM, January 7, 1755, 10–11.
59   **"combination" of setters-up**: TNA: WO 47/61: OM, May 13, 1763, 299, and May 20, 1763, 322–24.
59   **In March 1755**: BCA: MS3101/C/D/15/1/1: SG to JF, March [24?], 1755.
59   **The next day**: TNA: WO 47/45: OM, March 25, 1755, 266.
59   **The looming war**: JF to SG, March 26, 1755.
59   **He and Galton exchanged**: See, for instance, BCA: MS3101/C/D/15/5/25: JF to SG, March 27, 1755; MS3101/C/D/15/1/1: SG to JF, March 27, 1755; MS3101/C/D/15/5/26: JF to SG, March 31, 1755.
59   **Soon Richard Heely**: TNA: WO 47/45: OM, April 26, 1755, 399.
60   **Jordan's clerk divulged**: BCA: MS3101/C/D/15/1/2: SG to JF, May 26, 1755, and May 31, 1755.
60   **"prospect of sales"**: BCA: MS3101/C/D/15/1/2: SG to John Galton, May 22, 1755. See also SG to John Galton, June 3, 1755; MS3101/C/D/15/1/1: SG to John Galton, May [8], 1755; SG to JF, May 14, 1755.
60   **"staggers the merchants"**: BCA: MS3101/C/D/15/1/2: SG to JF, May 29, 1755.
60   **hope from the *Swallow***: BCA: MS3101/C/D/15/1/1: SG to Nicholas Atkinson, May 10, 1755.
60   **"scarce anything got"**: BCA: MS3101/C/D/15/1/2: SG to JF, June 7, 1755, and June 8, 1755. See also John Galton to SG, May 25, 1755; SG to John Galton, May 27, 1755; JF to SG, June 2, 1755; SG to John Parr, May 17, 1755.
60   **"If a war"**: BCA: MS3101/C/D/15/1/2: SG to James Johnson, September 17, 1755. See also October 12, 1755; SG to JF, October [12 or 13], 1755; MS3101/C/D/15/5/38: JF to SG, July 14, 1755.
60   **In October, Barclay**: BCA: MS3101/C/D/15/1/1: SG to JF, May 14, 1755; MS3101/C/D/15/1/2: SG to John Galton, July 15 and 17, 1755; SG to Mr. Plumsted, October 18, 1755; SG to James Johnson, October 2, 20, and 27, 1755; SG to Johnson, September 17, 1755, and October 12, 1755; SG to JF, May 29 and 31, 1755, July [7 or 17], 1755, October [12 or 13], 1755, and October 30, 1755; MS3101/C/D/15/5/29: JF to SG, May 24, 1755; MS3101/C/D/15/5/32: JF to SG, May 29, 1755; MS3101/C/D/15/5/33: JF to SG, June 2, 1755; MS3101/C/D/15/5/34: JF to SG, June 3, 1755;

MS3101/C/D/15/5/35: JF to SG, June 6, 1755; Richards, "The Birmingham Gun Manufactory of Farmer and Galton," 57, 63–64.

61 **"more orders of same kind":** BCA: MS3101/C/D/15/1/2: SG to John Galton, July 10[?], 1755.

61 **"determined to rest":** BCA: MS3101/C/D/15/1/2: SG to John Parr, September 6, 1755. See also SG to Nicholas Atkinson, November 20, 1755.

61 **"utmost Diligence and Expedition":** TNA: WO 47/46: Hirst to Ordnance Board, October 29, 1755, in OM, October 30, 1755, 383–85.

62 **"prevent any prejudice":** TNA: WO 47/46: OM, November 13, 1755, 432–33; GL: MS5220/9: CM, November 11 and 15, 1755, 357–68.

62 **"account of the small arms":** TNA: WO 47/46: OM, December 23, 1755, 564. For the accounts, see GL: MS5220/9: Brazier et al. to Ordnance Board, November 28, 1755, 364–66, and December 16, 1755, 367–68; TNA: WO 47/46: OM, December 2, 1755, 484–45.

62 **"most considerable persons":** TNA: WO 47/46: OM, December 23, 1755, 567–68.

62 **"give the workmen":** TNA: WO 47/46: OM, December 29, 1755, 585.

62 **"of great consequence":** TNA: WO 47/48: October 3[?], 1756, 319. See also TNA: WO 47/46: OM, December 19, 1755, 546.

62 **"Ironmongery and Birmingham Ware":** BCA: MS3101/C/D/15/1/2: SG to James Johnson, October 6, 1756.

62 **"for the Guinea trade":** BCA: MS3101/C/D/15/1/2: SG to John Galton, September [?], 1756.

62 **Farmer & Galton carried on:** BCA: MS3101/C/D/15/1/2: SG to John Galton, October 2, 1755, and November 4, 1755; SG to JF, October 30, 1755, November 12, 1755, and November 16, 1755; SG to Nicholas Atkinson, November 20, 1755; MS3101/C/D/15/5/40: JF to SG, November 12, 1755; Bannerman, *Merchants and the Military*, 62, 65.

63 **They took French:** The African Company undermined his plan, and the posts were ultimately returned to France. M. Berg, "In Pursuit of Luxury," 139–40.

63 **"great drafts of Arms":** BCA: MS3101/C/D/15/1/2: SG to JF, November 27, 1755.

63 **Demand from Africa:** BCA: MS3101/C/D/15/1/2: SG to JF, December 1, 1755, December [11 or 13], 1755, and December 21, 1755; SG to John Parr, December 17, 1755; SG to James Johnson, December 15, 1755; MS3101/C/D/15/5/44: JF to SG, December 4, 1755; MS3101/C/D/15/5/48: JF to SG, December 19, 1755.

63 **John Willets of Wednesbury:** TNA: WO 47/46: Willets, letter, November 27, 1755, in OM, November 28, 1755, [?].

63 **Jordan requested further orders:** TNA: WO 47/46: OM, December 8 and 9, 1755, 509, and December 26, 1755, 529. See also WO 47/45: OM, April 26, 1755, 399.

63 **Tower stocks had:** TNA: WO 47/47: OM, January 20, 1756, 59–64; Bailey, "Liège Muskets in the British Army," 284.

63 **Contracts for 25,000:** TNA: WO 47/47: OM, January 13, 1756, 36–39; Frederick to the Ordnance Board, OM, January 12, 1756, 27–29; WO 47/45: OM, March 25, 1755, 266; WO 47/47: OM, February 3, 1756, 131, and March 6, 1756, 241.

64 **"go wherever the Board":** TNA: WO 47/46: OM, November 18, 1755, 444, and November 25, 1755, 463–64.

64 **The London company's:** GL: MS5220/9: CM, August 5, 1755, 350.

64 **Contractors knew that:** TNA: WO 47/43: OM, January 17, 1754, 13.

64 **the Ordnance Board granted:** TNA: WO 47/48: OM, October 2, 1756, 300–301.

64 **In 1757, Farmer:** TNA: WO 47/50: OM, September 20, 1757, 199–200.

64 **the office knew that Hirst:** TNA: WO 47/45: OM, March 25, 1755, 257–58, and April 11, 1755, 335–36; WO 55/2: Paper report No. 43, April 10, 1755, 146.

64 **five thousand muskets:** TNA: WO 47/43: OM, January 17, 1754, 13.

64 **The Hanburys owed Farmer & Galton:** BCA: MS3101/C/D/15/1/2: SG to Freame & Barclay, [c. December 12, 1755].

65 **contractors' willingness to persist:** Conway, *War, State, and Society*, 47.

Chapter Two: Who Made Guns?

66 **set up a smith's shop:** Showell, *Dictionary of Birmingham*, 317; B. Smith, "The Galtons of Birmingham," 132–33.

66 **general label "ironmonger":** BCA: MS3101/A/C/3/1: Lease of water corn mill, iron mines and furnaces at Rushall, 1720; MS3101/C/C/3/1/6: Abigail Jepson to Joseph Farmer, September 10, 1737.

67 **at least thirty:** D. Williams, *The Birmingham Gun Trade,* 21.

67 **Many were also:** Wise, "On the Evolution of the Jewellery and Gun Quarters in Birmingham," 70.

67 **Each gun passed:** On the process of gun production, see Goodman, "The Birmingham Gun Trade," 388–93.

67 **metals-based industrial enlightenment:** P. Jones, *Industrial Enlightenment,* 130–31; M. Berg, *The Age of Manufactures,* 265.

67 **The Farmer & Galton firm:** BCA: MS3101/C/D/15/1/1: SG to JF, July 11, 1752; SG to John Galton, October 30, 1755; SG to JF, October 30, 1755; MS3101/C/D/15/5/18: JF to SG, March 3, 1755; SG to JF, March 22, 1755.

68 **In 1718, he traveled:** Pearson, *The Life, Letters and Labours of Francis Galton,* 1:38n1; Diggins, "Principio." George Washington's father, Augustine, was one of the partners in 1729.

68 **He rented the Town Mill:** D. Williams, "James Farmer and Samuel Galton," 120.

68 **Joseph testified before Parliament:** Joseph Farmer, quoted in PP: *Journals of the House of Commons* XXII, April 20, 1737, 853; Evans et al., "Baltic Iron and the British Iron Industry," 656–60. In the event, native ironmasters did not like the idea of duty-free American iron and called for higher duties on Baltic iron. The iron trade had an ambivalent response to American iron, since it encompassed both producers of iron and those who made other objects from iron, many in partnerships. Hyde, *Technological Change and the British Iron Industry,* 50–51.

69 **the biggest purchasers:** Evans et al., "Baltic Iron and the British Iron Industry," 645; PP: *Journals of the House of Commons* XXIII, March 21, 1737, 109, 111.

69 **The Quaker meetinghouse:** P. Jones, *Industrial Enlightenment,* 172–73, 193. Birmingham supported Parliament in the Civil War; Puritan sects possibly put down roots then. The first recorded Quaker presence was in 1682. S. Lloyd, *The Lloyds of Birmingham,* 120.

69 **his son Sampson II:** H. Lloyd, *The Quaker Lloyds in the Industrial Revolution,* 105–6.

70 **the Town Mill:** Stephens, ed., *The Victoria History of the County of Warwick,* 7:86, 89, 263.

70 **Quakers owned or managed:** Hyde, *Technological Change in the British Iron Industry,* 120. Quakers were only 1 percent of the population, but a third of the ironmasters in the town were Friends. Their networks of ironworking and commerce stretched to Bristol, Wales, and the southwest. P. Jones, *Industrial Enlightenment,* 162–69.

70 **a wealthy Quaker ironmonger:** Flinn, *Men of Iron,* 31; PP: *Journals of the House of Commons* XXIII, March 21, 1737, 111.

70 **"a celebrated beauty":** FHL: PORT 40/117, 3: Handwritten transcript of press note on the marriage of James Farmer and Priscilla Plumsted, copied from *London Daily Post,* April 30, 1743.

70 **James's cousin Molly:** BCA: MS3101/C/D/14/2/5: JF to Mary Farmer (later Galton), August 29, 1742.

70 **Assured of her father's:** BCA: MS3101/C/D/14/2/9: JF to Mary Farmer, December 5, 1742.

70 **"not sacrifice my happiness":** BCA: MS3101/C/D/14/2/7: JF to Mary Farmer, October 3, 1742.

70 **bringing a frisson:** BCA: MS3101/C/C/2/3/7: Mary Farmer (later Galton) to Joseph Farmer (the younger), March 26, 1743; MS3101/C/C/2/3/2: Joseph Farmer to Mary, March 26, 1743/4.

70 **the marriage portion:** Friends Historical Library of Swarthmore College (FHLS): Hanbury-Aggs Family Papers RG 5/058: Box 4: Estate Papers of Thomas Plumsted, Release by James Farmer and Priscilla Farmer, October 4, 1752; Release by JF and Priscilla Farmer, December 13, 1752. I thank Simon Smith for these references. They cashed out the legacy, some £3,000.

71 **"haberdasher of small wares":** Pearson, *The Life, Letters and Labours of Francis Galton,* 1:39–40. The first Galton Quaker was John Galton, who married into the Quaker Button family. We have a bronze mortar he made in Taunton (Somerset, bordering Bristol) in 1705. http://galton.org /ancestry/index.htm.

71 **He was worth:** BCA: MS3101/B/15/1: Apprenticeship indenture, 1735; MS3101/B/15/2: Admittance of Samuel Galton as freeman of Bristol, 1742.

71 **Robert and several prominent:** BCA: MS3101/B/10/4: Arbitration award by Christopher Devonshire, John Lidderdale, Samuel Munckley, and Isaac Elton of Bristol, merchants, in a dispute between John Galton and Hannah Galton [. . .] and John Page of Bristol, merchant, concerning money spent by Robert Galton on the "Duke," and paid to John Galton and Hannah Galton by John Page in respect of his twelfth share in the "Duke," 1757–58.

71   **consignment of slaves:** Pearson, *The Life, Letters and Labours of Francis Galton*, 1:40.

71   **"a few boy servants":** *Boston News Letter*, March 7, 1746, quoted in Weeden, *Economic and Social History of New England*, 2:696.

71   **"gentleman of good sense":** BCA: MS3101/C/D/14/3/3: Joseph Farmer to Mary Farmer, March 26, 1746.

72   **The marriage settlement:** BCA: MS3101/A/A/1/5: Indenture tripartite between Mary Farmer, James Farmer, and John Galton, September 8, 1746; D. Williams, "James Farmer and Samuel Galton," 123.

72   **Gunmaking sank roots:** This was true of non-Quakers, too, like John Whateley, who through marriage drew other toymakers into his concerns and vice versa. BCA: MS3602/434: Indenture between John Whately the elder of Birmingham, Joseph Porter of Birmingham, and Edmund Scotton of Shustoke . . . , being a settlement previous to the marriage of the said John Whately the younger and the said Mary Croxall of messuages . . . , January 1, [1736]; MS3602/435: Bond from Thomas Moore to John Whateley, June 10, 1746.

72   **John Galton began to:** BCA: MS3101/C/D/15/1/1: SG to John Galton, July 21, 1751; SG to JF, July 10 and July 24, 1751; MS3101/C/D/15/1/2: SG to John Galton, September 16, 1755.

72   **Prankard was the major:** Prankard's ships circled from South Carolina to Hamburg to Stockholm to Bristol. He brought 54 percent of the Baltic iron that entered Bristol in 1730. No less than 42 percent of the Russian iron he sold went to Sampson Lloyd's slitting mill. Richards, "The Birmingham Gun Manufactory of Farmer and Galton," 22; Evans et al., "Baltic Iron and the British Iron Industry," 647, 650, 656–58.

72   **"Bristol Steel" too "frenzy":** BCA: MS3101/C/D/15/1/1: SG to John Galton, July 28, 1751.

72   **Like his father:** PP: *Journals of the House of Lords* XXVII, April 5, 1750, 452. The legislation did not work as imagined. Imports stayed low; American ironmasters had local markets. Evans et al., "Baltic Iron and the British Iron Industry," 660–62.

72   **He was intrigued by:** BCA: MS3101/C/D/15/5/10: JF to SG, April 27, 1750.

72   **whose share in the gun business:** BCA: MS3101/C/D/15/1/1: SG to JF, July 10, 1751.

72   **"the start of the others":** BCA: MS3101/C/D/15/1/1: SG to JF, October 12, 1751.

73   **Erecting forges at:** BCA: MS3101/A/B/1/2: Articles of Copartnership in Belbroughton Forge Furnace, 1751. See also MS3101/C/D/15/1/1: SG to JF, October 20, 1751; MS3101/C/D/15/1/2: SG to John Galton, June 3, 1755.

73   **theirs was an old-fashioned:** Gunmakers in general thought coke-smelted iron was of inferior quality through the 1750s. Ashton, *Iron and Steel in the Industrial Revolution*, 35.

73   **"some forrest to work with":** BCA: MS3101/C/D/15/1/1: SG to JF, July 11, 1752. The arrangements for wood supplies are described in SG to JF, October 20 and October 31, 1751.

73   **Galton anticipated a fall:** BCA: MS3101/C/D/15/1/2: SG to John Parr, November 20, 1755, and SG to James Johnson, January 25, 1757.

73   **William and John Wood:** Richards, "The Birmingham Gun Manufactory of Farmer and Galton," 107–8; Rowlands, *Masters and Men*, 132–33.

73   **The first Birmingham man:** Stephens, ed., *The Victoria History of the County of Warwick*, 7:85–86, 89.

73   **Of those who took out:** M. Berg, "Inventors of the World of Goods," 27.

74   **Besides the Town Mill:** Stephens, ed., *The Victoria History of the County of Warwick*, 7:253, 257, 263–65, 267; *Aris's Birmingham Gazette*, November 14, 1774, 3; D. Williams, "James Farmer and Samuel Galton," 124.

74   **When the gun spring:** BCA: MS3101/C/D/15/1/1: SG to JF, October 31, 1751, and [March] 1752. See also November 2, 1751.

74   **Galton now urged Farmer:** SG to JF, April 19, 1752.

74   **Farmer tried to charm:** JF to SG, [February 1753?].

74   **Some of the firm's:** BCA: MS3101/C/D/15/1/2: SG to John Galton, October 2, 1755.

74   **When he, in turn:** BCA: MS3101/C/D/15/1/2: SG to Mary Sowden, May 22, 1755; SG to JF, May 29, 1755.

74   **"to put round":** BCA: MS3101/C/D/15/5/7: JF to SG, January 20, [1750]. See also MS3101/C/C/2/1/14: JF to Joseph Farmer, January 4, [1744]; MS3101/C/C/2/1/15: JF to Joseph Farmer, January 14, [1744]; MS3101/ C/D/15/5/6: JF to SG, January 8, 1750; MS3101/C/D/15/5/8: JF to SG, February 5, [1750]; MS3101/C/D/14/2/19: JF to Mary Galton, March 3, [1750]; MS3101/C/D/15/5/

52: JF to SG, [February 1753?]; MS3101/C/D/15/5/13: JF to SG, December 10, 1753; MS3101/C/D/15/1/1: SG to JF, July 8 and August 31, 1751; MS3101/C/D/15/1/2: SG to JF, June 11, 1755, and undated [June 23, 1755?]; JF to Mary Galton, March 3, [1750].

75 **"prodigious quantity of"**: BCA: MS3101/C/D/15/5/2: JF to SG, October 14, 1748.

75 **"quantities of ironmongery goods"**: BCA: MS3101/C/D/15/1/1: SG to JF, September 22, 1754.

75 **"Silversmiths jewellers and cutters"**: N. Brown, *British Gunmakers*, 2:50–52.

75 **furbisher Richard Wooldridge:** Neal and Black, *Great British Gunmakers*, 366–67.

75 **Birmingham gunmakers also:** Advertisements in *Aris's Birmingham Gazette*, December 29, 1788, 3, and September 13, 1762, 3; *Aris's Birmingham Gazette*, April 24, 1775, 3.

75 **"great profit and advantage":** BCA: MS3602/273: Articles of Dissolution of Buttonmaking Partnership between Whately and Thomas Dobbs, May 24, 1780, and MS3602/442: Deed Poll between Whateley and Dobbs, May 24, 1780.

75 **Whateley continued to ally:** BCA: MS3782/12/33/8: John Whateley to Matthew Boulton, January 15, 1788; MS3782/12/33/47: Henry Piddock Whateley to Boulton, April 11, 1788; MS3782/12/33/183: J. Whateley to Boulton, December 2, 1788; MS3782/12/33/19: J. Whateley to Boulton, January 31, 1788; TNA: C107/10: H. P. Whateley to Rogers, November 26, 1792.

75 **Such associations meant:** See, for instance, TNA: WO 47/29: OM, May 10, 1757, 456.

75 **A 1733 poem that a Birmingham mechanic:** A Letter from a Mechanick in the busy Town of Birmingham, to Mr. Stayner, a Carver, Statuary, and Architect, in the sleepy Corporation of Warwick, *Aris's Birmingham Gazette*, February 1751, quoted in J. Langford, *A Century of Birmingham Life*, 40–41. *Aris's Gazette* began appearing in 1741. Money, *Experience and Identity*, 53.

76 **for the Naval Brassfoundry:** Aitken, "Brass and Brass Manufactures," in *The Resources, Products, and Industrial History of Birmingham and the Midland Hardware District*, ed. Timmins, 352–53.

76 **the toymaker supplied:** List of articles manufactured at Soho, in *Aris's Birmingham Gazette*, September 13, 1773, 3; P. Jones, *Industrial Enlightenment*, 86.

76 **the Galton arms factory:** BCA: MS3782/12/33/28: William Bird to Matthew Boulton, March 5, 1788.

76 **workmen came around:** BCA: MS3101/C/D/15/1/1: SG to JF, October 20, 1751.

76 **toy goods continued:** BCA: MS3101/C/D/15/1/1: SG to JF, July 11 and August 8, 1752.

76 **workmen were threatening:** BCA: MS3101/C/D/15/1/1: SG to JF, April 10, 1752.

76 **the warehouse's "toy room":** BCA: MS3101/C/D/15/1/2: SG to JF, June 8, 1755.

77 **"anything in the gun":** BCA: MS3101/C/D/15/1/2: SG to John Kidd, October 29, 1756.

77 **also a "linen draper":** BCA: MS3101/B/10/2: Admittance of John Galton, linen draper, as freeman of the city of Bristol, 1735/6; MS3101/C/D/15/1/1: SG to John Galton, July 21, 1751; MS3101/C/D/15/1/2: SG to John Galton, July [10?], 1755.

77 **his cousin Hannah:** BCA: MS3101/C/A/1/6/1: Hannah Galton to Susannah Abrahams, April 9, 1751; MS3101/C/A/1/6/8: Hannah Galton to Susannah Abrahams, October 4, [1751–55]; *Boston Post Boy*, December 12, 1748, www.newspaperabstracts.com/link.php?action=detail&id=61555.

77 **He also dealt in:** BCA: MS3101/C/D/15/2/1: JF, Nerbel and Co. to Farmer & Galton, September 10, 1752; MS3101/C/D/15/5/11: JF to SG, July 8, 1751; MS3101/C/D/15/5/13: JF to SG, December 10, 1753.

77 **"little parcel of":** BCA: MS3101/C/D/15/1/1: SG to JF, May 10, 1755.

77 **the Liverpool merchant John Hardman:** Rawley and Behrendt, *The Transatlantic Slave Trade*, 172; Richards, "The Birmingham Gun Manufactory of Farmer and Galton," 52–54.

77 **East India goods:** BCA: MS3101/C/C/2/1/18: JF to Joseph Farmer, February 18, 1744.

77 **also borrowed from:** See, for instance, BCA: MS3101/C/D/15/6/1: Joseph Farmer to SG, September 5, 1750; MS3101/C/D/15/1/1: SG to Joseph Farmer, December 28, 1751.

77 **dabbling in his cousin:** BCA: MS3101/C/C/2/3/7: Mary Farmer (later Galton) to Joseph Farmer, October 8, 1743. See also MS3101/C/D/15/5/3: JF to SG, January 3, 1749.

77 **The cotton trade:** BCA: MS3101/C/D/15/1/1: SG to JF, July 6, 1751.

77 **When he lost more:** BCA: MS3101/C/D/15/5/11: JF to SG, July 8, 1751.

77 **the "battery" trade:** BCA: MS3101/C/D/15/1/1: Copy of JF to John Parr, July 7, 1752.

77 **"mercantile affairs on his account":** BCA: MS3101/C/D/15/1/1: SG to JF, December 2, 1753.

77 **"bring a reflection":** BCA: MS3101/C/D/15/1/2: SG to Nicholas Atkinson, September 6, 1755. See also MS3101/C/D/15/1/1: SG to Atkinson, May 10, 1755, SG to JF, May 19, 1755; MS3101/C/D/15/1/2: SG to JF, May 26, 29, and 31, 1755; MS3101/C/D/15/6/2: Joseph Farmer to SG,

December 30, 1753; MS3101/C/D/15/1/1: SG to Joseph Farmer, January 5, 1754; MS3101/C/D/15/5/15: JF to SG, January 8, 1754.

77 **he cleared his debts:** BCA: MS3101/B/7/3: Assignment of shares in 2 ships [. . .] by Joseph Farmer to SG, February 24, 1763.

78 **more than £2,000:** PP: *Journals of the House of Commons* XXVI, May 21, 1751, appendix 2, 250–51; BCA: MS3101/C/D/15/1/2: SG to James Johnson, July 5, 1756. See also MS3101/C/D/15/5/10: JF to SG, April 27, 1750.

78 **"good exclusive of":** BCA: MS3101/C/D/15/5/10: JF to SG, April 27, 1750.

78 **Haymaking took a:** BCA: MS3101/C/D/14/2/3: JF to Mary Farmer (later Galton), July 9, 1742, and MS3101/C/D/14/2/4: July 22, 1742.

78 **In lean years:** BCA: MS3101/C/D/15/5/5: JF to SG, December 15, 1749; MS3101/C/D/15/5/6: January 8, 1750; January 20, [1750]; February 5, 1750; MS3101/C/D/15/5/9: February 7, 1750.

78 **he acquired land and workshop:** BCA: MS3101/C/D/15/1/2: SG to Strickland, [November 12–20, 1755]; Williams, "James Farmer and Samuel Galton," 125; B. Smith, "The Galtons of Birmingham," 149; MS3101/A/A/1/3: Attornments between Galton and Thomas Acton, and between Galton and William Tongue, April 8, 1777; advertisement, *Aris's Birmingham Gazette,* June 22, 1772, 3; Pearson, *The Life, Letters and Labours of Francis Galton,* 1:45–46. In 1775, Galton transferred £10,000 to his son.

80 **The Whateleys also:** BCA: 608488[ZZ33]: Estates of Henry Piddock Whateley in the parish of Handsworth, 1794.

80 **Agriculture and industry:** Hudson, *The Industrial Revolution,* 95.

80 **Charitable investment in:** J. Langford, *A Century of Birmingham Life,* 1:155.

80 **He helped fund:** BCA: MS3782/12/38/3: SGII to Matthew Boulton, January 9, 1793. Galton Jr. published a paper on canals in 1817. Pearson, *The Life, Letters and Labours of Francis Galton,* 1:48.

80 **Both invested in the Rose Copper:** Uglow, *The Lunar Men,* 352; B. Smith, "The Galtons of Birmingham," 149–50.

81 **senior Galton died:** Pearson, *The Life, Letters and Labours of Francis Galton,* 1:40.

81 **The family was still:** BCA: MS3101/C/D/10/78: Edward Wakefield to John Howard Galton, September 4, 1820.

81 **After the Galton bank:** B. Smith, "The Galtons of Birmingham," 148–50. The banks absorbed in Midland Bank are listed in Crick and Wadsworth, *A Hundred Years of Joint-Stock Banking,* appendix B, 446–50.

81 **Even where their markings:** Bailey and Nie, *English Gunmakers,* 13.

81 **Many temporarily hired:** D. Williams, *The Birmingham Gun Trade,* 51.

81 **the first barrel maker:** Stephens, ed., *The Victoria History of the County of Warwick,* 7:85–86.

82 **Directories that began:** Bailey and Nie, *English Gunmakers,* 10–12. Sketchley's Birmingham directory of 1767 counted sixty-two workers in the trade: thirty-five gun and pistol makers; eight barrel makers and filers; five barrel polishers and finishers; eleven lockmakers, forgers, finishers and filers; and three gun-swivel makers and stockers. Cited in Chew, *Arming the Periphery,* 57–58.

82 **"in the toy way":** BCA: MS3101/C/D/15/1/1: SG to JF, July 4, 1752.

82 **"A man may have described":** Bailey and Nie, *English Gunmakers,* 17.

82 **Birmingham's population of masters:** Thompson, *The Making of the English Working Class,* 239; M. Berg, "Factories, Workshops, and Industrial Organisation," 138–39.

82 **An old Birmingham song:** Quoted in Selgin, *Good Money,* 131. A broadsheet with the lyrics was printed in Birmingham in 1826. See http://efdss-thefullenglish.blogspot.com/2013/11/folk-song-in-england-on-edge-of-leafy.html.

83 **especially women and children:** In gunmaking, women were common in "making off." There were also a few women in polishing and barrel boring. Goodman, "On the Progress of the Small Arms Manufacture," 497.

83 **James and Joseph Farmer plotted:** BCA: MS3101/C/C/2/1/9: JF to Joseph Farmer, November 29, 1743, and MS3101/C/C/2/1/11: December 10, 1743; MS3101/C/C/2/1/12: December 17, 1743; MS3101/C/C/2/1/13: December 31, 1743; MS3101/C/C/2/1/16: January 25, 1744; and MS3101/C/C/2/1/17: February 1, 1744.

83 **Lockmaking was the only:** Rowlands, *Masters and Men,* 132–33; Bailey and Nie, *English Gunmakers,* 20. Saint-Étienne's armorers also did not belong to a legally recognized guild—unique in France. The industry was socially fluid. Alder, *Engineering the Revolution,* 176.

83 **Galton fretted that:** BCA: MS3101/C/D/15/1/1: SG to John Parr, March 11, 1752. See also SG to JF, March 15, 1752, and SG to John Parr, March 18, 1752.

83 **"with every great apparent":** BCA: MS3101/C/D/15/1/1: SG to JF, March 22, 1752. See also MS3101/C/D/15/5/12: JF to SG, May 19, 1752; MS3101/C/D/15/1/1: SG to John Parr, June 14, 1752.

84 **Even gun masters could not:** Goodman, "The Birmingham Gun Trade," 391.

84 **John Whateley testified:** TNA: BT 6/10: Representation of Mr. John Whateley dated Birmingham 27 March 1788 on the importance of the manufacture of guns carried on there, 354.

84 **One scholarly estimate:** The town's population was seventy thousand in 1800. Hall, *Civilising Subjects,* 268–69.

84 **The poet Robert Southey:** [Southey], *Letters from England,* 2:58–59. More than 6,500 families worked on brass goods alone. Thompson, *The Making of the English Working Class,* 239.

84 **Lord Shelburne toured:** Cited in Koehn, *The Power of Commerce,* 59.

84 **half the gun manufacturers:** Wise, "On the Evolution of the Jewellery and Gun Quarters in Birmingham," 66, 68; Bailey and Nie, *English Gunmakers,* 17.

85 **"got into other business":** TNA: WO 47/45: OM, March 25, 1755, 257–58.

85 **Early in the American war:** Advertisements in *Aris's Birmingham Gazette,* February 2, 1767, 3, November 24, 1766, 3, and June 6, 1768, 3; TNA: WO 47/90: OM, December 9, 1777, 574–75, and December 20, 1777, 597–98; WO 47/46: OM, August 14, 1755, 158.

85 **By 1775, *Aris's*:** *Aris's Birmingham Gazette,* June 26, 1775, 3.

85 **Contractors made contracts:** TNA: WO 47/91: OM, March 23 and 24, 1778, 243.

85 **"Wanted immediately MEN":** Advertisement by Thomas Gill, *Aris's Birmingham Gazette,* May 11, 1778, 3.

85 **"that his men may not":** TNA: WO 47/46: OM, September 4, 1755, 212. See also WO 47/49: OM, June 17, 1757, 609.

86 **"men on the spot:** TNA: WO 47/91: OM, April 10, 1778, 299.

86 **"had got several of":** TNA: WO 47/49: OM, January 7, 1757, 24–26.

86 **for his "disinterested behavior":** TNA: WO 55/2: Paper report No. 43, April 10, 1755, 146; WO 47/45: OM, April 11, 1755, 335–36.

86 **"no unnecessary difficulties":** TNA: WO 47/46: OM, paraphrasing Hirst to Ordnance Board on October 29, October 30, 1755, 383–85.

86 **"entice or employ":** TNA: WO 47/47: OM, January 28, 1756, 110–11.

86 **"the least interruption":** TNA: WO 55/2: Charles Frederick to the Ordnance Board, June 6, 1757, [83?].

86 **At least one, Richard Molineux:** TNA: WO 47/48: OM, November 3, 1756, 406–7, 413.

87 **Galton complained about:** BCA: MS3101/C/D/15/1/2: SG to Charles Frederick, July 31, 1756.

87 **"referred to themselves":** Behagg, "Mass Production without the Factory," 5–6.

87 **The 1776 issue of:** TNA: WO 47/48: OM, November 1, 1776, 244.

87 **"Men being very scarce":** TNA: WO 47/90: Waller and Loder, letter, July 31, paraphrased, and OM, August 1, 1777, 143–44. See also Loder to the Board, paraphrased in OM, July 18, 1777, 91–92; Richard Trested to Ordnance Board, paraphrased in OM, November 28, 1777, 514; WO 47/91: Samuel Oakes to the Ordnance Board, March 15, paraphrased in OM, 20, 1778, 224; Thompson Davis to the Ordnance Board, March 25, paraphrased in OM, March 27, 1778, 258.

88 **His marriage to Priscilla:** BCA: MS3101/C/D/14/2/12: JF to Mary Farmer (later Galton), July 4, 1743; Pearson, *The Life, Letters and Labours of Francis Galton,* 1:32.

88 **The bank invested:** In the 1770s, banking became the major preoccupation as the American War of Independence forced the firm to reduce its activity in North America. Price, "The Great Quaker Business Families," 366–67, 376; Tuke, ed., *History of Barclays Bank Limited,* 35–40.

88 **James Farmer became utterly:** BCA: MS3101/C/C/2/3/8: Mary Farmer to Joseph Farmer, January 3, [1744].

88 **Plumsted conveyed gun orders:** See, for instance, BCA: MS3101/C/D/15/5/6: JF to SG, January 8, 1750, and MS3101/C/D/15/5/8: February 5, 1750.

88 **For Earl Daniel:** BCA: MS3101/C/D/15/5/27: JF to SG, May 14, 1755; MS3101/C/D/15/1/1: SG to JF, May 14, 1755.

88 **the African Company bought:** TNA: T70/1516: Bill from African Company for purchases from Thomas Plumsted and Son, March 14, 1750.

88 **Galton bought locks:** BCA: MS3101/C/D/15/1/1: SG to JF, May 10, 1755.
88 **Joseph Freame also bought:** BCA: MS3101/C/D/15/5/23: JF to SG, March 25, 1755.
89 **"mostly lies on our":** BCA: MS3101/C/D/15/1/1: [SG] to John Parr, July 20, 1754.
89 **he beseeched Farmer:** SG to JF, September 19, 1754.
89 **for ease of accounting:** BCA: MS3101/C/D/15/1/1: SG to Nerbel, December 15, 1751, and December 19, 1751; [SG] to John Parr, July 20, 1754.
89 **"a young fellow":** BCA: MS3101/C/D/15/1/1: SG to Nicholas Atkinson, March 22, 1755 (repeated in SG to John Parr, March 22, 1755). See also MS3101/C/D/15/5/1: JF to SG, August 23, 1748.
89 **"as bankers they never":** BCA: MS3101/C/D/15/1/1: SG to John Parr, May 17, 1755.
90 **Farmer's "dubious accounts":** BCA: MS3101/C/D/15/1/1: SG to JF, December 11, 1754. See also SG to JF, December 23, 1754; MS3101/D/1/1: JF and SG, handwritten contract, December 31, 1754.
90 **He had dealt with:** BCA: MS3101/C/D/15/5/10: JF to SG, April 27, 1750.
90 **his crew "barbarously used":** BCA: MS3101/C/D/15/5/16: JF to SG, September 10, 1754.
90 **Guns, too, were part:** Yale University Beinecke Rare Book and Manuscript Library (YU): Osborn Shelves FC160: Robert Plumsted Letter Book (1752–56): Robert Plumsted to Farmer & Montague, August 10, 1754 (or October 8, 1754), 160 (I thank Simon Smith for this reference); BCA: MS3101/C/D/15/1/2: SG to JF, [June 1755], SG to Montaignt, July 6, 1756, and October 28, 1756.
90 **Johnson was confident:** TNA: T70/1516: James Johnson to Royal African Company, December 28, 1750.
90 **Farmer owed him:** Richards, "The Birmingham Gun Manufactory of Farmer and Galton," 18, 148.
91 **"intimacy and interest":** BCA: MS3101/C/D/15/1/1: SG to Joseph Farmer, December 26, 1753. See also Alan J. Kidd, "Touchet, Samuel (c. 1705–1773)," *Oxford Dictionary of National Biography* online, accessed January 3, 2017, www.oxforddnb.com/view/article/57578.
91 **As gunmakers, Farmer:** BCA: MS3101/C/D/15/1/1: SG to John Galton, May 8, 1755; MS3101/C/D/15/1/2: SG to John Galton, May 27, 1755, and June 5, 1755.
91 **The Champions were also:** Raistrick, *Dynasty of Iron Founders*, 40; *Quakers in Science and Industry*, 190–200.
91 **Champion and George Hayley:** Richards, "The Birmingham Gun Manufactory of Farmer and Galton," 66; J. Harris, "Copper and Shipping in the Eighteenth Century," 552.
91 **"as a pledge":** BCA: MS3101/C/D/15/1/2: SG to John Galton, May 20, 1755.
91 **"one hundred of the thinnest":** BCA: MS3101/C/D/15/1/2: SG to George Pengree, June 5, 1756 (repeated July 13, 1756).
91 **Farmer also owed:** BCA: MS3101/C/D/15/1/2: SG to JF, May 26, 1755.
91 **He testified in Parliament:** PP: *Journals of the House of Commons* XXVI, March 14, 1753, 674; P. Jones, *Industrial Enlightenment*, 25. Before the first canals opened, Birmingham depended on roads. Turnpiking came early to the region, likely as a response to heavy road usage, especially for carriage of industrial raw materials.
91 **James's letters took:** See, for instance, BCA: MS3101/C/D/15/5/18: JF to SG, March 3, 1755.
92 **"with whom a secret":** BCA: MS3101/C/D/15/1/1: SG to JF, March 5, 1755.
92 **Freame & Barclay gave notice:** BCA: MS3101/D/1/2: Copy of James Farmer's answer to the bill of complaint brought against him and Samuel Galton by administrators representing Abraham James Hillhouse, c. 1757.
92 **made his "friends secure":** BCA: MS3101/C/D/15/5/20: JF to SG, March 21, 1755.
92 **"one of the best friends":** BCA: MS3101/C/D/15/5/21: JF to SG March 22, 1755.
92 **Samuel assured Freame:** BCA: MS3101/C/D/15/1/1: SG to Freame & Barclay, March 22, 1755; SG to JF, March 23, 1755.
92 **"so dismal a crisis":** BCA: MS3101/C/D/15/1/1: SG to Robert Plumsted, March 21, 1755.
92 **He hoped Freame & Barclay:** BCA: MS3101/C/D/15/1/1: SG to Messrs. Freame and Barclay, March 22, 1755.
93 **"relations of Mrs. Farmer":** BCA: MS3101/C/D/15/1/1: SG to Nicholas Atkinson, March 22, 1755. See also SG to John Parr, March 22, 1755.
93 **Farmer also applied:** See BCA: MS3101/C/D/15/5/22: JF to SG, March 24, 1755; MS3101/C/D/15/5/23: JF to SG, March 25, 1755; MS3101/C/D/15/5/24: JF to SG, March 26, 1755; MS3101/C/D/15/1/1: SG to John Spilsbury, [March 1756].

93 **"not hitting it off":** BCA: MS3101/C/D/15/5/25: JF to SG, March 27, 1755. Bankruptcy was often the unintentional consequence of the poor condition of most eighteenth-century account books. Hoppitt, *Risk and Failure in English Business,* 39.

93 **Freame informed the London banker:** BCA: MS3101/C/D/15/5/26: JF to SG, March 31, 1755.

93 **Drummond's bank served:** Philip Winterbottom, "Drummond, Andrew (1688–1769)," *Oxford Dictionary of National Biography* online, accessed January 3, 2017, www.oxforddnb.com/view/article /47581.

93 **"securing the gun trade":** BCA: MS3101/C/D/15/1/2: SG to John Galton, June [18–20?], 1755.

93 **So, too, did Farmer's:** BCA: MS3101/C/D/15/1/2: SG to Cousin Baskerville, June 24, 1755.

93 **The assignees were intent:** BCA: MS3101/C/D/15/5/33: JF to SG, June 2, 1755; MS3101/C/D/ 15/5/34: June 3, 1755; MS3101/C/D/15/1/2: SG to John Parr, September 6, 1755.

93 **His investments were bound:** BCA: MS3101/C/D/15/5/37: JF to SG, June 24, 1755; MS3101/ C/D/15/1/2: SG to Robert Plumsted, September 7, 1755; YU: Robert Plumsted Letter Book: Robert Plumsted to Farmer & Montague, June 24, 1755 (I thank Simon Smith for this reference). The Plumsteds indemnified Farmer. BCA: MS3101/C/D/15/5/44: JF to SG, December 4, 1755; FHLS: Bond of Indemnity, Mary Plumsted to Robert Plumsted, January 5, 1756 (I thank Simon Smith for this reference).

93 **This self-absorption may:** BCA: MS3101/C/D/15/1/2: SG to JF, March 8, 1756 (lined-out text).

94 **"Effects enough abroad":** BCA: MS3101/C/A/1/8/1: SG to Susannah Abrahams, May 24, 1755.

94 **In explaining the delay:** See BCA: MS3101/C/D/15/1/2: SG to John Galton, November [21–26], 1755; SG to JF, December 6, 1755; SG to John Parr, February 13, 1756; SG to Freame & Barclay, December [13?], 1755; MS3101/C/D/15/5/24: JF to SG, March 26, 1755; MS3101/C/D/15/10/2: John Galton to SG, August 9, 1757. Osgood Hanbury married Mary Lloyd, daughter of Sampson Lloyd II, in 1757, just after these proceedings. Sampson Lloyd II was married to the daughter of Nehemiah Champion. His other daughter, Rachel, married David Barclay.

94 **When Oswald later:** Hancock, *Citizens of the World,* 3, 253. Once he borrowed from the Bank of Scotland.

94 **In May 1755:** See BCA: MS3101/C/D/15/1/1: SG to JF, May 14, 1755; MS3101/C/D/15/5/29: JF to SG, May 24, 1755; MS3101/C/D/15/1/2: SG to JF, May 29, 1755; MS3101/C/D/15/5/32: JF to SG, May 29, 1755; MS3101/C/D/15/5/31: JF to SG, May 27, 1755.

94 **kept them in temper:** BCA: MS3101/C/D/15/5/28: JF to SG, May 22, 1755.

94 **the committee decided on:** BCA: MS3101/C/D/15/5/35: JF to SG, June 6, 1755. See also MS3101/C/D/15/5/33: June 2, 1755; MS3101/C/D/15/5/34: June 3, 1755.

94 **Barclay selected from:** BCA: MS3101/C/D/15/1/2: SG to JF, October 30, 1755.

94 **He loaned Farmer cash:** BCA: MS3101/C/D/15/10/3: John Galton to SG, August 11, 1757, and MS3101/C/D/15/10/4: August 23, 1757; MS3101/C/D/15/1/2: SG to James Johnson, May 3, 1756.

94 **as a "particular acquaintance":** BCA: MS3101/C/D/15/1/2: SG to JF, May 29, 1755.

94 **The Freames and Barclays:** BCA: MS3101/C/D/15/1/2: SG to Samuel Montaignt, July 6, 1756; SG to John Galton, November [21–26], 1755; SG to JF, December 6, 1755; SG to John Parr, February 13, 1756.

94 **"regular manner of living":** BCA: MS3101/C/D/15/5/32: JF to SG, May 29, 1755. See also MS3101/C/D/15/1/2: SG to JF, May 26, 1755; MS3101/C/D/15/1/1: SG to Nicholas Atkinson, May 10, 1755; SG to JF, May 19, 1755.

95 **"It will not suit":** BCA: MS3101/C/D/15/1/1: SG to JF, May 18, 1755.

95 **"man of assiduity":** BCA: MS3101/C/D/15/1/2: SG to JF, [June 6?], 1755. See also MS3101/C/ D/15/1/2: SG to JF, June 8, 1755.

95 **"pushing on the business":** BCA: MS3101/C/D15/1/2: SG to JF, May 31, 1755.

95 **"If his interest will":** BCA: MS3101/C/D/15/5/[?]: JF to SG, September 27, 1755.

95 **"advantage Mr. Farmer's presence":** BCA: MS3101/C/D/15/1/2: SG to Robert Plumsted, October 18, 1755.

95 **"if a war should":** BCA: MS3101/C/D/15/1/2: SG to James Johnson, September 17, 1755.

95 **"continued connection of":** BCA: MS3101/C/D/15/1/2: SG to James Johnson, October 12, 1755. See also SG to James Johnson, October 20, 1755.

95 **"an agreement between you":** BCA: MS3101/C/D/15/1/2: James Johnson to SG, quoted in SG to JF, October 26, 1755.

95 **By the end of the year:** BCA: MS3101/C/D/15/1/2: SG to James Johnson, December 15, 1755, and [March] 1756.

95 **His nephew purchased:** BCA: MS3101/C/D/15/1/2: SG to JF, December 1, 1755; MS3101/C/D/15/5/44: JF to SG, December 4, 1755.

95 **He tracked ship arrivals:** BCA: MS3101/C/D/15/1/2: SG to James Johnson, July 5, 1756, October 26, 1756, and February 27, 1757; SG to Samuel Beardsley, April 20, 1757; MS3101/C/D/15/10/2: John Galton to SG, August 9, 1757.

96 **He handled payments:** BCA: MS3101/C/D/15/1/2: SG to George Kitson, January 25, 1757, and SG to James Johnson, January 25, 1757.

96 **He addressed the surveyor:** BCA: MS3101/C/D/15/1/2: SG to James Johnson, September 8, 1756.

96 **He took on Galton's:** BCA: MS3101/C/D/15/1/2: SG to Capel Hanbury, May 30, 1757.

96 **He was involved in:** BCA: MS3101/C/D/15/1/2: SG to James Johnson, October 6, 1756.

96 **"the means of making":** BCA: MS3101/C/D/15/1/2: SG to JF, October 26, 1755. See also SG to James Johnson, October 27, 1755; SG to JF, July 7 [or 17], 1755, and October [12 or 13], 1755.

96 **"be so settled":** BCA: MS3101/D/1/1: Memorandum of the terms of partnership to be entered on between James Farmer and Samuel Galton. A duplicate of what Galton signed August 5, 1755, and Farmer signed January 1756, signed by JF, April 27, 1761.

96 **As 1756 wore on:** See BCA: MS3101/C/D/15/1/2: SG to James Johnson, October 26, 1756, and February 27, 1757; SG to Beardsley, April 20, 1757; John Galton to SG, August 9, 1757; SG to Samuel Montaignt, July 6, 1756, and October 28, 1756; SG to Joseph Manesty, March 26, 1756; SG to Daniel, July 30, 1756, and October 29, 1756; SG to John Davis Molineux and the Assembly Montserrat, July 30, 1756; SG to John Parr, October 15, 1756; SG to John Kidd, October 29, 1756; MS3101/C/D/15/1/1: SG to JF, October 20, 1751.

97 **"so good and obliging":** BCA: MS3101/C/D/15/1/1: SG to John Parr, March 18, 1752.

97 **"some allowance for":** BCA: MS3101/C/D/15/1/2: SG to Joseph Ward, July 20, 1756.

97 **"anything in the gun":** BCA: MS3101/C/D/15/1/2: SG to John Kidd, October 29, 1756.

97 **to "affluent circumstances":** BCA: MS3101/C/A/1/8/15: SG to Susannah Abrahams, June 18, 1760.

97 **"in high spirits":** FHL: Temp MSS 403/1/1/1/10: SG to Joseph Freame, quoted in Freame to Priscilla Farmer, December 14, 1762.

97 **With a 1766 agreement:** Pearson, *The Life, Letters and Labours of Francis Galton*, 1:40.

97 **By 1770, the most:** Stephens, ed., *The Victoria History of the County of Warwick*, 7:96.

97 **James's old friends:** BCA: MS3101/B/23/3: True copy [attested June 14, 1773] of James Farmer's will of May 15, 1772, with further note dated December 18, 1772.

97 **The following year:** Price, "The Great Quaker Business Families," 379–80.

97 **Barclay took charge:** FHL: Temp MSS 403/1/1/3/24: David Barclay to Priscilla Farmer, June 12, 1774. See also 403/1/1/3/19: July 22, 1773. Silvanus Bevan was the elder Freame's nephew, who joined the bank in 1766.

97 **Samuel Jr. married:** FHL: Temp MSS 403/3/6/1/1: Charles Lloyd to Mary Lloyd (née Farmer), October 21, 1777; BCA: MS3101/C/D/15/15/6: SG to William Bird, August 26–27, 1780; MS3101/B/16/1: Samuel Galton Jr.'s account of his mother's death, 1777; MS3101/C/D/15/15/5: SG to William Bird, August 24, 1780.

98 **"gentlemen of the first families":** Brooke, *Liverpool as It Was during the Last Quarter of the Eighteenth Century*, 290–94. See also BCA: MS3101/D/2/2: Articles of Agreement, March 1, 1776, between Samuel Galton, Samuel Galton Jnr., and James Forshaw; Baines, *History of the Commerce and Town of Liverpool*, 1:444; Picton, *Memorials of Liverpool, Historical and Topographical*, 296–97.

98 **"so amply rewarded":** Hutton, *An History of Birmingham* (1781), 79.

98 **Their sister Adèle's husband:** P. Jones, *Industrial Enlightenment*, 125; Hall and Davidoff, *Family Fortunes*, 264, 327. Tertius's other sister, Sophia, cared for their father in his old age. After his death, she married her father's trusted bank clerk, a match her brothers thought beneath her.

98 **He leased land:** John Whateley to Matthew Boulton, January 31, 1788; BCA: MS3782/12/39/250: H. P. Whateley to Boulton, September 13, 1794; MS3782/12/39/229: H. P. Whateley to Boulton, August 21, 1794; MS3602/445: Lease from Whateleys to Boulton, August 25, 1794; MS3782/12/39/236: H. P. Whateley to Boulton, August 30, 1794; H. P. Whateley to Boulton, January 15, 1788; MS3602/308: Lease, December 7, 1818.

98–99   **Matthews and Boulton also helped:** BCA: MS3782/12/39/320: James Alston to Matthew
          Boulton, November 24, 1794.
   99   **Boulton composed the differences:** Subcontractors like Archer took a 5 percent price cut
          when working through Galton on an East India Company order; they, in turn, had their own
          subcontractors making parts. B. Smith, "The Galtons of Birmingham," 142–43.
   99   **they avoided importing:** TNA: WO 46/12: T. Blomfield for George Townshend to George
          Crawford, [August 1780], [between 138 and 161].
   99   **The Worshipful Company of Gunmakers:** Worshipful Company of Gunmakers, *The Case of
          the Company of Gun-Makers.*

Chapter Three: The State and the Gun Industry, Part 2: 1756–1815

  102   **the war paved the way:** The British captured Louisburg in the summer of 1758, Quebec in
          September 1759, and Montreal in 1760. In West Africa, they took French colonies in 1758 and
          1759. In the West Indies, Guadeloupe, Dominica, Martinique, Grenada, St. Lucia, and St. Vin-
          cent fell to the British between 1759 and 1762. In India, the start of 1761 saw the fall of Pondi-
          cherry and the elimination of the French from the south. When Spain joined, its colonies became
          targets. The British took Spanish Havana (later traded for Florida). Late in 1762, they took
          Manila.
  102   **Britain provisioned 96 percent:** Hancock, *Citizens of the World,* 221–22.
  102   **Colonial governments in:** Colonial merchants also imported some 36,000 shoulder arms and
          four thousand pairs of pistols during the war, but these were not of a quality to sustain military
          forces in the field. Sweeney, "Firearms, Militias, and the Second Amendment," 336–37. The
          most commonly used weapon in this war was the musket. Pistols and shorter muskets such as the
          musketoon (a type of shotgun) were almost exclusively for mounted soldiers. Reloading them
          took two to three minutes; one needed at least a couple at the ready, and that extra weight did not
          make sense for an infantryman already burdened with sixty pounds of equipment. Leach, *Arms
          for Empire,* 4–8; Nester, *The Great Frontier War,* 124–28.
  103   **Galton waited for Davis:** BCA: MS3101/C/D/15/1/2: SG to JF, March 6, 1756.
  103   **He showed small lots:** BCA: MS3101/C/D/15/1/2: SG to JF, March 8, 1756.
  103   **In May 1756:** TNA: WO 47/47: OM, May 4, 1756, 469, and June 3, 1756, 607; WO 47/48: OM,
          July 15, 1756, 54, and August 12, 1756, 128. See also WO 47/48: OM, October 16, 1756, 347,
          and December 17, 1756, 569.
  103   **It was able to purchase:** Bailey, "Liège Muskets in the British Army," 284.
  103   **It accepted stranded:** TNA: WO 47/56: OM, August 5, 1760, 102, and September 4, 1760, 168;
          WO 47/58: OM, July 3, 1761, 8, July 10, 1761, 27, July 12, 1761, 30–31, August 21, 1761, 131, and
          September 29, 1761, 231; WO 47/59: OM, January 12, 1762, 27, and February 9, 1762, 122.
  103   **"alarmed by new contractors":** BCA: MS3101/C/D/15/1/2: SG to Charles Frederick, July 31,
          1756 [and undated redraft]. Galton redrafted the letter some days later; according to the OM, it
          was dated August 18. It is the same letter, as it mentions the same complaints. See also TNA:
          WO 47/48: OM, August 23, 1756, 171–72; WO 47/47: OM, February 17, 1756, 188.
  103   **He had James Johnson:** SG to James Johnson, September 8, 1756.
  104   **"barrel forgers and lockmakers":** TNA: WO 47/48: OM, October 2, 1756, 300–301.
  104   **"encourage us to proceed":** SG to James Johnson, October 6, 1756.
  104   **The office fulfilled its:** TNA: WO 55/2: SG to Ordnance Board, May 9, 1757, 73. See also
          WO 47/49: OM, May 13, 1757, 464–65; WO 47/51: OM, June 23, 1758, 653–54; WO 47/52:
          OM, July 7, 1758, 29; WO 47/48: OM, October 16, 1756, 341–42.
  104   **Thomas Hadley and the Jordans:** TNA: WO 47/47: OM, January 23, 1756, 83–84, and Jan-
          uary 28, 1756, 110–11; WO 47/53: OM, June 1, 1759, 576, March 6, 1759, 282, and March 20,
          1759, 350; WO 47/54: OM, July 11, 1759, 44.
  104   **reminding them not to:** TNA: WO 47/48: OM, November 3, 1756, 406–7, and November 16,
          1756, 466; WO 47/50: OM, October 8, 1757, 253–54; WO 47/53: OM, May 22, 1759, 545; GL:
          CM MS5220/9, March 31, 1749, 275.
  104   **Within weeks, Jordan:** TNA: WO 47/49: OM, January 7, 1757, 24–25.
  104   **"some quite foreign":** TNA: WO 47/48: JF to the Ordnance Board, October 12, 1756, and
          Joseph Hunt to Ordnance Board, October 13, 1756, referred to in OM, October 16, 1756, 338
          and 348. See also BCA: MS3101/C/D/15/1/2: SG to Ordnance Office, October 11, 1756.

104 **The Birmingham paper:** *Aris's Birmingham Gazette,* November 17, 1760, 3, August 31, 1761, 3, January 18, 1762, 3, and September 13, 1762, 3; advertisement, August 19, 1765, 3.
104 **The Ordnance Office was widening:** TNA: WO 47/48: OM, August 14, 1756, 138, October 23, 1756, 365, and October 28, 1756, 387.
104 **"in combination . . . did":** TNA: WO 47/61: OM, May 20, 1763, 322–24. See also WO 47/61: OM, May 13, 1763, 299. Quality mattered: Peter Gandon was denied further orders when many of his first hundred were "several times turned back" and finished "in an indifferent manner." WO 47/48: OM, December 17, 1756, 574; WO 47/49: OM, January 7, 1757, 24–26. Rough stocking was more tightly controlled—done mainly by the Wallers and Isaac Kelso. Abraham Griggs was refused but kept in reserve. WO 47/49: OM, March 19, 1757, 299; WO 47/51: OM, March 14, 1758, 261. Stocks from someone "not of the trade" were considered risky, given their propensity to warp and change after inspection. Moreover, the Wallers had declined private business to serve the office exclusively.
104 **"more precarious of reaching":** SG to Nicholas Atkinson, April 6, 1757. Prohibition against sending arms by water meant that many were transported overland. BCA: MS3101/C/D/15/1/2: SG to Nicholas Atkinson, October 19, 1756.
105 **"now settled with me":** BCA: MS3101/C/D/15/1/2: SG to Robert Lawrie, October 30, 1756. See also SG to John Parr, October 29, 1756; SG to Robert Lawrie, [summer 1757]; SG to George Kitson, December [c. 20], 1756, and January 25, 1757; Farmer & Galton to Oughston, February 16, 1757; SG to Honeyborne, October 30, 1756; SG to James Johnson, October 6, 1756, and October 26, 1756; SG to Tublay James, September 11, 1756; SG to Henry Bradley, February 16, 1757; SG to the Committee of the Company Trading to Africa, July 30, 1756; SG to Kendermason, November 20, 1756.
105 **"and [I] think [I] may assert":** BCA: MS3101/C/D/15/1/2: SG to Peter Farmer, February 16, 1757.
105 **old customer, "very safe":** BCA: MS3101/C/D/15/1/2: SG to James Johnson, February 27, 1757.
105 **"East Country ships":** BCA: MS3101/C/D/9/3/1: SG to John Galton, August 31, 1760. See also MS3101/C/D/15/1/2: SG to John Galton, February 22, 1757; John Galton to SG, August 9, 1757; John Galton to SG, August 23, 1757.
105 **"not quite so good":** TNA: WO 47/49: OM, February 26, 1757, 217. See also WO 47/49: OM, January 7, 1757, 29, and February 5, 1757, 130–31.
105 **By April, barrel production:** TNA: WO 47/49: OM, March 5, 1757, 241–42, May 6, 1757, 440, June 3, 1757, 545–46, and June 7, 1757, 567–68; WO 47/50: OM, July 5, 1757, 9, August 5, 1757, 91, September 2, 1757, 164–65, October 8, 1757, 253–54, August 12, 1757, 113, October 14, 1757, 271–72, November 3 and 4, 1757, 309–10, and December 6, 1757, 386–87.
105 **"extremely well being":** TNA: WO 55/2: Surveyor General Charles Frederick to the Board, June 6, 1757, 83. See also WO 55/2: Abstract of proposals, June 14, 1757, [?]; WO 47/49: OM, June 14, 1757, 591–92; WO 47/49: OM, April 5, 1757, 363, and April 19, 1757, 392–93; WO 47/50: OM, September 9, 1757, 179–80, and November 18, 1757, 347–48; WO 47/51: OM, February 3, 1758, 114, March 3, 1758, 223, April 7, 1758, 351, April 14, 1758, 372, and May 5, 1758, 461; WO 55/2: Surveyor General to the Ordnance Board, October 28, 1757, 95.
106 **"second sort of barrel":** TNA: WO 47/51: OM, April 25, 1758, 421. The short land musket, originating around 1750, enabled the tactical mobility the British Army needed in this war. Darling, *Red Coat and Brown Bess,* 31. On complaints from Bengal, see Harding, *Smallarms of the East India Company,* 1:11.
106 **Farmer & Galton was the first:** TNA: WO 47/51: OM, June 3, 1758, 570–71.
106 **Markbee's reports improved:** TNA: WO 47/52: OM, August 3, 1758, 117, July 4, 1758, 12–13, October 24 and 25, 1758, 353, November 8, 1758, 393, and December 5, 1758, 449; WO 47/53: OM, January 12 and 13, 1759, 46; January 5, 1759, 21, February 3, 1759, 148, February 6, 1759, 160, and February 9, 1759, 165.
106 **"hasten the Barrel Makers":** TNA: WO 47/53: OM, January 19, 1759, 86.
107 **Markbee passed 6,602:** TNA: WO 47/53: OM, April 3, 1759, 393, May 4, 1759, 488, and June 2, 1759, 589; WO 47/54: OM, July 3, 1759, 8.
107 **"great want of money":** TNA: WO 47/53: OM, April 3, 1759, 399. Interest was not allowed on debentures. Dickson, *The Financial Revolution in England,* 398.
107 **"greatly distressed for":** TNA: WO 47/54: OM, September 15, 1759, 262. See also WO 47/54: OM, August 3, 1759, 126, and September 7, 1759, 244–45; WO 47/97: OM, June 12, 1781, 602, 606.
107 **"masters of the gunlock trade":** *Aris's Birmingham Gazette,* June 28, 1759, quoted in Rowlands, *Masters and Men,* 162–63.

107 **"best Swedish iron":** TNA: WO 47/54: OM, December 4, 1759, 464–65; Blackmore, *British Military Firearms,* 50.

107 **when Wood asked:** TNA: WO 47/54: OM, November 24, 1759, 436. See also WO 47/53: OM, January 12 and 13, 1759, 46, February 6, 1759, 161, March 27, 1759, 367–68, and June 19, 1759, 645.

108 **"He is no Barrel or":** TNA: WO 47/53: OM, February 20, 1759, 215, 221. See also WO 47/53: OM, March 9 and 10, 1759, 289.

108 **Wilson continued to appear:** TNA: WO 47/53: OM, May 2, 1759, 480, and May 18, 1759, 538; WO 47/54: OM, July 3, 1759, 4, and July 17, 1759, 67. Wilson supplied the office in the next war, too, but was never popular, perhaps because his workforce struggled to work strictly to pattern. His power within the company also guaranteed the board's antagonism. His son William partnered with him in 1755. Bailey, "The Wilsons."

108 **After an abysmal 1,664:** TNA: WO 47/55: OM, February 5, 1760, 103, February 14, 1760, 134, and March 4, 1760, 197–98.

108 **Hirst extracted a price hike:** TNA: WO 47/55: OM, April 25, 1760, 335.

108 **From May through December:** TNA: WO 47/56: OM, July 4, 1760, 20–21, August 5, 1760, 99–101, September 5, 1760, 179–80, October 3, 1760, 244–45, November 4, 1760, 351–52, and December 4, 1760, 415–16; WO 47/57: OM, January 9, 1761, 17–18, February 27, 1761, 128–29, March 6, 1761, 150–51, April 3, 1761, 211–12, May 8, 1761, 309–10, and June 5, 1761, 375–76; WO 47/58: OM, July 3, 1761, 6–7, August 4, 1761, 91–92, September 4, 1761, 175–76, October 6, 1761, 248–49, October 8, 1761, 256, and November 3, 1761, 320–21; WO 47/59: OM, January 8, 1762, 18, and January 9, 1762, 23–24.

108 **"frequently obliged to make":** TNA: WO 47/59: OM, June 22, 1762, 541. See also WO 47/59: OM, June 30, 1762, 560; WO 47/60: OM, July 6, 1762, 11. Thomas Jordan died in March 1762. *Aris's Birmingham Gazette,* March 29, 1762, 3. Edward Jordan died in July 1758.

108 **"did throughout all the War":** TNA: WO 47/61: OM, May 20, 1763, 322–24. See also WO 47/60: OM, December 17, 1762, 432, and November 10, 1762, 331; WO 47/61: OM, January 28, 1763, 55, and May 13, 1763, 299.

109 **"The contract work":** Blackmore, *British Military Firearms,* 50–57.

109 **Nearly 305,000 arms:** Bailey, *British Board of Ordnance Small Arms Contractors,* 19.

109 **"an eminent Gun-Barrel-Maker":** *Aris's Birmingham Gazette,* July 25, 1763, 3.

109 **They, along with Farmer:** Subscribers listed in *Aris's Birmingham Gazette,* issues of September–December 1765.

109 **"a very considerable":** *Aris's Birmingham Gazette,* April 7, 1766, 3.

109 **Four gun workers were:** Advertisement, *Aris's Birmingham Gazette,* June 17, 1765, 3. See TNA: WO 47/63: OM, February 3, 1764, 59, February 8, 1764, 78–79, April 11, 1764, 249–50, and April 13, 1764, 262; S. N. to *Aris's Gazette,* September 26, 1763, 1.

109 **Contractors busily maintained:** TNA: WO 47/63: OM, February 24, 1764, 115, 118, and June 29, 1764, 489–90; WO 47/64: OM, November 27, 1764, 203; WO 47/65: OM, April 4, 1766, 229; WO 47/66: OM, October 29, 1765, 177; WO 47/67: OM, January 17, 1766, 15, and April 29, 1766, 309; WO 47/68: OM, October 14, 1766, 116.

109 **Some became piece men:** See, for instance, TNA: WO 47/62: OM, June 23, 1763, 417, and November 4, 1763, 211; WO 47/63: OM, January 25, 1764, 28.

109 **"forged work" for locks:** TNA: WO 47/58: OM, August 25, 1761, 138; WO 47/60: OM, July 9, 1762, 23; WO 47/63: OM, March 5, 1764, 149–50; WO 47/64: OM, December 6, 1764, 250; WO 47/65: OM, January 7, 1765, 2; WO 47/67: OM, March 21, 1766, 199; WO 47/70: OM, July 21, 1767, 63; WO 47/72: OM, August 4, 1768, 48; WO 47/76: OM, March 9, 1770, 118; WO 47/83: OM, April 29, 1774, 238.

109 **Markbee viewed thousands:** TNA: WO 47/62: OM, July 15, 1763, 11, August 30, 1763, 81, September 6, 1763, 103–4, October 11, 1763, 161, 170, December 2, 1763, 272, September 1, 1763, 89; WO 47/63: OM, January 20, 1764, 20, March 2, 1764, 138, March 9, 1764, 157–58, March 20, 1764, 185, March 30, 1764, 205, April 3, 1764, 216, April 13, 1764, 260, May 17, 1764, 348–49, and June 5, 1764, 407; WO 47/64: OM, September 6, 1764, 149–51, and December 11, 1764, 250–51.

110 **"who would otherwise be":** TNA: WO 47/65: OM, January 8, 1765, 3. See also January 25, 1765, 37; WO 47/66: OM, August 27, 1765, 95; WO 47/63: OM, May 10, 1764, 330.

110 **"a great Number of":** TNA: WO 47/65: February 9, 1765, 73. See also April 25, 1765, 293.

110 **Farmer and Galton estimated:** UCL: Galton/1/1/9/5/22: Statement of profits in place inventory for 1765, signed by Farmer and Galton.

110 **For 1766, the Ordnance Office:** See TNA: WO 47/66: OM, March 21, 1766, 198, and April 8, 1766, 248; WO 47/70: OM, July 10, 1767, 34–35, December 1, 1767, 238; WO 47/71: OM, April 15, 1768, 195, and June 7, 1768, 278.

110 **The Brown Bess was:** Bailey, *British Board of Ordnance Small Arms Contractors*, 19.

110 **In 1769, Hirst:** TNA: WO 47/73: OM, April 27, 1769, 213, June 13, 1769, 301, and June 20, 1769, 316; WO 47/74: OM, August 30, 1769, 113, September 6, 1769, 121, September 27, 1769, 131, October 25, 1769, 147; WO 47/75: OM, February 2, 1770, 58, and March 16, 1770, 134.

110 **French Protestants heading:** TNA: WO 47/62: OM, November 21, 1763, 249.

110 **Settlers provoked tensions:** See Black, *Britain as a Military Power*, 155–59.

110 **In 1767, returning:** TNA: WO 47/70: OM, November 2, 1767, 193.

111 **Calcutta officials prayed:** Fort William to Court of Directors, September 29, 1763, *Fort William–India House Correspondence*, 3:512.

111 **its bill for small arms:** Bowen, *The Business of Empire*, 285.

111 **In 1768–69, nearly:** Blackmore, *British Military Firearms*, 57.

111 **The company was:** Harding, *Smallarms of the East India Company*, 1:9, 13–14, 23–24.

111 **"proceeded in getting up":** TNA: WO 47/74: OM, July 12, 1769, 17. See WO 47/75: OM, March 9, 1770, 119.

112 **"useless as they are":** TNA: WO 47/75: OM, March 30, 1770, 170.

112 **Only Grice succeeded:** TNA: WO 47/76: OM, November 3, 1770, 206.

112 **Farmer & Galton was still:** TNA: WO 47/77: OM, February 22, 1771, 157.

112 **burdening gunmakers with:** BCA: MS3101/D/1/4: SG, Draft statement, "Reason for an allowance of bad debts," [post 1772].

112 **it wanted forty thousand:** Harding, *Smallarms of the East India Company*, 1:17–19. Some of these London makers supplied the company for decades, earning career payments of £100,000. Suppliers for 1771–1856 are listed in Harding, 1:293–304. The company experimented with putting smallarms supply out to public tender rather than contracting with the Worshipful Company collectively, but in 1774 it reverted to the old system.

112 **When the American war started:** TNA: WO 47/87: OM, May 10, 1776, 418; WO 47/86: OM, October 10 and 11, 1775, 170.

112 **Lord Shelburne noted:** B. Smith, "The Galtons of Birmingham," 139.

112 **The Ordnance Office still:** See TNA: WO 47/72: OM, December 16, 1768, 222–23.

113 **"clamorous and riotery":** Thomas Hadley, advertisement, *Aris's Birmingham Gazette,* June 8, 1772, 1.

113 **"obscure and malignant Charge":** Samuel Galton, advertisement, *Aris's Birmingham Gazette,* July 13, 1772, 3.

113 **"no Answer at all":** Thomas Hadley, advertisement, *Aris's Birmingham Gazette,* August 3, 1772, 3.

113 **Hadley resorted to:** BCA: MS3101/D/3/4: Thomas Hadley, printed leaflet, "To the Public," [c. 1772].

113 **Galton refused to:** BCA: MS3101/D/3/3: Account by Samuel Galton, [c. 1773].

114 **He accused Galton:** BCA: MS3101/D/3/2: Depositions of witnesses, 1772.

114 **"lads of spirit":** BCA: MS3101/D/3/1: Summary of case brought before court, [c. 1772].

114 **The next year:** TNA: WO 47/82: OM, July 13, 1773, 50.

114 **"distress attending people":** SG, Draft statement, "Reason for an allowance of bad debts."

115 **Among the fifty to sixty:** Advertisement, *Aris's Birmingham Gazette*, August 2, 1773, 1; advertisement, *Aris's Birmingham Gazette,* November 22, 1773, 3.

115 **Galton unloaded the most:** TNA: WO 47/85: OM, March 24, 1775, 242, April 7, 1775, 282, April 21, 1775, 310–11, and May 16, 1775, 384.

115 **Galton, Willets, Grice:** TNA: WO 55/5: Warrants recorded for July 11, 1775, 34.

115 **Within days, thousands:** TNA: WO 46/9: Ordnance Board to Lord Dartmouth, July 14, 1775, and another of same date to John Boddington, 132–33; WO 47/86: OM, July 11, 1775, 11, and July 25 and 26, 1775, 49.

116 **"for any other contractor":** TNA: WO 47/86: OM, August 8 and 9, 1775, 91. Matthias Barker and Joseph Harris (then Jane, widow of Joseph) dissolved their partnership in April. Advertisement, *Aris's Birmingham Gazette*, March 23, 1775, in April 3, 1775, 3.

116 **tried to coax workmen:** TNA: WO 47/86: OM, October 10 and 11, 1775, 170; Harding, *Smallarms of the East India Company*, 1:21, 29.

116 **When bayonet makers were:** TNA: WO 47/89: OM, February 18, 1777, 208–9, and March 20 and 21, 1777, 352–53; WO 47/90: OM, December 9, 1777, 574–75 and December 20, 1777, 597–98; WO 47/91: OM, January 6 and 7, 1778, 11; Office of Ordnance, advertisement, December 10, 1777, in *Aris's Birmingham Gazette,* December 15, 1777, 2.

116 **"particularly what Locks":** TNA: WO 47/86: OM, October 10 and 11, 1775, 172.

116 **"rely upon further orders":** TNA: WO 47/86: OM, October 25 and 26, 1775, 198. See also October 10 and 11, 1775, 178.

116 **William Holden of Birmingham:** TNA: WO 47/87: OM, January 30, 1776, 49.

116 **"demands we may expect":** TNA: WO 46/10: George Townshend to Sir Jeffrey Amherst, April 13, 1776, 105–7.

116 **Galton won a contract:** D. Williams, "James Farmer and Samuel Galton," 125.

116 **Birmingham was prolific:** See, for instance, TNA: WO 47/90: OM, October 9, 1777, 354; WO 47/91: OM, January 6 and 7, 1778, 11.

116 **A French traveler:** Barthélemy Faujas de Saint-Fond, 1777, cited in Ashton, *Iron and Steel in the Industrial Revolution,* 136.

116 **daymen worked from:** TNA: WO 47/89: OM, March 10, 1777, 299, and March 14, 1777, 312; WO 47/90: OM, December 17, 1777, 592; WO 47/91: OM, June 24, 1778, 572; WO 47/92: OM: December 18, 1778, 433. William Gameson was also from America. December 22, 1778, 444.

116 **an "Emergency" measure:** TNA: WO 47/87: OM, April 10, 1776, 315, and April 24, 1776, 354, 359. It is not clear whether the office followed through. Bailey thinks not. "Liège Muskets in the British Army," 287.

117 **"Indian trading guns":** TNA: WO 47/88: OM, October 11, 1776, 161.

117 **more than twenty thousand:** TNA: WO 47/89: OM, May 22 and 23, 1777, 587; WO 47/88: OM, October 29, 1776, 217.

117 **petitioned in vain:** GL: MS5220/10: CM, February 28, 1776, 589; Harding, *Smallarms of the East India Company,* 1:14–15.

117 **"small weak ill-temper'd":** Fort William to Court of Directors, March 20, 1776, *Fort William–India House Correspondence,* 7:413. See also Court of Directors to Fort William, March 25, 1776, 7:145–46.

117 **"as a Company":** TNA: WO 46/11: Ordnance Board to Master General, February 20, 1778, 10–11. See also WO 47/87: OM, April 29 and 30, 1776, 385.

117 **"in the country":** TNA: WO 47/87: OM, May 10, 1776, 418.

117 **The board refused William Sharp's:** TNA: WO 47/88: OM, July 5, 1776, 4, July 9 and 10, 1776, [?], August 1, 1776, 61, and November 1, 1776, 244.

118 **"singly and not in connection":** TNA: WO 47/88: OM, November 22, 1776, 293–94, and December 3, 1776, 343.

118 **The office did take locks:** TNA: WO 47/89: OM, February 18, 1777, 202.

118 **It also raised lock prices:** TNA: WO 47/89: OM, March 18, 1777, 336, May 27, 1777, 620–21, and June 10, 1777, 684–85.

118 **By July, Galton, Willets:** TNA: WO 47/89: OM, June 24 and 25, 1777, 736. See also WO 47/89: OM, June 10, 1777, 679–80; WO 46/10: John Courtney to John Boddington, June 20, 1777, 239.

118 **The consequent penalty:** TNA: WO 47/101: OM, May 3, 1783, 438–40.

118 **For the moment:** TNA: WO 47/90: OM, July 2, 1777, 11, July 18, 1777, 85–86, July 25, 1777, 119–20, and August 7, 1777, 174.

118 **"in the joint names":** TNA: WO 47/90: OM, August 7, 1777, 176–77, August 22, 1777, 239–40, and August 29, 1777, 261–63. See also WO 47/90: OM, December 12, 1777, 585.

118 **it would reduce the costs:** Blackmore, *British Military Firearms,* 268.

118 **"no place to inspect":** TNA: WO 47/90: OM, October 9, 1777, 364–65.

119 **"other contractors endeavoring":** TNA: WO 47/90: OM, November 4 and 5, 1777, 431.

119 **"all the support":** TNA: WO 47/91: OM, January 27, 1778, 80, and February 2 and 3, 1778, 94–95. See also WO 47/90: OM, November 20, 1777, 508, December 17, 1777, 592, and December 20, 1777, 597; WO 47/91: OM, January 6 and 7, 1778, 11.

119 **"Dissatisfaction of the Contractors":** TNA: WO 46/11: Board of Ordnance to Master General, February 20, 1778, 10–11.

119 **"proceed . . . with Harmony":** TNA: WO 47/91: OM, February 24, 1778, 156.

119 **consultation with the office:** TNA: WO 47/91: OM, February 23, 1778, 149.

119   **The office allowed:** TNA: WO 47/91: OM, February 24, 1778, 152.
119   **"the length of time":** TNA: WO 47/91: OM, January 23, 1778, 65.
119   **When Galton complained:** TNA: WO 47/91: OM, February 10, 1778, 113, and February 13, 1778, 125. The office still avoided favoritism: William Henshaw's offer of ten thousand arms was refused on the grounds that he required ready money, which would result in an "undue preference of him to the other contractors." March 3, 1778, 170.
119   **"from time to time":** TNA: WO 47/101: OM, May 3, 1783, 438–40. See also WO 47/91: OM, March 6, 1778, 181–82, March 16 and 17, 1778, 208, and March 20, 1778, 225.
119   **Now it directed:** GL: MS5220/10: CM, April 9, 1778, 615–16; TNA: WO 47/91: OM, March 27, 1778, 255; Harding, *Smallarms of the East India Company,* 1:15. In 1807, the East India Company repaid the favor by leasing the Worshipful Company of Gunmakers some of its land for a barrel warehouse. MS05220/11: CM, September 28, 1807, 259, and October 29, 1807, 264–65.
120   **Birmingham lockmakers tried:** TNA: WO 47/92: OM, August 21, 1778, 177.
120   **Fitzherbert was authorized:** TNA: WO 47/90: OM, December 27, 1777, 616; WO 47/93: OM, March 12, 1779, 192; WO 47/92: OM, July 24, 1778, 94; WO 47/92: OM, November 26, 1778, 395.
120   **A viewer from:** TNA: WO 47/94: OM, July 22, 1779, 38, September 11, 1779, 169.
120   **"great deficiency of arms":** TNA: WO 46/12: T. Blomfield to George Crawford, [August 1780], and John Courtenay [for the Master General] to Mr. Boddington, August 10, 1780, [?]; WO 46/13: Memorial on Mr. Crawford's affair about gunpowder and small arms, n.d. [1780–82] [loose page in bound volume]; WO 47/94: OM, September 4, 1779, 146, October 26, 1779, 286, and November 13, 1779, 327. See also Blackmore, *British Military Firearms,* 62.
120   **Crawford later provided:** TNA: WO 47/92: OM, December 22, 1778, 447; WO 47/94: OM, July 29, 1779, 61.
120   **Crawford also gathered:** TNA: WO 47/95: OM, February 1, 1780, 95.
120   **"the Enemy were intending":** TNA: WO 46/11: Memorandum on the State of Fire-Arms, June 24, 1779, 109. See WO 46/11: John Courtenay [for the Master General] to John Boddington, June 23, 1779, 109. See also Bailey, "Liège Muskets in the British Army," 288, 293.
121   **Thus the office canceled:** TNA: WO 47/91: OM, March 10, 1778, 189–90, March 20, 1778, 224, and March 31, 1778, 269.
121   **It gave successive contracts:** TNA: WO 47/92: OM, July 3, 1778, 13, [c. July 11–13, 1778], 51, July 22, 1778, 74, September 9, 1778, 217–18, and October 16, 1778, 313; WO 47/93: OM, January 16, 1779, 30, 35, and April 15, 1779, 286; WO 47/94: OM, November 13, 1779, 326.
121   **Michael Memory, a setter-up:** TNA: WO 47/89: OM, February 6 and 7, 1777, 153. See also WO 47/92: OM, December 18, 1778, 434–35.
121   **Pratt proposed bayonets:** TNA: WO 47/93: OM, November 13, 1778, 360–66; WO 47/91: OM, May 5, 1778, 390–91. See also WO 47/78: OM, September 3, 1771, 83; WO 47/90: OM, August 29, 1777, 254, December 12, 1777, 581, and December 22, 1777, 607; WO 47/93: OM, January 8, 1779, 10, and January 12, 1779, 21.
121   **he did work valued at:** TNA: WO 47/94: December 31, 1779, 406.
121   **The Worshipful Company's new:** GL: MS5220/10: CM, November 24, 1778, 631–36.
121   **"flat and longer":** TNA: WO 47/91: OM, March 23, 1778, 234, and March 23 and 24, 1778, 246.
121   **It accepted Daniel Moore's offer:** TNA: WO 47/91: OM, March 23 and 24, 1778, 240, and June 19, 1778, 557 and 561; WO 47/92: OM, September 9, 1778, 217–18, and November 6, 1778, 347.
121   **Leonard of Lichfield:** TNA: WO 47/94: OM, April 11, 1780, 259.
121   **Hirst asked Hines:** TNA: WO 47/91: OM, April 27, 1778, 363.
122   **Galton was initially:** TNA: WO 47/91: OM, June 3, 1778, 505.
122   **Galton now struggled:** BCA: MS3101/C/D/15/15/4: SG to William Bird, August 21, 1780, and MS3101/C/D/15/15/5: August 24, 1780; MS3101/C/D/15/15/2: SG to Bird, August 17, 1780; MS3101/C/D/15/14/1: SG to John Pratt, August 20, 1780. See also TNA: WO 47/94: OM, October 26, 1779, 284; WO 47/93: OM, January 8, 1779, 13; WO 47/91: OM, June 19, 1778, 557; WO 47/92: OM, September 23, 1778, [261?].
122   **Army gunfire killed:** Rudé, "The Gordon Riots," 99.
122   **During the turmoil:** TNA: WO 47/96: OM, July 15, 1780, 605.
122   **"nothing but necessity":** T. Blomfield to George Crawford, [August 1780]; John Courtenay to John Boddington, August 10, 1780. See also TNA: WO 47/96: OM, August 12, 1780, 687–88.

122 **"sensible of the complaints":** TNA: WO 46/12: Memo sent to Mr. Courtenay to be laid before the Board, [August 1780], 137.

122 **London contractors had:** TNA: WO 47/95: OM, May 18, 1780, 361, and June 10, 1780, 426.

123 **would be "too hazardous":** TNA: WO 47/96: OM, July 29, 1780, 651.

123 **"for the sake of the men":** BCA: MS3101/C/D/15/15/4: SG to William Bird, August 21, 1780; MS3101/C/D/15/15/1: SG to Bird, August 15, 1780.

123 **"Such a medley":** BCA: MS3101/C/D/15/6: SG to William Bird, August 26 and 27, 1780. See MS3101/C/D/15/15/5: SG to Bird, August 24, 1780; MS3101/C/D/15/15/2: J. Nottage to Bird, August 17, 1780; MS3101/C/D/15/15/3: SG to Bird, August 17, 1780.

124 **Doors remained closed:** TNA: WO 47/96: OM, November 7, 1780, 888.

124 **Galton produced a new:** TNA: WO 47/97: OM, May 2, 1781, 466, and June 12, 1781, 606; WO 47/98: OM, November 1, 1781, 1132–33.

124 **The office put out:** TNA: WO 47/98: OM, December 19, 1781, 1276, December 27, 1781, 1294–95; WO 47/99: OM, February 7, 1782, 114; WO 47/100: OM, July 1, 1782, 3, July 17, 1782, 87, August 21, 1782, 225, October 11, 1782, 456, October 23, 1782, 492, and October 30, 1782, 512, 515; WO 55/9: Pelham to Ordnance Board, September 30, 1782, [1?]; WO 47/101: OM, March 17, 1783, [274–86].

124 **But many of the 76,000:** Blackmore, *British Military Firearms*, 268; Bailey, "Liège Muskets in the British Army," 294.

124 **"no more stores":** TNA: WO 47/101: OM, February 7, 1783, 158–59.

124 **"if any viewer is":** TNA: WO 47/101: OM, March 14, 1783, 272–73.

124 **The "bad custom":** TNA: WO 46/12: Ordnance Board to Master General, September 23, 1780, 162–63; WO 47/92: OM, December 5, 1778, 409, and October 9, 1778, 292.

125 **It summarily dismissed:** TNA: WO 47/96: OM, November 25, 1780, 935. The only Pratt contract after this was May 12, 1781. He was paid imprests: WO 47/98: OM, July 3, 1781, 691, and July 26, 1781, 795. See also D. Williams, "James Farmer and Samuel Galton," 132.

125 **the East India Company:** Harding, *Smallarms of the East India Company*, 1:30.

125 **In the second half:** Inikori, "The Import of Firearms into West Africa," 345.

125 **the trade's "whole existence":** Representation of Mr. John Whateley dated Birmingham 27 March 1788, 354. See also TNA: BT 6/12: Minutes, April 26, 1788, [?]; Henry Whateley to Matthew Boulton, April 11, 1788.

126 **"greatly and extensively":** Advertisement, *Aris's Birmingham Gazette,* May 18, 1789, 3.

126 **would be "highly improper":** Advertisement, *Aris's Birmingham Gazette,* May 25, 1789, 2.

126 **on the "present precarious":** TNA: C107/9: John Whateley to James Rogers, July 4, 1789.

126 **revolutionaries stormed Paris's Bastille:** Two years earlier, Shays' Rebellion, in the new United States of America, had also offered a lesson on the importance of government mastery of arms stores. The rebels clutched old guns, clubs, swords, and bludgeons as they faced militiamen likewise "not more than half armed." The conflict centered on control of the muskets in the Springfield, Massachusetts, arsenal. Sweeney, "Firearms, Militias, and the Second Amendment," 356.

126 **In 1789, Guillaume Foucault:** P. Jones, *Industrial Enlightenment,* 206. Boulton and John Fothergill founded Soho in the 1760s to produce countless ornamental wonders, including buckles, japanned ware, ormolu, and silverware.

126 **The next year, France:** The standards imposed through inspection and proofing were, as in Birmingham, continually reformulated as merchants and artisans subverted them. State coercion played a part. Alder, *Engineering the Revolution,* 169–74. As in England, overlap between civilian and military production made the process difficult.

127 **In 1792, Saint-Étienne's:** Alder, *Engineering the Revolution,* 194, 218–20. In 1793, the government got 6,800 muskets from the city. As war began, wealthy citizens seized the Lyon government, which administered Saint-Étienne, days before the National Convention fell to the Jacobins. The defiant Lyonnais sent a battalion to Saint-Étienne to secure guns and the local government against Jacobins. The French state regained control over gun production by reasserting authority over local government structures and monopolizing purchases. It aligned itself with the artisans who had become pivotal in municipal affairs.

127 **When the news emerged:** *Aris's Birmingham Gazette,* November 14, 1791, 3; July 2, 1792, 3; *Aris's Birmingham Gazette,* October 29, 1792, cited in Money, *Experience and Identity,* 229–30; Goodwin,

The Friends of Liberty, 243, 254. In the end, the radicals opted to spend the subscription Maxwell initiated on shoes for the republican armies, rather than arms.

127 **In a House of Commons:** PP: *Journals of the House of Commons* XXXIV, December 28, 1792, 224; Money, *Experience and Identity*, 229–30.

127 **"they set to work":** TNA: C107/10: SG to James Rogers, June 23 and 27, 1792; H. P. Whateley to James Rogers, June 27, 1792, and November 26, 1792. See also William Grice to Rogers, June 27, 1792.

127 **"very full of Orders":** TNA: HO 42/23/88: Memorandum from Brooke (attorney) to Home Office, October [18?], 1792, 203–4.

127 **three hundred thousand from:** TNA: HO 42/23/83: Memorandum, 1792, 193. See also HO 42/23/84: Memorandum recording information about the export of arms to France, December 8, 1792, 194–95.

128 **Galton and Whateley did make:** See TNA: HO 42/29, e.g., 42/29/52, for accounts of Galton's and Whateley's sales of French-pattern guns to the Treasury, March 20, 1794, 130–31; HO 42/28/67: Galton to Evan Nepean, undersecretary of the Home Office, January 28, 1794, 155–56; HO 42/48/66: John Whateley to Nepean, January 28, 1794, 153–54.

128 **Brooke alleged that:** TNA: HO 42/22/121: John Brooke, Birmingham, November 8, 1792, 316–17.

128 **Brooke grew paranoid:** TNA: HO 42/22/74: John Brooke to Evan Nepean, October 27, 1792, from Birmingham, 190–92, enclosing David Blair to John Wallis, October 27, 1792.

128 **"I should not wonder":** TNA: HO 42/23/86: John Hudson to William Wilberforce, 200.

128 **The "old Gentleman":** TNA: HO 42/22/148: John Mason to HO, reporting information from Galton and others in Birmingham, November 14, 1792, 376–77.

129 **"The Arms made here":** HO 42/22/149: SG to Evan Nepean, November 14, 1792, 378–79.

129 **The Home Office deputed:** Collins was possibly part of the Birmingham military contracting world. In 1783, William Collins, in Birmingham, patented a method for making ship bolts (chap. 4). J. Harris, *The Copper King*, 558–62.

129 **"pursued the Object":** TNA: HO 42/23/93: William Collins, Birmingham, December 4, 1792, 214–15.

129 **"considerable quantities of arms":** TNA: HO 42/23/146: William Collins to Thomas Williams, Home Office, December 12, 1792, 343–45. The Levellers were a radical group who called for abolition of the monarchy, social and agrarian reforms, and religious freedom during the English Civil War.

130 **"the Manufacturer may not":** TNA: HO 42/23/92: John Hurd to Thomas Williams, Home Office, December 3, 1792, 212–13.

130 **"The government never interferes":** [Southey], *Letters from England,* 2:60–61.

131 **"Decline in the Gun Trade":** *Aris's Birmingham Gazette,* May 13, 1793, 3.

131 **As the Continent closed:** P. Jones, *Industrial Enlightenment,* 45–47.

131 **Advertisements promised "constant work":** Advertisement, *Aris's Birmingham Gazette,* February 18, 1793, 3; advertisement for Edward Payton, gunmaker, Shrewsbury, June 24, 1793, *Aris's Birmingham Gazette,* 3; advertisement, *Aris's Birmingham Gazette,* July 8, 1793, 3.

131 **the British army stood:** Cole, *Arming the Royal Navy,* 5.

131 **Volunteer units numbered:** Colley, *Britons,* 287.

131 **When war began:** Chew, *Arming the Periphery,* 64.

131 **Nock, in London:** Bailey and Harding, "From India to Waterloo," 49.

132 **"everything that could induce":** Quoted in Blackmore, *British Military Firearms,* 132–33.

132 **"who do not require the same":** TNA: HO/50/369: Richmond to Dundas, October 11, 1793, quoted in Harding, *Smallarms of the East India Company,* 1:30.

132 **could not work "to the pattern":** TNA: HO/50/371: Richmond to Dundas, January 24, 1794, quoted in Glover, *Peninsular Preparation,* 54.

132 **By the end of 1794:** Blackmore, *British Military Firearms,* 133.

133 **the Ordnance Office deemed:** Glover, *Peninsular Preparation,* 49–51.

133 **with its forces expanding:** B. Collins, *War and Empire,* 467.

133 **The company's cash:** Blackmore, *British Military Firearms,* 133–36; Harding, *Smallarms of the East India Company,* 1:31–32. In 1800, it supplied the Ordnance Office forty thousand muskets from Germany (while Ordnance officials also bought up guns in Hamburg and Copenhagen). Prussia withdrew from the war in 1795, making Central Europe a possible arms market for Britain.

133 **It also sold the Ordnance:** The company also supplied manpower and other financial and material resources. It exported iron, muskets, ordnance, copper, and textiles to maintain Britain's economic strength; imported food and gunpowder; transported troops to the West Indies; funded troops in India; and paid duties on Asian imports. Its accounts with the state were only settled in 1822. Knight, *Britain Against Napoleon*, 393.

133 **particularly for foreign units:** B. Collins, *War and Empire*, 114. Regular British Army troops got short land muskets; India-patterns went to Volunteers and militia; and trade and foreign arms went to foreign troops in British pay. Bailey and Harding, "From India to Waterloo," 54.

133 **It was increasingly seen:** Quoted in Bowen, "Mobilising Resources for Global Warfare," 108–10.

134 **"Checque upon the":** TNA: WO 46/24: Secretary of the Board of Ordnance (Crew) to Hadden, July 25, 1794, quoted in Blackmore, *British Military Firearms*, 271.

134 **a "loyal subject":** TNA: HO 42/30/71: Bristol subject to William Pitt, May 21, 1794, 169–80.

134 **the Home Office received:** TNA: HO 42/36/135: Acting Magistrate, West Riding, to Home Office, November 9, 1795, 284–85.

134 **"amalgam of private capitalism":** Alder, *Engineering the Revolution*, 329. See also 119, 255–58, 284–92.

134 **the Spanish government also:** Spain's original arms makers in Guipúzcoa had been situated close to iron and wood resources near the "traditional enemy's frontier" and fell under French control—the very risk that had driven diffusion of the British arms industry. Basque artisans from the occupied villages were moved to Oviedo. La Force, "The Supply of Muskets and Spain's War of Independence."

134 **"for the erecting and repairing":** Quoted in M. Smith, *Harpers Ferry Armory and the New Technology*, 28. The contract system was even more unreliable there.

135 **Its first superintendent:** Joseph Perkin left for America in 1774, finding work in Virginia "chiefly at Gunlocks" before setting up a gun shop in Philadelphia. He made arms for private and public patrons and inspected military stores before his assignment to Harpers Ferry. M. Smith, *Harpers Ferry Armory and the New Technology*, 38.

135 **The goal of interchangeable:** The artisans were unlikely to suggest substitution of machinery for their labor, and the social and political position of their managers depended on their loyalty. M. Smith, *Harpers Ferry Armory and the New Technology*, 84.

135 **Gunmakers and the office:** Advertisements in *Aris's Birmingham Gazette*, September 1, 1794, 3; November 3, 1794, 3; January 5, 1795, 3; January 26, 1795, 3; March 9, 1795, 3; Ordnance Office Notice, *Aris's Birmingham Gazette*, March 14, 1796, 1.

135 **Ordnance viewers persuaded:** Blackmore, *British Military Firearms*, 134.

135 **The office tapped:** Bailey, *British Board of Ordnance Small Arms Contractors*, 58.

135 **Office viewers staffed:** Parsons, *Observations on the Manufacture of Fire-Arms for Military Purposes*, 32. Within a few years, the volume of work exceeded the new proofhouse's capacity.

136 **Whole nations were pitted:** Parsons, *Observations on the Manufacture of Fire-Arms for Military Purposes*, 23–24.

136 **the Ordnance Office toyed:** Blackmore, *British Military Firearms*, 268; Goodman, "The Birmingham Gun Trade," 411.

136 **The Ordnance Office's vast stores:** Parsons, *Observations on the Manufacture of Fire-Arms for Military Purposes*, 14, 20.

136 **A hundred thousand:** Glover, *Peninsular Preparation*, 56–58.

136 **"ever prepared with warlike stores":** Parsons, *Observations on the Manufacture of Fire-Arms for Military Purposes*, 25 (quoting Baron Dupin).

136 **Contracts for stocking:** Blackmore, *British Military Firearms*, 138–39, 268–69.

137 **The Ordnance Office secured:** Glover, *Peninsular Preparation*, 60.

137 **The decade 1804–15:** Chew, *Arming the Periphery*, 64.

137 **These regulations resembled:** Beckert, *Empire of Cotton*, 43–45.

137 **The company mimicked:** Bowen, *The Business of Empire*, 285–86; Bailey and Harding, "From India to Waterloo," 55.

137 **In 1805, it created:** Bailey, *British Military Longarms*, 11. These mills had supplied rough plate for the Royal Armouries at Greenwich in the seventeenth century and tools for road construction in Scotland in the early eighteenth century.

137 **Birmingham workers staffed:** Knight, *Britain Against Napoleon*, 373. It only began producing in 1808.

137 **The factory was designed:** D. Williams, *The Birmingham Gun Trade*, 43, 84.

138 **"the greatest, and perhaps":** PP: *Journals of the House of Commons* LX, February 28, 1805, 100.

138 **"shut from the Market":** Blackmore, *British Military Firearms*, 139.

138 **"an immense demand":** BCA: MS3101/C/D/10/65/1: Richard Rathbone to John Howard Galton, October 4, 1807.

138 **a "contractors' cartel":** D. Williams, *The Birmingham Gun Trade*, 45–46.

138 **"in their own country":** Behagg, "Mass Production without the Factory," 10–11.

138 **the office donated:** Blackmore, *British Military Firearms*, 140.

138–39 **The committee renegotiated:** Behagg, "Mass Production without the Factory," 11–12.

139 **the general erosion of:** Thompson, *The Making of the English Working Class*, 252–53. Artisans reacted vigorously to the repeal, regarding the "mystery"—the skill they conveyed to an apprentice—as property.

139 **If a man bound himself:** Behagg, "Mass Production without the Factory," 12.

139 **According to one embittered:** Deakin, *Plain Narrative of the Circumstances That Have Occurred in the Transactions*, 22–23.

140 **A Prussian in town:** D. Williams, *The Birmingham Gun Trade*, 31–32.

140 **In 1811, the French:** Simond, *Journal of a Tour and Residence in Great Britain*, 120.

140 **Small workshops coexisted:** These large units controlled the credit and marketing facilities the small firms used. Hudson, *The Industrial Revolution*, 121–26.

140 **An English observer:** Richard Lovell Edgworth, quoted in P. Jones, *Industrial Enlightenment*, 39–40.

140 **"destined to supply":** A. Smith, *The Wealth of Nations*, 4, 14, 19.

141 **Birmingham's small workshops:** Concentration of market power in fewer firms was not the measure of modern industrial organization. See M. Berg, "Factories, Workshops and Industrial Organisation," 126–27, 136–37.

141 **Machinery, the contractors' cartel:** Behagg, "Mass Production without the Factory," 2, 9.

141 **The town produced:** D. Williams, *The Birmingham Gun Trade*, 43, 45–46, 84.

141 **The Ordnance India-pattern:** Harding, *Smallarms of the East India Company*, 1:32.

141 **Britain supplied its own:** Parsons, *Observations on the Manufacture of Fire-Arms for Military Purposes*, 23–24; PP: Accounts and Papers, 1806, 12:399, 4, and 12:443, 4. In 1808, Spain was desperate for muskets for the mass army it was raising against French occupation. Because of the Ordnance Office monopoly on purchases in Britain, the British government supplied Spain arms as grants-in-aid, purchasing the arms on its own account. Fearing dependency and indebtedness, Spain tried belatedly to build factories and diffuse gunmaking, but shortage of materials and skill, plus occupation, undermined those efforts. La Force, "The Supply of Muskets and Spain's War of Independence."

141 **"independent and mighty":** Parsons, *Observations on the Manufacture of Fire-Arms for Military Purposes*, 24.

141 **"put in execution":** Baron Dupin, quoted in Parsons, *Observations on the Manufacture of Fire-Arms for Military Purposes*, 13–14.

141 **France's ten state-controlled:** D. Williams, *The Birmingham Gun Trade*, 43; Hutton, *The History of Birmingham* (1835), 180–81; Goodman, "On the Progress of the Small Arms Manufacture," 501–2; Parsons, *Observations on the Manufacture of Fire-Arms for Military Purposes*, 12, 16, 22. Glover says France produced more than Britain from 1803 to 1815, citing Dupin, *Military Force of Great Britain* (1822), 2:175, which gives total French production of muskets, carbines, rifles, and pistol pairs at 3.9 million and British at 3.1 million. *Peninsular Preparation*, 47n4.

142 **The office itself grew:** Morriss, *The Foundations of British Maritime Ascendancy*, 190, 193–95, 221–22; Cole, *Arming the Royal Navy*, 7. Throughout the country, the office employed a much larger number.

142 **When Midlands ironmasters:** Birch, *The Economic History of the British Iron and Steel Industry*, 54.

142 **The town came together:** *Aris's Birmingham Gazette*, March 22, 1813, quoted in J. Langford, *A Century of Birmingham Life*, 2:326–27.

142 **Parliament made proving:** B. Smith, "The Galtons of Birmingham," 139.

143 **The office ordered:** Bailey and Nie, *English Gunmakers*, 21.
143 **Britain signed a treaty:** Parsons, *Observations on the Manufacture of Fire-Arms for Military Purposes*, 14, 24, 99. The French government imported barrels. Some gunmakers nevertheless, at great risk and expense, shipped arms to neutral ports for reshipment to South America, causing diplomatic strife.
143 **Thousands who had:** Hutton, *The History of Birmingham* (1835), 180–81.
143 **Many "industrious manufacturers":** *Aris's Birmingham Gazette*, April 29, 1816, quoted in J. Langford, *A Century of Birmingham Life*, 2:336.
144 **"properly roused to":** *Aris's Birmingham Gazette*, May 6, 1816, quoted in J. Langford, *A Century of Birmingham Life*, 2:336.
144 **"so many gentlemen who":** Quoted in J. Langford, *A Century of Birmingham Life*, 2:336–37.
144 **"the same proportion":** Parsons, *Observations on the Manufacture of Fire-Arms for Military Purposes*, 88–89.
144 **"severe privation" caused:** BCA: MS3101/C/D/10/9/64: SGII to Tertius Galton, Howard, and Hubert Galton, January 30, 1819.
144 **The Bengal government's suggestion:** Harding, *Smallarms of the East India Company*, 1:29.
145 **French imperial demand:** Alder, *Engineering the Revolution*, 128, 175, 184; Mokyr, "Technological Change," 33. The Dutch case offers a fascinating point of comparison, as does the Ottoman Empire, another land of partnerships in which state functions were "outsourced." Yaycioglu, *Partners of the Empire*.

Chapter Four: The State, War, and Industrial Revolution

146 **These distinguished neighbors:** The group first formed in 1765 at Matthew Boulton's home. Porter, *The Creation of the Modern World*, 427–28.
147 **This was why:** M. Brown, *Firearms in Colonial America*, 372–76.
147 **Bacon would have been familiar:** Wallace, *The Social Context of Innovation*, 7, 25, 28, 101.
147 **The Royal Brass Foundry:** P. Langford, *A Polite and Commercial People*, 634–35.
148 **tweaking was the driving force:** Particular engineering feats were perhaps less important than application of ingenuity over a wide area of economic activity—unpatented microinventions. See especially Mokyr and Meinsenzahl, "The Rate and Direction of Invention in the British Industrial Revolution."
148 **Iron furniture was:** M. Brown, *Firearms in Colonial America*, 228.
148 **tested how lacquered:** TNA: WO 47/38: OM, July 9 and 10, 1751, 8. All three rusted the bayonets.
148 **"stronger than the common":** TNA: WO 47/46: OM, December 23, 1755, 560–61.
148 **the Small Gun Office:** TNA: WO 47/71: OM, February 8, 1768, 64, February 12, 1768, 72, and February 15, 1768, 75.
148 **"safe method of making":** TNA: WO 46/10: George Townshend to Jeffrey Amherst, April 13, 1776, 105–7.
148 **the clockmaker Benjamin Huntsman:** Richards, "The Birmingham Gun Manufactory of Farmer and Galton," 104.
149 **Diderot's *Encyclopédie* of the 1750s:** D. Williams, *The Birmingham Gun Trade*, 29.
149 **Gunsmiths lured French:** Alder, *Engineering the Revolution*, 145.
149 **A Birmingham gunsmith:** Bailey and Nie, *English Gunmakers*, 21. The technique was still in use in 1770.
149 **He was allowed to patent:** TNA: WO 47/88: OM, November 22, 1776, 292. See WO 47/89: OM, February 4, 1777, 136; Blackmore, *British Military Firearms*, 71–72, 81–83.
149 **When John Pratt:** TNA: WO 47/89: OM, May 1 and 2, 1777, 503–4; WO 47/90: OM, December 20, 1777, 597; WO 47/91: OM, January 13, 1778, 30.
149 **The Ordnance Board let:** TNA: WO 47/94: OM, September 21, 1779, 193.
149 **Sir John Burgoyne:** TNA: WO 47/98: OM, October 4, 1781, 1054, and October 13, 1781, 1085, 1088.
149 **a "screwless lock":** Blackmore, *British Military Firearms*, 87–89.
149 **Nock was experimenting:** TNA: WO 47/102: OM, October 22, 1783, 448.
149 **He relied on a design:** D. Williams, *The Birmingham Gun Trade*, 56.
150 **"jigging the Barrel":** TNA: WO 55/11: James Luttrell to Ordnance Board, June 25, 1784, 147–49.

150 **He also instructed:** TNA: WO 55/11: James Luttrell to Ordnance Board, June 30, 1784, [151?].

150 **paid Durs Egg:** TNA: WO 55/11: James Luttrell to Ordnance Board, July 13, 1784, 155.

150 **"eminent compass maker":** *Aris's Birmingham Gazette,* May 24, 1784, 3.

150 **Soon Nock improved on:** M. Brown, *Firearms in Colonial America,* 372–76; Morriss, *The Foundations of British Maritime Ascendancy,* 194.

150 **some of Nock's innovations:** Blackmore, *British Military Firearms,* 136–37.

150 **an important supporter of:** See Millburn, "The Office of Ordnance and the Instrument-Making Trade," 292; TNA: WO 47/70: OM, August 25, 1767, 120–21; Timmins, *The Resources, Products, and Industrial History of Birmingham and the Midland Hardware District,* 533.

150 **Some instruments were:** TNA: WO 47/20A: OM, n.d. [1714–21?], 22 or 65.

151 **"very careful and proper person":** TNA: WO 47/83: OM, May 17, 1774, 282–84.

151 **The standard English lock:** M. Brown, *Firearms in Colonial America,* 376.

151 **Henry Osborne of Birmingham:** Blackmore, *British Military Firearms,* 115.

151 **Between 1806 and 1817:** Stephens, ed., *The Victoria History of the County of Warwick,* 7:96–97; *RSCSA,* 172–73; N. Brown, *British Gunmakers,* 2:391; Behagg, "Mass Production without the Factory," 10; Bailey and Nie, *English Gunmakers,* 20; D. Williams, *The Birmingham Gun Trade,* 41–42; Holtzapffel, *Turning and Mechanical Manipulation,* appendix T, 965–66.

152 **When he set his:** Goodman, "The Birmingham Gun Trade," 389.

152 **Incremental innovations maximized:** The Scottish minister and sportsman Alexander Forsyth invented the percussion lock while tinkering with his flintlock. He shared his experiments with the Tower in 1806–7 but was turned out by a regime change there just then. He patented his lock, fighting off infringements for years. During the Napoleonic Wars, a shift in the standard weapon was difficult; the project was shelved until 1834. Ffoulkes, *Arms & Armament,* 54–56.

152 **Birmingham button makers:** D. Williams, *Birmingham Gun Trade,* 27.

152 **One of them, Michael Alcock:** Alder, *Engineering the Revolution,* 235–36, 266, 321. The labor force for the Manufacture of Paris drew from local metal tradesmen, most of whom did not have gunsmithing skills, unlike their Birmingham counterparts. French welding, iron forging, and hardware manufacture were also poorer in Saint-Étienne.

152 **the French brought Alcock:** J. Harris, *Industrial Espionage and Technology Transfer,* chaps. 8 and 9, esp. 66, 208. Alcock went to France at the end of 1755 after going bankrupt. Many of the buttons were for military uniforms.

152 **"We can only be":** Jabez Maud Fisher, quoted in D. Williams, "James Farmer and Samuel Galton," 125.

153 **French spies in the 1780s:** P. Jones, *Industrial Enlightenment,* 152.

153 **The French launched their:** Alder, *Engineering the Revolution,* 235–36.

153 **Many of the improvements in lathes:** M. Brown, *Firearms in Colonial America,* 380.

153 **John Wyatt had experience:** See M. Berg, "In Pursuit of Luxury," 131, 137–38.

154 **Birmingham's William Osborne:** Gill, *History of Birmingham,* 1:98, 295.

154 **Surplus government musket:** Mokyr, *The Enlightened Economy,* 136. By 1829, two hundred public gas companies, plus private installations, existed.

154 **Small-arms manufacture was:** See also O'Brien, "The Contributions of Warfare with Revolutionary and Napoleonic France to the Consolidation and Progress of the British Industrial Revolution," 47.

154 **The first reverberatory furnace:** John, "War and the English Economy," 330.

154 **The Lloyds adopted the Darby:** Wallace, *The Social Context of Innovation,* 87, 97. John Kelsall, Lloyd's clerk, later served at Dolgyn furnace, which was connected to the Darbys of Coalbrookdale. His service ensured continuing close contact between Lloyd and Darby. Raistrick, *Quakers in Science and Industry,* 113–16.

154 **The War of the Austrian:** Hudson, *The Industrial Revolution,* 52, 56–57.

154 **Gunmakers' fussiness stimulated:** Richards, "The Birmingham Gun Manufactory of Farmer and Galton," 100–108.

154 **"made of the best sort":** TNA: WO 55/2: Charles Frederick to Ordnance Board, June 6, 1757, [83?]; WO 47/54: OM, December 4, 1759, 464–65.

155 **his sons John and William:** William Wilkinson set up a cannon foundry in Nantes before the American war, directing construction of a great coke-iron-making plant at Le Creusot. Knight, *Britain Against Napoleon,* 37; Chaloner, "Isaac Wilkinson, Potfounder."

155 **Darby and John Wilkinson:** Raistrick, *Quakers in Science and Industry*, 141, 344.
155 **"unexpected obstacles" in the way:** TNA: WO 46/10: George Townshend to Sir Jeffrey Amherst, April 13, 1776, 105–7.
155 **"This country is never":** TNA: WO 46/10: George Townshend to Sir Jeffrey Amherst, April 30, 1776, 122–23.
155 **mathematical instrument maker:** TNA: WO 47/88: OM, October 29, 1776, 217; WO 47/43: OM, January 16, 1754, 6.
155 **"unintentionally nourish" developments:** Wallace, *The Social Context of Innovation*, 7–8, 25, 28.
156 **canceled the patent:** P. Langford, *A Polite and Commercial People*, 634–35; Namier, "Anthony Bacon, M.P., an Eighteenth-Century Merchant," 20, 47–50.
156 **"cannot be exaggerated":** Roll, *An Early Experiment in Industrial Organisation*, 25, 157–59. Wilkinson bored the first eighteen-inch cylinder for the engine in April 1775. Darby also cast engine cylinders.
156 **he made the main engine:** R. Brown, "Guns Carried on East Indiamen," 19.
156 **He originated the Ordnance Survey:** Morriss, *The Foundations of British Maritime Ascendancy*, 194–95, 200–1.
156 **Under the Earl of Chatham:** Knight, *Britain Against Napoleon*, 41–47.
156 **When walnut supply:** Blackmore, *British Military Firearms*, 139.
157 **His first breakthrough:** J. Harris, *The British Iron Industry*, 39–40. The iron industry shifted to coal in response to changing fuel prices rather than because of a specific technological breakthrough. Coal was cheap in the Midlands and was used to reheat wrought iron to work into various goods. Over time, it was employed further back in the chain of production.
157 **a "plain Englishman":** Joseph Black to James Watt, 1784, quoted in Coleman and Macleod, "Attitudes to New Techniques," 602–3.
157 **Wilkinson installed fourteen:** Birch, *The Economic History of the British Iron and Steel Industry*, 35–36, 43. Cort heated pig iron in a reverberatory furnace, then puddled it to bring impurities to the surface. It was then squeezed and pressed by cylinders in a rolling mill.
157 **In the 1790s:** Shenhav, "At a Gun Point," 27.
158 **Benjamin Farmer was moved:** In Shropshire, a decade earlier, he had tried to manufacture bar iron by the "fire of pitt coal only." An old man had shown him a process for extracting sulfur from the coal, but the resulting iron was not of uniform quality. Benjamin dreamt up a way to purify the iron by processing its pure and impure parts separately so that "Iron of very different qualities . . . might be produced from the same Pigg." FHL: Temp MSS 403/1/2/1/56: Benjamin Farmer to Mary Lloyd, May 21, 1797.
158 **The Cort process freed:** Evans et al., "Baltic Iron and the British Iron Industry," 662.
158 **Foreign iron prices:** Ashton, *Iron and Steel in the Industrial Revolution*, 143. See also O'Brien, "The Contributions of Warfare with Revolutionary and Napoleonic France to the Consolidation and Progress of the British Industrial Revolution," 52–54. Britain's fraught relations with Russia were also important; Russians raised the terms on which they sold iron abroad.
158 **Coal-rich areas like:** In 1790, there were twenty-one coke blast furnaces in operation in South Staffordshire, fifteen in Wolverhampton. In 1806, forty-two furnaces were built in Staffordshire. G. Allen, *The Industrial Development of Birmingham*, 20–21. At first, the iron produced by Cort's process appeared too weak for arms making. Later investigations into the chemical properties of the ore improved its strength, enabling the use of puddled iron in arms. M. Brown, *Firearms in Colonial America*, 380.
158 **They, too, multiplied:** John, "War and the English Economy," 334.
158 **"Golden toys or ormolu":** Matthew Boulton, 1796, quoted in P. Jones, *Industrial Enlightenment*, 228.
158 **Thomas Malthus claimed:** Quoted in Crouzet, "The Impact of the French Wars on the British Economy," 209.
158 **Other big purchasers:** Shenhav, "At a Gun Point," 26.
159 **worth "unremitting exertions":** Deakin to Mulgrave, October 27, 1814, and Deakin to Ordnance Board, August 18, 1814, in Deakin, *Plain Narrative of the Circumstances That Have Occurred in the Transactions*, 16 and 24–26.
159 **the period's single most:** See, for instance, Duffy, "The Foundations of British Naval Power," 58–59, 62. Copper sheathing was first suggested in 1708. In 1761, the first naval ship bottom was sheathed. The sheathing was removed in 1766 because of its damage to the ship's iron bolts. Copper was tried again in 1769.

159 **early trials of brass sheathing:** J. Harris, "Copper and Shipping in the Eighteenth Century," 552. William Champion earned many patents. Raistrick, *Quakers in Science and Industry*, 193.

159 **In 1783, technicians:** Knight, *Britain Against Napoleon*, 36–37; J. Harris, *Industrial Espionage and Technology Transfer*, 271.

159 **partner, John Westwood:** *Aris's Birmingham Gazette*, January 17, 1780, 3.

159 **he had himself appointed:** Upon his death, he left half a million pounds. It was Boulton and other Birmingham men who accused Williams of monopolistic practices in 1799, prompting the inquiry.

160 **His innovations built on:** Knight, *Britain Against Napoleon*, 170–71, 320–21, 353.

160 **For this, Bentham worked:** Ibid., 321, 376–80, 472–73; Knight and Wilcox, *Sustaining the Fleet*, 15–16. The Admiralty also sent Samuel Bentham to Russia in 1805 to oversee building of British warships there. There he built a wooden Panopticon to manage thousands of unskilled workers operating machinery. Samuel also set the manufacture of navy biscuits on a production-line basis. Maudslay's factory at Lambeth set new standards of precision engineering using lathes but also made steam engines; he sold one to the Woolwich Arsenal in 1809.

161 **Boulton puzzled over:** P. Jones, *Industrial Enlightenment*, 89.

162 **In 1775, the Society:** *Aris's Birmingham Gazette*, December 25, 1775, 3.

162 **This is the primary:** Mathias, *The Transformation of England*, 65–66, 82–83.

162 **This community also:** See, for instance, BCA: MS3782/12/27/102: SGII to Matthew Boulton (and James Watt), [1782].

162 **"culture of apartness":** P. Jones, *Industrial Enlightenment*, 187–88.

162 **a range of devices:** Pearson, *The Life, Letters and Labours of Francis Galton*, 1:43–44, 47.

163 **He collected information:** Uglow, *The Lunar Men*, 352. Erasmus Darwin published some of his work in 1791, and Galton himself in 1799.

163 **He was a subscriber:** P. Jones, *Industrial Enlightenment*, 75.

163 **The Scotsman James Keir:** Ibid., 123–24, 230.

163 **He held trials:** J. Harris, "Copper and Shipping in the Eighteenth Century," 555–62.

164 **"Knowledge is Power":** SGII to Howard Galton, February 10, 1811, quoted in P. Jones, *Industrial Enlightenment*, 18–19 and 218.

164 **the town outdid:** P. Jones, *Industrial Enlightenment*, 19, 39.

165 **"fresh flow of new enterprises":** Ashton, *Iron and Steel in the Industrial Revolution*, 136–37.

165 **but also "national security":** Hutton, *An History of Birmingham* (1781), 64.

165 **naval dockyards employed:** Morriss, *The Foundations of British Maritime Ascendancy*, 193–95, 200–1.

165 **The 1,500 workers:** TNA: WO 46/10: George Townshend to the Ordnance Board, in Townshend to Amherst, April 23, 1777, 217–24.

166 **The Victualling Office ran:** M. Anderson, *War and Society in Europe*, 153.

166 **The Crowleys' nail manufactory:** Flinn, *Men of Iron*, 44.

166 **He wrote in 1705:** Ibid., 147–48, 253–54. Crowley brought workers who made nails in home smithies together into a single unit to supervise them. Each nail was still made separately by hand. He wanted consistent high quality for the cost advantage.

166 **the private sector outproduced the state:** Knight, *Britain Against Napoleon*, 357.

166 **Averting invasion involved:** O'Brien, "The Contributions of Warfare with Revolutionary and Napoleonic France to the Consolidation and Progress of the British Industrial Revolution," 35.

167 **roughly 80 percent:** O'Brien, *Power with Profit*, 12–13.

167 **Arms and ammunition:** O'Brien, "The Impact of the Revolutionary and Napoleonic War," 367.

167 **British military expenditures:** O'Brien, "Political Preconditions for the Industrial Revolution," 135.

167 **the Cornish tin industry:** D. Jones, *War and Economy in the Age of William III*, 89–90. Mention of such sales tended to depress prices abroad, so little came of these efforts. See also Craig, *The Mint*, 208, 216.

167 **cannonball casting in Sussex:** Raistrick, *Dynasty of Iron Founders*, 100.

167 **it languished from:** John, "War and the English Economy."

167 **the Sitwells of Derbyshire:** Ashton, *Iron and Steel in the Industrial Revolution*, 195.

167 **"made a mint":** Porter, *English Society in the Eighteenth Century*, 211–13.

167 **they went on to supply:** See, for instance, TNA: WO 47/35: OM, May 8, 1750, 363; WO 47/39: OM, June 5, 1752, 447; WO 47/51: OM, May 8, 1772, 288; WO 47/80: OM, November 9, 1773, 228.

167 **they supplied big guns:** R. Brown, "Guns Carried on East Indiamen," 18; Flinn, *Men of Iron,* 153–54, 224. See also TNA: WO 47/53: OM, April 3, 1759, 392–93.

168 **"guns, heads and fittings":** Raistrick, *Dynasty of Iron Founders,* 66–68.

168 **Eleven new smelting works:** Ashton, *Iron and Steel in the Industrial Revolution,* 132–33.

168 **It stimulated construction of:** In the first half of the nineteenth century, the area still had some forty-five water mills. Stephens, ed., *The Victoria History of the County of Warwick,* 7:253. Steady improvement in waterpower was part of the tinkering culture of industrial revolution. Mokyr, *The Enlightened Economy,* 127.

168 **"the easiest avenue to wealth":** Wallace, *The Social Context of Innovation,* 101, 218–19. The combined weight of government purchases accounted for 20 percent of total iron output during the Napoleonic Wars. Government orders were important to an industry whose annual pig iron output rose from 70,000 to 395,000 tons and bar iron from 32,000 tons to 150,000 tons between 1788 and 1815. Pig iron output did not return to 1815 levels for several years. Bowen, *War and British Society,* 71–80.

168 **pushed for elimination:** S. Lloyd, *The Lloyds of Birmingham,* 30.

168 **The end of the Napoleonic Wars:** Selgin, *Good Money,* 257–58.

168 **The Crowleys abandoned:** Flinn, *Men of Iron,* 154, 223.

168 **Stagnation in ironworks:** Birch, *The Economic History of the British Iron and Steel Industry,* 55.

168 **Cheap copper, in turn:** John, "War and the English Economy," 331, 333–35.

169 **copper hoops and rivets:** TNA: WO 47/2575: OM, June 13, 1803, 965, and July 1, 1803, 1094; Conway, *The British Isles and the American War of Independence,* 78–79.

169 **buckle-making village:** Pearce, *The History and Directory of Walsall,* 29.

169 **Clothier-contractors provided:** D. Smith, "Army Clothing Contractors and the Textile Industries in the 18th Century," 153–64.

169 **West Riding textile firms:** Hudson, *The Industrial Revolution,* 60.

169 **Daniel Defoe visited:** D. Jones, *War and Economy in the Age of William III,* 203. Only two European armies are known not to have used English textiles at the time: Austria and Sweden (126, 201–3). Government spending may have concentrated the textile business into fewer hands or regions.

169 **William Wilson, a London clothier:** Conway, *War, State, and Society,* 111–12.

170 **a tartan-manufacturing firm:** Conway, "Britain and the Impact of the American War," 134.

170 **paid "rich dividends":** P. Langford, *A Polite and Commercial People,* 539.

170 **the Navy Board purchased:** Brewer, *The Sinews of Power,* 37.

170 **the Victualling Board made:** Knight and Wilcox, *Sustaining the Fleet,* 2–5, 212–13. For agricultural growth during the Napoleonic Wars, see O'Brien, "The Contributions of Warfare with Revolutionary and Napoleonic France to the Consolidation and Progress of the British Industrial Revolution," 39–44.

170 **brought "great regret":** Quoted in Brewer, *The Sinews of Power,* 196.

170 **Duke of Montagu's shipyard:** Conway, *The British Isles and the American War of Independence,* 78. Parliament agreed to spend more than £2.6 million in private yards during the American war, and navy bills likely added more to this.

170–71 **71 percent of the tonnage:** Morriss, *The Royal Dockyards,* 28.

171 **Prices *fell* during:** Conway, *War, State, and Society,* 110.

171 **The East India Company created:** Fichter, *So Great a Proffit,* 174.

171 **it spent more than £70 million:** Bowen, *The Business of Empire,* 264–67, 295. Copper-mine owners like John Vivian and Thomas Williams said that ending copper exports to Asia would ruin England's mines and metal manufactures. Wool manufacturers in Cornwall and Devon said half the long ells they made were for China, consuming 800,000 sheep and giving employment to sixteen thousand.

171 **As early as 1726:** Bannerman, *Merchants and the Military,* 5, 102.

172 **As ordinary investors:** Joslin, "London Bankers in Wartime, 1739–64," 159.

172 **the breakthrough for Quaker:** Price, *Capital and Credit in British Overseas Trade,* 32, 34.

172 **John Eliot's insurance:** Dickson, *The Financial Revolution in England,* 505–6, 514.

172 **"load of business":** FHL: Temp MSS 403/1/1/1/1: Joseph Freame to Mary Plumsted, March 1, 1761.

172 **a committee of two dozen:** See FHL: Temp MSS 403/1/1/1/3: Joseph Freame to Mary Plumsted, October 30, 1761; 403/1/1/1/4: Joseph Freame to Mary Plumsted, December 25, 1761.

172 **The Hanburys, whose businesses:** See TNA: WO 47/42: OM, September 4, 1753, 125.

173 **major specie contractors:** See, for instance, YU: Osborn Shelves FC 160: Robert Plumsted Letter Book (1752–56): Robert Plumsted to William Plumsted, July 4, 1755, 380. Thanks to Simon Smith for this reference.

173 **He stood fifth:** Kidd, "Touchet, Samuel."

173 **Contractors like him:** Of twenty-two undertakers of the £8 million government loan of 1759, seven who subscribed nearly £3 million were also contractors. Of forty-six contractors employed during the American war, fourteen had partnerships with banking firms and were linked with government stock, and thirteen others subscribed nearly £350,000 to the public funds. Brewer, *The Sinews of Power*, 207–8.

173 **Oswald became biggest:** Hancock, *Citizens of the World*, 222, 224, 226, 386.

173 **"Nabob of the North":** Bannerman, *Merchants and the Military*, 128–29.

173 **ten Treasury contractors:** Baker, *Government and Contractors*, 175–83, 227–28.

174 **The bedding supplier John Trotter:** Knight, *Britain Against Napoleon*, 23–24, 394. In John Brewer's terms, they were "neither state fish nor society fowl." *The Sinews of Power*, 207–8.

174 **Birmingham submitted five:** P. Langford, *A Polite and Commercial People*, 539, 634–35.

174 **Galton and Lloyd were key:** Stephens, ed., *The Victoria History of the County of Warwick*, 7:291.

174 **a "disinterested gentleman":** Hall and Davidoff, *Family Fortunes*, 445.

175 **"men of movable property":** Koehn, *The Power of Commerce*, 18–19, 29.

175 **Weather caused more:** John, "War and the English Economy," 334–40.

175 **the American Continental Congress:** *Aris's Birmingham Gazette*, January 9, 1775, 3, January 16, 1775, 3, and January 23, 1775, 3; Samuel Elam to the printers, February 6, 1775, 1, and February 6, 1775, 3.

175 **But twice as many:** *Aris's Birmingham Gazette*, January 30, 1775, 3, and February 20, 1775, 3.

175 **Manchester merchants proudly:** *Aris's Birmingham Gazette*, September 11, 1775, 3.

175 **If monarchs saw:** Brewer, *The Sinews of Power*, xxi, 167, 189. See also Colley, *Britons*, 68. To be sure, the uncertainty caused by war could also cause depression and anxiety among businessmen. Bowen, *War and British Society*, 2, 59, 67–68.

175 **Its wars were of a piece:** BCA: MS3101/C/D/15/5/41: JF reported to SG, November 29, 1755, and MS3101/C/D/15/5/42: December 1, 1755; advertisement, *Aris's Birmingham Gazette*, September 3, 1781, 3.

175 **Parliament authorized the issue:** P. Jones, *Industrial Enlightenment*, 46.

176 **In 1737, English iron manufacturers:** PP: *Journals of the House of Commons* XXIII, March 21, 1737, 109–13.

176 **James Farmer spoke:** Richards, "The Birmingham Gun Manufactory of Farmer and Galton," 103; M. Brown, *Firearms in Colonial America*, 241.

176 **"sophisticated and dynamic":** Parthasarathi, *Why Europe Grew Rich and Asia Did Not*, 187–88.

177 **In 1787, its ruler:** Ibid., 207, 212–13, 255.

177 **But the Court of Directors frowned:** John Harrison, William James, Benjamin Booth, et al., London to Governor General and Council at Fort William in Bengal, March 25, 1776, in *Fort William–India House Correspondence*, 7:145–46; Letter to Court of Directors, March 20, 1776, 7:413.

178 **"the rendering a Colony":** NAI: G. Browne, remarks by Assistant Secretary at Fort William re consequences for EIC relations with Crown for trade, wealth here and at home, November 21, 1770, *Fort William–India House Correspondence*, Secret Committee, Consultation No. 2, 347–54 (italics added).

178 **"No Indian, black or":** Quoted in Young, *The East India Company's Arsenals and Manufactories*, 208.

179 **deputy commissary of ordnance:** Young, *The East India Company's Arsenals and Manufactories*, 224. There was also need to supply saddlery, harnesses, timber, carriages, and so on. The 1770 decision to forbid employment of Indians as gunners was not strictly enforced, partly because of the shortage of European recruits and their lack of skill and high desertion rates. Deserters often offered their skills to native princes. The company was prohibited from employing Eurasians in the 1790s, but the Marathas hired many "half-castes," mostly of Portuguese extraction, as gunners. Pemble, "Resources and Techniques in the Second Maratha War," 387.

179 **"the whole gamut of activities":** Parthasarathi, *Why Europe Grew Rich and Asia Did Not,* 255–57. This omission anticipated the similar policy of purchasing railroad materials in Britain.

Interlude: A Brief Lesson from African History

183 **guns came to Japan:** Howell, "The Social Life of Firearms in Tokugawa Japan," 65–80.

184 **These nonmilitary uses:** Kea, "Firearms and Warfare on the Gold and Slave Coasts," 204–7; J. Miller, *Way of Death,* 89, 92; G. White, "Firearms in Africa," 179. Eighteenth-century Africans preferred weak domestic gunpowder to the more powerful British product because it damaged the shoddy guns less and killed fewer of its users.

184 **Many Africans refused:** Beachey, "The Arms Trade in East Africa," 452; G. White, "Firearms in Africa," 174.

184 **Oyo cavalrymen preferred:** Reid, *Warfare in African History,* 88.

185 **Ashanti, near the coast:** Kea, "Firearms and Warfare on the Gold and Slave Coasts," 208–10.

185 **Gold Coast mercenaries:** Reid, *Warfare in African History,* 89, 103.

185 **In Yorubaland, for instance:** R. Smith, "Yoruba Armament."

186 **"The symbolic single volley":** J. Miller, *Way of Death,* 87.

186 **As far east as:** G. Berg, "The Sacred Musket."

186 **tight arrangement of troops:** Reid, *Warfare in African History,* 89. On the Dahomey's professionalized and centralized tactics, see Law, *The Slave Coast of West Africa,* 270–72.

186 **"very soul of commerce":** J. Miller, *Way of Death,* 93–94.

186 **Growing European shipments:** Warren Whatley, personal communication, June 23, 2012, and "Guns-for-Slaves."

186 **Slave gathering provoked:** Reid, *Warfare in African History,* 85, 89.

187 **pellets and stones were:** Tracy, *The Political Economy of Merchant Empires,* 167–68.

187 **Firearms were also likely:** J. Miller, *Way of Death,* 94.

187 **The average life of a gun:** Ibid., 91.

187 **Each formed alliances:** Kea, "Firearms and Warfare on the Gold and Slave Coasts," 188.

188 **"guns in a considerable number":** PP: Minutes reported to the House of Commons, March 19, 1790, *House of Commons Papers* LXXII, Minutes of Evidence on the Slave Trade, March 8, 1790, 586–87.

188 **Africans aboard the canoes:** Future scholars may assess the accuracy of these claims by examining images collected by Jerry Handler and Michael Tuitte, www.slaveryimages.org.

189 **"They are almost wholly":** J. Swanzy, in PP: *Report from the Select Committee on Papers Relating to the African Forts* (1816), 29–30. On the continuities in European slave trading despite the 1807 acts, see essays in the *William and Mary Quarterly* 66:4 (2009). I thank Joe Miller for this reference.

189 **their use value in the hands:** J. Miller, *Way of Death,* 89.

189 **"ordinary trading musquets":** TNA: WO 47/47: OM, May 11, 1756, 493–94. See also WO 47/ 48: OM, November 23, 1756, 509–10.

190 **generic "iron ordnance":** Inikori, "The Import of Firearms into West Africa," 345. The 1766 figure of more than 150,000 guns sent annually from Birmingham to the African coast is from Rowlands, *Masters and Men,* 129.

190 **"burst when fired":** [Southey], *Letters from England,* 2:60–61.

190 **"hardly be believed":** Parsons, *Observations on the Manufacture of Fire-Arms for Military Purposes,* 45–46. Complaints that the Birmingham Proof House passed bad guns reemerged in the 1840s. G. White, "Firearms in Africa," 180.

190 **Their presence in a warlord's:** J. Miller, *Way of Death,* 92.

Chapter Five: Guns and Money

191 **official commitment to:** Valenze, *The Social Life of Money,* 34.

192 **Retail depended heavily:** Finn, *The Character of Credit,* 6.

192 **Tobacco and sugar were:** Valenze, *The Social Life of Money,* 44–49.

192 **Brass wire was:** Aitken, "Brass and Brass Manufactures," 319–21.

192 **coast for "teeth wood or gold dust":** James Birchall, promissory note, February 14, 1752, in SG to Nicholas Atkinson, April 6, 1757.

193 **Customers in Montserrat:** SG to Molineux and the Assembly Montserrat, July 30, 1756.

193 **Galton received sugar:** SG to John Galton, February 22, 1757.

193　his relative David Barclay: Price, *Capital and Credit in British Overseas Trade*, 366–67.

193　They knew that arms were: Hirst, *The Quakers in Peace and War*, 79. See chap. 7.

193　In Quaker networks: Price, "The Great Quaker Business Families," 385.

193–94　"for the sake of ready money": Letter to the public, *Aris's Birmingham Gazette*, November 25, 1765, 1.

194　In the 1770s: *Aris's Birmingham Gazette*, October 26, 1778, 3.

194　"unreasonable long credits": BCA: MS3101/C/D/15/5/12: JF to SG, May 19, 1752.

194　Farmer and Galton felt pressured: SG to JF, May [?], 1752; JF to SG, June 24, 1755; SG to John Parr, September 6, 1755.

194　Galton was horrified: SG to JF, June 14, 1752.

194　Farmer's Liverpool agent: JF to Mary Farmer (later Galton), July 22, 1742.

194　Farmer toured the Continent: BCA: MS3101/C/D/15/7/1: Priscilla Farmer to SG, October 20, 1748.

194　reference to "mere promises": Poovey, *Genres of the Credit Economy*, 72.

194　Galton & Son even settled: BCA: MS3101/C/D/15/14: Galton & Son to Pratt's firm, August 25 [or 20], 1780.

195　"on a presumption we": Quoted in Bannerman, *Merchants and the Military*, 13.

195　the state usually owed: Bannerman, *Merchants and the Military*, 63, 143.

195　An act of Parliament was: TNA: WO 46/9: Treasury minutes, November 28, 1774, in Ordnance Board to George Townshend, [November 1774], 60; WO 46/11: Ordnance Board to Master General, February 20, 1778, 10–11.

195　besides government stock: Dickson, *The Financial Revolution in England*, 514.

195　Selling an old or broken: *Aris's Birmingham Gazette*, September 3, 1764, 3.

195　New instruments of currency: Poovey, *Genres of the Credit Economy*, 54.

196　"sold and lodged": SG to John Parr, May 17, 1755.

196　"pretends Mr. Farmer lodged": SG to John Galton, May 20, 1755.

196　He suggested that Pengree: BCA: MS3101/C/D/15/1/2: SG to George Pengree, January 31, 1756; SG to George Pengree, June 5, 1756. These debts remained unresolved at Farmer's death, decades later. See FHL: Temp MSS 403/1/1/3/21: David Barclay to Charles Lloyd, November 18, 1774.

197　Rates of exchange: Gunpowder contractors were also paid in saltpeter. When the "state of salt petre" did not admit of that arrangement, they were paid in ready money. TNA: WO 47/48: OM, September 23 and 24, 1756, 254–55.

197　when it acquired rusted: TNA: WO 47/62: OM, October 11, 1763, 161.

197　Richard Jones bid highest: TNA: WO 47/28: OM, April 14, 1715, 106, and May 6, 1715, 118. See also WO 47/33: OM, February 16, [1720], 97; WO 47/63: OM, January 20, 1764, 16 and 506, and March 9, 1764, 157–58.

197　Gunmakers also bought: See TNA: WO 47/29: OM, January 8, 1716, 24.

197　Old iron gunmetal: See, for instance, TNA: WO 47/46: OM, December 2, 1755, 488; WO 47/89: OM, February 4, 1777, 135.

197　money was more important: Muldrew, "'Hard Food for Midas,'" 82–84.

197　the Ordnance Office broke: TNA: WO 47/102: OM, October 13, 1783, 371, October 15, 1783, 377–78, and October 29, 1783, 522–23.

197　"conduct at the late sale": TNA: 47/102: OM, November 5, 1783, 582.

197　allowed to purchase: TNA: WO 47/102: OM, October 30, 1783, 553–54.

197　A servant to London gunmakers: TNA: WO 47/66: OM, December 13, 1765, 250.

198　A gun contractor sought: TNA: WO 47/69: OM, February 20, 1767, 85.

198　arms on a Spanish prize ship: TNA: WO 47/26: OM, December 29, 1781, 1306–7.

198　The good citizen thus lost: TNA: WO 47/48: OM, July 15, 1756, 52–54, and August 4, 1756, 105.

198　Ordnance officials judged: TNA: WO 47/38: OM, October 22, 1751, 270.

198　the office discovered that: TNA: WO 47/49: OM, January 27, 1757, 101–2.

198　A Tower employee: TNA: WO 47/55: OM, May 20, 1760, 424.

198　The office prosecuted: TNA: WO 47/56: OM, September 23, 1760, 210.

198　As the trial proceeded: TNA: WO 47/57: OM, January 27, 1761, 56.

199　in the seventeenth century: R. Brown, "Guns Carried on East Indiamen," 17.

199   **a 1764 list of:** W. Earle, Collector, advertisement, *Aris's Birmingham Gazette*, October 8, 1764, 3.

199   **the philosopher David Hume:** Hume, "Of Commerce," 1752, quoted in M. Berg, "In Pursuit of Luxury," 130–31.

199   **"Beside the prestige of":** M. Berg, *Luxury and Pleasure*, 155.

199   **all metals were preciously:** *Aris's Birmingham Gazette*, January 7, 1760, 3.

199   **Boulton & Fothergill lost:** *Aris's Birmingham Gazette*, November 12, 1770, 3.

199   **nailers who helped themselves:** *Aris's Birmingham Gazette*, April 9, 1770, 3. See also September 19, 1763, 3; April 15, 1765, 3; December 30, 1765, 3; June 8, 1789, 3; and March 25, 1776, 3.

199   **warehouse was robbed of:** *Aris's Birmingham Gazette*, April 30, 1787, 3.

199   **A workshop lost iron:** *Aris's Birmingham Gazette*, July 27, 1789, 3.

199   **another lost brass cocks:** *Aris's Birmingham Gazette*, August 14, 1797, 3.

199   **a third was robbed:** *Aris's Birmingham Gazette*, December 27, 1790, 3. See also February 22, 1773, 3; March 22, 1773, 3; April 16, 1787, 3; and October 28, 1793, 3.

199   **Button workshops were not:** *Aris's Birmingham Gazette*, February 10, 1794, 3; advertisement, June 8, 1788, 3.

199   **Wagons were robbed:** *Aris's Birmingham Gazette*, December 31, 1764, 3.

199   **Policing expanded in the town:** *Aris's Birmingham Gazette*, November 30, 1789, 3; August 12, 1776, 3.

199   **"dealer in metals":** BCA: MS3602/294: Will of Thomas Whateley of Birmingham, January 1, 1812.

199   **the Birmingham paper reported:** Advertisement, *Aris's Birmingham Gazette*, January 19, 1767, 3.

199   **a New Street warehouse:** *Aris's Birmingham Gazette*, December 26, 1768, 3.

199–200   **the workshop of Thomas Archer:** Advertisement, *Aris's Birmingham Gazette*, March 9, 1772, 3.

200   **he again lost:** Advertisement, *Aris's Birmingham Gazette*, May 25, 1789, 2.

200   **Gold dust, "touch-hole gold":** See *Aris's Birmingham Gazette*, November 7, 1785, 3, and advertisement, 2; October 30, 1786, 3; February 20, 1786, 3; March 12, 1787, 3; advertisement, May 25, 1789, 2; January 16, 1797, 3; January 23, 1797, 3; advertisement, September 2, 1799, 3; July 22, 1799, 3; March 17, 1783, 3; June 29, 1788, 3; October 29, 1764, 3; and March 9, 1767, 3.

200   **guns were also robbed:** See advertisement, *Aris's Birmingham Gazette*, January 16, 1769, 3; James Alcock, advertisement, October 25, 1762, 3. For instances of plate theft, see advertisement, July 27, 1788, 3; April 25, 1774, 3; and February 6, 1764, 3.

200   **Plate was melted:** Grassby, "English Merchant Capitalism in the Late Seventeenth Century," 90.

200   **"the simple price value":** Muldrew, "'Hard Food for Midas,'" 109.

200   **the government also prohibited:** *Aris's Birmingham Gazette*, July 25, 1785, 3.

201   **"Forging," which we take:** *Oxford English Dictionary* online, s.v. "forge *v.¹*," www.oed.com.

201   **"coining the gun carriages":** TNA: WO 47/34: OM, December 15, 1749, [470–72?].

201   **This is "to coin":** *Oxford English Dictionary* online, s.v. "coin *v.¹*," www.oed.com.

201   **the master smith of the Ordnance Office:** Craig, *The Mint*, 204, 207.

201   **Britain's first "milled" coins:** Selgin, *Good Money*, xvi, 12. From 1672 to 1713, the mint coined 548,327 guineas from Royal African Company gold. R. Hermann, "Money and Empire," 100, 104–5.

202   **"all the bad money":** Showell, *Dictionary of Birmingham*, 50, 313. Showell insisted that nearly all of the villains involved in that trade were supplied by London. Hammerstruck silver coins lacked raised, protective edges and uniformity and were often clipped while continuing to pass at face value.

202   **"synonym for anything":** J. Langford, *A Century of Birmingham Life*, 1:xx.

202   **"not properly money":** Quoted in Mathias, *The Transformation of England*, 194. In 1693, the mint briefly resumed copper coinage in place of tin (seen as entirely lacking in intrinsic value and easily counterfeited) but then contracted it out for a decade. A private combine coined blanks that were stamped at the mint. In 1713, the mint began to produce copper coins itself, motivated partly by the new reverberatory furnace. But production was delayed, and it fell back on buying copper strips to cut into blanks. The new issue began in 1718. Copper was coined again in 1729. Craig, *The Mint*, 182, 192, 201, 220, 248; Mathias, *English Trade Tokens*, 14.

202 **Legally, making such coins:** Craig, *The Mint*, 252; Porter, *English Society in the Eighteenth Century*, 151. After 1742, the punishment was two years of jail. But the state never had the power to search premises for illegal molds and dies. Mathias, "The People's Money in the Eighteenth Century," 194–96.

202–3 **"where 1,000 halfpennies":** Showell, *Dictionary of Birmingham*, 42–43.

203 **By 1787, genuine:** Symons, "The Mining and Smelting of Copper in England and Wales," 112.

203 **echoed the Worshipful Company:** See, for instance, GL: MS05220/8: CM, March 31, 1737, 94–96.

203 **Blame for counterfeiting:** J. Langford, *A Century of Birmingham Life*, 1:xx.

203 **"by good luck was":** [Southey], *Letters from England*, 2:61–65.

203 **For instance, in 1760:** *Aris's Birmingham Gazette*, June 23, 1760, 3, and February 26, 1770, 3. See also April 22, 1765, 2, November 17, 1766, 1, and December 29, 1777, 3.

203 **a resident of Wolverhampton:** *Aris's Birmingham Gazette*, February 16, 1761, 3; August 3, 1761, 3; October 3, 1763, 3; and April 15, 1765, 3. Cardan was tried for high treason but his sentence respited. If spared execution, coiners might be burned in the hand and imprisoned for a year. *Aris's Birmingham Gazette*, April 1, 1776, 3. In 1788, a Birmingham man was executed for counterfeiting copper coins and using them in payment. August 11, 1788, 3; July 28, 1788, 3; June 27, 1788, 3; and June 23, 1788, 3. Among the eight publicly executed in Birmingham in 1802, "some" were counterfeiters. Hutton, *The History of Birmingham* (1835), 419.

203 **"and several Things":** *Aris's Birmingham Gazette*, April 13, 1772, 3.

203 **policing only made:** *Aris's Birmingham Gazette*, March 13, 1786, 3.

203 **"Residence of Artists":** Samuel Garbett, in *Aris's Birmingham Gazette*, June 7, 1779, 3.

204 **the "important trade":** Arthur Ryland, "The Birmingham Assay Office," in *The Resources, Products, and Industrial History of Birmingham*, ed. Timmins, 503.

204 **"past associations with":** M. Berg, *Luxury and Pleasure*, 181.

204 **The first Soho objects:** *Aris's Birmingham Gazette*, September 13, 1773, 3.

204 **he called for a return:** Craig, *The Mint*, 263–64.

204 **his firm was among:** See, for instance, advertisements in *Aris's Birmingham Gazette*, September 27, 1773, 3; July 11, 1774, 3; January 16, 1775, 3; March 20, 1775, 1; April 24, 1775, 3; April 29, 1776, 3; and June 3, 1776, 3. Grice also sold standardized scales for weighing gold coin.

204 **Retailers cooperatively announced:** Advertisement to all those who come to the Birmingham Canal Company Wharf for coals, *Aris's Birmingham Gazette*, September 6, 1773, 3.

204 **execution of James Duckworth:** Showell, *Dictionary of Birmingham*, 66; *Aris's Birmingham Gazette*, August 23, 1773, 3.

205 **"a very poor Reason":** Letter to the printers, *Aris's Birmingham Gazette*, September 6, 1773, 3.

205 **"At what time [did]":** *Aris's Birmingham Gazette*, February 15, 1773, 3. See also February 8, 1773, 3; September 13, 1773, 3; and advertisements by retailers in issues of *Aris's Gazette*, September 1773 and April 1774.

205 **There was no need:** *Aris's Birmingham Gazette*, August 19, 1776, 3. See also March 1, 1773, 3; September 20, 1773, 3; September 23, 1776, 3; September 29, 1777, 3; and May 14, 1787, 3. Some shopkeepers earned a slight advantage by accepting guineas wanting one pence and sending them to London, where they passed for full value. April 4, 1774, 3.

205 **Counterfeiting, too, went on:** See, for instance, *Aris's Birmingham Gazette*, December 19, 1774, 3; July 10, 1775, 3; letter to *Aris's Birmingham Gazette*, January 29, 1776, 3; London trader to Birmingham correspondent, *Aris's Birmingham Gazette*, February 12, 1776, 3; *Aris's Birmingham Gazette*, February 19, 1776, 3, and advertisement, same page; December 7, 1778, 3; June 28, 1779, 3.

205 **Gold coins were current:** See Samuel Garbett in *Aris's Birmingham Gazette*, June 7, 1779, 3.

205 **A collective leap:** See *Aris's Birmingham Gazette*, September 2, 1776, 3; May 19, 1777, 3; September 1, 1777, 3; May 31, 1778, 3; November 27, 1780, 3; September 3, 1781, 3; November 11, 1782, 3; May 5, 1783, 3; May 24, 1784, 3; September 6, 1784, 3; and August 13, 1787, 3.

205 **"can be said to *stand for*":** Poovey, *Genres of the Credit Economy*, 66.

205 **Their report recommended:** Mathias, *The Transformation of England*, 193.

206 **He would adapt:** Craig, *The Mint*, 264; Selgin, *Good Money*, 63.

206 **The urgency of putting:** P. Jones, *Industrial Enlightenment*, 68; Craig, *The Mint*, 264; advertisement, *Aris's Birmingham Gazette*, February 6, 1786, 3.

206 **"to petition parliament":** Quoted in Selgin, *Good Money*, 70.

206 **He made coins for:** Selgin, *Good Money*, 64–65, 89. See also Whiting, *British Trade Tokens*, 22. He also made some Dutch coins. Craig, *The Mint*, 264. The sheet copper and round blanks were prepared at Soho with the company's own copper cake, but the coins were struck at a makeshift mint in a warehouse in London; they were not steam-struck. That innovation came with the next orders, from other industrialists.

206 **Wolverhampton's manufacturers, including some:** *Aris's Birmingham Gazette*, October 4, 1773, 3. Thomas Hadley resorted to fraudulent £10 notes of hand to prevent workmen from attending to Farmer & Galton's orders. Some manufacturers who became bankers, such as the Lloyds, also issued their own notes. See below. Small notes issued by country banks before 1775 (when notes smaller than £1 were declared illegal) filled an important gap. Mokyr, *The Enlightened Economy*, 223.

206 **Roughly four hundred:** Whiting, *British Trade Tokens*, 77–144.

206 **soon Boulton began:** J. Harris, *The Copper King*, 153.

206 **private issuers had minted:** Mokyr, *The Enlightened Economy*, 447.

206 **Wilkinson also printed:** Wallace, *The Social Context of Innovation*, 27, 228–32.

207 **possessed value only:** Wilkinson's countinghouse was robbed of copper coin worth more than a hundred thousand guineas. *Aris's Birmingham Gazette*, November 9, 1789, 3. Tokens were also used in the early seventeenth century.

207 **Royal Mint engravers:** Craig, *The Mint*, 252.

207 **Late in the summer:** BCA: MS3782/12/32/140: SGII to Matthew Boulton, August 1787.

207 **"a considerable consumption":** J. Whateley to Matthew Boulton, January 15, 1788, and January 31, 1788.

207 **"utmost expedition and":** J. Whateley to Matthew Boulton, April 11, 1788.

208 **Henry Whateley provided:** Whateley to Boulton, December 2, 1788.

208 **Erasmus Darwin exclaimed:** Reported in *Aris's Birmingham Gazette*, June 11, 1792, 3. See also *Aris's Birmingham Gazette*, April 3, 1792, 3.

208 **Soon after the Priestley Riots:** P. Jones, *Industrial Enlightenment*, 197, 207.

208 **He and Garbett supported:** *Aris's Birmingham Gazette*, August 26, 1792, 3, and advertisement, same page.

208 **Williams bought up good:** Selgin, *Good Money*, 178–79.

208 **By the 1790s:** Symons, "The Mining and Smelting of Copper in England and Wales," 114, 139–41.

208 **"best tough cake":** BCA: MS3782/12/39/225: Matthew Boulton to EIC directors, August 18, 1794.

209 **Boulton struck coins:** Selgin, *Good Money*, 107–11, 119.

209 **Charles Lloyd was astonished:** FHL: Temp MSS 403/3/6/63: Charles Lloyd to Priscilla Farmer, March 1, 1797.

209 **He received a contract:** Valenze, *The Social Life of Money*, 265–66; Selgin, *Good Money*, 156–59, 162–63, 171, 181.

209 **consumed twelve hundred tons:** Symons, "The Mining and Smelting of Copper in England and Wales," 113; Whiting, *British Trade Tokens*, 23.

209 **the Quaker Joseph Gibbins:** Crick and Wadsworth, *A Hundred Years of Joint-Stock Banking*, 50.

210 **they did not eliminate:** Showell, *Dictionary of Birmingham*, 42–43; *Aris's Birmingham Gazette*, February 4, 1799, 3. On Boulton's experiments with manufacturing techniques that might preclude counterfeiting, see S. Shaw, *The History and Antiquities of Staffordshire*, 2:119.

210 **Between 1797 and 1806:** P. Jones, *Industrial Enlightenment*, 57, 69, 209; Hutton, *The History of Birmingham* (1835), 398.

210 **He sold an entire mint:** Ralph Heaten, "Birmingham Coinage," in *The Resources, Products, and Industrial History of Birmingham and the Midland Hardware District*, ed. Timmins, 555.

210 **Between the Admiralty:** Selgin, *Good Money*, 183–84.

210 **it asked Boulton to:** Whiting, *British Trade Tokens*, 25.

210 **the Bank of England:** Selgin, *Good Money*, 199–202.

210 **Another Birmingham manufacturer:** Timmins, "Die-Sinking," in *The Resources, Products, and Industrial History of Birmingham and the Midland Hardware District*, ed. Timmins, 562.

211 **a few months after his death:** On Boulton's death, a funeral medal was struck at the Soho mint. P. Jones, *Industrial Enlightenment*, 236.

211 **It was taken seriously:** Tertius Galton, *A Chart, Exhibiting the Relation between the Amount of Bank of England Notes in Circulation, the Rate of Foreign Exchanges, and the Prices of Gold and Silver Bullion and of Wheat*; PP: House of Commons Papers: Report of the Select Committee on Petitions Complaining of Depressed State of Agriculture of United Kingdom: Minutes of Evidence, appendix, IX (1821), 209. Tertius Galton foretold the fall in the money market in 1825.

211 **Manufacture of "token money":** Whiting, *British Trade Tokens*, 31.

211 **commercial coiners went:** Selgin, *Good Money*, 201–2, 258.

212 **A coiner's machinery:** Heaten, "Birmingham Coinage," 555.

212 **Birmingham became a "financial centre":** M. Berg, *Luxury and Pleasure*, 213–14.

213 **The Freame & Gould bank:** Tuke, ed., *History of Barclays Bank Limited*, 32–34; Raistrick, *Two Centuries of Industrial Welfare*, 151.

213 **Joseph Freame shared his worries:** See FHL: Temp MSS 403/1/2/1/7: JF to Mary Farmer [later Lloyd], July 29, 1761; 403/1/1/1/1: Joseph Freame to Mary Farmer, August 31, [1761 or 1763]; 403/1/1/1/21: Joseph Freame to Mary Plumsted, March 13, 1764.

213 **Agatha Barclay, who became:** See, for instance, FHL: Temp MSS 403/1/1/2/35: Agatha Barclay to Mary Farmer, May 29, 1773.

214 **Private banking partnerships:** Joslin, "London Bankers in Wartime," 157.

214 **was a stepping-stone:** Neal, "The Finance of Business during the Industrial Revolution," 165–67.

214 **Instead, virtually all:** Hutton, *The History of Birmingham* (1835), 201; Wallace, *The Social Context of Innovation*, 228–32.

215 **Raising finance on:** Hudson, *The Industrial Revolution*, 95.

215 **Galton had to struggle:** BCA: MS3101/C/D/15/1/1: SG to John Galton, May 13, 1755.

215 **"entirely with the dealers":** BCA: MS3101/C/D/15/1/2: [John Galton?] to "Cousin," [n.d., mid-1756]. See Sayers, *Lloyds Bank in the History of English Banking*, 8.

215 **They took deposits:** Raistrick, *Quakers in Science and Industry*, 120, 325, 344.

215 **Notes smaller than one pound:** Mokyr, *The Enlightened Economy*, 223.

215 **"Opulent tradesmen," they found:** Hutton, *An History of Birmigham* (1781), 83.

215 **In 1770, the younger:** Raistrick, *Quakers in Science and Industry*, 325. The London bank merged with the Birmingham original in 1889, turning Lloyds into a national banker. Wallace, *The Social Context of Innovation*, 228–32.

216 **The Spooners evolved:** The partners also leased land, a mill, and a steam engine on behalf of James Watt from the Whateleys. BCA: MS3602/295: Lease, December 21, 1817; MS3602/308: Lease, December 7, 1818.

216 **two Quaker banks:** Price, "The Great Quaker Business Families," 384–85.

216 **there were no more than:** Joslin, "London Bankers in Wartime," 157.

216 **New country banks:** Neal, "The Finance of Business during the Industrial Revolution," 168. Country banks were rare in Lancashire, possibly because of early failures there in 1788 and because attorneys fulfilled the function of intermediaries. Older forms, such as inland bills of exchange, were used for payments (rather than banknotes). The very dominance of the cotton trade—compared with the more diverse range of goods in the Midlands—also shaped the difference in institutions.

216 **They were part:** Into the 1830s, many solicitors, tradesmen and manufacturers, clergymen, and doctors continued to perform banking functions, even if it was merely holding or investing the savings of a laborer who did not trust that new invention, the bank. Hall and Davidoff, *Family Fortunes*, 245.

216 **In 1811, Tertius's brother:** BCA: MS3101/C/D/10/2/19: Tertius Galton to Howard Galton, August 6, 1811; MS3101/C/D/10/2/109: Polly to John Howard Galton, April 15, 1813.

216 **"casualties of trade":** BCA: MS3101/C/D/10/10/21: Tertius Galton to Howard Galton, January 28, 1819; MS3101/C/D/10/9/64: SGII to Tertius Galton, Howard Galton, and Hubert Galton, January 30, 1819.

217 **All but one survived the crisis:** Gill, *History of Birmingham*, 1:314. The one that failed was Gibbins, Smith, and Goode. Crick and Wadsworth, *A Hundred Years of Joint-Stock Banking*, 53.

217 **sheer "commercial wearyness":** Elizabeth Anne Wheler (née Galton), quoted in Hall and Davidoff, *Family Fortunes*, 226.

217 **Henry Drummond joined:** Philip Winterbottom, "Drummond, Henry (c. 1730–1795)," *Oxford Dictionary of National Biography* online, accessed January 9, 2017, www.oxforddnb.com/view/article/48025. See also Baker, *Government and Contractors*, 175–83.

217 **he partnered with Richard Cox:** John Booker, "Cox, Richard (1718–1803)," *Oxford Dictionary of National Biography* online, accessed January 9, 2017, www.oxforddnb.com/view/article/45706.

217 idea of "the economy": See Mitchell, *Rule of Experts*, 99.
218 Conservatism about monetary: D. Carey, "An Empire of Credit," 3.
218 increase of "real money": Letter to *Aris's Birmingham Gazette*, October 20, 1766, 3.
218 "acts all Substance": Defoe, 1710, quoted in Wahrman, *The Making of the Modern Self*, 209–10.
218 Drummond bought some: Bolitho and Peel, *The Drummonds of Charing Cross*, 76.

Chapter Six: Guns in Arms, Part 1: Home

219 Though different sorts: The same basic models were available across the century (especially pistols, muskets, fowlers). The gun's place in eighteenth-century violence formed independently of technological advances (amply covered by others). This is not a study of the cult or culture of guns, which would require different types of evidence.

219–20 But shopkeepers and stockholders: Porter, *English Society in the Eighteenth Century*, 371.

220 The British Crown regulated: Charles, "The Faces of the Second Amendment outside the Home," 1, 7–8, 14–15, 21–22. For instance, an act of Parliament in 1523 forbade those with less than a £100 income from possessing firearms. Guns were only for the upper gentry, a very small group. Enforcement was another matter, and laws changed as peace and war came. Perrin, *Giving Up the Gun*, 58–62; Schwoerer, *Gun Culture in Early Modern England*, chap. 3. Laws against concealed firearms date to 1541 and associated them with theft. Cockburn, "Patterns of Violence in English Society," 85.

220 Militia Acts of 1661–63: Western, *The English Militia in the Eighteenth Century*, 3–5, 11, 71.
220 A statute of 1670: Kennett and Anderson, *The Gun in America*, 24.
220 The phrases "Suitable to": Schwoerer, "To Hold and Bear Arms," 48–56, 59–60; *Gun Culture in Early Modern England*, chap. 10; Charles, "The Faces of the Second Amendment," 23–30; *Historicism, Originalism, and the Constitution*, 134–39.
220 framework for game laws: Sharpe, *Crime in Early Modern England*, 180; Munsche, *Gentlemen and Poachers*, chap. 1.
221 even when farmers: Schwoerer, *Gun Culture in Early Modern England*, 166; Munsche, *Gentlemen and Poachers*, chap. 4.
221 powers of search and seizure: Kennett and Anderson, *The Gun in America*, 25; Charles, "The Faces of the Second Amendment," 6.
221 Searches eventually revealed: Western, *The English Militia in the Eighteenth Century*, 72.
221 laws prohibited Highlanders: Kennett and Anderson, *The Gun in America*, 22.
221 word came that two: TNA: WO 47/30: OM, March 27, 1718/9, 124, and May 26, 1719, 225.
221 This recognition came: Black, *Britain as a Military Power*, 24–25.
221 the rebellion had shown how: See Conway, *War, State, and Society*, 86; TNA: WO 47/34: OM, April 18, 1749, 146; March 21, 1748, 95; and February 14, 1748, [18?]; WO 47/73: OM, February 7, 1769, 48, and February 21, 1769, 89.
221 Samuel Johnson remarked: Johnson, *A Journey to the Western Islands of Scotland*, 207.
221 the Smuggling Act of 1736: P. Langford, *A Polite and Commercial People*, 301.
222 militia's last real success: Western, *The English Militia in the Eighteenth Century*, 29, 68, 102.
222 Through the 1740s: Kennett and Anderson, *The Gun in America*, 11; Western, *The English Militia in the Eighteenth Century*, 52, 57, 71–73.
222 London gunsmiths took: See, for instance, TNA: WO 47/46: OM, December 6, 1753, 307–8.
222 "they were for some desperate": Winslow, "Sussex Smugglers," 161.
222 firearms were not particularly easy: Derek Stimpson, archivist at the Worshipful Company of Gunmakers, supports this view. Personal communication, November 14, 2016.
222 The much maligned ignorance: TNA: WO 47/38: OM, August 9, 1751, 134–35.
222 Ordnance Office records contain: TNA: WO 47/46: OM, July 25, 1755, [?], July 28, 1755, 100, August [8?], 1755, 144, and August 26, 1755, 193; WO 47/31: OM, August 9, 1751, 134–35, December 3, 1751, 415, and December 19, 1751, 480; WO 47/39: January 30, 1752, 91; WO 46/10: Ordnance Board to Lord Townshend, December 8, 1775, in Townshend to Lord Weymouth, January 12, 1766, 32.
223 The government sent: TNA: WO 47/42: OM, August 3, 1753, 60; August 9, 1753, 78; August 17, 1753, 100–1.
223 In 1755, a Tory polemicist: Schwoerer, *Gun Culture in Early Modern England*, 166.

223 **Another pamphleteer echoed:** "A True-Born Englishman," *An Alarm to the People of England,* 7–9.

223 **Participation depended on:** P. Langford, *Public Life and the Propertied Englishman,* 296–98.

223 **Decades of disarmament:** The new militia was to be two thirds the size of the original (sixty thousand), based on a census of men aged eighteen to fifty who would serve three years or pay a fine of £10 or find a substitute. There was a provision for general training by rotation in service, but no insistence on personal service even then. The opposition scheme was to raise a militia only in the towns to ensure that they would be concentrated and prevent disorderly marches to and from exercises and scattering of arms among the parishes. Each town would have a magazine under the eye of the adjutant. They did not want arms in the hands of churchwardens to be seized by rioters. Two changes resulted from these demands: arms would be in the care of sergeants, and lord lieutenants would have the power to order their removal in emergency. Western, *The English Militia in the Eighteenth Century,* 107, 117, 120, 129, 146, 135–36, 441.

223 **he threatened that if:** *An Alarm to the People of England,* 26, 34, 41. The last eleven names are capitalized and spell out a message: "ARTFUL ROBBERS esq, etc. TOGETHER JOINED PLOT TO OVERTURN AND PLUNDER US OF OUR LIBERTY."

223 **T. Richards, a Birmingham gunmaker:** *Aris's Birmingham Gazette,* August 2, 1779, 3; September 20, 1779, 3; August 14, 1780, 3; and August 9, 1784, 3.

224 **proliferation of accidental:** HVD: Data for Gloucester, 1760s–'80s: four accidental gun deaths. In Birmingham from 1760 to 1793, twenty-five gun-related deaths were reported in the local paper, all but one accidents in the course of hunting with, playing with, or caring for a gun. See, for instance, *Aris's Birmingham Gazette,* January 17, 1763, 3; July 25, 1763, 3; December 29, 1766, 3; December 21, 1772, 3; January 8, 1776, 3; January 22, 1776, 3; September 3 and 15, 1777, 3; January 12, 1789, 3; October 19, 1789, 3; October 24, 1791, 3; November 14, 1791, 3; February 13, 1792, 3; and July 1, 1793, 3. Future scholars might perform more robust quantitative analysis of these reports.

224 **The Birmingham newspaper had:** *Aris's Birmingham Gazette,* January 12, 1789, 3. See also April 17, 1797, 3.

224 **The Ordnance Office diligently:** TNA: WO 47/61: OM, May 26, 1763, 341, May 28, 1763, 344, and June 1, 1763, 350; WO 47/62: OM, July 16, 1763, 16, and September 1, 1763, 89; WO 47/63: OM, April 11, 1764, 241, January 20, 1764, 16, and March 9, 1764, 157; WO 47/74: OM, November 10, 1769, 167, and December 5, 1769, 213–14; WO 47/75: OM, January 12, 1770, 11; WO 47/97: OM, March 1, 1781, 211.

224 **During the Gordon Riots:** Schwoerer, *Gun Culture in Early Modern England,* 167–69; Malcolm, *Guns and Violence,* 86–88.

224 **"as afraid of its own people":** Colley, "The Reach of the State, the Appeal of the Nation," 168.

224 **Radicals urging crowds:** See, for instance, *Aris's Birmingham Gazette,* July 27, 1795, 3.

224 **"I wished they had":** Quoted in Bohstedt, *The Politics of Provision,* 197. It is unclear whether the king was shot at—either a bullet or a stone passed through the windows of the state coach, fired from an air gun. The king reportedly said in the House of Lords, "My Lord I have been shot at." J. Langford, *A Century of Birmingham Life,* 2:60.

224 **fear of rebellion drove:** B. Collins, *War and Empire,* 130.

225 **"defend our government":** *Aris's Birmingham Gazette,* May 7, 1798, 3.

225 **Within weeks came:** Advertisement, *Aris's Birmingham Gazette,* May 21, 1798, 2.

225 **wall graffiti in Birmingham:** Bohstedt, *The Politics of Provision,* 197.

225 **Through the 1790s, the British state:** Kennett and Anderson, *The Gun in America,* 26, 28–30.

225 **"A good fowling-piece":** Quoted in Knight, *Britain Against Napoleon,* 263.

226 **The rioters wielded:** *Aris's Birmingham Gazette,* July 25, 1791, 3; Hutton, *The History of Birmingham* (1835), 427–29. Firing of a pistol temporarily dispersed the assailants against one house. The king sent troops to relieve the town. Watt traveled to the next Lunar Society meeting with loaded pistols in coat pockets. P. Jones, *Industrial Enlightenment,* 201. Birmingham's riots of 1715 and 1751 also focused on destruction of houses of worship. Showell, *Dictionary of Birmingham,* 271–72.

226 **in Machynlleth around 1739:** Guldi, *Roads to Power,* 162.

226 **in Birmingham in 1789:** *Aris's Birmingham Gazette,* March [?], 1789, 3. One instance of an armed crowd firing on authorities appears in Gilmour, *Riot, Risings and Revolution,* 135–232. A weaver shot a soldier raiding the Dolphin Ale-House in London in 1769, but this was not part of a riot. Rudé, *Wilkes and Liberty,* 102.

226 **"Mobs" did not use guns:** See also Kennett and Anderson, *The Gun in America*, 29–30.

226 **The night before:** *Account of the Cruel Massacre Committed by John Porteous, Captain of the City Guard of Edinburgh.*

227 **Going by evidence from Gloucester:** HVD: Gloucester, 1724–29; 1730s; 1740s; 1750s. There was one instance in 1724–29 of accidental death by pistol.

227 **a dispute between two men:** HVD: Gloucester Inquests: February 3, 1741.

227 **"through his body":** HVD: Gloucester Inquests: February 2 and 16, 1742.

227 **the steward to Lord Bathurst:** HVD: Gloucester Inquests: July 29, 1755. On earlier gun suicides, see Schwoerer, *Gun Culture in Early Modern England*, 123.

227 **In London, too:** See POB: Records for 1700–1760.

227 **Data from Coventry:** HVD: Coventry: 1755–63. Between 1720 and 1810 in Kent, 21 percent of violent deaths were due to gunshot wounds, as compared with 14 percent from blunt instruments and 12 percent from bladed weapons. Shootings caused less than 3 percent of fatal violence between 1560 and 1660, but 26 percent from 1720 to 1729. Between 1720 and 1810, more than 20 percent of Kent homicides were committed by firearms, although the average rarely exceeded one per year. Cockburn, "Patterns of Violence in English Society," 82–83, 86, 87, 88.

228 **In 1760s–'80s Gloucester:** HVD: Gloucester: 1760s–'80s. Quote from Inquest of December 22, 1766.

228 **reported murders involved:** See, for instance, *Aris's Birmingham Gazette*, February 16, 1767, 3; June 23, 1766, 3; January 22, 1770, 3; June 10, 1771, 3; and June 17, 1776, 3.

228 **A recruiting sergeant:** *Aris's Birmingham Gazette*, April 21, 1788, 3.

228 **one accidental gun slaying:** *Aris's Birmingham Gazette*, November 4, 1776, 3.

228 **The homicide rate remained:** L. Stone, "Interpersonal Violence in English Society"; Sharpe, "Crime in England."

228 **The British were not too different:** Howell, "The Social Life of Firearms in Tokugawa Japan," 73–74.

228 **The sheer inefficiency:** As the Australian comedian Jim Jefferies puts it, "You know what's good about the musket? It gives you a lot of time to calm down."

229 **like bows, which:** See Malcolm, *Guns and Violence*, 30–31. On gun use in earlier periods, see Schwoerer, *Gun Culture in Early Modern England*. Gun violence in the name of religion, for instance, was more common in the sixteenth century (104).

229 **a man endeavoring to:** A. G. Esq., *The Impetuous Love, or the Guiltless Parricide*, 1:167–68, 2:47–48.

229 **In Birmingham in 1765:** *Aris's Birmingham Gazette*, January 21, 1765, 3.

229 **six robbers entered:** *Aris's Birmingham Gazette*, January 22, 1770, 3.

229 **At times, the robber:** See, for instance, *Aris's Birmingham Gazette*, October 23, 1775, 3; November 15, 1779, 3; December 6, 1779, 3; January 24, 1780, 3; and November 27, 1780, 3.

229 **threat of "instant Death":** *Aris's Birmingham Gazette*, January 18, 1790, 3.

230 **In some instances:** See *Aris's Birmingham Gazette*, May 11, 1789, 3.

230 **But he had kept his gun:** POB: Mr. Raine, trial for John Sellers, Elizabeth Jones, and Richard Footner, September 14, 1796, available at: www.oldbaileyonline.org/browse.jsp?id=t17960914-5 -defend95&div=t17960914-5#highlight.

230 **Those who wielded:** POB: William Shields, testimony, trial of Thomas Robinson, September 16, 1778, available at: www.oldbaileyonline.org/browse.jsp?id=t17780916-51–off248&div=t17780916 -51&terms=robinson#highlight.

230 **The flintlock's more efficient:** Darling, *Red Coat and Brown Bess*, 10–11. The flintlock produced a spark by striking flint against steel; the spark ignited the priming powder, which ignited the main charge. Reloading still took minutes—powder had to be reloaded and rammed down, the pan primed, the flint checked. Linear tactics were first developed by Sweden's Gustavus Adolphus and later refined in France. Essentially, infantry troops armed with muskets were deployed in long, tight lines, (typically) in three ranks, which fired rank by rank to maximize the number of volleys.

230 **"noise of fire-arms":** A. Smith, *The Wealth of Nations*, 755–56.

231 **Experienced officers had:** M. Brown, *Firearms in Colonial America*, 165–66; Harding, *Smallarms of the East India Company*, 3:355, 386.

231 **"A soldier's musket":** Hanger, *A Letter to the Right Hon. Lord Castlereagh*, 78. Hanger repeated this line in his pamphlet of shooting advice. *To All Sportsmen, and Particularly to Farmers, and Gamekeepers,*

205. There is no evidence to support Hanger's assertion that most muskets were so badly bored; he likely misunderstood the true causes of their inaccuracy at the moment when military thinking had begun to shift. Harding, *Smallarms of the East India Company,* 3:292.

231 Lieutenant Colonel Lee: Ffoulkes, *Arms & Armament,* 54–55.

231 ex-master of the Tower Armouries: Ibid., 80.

232 In Birmingham from 1760 to 1799: See, for instance, *Aris's Birmingham Gazette,* January 3, 1763, 3; February 28, 1763, 3; June 6, 1763, 3; October 17, 1768, 3; November 28, 1768, 3; December 21, 1772, 3; January 18, 1773, 3; advertisement, January 30, 1775, 3; October 16, 1776, 3; March 15, 1773, 3; August 19, 1776, 3; December 11, 1780, 3; January 8, 1781, 3; August 19, 1781, 3; December 9, 1782, 3; September 26, 1785, 3; September 28, 1789, 3; October 5, 1789, 3; December 28, 1789, 3; January 18, 1790, 3; November 19, 1792, 3; February 11, 1793, 3; January 27, 1794, 3; January 18, 1796, 3; February 15, 1796, 3; October 31, 1796, 3; December 19, 1796, 3; September 4, 1797, 3; January 29, 1798, 3; February 7, 1799, 3; February 25, 1799, 3; March 25, 1799, 3; September 2, 1799, 3; September 9, 1799, 3; and November 25, 1799, 2.

232 A gentleman in Ayrshire: Thompson, "The Crime of Anonymity," 266.

232 "People of property": *Gentleman's Magazine* 33 (1763), 410–11, quoted in Conway, *War, State, and Society,* 134.

232 A reader of the Birmingham newspaper: *Aris's Birmingham Gazette,* January 13, 1777, 3.

232 The paper later blamed: *Aris's Birmingham Gazette,* July 22, 1793, 3.

232 popular contemporary historian: Hutton, *The History of Birmingham* (1835), 413.

232 The Birmingham newspaper hoped: *Aris's Birmingham Gazette,* January 25, 1790, 3.

232 Colonel Hanger published: Hanger, *To All Sportsmen, and Particularly to Farmers, and Gamekeepers,* 149–50.

232 Homeowners waved their: See, for instance, *Aris's Birmingham Gazette,* July 15, 1776, 3, and January 18, 1773, 3. I will have more to say on masculinity and gun use in the next chapter, but future scholars will have to relate the fuller gender story about gun use—the infrequency with which guns were found in the hands of women and emerging notions of gun-toting masculinity.

232 Samuel Johnson insisted: Johnson, *A Journey to the Western Islands of Scotland,* 208–11.

233 The circumstances of the remaining: *Aris's Birmingham Gazette,* October 17, 1768, 3; June 23, 1766, 3; May 11, 1766, 3; April 20, 1772, 3; March 15, 1773, 3; January 29, 1776, 3; February 18, 1781, 3; October 28, 1793, 3; May 12, 1794, 3; May 4, 1795, 3; February 1, 1796, 3; September 19, 1796, 3; September 9, 1799, 3; November 11, 1799, 3; June 29, 1795, 3; March 17, 1788, 3; March 2, 1761, 3; and March 29, 1773, 3.

233 In reported nonlethal: *Aris's Birmingham Gazette,* February 16, 1767, 3; January 28, 1793, 3; September 11, 1797, 3; and May 13, 1793, 3.

233 "discharged a pistol": *Aris's Birmingham Gazette,* March 18, 1776, 3.

233 A young man masquerading: *Aris's Birmingham Gazette,* November 7, 1791, 3.

233 "fit of jealousy": *Aris's Birmingham Gazette,* June 17, 1793, 3.

233 "shot her with a brace": *Aris's Birmingham Gazette,* December 15, 1788, 3.

233 In Kent in 1778: Cockburn, "Patterns of Violence in English Society," 87. See *Aris's Birmingham Gazette,* July 27, 1795, 3, for an incident in Surrey.

234 London trials involving guns: POB: Records for 1700–1800.

234 She had refused Hackman's heart: McLynn, *Crime and Punishment in Eighteenth-Century England,* 49; POB: Trial of James Hackman, April 1779, available at: www.oldbaileyonline.org /browse.jsp?id=t17790404-3&div=t17790404-3&terms=hackman#highlight.

234 In 1797 in Staffordshire: *Aris's Birmingham Gazette,* August 28, 1797, 3. In the seventeenth century, men went armed with the "dag," the small, easily concealable gun, and used it in moments of passion. Lois Schwoerer, personal communication, October 29, 2016.

234 Objects do not merely: D. Miller, *Stuff,* 10, 59–60, 75, 135.

234 Bruno Latour explains: Latour, *Pandora's Hope,* 178–80.

234 The tension and fear: See R. Collins, *Violence,* 58–59.

235 Archery required too much: Archery remained a robust English tradition. Birmingham had its share of popularly attended archery tournaments. See, for instance, *Aris's Birmingham Gazette,* July 4, 1791, 3.

235 the "relative restraint": Elias, *The Civilizing Process,* 1:200–202.

235 inventor of a double-shot: Aitken, *A Description of Double-Shot Fire-Arms,* preface, vii.

236 **"He who shoots a bird":** A. Smith, *The Theory of Moral Sentiments,* 92–93, 100.
236 **"polite and commercial people":** P. Langford, *A Polite and Commercial People,* 6. Guns may have been used in earlier property disputes, too, but changes in their material nature and availability and in the relationship of property to the state meant that they became entwined with the eighteenth-century regime of property in a new way.
237 **Crimes were directed:** L. Stone, "Interpersonal Violence in English Society," 25–30, 33. See also Emsley, *Hard Men,* chap. 1.
237 **"Forks transformed table manners":** Hall, *Civilising Subjects,* 271, 289.
237 **As war became more:** Elias, *Power & Civility: The Civilizing Process,* 2:237, 299–300; *The Civilizing Process,* 1:200–202.
237 **"a mode of execution":** Paley, "Of Crimes and Punishments," in *The Principles of Moral and Political Philosophy* (1785), quoted in Rabin, *Identity, Crime, and Legal Responsibility,* 56.
237 **Gruesome public executions:** Burning at the stake ended in 1790; drawing and quartering in 1820; dissection in 1832; gibbeting in 1834. Cockburn, "Patterns of Violence in English Society," 101, 104; McLynn, *Crime and Punishment in Eighteenth-Century England,* 297.
238 **Rules of engagement:** Banks, *A Polite Exchange of Bullets,* esp. 126–27, 206, 208. In London, wearing swords remained fashionable among elites, with some imitation down the social ladder. Dueling was abolished in 1840.
238 **A man killed in:** *Aris's Birmingham Gazette,* June 26, 1797, 3.
238 **Quarreling sailors used:** *Aris's Birmingham Gazette,* September 29, 1794, 3.
239 **poachers and smugglers carried:** In John Locke's well-known formulation, published just after that regime came to power, government's end is the preservation of property.
239 **not all poachers:** See Sharpe, *Crime in Early Modern England,* 175–88.
239 **Poaching remained rampant:** McLynn, *Crime and Punishment in Eighteenth-Century England,* 207–9. See also *Aris's Birmingham Gazette,* October [18 or 25], 1790, entire issue; advertisement and list of game certificates, September 19, 1791, [3?].
239 **as "excellent marksmen":** *Aris's Birmingham Gazette,* October 24, 1796, 1.
239 **why free imports:** Porter, *English Society in the Eighteenth Century,* 114–15. Ordinary thieves got less sympathy than gang leaders like Jonathan Wild, who achieved glory as the minnow who got caught while elite sharks like Walpole got away.
240 **many smugglers declared:** Brewer, *The Sinews of Power,* 54.
240 **Many of these gentlemen:** Emsley, *Hard Men,* 29.
241 **"We swarm with highwaymen":** Walpole, quoted in McLynn, *Crime and Punishment in Eighteenth-Century England,* 79.
241 **By choking off outlets:** McLynn, *Crime and Punishment in Eighteenth-Century England,* 79–80.
241 **"they would have been":** *Aris's Birmingham Gazette,* February 13, 1797, 3.
241 **He was a mobile stranger:** Guldi, *Roads to Power,* 82, 154–55, 170–71.
241 **a "Jacobite flavor":** McLynn, *Crime and Punishment in Eighteenth-Century England,* 57.
241 **Their use of firearms:** The gun's close association with the highwayman is buried in its very name: "Snaphance" was a Dutch borrowing for "firearm," but the word also referred to an armed robber or highwayman. *Oxford English Dictionary* online, s.v. "snaphance, snaphaunce," accessed September 12, 2017, www.oed.com. "Snaphance" is also related to the German *Schnapphahn,* meaning "poultry thief." Ffoulkes, *Arms & Armament,* 54.
241 **an "inhuman miscreant":** *Aris's Birmingham Gazette,* August 27, 1798, 3.
242 **Crowd action was:** Sharpe, *Crime in Early Modern England,* 198. The aims of French revolutionaries of 1789 were more politically radical; that is why the storming of the Bastille was a seizure of thirty thousand arms.
242 **some who attacked:** Rudé, "The Gordon Riots," 97.
242 **There was not a single:** McLynn, *Crime and Punishment in Eighteenth-Century England,* 234–38.
243 **Under the Mutiny Act:** O'Brien, "Central Government and the Economy," 226. The first Mutiny Act passed in 1689; the last in 1879.
243 **"this instead of intimidating":** *Aris's Birmingham Gazette,* June 29, 1795, 3.
243 **Two months later:** *Aris's Birmingham Gazette,* August 10, 1795, 3.
243 **The "humane conduct":** *Aris's Birmingham Gazette,* April 18, 1796, 3.
243 **troops shot a boy:** *Aris's Birmingham Gazette,* May 2, 1796, 3.

243 **the idea of a "military" world:** D. Bell, *The First Total War,* 11.
243 **"his castle of defence":** POB: James Ripley's Defence, trial of Ripley, Robert Herbert, Richard Burton, Richard Matthews, April 1815, available at: www.oldbaileyonline.org/browse.jsp?id =t18150405-13–defend169&div=t18150405-13#highlight.
244 **defense of property on a national scale:** Hutton, *The History of Birmingham* (1835), 413–15.
244 **"A Man is not suffered":** *An Alarm to the People of England,* 21, 24–26 (italics added).
244 **"patriotic British Heroine":** *Aris's Birmingham Gazette,* June 28, 1779, 3.
244 **"the dreadful energy of a State":** Edmund Burke, "Letters on a Regicide Peace," quoted in P. Langford, *Public Life and the Propertied Englishman,* 583.
245 **"What was now to be punished":** Thompson, *Whigs and Hunters,* 206–7.
245 **was "really instituted for":** A. Smith, *The Wealth of Nations,* 771.
245 **"not suffer at all":** Hale, quoted in Malcolm, *Guns and Violence,* 70.
245 **fifty capital offenses:** Porter, *English Society in the Eighteenth Century,* 151. There were new capital offenses against being out at night with blackened face, destroying turnpikes or silk on looms, and so on. Poachers who fired at keepers committed a capital offense.
245 **"by *unpredictable* example":** P. Langford, *A Polite and Commercial People,* 297 (italics added). The dreadful penalties made victims reluctant to press charges and juries reluctant to convict.
245 **The Riot Act of 1715:** O'Brien, "Central Government and the Economy," 226.
245 **"If we diminish the terror":** Quoted in Hay, "Property, Authority and the Criminal Law," 18.
245 **private citizens formed associations:** O'Brien, "Central Government and the Economy," 217.
246 **It existed in tension and continuity with:** Braddick, "The Early Modern English State," 111.
246 **"*signal credibly* that property":** Mokyr, *The Enlightened Economy,* 411, 413 (italics added).
246 **Such was the outcome:** POB: Trial of Thomas Gilberthorp and John Green, May 1768, available at: www.oldbaileyonline.org/browse.jsp?id=t17680518-38&div=t17680518-38&terms=gilberthorp #highlight; Rudé, *Wilkes and Liberty,* 96–97.
246 **"wanton disregard for":** POB: Trial of Porter Ridout, October 1784, available at: www.oldbai leyonline.org/browse.jsp?id=t17841020-1&div=t17841020-1&terms=porter|ridout#highlight.
246 **killing three: "justifiable defence":** In Wiltshire County coroners' records, this was the only incident from 1752 to 1796 in which a gun was noted as a weapon used deliberately to kill another human being. There were numerous accidental deaths and seven suicides with guns. In many records, no weapon is named. Bills 1772–1774, for May 16, 1791, in Hunnisett, *Wiltshire Coroners' Bills,* 114–15; *Aris's Birmingham Gazette,* May 23, 1791, 3. After firing, the clothier handed the machine over to the crowd, who burned it and dispersed on the arrival of the constables.
246 **"considered chancel-medley":** See, for instance, POB: Trial of Francis Kettleby, December 1710, available at: www.oldbaileyonline.org/browse.jsp?id=t17101206-42&div=t17101206-42&terms= francis|kettleby#highlight.
247 **"No man has a right":** *Aris's Birmingham Gazette,* June 2, 1788, 3.
247 **For most of the century:** McLynn, *Crime and Punishment in Eighteenth-Century England,* 41.
247 **"reason has assumed its office":** POB: Trial of Richard England, February 1746, available at: www.oldbaileyonline.org/browse.jsp?id=t17960217-27-off157&div=t17960217-27&terms=passion |reason#highlight. See also Trial of James Annesley and Joseph Redding, July 1742, available at: www.oldbaileyonline.org/browse.jsp?id=t17420715-1&div=t17420715-1&terms=james |annesley#highlight.
247 **a "manslaughter" verdict became:** Rabin, *Identity, Crime, and Legal Responsibility,* 55.
248 **"There was a time":** Pitt, quoted in Colley, *Britons,* 310.
248 **"being drawn in the militia":** Hutton, *The History of Birmingham* (1835), 415.
248 **enlisted men made up:** Knight, *Britain Against Napoleon,* 260.
248 **Half a million civilians:** Colley, *Britons,* 312.
248 **"A determination on the part":** Quoted in ibid., 309.
248 **Average enrollment during:** Guldi, *Roads to Power,* 155. See also note for p. 2.
248 **hundreds of thousands of Volunteers:** Bohstedt, *The Politics of Provision,* 227, 228, 230.
248 **"the most common collective working class":** Colley, *Britons,* 312.
249 **Village artisans became:** Guldi, *Roads to Power,* 168.
249 **Mass arming exposed:** Banks, *A Polite Exchange of Bullets,* 237.
249 **Duke of Wellington extended:** D. Bell, *The First Total War,* 140–41, 254.

249 **Madras Army soldiers aiming:** Harding, *Smallarms of the East India Company*, 3:292, 355. In civilian realms, too, precision seems to have become an objective on the eve of the French Revolution. The first trace I have found of appreciation for marksmanship appeared in 1788, in relation to a tradesman who wagered he could shoot a bullet through a butcher's cleaver in three tries and succeeded. It was newsworthy because of its novelty. *Aris's Birmingham Gazette*, December 1, 1788, 3. Two years later, a military officer reputed to be one of the kingdom's "best shots" wagered that he could put nineteen out of twenty balls into an orange sixty-one feet away. He won. July 19, 1790, 3. Under the heading "extraordinary shot," in 1793, a clergyman killed a partridge, shot a man, a hog, and a hog sty, broke fourteen panes of glass, and knocked down six gingerbread kings and queens in the window with a single discharge of his gun. October 7, 1793, 3.

249 **Toward the end of:** The 1797 Bengal standing orders reminded men not to hurry in firing and called on rear officers to ensure that men loaded and leveled their arms properly. Harding, *Smallarms of the East India Company*, 3:265, 387.

249 **"Look along the barrel":** Quoted in ibid., 3:263.

250 **"precision and coolness":** Quoted in ibid. In 1803, sepoys, too, received a general order to improve accuracy of aim while triggering on command. From this time, the company's special light infantry muskets had backsights to facilitate aimed fire. The pause came to the Madras Army in 1805 and to the other presidencies in short order. Ibid., 3:265, 387.

250 **the order "Fire" was:** Ibid., 3:264.

250 **The emphasis on effective:** Ibid., 4:276. All agreed that the objective of musketry fire was the shocking impact of heavy casualties on the enemy's front ranks, which would open up the opportunity to close in with the bayonet. But they differed on the best means of achieving that impact.

250 **military thinkers brainstormed:** See Butler, *A Letter to the Right Honorable William Pitt, on the Defence of the Country* (1804), 5, 17, 21; Hanger, *To All Sportsmen, and Particularly to Farmers, and Gamekeepers*, 186–89.

250 **in 1805, Napoleon:** Alder, *Engineering the Revolution*, 111.

250 **The unique British interest:** On Native American marksmanship, see Starkey, "Conflict and Synthesis." On the Marathas, see Cooper, *The Anglo-Maratha Campaigns*, 40–41, 63.

250 **The gun did not:** Japanese understanding of guns also shifted as a result of social transformation, in the 1840s. Howell, "The Social Life of Firearms in Tokugawa Japan," 65–80. Likewise, while the musket remained constant, French infantry tactics changed rapidly from the 1750s to the 1790s. Alder, *Engineering the Revolution*, 109.

250 **British military manuals':** See Foucault, *Discipline and Punish*, 157–59.

250–51 **newspapers reminded readers:** HVD: Gloucester Inquests, October 28, 1805; *Aris's Birmingham Gazette*, April 17, 1797, 3. Other accidents reported in *Aris's Birmingham Gazette*, January 19, 1795, 3; January 26, 1795, 3; February 23, 1795, 3; May 4, 1795, 3; November 23, 1795, 3; June 20, 1796, 3; and August 29, 1796, 3.

251 **"frightened to death":** HVD: Gloucester Inquests, November 25, 1805.

251 **Despite official precautions:** HVD: Gloucester Inquests, November 9, 1807.

251 **The years 1811–15:** HVD: Gloucester Inquests, 1811–15.

251 **"old man of considerable property":** HVD: Gloucester Inquests, August 11, 1800.

251 **"without even knowing":** *Aris's Birmingham Gazette*, September 15, 1794, 3. Casual violence existed apart from guns, such as the reported "monster" who stabbed a lady in the street and ran off. *Aris's Birmingham Gazette*, January 26, 1794, 3. Earlier periods also saw instances of random gun violence probably related to mental illness. Schwoerer, *Gun Culture in Early Modern England*, 104. It is conceivable that war drove such instances of mental illness. Certainly, what we see in the early 1800s is more intense and marked than rarer earlier instances.

251 **a man stopped a woman:** *Aris's Birmingham Gazette*, July 21, 1794, 3.

251–52 **"with coolness and deliberation":** *Aris's Birmingham Gazette*, June 15, 1795, 3. See McLynn, *Crime and Punishment in Eighteenth-Century England*, 48.

252 **In Gloucester in 1797:** HVD: Gloucester Inquests, October 2, 1797.

252 **one currier shot:** HVD: Gloucester Inquests, January 18, 1802.

252 **"imprudently pointed towards":** HVD: Gloucester Inquests, September 27, 1802.

252 **Birmingham man was hanged:** Hutton, *The History of Birmingham* (1835), 419.

252 **When a coal carrier:** HVD: Gloucester Inquests, September 12, 1814.

252 **In Greater London between:** POB: Records for 1800–1815.

252 **in Leicestershire in 1795:** *Aris's Birmingham Gazette,* August 10, 1795, 3. In Sheffield, too, Volunteers fired on rioters, killing two and wounding more.

252 **Navvies and colliers:** Bohstedt, *The Politics of Provision,* 184.

252 **the radical John Thelwall:** *Aris's Birmingham Gazette,* March 13, 1797, 3.

252 **In Carlisle in 1812:** Bohstedt, *The Politics of Provision,* 241.

253 **the 1763 attempt:** Colley, *Britons,* 106. Later that year, Wilkes was seriously wounded by a bullet in the groin during a duel. He began to retire from the political scene. Rudé, *Wilkes and Liberty,* 34.

253 **"had not attempted to kill":** J. Langford, *A Century of Birmingham Life,* 2:99–100.

253 **He was acquitted:** Passage of the Criminal Lunatics Act within days of his trial led to his incarceration for life, unlike earlier defendants acquitted on similar grounds. Rabin, *Identity, Crime, and Legal Responsibility in England,* 1–2.

253 **"Mr. Perceval has unfortunately":** POB: Trial of Bellingham, May 1812, available at: www.oldbaileyonline.org/browse.jsp?id=t18120513-5-off22&div=t18120513-5&terms=bellingham#highlight. In the same period in the United States, Thomas Selfridge was tried for a different sort of gun murder. Charles Austin attacked him in the street with a stick, and Selfridge shot him—impulsively. His defense argued that the pistol was not the best weapon for such a purpose, given its liability to misfire in emotionally driven conflict; a sword would have served him better. Cornell, *A Well-Regulated Militia,* 112. To be sure, earlier political assassinations with guns had been plotted, too—including the Rye House Plot to shoot King Charles II. On these, see Schwoerer, *Gun Culture in Early Modern England,* 105.

254 **In Kent, bladed weapons:** Cockburn, "Patterns of Violence in English Society," 82–88.

254 **A fatal contest:** *Aris's Birmingham Gazette,* April 1, 1799, 3.

254 **Soldiers still scuffled:** See, for instance, *Aris's Birmingham Gazette,* January 4, 1796, 3; February 29, 1796, 3; and October 10, 1796, 3.

254 **That was the cultural work:** By contrast, in Japan, even when peasants began to see guns as weapons in the 1840s, they still did not use them to shoot "bad guys." Howell, "The Social Life of Firearms in Tokugawa Japan," 77.

254 **"emotionally repressed nation":** Dixon, "Forgotten Feelings."

255 **"sometimes took out a gun":** Austen, *Persuasion,* 30.

255 **"man of feeling":** Rabin, *Identity, Crime, and Legal Responsibility in England,* 169.

255 **Victorian citizenry surrendered:** Emsley, *Hard Men,* 158–59.

255 **With dress, house address:** Mokyr, *The Enlightened Economy,* 377–79, 385.

255 **Highwaymen also disappeared:** Guldi, *Roads to Power,* 155. The last mounted highway robbery took place in 1831. McLynn, *Crime and Punishment in Eighteenth-Century England,* 81.

256 **"The English, they do not stab":** Christie, *Murder on the Orient Express,* 153.

256 **The "horrid spectacle":** HVD: Gloucester Inquests, November 19, 1810. See also *Aris's Birmingham Gazette,* January 8, 1776, 3.

256 **"quite open to the windpipe":** *Aris's Birmingham Gazette,* May 26, 1766, 3, and June 1, 1766, 3.

256 **"he received the entire contents":** HVD: Gloucester Inquests, *Gloucester Herald,* September 2, 1815. Industrial accidents also introduced new forms of mechanically produced bodily mutilation.

256 **"mystery in the business":** J. Bell, *Discourses on the Nature and Cure of Wounds,* 1:131. See also Hunter, *A Treatise on the Blood, Inflammation, and Gun-Shot Wounds,* 2:246.

257 **"Where fallen Cruelty":** Aldington, *A Poem on the Various Scenes of Shooting.* The 1768 edition was titled "A Poem on the Cruelty of Shooting with Some Tender Remarks on the 10th of May 1768, Particularly on Young Mr. Allen." See McKnight, "Rural Sports," chap. 7.

258 **"so frightful as to exceed":** Quoted in Headrick, *Tools of Empire,* 85–86.

259 **"The ambition of the Sportsman":** [Pye], *Shooting.*

259 **"as he had liv'd with a pistol":** *An Account of the Lives of the Most Notorious Murderers and Robbers,* 24.

259 **Evidence submitted to Parliament:** PP: *An Abstract of the Evidence Delivered before a Select Committee of the House of Commons in the Years 1790, and 1791; on the Part of the Petitioners for the Abolition of the Slave Trade* (London, 1791), 73.

259 **Abolitionist evidence in 1805:** Advocate General to Lord Seaforth, October 25, 1804, in PP: House of Commons Papers X: *Papers Presented to the House of Commons Respecting the Slave Trade; &c.* (1805), 9.

Chapter Seven: Guns in Arms, Part 2: Abroad

261 **Sure enough, within days:** Hirst, *The Quakers in Peace and War*, 79.

261 **But at other times:** See Colley, *Captives*, 68; Blackmore, *British Military Firearms*, 26.

261 **Property was not an abstract:** Mitchell, *Rule of Experts*, 57, 297–98.

262 **Guns for trade were:** Bailey and Nie, *English Gunmakers*, 8.

263 **engaged in "assortment bargaining":** R. Hermann, "Money and Empire," 100, 104–5; Joseph Miller, personal communication, October 18, 2013 (citing the work of Marion Johnson and Philip Curtin).

263 **The Ordnance Office allowed the sales:** The Worshipful Company protested only sale of unproved guns. See also GL: MS5220/7: CM, March 28, 1723, 106–7, for an early company effort to ensure proving of old guns sold from the Tower for resale.

263 **The Royal African Company also armed:** Kea, "Firearms and Warfare on the Gold and Slave Coasts," 188, 194; R. Hermann, "Money and Empire," 109–10.

263 **"cocked it and holding it up":** Entry for May 13, 1769, in J. Banks, *The Endeavour Journal*, 87.

264 **"the necessity of keeping the Indians":** Robinson, *Beauties of Nature and Art Displayed*, 11:211. Volumes 11–13 comprise the voyages in the Southern Hemisphere by Commodore Byron, Captain Wallis, Captain Carteret, and Captain Cook. The official account of the second voyage, ending in 1775, was published in 1777, but an anonymous unauthorized account by the gunner's mate John Marra that appeared in 1775 was probably the source of this account.

264 **preserving that aura was essential:** A similar logic guided imperial use of later technologies. On airpower, see Satia, *Spies in Arabia*, chap. 8.

264 **"had been about the ship":** Robinson, *Beauties of Nature and Art Displayed*, 12:150–51.

264 **Incidents abound during:** See, for instance, Robinson, *Beauties of Nature and Art Displayed*, 11:115, 132.

264 **"were not accustomed to":** A. Anderson, *A Narrative of the British Embassy to China*, 65–66.

265 **"They seemed . . . in less fear":** Robinson, *Beauties of Nature and Art Displayed*, 13:162–63. See also 11:132.

265 **The Earl of Shaftesbury:** Quoted in Wennerlind, *Casualties of Credit*, 198.

266 **"had been more to blame":** Robinson, *Beauties of Nature and Art Displayed*, 11: 144–45, 194–95, 210.

267 **"as leave shoot them":** Cocker, *Rivers of Blood, Rivers of Gold*, 124–26, 133–37.

267 **a group aspiring to settlement abroad:** TNA: WO 47/77: OM, March 26, 1771, 271.

267 **Their instructions said nothing:** Steele, *Warpaths*, 39–45, 64–65.

268 **"presume and provoke unfriendliness":** Ibid., 85–86.

268 **Settlers typically used:** Peterson, *Arms and Armor in Colonial America*, 69.

269 **A Quaker in Maryland struggled:** FHL: Temp MSS 403/1/2/2/12: Mary Thomas of Maryland to Priscilla Farmer, [1760–61].

269 **After several attempts at:** Kennett and Anderson, *The Gun in America*, 52–54. See also Puype, "Dutch 17th-Century Flintlocks Recovered from Seneca Iroquois Sites in New York State," 232–34.

271 **the company traded 10,100:** Steele, *Warpaths*, 76–77, 106, 153, 167.

271 **From 1713 to 1730:** Rich, *The History of the Hudson's Bay Company*, 1:311, 511–12, 639–40.

271 **Native American purchases remained:** Carlos and Lewis, *Commerce by a Frozen Sea*, 140, 142.

271 **when Lewis and Clark were:** Fichter, *So Great a Proffit*, 212–13.

271 **The Ordnance Office contractor:** Bailey, "The Wilsons," 15–16.

272 **At the outbreak:** See, for instance, instructions to Albany Fort in 1744 and to Prince of Wales Fort in 1748, in Willson, *The Great Company*, 1:325, 337.

272 **The English again armed them:** See, for instance, TNA: WO 47/47: OM, May 11, 1756, 495.

272 **The department bought guns:** Bailey, "The Wilsons," 17, 19.

272 **When officials discontinued gifts:** Russell, *Guns on the Early Frontiers*, 47–48.

273 **sent by packtrain:** Ibid., 49–50.

273 **The governor of East Florida:** Bailey, "The Wilsons," 20, 24.

273 **John Jay's Treaty:** Russell, *Guns on the Early Frontiers*, 52–55.

273 **Their goods included:** Hanson, *The Northwest Gun*, 16–17, 53. Birmingham gunsmiths, the Ketlands especially, also supplied these arms. M. Brown, *Firearms in Colonial America*, 368.

274 **They refused obsolete guns:** M. Brown, *Firearms in Colonial America*, 156.

274 **Woodland Native Americans persuaded the company:** Ray, *Indians in the Fur Trade*, 73.

274 **In the 1740s:** Carlos and Lewis, *Commerce by a Frozen Sea*, 101.

274   **"frequently burst, not from the Fault"**: Quoted in Rich, *The History of the Hudson's Bay Company*, 594.
274   **"killed by the bursting"**: Letter, November 26, 1776, in Anburey, *Travels through the Interior Parts of America*, 1:128.
274   **English arms were the most favored**: Russell, *Guns on the Early Frontiers*, 55.
275   **"Many thousand Families of the Natives"**: Rich, *The History of the Hudson's Bay Company*, 494.
275   **"nations of hunters"**: Willson, *The Great Company*, 2:123–26.
275   **Shorter guns (three and a half feet)**: Steele, *Warpaths*, 179–82.
275   **guns were not used to hunt**: Carlos and Lewis, *Commerce by a Frozen Sea*, 140. The new, perhaps definitive, account of Native American gun trading and gun use can be found in Silverman, *Thundersticks*.
276   **Native Americans valued them**: Starkey, "Conflict and Synthesis," 64–65, 68–71; Silverman, *Thundersticks*, 8–9, 28–29.
276   **Native Americans' distinct tactical uses**: Malone, *The Skulking Way of War*, 35–36, chap. 4.
276   **most accounts of Native American**: This problem applies equally to British accounts of South Asian marksmanship.
276   **Parts of useless guns were used**: M. Brown, *Firearms in Colonial America*, 157.
276   **He had learned to do all**: Adams, *Modern Voyages*, chap. 24, 66–67.
277   **The Virginia Company and**: Sweeney, "Firearms, Militias, and the Second Amendment," 314, 329, 339–41.
277   **In 1737 and 1741**: Bailey, "The Wilsons," 15, 17, 19, 24.
277   **Gun ownership was widespread**: Sweeney, "Firearms, Militias, and the Second Amendment," 312, 326–27, 334–35, 338–39, 348–49, 352–55, 362–63. In the 1770s, rates of private ownership were somewhat lower in the northeast but remained consistent elsewhere. Churchill, "Gun Ownership in Early America." Early on, slaves were also armed at times to confront external threats, as in the war against the Yamasees in 1715–17.
278   **In 1823, the U. S. Army**: Russell, *Guns on the Early Frontiers*, 150–51.
278   **A mob came whistling**: Fichter, *So Great a Proffit*, 9–10.
278   **Guns were also important**: Russell, *Guns on the Early Frontiers*, 82–83.
278   **The American long rifle**: Sweeney, "Firearms, Militias, and the Second Amendment," 342.
278   **Homicide rates were**: Roth, "Guns, Gun Culture, and Homicide," esp. 232–36.
278   **They might be displayed**: See, for instance, Willson, *The Great Company*, 1:98, 103, 110, 143, 202.
279   **return of long-lost**: See, for instance, Bryce, *The Remarkable History of the Hudson's Bay Company*, 130.
279   **frontiersmen also subscribed to**: M. Brown, *Firearms in Colonial America*, 280.
279   **These "Northwest Guns"**: Hanson, *Northwest Gun*, 15–16.
279   **The Coercive Acts of 1774**: Sweeney, "Firearms, Militias, and the Second Amendment," 343, 346. The Massachusetts Provincial Congress ordered fifteen thousand from France. Connecticut and Massachusetts ordered recovery of public arms from the private hands into which they had drifted and impressed private arms.
279   **James Adair, an "English Chikkasaw"**: Adair, *The History of the American Indians*, 276, 300.
279   **This was a land in which**: Bryce, *The Remarkable History of the Hudson's Bay Company*, 290.
279   **"How vain and fruitless"**: Peter Williamson, "Sufferings of Peter Williamson, One of the Settlers in the Back Parts of Pennsylvania," in *Affecting History of the Dreadful Distresses*, 20–21.
280   **Such narratives offered**: Colley, *Captives*, 177.
280   **"just between his eyes"**: Adair, *History of the American Indians*, 336–38, 357, 393.
280   **after burying a knife**: Letter to a gentleman of Philadelphia, April 26, 1779, in *Affecting History of the Dreadful Distresses*, 9–10.
281   **In regions like**: Fichter, *So Great a Proffit*, 221. See also Roth, *American Homicide*, chaps. 1–2.
281   **North West Company men broke**: Willson, *The Great Company*, 2:117, 120, 133.
281   **An explorer from Winnipeg**: Bryce, *Remarkable History of the Hudson's Bay*, 224, 232.
281   **For colonials, too**: Kennett and Anderson, *The Gun in America*, 43.
281   **But Native Americans**: Leach, *Arms for Empire*, 10.
282   **Guns were adapted**: Blackmore, *British Military Firearms*, 58–59. The Madras Presidency Army used rifles as early as 1711. Cooper, Review of *Smallarms of the East India Company*, 3:761.
282   **Light infantry units**: Steele, *Warpaths*, 209.

282 **British soldiers were in the line:** TNA: WO 46/10: Ordnance Board to Major General Howe, March 12, 1776, 83–84. See also Blackmore, *British Military Firearms*, 69–70.

282 **Grice fashioned a rifle barrel:** TNA: WO 47/87: OM, May 7, 1776, 402.

282 **He, Barker, Willets:** M. Brown, *Firearms in Colonial America*, 340.

282 **The Ordnance Office inspector:** TNA: WO 47/87: OM, May 3, 1776, 393.

282 **Others arrived to proof:** TNA: WO 47/88: OM, August 28, 1776, 106.

282 **But many British officers:** Peterson, *Arms and Armor in Colonial America*, 200–201, 218–20. Ferguson was killed in 1780 in the Carolinas. His corps suffered high casualties on the front lines and was disbanded.

282 **The British governor:** Fichter, *So Great a Proffit*, 222.

282 **British commander General Amherst:** R. White, *The Middle Ground*, 258–59; Hamilton, "In the King's Service," 332.

282 **Belated British attempts:** B. Collins, *War and Empire*, 130.

283 **several thousand Maroons fought:** Blackburn, *The Making of New World Slavery*, 404.

283 **the Ordnance Office later readily agreed:** TNA: WO 47/75: OM, March 30, 1770, 170.

283 **a report emerged:** *Aris's Birmingham Gazette*, October 12, 1795, 3.

283 **capture of the *Olive Branch*:** I. Allen, *Particulars of the Capture of the Ship* Olive Branch, esp. preface, 3–12.

285 **The Ottomans traded guns:** Chew, *Arming the Periphery*, 32–33; Casale, *The Ottoman Age of Exploration*, 146. Ottoman skill in gun manufacture owed a great deal to contact with Europe. It is unclear whether the first matchlocks there (in the fifteenth century) were made locally or imported. Agoston, *Guns for the Sultan*, 89; Elgood, *Firearms of the Islamic World*, 52–55.

285 **The Mughals used guns:** Khan, "The Indian Response to Firearms," 56–58, 62.

286 **In Mughal combat:** Elgood, *Firearms of the Islamic World*, 135–38, 142–43; Gommans, *Mughal Warfare*, 147–49, 154–55, 159, 161–62. Zamindars and tribal chiefs entrenched in forts and jungles without horses did use them in infantry tactics.

286 **In 1615, Sir Thomas Roe:** Young, *The East India Company's Arsenals and Manufactories*, 129.

287 **By the 1690s, the East India Company:** R. Brown, "Guns Carried on East Indiamen."

287 **"Hardly a ship came":** Col. H. Munro, quoted in Chew, *Arming the Periphery*, 28.

287 **the Board of Customs:** Chew, *Arming the Periphery*, 29.

287 **Muskets were ordered:** Young, *The East India Company's Arsenals and Manufactories*, 222.

287 **"against the Sumatrians, Madagascar Blacks":** Quoted in Harding, *Smallarms of the East India Company*, 4:150–55.

287 **"If you could perswade":** Quoted in Harding, *Smallarms of the East India Company*, 4:311–13.

288 **In western India:** Harding, *Smallarms of the East India Company*, 4:347.

288 **the Select Committee at Calcutta:** Elgood, *Firearms of the Islamic World*, 145.

288 **British Army units often:** Harding, *Smallarms of the East India Company*, 4:499.

288 **In 1771, it hired:** Ibid., 1:18.

288 **The company's bureaucracy for:** Young, *The East India Company's Arsenals and Manufactories*, 12–15, 32–33, 36–37, 42, 47–48, 53–54, 57. In 1788, the staff under the commissary of stores at Fort William, in Calcutta, apart from the foundry, included an assistant commissary, four conductors, three park and lab sergeants, six European laborers, two European smiths, a carpenter, and a cooper. Among Indians, the department had five coopers, fifty-three smiths, sixty-five carpenters, thirteen sawyers, eleven painters, twenty-two brass men, 204 sicklegars (polishers or cleaners of small arms), eleven sailmakers, thirty-two armorers, thirteen chucklers (leatherworkers), and 344 magazine men. Magazines were also opened at Vellore, Tanjore, and elsewhere.

288 **short-lived European militia:** Harding, *Smallarms of the East India Company*, 4:424.

289 **British arms were provided:** Ibid., 4:421.

289 **During the Second Anglo-Mysore War:** Ibid., 4:320.

290 **The Marathas struggled to:** Ibid., 4:583–85.

290 **In 1763, Hyder Ali:** Ibid., 4:580–81.

290 **ships' captains and merchants:** Fort William to Court of Directors, March 20, 1776, *Fort William–India House Correspondence*, 7:413–55.

290 **Thus, in 1723:** Harding, *Smallarms of the East India Company*, 4:92–93, 592–93.

290 **many were shipped to London:** Elgood, *Firearms of the Islamic World*, 146.

291 **It refused Mir Jafar's:** Fort William to Court of Directors, September 29, 1763, *Fort William–India House Correspondence*, 3:515–20.

291 **"falling into Hands who may":** Quoted in Harding, *Smallarms of the East India Company*, 4:579.

291 **While ordering thousands:** Elgood, *Firearms of the Islamic World*, 145.

291 **This plea faltered:** Harding, *Smallarms of the East India Company*, 1:8–9.

291 **The company did purchase:** Young, *The East India Company's Arsenals and Manufactories*, 222–23. A 1771 report on Patna magazine stores showed that nearly a third of the swords were Indian-made and of very good quality.

291 **Its guns were said to be:** Young, *The East India Company's Arsenals and Manufactories*, 224.

291 **European mercenaries started:** Elgood, *Firearms of the Islamic World*, 86–87, 123, 135–38, 142, 147–49, 151, 158, 164–65, 166–68, 170, 177, 179; Chew, *Arming the Periphery*, 213–14.

292 **After Buxar, the nawab:** NAI: *Fort William–India House Correspondence:* Foreign and Political: Secret and Select Committee, vol. 14: Richard Smith, August 3, 1768, 356–64 and 366–77.

292 **Smith suspected that the nawab:** Elgood, *Firearms of the Islamic World*, 158. See also NAI: *Fort William–India House Correspondence*: Foreign and Political: Secret and Select Committee, vol. 14: Harper, May 20, 1768, 378–79.

292 **Shuja also employed:** NAI: *Fort William–India House Correspondence:* Foreign and Political: Secret and Select Committee, vol. 14: Aga Reza Moghul's account and translation of letter from Shuja-ud-Dowlah, in Thomas Rumbold to H. Verelst, June 30, 1768, 322–24.

292 **The boat passed all:** NAI: *Fort William–India House Correspondence:* Foreign and Political: Secret and Select Committee, vol. 14: H. Verelst, minute on letters re. the arms, July 23, 1768, 317–18; Thomas Rumbold to Verelst, June 19, 1768, with list dated June 12, 1768, 319; Wallen to Rumbold, June 10, 1768, 320; Rumbold to Wallen, June 19, 1768, 321; Gabriel Harper to Verelst, June [26?], 1768, 326–28.

293 **"folly and evil imaginations":** NAI: *Fort William–India House Correspondence:* Foreign and Political: Secret and Select Committee, vol. 14: translation of letter from Presidency to Shuja-ud-Dowlah, in minutes of committee meeting, July 27, 1768, 346–47.

293 **Calcutta now amiably:** Harding, *Smallarms of the East India Company*, 4:582.

293 **He received five thousand:** NAI: *Military Board of Ordnance Proceedings 1777 Feb.–Apr.*: Governor General and Council to the Ordnance Board, December 23, 1776, in minutes of February 8, 1777, 61–62; J. Baugh, secretary of the Board of Inspection to the Board of Ordnance, February 20, 1777, in minutes of April 5, 1777, 13.

293 **This began to grate:** Harding, *Smallarms of the East India Company*, 4:582–83; Elgood, *Firearms of the Islamic World*, 145.

293 **They allowed construction:** Elgood, *Firearms of the Islamic World*, 159–64.

294 **In the Second Anglo-Mysore War:** Harding, *Smallarms of the East India Company*, 4:579, 581.

294 **In nearly a dozen:** Young, *The East India Company's Arsenals and Manufactories*, 134; Elgood, *Firearms of the Islamic World*, 157–58, 164–65; Chew, *Arming the Periphery*, 213–14.

294 **After the British restored:** On collection of Tipu's weapons, see Jasanoff, *The Edge of Empire*, 183.

294 **Maratha military culture derived:** Cooper, *The Anglo-Maratha Campaigns*, 19, 40–41, 47, 50–51.

295 **But buyers complained that:** Unserviceable artillery guns were sold as river buoys and posts for the gates of Fort William. NAI: *Military Board of Ordnance Proceedings 4 November 1775 to January 1776*: Military Storekeeper to Warren Hastings and Board of Ordnance, December 16, 1775, in minutes of December 23, 1775, 534–35.

295 **"may for a time prevent":** William Henry Tone, 1800, quoted in Cooper, *The Anglo-Maratha Campaigns*, 47n100; Personal communication with Randolf Cooper, October 24, 2012. See also Elgood, *Firearms of the Islamic World*, 147.

295–96 **Company arms spread:** Harding, *Smallarms of the East India Company*, 4:586, 590–91; Chew, *Arming the Periphery*, 104.

296 **From the 1790s:** Prestholdt, *Domesticating the World*, 26; Chew, *Arming the Periphery*, 41.

296 **His admiration for this:** Twining, *Travels in India a Hundred Years Ago*, 182, 296–300.

297 **three British men forced their way:** Kolsky, *Colonial Justice in British India*, 50–53.

297 **"Here shooting of tigers":** Quoted in ibid., 19.

298 **English arms were standard:** Chew, *Arming the Periphery*, 104, 130.
298 **In South Africa, British:** Storey, *Guns, Race, and Power in Colonial South Africa*, 2.
298 **In Southeast Asia, too:** Tagliacozzo, *Secret Trades, Porous Borders;* Chew, *Arming the Periphery*, 193.
298 **Imperial expansion was fundamentally:** Today drone warfare is understood similarly: "People are a lot more comfortable with a Predator strike that kills many people than with a throat-slitting that kills one." Vicki Divoll, former CIA lawyer, quoted in Mayer, "The Predator War."
298 **"opulent and civilized over a poor":** A. Smith, *The Wealth of Nations*, 765, 675–76.
299 **"civility and humanity":** Hutton, *The History of Birmingham* (1835), 160. The surgeon John Hunter viewed the spread of firearms more cynically: "It is curious to observe that fire-arms and spirits are the first of our refinements that are adopted in uncivilized countries; and, indeed, for ages they have been the only objects that have been at all noticed or sought after by rude nations." *A Treatise on the Blood, Inflammation, and Gun-Shot Wounds*, 2:245.

Interlude: A Brief Account of the Society of Friends

303 **His influence spread:** Hirst, *Quakers in Peace and War*, chaps. 2–6.
304 **From 1682, the Society's:** Ibid., 185–89.
304 **The state was actively:** Flinn, *Men of Iron*, 65–66.
304 **Even Abraham Darby II:** In the next war, he and his partner, Richard Reynolds, refused orders for guns and armaments (although benefiting from the boom in iron demand). Reynolds's pacifism would induce him to refuse to pay taxes in 1798. Wallace, *The Social Context of Innovation*, 218.
304 **Ambrose Crowley III was:** He married in the Church of England in 1682. Flinn, *Men of Iron*, 153, 224.
305 **Hanburys also transported:** Price, "English Quaker Merchants and War at Sea," 73, 77, 79, 81.
305 **The Quaker banker Samuel Hoare:** Raistrick, *Quakers in Science and Industry*, 341.
305 **"a settled maxim, that":** Quoted in P. Langford, *A Polite and Commercial People*, 622.
305 **Many Quaker fortunes went:** Price, "The Great Quaker Business Families," 384–85.
305 **"yet they contribute to them":** Volunteer, quoted in Hirst, *Quakers in Peace and War*, 185–89.
305 **"love of one's country":** BCA: MS3101/C/D/14/3/1: Joseph Farmer to Mary Galton, [1745].
305 **"indispensible duty of every":** BCA: MS3101/C/D/14/3/2: Joseph Farmer to Mary Galton, December 1745.
305 **his cousin Thomas Farmer:** BCA: MS3101/C/C/2/2/1: Thomas Farmer to Joseph Farmer, November 30, 1745.
306–07 **"as an Englishman":** Quoted in Conway, *War, State, and Society*, 173.
306 **army life gave him:** In his will of 1763, Joseph identified himself as a "merchant of Liverpool" and "Lt. in HM's 31st Regiment of Foot," commanded by Colonel James Adolphus Oughton. BCA: MS3101/B/7/2: Will of Joseph Farmer, 1763; MS3101/B/7/3: Joseph Farmer to SG, assignment, February 24, 1762.
306 **"Do you bear a faithful":** Hirst, *Quakers in Peace and War*, 195, 202.
306 **"any gain or advantage":** Skeel, "The Letter-book of a Quaker Merchant," 140–41; S. Smith and T. R. Wheeley, "'Requisites of a Considerable Trade,'" 562.
307 **"little dirty disagreeable":** FHL: Temp MSS 403/1/2/1/12: Joseph Farmer to Mary Farmer, February 6, 1764.
307 **He protested to his:** FHL: Temp MSS 403/1/2/1/13: Joseph Farmer to Priscilla Farmer, April 26, 1765.
307 **Gun ownership rates in American colonies:** Sweeney, "Firearms, Militias, and the Second Amendment," 322–25.
307 **The Gurneys had guns:** "Summary" of *Gurney Times* collection of the National Trust, www.nationaltrustcollections.org.uk; Bidwell, *Annals of an East Anglian Bank*, 360.
307 **"went to a Quaker's to see":** Quoted in Williams, "James Farmer and Samuel Galton," 125.
307 **An American Quaker at Galton's:** Jabez Maud Fisher, quoted in William, "James Farmer and Samuel Galton," 125.
308 **one expression of concern:** FHL: Temp MSS 403/1/2/3/2: Mercy Bell to JF, [1756].
308 **"most unhappy man living":** JF to SG, March 25, 1755.

308 **even though the very security:** Price, "The Great Quaker Business Families," 385. Overly risky trade and bankruptcy could lead to temporary exclusion or disownment. Hoppit, *Risk and Failure in English Business*, 31.

308 **he had not dragged:** JF to SG, March 31, 1755.

308 **He had committed no:** JF to SG, June 2, 1755, and June 3, 1755. Other bankrupt Friends were more self-critical. See BCA: MS695/22/2: Papers of Mary Capper: Handwritten testimony of GW of G, June 30, 1759.

308 **Society's leniency may have:** Raistrick, *Quakers in Science and Industry*, 116–18.

308 **"My Brother Farmer not":** SG to Nicholas Atkinson, March 22, 1755 (repeated in SG to John Parr, March 22, 1755). See also BCA: MS3101/C/D/15/1/1: SG to John Parr, March 29, 1755.

308 **His wife (Farmer's sister):** BCA: MS3101/C/A/1/7/7: Mary Galton to Susannah Abrahams, May 9, 1755.

308 **Freame did hope:** SG to JF, March 24, 1755; John Galton [based on a draft by SG] to JF, March [25 or 26], 1755.

308 **but also as eighteenth-century men:** Rothschild, *The Inner Life of Empires*, 288–89.

309 **"with a man of his Cast":** Barclay to Lloyd, November 18, 1774.

309 **Galton, like Lloyd, was:** P. Jones, *Industrial Enlightenment*, 187–88; Wallace, *The Social Context of Innovation*, 225.

309 **"Chosen Overseer of":** D. Williams, "James Farmer and Samuel Galton," 124.

309 **He and Farmer contributed:** Advertisements, *Aris's Birmingham Gazette*, November 18, 1765, 3; November 25, 1765, 3; December 2, 1765, 3; December 9, 1765, 3; and December 16, 1765, 3.

309 **The 1769 Improvement Act:** Gill, *History of Birmingham*, 1: 157. Birmingham's Dissenters were not excluded from local government or the magistrate's bench. P. Jones, *Industrial Enlightenment*, 190–91.

309 **Theirs were "pretended scruples":** Paine, "To the Representatives of the Religious Society of the People called Quakers, or to so many of them as were concerned in publishing a late piece, entitled 'The ANCIENT TESTIMONY AND PRINCIPLES of the people called QUAKERS renewed, with Respect to the KING and GOVERNMENT, and touching the COMMOTIONS now prevailing in these and other parts of AMERICA, addressed to the PEOPLE IN GENERAL,'" in Appendix to *Common Sense*, 94–95. I thank Keith Baker for this reference.

309 **Adam Smith noted that military:** A. Smith, *The Wealth of Nations*, 883.

310 **Abolitionism was part of:** Thomas Haskell, "Capitalism and the Origins of the Humanitarian Sensibility, Part 2," in *The Antislavery Debate*, ed. Bender, 145–46.

310 **The worst abuses could be:** C. Brown, *Moral Capital*, 52–53.

310 **Investigation into East India:** Dirks, *The Scandal of Empire*.

311 **"exact in performing promises":** BCA: MS695/26/6: *Epistle from the Yearly Meeting in London to the Quarterly Meetings*, May 24, 1779.

311 **Taking up this political:** C. Brown, *Moral Capital*, 24, 88–89, 394–96, 406.

311 **The new venture was:** FHL: Temp MSS 403/1/1/3/32: David Barclay to Priscilla Farmer, July 10, 1781. Upon his death, he left small legacies for "the Blacks whom he so kindly liberated." MSS 403/4/7/1/28: Lloyd to Mary Lloyd (née Farmer), June 10, 1809.

312 **he led a delegation:** C. Brown, *Moral Capital*, 402, 405–6, 409, 419–20, 423.

312 **as "unusually virtuous":** Ibid., 424. See also 24, 391–96.

312 **If wealthy families like:** David Brion Davis, "The Quaker Ethic and the Antislavery International," in *The Antislavery Debate*, ed. Bender, 57.

312 **the Birmingham Meeting of 1789:** FHL: *Minutes of the Yearly Meeting Held in London Beginning the 5th of 6 mo 1786*, Quarterly Meetings Answers to the Yearly Meetings Queries: Warwickshire (March 23, 1789), No. 27, 493–94; London and Middlesex, 478–79; Berkshire, 435.

313 **"preserve and edify the body in love":** FHL: General Epistle, May 25, 1790, last entry in *Minutes of the Yearly Meeting Held in London Beginning the 5th of 6 mo 1786*.

313 **The Yearly Meeting's Written Epistle:** FHL: Written Epistle to Monthly and Quarterly Meetings, May 25, 1790, in *Minutes of the Yearly Meeting Held in London Beginning the 5th of 6 mo 1786*, 602–3.

313 **In 1795, the Society also:** Price, "The Great Quaker Business Families," 387.

313 **"to prevent . . . their being made":** Quoted in Hirst, *Quakers in Peace and War*, 217–18.

314 **Joseph Robinson wrote to:** Quoted in ibid., 233–34.

314 **"We believe Friends are"**: BSMH: *Warwickshire North Monthly Meeting Book from 12th of 1st mo 1791 to 11th of 12 mo 1799*, vol. 11, shelf number 23: Answers to Queries for Yearly Meeting for 1793: 8th query, March 13, 1793.

314 **the "private admonition"**: As noted by FHL: Box 11 1/12: Temp MSS 715.E97: Morris Birkbeck, Cursory remarks on some passages titled "Facts" contained in an address "To the Friends of the Monthly Meeting at Birmingham," printed and dispersed by SGII, 1795.

314 **"*sole*, and *entire*"**: BCA: MS3101/B/16/2: SGII, "To the Friends of the Monthly Meeting at Birmingham," 1795.

314 **"a genteel family"**: FHL: Temp MSS 403/7/15/3/32: J. and L. Delworth to Charles and Mary Lloyd, April 27, 1787.

315 **frequent admonishment against paying rates**: Hirst, *Quakers in Peace and War*, 209, 214.

315 **Friends were disowned**: BSMH: *Warwickshire North Monthly Meeting Book from 12th of 1st mo 1791 to 11th of 12 mo 1799*, vol. 11, shelf number 23: Meeting, March 12, 1794, minute 3; Meeting June 10, 1795, minute on Cornelius Aston.

315 **"at this and some former"**: BSMH: *Warwickshire North Monthly Meeting Book from 12th of 1st mo 1791 to 11th of 12 mo 1799*, vol. 11, shelf number 23: Tamworth Meeting, April 8, 1795, minute 8. The minute was continued: Hartshill Meeting, May 13, 1795, minute 6; Birmingham Meeting, June 10, 1795, minute 5.

315 **The Yearly Meeting sent**: Hirst, *Quakers in Peace and War*, 234–35.

315 **In July came the happy**: BSMH: *Warwickshire North Monthly Meeting Book from 12th of 1st mo 1791 to 11th of 12 mo 1799*, vol. 11, shelf number 23: Tamworth Meeting, July 18, 1795, minute 7.

Chapter Eight: Galton's Disownment

316 **He mediated a dispute**: Advertisement, *Aris's Birmingham Gazette*, December 13, 1790, 2.

316 **During the riots of**: P. Jones, *Industrial Enlightenment*, 196; Uglow, *The Lunar Men*, 446.

317 **finding a doctor courting**: S. Lloyd, *The Lloyds of Birmingham*, 130.

317 **The minute relating to**: BSMH: *Warwickshire North Monthly Meeting Book from 12th of 1st mo 1791 to 11th of 12 mo 1799*, vol. 11, shelf number 23: Monthly Meeting, August 12, 1795, minute 7; Monthly Meeting, September 9, 1795, minute 7; Monthly Meeting, October 14, 1795, minute 5; Monthly Meeting, November 11, 1795, minute 5; Monthly Meeting, December 9, 1795, minute 5.

317 **"candid and liberal conduct"**: SGII, "To the Friends of the Monthly Meeting at Birmingham," 1795.

317 **"pure religion includes the purest"**: BCA: MS3101/C/D/10/9/53: SGII to John Howard Galton, December 11, 1815.

319 **He confided to his**: BCA: MS3101/C/D/1/1/1: SGII to Adèle Galton, August 17, 1818.

323 **it might have been easy**: As noted by B. Smith, "The Galtons of Birmingham," 145.

323 **Galton Jr. was worth**: Pearson, *The Life, Letters and Labours of Francis Galton*, 1:46.

323 **accumulation over several**: Price, "The Great Quaker Business Families," 385.

323 **"significantly complicated—and not"**: Finn, *The Character of Credit*, 76.

323 **hoarding money would**: Muldrew, "'Hard Food for Midas,'" 98, 119–20. Late-century loosening of such constraints on the use of capital may have fueled the need for another means of assessing Galton's moral compass.

323 **Nor did wealth necessarily**: Levy, "The History of Profit."

323 **Accounting practices did not**: Mokyr, *The Enlightened Economy*, 351.

323 **as "engrossing temper"**: SG to JF, June 14, 1752. See also June 8, 1755.

324 **"being determined to rest"**: SG to John Parr, September 6, 1755. The firm's profits out of the slave trade were likely more modest than those of other slave-trading merchants. Richards, "The Birmingham Gun Manufactory of Farmer and Galton," 123.

324 **"hurrying guns through"**: SG to JF, June 7, 1755. See also SG to JF, [c. December 6 to 10, 1754] and December 12, 1754; SG to John Galton, May 22, 1755.

324 **the humble refuge**: JF to SG, March 25, 1755, and March 27, 1755.

324 **"private desire for profit"**: Muldrew, "Interpreting the Market," 177.

324 **Even fantastically successful**: Raistrick, *Quakers in Science and Industry*, 340.

324 **"those apparently in a prosperous"**: FHL: Temp MSS 403/1/1/2/35: Agatha Barclay to Mary Farmer, May 29, 1773.

324 **Freame bemoaned that:** FHL: Temp MSS 403/1/1/1/6: Joseph Freame to Mary Farmer, June 16, 1762.

324 **"our hurry in business":** FHL: Temp MSS: 403/1/1/1/8: Joseph Freame to Mary Plumsted, August 19, 1762. See also 403/1/1/1/3: October 30, 1761.

324 **he grumbled in 1762:** FHL: Temp MSS 403/1/1/1/10: Joseph Freame to Priscilla Farmer, December 14, 1762.

325 **Charles Lloyd complained:** FHL: Temp MSS 403/3/6/2/7: Charles Lloyd to Mary and Priscilla Farmer, May 5, 1777.

325 **Lloyd praised his:** FHL: Temp MSS 403/4/7/1/28: Charles Lloyd to Mary Farmer, June 10, 1809.

325 **as he explained to:** BCA: MS3101/C/D/10/9/64: SGII to Tertius, Hubert, and Howard Galton, January 30, 1819. See also MS3101/C/D/16/5/1: SGII to Joseph Strutt, October 12, 1819. Galton Jr. held to partible inheritance, dividing his land and liquid capital among his sons and leaving his daughters equally lucrative trusts. Hall and Davidoff, *Family Fortunes*, 206.

325 **it was also an industry:** The state struck a bargain with wealthy brewers and other powerful local interests after 1714: in return for protection against French wine, brewers agreed to be taxed at high rates. The government encouraged concentration in the industry to ease tax collection (an interesting counterpoint to its diffusion of the gun industry). Beer, hops, malt, and related products accounted for about 75 percent of all excise taxes. Mokyr, *The Enlightened Economy*, 436. On brewing and agriculture, see Mathias, *The Transformation of England*, 252.

326 **"above Twenty thousand Hands":** Quoted in Finn, *The Character of Credit*, 203.

326 **"great wants of the great body":** A. Smith, *The Wealth of Nations*, 4.

326 **His father had always agonized over:** SG to John Galton, May 13, 1755.

326 **the abolition movement illuminated:** Thomas Haskell, "Capitalism and the Origins of the Humanitarian Sensibility, Part I," in *The Antislavery Debate*, ed. Bender, 110–11; "Capitalism and the Origins of the Humanitarian Sensibility, Part 2," in *The Antislavery Debate*, ed. Bender, 140.

327 **Cognizance of the impersonal:** As David Brion Davis notes, "The knowledge that our economic acts are related in some way to most of the world's crime and oppression can blunt any sense of complicity." "Reflections on Abolitionism and Ideological Hegemony," in *The Antislavery Debate*, ed. Bender, 177–78. See also Blackburn, *The Making of New World Slavery*, 15–16.

327 **"intricate web of mutual":** John Ashworth, "The Relationship between Capitalism and Humanitarianism," in *The Antislavery Debate*, ed. Bender, 186–87.

327 **The Napoleonic Wars would:** Colley, *Britons*, 99–100.

327 **Galton could not conceive:** In 1710, the Quaker John Bellers had conceived of such a universe, pointing to the waste of treasure in the War of the Spanish Succession, which might otherwise have been invested in "palaces, hospitals, bridges, and [making] rivers navigable." Quoted in Hirst, *Quakers in Peace and War*, 167. The idea that war's moral liabilities included its developmental cost to the realm became typical of liberal political economy.

328 **The quandary faced by:** Porter, *English Society in the Eighteenth Century*, 199.

328 **The Society of Friends routinely urged:** Walvin, *The Quakers*, 77.

328 **his daughters' participation in the sugar:** They later served as committee members of the West Bromwich, Birmingham and District Ladies Society for the Relief of Negro Slaves (founded 1825).

328 **"the relation of one thing to":** Quoted in Thomas Haskell, "Capitalism and the Origins of the Humanitarian Sensibility, Part 2," in *The Antislavery Debate*, ed. Bender, 158.

329 **"we had the good fortune":** FHL: Temp MSS 403/1/1/1/9: Joseph Freame to Mary Plumsted, October 15, 1762.

329 **In 1782, Quaker homes:** P. Jones, *Industrial Enlightenment*, 187–89.

329 **In 1789, they were:** *Aris's Birmingham Gazette*, March [?], 1789, 3.

329 **town's abolition petition:** *Aris's Birmingham Gazette*, February 4, 1788, 3. See also January 28, 1788, 3, and February 11, 1788, 3.

329 **He dined with plantation owners:** Uglow, *The Lunar Men*, 413–14.

329 **"famous Birmingham names":** As reported in J. Langford, *A Century of Birmingham Life*, 1:440.

329 **Priestley's sermons envisioned:** C. Brown, *Moral Capital*, 328–29.

330 **a descendant of the Apologist:** He was not above joking about her ancestry: accepting Matthew Boulton's dinner invitation, he explained that he would convey his wife's apologies for not having called

on their family earlier but that, since "she is herself descended from a famous Apologist," he would "do much better in giving her the opportunity of making her own." SGII to Boulton, August 1787.

330 **described Galton Jr. as practically a Deist:** Hirst, *Quakers in Peace and War*, 240.

330 **"habits of regularity":** Reported in BCA: MS3101/C/E/5/8/1: Tertius Galton to Joseph Strutt, June 4, 1810.

330 **Galton's experience with:** John Howard Galton to Friends of Warwickshire North Monthly Meeting, draft letter edited by SGII, enclosed in BCA: MS3101/C/D/10/9/65: SGII to John Howard Galton, December 5, 1819.

330 **Sampson Lloyd III also:** Price, "The Great Quaker Business Families," 379.

331 **The Society dwindled:** P. Jones, *Industrial Enlightenment*, 169.

331 **marriage took many:** Raistrick, *Quakers in Science and Industry*, 341.

331 **Patriotism also caused:** Price, "The Great Quaker Business Families," 387, 389.

331 **The family curated its Quaker:** FHL: Temp MSS 403/1/1/3/58: David Barclay to "My Dear Sister," February 12, 1802; 403/1/13/59: David Barclay to Charles Lloyd, February 17, 1802.

331 **Galton Jr. had his ancestors':** BCA: MS3101/B/16/3: SGII, "Tombs of My Ancestors," 1809.

331 **The family cellars were:** P. Jones, *Industrial Enlightenment*, 186–88.

331 **the house and grounds were:** S. Lloyd, *The Lloyds of Birmingham*, 130.

331 **dress became less crucial:** Wahrman, *The Making of the Modern Self*, 274–76, 279.

332 **the "shrine of morality":** Porter, *English Society in the Eighteenth Century*, 323.

332 **"decidedly statistical bent":** F. Galton, *Memories of My Life*, 3. He reserved for his father, Tertius, what was surely his highest form of compliment: a man "eminently statistical by disposition." The tables in his tract on currency attested to his "scientific bent. . . . A sliding rule . . . was his constant companion" (8).

333 **"the idea of a distinctive":** Rothschild, *The Inner Life of Empires*, 123–24. See also 132–33 and 150–53.

333 **the government's right and:** Brewer, *The Sinews of Power*, 167.

333 **It was difficult for:** Muldrew, "Interpreting the Market," 169, 177, 181–82.

334 **"should attempt to vindicate":** BSMH: *Warwickshire North Monthly Meeting Book from 12th of 1st mo 1791 to 11th of 12 mo 1799*, vol. 11, shelf number 23: Birmingham Meeting, February 10, 1796, minute 7. See also Birmingham Meeting, January 13, 1796, minute 8.

334 **He questioned the modest:** Morris Birkbeck, cursory remarks on some passages titled "Facts," contained in an address "To the Friends of the Monthly Meeting at Birmingham," printed and dispersed by SGII, 1795. This is a member of the family of George Birkbeck, founder of Birkbeck College in London—probably the influential Quaker minister Morris Birkbeck (1734–1816). Interestingly, his son by the same name (1764–1825) left the Quaker fold in 1802. Annoyed at being taxed by a government that denied him a vote because of his religion, he established a utopian community in the United States. Charlotte Erickson, "Birkbeck, Morris (1764–1825)," *Oxford Dictionary of National Biography* online, accessed January 12, 2017, www.oxforddnb.com/view/article/59873.

336 **"to receive any further Collection":** BSMH: *Warwickshire North Monthly Meeting Book from 12th of 1st mo 1791 to 11th of 12 mo 1799*, vol. 11, shelf number 23: Birmingham Meeting, March 9, 1796, minute 9.

336 **their London counterparts:** FHL: *Minutes of the Yearly Meeting Held in London, 1791–1800*, Answers to the Queries, 8th Query, from Warwickshire, May 18, 1796, 287–88.

336 **the regional Quarterly Meeting:** BSMH: *Warwickshire North Monthly Meeting Book from 12th of 1st mo 1791 to 11th of 12 mo 1799*, vol. 11, shelf number 23: Tamworth Meeting, April 13, 1796, minute 6, 148. The five were John Cash, Thomas Harris, Joseph Burgess, Joseph Seymour, and Jeffery Beavington.

336 **without appreciable results:** See BSMH: *Warwickshire North Monthly Meeting Book from 12th of 1st mo 1791 to 11th of 12 mo 1799*, vol. 11, shelf number 23: Hartshill Meeting, May 11, 1796, minute 3; Birmingham Meeting, June 8, 1796, minute 3.

336 **In July, the Birmingham Meeting:** BSMH: *Warwickshire North Monthly Meeting Book from 12th of 1st mo 1791 to 11th of 12 mo 1799*, vol. 11, shelf number 23: Birmingham Meeting, July 13, 1796, minute 8; Hirst, *Quakers in Peace and War*, 239.

336 **"that part of the concern":** BSMH: *Warwickshire North Monthly Meeting Book from 12th of 1st mo 1791 to 11th of 12 mo 1799*, vol. 11, shelf number 23: Hartshill Meeting, August 10, 1796, minute 3.

336 **Lloyd and Gibbins:** BSMH: *Warwickshire North Monthly Meeting Book from 12th of 1st mo 1791 to 11th of 12 mo 1799,* vol. 11, shelf number 23: Birmingham Meeting, September 14, 1796, minute 3.

336 **"excellent common sense":** Quoted in Hirst, *Quakers in Peace and War,* 236.

337 **He continued to donate:** *Aris's Birmingham Gazette,* September 28, 1795, 3; Gill, *History of Birmingham,* 1:131; BSMH: Birmingham Preparative Meeting Minutes, 1783–1807, vol. 2, shelf number 80: School contributions for 1792, 152; for 1795, 155; for 1796, 159.

337 **While the controversy unfolded:** *Aris's Birmingham Gazette,* September 27, 1790, 3; December 22, 1794, 3; December 29, 1794, 3; July 13, 1795, 3; July 27, 1795, 3; and August 10, 1795, 3; J. Langford, *A Century of Birmingham Life,* 2:46.

337 **In 1798, he promoted:** *Aris's Birmingham Gazette,* March 5, 1798, 3.

337 **He subscribed to:** BSMH: Birmingham Preparative Meeting minutes, 1783–1807, vol. 2, shelf number 80: Meeting, March 6, 1796, 157.

337 **He participated in the plan:** BSMH: Birmingham Preparative Meeting minutes, 1783–1807, vol. 2, shelf number 80: Meetings, March 11, 1792, 153; March 6, 1796, 156; November 6, 1796, 158.

337 **"profit by any concern in":** BCA: MS695/26/11: *Epistle from the Yearly Meeting in London to the Quarterly Meetings,* May 1798, 3.

337 **"gentleman peculiarly distinguished by":** *Aris's Birmingham Gazette,* July 1, 1799, 3.

337 **"sound and acute understanding":** *Gentleman's Magazine,* 1799, 63, quoted in Pearson, *The Life, Letters and Labours of Francis Galton,* 1:41.

338 **"larger concourse of spectators":** J. Langford, *A Century of Birmingham Life,* 2:91–92, quoting an account dated July 15, 1799. See also *The Monthly Magazine,* August 1, 1799, copied in UCL: Galton/1/1/10/4.

338 **he engaged workshops in:** Galton to Ordnance, June 4, 1803, paraphrased in TNA: WO 47/2575: OM, June 6, 1803, 916–17.

338 **Rising fortunes in town:** S. Lloyd, *The Lloyds of Birmingham,* 64.

338 **He joined the copper business:** Ann Prior, "Gibbins family (per. c. 1770–1919)," *Oxford Dictionary of National Biography* online, accessed January 12, 2017, www.oxforddnb.com/view/article/48023.

339 **his son would open:** There is some dispute on how the Galton bank came to be absorbed between 1829 and 1831: See B. Smith, "The Galtons of Birmingham," 148n10.

339 **"As I really am":** BCA: MS3101/C/D/10/65/1: Richard Rathbone to John Howard Galton, October 4, 1807.

339 **scribbling at the top, "Burn this":** BCA: MS3101/C/D/10/5/24: Hubert Galton at Duddeston to John Howard Galton at Oxford, April 1806–10.

339 **They were typical of Quakers:** Porter, *English Society in the Eighteenth Century,* 199.

339 **Tertius held the title of overseer:** Gill, *History of Birmingham,* 1:132.

339 **He and Tertius served:** J. Langford, *A Century of Birmingham Life,* 2:406.

339 **Tertius was high bailiff:** B. Smith, "The Galtons of Birmingham," 140, 147.

340 **"Friends everywhere against keeping":** Quoted in Hirst, *Quakers in Peace and War,* 214.

341 **the verb *bore*:** Majumdar, *Prose of the World,* 19.

341 **"The great importance of trade":** Quoted in Colley, *Britons,* 323.

342 **"the other paraphernalia of military metallic":** Hall, *Civilising Subjects,* 273.

342 **"system of government":** A. Smith, *The Wealth of Nations,* 693.

342 **Nineteenth-century evangelicals:** I thank Alex Owen for this observation.

343 **"an old Birmingham worthy":** J. Langford, *A Century of Birmingham Life,* 2:91–92. See also Stephens, ed., *The Victoria History of the County of Warwick,* 7:96.

343 **"our adviser and sympathiser":** Quoted in Hall and Davidoff, *Family Fortunes,* 333.

343 **thought it "very able":** "Notes on the Disownment of Samuel Galton," *Quakeriana* 1:5 (July 1894), 74; Hirst, *Quakers in Peace and War,* 236.

343 **"clear, argumentative, and able statement":** S. Lloyd, *Lloyds of Birmingham,* 120–29.

344 **he reported on:** Storey, *Guns, Race, and Power in Colonial South Africa,* 93, 99–100. Livingstone himself delivered hundreds of pounds of powder and lead to the Kololo chief Sekeletu in 1852, months after creation of the South African Republic prohibited arms trading to Africans north of the Orange River.

344 **two gunmakers publicly criticized:** Artifex and Opifex, *The Causes of Decay in a British Industry,* v, 31, 56.

Chapter Nine: The Gun Trade after 1815

345 Tertius carried on: See J. Langford, *A Century of Birmingham Life,* 2:411, 457–58, 471, 495, 501.

345 The Steelhouse Lane premises: Pearson, *The Life, Letters and Labours of Francis Galton,* 1:51.

345 Galton Bridge, in Smethwick: D. Williams, "James Farmer and Samuel Galton," 127–28.

345 Another cousin of Francis: S. Lloyd, *The Lloyds of Birmingham,* 130–31.

346 Assimilation often entailed: Price, "The Great Quaker Business Families," 380, 387.

346 His children carried on: Inikori, *Africans and the Industrial Revolution,* 465–67. On the Whateleys, see also BCA: MS3602/304, 309 (1818) and 460 (1851).

346 Of thirty-one men who called: Behagg, "Mass Production without the Factory," 5–6.

346 Britain's historic prosperity: The wealth of many of Britain's most powerful families is traceable to state compensation for lost property in slaves after abolition. Sanchez Manning, "Britain's Colonial Shame: Slave-Owners Given Huge Payouts after Abolition." *The Independent,* February 24, 2013, www.independent.co.uk/news/uk/home-news/britains-colonial-shame-slaveowners-given-huge -payouts-after-abolition-8508358.html. The database is available at www.ucl.ac.uk/lbs.

346 "old-established families of bankers": Quoted in Thompson, "The Peculiarities of the English," 265.

346 "nearly the whole of": Hall, *Civilising Subjects,* 271–73.

347 the storekeeper George Lovell: Blackmore, *British Military Firearms,* 273.

347 Continuing friction with Spain: Parsons, *Observations on the Manufacture of Fire-Arms for Military Purposes,* 99–104.

347 the Seizure of Arms Act: Greenwood, *Firearms Control,* 14–15, 17–24.

347 In Ireland, annual: Storey, *Guns, Race, and Power in Colonial South Africa,* 245.

347 The Ordnance Board issued: Bailey, *British Board of Ordnance,* 22.

348 contemporary account reports: Goodman, "On the Progress of the Small Arms Manufacture," 500, 503.

348 The Birmingham trade was: J. Langford, *A Century of Birmingham Life,* 2:579.

348 Two years later: *RSCSA,* 344.

348 The "Musket Wars": Storey, *Guns, Race, and Power in Colonial South Africa,* 332.

348 The Ordnance Office sold: Parsons, *Observations on the Manufacture of Fire-Arms for Military Purposes,* 30, 31, 41–42, 50, 63, 64, 66, 68, 70–76, 79, 81–95.

350 "become the manufactory and": Ibid., 96–106.

350 In 1838, British forces were: PP: *Second Report from the Select Committee on Army and Ordnance Expenditure,* July 12, 1849, 145, 308, 499.

350 "the great school in": Quoted in D. Williams, *The Birmingham Gun Trade,* 84–85.

350 The old system was: Memorandum re. small arms, February 18, 1854, appendix of *RSCSA,* 451–52; PP: *Second Report from the Select Committee on Army and Ordnance Expenditure,* July 12, 1849, xxxv, 499.

350 The home secretary took: Greenwood, *Firearms Control,* 16.

350 Enfield adopted machinery: Blackmore, *British Military Firearms,* 275.

350 a movement to revive: See W. C. Aitken, "The Revived Art of Metal-Working in the Precious Metals, Brass and Iron, on Mediæval, or True Principles," in *The Resources, Products, and Industrial History of Birmingham and the Midland Hardware District,* ed. Timmins, 536–51.

350 the local press warned: *RSCSA,* 458–59.

351 Lovell mediated price fixing: PP: *Second Report from the Select Committee on Army and Ordnance Expenditure,* July 12, 1849, 309–11, 625–27.

351 Railways had brought: Blackmore, *British Military Firearms,* 275.

351 Together they accused: PP: *Second Report from the Select Committee on Army and Ordnance Expenditure,* July 12, 1849, 290–92, 295, 298, 300, 301, 305, 499.

351 after all, they produced: *RSCSA,* 344.

351 the Ordnance Office observed: Blackmore, *British Military Firearms,* 275.

352 newspapers were alarmingly: Greenwood, *Firearms Control,* 16–17. The return showed that 378 guns, 467 pistols, and 71 swords had been sold to "Gentlemen, Respectable Tradesmen, Gamekeepers, etc." But 122 guns, 162 pistols, 22 swords, and 18 other weapons had been sold to "Mechanics, Labourers, etc., who are believed to be, and others known to be Chartists."

352 "In some Cases Advertizing": Quoted in Bannerman, *Merchants and the Military,* 121, 129, 140, 145.

352 **The committee decided:** PP: *Second Report from the Select Committee on Army and Ordnance Expenditure,* July 12, 1849, xxxvi, 312, 499, 621–22.

352 **"in opposition to the trade":** Ibid., xxxv, 302, 307.

353 **the "evil tendency":** Lovell, 1848, quoted in appendix to *RSCSA,* 454–55.

353 **The manner of welding barrels:** M. Smith, *Harpers Ferry Armory and the New Technology,* 115.

353 **Blanc's shops hosted:** Merritt Roe Smith, "Army Ordnance and the 'American System' of Manufacturing, 1815–1861," in *Military Enterprise and Technological Change,* 44–47.

354 **In 1798, the U.S. government:** M. Brown, *Firearms in Colonial America,* 383–87.

354 **Decius Wadsworth was:** Merritt Roe Smith, "Army Ordnance and the 'American System' of Manufacturing," in *Military Enterprise and Technological Change,* 49–54, 56, 60–63, 76–77, 86.

354 **It took time:** M. Smith, *Harpers Ferry Armory and the New Technology,* 107, 322, 328, 334.

354 **Legally, arms for:** Ruttan, *Is War Necessary for Economic Growth?,* 24, 30–31.

354 **This "American system of manufacture":** Rosenbloom, "Anglo-American Technological Differences in Small Arms Manufacturing," 684–85, 687.

355 **In 1850, tenders for:** *RSCSA,* iv, viii, 7.

355 **barrel welders won:** Artifex and Opifex, *The Causes of Decay in a British Industry,* 7, 24.

355 **"the greatest mart":** *RSCSA,* 420.

355 **Nasmyth's steam hammer:** *RSCSA,* 7, 17.

355 **The Ordnance Office turned:** *RSCSA,* 21, 103–5.

355 **Private barrel makers:** *RSCSA,* 58.

355 **Lovell affirmed that:** *RSCSA,* 450–51.

356 **They asked for an official:** *RSCSA,* 58.

356 **until "fair competition":** *RSCSA,* 103–4, 300.

356 **"Cheapest, most Expeditious":** *RSCSA,* iii, v.

356 **memorandum of February 1854:** Memorandum re. small arms, February 18, 1854, appendix of *RSCSA,* 451–52.

356 **"at any moment with":** *RSCSA,* 134.

357 **Lord Seymour assured:** *RSCSA,* 10.

357 **Sir Thomas Hastings:** *RSCSA,* 15–16.

357 **Besides displaying his guns:** Williams, *The Birmingham Gun Trade,* 73.

357 **All of Birmingham's gunmakers:** *RSCSA,* 8.

357 **To the concern that:** *RSCSA,* 17.

357 **A delegation that had:** D. Williams, *The Birmingham Gun Trade,* 78.

358 **A machine maker contended:** *RSCSA,* 29, 46, 68–69, 120.

358 **"under a kind of":** *RSCSA,* 110.

358 **Hastings explained that:** *RSCSA,* 53–54.

358 **A machine maker added:** *RSCSA,* 120.

359 **a government factory would:** *RSCSA,* xxvi.

359 **Others cited as evidence:** *RSCSA,* 103–5, 201. His son Francis died in 1845 while purchasing gunstocks on the Continent. During a strike at Enfield the next year, a worker attacked George Lovell. The year 1847 brought conflict with the contractors and their workmen. Much of this was triggered by Francis Lovell's indiscretions as assistant inspector of small arms—he was accused of falsifying the accounts for gunstocks. Francis was dismissed. Pam, *The Royal Small Arms Factory,* 43.

359 **far from inefficient:** *RSCSA,* 214–17, 223.

359 **Others tallied fowling:** *RSCSA,* 17, 228, 243, 315–16, 344.

359 **Colonel Bonner, who:** *RSCSA,* viii, 361–70.

359 **Westley Richards of Birmingham:** *RSCSA,* 431, 436, 441–42.

360 **Others argued that:** *RSCSA,* 326, 378, 423.

360 **"made to appear in":** *RSCSA,* 406. See also 201.

360 **Others reported bad:** *RSCSA,* xxv, 79, 260.

360 **But they needed:** *RSCSA,* xix–xxi, 173, 308.

360 **with half a dozen:** *RSCSA,* 431.

360 **The state countered:** *RSCSA,* x.

360 **Some gunmakers insisted:** *RSCSA,* xix–xxi, 253.

360 **They met sudden demand:** *RSCSA,* 157, 314, 327–28.

361 "different parts of the country": *RSCSA*, 254.
361 Many had had nothing to do: *RSCSA*, 253–54, 418.
361 "walking about and leaving": *RSCSA*, 335.
361 Many were in wool: *RSCSA*, 319, 328, 379.
361 Most agreed that: *RSCSA*, 224, 337, 379. According to Chew, in 1852, Birmingham had 5,167 of Britain's 7,731 gunsmiths and workers. *Arming the Periphery*, 57.
361 the superintendent at Enfield: *RSCSA*, 290–91.
361 Hastings called for: *RSCSA*, 56.
362 Whitworth, impressed as he was: *RSCSA*, v.
362 Colt, too, urged: *RSCSA*, 88–89.
362 "the advantage of an increased": *RSCSA*, vii.
362 "as a check upon": *RSCSA*, ix–x.
362 Birmingham possessed rolling: *RSCSA*, 7.
363 "must wholly depend": Ibid.
363 Critics spoke of: *RSCSA*, 21.
363 "on the banks of": Parsons, *Observations on the Manufacture of Fire-Arms for Military Purposes*, 22.
363 They united as: Page, ed., *The Victoria History of the County of Warwick*, 2:228.
363 Those who carried on: Goodman, "On the Progress of the Small Arms Manufacture," 501.
363 Workmen did not: Artifex and Opifex, *The Causes of Decay in a British Industry*, 5.
363 scandalous inefficiencies affecting: Skentelbery, *Arrows to Atom Bombs*, 18–20, 27.
363 The *Times* of London: "The Manufacture of Small Arms and Artillery," *Times* (London), July 13, 1855, 5.
364 Goodman, as chairman: John Goodman to the *Times* (London), August 2, 1855, 6.
364 The *Birmingham Journal*: Cited in D. Williams, *Birmingham Gun Trade*, 95.
364 One contractor established: Goodman, "The Birmingham Gun Trade," 388.
364 They persuaded the master: Blackmore, *British Military Firearms*, 275–76.
364 The sixty-odd parts: Goodman, "On the Progress of the Small Arms Manufacture," 500.
364 The factory could make: Ffoulkes, *Arms & Armament*, 55.
365 Its turn-of-the-century range: Vernon, *Distant Strangers*, 67; Headrick, *Tools of Empire*, 84.
365 Army officers drew on: *RSCSA*, 157, 438.
365 Richards's carbine became: Richards (and contemporary gunmakers) had numerous patents. See Page, ed., *The Victoria History of the County of Warwick*, 2:231; entry on "Westley Richards & Co." in McIntosh, *Best Guns*.
365 fifteen of the largest contractors: Fries, "British Response to the American System," 386–87, 398.
365 It could produce: Behagg, "Mass Production without the Factory," 13.
365 Its first government contract: D. Williams, *The Birmingham Gun Trade*, 97.
365 The northern states and: Goodman, "On the Progress of the Small Arms Manufacture," 503–4.
366 Goodman repeated in 1865: Ibid., 497.
366 Much skilled labor: Chew, *Arming the Periphery*, 83.
366 The London Armoury Company: D. Williams, *The Birmingham Gun Trade*, 97.
366 Street improvements demolished: Page, ed., *The Victoria History of the County of Warwick*, 2:230.
366 The Birmingham School: Artifex and Opifex, *The Causes of Decay in a British Industry*, 58.
366 The manual trade: Wise, "On the Evolution of the Jewellery and Gun Quarters in Birmingham," 71–72.
366 Phipson noted wryly: Thomas Phipson, "The Pin Trade," in *The Resources, Products, and Industrial History of the Birmingham and Midland Hardware District*, ed. Timmins, 601.
366 "as a response to": Fries, "British Response to the American System," 379, 385, 403.
367 The twentieth century: Edgerton, *Warfare State*, 1, 7.
367 The Cape and Natal: Storey, *Guns, Race, and Power in Colonial South Africa*, 75, 111, 182, 184. Regulations were widely disregarded and evaded.
367 His son John deemed: Ibid., 99–101.
367 Between the 1860s and the 1890s: Chew, *Arming the Periphery*, 87.
367 An 1874 report by: Storey, *Guns, Race, and Power in Colonial South Africa*, 182, 196.
368 New tariffs undermining: Page, ed., *The Victoria History of the County of Warwick*, 2:230.

368 **clear technological hierarchy:** Headrick, *Tools of Empire*, 84. "The disparity between the rifle of World War One and the Napoleonic musket was greater than between the musket and the bow and arrow."

368 **The Crimean War inspired:** Birch, *The Economic History of the British Iron and Steel Industry*, 320–23, 328.

368 **John Brown of Sheffield:** Ibid., 313.

369 **The British government took over:** McNeill, *The Pursuit of Power*, 238–41.

369 **The navy leaked:** Ibid., 268–70.

370 **In 1886, as director:** Ibid., 270–72.

370 **In 1897, Armstrong:** Shenhav, "At a Gun Point," 56.

371 **"Practically all mechanical progress":** Quoted in Trebilcock, "'Spin-off' in British Economic History," 485–86.

371 **Though much government work:** Artifex and Opifex, *The Causes of Decay in a British Industry*, 21; Bailey and Nie, *English Gunmakers*, 25–26.

371 **BSA was the largest:** D. Williams, *The Birmingham Gun Trade*, 130; Ball, "The Decline of the International Control of Small Arms," 830.

372 **In 1896, the Birmingham:** Stephens, ed., *Victoria History of the County of Warwick*, 7:185–86.

372 **Two gunmakers analyzing:** Artifex and Opifex, *The Causes of Decay in a British Industry*, 21–22. The authors were likely W. W. Greener and Charles Edward Greener.

372 **Government aid fostered:** Grant, *Rulers, Guns, and Money*, 4, 12.

372 **Birmingham's manufacturers did not:** Artifex and Opifex, *The Causes of Decay in a British Industry*, 37.

372 **European states unloaded:** Grant, *Rulers, Guns, and Money*, 37–38, 198, 232–34.

372 **Britain futilely opposed:** Ibid., 38, 63–73, 77, 237.

373 **They also finally set up:** Young, *The East India Company's Arsenals and Manufactories*, 224.

373 **Consumers from the Middle East:** Crews, "Trafficking in Evil?," 121, 137.

373 **It was in this context:** Artifex and Opifex, *The Causes of Decay in a British Industry*, v, 31, 56.

374 **By 1930, it was:** Ball, "Britain and the Decline of the International Control of Small Arms," 830–31. Vickers, the Birmingham revolver company Webley & Scott, and other arms manufacturers also made cars and motorcycles. The Royal Enfield motorcycle brand logo today depicts a cannon and the motto "Made Like a Gun."

374 **In 1919, Birmingham gunmakers:** Stephens, ed., *The Victoria History of the County of Warwick*, 7:186.

374 **the British journalist Vera Brittain:** Brittain, *Testament of Youth*, 632–33, 638.

374 **The ten years following:** Edgerton, *Warfare State*, 46, 154.

374 **British-based arms trader:** Sampson, *The Arms Bazaar*, chap. 1.

375 **Brown's British Defence:** Collier, *Arms and the Men*, 271–72, 275, 277.

375 **protestations of concern:** See, for instance, TNA: DO 35/8262: CRO, brief, Supply of Armaments to India and Pakistan, Cabinet Paper, December 17, 1917, for PM's Commonwealth tour, January–February 1958. The American approach to arms sales after the war was more subject to diplomatic concerns; they also gave arms away, something the British could not countenance in their straitened circumstances. Sampson, *The Arms Bazaar*, 106–7.

375 **British Aerospace (BAe), determined:** Pam, *The Royal Small Arms Factory*, chap. 9.

375 **There are roughly:** Wood and Hillier, *Shattered Lives*, chap. 4.

376 **In 2003, there were:** Owen Bowcott and Richard Norton-Taylor, "War on Terror Fuels Small Arms Trade," *Guardian*, October 10, 2003, www.guardian.co.uk/armstrade/story/0,10674, 1059843,00.html.

376 **Global arms exports:** Theohary, "Conventional Arms Transfers to Developing Nations."

376 **Even as sales of large:** Chew, *Arming the Periphery*, 9, 11.

376 **It is managed by:** Wood and Peleman, *The Arms Fixers*.

376 **nano drones, tiny weapons:** David Wood, "American Drones Ignite New Arms Race from Gaza to Iran to China," *Huffington Post*, November 27, 2012, www.huffingtonpost.com/2012/11/27 /american-drones_n_2199193.html.

376 **Britain is the world's:** Jon Stone, "Britain Is Now the Second Biggest Arms Dealer in the World," *The Independent*, September 5, 2016, www.independent.co.uk/news/uk/home-news/britain-is-now -the-second-biggest-arms-dealer-in-the-world-a7225351.html.

376 **After Foreign Minister Robin Cook's:** Sampson, *The Arms Bazaar*, 297, 299, 329.

376 **Under David Cameron:** Rowena Mason, "David Cameron Boasts of 'Brilliant' UK Arms Exports to Saudi Arabia," *Guardian,* February 25, 2016, www.theguardian.com/world/2016/feb/25/david-cameron-brilliant-uk-arms-exports-saudi-arabia-bae.

376 **Industry spokesmen continue:** Paul Everitt, quoted in Jamie Doward, "Does UK's Lucrative Arms Trade Come at the Cost of Political Repression?," *Guardian,* February 12, 2017, www.theguardian.com/world/2017/feb/12/british-arms-deals-with-saudi-arabia-high-court.

376 **"new, and entirely different":** Thompson, "The Peculiarities of the English," 266.

377 **"jobs for generals" scandal:** Nick Hopkins, Rob Evans, and Richard Norton-Taylor, "MoD Staff and Thousands of Military Officers Join Arms Firms," *Guardian,* October 15, 2012, www.guardian.co.uk/uk/2012/oct/15/mod-military-arms-firms.

377 **"no manufacturing industry":** Artifex and Opifex, *The Causes of Decay in a British Industry,* 33.

378 **"as all new mechanics":** *RSCSA,* 14, 86, 88.

378 **The British state forged conditions:** Beckert, *Empire of Cotton,* 155.

378 **This narrative does not:** Scholarship based on recent U.S. data shows that government demand has a significant impact on corporate R&D activity and should be considered in debates on innovation policy. Slavtchev and Wiederhold, "Technological Intensity of Government Demand and Innovation."

379 **"They are commonly dissatisfied":** A. Smith, *The Wealth of Nations,* 884, 996.

379 **a "discursive machine-gun":** Kittler, *Gramophone, Film, Typewriter,* 14, 190–92.

Chapter Ten: Opposition to the Gun Trade after 1815

380 **"with the eyes of other":** A. Smith, *The Theory of Moral Sentiments,* 110.

380 **The final version:** Wahrman, *The Making of the Modern Self,* 188–89, 272, 308.

380 **The eighteenth-century man:** Thomas Haskell, "Capitalism and the Origins of the Humanitarian Sensibility, Part 2," in *The Antislavery Debate,* ed. Bender, 152.

381 **Meticulous study of his:** See, for instance, his notes in UCL: Galton/1/1/10/1.

381 **The younger Lloyd likewise:** S. Lloyd, *The Lloyds of Birmingham,* 122.

381 **"being gifted and full":** Quoted in Pearson, *The Life, Letters and Labours of Francis Galton,* 3:32.

381 **There is a strange poetry:** Stephens, ed., *The Victoria History of the County of Warwick,* 7:62n.

381 **"animals of a greedy":** Colonel Barré, 1778, quoted in Baker, *Government and Contractors,* 242.

382 **Laws such as the:** Greenwood, *Firearms Control,* 17–19.

382 **Henry Bartle Frere:** Storey, *Guns, Race, and Power in Colonial South Africa,* 232, 234.

382 **As the trade grew:** Ibid., 75, 111, 182, 184, 245, 282–84, 316–18, 332–34.

383 **Imperial authorities also blamed:** Crews, "Trafficking in Evil?," 121.

384 **"British influence in the Persian Gulf":** *Times of India,* May 28, 1898, quoted in Noel-Baker, *The Private Manufacture of Armaments,* 108.

384 **"Government maintains warships":** Report by C. A. Kemball, quoted in *Times of India,* August 24, 1901, quoted in Noel-Baker, *The Private Manufacture of Armaments,* 108.

384 **Gunmakers complained that:** Artifex and Opifex, *The Causes of Decay in a British Industry,* 196–97, 200.

385 **"a very necessary article":** G. Shaw, *Major Barbara,* 110–11, 127.

385 **"all who wish to":** Artifex and Opifex, *The Causes of Decay in a British Industry,* v, 210–11.

386 **"at least as great a public":** Lorimer, *Gazetteer of the Persian Gulf, Oman, and Central Arabia,* vol. 1, part 2, 2586–87.

386 **slowly building paranoia:** Satia, *Spies in Arabia,* chap. 6.

386 **the Hague Convention also:** D. Stone, "Imperialism and Sovereignty," 215–16.

386 **The British resorted to unilateral:** Ball, "Britain and the Decline of the International Control of Small Arms," 818.

386 **He explained the logic:** Keppel, *Gun-Running and the Indian North-West Frontier,* xi–xiii, 50–54, 79, 125–26.

388 **Instead of the Pistols Bill:** Greenwood, *Firearms Control,* 27–33.

388 **Labour MP Philip Snowden:** Ball, "Britain and the Decline of the International Control of Small Arms," 815–18, 820–21.

389 **The imperial anxieties:** Satia, *Spies in Arabia,* chap. 7.

389 **It consulted with the chief:** Greenwood, *Firearms Control,* 34–38.

389 **Sir Edward Grey:** Noel-Baker, *The Private Manufacture of Armaments,* 395.

389 **"high moral issue":** Ball, "Britain and the Decline of the International Control of Small Arms," 821.

390 **the convention forbade export:** D. Stone, "Imperialism and Sovereignty," 218.

390 **"moral duty of all":** Quoted in ibid., 218.

390 **its Temporary Mixed Commission:** Ball, "Britain and the Decline of the International Control of Small Arms," 824.

390 **The United States recognized:** D. Stone, "Imperialism and Sovereignty," 219–21.

390 **"adapted both to warlike":** PP: Cmd. 414: Treaty Series No. 12 (1919), Convention for the Control of the Trade in Arms and Ammunition, and Protocol, signed September 10, 1919, chap. 1, 45.

390 **All the signees:** Ball, "Britain and the Decline of the International Control of Small Arms," 823.

391 **After the war:** Lawrence, "Forging a Peaceable Kingdom," 562, 569–70.

391 **the Firearms Bill passed:** Greenwood, *Firearms Control*, chap. 3.

391 **Belgian representatives argued:** Ball, "Britain and the Decline of the International Control of Small Arms," 825–27.

392 **Nearly forty nations:** Collier, *Arms and the Men*, 184. See PP: Cmd. 3448: Miscellaneous No. II (1929): International Convention for the Supervision of the International Trade in Arms and Ammunition with Declaration Regarding the Territory of Ifni, Geneva, June 17, 1925.

392 **Britain reversed even:** Ball, "Britain and the Decline of the International Control of Small Arms," 831.

392 **Then the leftist MP:** *Times* (London), March 13, 1928, 8.

392 **in the Commons, Hugh Dalton:** Quoted in Union of Democratic Control, *The Secret International*, 7n1.

392 **During the debate:** *Times* (London), March 9, 1926, 8.

392 **In 1931, an order-in-council:** Collier, *Arms and the Men*, 184.

393 **"thousands of persons of all":** Wells, cited in Union of Democratic Control, *The Secret International*, 43–45.

393 **The 1929 stock market:** Collier, *Arms and the Men*, 4–7.

393 **exposé on the "secret international":** Union of Democratic Control, *The Secret International*, preface, 5–6, 25–26, 32, 11–13, 27, 48.

394 **establishing an export licensing:** D. Anderson, "British Rearmament and the 'Merchants of Death,'" 8–9.

394 **"Food of the Gods":** Ashton, *Iron and Steel in the Industrial Revolution*, chap. 6, 128–29, 136.

395 **the interwar peace movement's:** Edgerton, *Warfare State*, 25.

395 **All existing firearms:** Greenwood, *Firearms Control*, chap. 4 and 60, 69, 70.

396 **Christopher Addison (minister):** Collier, *Arms and the Men*, 172–80.

396 **In October 1934:** D. Anderson, "British Rearmament and the 'Merchants of Death,'" 11.

396 **high-ranking Conservative politician:** Quoted in PP: Cmd. 5292: *Report of the Royal Commission on the Private Manufacture of and Trading in Arms* (1936), appendix 1, 55.

396 **massive public outpouring:** See ibid., 76–83.

396 **Communist Party General Secretary:** D. Anderson, "British Rearmament and the 'Merchants of Death,'" 15, 17–18; Edgerton, *Warfare State*, 46. The commission excluded warships and military aircraft from its definition of arms.

396 **Addison and Lloyd George:** Collier, *Arms and the Men*, 182.

397 **If exporting meant:** D. Anderson, "British Rearmament and the 'Merchants of Death,'" 25–26.

397 **Charles Craven of Vickers:** Ibid., 20.

397 **Abolition would also harm:** *Report of the Royal Commission on the Private Manufacture of and Trading in Arms*, 18, 27–28.

398 **"the whole field of industrial":** Ibid., 29–31, 33, 65.

398 **The Labour Party's interest:** Curiously, in 1926, Harry Pollitt had sought a job as a boilersmith at Woolwich Arsenal but was fired after a day when he was recognized as a convicted seditionist. In fact, his purpose was probably not subversive, but simply to log enough time in a union job to qualify for Boilermakers' Society membership and delegate slots to the Trade Unions Congress and the Labour Party. TNA: KV 2/1034 and KV 3/18. I thank Jennifer Luff for this story and references.

398 **"the fact that under":** *Report of the Royal Commission on the Private Manufacture of and Trading in Arms*, 18, 45, 51.

399 **commission also criticized:** Ball, "Britain and the Decline of the International Control of Small Arms," 831–32; PP: Cmd. 5451: *Statement Relating to Report of the Royal Commission on the Private Manufacture of and Trading in Arms, 1935–36* (1937), 20.

399 **the report was buried:** D. Anderson, "British Rearmament and the 'Merchants of Death,'" 6, 28, 30–31.

399 **the subsidy to ensure:** Ball, "Britain and the Decline of the International Control of Small Arms," 833–34.

400 **"whole industry of metallurgy":** Noel-Baker, *The Private Manufacture of Armaments*, 52–53, 55–57, 62–64, 68, 73, 81, 93–94.

401 **Ministry of Supply emerged:** D. Anderson, "British Rearmament and the 'Merchants of Death,'" 30. The title master general had been resurrected as a War Office position in 1904. In 1938, the Ordnance Board absorbed the small-arms committee of that time. In 1939, with the Ministry of Supply, the position of master general lapsed again, returning in 1959 when the ministry ended. Skentelbery, *Arrows to Atom Bombs*, 10, 141.

401 **the 1937 Firearms Act was:** Greenwood, *Firearms Control*, 70–71, 92–93, 183.

401 **"Thing" that E. P. Thompson:** Edgerton, *Warfare State*, 225–26.

402 **the Hungerford massacre:** Collier, *Arms and the Men*, 271–72, 277, 282. Laws are different in Northern Ireland and Scotland.

402 **That year, the United States:** Wood and Peleman, *The Arms Fixers*, chaps. 8–9.

402 **successive reviews of:** House of Commons, Committees on Arms Export Controls, *Scrutiny of Arms Export Controls (2013)*, 9–10; Curtis, Close, Dury, and Isbister, *The Good, the Bad, and the Ugly*, 3–5.

403 **Of the 140 states:** Ball, "Britain and the Decline of the International Control of Small Arms," 835–36. A consortium of nongovernmental organizations (the Control Arms Campaign) launched this United Nations conversation.

403 **the United Nations General Assembly:** "Containing the Conventional Arms Trade," *New York Times*, October 1, 2013, www.nytimes.com/2013/10/01/opinion/containing-the-conventional-arms-trade.html.

404 **notions of "moral economy":** Thompson, "The Peculiarities of the English," 292–93.

404 **"constitutively guilty in conscience":** Baucom, *Specters of the Atlantic*, 239, 245.

405 **urged the United States:** "Containing the Conventional Arms Trade," *New York Times*, October 1, 2013, www.nytimes.com/2013/10/01/opinion/containing-the-conventional-arms-trade.html.

406 **The newspaper challenged:** Michael Luo and Mike McIntire, "Children and Guns: The Hidden Toll: Accidental Shooting Deaths Are Widely Undercounted," *New York Times*, September 29, 2013, 1, 20–21.

406 **In literature, they remain:** One author determined after the Sandy Hook shootings to avoid putting guns in the hands of her fictional villains, realizing that they were too easy, and their fictional ubiquity perhaps desensitized Americans to them. Renn, "Unarmed and Dangerous."

407 **"Everybody wants a gun":** *RSCSA*, 17, 136.

408 **"such firelocks as they":** Quoted in Sweeney and Cornell, "All Guns Are Not Created Equal." Political leaders were talking about arming or rearming existing state militias, not disarming some imaginary 'citizens' militia." The militias had come to depend on public arms, not privately owned arms. How to supply those was the question.

408 **The Second Amendment was:** Sweeney and Cornell, "All Guns Are Not Created Equal."

408 **In the seventeenth century:** Perrin, *Giving Up the Gun*, 81.

409 **Even France forgot:** Alder, *Engineering the Revolution*, 19, 319.

409 **"how an agent of death":** Amanda Froelich, "Artist Melts 1,527 Guns and Turns Them into Shovels for Planting Trees," *True Activist*, August 17, 2015, www.trueactivist.com/artist-melts-1527-guns-and-turns-them-into-shovels-for-planting-trees.

409 **"The fire-arms industry established":** Artifex and Opifex, *The Causes of Decay in a British Industry*, 252.

409 **The 1908 history:** Page, ed., *The Victoria History of the County of Warwick*, 2:391–93.

410 **"There's nothing intrinsically evil":** Mike McIntire and Michael Luo, "Gun Makers Saw No Role in Curbing Improper Sales," *New York Times*, May 27, 2013, www.nytimes.com/2013/05/28/us/gun-makers-shun-responsibility-for-sales-suits-show.html.

410 **In 1862, the son:** "Sarah Winchester, Woman of Mystery," https://web.archive.org/web/2017050 1061643/http://www.winchestermysteryhouse.com/sarahwinchester.cfm.

BIBLIOGRAPHY

UNPUBLISHED PRIMARY SOURCES

Birmingham City Archives

Galton Papers
Boulton Correspondence
Pyddoke Family Papers
Records of Mary Capper
Josiah Goodwin, "Notes on the History of Birmingham with Special References to the Battle of Birmingham, the Gun Trade, the Button Trade, Thread and Linen," MS, c. 1850.

The National Archives, Kew

Records of the War Office (WO), Board of Trade (BT), Treasury (T), Home Office (HO), Dominions Office (DO), Chancery (C), Security Service (KV)

Guildhall Library, London

Papers of the Worshipful Company of Gunmakers

National Archives of India, New Delhi

Proceedings of the Military Board of Ordnance
Fort William–India House Correspondence

Records of the Friends House Library, London

Records of the Society of Friends, Bull Street Meeting House, Birmingham

Proceedings of the Old Bailey

Available at www.oldbaileyonline.org.

Special Collections, University College London

Galton Papers

Historical Violence Database, Ohio State University
Inquests in Gloucester, Bristol, and Coventry, England 1500–1838, available at https://cjrc.osu.edu /research/interdisciplinary/hvd/europe/bristol-and-gloucester.

State Library, New South Wales
Papers of Sir Joseph Banks, Series 84, available at http://www2.sl.nsw.gov.au/banks/series_84/84 _view.cfm.

PUBLISHED PRIMARY SOURCES

Account of the Cruel Massacre Committed by John Porteous, Captain of the City Guard of Edinburgh, at the Execution of Andrew Wilson Merchant, upon the 14th of April 1736 [. . .] Glasgow, 1789.
An Account of the Lives of the Most Notorious Murderers and Robbers: Edward Burnworth Alias Frazier, William Blewet, Emanuel Dickenson, Thomas Berry alias Teague, John Higgs, and John Legee [. . .] London: Printed for J. Roberts, 1726.
Adair, James. *The History of the American Indians; Particularly Those Nations Adjoining to the Missisippi* [sic], *East and West Florida, Georgia, South and North Carolina, and Virginia* . . . London: Printed by Edward and Charles Dilly, 1775.
Adams, John. *Modern Voyages: Containing a Variety of Useful and Entertaining Facts, Respecting the Expeditions and the Principal Discoveries of Cavendish* . . . Dublin, 1790.
Affecting History of the Dreadful Distresses of Frederic Manheim's Family [. . .] Philadelphia: D. Humphreys, 1794.
Aitken, John, M.D. *A Description of Double-Shot Fire-Arms*. London, 1781.
An Alarm to the People of England; Shewing Their Rights, Liberties, and Properties, to Be in the Utmost Danger from the Present Destructive, and Unconstitutional Association, for the Preservation of the Game All over England, Which Is Proved to Be Illegal. London: Printed for J. Scott, at the Black Swan, 1757.
Aldington, John. *A Poem on the Cruelty of Shooting with Some Tender Remarks on the 10th of May 1768, Particularly on Young Mr. Allen*. London, 1768.
———. *A Poem on the Various Scenes of Shooting. On a New Plan*. London, 1767.
Allen, Ira. *Particulars of the Capture of the Ship* Olive Branch, *Laden with a Cargo of Arms, &c, the Property of Major-General Ira Allen, Destined for Supplying the Militia of Vermont, and Captured by HM's Ship of War,* Audacious. London, 1798.
Anburey, Thomas. *Travels through the Interior Parts of America. In a Series of Letters by an Officer*. 2 vols. London: Printed for W. Lane, 1789.
Anderson, A. *An Historical and Chronological Deduction of the Origins of Commerce: From the Earliest Accounts*. 4 vols. London: Printed by J. Walter, 1787–89.
Anderson, Aenaes. *A Narrative of the British Embassy to China, in the Years 1792, 1793, & 1794*. Dublin, 1795.
Aris's Birmingham Gazette (1760 through 1800).
Artifex and Opifex [pseud.]. *The Causes of Decay in a British Industry*. London: Longmans, Green, 1907.
Austen, Jane. *Persuasion*. Amersham, UK: Transatlantic, 2012. First published 1817.
Baines, Thomas. *History of the Commerce and Town of Liverpool and of the Rise of Manufacturing Industry in the Adjoining Counties*. London: Brown, Green, Longmans, 1852.
Banks, Joseph. *The Endeavour Journal of Sir Joseph Banks, 1768–1771*. [Sydney], 1769.
Bell, John. *Discourses on the Nature and Cure of Wounds in Two Volumes*. 1st American Edition. Vol. 1, *Of Wounds in General* . . . Walpole, N.H.: Printed for Thomas & Thomas and Justin Hinds, by George W. Nichols, 1807.
Brittain, Vera. *Testament of Youth: An Autobiographical Study of the Years 1900–1925*. New York: Penguin, 2004. First published 1933.
Brontë, Emily. *Wuthering Heights*. London: Thomas Cautley Newby, 1847.
Brooke, Richard. *Liverpool as It Was during the Last Quarter of the Eighteenth Century, 1775 to 1800*. Liverpool: J. Mawdsley, 1853.
Butler, John. *A Letter to the Right Honorable William Pitt, on the Defence of the Country, with a Detail of Improvements in the Construction and Use of Fire-Arms, Great and Small, by Which the Effect of Both*

May Be Rendered Incomparably More Destructive than Heretofore, and by Such Simple Means as to Be within the Reach of Every Individual Who Carries a Musquet. Dublin: Printed by Charles Downes, 1804.

Christie, Agatha. *Murder on the Orient Express.* New York: Pocket, 1976. First published 1934.

Darwin, Erasmus. *The Collected Letters of Erasmus Darwin.* Edited by Desmond King-Hele. Cambridge: Cambridge University Press, 2007.

Deakin, Francis. *Plain Narrative of the Circumstances That Have Occurred in the Transactions between the Honourable Board of Ordnance and Mr. Francis Deakin of Birmingham, One of Their Manufacturers.* Birmingham, 1816.

Defoe, Daniel. *The Life and Strange Surprizing Adventures of Robinson Crusoe of Tork, Mariner.* London: W. Taylor, 1719.

Engelbrecht, H. C., and F. C. Hanighen. *Merchants of Death: A Study of the International Armament Industry.* New York: Dodd, Mead, 1934.

Ffoulkes, Charles. *Arms & Armament: An Historical Survey of the Weapons of the British Army.* London: G. G. Harrap, 1945.

Fort William–India House Correspondence and Other Contemporary Papers Relating Thereto. Vol. 3 (Public series): 1760–1763, edited by R. R. Sethi, and vol. 7 (Public, select, and secret): 1773–1776, edited by R. P. Patwardham. Delhi: Manager of Publications, 1949–58.

G., A. *The Impetuous Love, or the Guiltless Parricide, Shewing, to What Lengths Love May Run, and the Extream Folly of Forming Schemes for Futurity.* 2 vols. London: E. Ross, 1757.

Galton, Francis. *Memories of My Life.* New York: E. P. Dutton, 1909.

Galton, Samuel Tertius. *A Chart, Exhibiting the Relation between the Amount of Bank of England Notes in Circulation, the Rate of Foreign Exchanges, and the Prices of Gold and Silver Bullion and of Wheat; Accompanied with Explanatory Observations.* London: J. Johnson, 1813.

Goodman, John D. "On the Progress of the Small Arms Manufacture." *Journal of the Statistical Society of London* 28 (1865): 494–506.

———. "The Birmingham Gun Trade." In *The Resources, Products, and Industrial History of Birmingham and the Midland Hardware District: A Series of Reports, Collected by the Local Industries Committee of the British Association at Birmingham, in 1865,* edited by Samuel Timmins, 381–431. London: Robert Hardwicke, 1866.

Hanger, Col. George. *A Letter to the Right Hon. Lord Castlereagh, Secretary of State.* London: Kessinger, 1808.

———. *To All Sportsmen, and Particularly to Farmers, and Gamekeepers. Above Thirty Years' Practice in Horses and Dogs.* London: Printed for the author, sold by J. J. Stockdale, Pall Mall, 1814.

Hawkesworth, John. *An Account of the Voyages Undertaken by the Order of His Present Majesty, for Making Discoveries in the Southern Hemisphere [. . .] Drawn Up from the Journals Which Were Kept by the Several Commanders, and from the Papers of Joseph Banks, Esq.* Dublin: printed for James Williams, 1775.

Hicks, Edward. "Notes on the Disownment of Samuel Galton." *Quakeriana* 1, No. 5 (July 1894): 72–76.

Hobson, J. A. *Imperialism: A Study.* London: J. Nisbet, 1902.

Hunter, John. *A Treatise on the Blood, Inflammation, and Gun-Shot Wounds, by the late John Hunter, to Which Is Prefixed a Short Account of the Author's Life, by His Brother-in-Law, Everard Home.* Vol. 1. Philadelphia: Thomas Bradford, 1796.

Hutton, William. *An History of Birmingham, to the End of the Year 1780.* Birmingham: Pearson and Rollason, 1781.

———. *The History of Birmingham.* 6th ed. London: G. Berger, 1835.

Johnson, Samuel. *A Journey to the Western Islands of Scotland.* London: Strahan and Cadell, 1785. First published 1775.

Keppel, Arnold. *Gun-Running and the Indian North-West Frontier.* London: John Murray, 1911.

Lorimer, J. G. *Gazetteer of the Persian Gulf, Oman, and Central Arabia.* Vol. 1, *Historical,* part II. Calcutta: Superintendent Government Printing, 1915. Reprint 1970.

Newdegate-Newdigate, Anne Emily Garnier. *Cavalier and Puritan in the Days of the Stuarts: Compiled from the Private Papers and Diary of Sir Richard Newdigate, Second Baronet, with Extracts from MS. News-letters Addressed to Him between 1675 and 1689.* London: Smith, Elder, 1901.

Newton, John. *Memoirs of the Rev. John Newton, with Selections from His Correspondence.* London: R.B. Seeley and W. Burnside, 1835.

Noel-Baker, Philip. *The Private Manufacture of Armaments.* London: V. Gollancz, 1936.

Paine, Thomas. *Common Sense.* Philadelphia: W. & T. Bradford, 1776.

ProQuest U.K. Parliamentary Papers

Parsons, B. [attributed] [King, S.]. *Observations on the Manufacture of Fire-Arms for Military Purposes; on the Number Supplied from Birmingham to the British Government, during the Late War; on the Proof to Which the Barrels are Subjected; and on the Birmingham Proof-House: Together with Some Remarks upon the Inexpediency of the Ordnance Department Fabricating Small Arms and upon the Obstacles to the Free Export of Arms.* London: Longmans, 1829.

Pearce, Thomas. *The History and Directory of Walsall, Containing Its Antiquities, Modern Survey of Its Improvements, a Description of Its Public Edifices, and an Enumeration of Its Local and Commercial Advantages.* Birmingham, UK: Thomson and Wrightson, 1813.

Pearson, Karl. *The Life, Letters and Labours of Francis Galton.* 3 vols. Cambridge: Cambridge University Press, 1914–30.

Picton, James Allanson. *Memorials of Liverpool, Historical and Topographical, Including a History of the Dock Estate.* 2nd ed. London, 1875.

Polier, Henri. *A European Experience of the Mughal Orient: The Ijaz-I Arsalani (Persian Letters) of Antoine-Louis Henri Polier.* Delhi: Oxford University Press, 2001.

[Pye, Henry James]. *Shooting, a Poem.* London: J. Davis, 1784.

Robinson, G. *Beauties of Nature and Art Displayed, in a Tour through the World.* 2nd ed. Vols. 11–13. London: G. Robinson, 1774–75.

Schimmelpenninck, Mary Anne. *Life of Mary Anne Schimmelpenninck.* Edited by Christiana Hankin. 2 vols. London: Longmans, Green, 1858.

Shaw, George Bernard. *Major Barbara: With an Essay as First Aid to Critics.* New York: Brentano's, 1917. First published 1907.

Shaw, Stebbing. *The History and Antiquities of Staffordshire.* Vol. 2, part 1. London: J. Nichols, 1798.

Showell, Walter. *Dictionary of Birmingham.* Birmingham, UK: J. G. Hammond, 1885.

Simond, Louis. *Journal of a Tour and Residence in Great Britain: During the Years 1810 and 1811.* Vol. 2. Edinburgh: J. Ballantyne, 1817.

Smiles, Samuel. *Lives of Boulton and Watt: Principally from the Original Soho MSS.* London: John Murray, 1865.

———. *Self-Help; with Illustrations of Character and Conduct.* London: John Murray, 1859.

Smith, Adam. *An Enquiry into the Nature and Causes of the Wealth of Nations.* Edited by Edwin Cannan. New York: Modern Library, 1994. First published 1776.

———. *The Theory of Moral Sentiments.* Edited by D. D. Raphael and A. L. Macfied. Indianapolis: Liberty Fund, 1982. First published 1759–61.

———. *Lectures on Jurisprudence.* Edited by R. L. Meek, D. D. Raphael, and P. G. Stein. Oxford: Clarendon, 1978. First published 1763.

Southey, Robert [Don Manuel Alvarez Espriella]. *Letters from England.* Vol. 2. London: Longmans, Hurst, Rees, Orme, 1807.

The Times (London).

Timmins, Samuel, ed. *The Resources, Products, and Industrial History of Birmingham and the Midland Hardware District: A Series of Reports, Collected by the Local Industries Committee of the British Association at Birmingham, in 1865.* London: Robert Hardwicke, 1866.

Twining, Thomas. *Travels in India a Hundred Years Ago, with a Visit to the United States . . .* Edited by William Twining. London: James R. Osgood, McIlvaine, 1893.

Union of Democratic Control. *The Secret International: Armament Firms at Work.* London: The Union of Democratic Control, 1932.

Worshipful Company of Gunmakers. *The Case of the Company of Gun-Makers of the City of London.* London, 1711.

SECONDARY SOURCES

Agoston, Gabor. *Guns for the Sultan: Military Power and the Weapons Industry in the Ottoman Empire.* New York: Cambridge University Press, 2005.

Ajayi, J. F. Ade, and Robert Smith. *Yoruba Warfare in the Nineteenth Century.* Cambridge: Cambridge University Press, 1964.

Alder, Ken. *Engineering the Revolution: Arms and Enlightenment in France, 1763–1815.* Princeton, N.J.: Princeton University Press, 1997.

Allen, G. C. *The Industrial Development of Birmingham and the Black Country, 1860–1927.* London: G. Allen & Unwin, 1929.

Allen, Robert. *The British Industrial Revolution in Global Perspective.* New York: Cambridge University Press, 2009.

———. *The Industrial Revolution: A Very Short Introduction.* Oxford: Oxford University Press, 2017.

Alpern, Stanley. "What Africans Got for Their Slaves: A Master List of European Trade Goods." *History in Africa* 22 (1995): 18–21.

Alpers, Edward. *Ivory & Slaves in East Central Africa: Changing Patterns of International Trade to the Late Nineteenth Century.* London: Heinemann, 1975.

Ames, Edward, and Nathan Rosenberg. "The Enfield Arsenal in Theory and History." *Economic Journal* 78, no. 312 (1968): 827–42.

Amussen, Susan Dwyer. "Punishment, Discipline, and Power: The Social Meanings of Violence in Early Modern England." *Journal of British Studies* 34 (1995): 1–34.

Anderson, David. "British Rearmament and the 'Merchants of Death': The 1935–36 Royal Commission on the Manufacture of and Trade in Armaments." *Journal of Contemporary History* 29 (1994): 5–37.

Anderson, Fred. *Crucible of War: The Seven Years' War and the Fate of Empire in British North America, 1754–1766.* New York: Knopf, 2001.

Anderson, J. L. "Aspects of the Effect on the British Economy of the Wars against France, 1793–1815." *Australian Economic Review* 12 (1972): 1–20.

Anderson, M. S. *War and Society in Europe of the Old Regime, 1618–1789.* Stroud, UK: Sutton, 1989.

———. *The War of the Austrian Succession, 1740–1748.* New York: Longmans, 1995.

Annan, Noel. "The Intellectual Aristocracy." In *The Dons: Mentors, Eccentrics, and Geniuses,* 304–41. Chicago: University of Chicago Press, 1955.

Anon. "Moses Franks." Twickenham Museum. www.twickenham-museum.org.uk/detail.asp?Content ID=101.

Appadurai, Arjun, ed. *The Social Life of Things: Commodities in Cultural Perspective.* Cambridge: Cambridge University Press, 1988.

Arendt, Hannah. *The Human Condition.* Chicago: University of Chicago Press, 1958.

Ashton, T. S. *Economic Fluctuations in England, 1700–1800.* Oxford: Clarendon, 1959.

———. *Iron and Steel in the Industrial Revolution.* 3rd ed. New York: Barnes and Noble, 1963. First published 1924.

Ashworth, William. *Customs and Excise: Trade, Production and Consumption in England, 1640–1845.* New York: Oxford University Press, 2003.

Atmore, Anthony, and Peter Sanders. "Sotho Arms and Ammunition in the Nineteenth Century." *Journal of African History* 4 (1971): 1971: 535–44.

Austen, Ralph A., and Woodruff D. Smith. "Private Tooth Decay as Public Economic Virtue: The Slave-Sugar Triangle, Consumerism, and European Industrialization." In *The Atlantic Slave Trade: Effects on Economies, Societies, and Peoples in Africa, the Americas, and Europe,* edited by Joseph Inikori and Stanley Engerman, 183–203. Durham, N.C.: Duke University Press, 1992.

Bagehot, Walter. *Lombard Street: A Description of the Money Market.* New York: Wiley, 1999. First published 1873.

Bailey, De Witt. *British Military Longarms, 1715–1815.* Harrisburg, Pa.: Stackpole, 1972.

———. *British Board of Ordnance Small Arms Contractors, 1689–1840.* Rhyl, UK: W. S. Curtis, 1999.

———. "Liège Muskets in the British Army, 1740–1783." In *Aspects of Dutch Gunmaking,* edited by H. L. Visser and D. W. Bailey, 281–94. Zwolle, Netherlands: Waanders, 1997.

———. "The Wilsons: Gunmakers to Empire, 1730–1832." *American Association of Arms Collectors Bulletin* 85 (Spring 2002): 11–24.

Bailey, De Witt, and David Harding. "From India to Waterloo: The 'India Pattern' Musket." In *The Road to Waterloo: The British Army and the Struggle against Revolutionary and Napoleonic France, 1793–1815,* edited by Alan Guy, 48–57. London: National Army Museum, 1990.

Bailey, De Witt, and A. Nie. *English Gunmakers: The Birmingham and Provincial Gun Trade in the 18th and 19th Century.* New York: Arco, 1978.

Baker, Norman. "Changing Attitudes towards Government in Eighteenth-Century Britain." In *Statesmen, Scholars and Merchants: Essays in Eighteenth-Century History Presented to Dame Lucy Sutherland,* edited by A. Whiteman, J. S. Bromley, and P. G. M. Dickson, 203–19. Oxford: Clarendon, 1973.

————. *Government and Contractors: The British Treasury and War Supplies, 1775–1783*. London: Athlone, 1971.

————. "The Treasury and Open Contracting, 1778–1782." *Historical Journal* 15, no. 3 (1972): 433–54.

Banks, Stephen. *A Polite Exchange of Bullets: The Duel and the English Gentleman, 1750–1850*. Woodbridge, UK, and Rochester, N.Y.: Boydell, 2010.

Bannerman, Gordon. *Merchants and the Military in Eighteenth-Century Britain: British Army Contracts and Domestic Supply, 1739–1763*. London: Pickering & Chatto, 2007.

————. "The 'Nabob of the North': Sir Lawrence Dundas as Government Contractor." *Historical Research* 83, no. 210 (February 2010): 102–23.

Barker-Benfield, G. J. *The Culture of Sensibility: Sex and Society in Eighteenth-Century Britain*. Chicago: Chicago University Press, 1992.

Barrell, John. *Imagining the King's Death: Figurative Treason, Fantasies of Regicide, 1793–1796*. New York: Oxford University Press, 2000.

Bates, David William. *States of War: Enlightenment Origins of the Political*. New York: Columbia University Press, 2012.

Baucom, Ian. *Specters of the Atlantic: Finance Capital, Slavery, and the Philosophy of History*. Durham, N.C.: Duke University Press, 2005.

Baugh, D. A. *Naval Administration in the Age of Walpole*. Princeton, N.J.: Princeton University Press, 1965.

Beachey, R. W. "The Arms Trade in East Africa in the Late Nineteenth Century." *Journal of African History* 3 (1962): 451–67.

Beckert, Sven. *Empire of Cotton: A Global History*. New York: Knopf, 2015.

Behagg, C. "Mass Production without the Factory: Craft Producers, Guns and Small Firm Innovation, 1790–1815." *Business History* 40, no. 3 (1998): 1–15.

Bell, David. "In Defense of Drones: A Historical Argument." *New Republic,* January 26, 2012, www.tnr.com/article/politics/100113/obama-military-foreign-policy-technology-drones.

————. *The First Total War: Napoleon's Europe and the Birth of Warfare as We Know It*. Boston: Houghton Mifflin, 2007.

Bellesiles, Michael. *Arming America: The Origins of a National Gun Culture*. New York: Knopf, 2000.

————. "Exploring America's Gun Culture." *William and Mary Quarterly* 59 (2002): 241–68.

Bender, Thomas, ed. *The Antislavery Debate: Capitalism and Abolitionism as a Problem in Historical Interpretation*. Berkeley: University of California Press, 1992.

Benjamin, Walter. "The Work of Art in the Age of Mechanical Reproduction." In *Illuminations: Walter Benjamin Essays and Reflections,* edited by Hannah Arendt. New York: Schocken, 1968. Article first published 1937.

Berg, Gerald. "The Sacred Musket: Tactics, Technology, and Power in Eighteenth-Century Madagascar." *Comparative Studies in Society and History* 27 (1985): 261–79.

Berg, Maxine. *The Age of Manufactures, 1700–1820: Industry, Innovation and Work in Britain*. 2nd ed. London: Routledge, 1994.

————. "Commerce and Creativity in Eighteenth-Century Birmingham." In *Markets and Manufacture in Early Industrial Europe,* edited by Berg, 173–202. London: Routledge, 1991.

————. "Factories, Workshops and Industrial Organisation." In *The Economic History of Britain since 1700*. Vol. 1, *1700–1860,* edited by Roderick Floud and Deirdre McCloskey, 123–50. New York: Cambridge University Press, 1981.

————. "In Pursuit of Luxury: Global History and British Consumer Goods in the Eighteenth Century." *Past & Present* 182 (2004): 85–142.

————. "Inventors of the World of Goods." In *From Family Firms to Corporate Capitalism: Essays in Business and Industrial History in Honour of Peter Mathias,* edited by Kristine Bruland and Patrick O'Brien, 21–50. Oxford: Clarendon, 1998.

————. *Luxury and Pleasure in Eighteenth-Century Britain*. New York: Oxford University Press, 2005.

————. "Product Innovation in Core Consumer Industries." In *Technological Revolutions in Europe: Historical Perspectives,* edited by Berg and Kristine Bruland, 138–57. Northampton, Mass.: Edward Elgar, 1988.

————. "Revisions and Revolutions: Technology and Productivity Change in Manufacture in Eighteenth-Century England." In *Innovation and Technology in Europe: From the Eighteenth Century to the Present Day,* edited by Peter Mathias and John A. Davis, 43–64. Oxford: Blackwell, 1991.

Berg, Maxine, and Pat Hudson. "Rehabilitating the Industrial Revolution." *Economic History Review* 45, no. 1 (1992): 24–50.

Berry, H., and J. Gregory, eds. *Creating and Consuming Culture in North-East England, 1660–1830.* Burlington, Vt.: Ashgate, 2004.

Bidwell, W. H. *Annals of an East Anglian Bank.* Norwich, UK: Agas H. Goose, 1900.

Binney, J. E. D. *British Public Finance and Administration, 1774–92.* Oxford: Clarendon, 1958.

Birch, A. *The Economic History of the British Iron and Steel Industry, 1784–1879: Essays in Individual and Economic History with Special Reference to the Development of Technology.* New York: A. M. Kelly, 1967.

Birmingham Gun Museum. "Birmingham Gunmakers Pre-1800," www.birminghamgunmuseum.com /Birmingham_Gun_makers_pre-1800.php.

Black, Jeremy. *Britain as a Military Power, 1688–1815.* London: Routledge, 1999.

———. "Eighteenth-Century Warfare Reconsidered." *War in History* 1 (1994): 215–32.

———. "European Overseas Expansion and the Military Revolution." In *Technology, Disease and Colonial Conquests, Sixteenth to Eighteenth Centuries: Essays Reappraising the Guns and Germs Theories,* edited by George Raudzens, 1–30. Boston: Brill, 2001.

———. *European Warfare, 1660–1815.* New Haven, Conn.: Yale University Press, 1994.

———. "The Industrial Revolution." *In Our Time,* BBC Radio 4, December 2010, www.bbc.co.uk /programmes/b00wqdc7.

Blackburn, Robin. *The Making of New World Slavery: From the Baroque to the Modern, 1492–1800.* London: Verso, 1997.

Blackmore, Howard L. *British Military Firearms, 1650–1850.* London: Arco, 1961.

Blaney, Tom. *The Chief Sea Lion's Inheritance: Eugenics and the Darwins.* Leicester, UK: Troubador, 2011.

Bohstedt, John. *The Politics of Provision: Food Riots, Moral Economy, and Market Transition in England, c. 1550–1850.* Burlington, Vt.: Ashgate, 2010.

Bolitho, H., and D. Peel. *The Drummonds of Charing Cross.* London: Allen & Unwin, 1967.

Bourke, Joanna. *Deep Violence: Military Violence, War Play and the Social Life of Weapons.* Berkeley, Calif.: Counterpoint, 2015.

———. *An Intimate History of Killing: Face-to-Face Killing in Twentieth-Century Warfare.* London: Granta, 1999.

Bowen, H. V. *The Business of Empire: The East India Company and Imperial Britain: 1756–1833.* Cambridge: Cambridge University Press, 2006.

———. "Mobilising Resources for Global Warfare: The British State and the East India Company, 1756–1815." In *Mobilising Resources for War: Britain and Spain at Work during the Early Modern Period,* edited by Bowen and A. González Enciso, 81–110. Pamplona, Spain: Ediciones Universidad de Navarra, 2006.

———. *War and British Society, 1688–1815.* Cambridge: Cambridge University Press, 1998.

Bowen, H. V., and A. Gonzalez Enciso, eds. *Mobilising Resources for War: Britain and Spain at Work during the Early Modern Period.* Pamplona, Spain: Ediciones Universidad de Navarra, 2006.

Braddick, M. J. "The Early Modern English State and the Question of Differentiation, from 1550–1700." *Comparative Studies in Society and History* 38, no. 1 (1996): 92–111.

———. "An English Military Revolution?" *Historical Journal* 36, no. 4 (1994): 965–75.

Brewer, John. *The Sinews of Power: War, Money, and the English State, 1688–1783.* Cambridge, Mass.: Harvard University Press, 1989. First published 1988.

Brief of Jack Rakove, Saul Cornell, David Konig, William Novak, Lois Schwoerer et al. as Amici Curiae, *District of Columbia, et al., v. Dick Anthony Heller,* 554 U.S. 570, No. 07-290 (2008), www.scotusblog .com/wp-content/uploads/2008/01/07-290_amicus_historians.pdf.

Brock, Peter. *Pacifism in Europe to 1914.* Princeton, N.J.: Princeton University Press, 1972.

Brown, Christopher Leslie. *Moral Capital: Foundations of British Abolitionism.* Chapel Hill: University of North Carolina Press, 2006.

Brown, Christopher Leslie, and Philip D. Morgan, eds. *Arming Slaves: From Classical Times to the Modern Age.* New Haven, Conn.: Yale University Press, 2006.

Brown, M. L. *Firearms in Colonial America: The Impact on History and Technology, 1492–1792.* Washington, D.C.: Smithsonian Institute Press, 1980.

Brown, Nigel. *British Gunmakers: Historical Data on the Birmingham, Scottish and Regional Gun Trade in the 19th and 20th Centuries.* Vol. 2. Shewsbury, UK: Quiller, 2005.

Brown, Ruth Rhynas. "Guns Carried on East Indiamen, 1600–1800." *International Journal of Nautical Archaeology and Underwater Exploration* 19 (1990): 17–22.

Browning, Christopher. *Ordinary Men: Reserve Police Battalion 101 and the Final Solution in Poland*. New York: Harper Perennial, 1998.

Browning, Reed. "The Duke of Newcastle and the Financing of the Seven Years' War." *Journal of Economic History* 31, no. 2 (1971): 344–77.

———. *The War of the Austrian Succession*. New York: St. Martin's, 1993.

Bryce, George. *The Remarkable History of the Hudson's Bay Company, Including That of the French Traders of North-Western Canada and of the North-West, XY, and Astor Fur Companies*. London: S. Low, Marston & Co, 1900.

Buchanan, Brenda J. *Gunpowder: The History of an International Technology*. Bath, UK: Bath University Press, 1996.

———, ed. *Gunpowder, Explosives and the State: A Technological History*. Aldershot, UK: Ashgate, 2006.

Cain, P. J., and A. G. Hopkins. *British Imperialism: Innovation and Expansion, 1688–1914*. New York: Longmans, 1993.

Carey, A. Merwyn. *English, Irish, and Scottish Firearms Makers: When, Where, and What They Made from the Middle of the Sixteenth Century to the End of the Nineteenth Century*. 2nd. ed. New York: Arco, 1956. First published 1954.

Carey, Daniel. "An Empire of Credit: English, Scottish, Irish, and American Contexts." In *The Empire of Credit: The Financial Revolution in the British Atlantic World, 1688–1815*, edited by Daniel Carey and Christopher Finlay, 1–24. Portland, Ore.: Irish Academic Press, 2011.

Carlos, Ann M., and Frank D. Lewis. *Commerce by a Frozen Sea: Native Americans and the European Fur Trade*. Philadelphia: University of Pennsylvania Press, 2010.

Carman, W. Y. *A History of Firearms, from Earliest Times to 1914*. London: Routledge, 1955.

Carruthers, Bruce. *City of Capital: Politics and Markets in the English Financial Revolution*. Princeton, N.J.: Princeton University Press, 1996.

Casale, Giancarlo. *The Ottoman Age of Exploration*. New York: Oxford University Press, 2010.

Chaloner, W. H. "Isaac Wilkinson, Potfounder." In *Studies in the Industrial Revolution: Presented to T. S. Ashton*, edited by L. S. Pressnell, 23–51. London: Athlone, 1960.

Chandler, David. *The Art of Warfare in the Age of Marlborough*. New York: Hippocrene, 1976.

Chaplin, Joyce. *Subject Matter: Technology, the Body, and Science on the Anglo-American Frontier, 1500–1676*. Cambridge, Mass.: Harvard University Press, 2003.

Charles, Patrick. "The Faces of the Second Amendment outside the Home: History versus Ahistorical Standards of Review." *Cleveland State Law Review* 60 (2012): 1–55.

———. *Historicism, Originalism, and the Constitution: The Use and Abuse of the Past in American Jurisprudence*. Jefferson, N.C.: McFarland, 2014.

Chew, Emrys. *Arming the Periphery: The Arms Trade in the Indian Ocean during the Age of Global Empire*. Houndsmills, UK: Palgrave, 2012.

Childs, John. "The Army and the State in Britain and Germany during the Eighteenth Century." In *Rethinking Leviathan: The Eighteenth-Century State in Britain and Germany*, edited by John Brewer and Eckhart Hellmuth, 53–70. Oxford: Oxford University Press, 1999.

Churchill, Robert H. "Gun Ownership in Early America: A Survey of Manuscript Militia Returns." *William and Mary Quarterly* 60 (2003): 615–42.

———. "Guns and the Politics of History." *Reviews in American History* 29 (2001): 329–37.

Cipolla, Carlo M. *Guns, Sails, and Empires: Technological Innovation and the Early Phases of European Expansion, 1400–1700*. New York: Minerva, 1965.

Clark, Anna, and Aaron Windel. "The Early Roots of Liberal Imperialism: 'The Science of a Legislator' in Eighteenth-Century India." *Journal of Colonialism and Colonial History* 14, no. 2 (2013), https://muse.jhu.edu.

Clifford, Helen. "A Commerce with Things: The Value of Precious Metal in Early Modern England." In *Consumers and Luxury: Consumer Culture in Europe, 1650–1850*, edited by Maxine Berg and Helen Clifford, 147–67. Manchester: Manchester University Press, 1999.

———. "Concepts of Invention, Identity and Imitation in the London and Provincial Metal-Working Trades, 1750–1800." *Journal of Design History* 12, no. 3 (1999): 241–55.

Cockburn, J. S. "Patterns of Violence in English Society: Homicide in Kent, 1560–1985." *Past and Present* 130 (1991): 70–106.

Cocker, Mark. *Rivers of Blood, Rivers of Gold: Europe's Conquest of Indigenous Peoples.* London: Jonathan Cape, 1998.

Cole, Gareth. *Arming the Royal Navy, 1793–1815: The Office of Ordnance and the State.* London: Pickering & Chatto, 2012.

Coleman, D. C., and Christine Macleod. "Attitudes to New Techniques: British Businessmen, 1800–1950." *Economic History Review* 39 (1986): 588–611.

Colley, Linda. *Britons: Forging the Nation, 1707–1837.* New Haven, Conn.: Yale University Press, 1994.

———. *Captives: Britain, Empire and the World, 1600–1850.* New York: Anchor, 2004.

———. "The Reach of the State, the Appeal of the Nation." In *An Imperial State at War: Britain from 1689–1815,* edited by Lawrence Stone, 165–84. London: Routledge, 1993.

Collier, Basil. *Arms and the Men: The Arms Trade and Governments.* London: H. Hamilton, 1980.

Collins, Bruce. *War and Empire: The Expansion of Britain, 1790–1830.* New York: Longmans, 2010.

Collins, Randall. *Violence: A Micro-Sociological Theory.* Princeton, N.J.: Princeton University Press, 2008.

Conway, Stephen. "Britain and the Impact of the American War, 1775–1783." *War in History* 2 (1995): 127–50.

———. *The British Isles and the American War of Independence.* New York: Oxford University Press, 2000.

———. *War, State, and Society in Mid-Eighteenth-Century Britain and Ireland.* New York: Oxford University Press, 2006.

Cooper, John S. *For Commonwealth and Crown: English Gunmakers of the Seventeenth Century.* Dorset, UK: W. Hunt, 1993.

Cooper, Randolf G. S. *The Anglo-Maratha Campaigns and the Contest for India: The Struggle for Control of the South Asian Military Economy.* Cambridge: Cambridge University Press, 2003.

———. "Review of *Smallarms of the East India Company 1600–1865.* Vol. 1, *Procurement and Design,* and vol. 2, *Catalogue of Patterns,* by D. F. Harding." *Modern Asian Studies* 33 (1999): 759–67.

———. "Review of *Smallarms of the East India Company 1600–1856.* Vol. 3, *Ammunition and Performance,* and vol. 4, *The Users and Their Smallarms,* by D. F. Harding." *Modern Asian Studies* 36 (2002): 758–64.

Cornell, Saul. *A Well-Regulated Militia: The Founding Fathers and the Origins of Gun Control in America.* Oxford: Oxford University Press, 2006.

Corvisier, A. *Armies and Societies in Europe, 1494–1789.* Bloomington: Indiana University Press, 1979.

Crafts, Nicholas. "British Economic Growth, 1700–1850: Some Difficulties of Interpretation." *Explorations in Economic History* 24 (1987): 245–68.

———. *British Economic Growth during the Industrial Revolution.* New York: Oxford University Press, 1985.

Craig, Sir John. *The Mint: A History of the London Mint from A.D. 287 to 1948.* Cambridge: Cambridge University Press, 1953.

Cramer, Clayton, and Joseph Edward Olson. "Pistols, Crime, and Public: Safety in Early America." *Willamette Law Review* 44, no. 4 (2008): 699–722.

Cressy, David. *Saltpeter: The Mother of Gunpowder.* New York: Oxford University Press, 2013.

Crews, Robert. "Trafficking in Evil? The Global Arms Trade and the Politics of Disorder." In *Global Islam in the Age of Steam and Print, 1850–1930,* edited by James Gelvin and Nile Green, 121–42. Berkeley: University of California Press, 2014.

Crick, W. F., and J. E. Wadsworth. *A Hundred Years of Joint-Stock Banking.* 2nd ed. London: Hodder & Stoughton, 1938. First published 1936.

Crouzet, François. "The Impact of the French Wars on the British Economy." In *Britain and the French Revolution, 1789–1815,* edited by H. T. Dickinson, 189–209. Houndmills, UK: Macmillan, 1989.

Curtis, E. E. *The Organization of the British Army in the American Revolution.* New Haven, Conn.: Yale University Press, 1926.

Curtis, Mark, Helen Close, Vanessa Dury, and Roy Isbister. *The Good, the Bad, and the Ugly—A Decade of Labour's Arms Exports.* London: Saferworld, 2007.

Daaku, Kwame. *Trade and Politics on the Gold Coast, 1600–1720: A Study of the African Reaction to European Trade.* London: Clarendon, 1970.

Dale, Stephen. *The Muslim Empires of the Ottoman, Safavids, and Mughals.* New York: Cambridge University Press, 2010.

Dalrymple, William. *White Mughals: Love and Betrayal in Eighteenth-Century India.* New York: Penguin, 2004.

Daly, Gavin. *The British Soldier in the Peninsular War: Encounters with Spain and Portugal, 1808–1814.* New York: Palgrave Macmillan, 2013.

Darling, Anthony. *Red Coat and Brown Bess.* Historical Arms Series no. 12. Bloomfield, Ont.: Museum Restoration Service, 1971.

Daunton, Martin. *Progress and Poverty: An Economic and Social History of Britain, 1700–1850.* New York: Oxford University Press, 1995.

Davey, James. *The Transformation of British Naval Strategy: Seapower and Supply in Northern Europe, 1808–1812.* Rochester, N.Y.: Boydell, 2012.

Davies, K. G. *The Royal African Company.* New York: Longmans, Green, 1957.

Davis, Natalie Zemon. *The Return of Martin Guerre.* Cambridge, Mass.: Harvard University Press, 1983.

de Goede, Marieke. *Virtue, Fortune, and Faith: A Genealogy of Finance.* Minneapolis: University of Minnesota Press, 2005.

de Jong, Staat van Oorlog: *Wapenbedrijf en militaire hervorming in de Republiek der veredigde Nederlanded, 1585–1621.* Hilversum, Netherlands: Verloren, 2005.

de Vries, Jan. "The Industrial Revolution and the Industrious Revolution." *Journal of Economic History* 54, no. 2 (1994): 249–270.

Deane, Phyllis. "War and Industrialisation." In *War and Economic Development: Essays in Memory of David Joslin,* edited by J. M. Winter, 91–102. New York: Cambridge University Press, 1975.

Dent, Robert Kirkup. *Old and New Birmingham: A History of the Town and Its People.* Birmingham: Houghton and Hammond, 1880.

Devereaux, Simon. "The Historiography of the English State during 'The Long Eighteenth Century': Part I—Decentralized Perspectives." *History Compass* 7 (2009): 742–64.

———. "The Historiography of the English State during 'The Long Eighteenth Century': Part Two—Fiscal-Military and Nationalist Perspectives." *History Compass* 8 (2010): 843–65.

———. "Recasting the Theatre of Execution: The Abolition of the Tyburn Ritual." *Past and Present* 202 (2009): 127–74.

Dick, Malcolm. "The Lunar Society and the Anti-Slavery Debate." *Revolutionary Players.* www .revolutionaryplayers.org.uk/the-lunar-society-and-the-anti-slavery-debate.

Dickson, P. G. M. *The Financial Revolution in England: A Study in the Development of Public Credit, 1688–1756.* New York: St. Martin's, 1967.

Diggins, Milt. "Principio." Historical Society of Cecil County. www.cchistory.org/Principio.htm.

Diouf, Sylviane A., ed. *Fighting the Slave Trade: West African Strategies.* Oxford: James Currey, 2003.

Dirks, Nicholas. *The Scandal of Empire: India and the Creation of Imperial Britain.* Cambridge, Mass.: Harvard University Press, 2008.

Dixon, Thomas. "Forgotten Feelings: Our Emotional Past." *Huffington Post,* December 1, 2012. www .huffingtonpost.co.uk/thomas-dixon/british-stiff-upper-lip-our-emotional-past_b_1929511.html.

Duffy, M. "The Foundations of British Naval Power." In *The Military Revolution and the State, 1500–1800,* edited by Duffy, 49–85. Exeter, UK: University of Exeter, 1980.

———. "Introduction: The Military Revolution and the State, 1500–1800." In *The Military Revolution and the State, 1500–1800,* edited by M. Duffy, 1–9. Exeter, UK: University of Exeter, 1980.

E., J. H. "Richard Oswald." *Notes and Queries* 8, no. 324 (1853): 549.

Edgerton, David. *Warfare State: Britain, 1920–1970.* Cambridge: Cambridge University Press, 2006.

Elias, Norbert. *The Civilizing Process: The Development of Manners.* Vol. I, translated by Edmund Jephcott. New York: Urizen, 1978.

———. *Power & Civility: The Civilizing Process.* Vol. II, translated by Edmund Jephcott. New York: Pantheon, 1982.

Elgood, Robert. *Firearms of the Islamic World in the Tareq Rajab Museum, Kuwait.* London: I. B. Tauris, 1995.

Ellis, John. *The Social History of the Machine Gun.* Baltimore: Johns Hopkins University Press, 1986.

Emsley, Clive. *Crime and Society in England, 1750–1900.* London: Longmans, 1987.

———. *Hard Men: The English and Violence since 1750.* London: Hambledon and London, 2005.

Engerman, Stanley. "Mercantilism and Overseas Trade, 1700–1800." In *The Economic History of Britain since 1700.* Vol. 1, *1700–1860,* edited by Roderick Floud and Deirdre McCloskey, 182–204. 2nd ed. New York: Cambridge University Press, 1981.

Evans, Chris, Owen Jackson, and Göran Rydén. "Baltic Iron and the British Iron Industry in the Eighteenth Century." *Economic History Review* 55, no. 4 (2002): 642–65.

Faber, Eli. *Jews, Slaves and the Slave Trade: Setting the Record Straight.* New York: New York University Press, 1998.

Ffoulkes, Charles. *The Gun-Founders of England, with a List of English and Continental Gun-Founders from the XIV to the XIX Centuries.* Cambridge: Cambridge University Press, 1937.

Fichter, David. *So Great a Proffit: How the East Indies Trade Transformed Anglo-American Capitalism.* Cambridge, Mass.: Harvard University Press, 2010.

Finn, Margot. *The Character of Credit: Personal Debt in English Culture, 1740–1914.* Cambridge: Cambridge University Press, 2003.

Fisher, Humphrey J., and Virginia Rowland. "Firearms in the Central Sudan." *Journal of African History* 13 (1971): 591–607.

Fletcher, Robert. *British Imperialism and 'The Tribal Question': Desert Administration and Nomadic Societies in the Middle East, 1919–1936.* Oxford: Oxford University Press, 2015.

Flinn, Michael. *Men of Iron: The Crowleys in the Early Iron Industry.* Edinburgh: Edinburgh University Press, 1962.

———. "Sir Ambrose Crowley, Ironmonger, 1658–1713." In *Explorations in Enterprise*, edited by H. G. J. Aitken, 241–58. Cambridge, Mass.: Harvard University Press, 1965.

———. "Trends in Real Wages, 1750–1850." *Economic History Review* 27 (1974): 395–413.

Forbes, A. *A History of the Army Ordnance Services.* 3 vols. London: Medici Society, 1929.

Foster, Herbert J. "Partners or Captives in Commerce? The Role of Africans in the Slave Trade." *Journal of Black Studies* 6 (1976): 421–34.

Foucault, Michel. *Discipline and Punish: The Birth of the Prison.* New York: Pantheon, 1977.

Frank, Zephyr, Steven Topik, and Carlos Marichal, eds. *From Silver to Cocaine: Latin American Commodity Chains and the Building of the World Economy, 1500–2000.* Durham, N.C.: Duke University Press, 2006.

Fries, Russell. "British Response to the American System: The Case of the Small-Arms Industry after 1850." *Technology & Culture* 16 (1975): 377–403.

Fullagar, Kate. *The Savage Visit: New World People and Popular Imperial Culture in Britain, 1710–1795.* Berkeley: University of California Press, 2012.

Gaskill, Malcolm. *Crime and Mentalities in Early Modern England.* Cambridge: Cambridge University Press, 2000.

Gattrell, Vic. *The Hanging Tree: Execution and the English People, 1770–1868.* New York: Oxford University Press, 1996.

Genç, Mehmet. "Ottoman Industry in the 18th Century." In *Manufacturing in the Ottoman Empire and Turkey,* edited by Donald Quataert, 59–86. Albany: State University of New York Press, 1994.

Ghosh, Durba. *Sex and the Family in Colonial India: The Making of Empire.* New York: Cambridge University Press, 2008.

Gill, Conrad. *History of Birmingham.* Vol. 1, *Manor and Borough to 1865.* London: Oxford University Press, 1952.

Gillham, Nicholas Wright. *A Life of Sir Francis Galton: From African Exploration to the Birth of Eugenics.* New York: Oxford University Press, 2001.

Gilmour, Ian. *Riot, Risings and Revolution: Governance and Violence in Eighteenth-Century Britain.* London: Hutchinson, 1992.

Glover, Richard. *Peninsular Preparation: The Reform of the British Army, 1795–1809.* Cambridge: Cambridge University Press, 1963.

Gommans, Jos. *Mughal Warfare: Indian Frontiers and Highroads to Empire, 1500–1700.* London: Routledge, 2002.

Goodwin, Albert. *The Friends of Liberty: The English Democratic Movement in the Age of the French Revolution.* Cambridge, Mass.: Harvard University Press, 1979.

Grant, Jonathan. *Rulers, Guns, and Money: The Global Arms Trade in the Age of Imperialism.* Cambridge, Mass.: Harvard University Press, 2007.

Grassby, R. "English Merchant Capitalism in the Late Seventeenth Century: The Composition of Business Fortunes." *Past and Present* 46 (1970): 87–107.

Greenwood, Colin. *Firearms Control: A Study of Armed Crime and Firearms Control in England and Wales.* London: Routledge & Kegan Paul, 1972.

Griffiths, Paul, Adam Fox, and Steve Hindle, eds. *The Experience of Authority in Early Modern England.* New York: St. Martin's, 1996.

Gruber, Ira. "Of Arms and Men: 'Arming America' and Military History." *William and Mary Quarterly* 59 (2002): 217–22.

Guldi, Jo. *Roads to Power: Britain Invents the Infrastructure State.* Cambridge, Mass.: Harvard University Press, 2012.

Gutmann, Myron P. "War and Industrial Development." In *Proto-Industrialisation: Recherches Recentes et Nouvelles Perspectives,* edited by Rene Leboutte, 152–180. Geneva: Droz, 1996.

Guy, J. J. "A Note on Firearms in the Zulu Kingdom with Special Reference to the Anglo-Zulu War, 1879." *Journal of African History* 12 (1971): 557–70.

Hall, Catherine. *Civilising Subjects: Metropole and Colony in the English Imagination, 1830–1867.* Oxford: Polity, 2002.

Hall, Catherine, and Leonore Davidoff. *Family Fortunes: Men and Women of the English Middle Class, 1780–1850.* London: Hutchinson, 1987.

Hall, Catherine, Nicholas Draper, Keith McClelland, Katie Donington, and Rachel Long. *Legacies of British Slave-Ownership.* Cambridge: Cambridge University Press, 2014.

Hamilton, Michelle. "In the King's Service." In *English Atlantics Revisited: Essays Honouring Professor Ian K. Steel,* edited by Nancy L. Rhoden, 310–44. Ithaca, N.Y.: McGill-Queen's University Press, 2007.

Hancock, David. *Citizens of the World: London Merchants and the Integration of the British Atlantic Community, 1735–1785.* New York: Cambridge University Press, 1997.

———. "'Domestic Bubbling': Eighteenth-Century London Merchants and Individual Investment in the Funds." *Economic History Review* 47, no. 4 (1994): 679–702.

———. "Scots in the Slave Trade." In *Nation and Province in the First British Empire: Scotland and the Americas, 1600–1800,* edited by Ned C. Landsman, 60–93. Cranbury, N.J.: Associated University Presses, 2001.

Handler, Jerome S., and Michael L. Tuite Jr. "The Atlantic Slave Trade and Slave Life in the Americas: A Visual Record." Virginia Foundation for the Humanities. http://slaveryimages.org.

Hanson, Charles E., Jr. *The Northwest Gun.* Lincoln: Nebraska State Historical Society, 1955.

Harding, D. F. *Smallarms of the East India Company, 1600–1856.* 4 vols. London: Foresight, 1997.

Harling, Philip. *The Waning of 'Old Corruption': The Politics of Economical Reform in Britain, 1779–1846.* New York: Clarendon, 1996.

Harling, Philip, and Peter Mandler. "From 'Fiscal-Military' State to Laissez-Faire State, 1760–1850." *Journal of British Studies* 32 (1993): 44–70.

Harris, J. R. *The British Iron Industry, 1700–1850.* Basingstoke, UK: Macmillan, 1988.

———. "Copper and Shipping in the Eighteenth Century." *Economic History Review* 19, no. 3 (1966): 550–68.

———. *The Copper King: A Biography of Thomas Williams of Llanidan.* Toronto: University of Toronto Press, 1964.

———. *Industrial Espionage and Technology Transfer: Britain and France in the 18th Century.* Brookfield, Vt.: Scolar, 1998.

Harris, Ron. "Government and the Economy, 1688–1850." In *The Cambridge Economic History of Modern Britain.* Vol. 1, *Industrialisation, 1700–1860,* edited by Roderick Floud and Paul Johnson, 204–37. Cambridge: Cambridge University Press, 2004.

Hattendorf, J. B. *England in the War of the Spanish Succession: A Study of the English View and Conduct of Grand Strategy, 1702–1712.* New York: Garland, 1987.

Hawke, Gary. "Reinterpretations of the Industrial Revolution." In *The Industrial Revolution and British Society,* edited by Patrick O'Brien and Roland Quinault, 54–78. Cambridge: Cambridge University Press, 1993.

Hay, Douglas. "Property, Authority and the Criminal Law." In *Albion's Fatal Tree: Crime and Society in Eighteenth-Century England,* edited by D. Hay, E. P. Thompson, and P. Linebaugh, 17–63. New York: Pantheon, 1975.

———. "War, Dearth and Theft in the Eighteenth Century: The Record of the English Courts." *Past and Present* 95 (1982): 117–60.

Headrick, Daniel. *Tools of Empire: Technology and European Imperialism in the Nineteenth Century.* New York: Oxford University Press, 1981.

Hermann, Robin. "Money and Empire: The Failure of the Royal African Company." In *The Empire of Credit: The Financial Revolution in the British Atlantic World, 1688–1815,* edited by Daniel Carey and Christopher Finlay, 97–119. Portland, Ore.: Irish Academic Press, 2011.

Herrmann, David. *The Arming of Europe and the Making of the First World War.* Princeton, N.J.: Princeton University Press, 1996.

Hirst, M. E. *The Quakers in Peace and War: An Account of Their Peace Principles and Practice.* New York: J. S. Ozer, 1972.

Hobsbawm, Eric. *Industry and Empire: From 1750 to the Present Day.* New York: Pantheon, 1968.

Hoff, Arne. "The Term Snaphaunce." In *Aspects of Dutch Gunmaking,* edited by H. L. Visser and D. W. Bailey, 138–44. Zwolle, Netherlands: Waanders, 1997.

Hoffman, Philip. "Prices, the Military Revolution, and Western Europe's Comparative Advantage in Violence." *Economic History Review* 64 (2011): 39–59.

———. *Why Did Europe Conquer the World?* Princeton, N.J.: Princeton University Press, 2015.

Holtzapffel, Charles. *Turning and Mechanical Manipulation, Intended as a Work of General Reference and Practical Instruction on the Lathe and the Various Mechanical Pursuits Followed by Amateurs.* Vol. 2. London: Holtzapffel, 1856.

Hopkins, Eric. *Birmingham: The First Manufacturing Town in the World, 1760–1840.* London: Weidenfeld & Nicolson, 1989.

———. "Working Hours and Conditions during the Industrial Revolution: A Re-Appraisal." *Economic History Review* 35 (1982): 52–66.

Hoppit, Julian. "Attitudes to Credit in Britain, 1680–1790." *Historical Journal* 33, no. 2 (1990): 305–22.

———. *Risk and Failure in English Business, 1700–1800.* New York: Cambridge University Press, 1987.

———. "The Use and Abuse of Credit in 18th-Century England." In *Business Life and Public Policy: Essays in Honour of D. C. Coleman,* edited by Neil McKendrick and R. B. Outhwaite, 64–78. New York: Cambridge University Press, 1986.

House of Commons, Committees on Arms Export Controls. *Scrutiny of Arms Export Controls (2013): Scrutiny of the Government's UK Strategic Export Controls Annual Report 2011.* London: The Stationery Office, 2013.

Howell, David. "The Social Life of Firearms in Tokugawa Japan." *Japanese Studies* 29 (2009): 65–80.

Hudson, Pat. *The Industrial Revolution.* London: Edward Arnold, 1992.

Hudson, Peter. "The National City Bank of New York and Haiti, 1909–1922." *Radical History Review* 115 (2013): 91–114.

Hueckel, G. "War and the British Economy, 1793–1815: A General Equilibrium Analysis." *Explorations in Economic History* 10 (1973): 365–97.

Hughes, B. P. *Firepower: Weapons Effectiveness on the Battlefield, 1630–1850.* New York: Scribner, 1974.

Hunnisett, R. F. *Wiltshire Coroners' Bills, 1752–1796.* Stoke-on-Trent, UK: Wiltshire Record Society, 1981.

Hyde, C. K. *Technological Change and the British Iron Industry, 1700–1870.* Princeton, N.J.: Princeton University Press, 1977.

Hyslop, J. "Guns, Drugs and Revolutionary Propaganda: Indian Sailors and Smuggling in the 1920s." *South African Historical Journal* 61 (2009): 838–46.

Ignatieff, Michael. *A Just Measure of Pain: The Penitentiary in the Industrial Revolution, 1750–1850.* New York: Pantheon, 1978.

Inalcik, Halil. "The Socio-Political Effects of the Diffusion of Fire-arms in the Middle East." In *War, Technology and Society in the Middle East,* edited by V. J. Parry and M. E. Yapp, 195–217. London: Oxford University Press, 1975..

Inikori, Joseph. *Africans and the Industrial Revolution in England: A Study in International Trade and Economic Development.* New York: Cambridge University Press, 2002.

———. "The Import of Firearms into West Africa, 1750–1807: A Quantitative Analysis." *Journal of African History* 18 (1977): 339–68.

———. "Slavery and the Revolution in Cotton Textile Production in England." In *The Atlantic Slave Trade: Effects on Economies, Societies, and Peoples in Africa, the Americas, and Europe,* edited by Inikori and Stanley Engerman, 145–81. Durham, N.C.: Duke University Press, 1992.

Jackson, R. V. "Government Expenditure and British Economic Growth in the 18th Century: Some Problems of Measurement." *Economic History Review* 43 (1990): 217–35.

James, Harold. *Family Capitalism: Wendels, Haniels, Falcks, and the Continental European Model.* Cambridge, Mass.: Belknap Press, 2006.

Jasanoff, Maya. *The Edge of Empire: Lives, Culture, and Conquest in the East, 1750–1850.* New York: Knopf, 2005.

John, A. H. "Farming in Wartime, 1793–1815." In *Land, Labour and Population in the Industrial Revolution: Essays Presented to J. D. Chambers,* edited by E. L. Jones and G. E. Mingay, 28–47. London: Arnold, 1967.

———. "War and the English Economy, 1700–1763." *Economic History Review* 7, no. 3 (1755): 329–44.

Jones, Colin. "The Military Revolution and the Professionalization of the French Army Under the Ancien Régime." In *The Military Revolution Debate: Readings on the Military Transformation of Early Modern Europe,* edited by C. Rogers, 149–67. Boulder, Colo.: Westview, 1995.

Jones, D. W. *War and Economy in the Age of William III and Marlborough.* Oxford: Basil Blackwell, 1988.

Jones, Peter. *Industrial Enlightenment: Science, Technology and Culture in Birmingham and the West Midlands, 1760–1820.* Manchester: Manchester University Press, 2009.

Jones, W. J. "The Foundations of English Bankruptcy: Statutes and Commission in the Early Modern Period." *Transactions of the American Philosophical Society* 68 (1979): 1–63.

Joslin, David. "London Bankers in Wartime, 1739–64." In *Studies in the Industrial Revolution: Presented to T. S. Ashton,* edited by L. S. Pressnell, 156–76. London: Athlone, 1960.

Kea, R. A. "Firearms and Warfare on the Gold and Slave Coasts from the Sixteenth to the Nineteenth Centuries." *Journal of African History* 12, no. 2 (1971): 185–213.

Kennedy, Paul. *The Rise and Fall of the Great Powers.* New York: Random House, 1987.

Kennett, Lee. *The French Armies in the Seven Years' War: A Study in Military Organisation and Administration.* Durham, N.C.: Duke University Press, 1976.

Kennett, Lee, and James LaVerne Anderson. *The Gun in America: The Origins of a National Dilemma.* Westport, Conn.: Greenwood, 1975.

Khan, Iqtidar Alam. "The Indian Response to Firearms, 1300–1750." In *Gunpowder, Explosives and the State: A Technological History,* edited by Brenda Buchanan, 51–66. Aldershot, UK: Ashgate, 2006.

King, Peter. *Crime, Justice, and Discretion in England, 1740–1820.* New York: Oxford University Press, 2000.

Kittler, Friedrich. *Gramophone, Film, Typewriter.* Stanford, Calif.: Stanford University Press, 1999.

Knight, Roger. *Britain Against Napoleon: The Organization of Victory, 1793–1815.* New York: Allen Lane, 2013.

Knight, Roger, and Martin Wilcox. *Sustaining the Fleet, 1793–1815: War, the British Navy and the Contractor State.* Rochester, N.Y.: Boydell, 2010.

Koehn, Nancy. *The Power of Commerce: Economy and Governance in the First British Empire.* Ithaca, N.Y.: Cornell University Press, 1994.

Kolsky, Elizabeth. *Colonial Justice in British India: White Violence and the Rule of Law.* New York: Cambridge University Press, 2011.

La Force, J. Clayburn. "The Supply of Muskets and Spain's War of Independence." *Business History Review* 43 (1969): 523–44.

Langford, J. A. *A Century of Birmingham Life: A Chronicle of Local Events, 1741–1841.* 2 vols. Birmingham: W. G. Moore, 1868.

Langford, Paul. "Manners and the Eighteenth-Century State: The Case of the Unsociable Englishman." In *Rethinking Leviathan: The Eighteenth-Century State in Britain and Germany,* edited by John Brewer and Eckhart Hellmuth, 281–316. Oxford: Oxford University Press, 1999.

———. *A Polite and Commercial People: England, 1727–1783.* New York: Oxford University Press, 1994.

———. *Public Life and the Propertied Englishman, 1689–1798.* Oxford: Clarendon, 1991.

Landes, David. *The Unbound Prometheus: Technological Change and Industrial Development in Western Europe from 1750 to the Present.* Cambridge: Cambridge University Press, 1969.

Laqueur, Thomas W. "Crowds, Carnivals, and the State in English Executions." In *The First Modern Society: Essays in English History in Honour of Lawrence Stone,* edited by Lawrence Stone, A. L. Beier, David Cannadine, and James M. Rosenheim, 305–55. New York: Cambridge University Press, 1989.

———. *Solitary Sex: A Cultural History of Masturbation.* New York: Zone, 2003.

Latour, Bruno. *Pandora's Hope: Essays on the Reality of Science Studies.* Cambridge, Mass.: Harvard University Press, 1999.

Law, Robin. "Horses, Firearms and Political Power in Pre-Colonial West Africa." *Past and Present* 72 (1976): 112–32.

———. *The Slave Coast of West Africa, 1550–1750: The Impact of the Atlantic Slave Trade on an African Society.* New York: Oxford University Press, 1991.

Lawrence, Jon. "Forging a Peaceable Kingdom: War, Violence, and Fear of Brutalization in Post–First World War Britain." *Journal of Modern History* 75 (2003): 557–89.

Leach, Douglas Edward. *Arms for Empire: A Military History of the British Colonies in North America, 1607–1763.* New York: Macmillan, 1973.

———. *Roots of Conflict: British Armed Forces and Colonial Americans, 1677–1763.* Chapel Hill: University of North Carolina Press, 1986.

Lemmings, David, ed. *The British and Their Laws in the 18th Century.* Rochester, N.Y.: Boydell, 2005.

Lenman, B. *Britain's Colonial Wars, 1688–1783.* Harlow, UK: Longmans, 2001.

Lepore, Jill. "Battleground America: One Nation, under the Gun." *The New Yorker,* April 23, 2012, www .newyorker.com/magazine/2012/04/23/battleground-america.

Lloyd, Humphrey. *The Quaker Lloyds in the Industrial Revolution.* London: Hutchinson, 1975.

Lloyd, Samuel. *The Lloyds of Birmingham.* 2nd ed. Birmingham: Cornish Brothers, 1907.

Macdonald, Janet. *The British Navy's Victualling Board, 1793–1815: Management Competence and Incompetence.* Rochester, N.Y.: Boydell, 2010.

Macfarlane, Alan. *Marriage and Love in England: Modes of Reproduction, 1300–1840.* New York: Blackwell, 1986.

Mack, Phyllis. "Religion, Feminism, and the Problem of Agency: Reflections on Eighteenth-Century Quakerism." *Signs* 29, no. 1 (2003): 149–77.

Macleod, Christine. *Inventing the Industrial Revolution: The English Patent System, 1660–1800.* New York: Cambridge University Press, 1988.

Madley, Benjamin. *An American Genocide: The United States and the California Indian Catastrophe.* New Haven, Conn.: Yale University Press, 2016.

Magnier, Mark. "Gun Culture Spreads in India." *Los Angeles Times,* February 20, 2012, http://articles .latimes.com/2012/feb/20/world/la-fg-india-guns-20120221.

Main, Gloria L. "Many Things Forgotten: The Use of Probate Records in 'Arming America.'" *William and Mary Quarterly* 59 (2002): 211–16.

Majumdar, Saikat. *Prose of the World: Modernism and the Banality of Empire.* New York: Columbia University Press, 2013.

Malcolm, Joyce Lee. "The Creation of a 'True Antient and Indubitable' Right: The English Bill of Rights and the Right to Be Armed." *Journal of British Studies* 32 (1993): 226–49.

———. *Guns and Violence: The English Experience.* Cambridge, Mass.: Harvard University Press, 2002.

———. *To Keep and Bear Arms: The Origins of an Anglo-American Right.* Cambridge, Mass.: Harvard University Press, 1994.

Malone, P. M. *The Skulking Way of War: Technology and Tactics Among the Indians of New England.* Lanham, Md.: Madison Books, 1991.

Mann, Bruce. *Republic of Debtors: Bankruptcy in the Age of American Independence.* Cambridge, Mass.: Harvard University Press, 2002.

Martin, Phyllis. "The Trade of Loango in the Seventeenth and Eighteenth Centuries." In *Pre-Colonial African Trade,* edited by Richard Gray and David Birmingham, 139–61. London: Oxford University Press, 1970.

Masco, Joseph. *The Nuclear Borderlands: The Manhattan Project in Post–Cold War New Mexico.* Princeton, N.J.: Princeton University Press, 2006.

Mathias, Peter. *English Trade Tokens: The Industrial Revolution Illustrated.* London: Abelard-Schuman, 1962.

———. *The Transformation of England: Essays in the Economics and Social History of England in the Eighteenth Century.* New York: Columbia University Press, 1979.

Mayer, Jane. "The Predator War: What Are the Risks of the CIA's Covert Drone Program?" *The New Yorker,* October 26, 2009, www.newyorker.com/magazine/2009/10/26/the-predator-war.

McCloskey, Deirdre. "1780–1860: A Survey." In *The Economic History of Britain since 1700.* Vol. 1, *1700–1860,* edited by Roderick Floud and McCloskey, 242–70. 2nd ed. New York: Cambridge University Press, 1981.

McIntosh, Michael. *Best Guns.* Traverse City, Mich.: Countrysport, 1989.

McLynn, Frank. *Crime and Punishment in Eighteenth-Century England.* London: Routledge, 1989.

McNeill, William. *The Pursuit of Power: Technology, Armed Force, and Society since A.D. 1000.* Chicago: Chicago University Press, 1983.

Metcalf, George. "A Microcosm of Why Africans Sold Slaves: Akan Consumption Patterns in the 1770s." *Journal of African History* 28 (1987): 377–94.

Millburn, John R. "The Office of Ordnance and the Instrument-Making Trade in the Mid-Eighteenth Century." *Annals of Science* 45, no. 3 (May 1988): 221–93.

Miller, Daniel. *Stuff.* Malden, Mass.: Polity, 2010.

———, ed. *Materiality.* Durham, N.C.: Duke University Press, 2005.

Miller, Joseph C. *Way of Death: Merchant Capitalism and the Angolan Slave Trade, 1730–1830.* Madison: University of Wisconsin Press, 1996.

Minchison, W. E. "The Merchants in England in the Eighteenth Century." In *Explorations in Enterprise,* edited by H. G. J. Aitken, 278–95. Cambridge, Mass.: Harvard University Press, 1965.

Mitchell, Timothy. *Rule of Experts: Egypt, Techno-Politics, Modernity.* Berkeley: University of California Press, 2002.

Mokyr, Joel. *The Enlightened Economy: Britain and the Industrial Revolution, 1700–1850.* New York: Penguin, 2009.

———. "Has the Industrial Revolution Been Crowded Out? Some Reflections on Crafts and Williamson." *Explorations in Economic History* 24 (1987): 293–319.

———. "The Intellectual Origins of Modern Economic Growth." *Journal of Economic History* 65 (2005): 285–351.

———. "Technological Change, 1700–1830." *The Economic History of Britain since 1700.* Vol. 1, *1700–1860,* edited by Roderick Floud and Deirdre McCloskey, 12–43. 2nd ed. New York: Cambridge University Press, 1981.

Money, John. *Experience and Identity: Birmingham and the West Midlands, 1760–1800.* Manchester: Manchester University Press, 1993.

Moreman, Tim. "The Arms Trade and the North-West Frontier Pathan Tribes, 1890–1914." *Journal of Imperial and Commonwealth History* 22 (1994): 187–216.

Morgan, Kenneth. *Bristol and the Atlantic Trade in the Eighteenth Century.* New York: Cambridge University Press, 1993.

———. "Bristol West India Merchants in the Eighteenth Century." *Transactions of the Royal Historical Society* 6, no. 3 (1993): 185–208.

———. "James Rogers and the Bristol Slave Trade." *Historical Research* 76 (2003): 189–216.

Morriss, Roger. *The Foundations of British Maritime Ascendancy: Resources, Logistics and the State, 1755–1815.* New York: Cambridge University Press, 2011.

———. *The Royal Dockyards during the Revolutionary and Napoleonic Wars.* Leicester, UK: Leicester University Press, 1983.

Muldrew, Craig. *The Economy of Obligation: The Culture of Credit and Social Relations in Early Modern England.* New York: Palgrave, 2001. First published 1998.

———. "'Hard Food for Midas': Cash and Its Social Value in Early Modern England." *Past and Present* 170 (2001): 78–120.

———. "Interpreting the Market: The Ethics of Credit and Community Relations in Early Modern England." *Social History* 18 (1993): 163–83.

Munsche, P. B. *Gentlemen and Poachers: The English Game Laws, 1671–1831.* New York: Cambridge University Press, 1981.

Namier, Lewis B. "Anthony Bacon, M.P., an Eighteenth-Century Merchant." *Journal of Economic and Business History* 2, no. 1 (1929): 20–70.

———.*The Structure of Politics at the Accession of George III.* London: Macmillan, 1957.

National Trust Collections. "Gurney Times, Celebrating 200 Years of Banking 1775–1975." www.nationaltrustcollections.org.uk/object/782485.

Neal, Larry. "The Finance of Business during the Industrial Revolution." In *The Economic History of Britain since 1700.* Vol. 1, edited by Roderick Floud and Deirdre McCloskey, 151–81. 2nd ed. New York: Cambridge University Press, 1981.

———. *The Rise of Financial Capitalism: International Capital Markets in the Age of Reason.* Cambridge: Cambridge University Press, 1990.

Neal, W. Keith, and D. H. L. Black. *Great British Gunmakers, 1540–1740.* Norwich, UK: Historical Firearms, 1984.

Ness, Gayl D., and William Stahl. "Western Imperialist Armies in Asia." *Comparative Studies in Society and History* 19 (1977): 2–29.

Nester, William. *The Great Frontier War: Britain, France, and the Imperial Struggle for North America, 1607–1755.* Westport, Conn.: Praeger, 2000.

Nicholls, James Fawckner, and John Taylor. *Bristol Past and Present: Civil and Modern History.* Bristol, UK: J. W. Arrowsmith, 1882.

Norman, Neil, and Ken Kelly. "Landscape Politics: The Serpent Ditch and the Rainbow in West Africa." *American Anthropologist* 106 (2008): 98–110.

O'Brien, Patrick. "Central Government and the Economy, 1688–1815." In The *Economic History of Britain since 1700.* Vol. 1, edited by Roderick Floud and Deirdre McCloskey, 205–41. 2nd ed. New York: Cambridge University Press, 1981.

———. "The Impact of the Revolutionary and Napoleonic Wars, 1793–1815, on the Long-Run Growth of the British Economy." *Fernand Braudel Center Review* 12 (1989): 335–95.

———. "Introduction: Modern Conceptions of the Industrial Revolution." In *The Industrial Revolution and British Society,* edited by O'Brien and Roland Quinault, 1–30. Cambridge: Cambridge University Press, 1993.

———. "Political Preconditions for the Industrial Revolution." In *The Industrial Revolution and British Society,* edited by O'Brien and Roland Quinault, 124–55. Cambridge: Cambridge University Press, 1993.

———. *Power with Profit: The State and the Economy, 1688–1815.* London: Institute of Historical Research, 1991.

———. "Public Finance in the Wars with France, 1793–1815." *Britain and the French Revolution, 1789–1815,* edited by H. T. Dickinson, 165–87. Houndmills, UK: Macmillan, 1989.

O'Brien, Patrick, and Roland Quinault, eds. *The Industrial Revolution and British Society.* Cambridge: Cambridge University Press, 1993.

Ogborn, Miles. *Indian Ink: Script and Print in the Making of the English East India Company.* Chicago: Chicago University Press, 2007.

Orwell, George. *The Road to Wigan Pier.* London: V. Gollancz, 1937.

Oxford Dictionary of National Biography online. www.oxforddnb.com.

Page, William, ed. *The Victoria History of the County of Warwick.* Vol. 2. London: Archibald Constable, 1908.

Pam, David. *The Royal Small Arms Factory: Enfield and Its Workers.* London: David Pam, 1998.

Pares, Richard. *War and Trade in the West Indies, 1739–1763.* Oxford: Clarendon, 1963.

Parker, Geoffrey. *The Military Revolution: Military Innovation and the Rise of the West, 1500–1800.* Cambridge: Cambridge University Press, 1988.

Parthasarathi, Prasannan. *Why Europe Grew Rich and Asia Did Not: Global Economic Divergence, 1600–1850.* New York: Cambridge University Press, 2011.

Peers, Douglas M. *Between Mars and Mammon: Colonial Armies and the Garrison State in Early Nineteenth Century India.* New York: St. Martin's, 1995.

Pemble, John. "Resources and Techniques in the Second Maratha War." *Historical Journal* 19 (1976): 375–404.

Perrin, Noel. *Giving Up the Gun: Japan's Reversion to the Sword, 1543–1879.* Boston: D. R. Godine, 1979.

Person, Yves. "Guinea-Samori." In *West African Resistance: The Military Response to Colonial Occupation,* edited by Michael Crowder, translated by Joan White, 111–443. New York: Africana, 1971.

Peterson, Harold. *Arms and Armor in Colonial America: 1526–1783.* Harrisburg, Pa.: Stackpole, 1956.

Petrović, Djurdjica. "Fire-Arms in the Balkans on the Eve of and after the Ottoman Conquests of the Fourteenth and Fifteenth Centuries." In *War, Technology and Society in the Middle East,* edited by V. J. Parry and M. E. Yapp, 164–94. London: Oxford University Press, 1975.

Phipps, William E. *Amazing Grace in John Newton: Slave-Ship Captain, Hymnwriter, and Abolitionist.* Macon, Ga.: Mercer University Press, 2001.

Pick, Daniel. *War Machine: The Rationalisation of Slaughter in the Modern Age.* New Haven, Conn.: Yale University Press, 1993.

Pincus, Steve. *1688: The First Modern Revolution.* New Haven, Conn.: Yale University Press, 2009.

Pollard, H. B. C. *A History of Firearms.* New York: Macmillan, 1983. First published 1926.

Pool, B. *Navy Board Contracts 1660–1832: Contract Administration under the Navy Board.* London: Longmans, 1966.

Poovey, Mary. *Genres of the Credit Economy: Mediating Value in Eighteenth- and Nineteenth-Century Britain.* Chicago: University of Chicago Press, 2008.

Porter, Roy. *The Creation of the Modern World: The Untold Story of the British Enlightenment.* New York: Norton, 2001.

———. *English Society in the Eighteenth Century.* New York: Penguin, 1982.

———. "Science, Provincial Culture and Public Opinion in Enlightenment England." *British Journal for Eighteenth-Century Studies* 3 (1980): 20–46.

Prestholdt, Jeremy. *Domesticating the World: African Consumerism and the Genealogies of Globalization.* Berkeley: University of California Press, 2008.

Price, J. M. *Capital and Credit in British Overseas Trade: The View from the Chesapeake, 1700–1776.* Cambridge, Mass.: Harvard University Press, 1980.

———. "English Quaker Merchants and War at Sea, 1689–1783." *West India Accounts: Essays on the History of the British Caribbean and the Atlantic Economy in Honour of Richard Sheridan,* edited by Richard B. Sheridan and Roderick Alexander McDonald, 64–86. Barbados: University of the West Indies Press, 1996.

———. "The Great Quaker Business Families of Eighteenth-Century London." In *The World of William Penn,* edited by R. S. Dunn and M. M. Dunn, 363–99. Philadelphia: University of Pennsylvania Press, 1986.

———. "What Did Merchants Do? Reflections on British Overseas Trade, 1660–1790." *Journal of Economic History* 49 (1989): 267–84.

Puype, Jan Piet. "Dutch 17th-Century Flintlocks Recovered from Seneca Iroquois Sites in New York State." In *Aspects of Dutch Gunmaking,* edited by H. L. Visser and D. W. Bailey, 204–34. Zwolle, Netherlands: Waanders, 1997.

Puype, Jan Piet, and Marco van der Hoeven, eds. *The Arsenal of the World: The Dutch Arms Trade in the Seventeenth Century.* Amsterdam: Batavian Lion International, 1996.

Rabin, Dana. *Identity, Crime, and Legal Responsibility in Eighteenth-Century England.* London: Palgrave, 2004.

Raistrick, Arthur. *Dynasty of Iron Founders: The Darbys and Coalbrookdale.* New York: Longmans, Green, 1953.

———. *Quakers in Science and Industry: Being an Account of the Quaker Contributions to Science and Industry during the 17th and 18th Centuries.* London: Bannisdale, 1950.

———. *Two Centuries of Industrial Welfare: The London (Quaker) Lead Company, 1692–1905: The Social Policy and Work of the Governor and Company for Smelting Down Lead with Pit Coal and Sea Coal; Mainly in Alston Moor and the Pennines.* Buxton, UK: Moorland, 1977.

Rakove, Jack. "The Second Amendment: The Highest Stage of Originalism." *Chicago-Kent Law Review* 76 (2000): 103–66.

———. "Words, Deeds, and Guns: 'Arming America' and the Second Amendment." *William and Mary Quarterly* 59 (2002): 205–10.

Randell, Jacqueline. "Colt Culture: Examining Representations of the American West in Victorian London." *Columbia University Journal of Politics & Society* 25 (Fall 2014): 6–26.

Raudzens, George. "Military Revolution or Maritime Evolution? Military Superiorities or Transportation Advantages as Main Causes of European Colonial Conquests to 1788." *Journal of Military History* 63 (1999): 631–41.

———. "War-Winning Weapons: The Measurement of Technological Determinism in Military History." *Journal of Military History* 54 (1990): 403–34.

———, ed. *Technology, Disease and Colonial Conquests, Sixteenth to Eighteenth Centuries: Essays Reappraising the Guns and Germs Theories.* Boston: Brill, 2001.

Rawley, James A., and Stephen D. Behrendt. *The Transatlantic Slave Trade: A History.* New York: Norton, 1981.

Ray, Arthur. *Indians in the Fur Trade: Their Role as Trappers, Hunters, and Middlemen in the Lands Southwest of Hudson Bay, 1660–1870.* Toronto: University of Toronto Press, 1974.

Reid, Richard. *Warfare in African History.* New York: Cambridge University Press, 2012.

Renn, Diana. "Unarmed and Dangerous: On Writing a Thriller with No Guns." *Huffington Post,* July 9, 2014, www.huffingtonpost.com/diana-renn/unarmed-and-dangerous-on-_b_5568724.html.

Rich, E. E. *The History of the Hudson's Bay Company, 1670–1870.* 2 vols. London: Hudson's Bay Record Society, 1958–59.

Richards, R. D. *The Early History of Banking in England.* New York: A. M. Kelley, 1965.

Richards, W. A. "The Import of Firearms into West Africa in the Eighteenth Century." *Journal of African History* 21 (1980): 43–59.

Richardson, David. "West African Consumption Patterns and Their Influence on the Eighteenth-Century English Slave Trade." In *The Uncommon Market: Essays in the Economic History of the Atlantic Slave Trade*, edited by Henry Gemery and Jan Hogendorn, 303–30. New York: Academic Press, 1979.

Riden, P. "The Output of the British Iron Industry before 1870." *Economic History Review* 30 (1977): 442–59.

Riding, Jacqueline. *Jacobites: A New History of the '45 Rebellion*. London: Bloomsbury, 2016.

Riello, Giorgio. "Things That Shape History: Material Culture and Historical Narratives." In *History and Material Culture: A Student's Guide to Approaching Alternative Sources*, edited by Karen Harvey, 24–47. New York: Routledge, 2009.

Roll, E. *An Early Experiment in Industrial Organisation: Being a History of the Firm Boulton & Watt, 1775–1805*. New York: A. M. Kelley, 1968. First published 1930.

Rosenbloom, Joshua L. "Anglo-American Technological Differences in Small Arms Manufacturing." *Journal of Interdisciplinary History* 23 (1993): 683–98.

Roth, Randolph. *American Homicide*. Cambridge, Mass.: Belknap Press, 2009.

———. "Guns, Gun Culture, and Homicide: The Relationship between Firearms, the Uses of Firearms, and Interpersonal Violence." *William and Mary Quarterly* 59 (2002): 223–40.

———. "Homicide in Early Modern England, 1549–1800: The Need for a Quantitative Synthesis." *Crime, Histories, and Societies* 5 (2001): 33–67.

Rothschild, Emma. *The Inner Life of Empires: An Eighteenth-Century History*. Princeton, N.J.: Princeton University Press, 2011.

Rowlands, Marie B. *Masters and Men: The West Midlands Metalware Trade before the Industrial Revolution*. Manchester: Manchester University Press, 1975.

Rudé, George. "The Gordon Riots: A Study of the Rioters and Their Victims: The Alexander Prize Essay." *Transactions of the Royal Historical Society* 6 (1956): 93–114.

———. *Wilkes and Liberty: A Social Study of 1763–1774*. Oxford: Clarendon, 1962.

Russell, Carl. *Guns on the Early Frontiers: A History of Firearms from Colonial Times through the Years of the Western Fur Trade*. Berkeley: University of California Press, 1957.

Ruttan, Vernon. *Is War Necessary for Economic Growth? Military Procurement and Technology Development*. New York: Oxford University Press, 2005.

Sampson, Anthony. *The Arms Bazaar: From Lebanon to Lockheed*. New York: Viking, 1977.

Sargent, Thomas, and Francois R. Velde. *The Big Problem of Small Change*. Princeton, N.J.: Princeton University Press, 2002.

Satia, Priya. "Developing Iraq: Britain, India and the Redemption of Empire and Technology in the First World War." *Past and Present* 197 (2007): 211–55.

———. "Drones: A History from the British Middle East." *Humanity* 5 (2014): 1–31.

———. *Spies in Arabia: The Great War and the Cultural Foundations of Britain's Covert Empire in the Middle East*. New York: Oxford University Press, 2008.

Satre, Lowell. *Chocolate on Trial: Slavery, Politics, and the Ethics of Business*. Athens: Ohio University Press, 2005.

Satz, Debra. *Why Some Things Should Not Be for Sale: The Moral Limits of Markets*. New York: Oxford University Press, 2010.

Sayers, R. S. *Lloyds Bank in the History of English Banking*. Oxford: Clarendon, 1957.

Schofield, Robert. *The Lunar Society of Birmingham: A Social History of Provincial Science and Industry in Eighteenth-Century England*. Oxford: Clarendon, 1963.

Schwoerer, Lois. *Gun Culture in Early Modern England*. Charlottesville: University of Virginia Press, 2016.

———. "To Hold and Bear Arms: The English Perspective." *Chicago-Kent Law Review* 76 (2000): 27–60.

Scouller, R. E. *The Armies of Queen Anne*. Oxford: Clarendon, 1996.

Searing, James. *West African Slavery and Atlantic Commerce: The Senegal River Valley, 1700–1860*. New York: Cambridge University Press, 1993.

Searle, G. R. *Corruption in British Politics, 1895–1930*. Oxford: Clarendon, 1987.

Selgin, George. *Good Money: Birmingham Button Makers, the Royal Mint, and the Beginnings of Modern Coinage, 1775–1821*. Ann Arbor: University of Michigan Press, 2008.

Sen, Sudipta. *Empire of Free Trade: The East India Company and Making of the Colonial Marketplace.* Philadelphia: University of Pennsylvania Press, 1998.

Sharpe, James A. *Crime in Early Modern England, 1550–1750.* 2nd ed. London: Longmans, 1999. First published 1984.

———. "Crime in England: Long-Term Trends and the Problem of Modernization." In *The Civilization of Crime: Violence in Town and Country since the Middle Ages,* edited by Eric Johnson and Eric Monkkonen, 17–34. Urbana: University of Illinois Press, 1996.

Shumway, Rebecca. *The Fante and the Transatlantic Slave Trade.* Rochester, N.Y.: University of Rochester Press, 2011.

Sifton, John. "A Brief History of Drones." *The Nation,* February 7, 2012, www.thenation.com/article /brief-history-drones.

Silverman, David. *Thundersticks: Firearms and the Violent Transformation of Native America.* Cambridge, Mass.: Belknap Press, 2016.

Skeel, C. A. J. "The Letter-book of a Quaker Merchant, 1756–8." *English Historical Review* 31 (1916): 137–43.

Skentelbery, Norman. *Arrows to Atom Bombs: A History of the Ordnance Board.* London: HMSO, 1975.

Skocpol, Theda. "Bringing the State Back In: Strategies of Analysis in Current Research." In *Bringing the State Back In,* edited by P. Evans, D. Rueschemeyer, and Skocpol, 3–38. New York: Cambridge University Press, 1985.

Smith, Barbara M. D. "The Galtons of Birmingham: Quaker Gun Merchants and Bankers, 1702–1831." *Business History* 9, no. 2 (1967): 132–50.

Smith, Crosbie, and Ben Marsden. *Engineering Empires: A Cultural History of Technology in Nineteenth-Century Britain.* New York: Palgrave, 2005.

Smith, D. J. "Army Clothing Contractors and the Textile Industries in the 18th Century." *Textile History* 14 (1983): 153–64.

Smith, Merritt Roe. *Harpers Ferry Armory and the New Technology: The Challenge of Change.* Ithaca, N.Y.: Cornell University Press, 1977.

———, ed. *Military Enterprise and Technological Change: Perspectives on the American Experience.* Cambridge, Mass.: MIT Press, 1985.

Smith, Robert. "Yoruba Armament." *Journal of African History* 8 (1967): 87–106.

Smith, Simon D., and T. R. Wheeley. "'Requisites of a Considerable Trade': The Letters of Robert Plumsted, Atlantic Merchant, 1752–58." *English Historical Review* (2009): 545–70.

Stanziani, Alessandro. *After Oriental Despotism: Eurasian Growth in a Global Perspective.* London: Bloomsbury, 2014.

Starkey, Armstrong. "Conflict and Synthesis: Frontier Warfare in North America, 1513–1815." In *Technology, Disease and Colonial Conquests, Sixteenth to Eighteenth Centuries: Essays Reappraising the Guns and Germs Theories,* edited by George Raudzens, 59–84. Boston: Brill, 2001.

Stears, Marc. *Progressives, Pluralists, and the Problems of the State: Ideologies of Reform in the United States and Britain, 1909–1926.* New York: Oxford University Press, 2002.

Steele, Ian. *Warpaths: Invasions of North America.* New York: Oxford University Press, 1995.

Stephens, W. B., ed. *The Victoria History of the County of Warwick.* Vol. 7, *The City of Birmingham.* London: Oxford University Press, 1964.

Stern, Philip. *The Company-State: Corporate Sovereignty and the Early Modern Foundations of the British Empire in India.* New York: Oxford University Press, 2011.

Stern, Walter. "Gunmaking in Seventeenth-Century London." *Journal of the Arms and Armour Society* 1 (1954): 66–75.

Stevenson, David. *Armaments and the Coming of War: Europe, 1904–14.* New York: Oxford University Press, 1996.

Stewart, Richard W. *The English Ordnance Office: A Case-Study in Bureaucracy, 1585–1625.* Woodbridge, UK: Royal Historical Society, 1996.

Stoker, Donald, and Jonathan Grant, eds. *Girding for Battle: The Arms Trade in Global Perspective, 1815–1940.* Westport, Conn.: Praeger, 2003.

Stone, David. "Imperialism and Sovereignty: The League of Nations' Drive to Control the Global Arms Trade." *Journal of Contemporary History* 35 (2000): 213–30.

Stone, Lawrence. "Interpersonal Violence in English Society, 1300–1980." *Past and Present* 101 (1983): 22–33.

———, ed. *An Imperial State at War: Britain from 1689–1815*. London: Routledge, 1993.

Stone, Lawrence, and J. C. F. Stone. *An Open Elite? England 1540–1880*. Oxford: Clarendon Press, 1984.

Storey, William. *Guns, Race, and Power in Colonial South Africa*. New York: Cambridge University Press, 2008.

Storrs, Christopher, ed. *The Fiscal-Military State in Eighteenth Century Europe*. Burlington, Vt.: Ashgate, 2008.

Strachan, Hew. *European Armies and the Conduct of War*. Winchester, Mass.: Allen & Unwin, 1983.

Streets, Heather. *Martial Races: The Military, Race and Masculinity in British Imperial Culture, 1857–1914*. Manchester: Manchester University Press, 2005.

Styles, John. *The Dress of the People: Everyday Fashion in Eighteenth-Century England*. New Haven, Conn.: Yale University Press, 2008.

———. "Manufacture, Consumption, and Design in Eighteenth-Century England." In *Consumption and the World of Goods*, edited by John Brewer and Roy Porter, 527–54. London: Routledge, 1993.

———. "'Our Traitorous Money Makers': The Yorkshire Coiners and the Law, 1760–83." In *An Ungovernable People: The English and Their Law in the Seventeenth and Eighteenth Centuries*, edited by John Brewer and John Styles, 172–249. London: Hutchinson, 1980.

Sweeney, Kevin M. "Firearms, Militias, and the Second Amendment." In *The Second Amendment on Trial: Critical Essays on District of Columbia v. Heller*, edited by Saul Cornell and Nathan Kozuskanich, 310–82. Amherst and Boston: University of Massachusetts Press, 2013.

Sweeney, Kevin M., and Saul Cornell. "All Guns Are Not Created Equal." *Chronicle of Higher Education*, January 28, 2013, www.chronicle.com/article/All-Guns-Are-Not-Created-Equal/136805.

Tagliacozzo, Eric. *Secret Trades, Porous Borders: Smuggling and States along a Southeast Asian Frontier, 1865–1915*. New Haven, Conn.: Yale University Press, 2005.

Tazzara, Correy. "Capricious Demands: Artisanal Goods, Business Strategies, and Consumer Behavior in Seventeenth-Century Florence." In *Early Modern Things: Objects and Their Histories*, edited by Paula Findlen, 204–24. London: Routledge, 2013.

Theohary, Catherine A. "Conventional Arms Transfers to Developing Nations, 2007–2014." Congressional Research Service, December 21, 2015. https://fas.org/sgp/crs/weapons/R44320.pdf.

Thomas, Hugh. *The Slave Trade: The Story of the Atlantic Slave Trade, 1440–1870*. New York: Simon & Schuster, 1997.

Thompson, E. P. "The Crime of Anonymity." In *Albion's Fatal Tree: Crime and Society in Eighteenth-Century England*, edited by D. Hay, E. P. Thompson, and P. Linebaugh, 255–344. New York: Pantheon, 1975.

———. *The Making of the English Working Class*. New York: Pantheon, 1963.

———. "The Moral Economy of the Crowd." *Past and Present* 50 (1971): 76–136.

———. "The Peculiarities of the English." In *The Poverty of Theory & Other Essays*, 245–301. New York: Monthly Review Press, 1978. Essay first published 1965.

———. *Whigs and Hunters: The Origin of the Black Act*. New York: Pantheon, 1975.

Thornton, John. "The Art of War in Angola, 1575–1680." *Comparative Studies in Society and History* 30 (1988): 360–78.

Tilly, Charles. "War Making and State Making as Organized Crime." In *Bringing the State Back In*, edited by Peter Evans, Dietrich Rueschemeyer, and Theda Skocpol. Cambridge: Cambridge University Press, 1985.

———. *Warfare in Atlantic Africa, 1500–1800*. London: UCL Press, 1999.

Tomlinson, H. C. *Guns and Government: The Ordnance Office under the Stuarts*. London: Royal Historical Society, 1979.

Tracy, James D. *The Political Economy of Merchant Empires*. New York: Cambridge University Press, 1991.

Trebilcock, Clive. "'Spin-off' in British Economic History: Armaments and Industry, 1760–1914." *Economic History Review* 22 (1969): 474–90.

Tredoux, Gavan, ed. Galton.org (Web site about Francis Galton).

Tuke, Anthony, ed. *History of Barclays Bank Limited, Including Many Private and Joint Stock Banks Amalgamated and Affiliated with It*, compiled by P. W. Matthews. London: Blades, East & Blades, 1926.

Uglow, Jenny. *The Lunar Men: The Friends Who Made the Future, 1730–1810*. New York: Farrar, Straus and Giroux, 2002.

Valenze, Deborah. *The Social Life of Money in the English Past*. New York: Cambridge University Press, 2006.

van Creveld, Martin. *Supplying War: Logistics from Wallenstein to Patton.* 2nd ed. New York: Cambridge University Press, 2004. First published 1977.

Vandervort, Bruce. *Wars of Imperial Conquest in Africa, 1830–1914.* London: UCL Press, 1999.

Vernon, James. *Distant Strangers: How Britain Became Modern.* Berkeley: University of California Press, 2014.

Vickery, Amanda. *Behind Closed Doors: At Home in Georgian England.* New Haven, Conn.: Yale University Press, 2009.

Wahrman, Dror. *The Making of the Modern Self: Identity and Culture in Eighteenth-Century England.* New Haven, Conn.: Yale University Press, 2004.

Wainwright, Peter S. "Henry Nock, Innovator, 1741–1804." *The American Society of Arms Collectors* 88 (2003): 1–20.

Walvin, James. *The Quakers: Money and Morals.* London: John Murray, 1997.

Wallace, Anthony F. C. *The Social Context of Innovation: Bureaucrats, Families, and Heroes in the Early Industrial Revolution, as Foreseen in Bacon's "New Atlantis."* Princeton, N.J.: Princeton University Press, 1982.

Weatherill, Lorna. *Consumer Behaviour and Material Culture in Britain, 1660–1760.* London: Routledge, 1996.

Weeden, William Babcock. *Economic and Social History of New England, 1620–1789.* Vol. 2. Boston: Houghton Mifflin, 1899.

Wennerlind, Carl. *Casualties of Credit: The English Financial Revolution, 1620–1720.* Cambridge, Mass.: Harvard University Press, 2011.

West, Jenny. *Gunpowder, Government and War in the Mid-Eighteenth Century.* Rochester, N.Y.: Boydell, 1991.

Western, John. *The English Militia in the Eighteenth Century: The Story of a Political Issue, 1660–1802.* London: Routledge, 1965.

White, Gavin. "Firearms in Africa: An Introduction." *Journal of African History* 12 (1971): 173–84.

White, Richard. *The Middle Ground: Indians, Empires, and Republics in the Great Lakes Region, 1650–1815.* New York: Cambridge University Press, 2011.

Whiting, J. R. S. *British Trade Tokens: A Social and Economic History.* New York: Drake, 1972.

Williams, David. *The Birmingham Gun Trade.* Stroud: Tempus, 2004.

———. "James Farmer and Samuel Galton: The Reality of Gun Making for the Board of Ordnance in the Mid-18th Century." *Arms & Armour* 7 (2010): 119–41.

Williams, Gomer. *History of the Liverpool Privateers and Letters of Marque, with an Account of the Liverpool Slave Trade.* New York: A. M. Kelley, 1966.

Williamson, J. G. "Why Was British Growth So Slow during the Industrial Revolution?" *Journal of Economic History* 44 (1984): 687–712.

Willson, Beckles. *The Great Company, 1667–1871: Being a History of the Honorable Company of Merchants-Adventurers Trading into Hudson's Bay.* 2 vols. Toronto: Copp Clark, 1899.

Wilson, Kathleen. *The Sense of the People: Politics, Culture, and Imperialism in England, 1715–1785.* New York: Cambridge University Press, 1995.

Winchester Mystery House Museum. "Sarah Winchester, Woman of Mystery." www.winchester mysteryhouse.com.

Winslow, Cal. "Sussex Smugglers." In *Albion's Fatal Tree: Crime and Society in Eighteenth-Century England,* edited by D. Hay, E. P. Thompson, and P. Linebaugh, 119–66. New York: Pantheon, 1975.

Wise. Michael J. "On the Evolution of the Jewellery and Gun Quarters in Birmingham." *Transactions and Papers* 15 (1949): 59–72.

———. "Some Factors Influencing the Growth of Birmingham." *Geography* 33, no. 4 (1948): 176–90.

Wolf, Eric. *Europe and the People without History.* Berkeley: University of California Press, 1983.

Wood, Brian, and Debbie Hillier. *Shattered Lives: The Case for Tough International Arms Control.* Oxfam, 2003. http://policy-practice.oxfam.org.uk/publications/shattered-lives-the-case-for-tough -international-arms-control-112366.

Wood, Brian, and Johan Peleman. *The Arms Fixers: Controlling the Brokers and Shipping Agents.* Peace Research Institute. Oslo, 2000. www.prio.org/Publications/Publication/?x=658.

Yaycioglu, Ali. *Partners of the Empire: The Crisis of the Ottoman Order in the Age of Revolutions.* Stanford, Calif.: Stanford University Press, 2016.

Young, H. A. *The East India Company's Arsenals and Manufactories.* Oxford: Clarendon, 1937.

UNPUBLISHED SECONDARY SOURCES

Levy, Jonathan. "The History of Profit." Lecture at Stanford University, June 4, 2013.

McKnight, Philip. "Rural Sports: The Poetry of Fishing, Fowling, and Hunting, 1650–1800." Ph.D. thesis, University of Ottawa, 2011.

Mokyr, Joel, and Ralf Meinsenzahl. "The Rate and Direction of Invention in the British Industrial Revolution: Incentives and Institutions." Working paper, 2011, http://papers.nber.org/papers /w16993.

O'Brien, Patrick. "The Contributions of Warfare with Revolutionary and Napoleonic France to the Consolidation and Progress of the British Industrial Revolution." Working paper, 2011, http://eprints .lse.ac.uk/31741/1/WP150.pdf.

Richards, W. A. "The Birmingham Gun Manufactory of Farmer and Galton and the Slave Trade in the Eighteenth Century." M.A. thesis, University of Birmingham, 1972.

Shenhav, Rivka. "At a Gun Point: How Demand for Armament Advanced Technology: 1450–1914." Unpublished paper, 2011.

Slavtchev, Viktor, and Simon Wiederhold. "Technological Intensity of Government Demand and Innovation." Working paper, 2012.

Symons, J. C. "The Mining and Smelting of Copper in England and Wales, 1760–1820." M.A. thesis, Coventry University, 2003.

Whatley, Warren. "Guns-for-Slaves: The 18th Century British Slave Trade in Africa." Unpublished paper, 2008, www.iga.ucdavis.edu/Research/All-UC/conferences/2008-spring/Whatley%20paper.pdf.

CREDITS

INDEX

Page numbers in *italics* refer to illustrations.